HARVARD STUDIES IN BUSINESS HISTORY

HARVARD STUDIES IN BUSINESS HISTORY
XXI

Edited by
ALFRED D. CHANDLER, JR.

Isidor Straus Professor of Business History
Graduate School of Business Administration
George F. Baker Foundation
Harvard University

Cosimo de' Medici

THE RISE AND DECLINE OF
THE MEDICI BANK

1397–1494

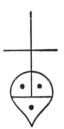

Raymond de Roover

HARVARD UNIVERSITY PRESS

Cambridge, Massachusetts

London, England

Library of Congress Catalog Card Number 63–11417

ISBN 0-674-77145-1

Printed in the United States of America

To

Abbott Payson Usher

EDITOR'S INTRODUCTION

The Rise and Decline of the Medici Bank marks a new departure for the *Harvard Studies in Business History*. It is the first in the series dealing wholly with business in Europe and it records the operations of an enterprise centuries ahead in time of the subjects of the other volumes. However, it is concerned with an institutional development, that of banking, which is represented by four earlier volumes in the *Studies*, and, like them, its emphasis is on the process of administration.

The Medici Bank was the most powerful banking house of the fifteenth century. It served as financial agent of the Church, extended credit to rulers, and facilitated international trade in Western Europe. By their personal influence and the use of their profits, the leading owners and administrators of the bank contributed to the development of Florence as the greatest center of the Renaissance. The history of this medieval business enterprise contributes to our knowledge of one of the great eras of European economic and cultural growth.

The special value of this volume to the *Studies* derives from the fact that the Medici Bank was close to the historical source of modern investment and commercial banking. Indeed, it conducted a type of business that was the medieval ancestor of that performed centuries later by a British and an American banking house represented by two volumes in the *Studies: The House of Baring in American Trade* and *Jay Cooke, Private Banker.*

The economic system within which the Medici operated was far different from that of the Barings or of Jay Cooke and his associates. These nineteenth-century firms worked in an international and a rapidly developing industrial and commercial economy with a broad market base. The fifteenth-century bankers also operated internationally, but within a business system made up largely of merchants and bankers serving principally Church, State, and Aristocracy.

Although operating in a different world, this medieval firm was in many respects similar to the Barings' and the Cookes' of the modern era. Like them, the Medici banking house was built by strong and creative entrepreneurs. It had a principal partnership with branches or correspondents in leading business centers. It had centralized policy making, at least in theory, and decentralized management of operations, with resulting problems of control. It largely worked with other people's money, and at times it took high risks in employing capital profitably. Indeed, it ran into serious difficulties from a complexity of causes. All three concerns, regardless of time or circumstance, demonstrated the importance of wise judgments in decision making and of a workable balance between centralized policy making and control and decentralized management of operations.

Although the author of *The Rise and Decline of the Medici Bank* is well known to historians, a brief introduction may be of interest to other readers. Belgian by birth, by early academic training, and by business experience (as an accountant, successively, in a bank and in the largest shipping firm in Antwerp), Raymond de Roover came to the United States to attend the Harvard Graduate School of Business Administration, where he received the M.B.A. degree in 1938. While at Harvard he studied business history with N. S. B. Gras and economic history with A. P. Usher. Later he studied economic history and economic theory at the University of Chicago, where he received the Ph.D. degree. He is Professor of History at Brooklyn College.

Professor de Roover has published several books and many articles on the history of banking, negotiable instruments, accounting, and economic thought. His earlier and shorter version of the history of the Medici Bank, which was published by the New York University Press, received the Herbert Baxter Adams Prize of the American Historical Association. His *Money, Banking and Credit in Medieval Bruges* was awarded the Charles Homer Haskins Medal of the Mediaeval Academy of America. His *Gresham on Foreign Exchange; an Essay in Early Mercantilism* was sponsored by the Harvard Graduate School of Business Administration and published by the Harvard University Press. A book in French on the history of the bill of exchange was published by the Ecole Pratique des Hautes Etudes with a subsidy from the government of France. For his contributions as a scholar, Professor de Roover, a naturalized citizen of the United States, was elected a foreign member of his native land's Royal Flemish Academy of Sciences, Letters, and Fine Arts.

In a publication of the Harvard Graduate School of Business Administration, it is especially appropriate to note, as suggested by Professor de Roover, the contribution of Dr. Florence Edler de Roover to this study of the Medici Bank. It was at this School that Mrs. de Roover, as a member of the business history group, first worked in the business records of the Medici family, of a branch engaged in manufacturing. It was she who later introduced her husband to the rich records in Italy of the banking house of the Medici. Although she disclaims participation in the authorship of the volume, Mrs. de Roover, as a Renaissance scholar, a student of Florentine and Lucchese history, and the author of the *Glossary of Mediaeval Italian Terms of Business* (published by the Mediaeval Academy), contributed ideas and criticism and assisted in the research in the records of the Medici Bank.

The cost of publishing this volume has been underwritten by the Harvard Graduate School of Business Administration. This is further evidence of the value placed by the administrators of this school on research and publication in the history of business as a contribution to business education and to knowledge of the historical background of our economic system and of the society which it serves.

Henrietta M. Larson

April 24, 1962

AUTHOR'S PREFACE

This book is the outcome of three years of research in the Florentine archives and supplants a much shorter essay on the same subject published in 1948 by the New York University Press. As this earlier publication was based on secondary sources which were not always reliable, it contains quite a few factual inaccuracies, but it gives nevertheless a general picture which is substantially correct and has not been altered very much in this new version. Therefore, libraries possessing the older version should not discard it, since it may be useful for readers who are pressed for time and who want to gather a general impression without bothering much about details. Moreover, the appendices, mainly abstracts from an account book kept by the Medici Bank in Bruges, are not reproduced in this new volume.

The first version was little more than a sketch. Systematic research has uncovered so much source material that it became possible to redo the job entirely and to write a new book which tells the story in greater detail, fills in many of the gaps, and uses the quantitative data brought to light by the discovery of the *libri segreti,* or the secret account books of the Medici Bank (1397–1450). The overall picture of the Bank as a going concern has been brought into better focus and mistakes based on inadequate information have been corrected. Hypothesis, to a large extent, has been replaced by certitude, especially with regard to the structure of the Bank, which, from 1397 to 1455, foreshadowed the modern holding company, with the understanding that it was an agglomerate of partnerships rather than of corporations. The new evidence proves that the Medici Bank may properly be called a bank, because it emphasized banking more than trade and trade more than manufacturing. The statistical data now available settle this question once and for all.

After this book went to press Dr. Gino Corti reported the discovery in the Florentine Archives (Conventi soppressi, Archivio 79, vol. 119) of the *libro segreto,* or personal account book, kept by Ilarione di Lippaccio de' Bardi, who was general manager of the Medici Bank from 1420 until his death around Christmas 1432. A microfilm copy of this manuscript reached me too late to make many changes, but it does not matter much. Although the *libro segreto* of Ilarione de' Bardi furnishes new and valuable information about the management of his household and estate, it contains little that is new concerning the Medici Bank and gives the same data about capital structure and allocation of profits that are found in *Libro segreto* No. 2 of the Bank itself. This is not surprising, since both manuscripts are in Ilarione's own hand with the exception of a few posthumous additions.

In recent years our knowledge of medieval banking has advanced with great strides. In no small measure, this progress is due to the pioneering efforts of Professor A. P. Usher who pointed the way leading to the final solution of many perplexing problems, especially those connected with the use of the bill of exchange as a transfer and credit instrument. As my teacher at Harvard, he urged me to enter this field, advice which I followed and never regretted. It is, therefore, proper that this book be dedicated to him.

This project would never have been carried out without the grant of a Fulbright Research Fellowship and the generous aid of the John Simon Guggenheim Memorial Foundation. This assistance enabled me to spend three full years in Italy, one year as a Fulbright Research Fellow (1951–1952) and two years as a Guggenheim Fellow (1949–1950 and 1952–1953).

My greatest debt is to my wife, Dr. Florence Edler de Roover ("Signora Fiorenza" to all our Italian friends), whose name should perhaps appear on the title page, but she steadfastly declines to assume any responsibility for a work bristling with statistical tables. (Her horror of them is unjustified, since I prepared and typed all the tables, leaving to her the easier job of the regular text, the footnotes, and the bibliography!)

The idea of rewriting my first and rather superficial essay really originated with *la Signora*. While I was visiting relatives in Belgium during the Christmas season of 1949, she wrote me from Florence that she had made a little exploratory tour of the Medici archives and that there was plenty of material which was still untouched and had been overlooked by earlier historians. The letter contained a summons to rush back to Italy and to abandon all other projects in order to delve into the records of the Medici Bank. From then on, my wife took charge of all the research involved in this new scheme. With her usual efficiency in such matters, she proceeded to go systematically through the inventory of the Medici Archives prior to the Principate (*Mediceo avanti il Principato*), quite a job, since there are thousands of cards or *schede*. Without this laborious process, it would have been impossible to find one's way through the jungle of the Medici papers. It was also my wife who discovered the secret account books of the Medici Bank in a mislabeled bundle (No. 153). At a later stage, when it came to writing the book, my wife continued to give me invaluable help with advice and criticism in matters of style and arrangement.

Next to the Signora Fiorenza, my greatest debt is to Dr. Gino Corti who acted as our research assistant and gave us devoted service in transcribing many of the letters and other documents. His flair for unearthing relevant material in unexpected places made available information that otherwise would have escaped our attention.

We wish to remember the late Dr. Ferdinando Sartini, Director of the State Archives in Florence, and to thank the present archivist, Dr. Sergio Camerani, and his wife, Dr. Giulia Camerani Marri, and the other staff members who, by the flexible application of regulations, greatly facilitated our research. Professor Federigo Melis deserves our gratitude for calling my wife's attention to Bundle No. 153 which, upon close inspection, proved to contain the secret account books of the Medici Bank instead of miscellaneous fragments.

In the course of my research, several persons kindly made helpful suggestions or supplied additional information. They are so numerous that it would be difficult to mention all of them. In particular, I am grateful to Professors Frederic C. Lane and Armando Sapori for raising stimulating questions, to Louis Marks for calling our attention to Parenti's chronicle and the documents in the Strozzi papers concerning Lorenzo's misappropriation of public funds, to Peter Partner for helping me with the identification of some members of the Roman Curia under Martin V, and to Warman Welliver for calling my attention to Lorenzo's correspondence with his ambassador, or *orator*, in Milan.

Professor Ralph W. Hidy read the manuscript before it went to press and wisely suggested that Chapter II be condensed. Professor Henrietta M. Larson, the editor of this series and an old friend, generously gave me the benefit of her long editorial experience. She read the manuscript throughout and made numerous suggestions for improvement. Chapter I was added and other chapters were cut or partly rewritten in accordance with her recommendations. I am greatly indebted to her not only for her editorial work on the manuscript but also for making arrangements for publication.

Mention should also be made of Miss E. Louise Lucas of the Fogg Art Museum, who was helpful in selecting the illustrations.

The completion of this manuscript relieves me of a burden which I have carried for ten years. It is true that other projects repeatedly interfered and slowed up my progress on the Medici Bank. I am glad that my task is finished and I only hope that my labors will not be in vain but will contribute something to a better knowledge of the economic background of the Italian Renaissance.

Raymond de Roover

Brooklyn College of the City University of New York
Brooklyn, New York
November 18, 1961

CONTENTS

TABLES

ILLUSTRATIONS

COSIMO DE' MEDICI, PATER PATRIAE, HEAD OF THE
MEDICI BANK, 1429–1464. Marble relief by Andrea del Ver-
rocchio. Formerly in Kaiser Friedrich Museum, Berlin   Frontispiece

DIAGRAMS

CHART

The Rise and Decline of the Medici Bank

1397–1494

I

INTRODUCTION

Modern capitalism based on private ownership has its roots in Italy during the Middle Ages and the Renaissance. From the Crusades to the Great Discoveries, Italy was the dominant economic power in the western world, and its merchants were the leading business men. They were the middlemen whose trade relations linked the Levant to the shores of the North Sea. As in Roman times, the Mediterranean had once more become the Mare Nostrum, the Italian sea over which the flags of Genoa, Pisa, and Venice held undisputed sway. Spices from the Orient were perhaps the backbone of the Italian trade, since there was always a market for them in the West, but the merchants of Italy handled other goods, among which silkstuffs, cloth, and wool were the principal ones. Gauged by modern standards, the volume of international trade was small, since it was more or less confined to luxury products, although it was by no means exceptional for cheap and bulky products, such as wheat or timber, to travel long distances.

The Italians were not only the principal merchants but also the principal bankers. In this field, their monopoly was nearly complete, the Catalans being only distant competitors. By far the best customer of the Italian banking and mercantile companies was the Church. The flow of papal remittances was scarcely less important than currents of trade and, according to circumstances, might either promote equilibrium or tend to disrupt it. Pawnbrokers and money-changers served local needs for credit accommodation, but foreign banking, that is, dealing in bills of exchange, was primarily in the hands of the Italian merchant-bankers.

This hegemony of the Italians rested largely upon superior business organization. As a matter of fact, they laid the foundations for most of the business institutions of today. Not only did they create the partnership, but they developed means for managing companies which had branches in foreign lands, thus overcoming the handicap of distance by forms of remote control. Joint-stock companies did not originate until the beginning of the seventeenth century, but the Medici Bank already foreshadowed the holding company in certain respects. The Italian merchants also developed double-entry bookkeeping (the first unquestionable examples in 1340), invented the bill of exchange in draft form, and experimented with marine insurance. In the field of banking, the

Italians did not discover the bank note, but they mastered the art of making payments by book transfer on the strength of oral or written orders. Since medieval banks operated on a fractional reserve principle, they created fiduciary money to the extent that transferable deposits were not entirely covered by cash in till or in vault. Another noteworthy contribution is that the Italian merchants evolved a body of mercantile law, customary at first, but codified later in ordinances, such as the famous *Ordonnance du Commerce* promulgated in 1673 by Louis XIV. Its rules, more or less universally adopted, still form the basis of commercial, or business, law today.

In the fourteenth and fifteenth centuries, the major Italian trading centers were Florence, Genoa, and Venice. As Genoa and Venice were coastal cities, their activity was oriented toward the sea, especially the trade with the Levant, though they also sent ships to England and Flanders through the Straits of Gibraltar. During the same two centuries, Florence, located inland, was perhaps the leading banking place. It also possessed flourishing woolen and silk industries and traded in spices and other luxury products. In 1406 it conquered Pisa and its port, Porto Pisano, and thus acquired direct access to the sea.[1]

A distinctive feature of Florentine business organization was the existence of large mercantile and banking companies which controlled a network of branches abroad. These "companies," of course, were partnerships rather than corporations. Large companies of this type, mostly Sienese, had been established as early as the first quarter of the thirteenth century. Siena, at the present time a sleepy Tuscan town, was perhaps for seventy-five years the main banking center in Europe, with Piacenza, another inland town, as a close rival. The largest of Sienese companies was the *Gran Tavola* (great table or bank) of the Bonsignori. It failed in 1298, and it is said that Siena never completely recovered from this blow. Its place was taken by Florence.

Between 1300 and 1345, the most powerful Florentine companies were those of the Bardi, the Peruzzi, and the Acciaiuoli. The Florentine chronicler, Giovanni Villani (1276–1348), who had been for a while a partner of the Peruzzi company, called them "the pillars of Christian trade," by which he meant presumably the main supports of the western trade in the Mediterranean area.[2] All three companies collapsed shortly before the Black Death (1348), which is believed to have wiped out one third of the population of Europe. The crash was probably caused by overextension of credit and excessive loans to sovereigns, especially to Edward III (reigned 1327–1377), King of England, and to Robert (1309–1343), the Angevin King of Naples. Such loans were a perennial threat to the solvency of medieval companies. Yet, the Italian companies always became involved in them, probably because it was difficult to avoid doing business with courts, a major outlet for the luxury products in which they were dealing.

As a measure of the size of these companies, it may be noted that in 1336, the Peruzzi, the second largest of the "big three," had fifteen branches scattered all over Western Europe and the Levant, from London to Cyprus, and employed a staff of about ninety clerks, or "factors." [3] In 1310 its capital amounted to nearly 103,000 gold florins, or approximately $412,000 at the present valuation of gold at $35 an ounce.[4] This was a considerable sum, especially since the purchasing power of money was then much greater than it is today. According to Villani, when the Peruzzi company failed in 1343, Edward III of England owed them "the value of a realm." [5] The Acciaiuoli, the smallest of the three companies, in 1341 had a staff of forty-three factors residing abroad.

After the disappearance of the three companies, the Pope was unable to find a banking firm that offered him the same facilities for the transfer of papal revenues or subsidies. Eventually the Alberti, a Florentine firm that had weathered the storm successfully, took advantage of the elimination of its rivals and succeeded in capturing the papal business. However, the Alberti company soon split into several rival firms because of family quarrels and, thereby, was greatly weakened. Moreover, some of the leading members of the family fell into disgrace with the ruling Florentine oligarchs, with the result that, from 1382 to 1434, the entire Alberti clan was sent into exile. The place of the Alberti was taken by the Medici, the Pazzi, the Rucellai, and the Strozzi. Although the Medici succeeded in overshadowing their competitors, they never attained the size of the Bardi or the Peruzzi, the giants of the fourteenth century. The year 1397 may be regarded as the founding date of the Medici Bank, for in that year Giovanni di Bicci de' Medici,[6] who had been managing a bank in Rome, decided to transfer his headquarters to Florence. The Bank lasted for nearly a hundred years, until 1494, when the Medici were expelled from Florence and all their property, business investments as well as real estate, was sequestered and put into the hands of receivers. In the course of that century, the Medici Bank went through a period of expansion, which ended with Cosimo's death in 1464, and a period of decline, which, slow and gradual at first, gained momentum after 1478, the year of the Pazzi conspiracy, which shook the Medici edifice to its foundation. As we shall see, the downfall was caused by a combination of poor management, ill-advised policies, structural weaknesses, and adverse business conditions which certainly worsened after 1470 owing to the shrinking volume of international trade, a contraction probably caused by disturbances in the Levant and transfer difficulties in settling Italian claims on Northern Europe.

Fortunately, the business records of the Medici Bank have been preserved in sufficient quantity to give a fairly detailed picture and to illuminate the inner workings of the Bank, the crucial problems of management and control and the formulation of policies, whether good or bad. True, the extant material is uneven and full of gaps, but it is more nearly complete than for any other medieval firm, the Datini business archives in Prato (Tuscany) excepted.[7]

For the period prior to 1451, one of the major sources is a set of *libri segreti* (confidential ledgers) discovered in 1950 in a mislabeled bundle.[8] These account books are three in number and, without a breach of continuity, cover a period of more than half a century, from March 26, 1397, when the Medici Bank was established, to March 24, 1451. Such libri segreti were usually kept by one of the partners and not entrusted to a bookkeeper. They contained the partners' accounts concerning investments and withdrawals, the accounts for operating results, the accounts of capital allocated to branches, and sometimes the salary accounts of the factors and clerks. Since the Medici libri segreti follow this same pattern, they give us valuable information on the capital structure of the firm as a whole and the profits earned by the different branches from year to year. These data, however valuable, are mainly statistical and give little information about policy. Business letters would have filled this gap. Unfortunately, few have survived for the period before 1450.

After 1450, the reverse is true: the correspondence becomes more abundant, but account books, with the exception of a few rather unimportant fragments, are missing. As a result, there are no quantitative data that would portray in expressive graphs the waning fortunes of the Medici Bank. The letters, however, unfold the tragedy in even more eloquent, if less precise, language. They show how matters slowly but inexorably went from bad to worse, how one branch after another ran onto the rocks or was refloated with great difficulty, how the Bank incurred huge losses because of insubordinate and prevaricating branch managers, how the top management failed to curb their activities, and how rifts over policy led to bickerings and mutual recrimination which hastened the downfall by preventing the application of efficacious remedies.

Besides letters and account books, the surviving records include a fair sample of partnership agreements, several balance sheets, and miscellaneous documents, such as bills of exchange, protests, deposit certificates, confidential reports and memoranda, and even a reorganization plan which was never carried into effect. Although incomplete, these records tell a story which may be amended in details, but which, on the whole, will not need revision.

Why study the Medici Bank? There are a number of reasons why such a study should be rewarding.

The Medici are well known in history because of the prominent rôle they played in the Italian Renaissance as political figures or as patrons of letters and fine arts. However, their activity as bankers and traders did not attract the same degree of attention. Yet, it was economic power that made it possible for the Medici to seize political power and that also provided the financial resources which enabled them to commission artists, to promote humanism, to collect a magnificent and unique library (the Laurenziana, still existing), and to spend huge amounts on monumental buildings, such as the church of San Lorenzo, the Dominican friary of San Marco, or the Badia of Fiesole. The Medici, from Giovanni di Bicci down, were not of the middle class, as some sociological historians have held, since the tax records show that they were by far the richest family in the entire city of Florence and occupied the upper rung of the social ladder.[9]

The history of the Medici Bank adds to our knowledge of the roots of modern business. From the standpoint of business history, this study brings out one main point: techniques have changed, but human problems have remained the same. How to pick out the right person and put him in the right place was as much a problem for the Medici as it is in business today.

Because of easier communications, the problem of control has taken different aspects, but it has not, therefore, been eliminated. The Medici Bank, especially after 1464, suffered from lack of coordination, and branch managers were at odds because they failed to understand each other's problems. How to coordinate different branches or departments continues to be a major issue confronting administrators in business as well as in government. As in the case of the Medici, mounting losses often sharpen conflicts, which then stand in the way of necessary adjustments to new conditions.

Although a midget by modern standards, the Medici Bank was the largest banking house of its time. Nevertheless, it failed to match the size of the Bardi and Peruzzi companies of earlier years, probably because conditions had ceased to be as favorable to large concerns. In contrast to the two or three centuries preceding the Black Death, which were characterized by almost continuous growth, historians now regard the fifteenth century as a period of stagnation, if not of regression. Of course there were ups and downs, but the troughs were more numerous than the peaks, and the Medici records suggest that the depression deepened after 1470 and lasted two or three decades.

Despite a declining volume of trade, organizational techniques continued to improve, perhaps because keener competition and falling profit margins put a premium on efficiency. The Medici Bank, its records show, certainly used the best methods available. From this standpoint, it was probably not typical, but rather represents the optimum that was achieved in the Middle Ages and the Renaissance. However, there is no evidence that Giovanni di Bicci and his son Cosimo were so successful because they were "innovating entrepreneurs" who introduced new products or new ways of doing business. On the contrary, their success was mainly due to the efficient use of existing methods and proven techniques. It is, for example, decidedly a legend that the Medici ever invented the bill of exchange. Perhaps they were creative in devising the "holding company" form of organization and in forming the alum cartel.

From the point of view of economic history, this study may perhaps be termed microeconomic, since it focuses its attention on a single firm. This firm, however, must be considered in its proper setting. For example, the Medici, like everyone else, had to observe the rules of the game when operating in the money market. In spite of the fact that they had a quasi monopoly of the alum trade, they were unable to exploit their advantage to the full because they ran afoul of organized consumer groups. In Milan, their main customer was the Sforza court, but in England the situation was entirely different and they were mainly concerned with wool, which they needed as much to fill the galleys on their homeward trip as to feed the Florentine looms and to provide employment for a restless proletariat. Frequently the Medici had no control whatsoever over economic conditions or political forces: all they could do was to set their sails to the wind and to make the best of a given situation, such as the War of the Roses in England or the crisis touched off by the Pazzi conspiracy. "God help it" is a favorite expression used in the Medici letters whenever political events or business prospects took an unexpected or unfavorable turn.

As this study will show, the Medici reached a highly developed and capitalistic form of organization, if "capitalistic" means that their aim was to make profits and that ultimate control rested with the owners of the capital invested in the business. In actual practice, however, major or strategic decisions, such as the establishment of a new branch or the renewal of a partnership contract, were always made in consultation with the general manager, who was very powerful, although he had only a minor share in capital and profits. Managerial or operational decisions were usually delegated to him and he did not need to consult the partners belonging to the Medici family in routine matters or day-to-day administration. One of the general manager's main tasks was the supervision of the branch managers in order to prevent their making undue commitments or unwise investments. Not an easy task! Because of slow communications and great distances, branch managers enjoyed quite a bit of autonomy; it was perhaps a weakness of the Medici Bank that they had too much leeway. Cosimo ruled his branch managers with a firm hand, but his successors relaxed their grip — with disastrous consequences.

There is no doubt that men such as Giovanni di Bicci and Cosimo di Giovanni were imbued with a capitalistic spirit of acquisitiveness and were bent upon accumulating great wealth. They actually built up a huge fortune which, after the manner of the time, was mostly invested in landed property, that is, in extensive holdings in the Mugello and farms scattered all over the surrounding countryside, especially in the direction of Prato and Signa, where Lorenzo the Magnificent built the villa of Poggio a Caiano. The Medici certainly were not satisfied with a modest living befitting their rank of simple citizens. Their social aspirations grew with each succeeding generation. Soon they strove to achieve princely status, although even Lorenzo the Magnificent continued to affect republican simplicity in his dress. The ascent of the family is perhaps better illustrated by their marriage alliances: the leading Florentine families first, the high nobility next, and finally the sovereign houses of Europe.

The results of this investigation belie the Max Weber thesis, according to which the capitalistic spirit is supposed to be a product of the Calvinist Reformation. The Medici antedated the reform movement by several decades, but to deny that they were capitalists engaged in the pursuit of wealth would be doing them more than slight injustice.

Capitalism in the age of the Medici meant, of course, commercial capitalism. As balance sheets show, the assets of the Medici Bank consisted primarily either of claims or of goods in stock, very little being invested in equipment. This is even true of the manufacturing establishments controlled by the Medici, since only simple tools were used in the production process, and, for the most part, they were owned by the workers themselves. What the employers supplied was the materials with which to work. Depreciation was known and bookkeepers sometimes made provisions for this purpose, but such items, it should be emphasized, were never more than a negligible fraction of operating cost. Industrial capitalism does not appear until the Industrial Revolution led to heavy investment in machinery and hence to high depreciation charges. In the Middle Ages, with the possible exception of mining and shipping, investment in fixed capital was small.

Industrialism is a recent phenomenon; it did not emerge in the age of the Medici. Theirs was an age in which big business — according to the standards of the time — was still confined to trade and banking. While the Medici emphasized banking rather than trade, they still combined both, a typical combination. Apparently the volume of international trade was not large enough to justify specialization in one line of business. Besides, high risks and unstable conditions were further inducements to diversify. As professor N. S. B. Gras once wrote, "scratch an early private banker and you find a merchant." [10] There was regional specialization. The Medici, unlike the Bardi and the Peruzzi, never operated in the Levant; their sphere of action was confined to Western Europe with the exclusion of Spain and Portugal. They made a timid attempt to penetrate into the Baltic, but they failed. There the Hanseatic League reigned supreme and did not brook any invasion of its territory. The domain of the Italian merchant-bankers did not extend east of the Rhine. West of it, they were in exclusive control. While competition between Florentines, Genoese, and Venetians was strong enough to prevent the transformation of this vast area into a colonial territory, Italian hegemony had nevertheless the beneficial effect of welding it into something like a common market.

II

THE MEDICI BANK AND ITS
INSTITUTIONAL BACKGROUND

Before entering into the heart of the subject, there are four topics of general import which may best be considered in the beginning as they provide threads running through the entire fabric of this book.

The first question to be considered is simply this: since the Church forbade the taking of interest, how did it happen that the Medici and other bankers were able to operate and lend money at a profit without laying themselves wide open to charges of usury? An answer to this question involves, of course, the entire problem of the relationship between the Church and the business world at the time of the Medici. An attempt will be made to determine whether the teachings of the Church actually influenced business practices; if so, how and to what extent.

The next problem deals with the place of the Medici Bank within the Florentine gild system. As bankers, the Medici came under the jurisdiction of the Arte del Cambio, or the Money-changers' Gild. It will be shown that the gild's regulatory powers were rather limited and did not carry great weight in the ordinary course of business.

Another topic deserving consideration is that of the *catasto*, a Florentine direct tax, which was based on individual returns filed with the tax officials, a procedure very much like that in use today in connection with the income tax in the United States, Great Britain, and other countries. Thousands and thousands of these returns, with almost no gaps, are still preserved in the Florentine archives. In this book extensive use has been made of the tax reports, not only of the Medici but also of their connections. These reports have been useful in many ways, for genealogical and biographical details as well as for quantitative or economic data. It is necessary, therefore, to introduce the reader to this important source of information and to tell him something about the origins and the administration of the catasto and the Florentine public debt.

A fourth topic which calls for comment is money. The purpose is not to write a treatise on medieval money, but to give the reader some guidance concerning the monetary units and symbols which appear in the Medici records and which will be used in subsequent chapters.

If the reader is pressed for time or eager to dip into the main theme of this book, he may skip this chapter for the present and postpone reading it until he comes across some puzzling difficulty. However, it is preferable to be systematic; pains have been taken to reduce this background material to a minimum compatible with an orderly presentation of each subject.

1. The Church's Usury Doctrine and the Business World

Medieval banking cannot be understood without keeping in mind the usury doctrine of the Church. Since the bankers, in this regard, tried as much as possible to comply with religious precepts, they had to operate without incurring the censure of the theologians. As a result, banking in the Middle Ages and even much later — on the Continent until far into the eighteenth century — was quite different from what it is today. It would be erroneous to believe that the usury doctrine was simply disregarded and had scarcely any effect on banking practices: on the contrary, as the available evidence proves, it exerted an enormous influence. First of all, the need for evading the usury prohibition, by legitimate means if possible, affected the entire structure of medieval banking. Second, it determined how the banks operated. And third, the usury doctrine, by recognizing certain transactions as licit and declaring others to be illicit, influenced business ethics and public opinion.

Medieval bankers, such as the Medici, might have conceded that some of their practices were on the fringe of legitimate business, but they would have disclaimed vigorously that they were manifest usurers; actually, they were not so regarded by the public. The more rigorous theologians, however, might have made reservations, but theological opinion did not necessarily agree with the views commonly held by practical men ignorant of casuistic subtleties.

To understand fully the scholastic position it is best to follow the same method of analysis as that used by the scholastic writers. What was usury? According to canon law, usury consisted in any increment, whether large or small, demanded above the principal solely on the strength of a *mutuum,* the legal term for a straight loan.[1] *Quidquid sorti accedit, usura est* (whatever exceeds the principal is usury). In this definition, each word has its importance. Consequently, usury in the Middle Ages did not apply to exorbitant rates only, but extended to *all* interest, whether high or low, excessive or moderate. By definition, a loan was a gratuitous contract. If it ceased to be such, it *ipso facto* became a usurious contract.[2] The dictum was: *usura solum in mutuo cadit.*[3] In other words, usury occurred only in a loan, whether a straight loan (overt usury) or a loan concealed under the color of another contract (palliate usury).[4] If it could be shown that a given contract was neither explicitly nor implicitly a loan, there was no usury involved. No reward could be claimed for lending in itself, but it was licit to demand *damnum et interesse,* or damages and interest, for other reasons not inherent in a loan, such as failure to repay the principal at maturity. Thus arose the doctrine of extrinsic titles which, because of its many loopholes, involved the theologians in endless difficulties.

It is impossible to go now into all the aspects of the usury problem: an exhaustive treatment would require volumes. Moreover, the Italian merchants — it is less true of the Spaniards — paid scant attention to the fine distinctions which the scholastic writers relished so much. According to the simplified and somewhat distorted version in circulation among the laity, usury was any *certain* gain exacted by virtue of a loan, especially if fully secured by pledges.[5] On the other hand, it was considered legitimate to receive compensation whenever a credit transaction was speculative or involved any risk or compulsion. Rightly or wrongly, interest was often passed off as a gift or a share in the profits of a business venture.[6] In fact, there were innumerable ways of circumventing the usury prohibition and, it must be said, they were encouraged by the quibbles of the Doctors. Approaching the problem from a legal point of view, the latter, unwittingly, gave the merchants a chance to make the most of technicalities.

The ban against usury did not halt the growth of banking, but recent research has shown that it certainly diverted the course of this development. Since the taking of interest was ruled out, the bankers had to find other ways of lending at a profit. The favorite method was by means of exchange by bills (*cambium per litteras*).[7] It did not consist in discounting as practiced today, but in the negotiation of bills payable in another place and usually in another currency. Interest, of course, was included in the price of the bill which was fittingly called a "bill of exchange." Although the presence of concealed interest is undeniable, the merchants argued — and most of the theologians accepted these views — that an exchange transaction was not a loan (*cambium non est mutuum*) but either a commutation of moneys (*permutatio*) or a buying and selling of foreign currency (*emptio venditio*).[8] In other words, the exchange transaction was used to justify the credit transaction, and speculative profits on exchange served as a cloak to cover interest charges. Nevertheless, it was argued that cambium was not usurious, since there could be no usury where there was no loan.[9]

The practical consequence was to tie banking to exchange, be it manual exchange or exchange by bills. It is perhaps significant that the bankers' gild of Florence was called the Arte del Cambio, or the Moneychangers' Gild. In the account books of the Italian merchant-bankers, including those of the Medici, one rarely, if ever, finds traces of discount, but there are thousands and thousands of entries relating to exchange transactions. There is no account for interest income, but an account entitled *Pro e danno di cambio* (Profit and Loss on Exchange). If this matter had not been so important because of the link with banking, there would have been no point to the elaborate discussion which most treatises on moral theology devote to licit and illicit exchange.[10] In the fifteenth century the subject was already receiving considerable attention in the works of Messer (Sir) Lorenzo Ridolfi (1360–1442), San Bernardino of Siena (1380–1444), and San Antonino (1389–1459), archbishop of Florence, all three contemporaries of Giovanni di Bicci and Cosimo de' Medici.[11] Later on, it was discussed with great competence by Fra Santi (Pandolfo) Rucellai (1437–1497), who became a Dominican friar in his old age after being widowed.[12] Since he was the son of a banker and had been in business himself, one must assume that he knew well how banks operated.[13] Hence, his emphasis on exchange dealings is significant. One even finds chapters dealing with this matter in merchant manuals, such as the curious treatise of Benedetto Cotrugli written in 1458.[14] In view of these discussions, there is no doubt that the Church's position toward usury had a real influence upon the conduct of business.

It is untrue that the bankers openly disregarded the teachings of the Church.[15] To be sure, they were not always consistent and often violated the precept against usury in private contracts. It does not follow, however, that there were many who pertinaciously questioned a doctrine erected into a dogma by the Church.[16] On the contrary, many a banker had an uneasy conscience about his unholy deals. Overwhelming evidence is given in the numerous medieval testaments in which the testator ordered restitution of all usury and ill-gotten gains.[17] True, such clauses became scarcer after 1350 because the merchant-bankers, while still continuing to make bequests to the Church for the salvation of their souls, were less and less eager to be branded as self-confessed usurers by referring specifically to restitution in their wills.

Moreover, they contended, with a semblance of truth, that they were engaged in legitimate business and not in usurious activities. In fact, they did shun illicit contracts as much as possible. Even the Pratese merchant-banker, Francesco di Marco Datini (1335–1410), although ruthless and grasping, boasted in letters to his wife that he had never made illicit profits. When his branch manager in Barcelona became involved in questionable exchange dealings, he was promptly rebuked by an irate master and told to desist.[18] The same attitude reveals itself in the correspondence of ser Lapo Mazzei (1350–1412), Datini's advisor and notary. In the partnership agreements of the Medici, illicit exchange was as a rule expressly forbidden, although this provision was not always carried out, as account books and other records prove. It is, therefore, understandable that Cosimo de' Medici himself was troubled by qualms about ill-acquired wealth and secured a papal bull which allowed him to atone for his covetousness by endowing the monastery of San Marco in Florence.[19]

These attitudes persist into the sixteenth century and even later. In 1517 and again in 1532, a group of Spanish merchants in Antwerp decided to consult theologians about the licitness of certain exchange dealings.[20] The Spaniard, Simon Ruiz (1526–1597), one of the leading bankers in Medina del Campo, refused to participate in any dubious contracts.[21] As late as the reign of Louis XIV, the draper, Jacques Savary (1622–1690), author of *Le Parfait Négociant*, a celebrated merchant manual, warns his readers against including interest in the face value of a bill or a note; this is usury, he contends, but it is permissible to speculate on the exchange.[22]

If it had not been for the usury doctrine, why would the merchants have adopted a cumbersome procedure when simpler methods were available? It is far easier to discount instruments of debt than to work with bills of exchange payable abroad in foreign currencies. First of all, this procedure complicates bookkeeping.[23] Next, it requires the bankers to operate with a network of correspondents in other places. Another drawback is that lenders, as well as borrowers, have to speculate and to run the risks of adverse exchange fluctuations. Moreover, the purchaser of a bill is exposed to loss not only through the insolvency of his debtor, but also through the failure of the correspondent to whom he sends a remittance. This is perhaps why the big bankers preferred to operate with their own branches. As for the borrower, if he had no funds standing to his credit in another place, he had to find some one willing to accept his drafts and to pay them when due. The drawee or payor would then have to recover his outlay at his own risk. The use of the bill of exchange thus increased both trouble and expense, so that the practical result of the usury prohibition, intended to protect the borrower, was to raise the cost of borrowing. To this extent the Church's legislation on usury may have retarded economic growth.

As Professor A. P. Usher has pointed out, the bill of exchange, or "letter of payment," introduced by the Italian merchants in the fourteenth century "was a distinctively new instrument."[24] Its extensive use was doubtless favored by the usury doctrine. From the point of view of commercial law, the effects were beneficial because the popularity of the bill of exchange led to the emergence of mercantile customs and legal rules which eventually culminated in the general acceptance of the principle of negotiability. One should not underestimate the legal and economic consequences of the toleration of the exchange contract by the moralists.[25] This toleration, by involving them in so many contradictions, contributed a great deal to the breakdown of their whole position.

By operating on the exchange, the bankers, taking advantage of a permissible form of contract, succeeded in evading the ban against usury. The important result was that bankers were not stigmatized as usurers. On the contrary, they lived as respected citizens and often played leading rôles in their communities. The great Italian bankers prided themselves on being called the Pope's money-changers. Their sons, if they went into holy orders, received preferment and became popes, cardinals, or bishops. The Medici family offers several examples, but they are by no means the only ones. The odium attached to usury swerved around the merchant-bankers to fall with all its impact on petty money-lenders and pawnbrokers.[26] In Florence, as elsewhere, they were branded as manifest usurers and ostracized by all respectable citizens. In accordance with canon law, the poor wretches lived under the ban of the Church, were deprived of the sacraments and of Christian burial, and were even unable to make valid testaments.[27]

Paradoxically, no such dreadful fate befell big bankers like the Medici because they professed not to engage in moneylending, but to confine their activities to licit contracts. Indeed, according to scholastic doctrine, this position was justifiable since there existed no usury save in loans.

2. THE MONEY-CHANGERS' GILD AND THE MEDICI BANK

In Florence, in the fifteenth century, there were three different kinds of credit institutions, all of them called banks in Italian: (1) *banchi di pegno* or *banchi a pannello* (pawnshops), (2) *banchi a minuto* (small banks), and (3) *banchi grossi* (great banks). In order to avoid confusion, it seems desirable to establish clear distinctions between these three categories.

The first group were not really banks in the ordinary acceptation of the word, but pawnshops managed by licensed usurers and called banchi a pannello because they were recognizable by a red hanging in the doorway.[28] They lent money on pledges of personal property and specialized in what is called today the "small loan" business.[29] Like houses of prostitution, pawnshops were regarded as the lesser of two evils. In accordance with canon law, their operators were branded as manifest usurers.[30] In principle, the public authorities were not supposed to grant licenses to such public sinners.[31] In practice, the Florentine city fathers managed to evade this canon by fining the pawnbrokers as a group 2,000 florins for committing "the detestable sin of usury." However, by paying this amount once a year, they were "to be free and absolved from any further censure, penalty, or exaction." [32] Actually, the so-called fine was a license fee and the real purpose of the grants was to allow public usury rather than to proscribe it.[33]

In the fourteenth century, the Florentine pawnbrokers were mostly

Christians, but it seems that from 1437 onward licenses were granted only to Jews. Whether Christians or Jews, pawnbrokers, being manifest usurers, were rigorously debarred from membership in any gild and, in particular, they were excluded from the Arte del Cambio.[34]

The Medici occasionally made loans secured by pledges. Thus, Giovanni di Bicci held as security a rich bejeweled miter belonging to Pope John XXIII (Baldassare Cossa) and later claimed by the latter's successor, Martin V.[35] But the Medici Bank was not a pawnshop: although it made loans to princes on the security of crown jewels and other articles of great value, it never advanced small sums to poor men who pawned their clothing or their tools.

Incidentally, there is no connection, however remote, between the three golden balls, the symbol of the pawnbrokers in Anglo-Saxon countries, and the torteaux (red roundels) of the Medici coat of arms.[36] It is probable that the Medici family used these armorial bearings long before it became connected with banking. It is true that bezants (gold roundels) are an heraldic representation of money. The Arte del Cambio of Florence, for example, bore as arms: gules, semée of bezants. If the pawnbrokers use three golden balls, the reason is simply because bezants are the traditional symbol of money in art and heraldry.

Since pawnshops were regulated directly by the *Signoria* (Florentine government) and remained outside the control of the gilds, the Arte del Cambio had jurisdiction over only two kinds of banks: the banchi a minuto and the banchi grossi. Bankers in Florence were called indiscriminately *banchieri* or *tavolieri* because they conducted their business seated behind a bank (*banco*) or table (*tavola*). This terminology was already used in Ancient Greece where bankers were designated by the word *trapeziti,* a derivation from τράπεζα (*trapeza* or table).[37]

Banchi a minuto were few and unimportant. There is little exact information available concerning their activity. Francesco di Giuliano de' Medici (1450–1528), a distant cousin of the rulers of Florence, was connected with two different banks of this description during the period from 1476 to 1491. From their extant account books, it appears that the business of a banco a minuto consisted chiefly in the sale of jewelry on credit, according to an installment plan.[38] Loans secured by jewelry were also made. Besides, money-changing and trading in bullion were part of the bank's activity. Time deposits bearing interest at the rate of nine or ten percent were accepted, but the ledgers contain no entries relating to deposits "payable on demand." Consequently, a banco a minuto was not a deposit bank.

There are more references to banchi a minuto in the archives of the Mercanzia, *Libro delle Accomandite,* which recorded all silent partnerships with limited liability.[39] Thus in 1471, Andrea di Lotteringo della

Stufa invested five hundred florins as a sleeping partner in a company managed by Piergiovanni d'Andrea Masini. The purpose of this partnership was to do business in Florence and to practice the art of banchiere a minuto. The managing partner, it is expressly stated, could not deal in exchange (cambiare in grosso) with or without bills. It is clear, therefore, that a banco a minuto was strictly a local bank doing a kind of business bordering on the jewelry trade. In Florence, however, goldsmiths did not belong to the Arte del Cambio but to the Arte di Por Santa Maria (the Gild of St. Mary's Gate), composed of gold and silversmiths, silk merchants, retail sellers of cloth and clothing, tailors, hosiers, doublet-makers, and embroiderers.[40]

The Medici Bank was certainly not a banco a minuto but one of the banchi grossi, which usually combined money-changing and local deposit banking with dealings in bills of exchange and foreign banking.[41] As the name Arte del Cambio intimates, banking, whether local or international, was still closely linked to exchange, either money-changing, which was local by nature, or exchange by bills, which necessarily postulated connections with other banking places.

Around 1338, there were, according to Giovanni Villani's famous chronicle, 80 banks of money-changers in Florence.[42] In 1350, two years after the Black Death, the number of firms had dropped to 57 with 120 partners. By 1356, they had increased slightly to 61.[43] In 1399, there were 71 banking houses, according to the gild's own records, the Libro di compagnie.[44] This figure fell to 33 in 1460.[45] Twelve years later, in 1472, the total was still the same, according to the chronicler, Benedetto Dei (1418–1492), which must be considered accurate, since it agrees with the records kept by the gild.[46] Then came a precipitate decline. By 1490, there were no longer enough members to fill the offices of the gild, and the records ceased to be kept up to date. Giovanni Cambi, another chronicler, asserts that there were only eight tavole left in 1516 and relates that one of them, the Da Panzano Bank, failed on December 29, 1520.[47] In other words, the Florentine banking system collapsed and this collapse also involved the Medici Bank.

The steady drop in the number of banks during the fifteenth century was, in the author's opinion, not due to greater concentration, but to a gradual, and after 1470 a rapid, decline in the volume of business. This phenomenon is by no means limited to Florence. In Bruges and Venice, too, the private transfer banks were hit by a major crisis during the last years of the fifteenth century.[48] Only in Spain did these banks survive for some unexplained reason.[49] What caused the crisis remains a mystery, but deposit banking was nearly destroyed until it was revived around 1575 with the creation of public banks in Palermo, Naples, Venice, Genoa, and other trading centers.[50]

What were the functions of the gild? They were chiefly regulatory and were confined to *local* banking.[51] Foreign banking was outside the gild's jurisdiction and, in fact, was ruled exclusively by merchant custom. Membership in the Arte del Cambio was compulsory for everyone operating a bank in Florence or being a partner in such a bank.[52] In accordance with the gild statutes, the head of each firm was required to declare the names of all partners or sons who assisted him in running the table or bank, but this requirement did not extend to partners who managed branches outside the city of Florence.[53] The correctness of this statement is confirmed by an analysis of the gild's matriculation list. Thus, in 1470, it mentions the firm, Pierfrancesco and Giuliano de' Medici & Co., as operating a tavola and lists as partners: Lorenzo de' Medici, Lodovico Masi, Francesco Nori, and Francesco Inghirami.[54] No reference is made to Francesco Sassetti, who, although general manager of the Medici Bank as a whole, was not a partner in the Florentine Tavola. Neither does the list include Giovanni Tornabuoni, who was in charge of the Rome office or any other of the Medici branch managers. Hence, the evidence is so conclusive that there is no need to belabor this point any further.

In the gild statutes, the tavolieri of Florence are portrayed as leading a rather sedentary existence and as conducting their business while sitting behind a table covered with a green cloth, an account book open in front of them, and a money pouch within reach (*sedentes ad tabulam cum tasca, libro et tappeto*).[55] Apparently, they always stood ready to change moneys and to make payments by transfer and these were the only two functions which the Arte del Cambio attempted to regulate.

Because of the intricacies of the Florentine monetary system, money-changing, that is petty exchange, remained an important function of the Florentine bankers and one of their principal sources of profit. They charged a commission not only on the exchange of foreign coin into local currency, but also on the exchange of gold florins for the silver pennies current in Florence.[56] The bankers were also dealers in bullion and presumably the main purveyors of the Mint.

The authorities used the gild as an enforcing agency and it is, therefore, not surprising that several rubrics of the statutes deal with monetary matters. Of course, any banker guilty of clipping or diminishing the current coins was heavily fined, expelled from the gild, and denounced to the public authorities as a counterfeiter.[57] A fine was also imposed upon any money-changer who would utter, or re-issue, false, counterfeit, and clipped coins except that he could buy them as bullion and cut them in two to withdraw them from circulation.[58] The same fate threatened anyone who put light florins into sealed bags and issued them to the public.[59] As these sanctions appeared insufficient, the statute of 1313 gave the consuls discretionary powers to punish as they saw fit any member of the gild who acquired illegal money without cutting it.[60] Similar enactments are found in public ordinances all over medieval Europe.[61] Perhaps they were no more effective in Florence than elsewhere for the purpose of maintaining the standard of the currency.

In the banking field, gild regulations did not go beyond the setting of professional standards and the protection of depositors against fraudulent practices. Insolvent or bankrupt money-changers were, of course, excluded from membership until creditors had been fully satisfied.[62]

Business procedure was not the same as today: transfers and withdrawals of cash were carried out by the banker on the strength of oral orders rather than of *polizze* (checks).[63] Otherwise, why are money-changers or bankers described as doing business sitting at a table with their books in front of them, ready to take orders from the lips of their customers? Since the entries in the journal of a money-changer or banker were the only records of otherwise oral proceedings, it is quite natural that the gild statutes threatened with heavy fines, expulsion, and other penalties any member found guilty of wilfully destroying his records, of erasing entries, or of fraudulently tampering with his books.[64] In order to prevent deception, the use of Arabic numerals in the extension columns was forbidden: amounts were to be written in Roman numerals.[65] Special provisions dealt with the preservation of records. Books of defunct or bankrupt money-changers were to be kept in the custody of the gild, which acquired for the purpose a large chest with three locks, so that it could be opened only in the presence of three gild officials, each of whom had a different key.[66] A money-changer exposed himself to expulsion and boycott, if he failed to pay any sum rightfully claimed by a depositor.[67] In case of litigation, a money-changer could not refuse to exhibit his account books and to deliver copies of his entries, if so requested by the gild's officers.[68]

One of the characteristic features of medieval banking, as Usher was first to emphasize, was the marked preference given to the oral order of transfer over the written assignment, later called check or cheque. In Barcelona, the regulations of the *taula* (municipal bank) forbade the use of the check (*polissa* in Catalan) as late as 1567, although this rule was relaxed soon thereafter.[69] In Venice, a conservative business center, it was still in full force in the eighteenth century, and the bookkeepers of the Banco del Giro were not allowed to enter any transfers unless the order was "dictated" to them by the depositor himself or his lawful attorney.[70] A few checks, dating from 1374, were discovered recently in Pisa.[71] Others of a slightly later date (1399–1400) are extant in the Datini archives in Prato.[72] Professor Federigo Melis, who has examined these documents carefully, maintains with reason that most of them are genuine checks drawn on a banker by his customer and made out in favor of a third party.[73] Consequently, it is clear that by 1400 checks were used in Tuscany, but it is still doubtful to what extent they had displaced the transfer order given orally to the banker sitting behind his desk or counter.[74]

One legal point requires clarification. According to the postglossators, payment by transfer in bank, whether by written or oral assignment, was final and, if accepted by the creditor, discharged the debtor completely.[75] This rule, however, did not apply to an assignment out of bank, and the debtor remained responsible until the creditor had been fully satisfied.[76]

It is possible that the Florentine banks were too numerous to permit the organization of an efficient clearing system, such as existed in Venice or in Bruges. To remedy this situation, a projector named Andrea di Francesco Arnoldi proposed, around 1432, to create a public transfer bank and to make payment in bank compulsory for all business transactions.[77] The project also involved monetizing the public debt, which would have been highly inflationary. It is fortunate, therefore, that the project came to naught.

In Florence, the banks were concentrated near the Mercato Nuovo (New Market), near the Mercato Vecchio (Old Market), in the vicinity of Or San Michele, the beautiful gild chapel, and Oltr'Arno, the quarter on the left bank of the Arno. According to all the catasto reports from 1427 to 1480, the Tavola of the Medici was located near the Mercato Nuovo in the Cavalcanti palace at the corner of the present via di Porta Rossa and the via dell'Arte della Lana, formerly called sdrucciolo dei Cavalcanti or d'Or San Michele.[78] The Tavola and two adjoining shops on the ground floor of the Cavalcanti palace belonged in one-third part to Lorenzo di Giovanni de' Medici, Cosimo's brother, who had acquired them as part of the dowry of his wife, Ginevra di Giovanni Cavalcanti. The rent on the one-third belonging to Lorenzo amounted to ten florins, corresponding to a total of thirty florins a year — rather high, but shops in this vicinity, the business center of Florence, were not let for a mere song. The Tavola, or Banco, in the Cavalcanti palace is also mentioned in a decision of 1451 when arbitrators divided the joint possessions of Cosimo and his nephew, Pierfrancesco di Lorenzo.[79] Perhaps it should be made clear that the Medici had their central office in their palace in via Larga and that only the Tavola in Florence was located in via Porta Rossa.

Because of the location, the Medici were sometimes called "tavolieri in Mercato Nuovo," as in the account book of Lazzaro di Giovanni di Feo Bracci (d. 1425), a merchant from Arezzo established in Florence. Incidentally, on November 8, 1415, he bought from them a bill of exchange on Barcelona, which proves that their Tavola did not confine its activity to local banking.[80] The Tavola of Cosimo and Lorenzo de' Medici is also mentioned in the private record of Rosso di Giovanni di Niccolò de' Medici, a very distant relative, who, in 1427, had with them a current account on which he drew to make local payments.[81]

Because the Medici operated a Tavola within the city of Florence, they were, generation after generation, members of the Arte del Cambio. According to Florentine custom, however, membership in one gild was not an impediment to membership in another gild. It was common for prominent merchants with a variety of interests to be enrolled in more than one gild. Thus, Francesco di Marco Datini (1335–1410) was simultaneously a member of the Silk Gild, known either as Arte di Por Santa Maria or Arte della Seta (1388), the Money-changers' Gild (1399), and the Calimala Gild (1404).[82] The same was true of the Medici. Giovanni di Bicci, the founder of the Medici Bank, joined the Money-changers' Gild in 1386 while he was still in the service of his distant relative Messer Vieri di Cambio de' Medici; in 1403, he added to this a membership in the Wool Gild (Arte della Lana).[83] His son, the famous Cosimo, *pater patriae,* matriculated both in the Arte del Cambio (1420) and the Arte della Seta (1433), but he apparently never belonged to either the Arte di Calimala or the Arte della Lana.[84] Cosimo's sons, however, were admitted to the latter as early as 1435, while still adolescents of nineteen and fourteen years.[85] They were already enrolled in the Arte del Cambio: Piero di Cosimo since 1425, and his brother Giovanni since 1426.[86] Later, Piero joined the Silk (1436) and the Calimala (1439) gilds.[87] Thus he eventually acquired membership in four gilds.

The next generation, Lorenzo the Magnificent and his brother Giuliano, followed in the footsteps of their elders. They were admitted to the Calimala Gild on January 15, 1459, despite the fact that they were only boys of ten and six.[88] Nearly seven years later, their father had them both matriculated in the Money-changers' Gild (December 30, 1465).[89] Lorenzo alone became, in 1469, a member of the Silk Gild.[90] There is no record of his being on the roster of the Wool Gild, but this may be an omission or an oversight.

The Medici, it is clear from the records, did not stand aloof from the gild system. Although the latter was rapidly disintegrating under the impact of changing conditions, it still retained regulatory powers which determined professional standards and set certain limits to the scope of individual initiative. It would, however, be wrong to exaggerate the rôle of the gilds: their influence was not as great as is often assumed by historians, because gild records have survived, whereas business records, which might bring the picture into better focus, have often been destroyed.

3. The Florentine Catasto

A much neglected source for the economic and social history of Florence is the unrivaled series of catasto records. They have been used mostly by art historians in order to find data concerning famous artists, but thus far this mine of information has not been exploited by other diggers with the exception of a few genealogists and a couple of pioneers, such as Heinrich Sieveking and Alfred Doren. Gianfrancesco Pagnini, far back in the eighteenth century, pointed the way, but few followed in his footsteps. Yet, the archives of the catasto are unusually rich in all kinds of data on demographic, social, and economic conditions, including the distribution of wealth and income, the class structure, the institution of slavery, the public debt, family life, urban and rural property, agrarian problems, business organization, and other topics.

In Florence, as elsewhere in medieval Europe, the government at first derived most of its income from indirect taxes: *gabelle* (excise duties) and tolls. They, of course, had the serious defect of violating the ability-to-pay principle because they weighed more heavily on the poor than on the well-to-do. Inasmuch as income from these indirect taxes proved insufficient to cover public expenditures, a direct tax called the *estimo* (estimate) was introduced in the course of the thirteenth century. It was a kind of property tax based on the assessed value of real and personal property. The purpose of these assessments was less to determine real value than to arrive at a figure which could be used as an individual quota for the allotment of the sum to be levied in each quarter, *gonfalone* (ward), or parish.[91] In other words, the estimo was what the French call *un impôt de répartition*.

Since assessment was based on rather arbitrary rules, there were loud complaints about the inequities of the tax system which burdened one person more than another, usually the poor for the benefit of the rich or political opponents for the benefit of those in power and their supporters. Repeated reforms, as for example in 1285, did not allay discontent.[92]

After being abolished in 1315, the estimo was reintroduced in 1325 because the government, as usual, needed more revenue to finance a campaign, this time against Castruccio Castracani (d. 1328), the lord of Lucca.[93] Under the pressure of the populace, a more thorough attempt was made to eliminate the injustices and inequalities of the estimo and to tax everyone "according to his capacity and his possibilities." [94] Assessments were based on sworn statements made by the taxpayers. Thus the foundation was laid for the future catasto.[95] Another feature of the reform of 1325 was that the tax rate on property was proportional to assessed value, but professional income was taxed according to a progressive scale.[96]

Because the estimo was contrary to the class interests of the *popolo grasso,* or the rich merchants and cloth manufacturers, it was consistently opposed by them. During the fourteenth century, the estimo became one of the main issues in the conflict between the oligarchy and the *popolo minuto,* that is, the artisans of the lesser gilds rather than the working class.[97] Depending upon the vicissitudes of this struggle for power and the needs for revenue, the estimo was alternately abolished and re-established; the government, however, relied as much as possible on indirect taxes, of which the incidence fell more heavily upon the poor.

Extraordinary expenses were financed by means of another device: the *prestanze,* or forced and voluntary loans. At first, such loans were secured by assignments on specific sources of revenue, but this method proved unsatisfactory, since it resulted in impounding future income. In November, 1342, the Duke of Athens (Walter de Brienne), who ruled Florence as dictator, found himself in such desperate straits that he cancelled all assignments in order to have the tax money flow into the public treasury instead of into the pockets of the state creditors.[98]

The floating debt had grown to such proportions that funding it appeared as the only solution. A law of December 29, 1343, ordered that all outstanding obligations be consolidated and entered into a ledger of the public debt. Within a few months, another decree declared that credits in this book would be transferable and entitle the beneficiary to interest at the rate of five percent. Thus the Monte Comune — literally "public fund" — came into existence between 1343 and 1345.[99] The theologians immediately began to quarrel over the point whether it was licit to receive interest on state loans and whether it was permissible to buy or sell stock in the Monte Comune.[100] The Franciscans said "yes," and the Dominicans and the Augustinians said "no." This controversy served only to trouble the conscience of overscrupulous persons, but did not prevent the rise of a market in Monte Comune stock, or in government bonds, as we would say today.

Everything went well for a few years. However, as the public debt grew, it became more and more difficult to pay interest punctually. As interest payments (*paghe*) were soon in arrears, they gave rise to a highly speculative market in overdue claims. As arrears accumulated, the price of the Monte Comune stock fell to 60 percent in 1427, 35 percent in 1431, and 20 percent in 1458.[101]

Matters were made worse by expedients used by the government in order to induce investors to lend money voluntarily. As early as 1358, three hundred florins in stock were offered for one hundred florins in cash to new subscribers, a device which raised the interest from 5

to 15 percent, in theory at least.[102] In 1362, the authorities again resorted to the same expedient in order to finance the war with Pisa.[103]
Peace was scarcely concluded when, in 1369, Florence became involved in
another campaign for the annexation of San Miniato al Tedesco. This
was a minor skirmish, however, and the money needed was easily raised:
instead of getting three to one, lenders received stock for money in the
proportion of only two to one. Thus originated the *Monte dell'uno tre*
and the *Monte dell'uno due,* which were merged with the old Monte in
1380.[104]

Of course, the Florentine government continued to rely on forced
loans when voluntary subscriptions were not forthcoming. Especially
in time of war, prestanze were numerous, sometimes several within the
same year. The popular poet, Antonio Pucci (c. 1310–1388), writing in a
satirical vein around 1373, even proclaims that there was one every
month.[105] The method of assessment varied in the course of time, but
followed more or less the precedent set by the estimo and was based on
property criteria. As the rules were arbitrary to a certain extent, they gave
rise to the usual grumblings about favoritism and injustice.

When, in 1390, war broke out anew with Milan, a law was passed to
allay this kind of criticism.[106] Individual quotas were set by commissioners in each ward, but this time elaborate rules were devised to insure fairness and to take into account ability to pay. Those assessed were
given the choice of paying the quota in full and receiving stock in the
Monte Comune (*animo rehabendi solvit*) or of paying only half and
giving up any further claim (*pro dimidia ad perdendum*).[107] This was
reintroducing the estimo through the back door.

In the beginning of the fifteenth century, the Florentine republic became involved in a succession of armed conflicts: the conquest of Pisa
(1404–1406), the war with Milan (1422–1428), and the unsuccessful
attempt to take Lucca (1429–1430) which brought about a second war
with Milan (1430–1433). These campaigns fought by greedy condottieri
and their mercenary troops required much money. The prolonged war
with Milan, especially, entailed a heavy drain on Florentine finances, so
that existing indirect taxes were by far insufficient to fill the deficit.[108]
To raise additional revenue became an unavoidable necessity. Despite the
oligarchy's aversion to direct taxes, Rinaldo degli Albizzi and the ruling
clique saw no other alternative than to propose the institution of the
catasto (1427).[109]

Whether the catasto should be regarded as a property tax or an income
tax may be a moot question, since it has some of the characteristics of
both. In contrast to the estimo which, as the name suggests, rested on an
estimate made by a board of assessors, the catasto, similar to modern
income taxes, was based on individual returns, called *portate,* which

were filed by the taxpayer with the tax collectors, or officials of the catasto.[110] The law required each head of a household to prepare a report listing all his property, real as well as personal, his stock in the Monte Comune, and all his business investments at home and abroad. In order to ascertain the income from such investments, the taxpayer was expected to add to his report a copy of the latest balance sheet or financial statement of each company or firm in which he was a partner.[111] Thus several balance sheets are still attached to the catasto reports of the Medici for 1427 and 1433.

There are in the Florentine archives thousands and thousands of portate neatly classified by quarter and gonfalone of the City. It is this collection, unique for the Middle Ages, which is such a precious source of information on all aspects of social and economic life. After having been examined and approved by the officials, the portate were transcribed with some abridgements in huge bound volumes called *campioni*. Most of them are still extant and are often more useful than the portate because they are easier to read and give the amount due by the taxpayer who made the return. The data recorded in the campioni were then summarized in the *sommario* which is merely a list giving the name of each taxpayer and the amount of his tax. There were originally separate summary volumes for each quarter of the city, but today only the set for the catasto of 1457 is complete.

The law of May 22, 1427, provided that returns were to be made every three years and that the amount due by each taxpayer was to be revised accordingly.[112] This provision was actually carried out in 1430 (second catasto) and in 1433 (third catasto). From then on, the rule was relaxed, perhaps because each catasto was such a tremendous job. A new revision was not made until 1442 (fourth catasto), followed by those of 1446 (fifth catasto), 1451 (sixth catasto), 1457 (seventh catasto), 1469–1470 (eighth catasto), and 1480–1481 (ninth and last catasto). The catasto was abolished in 1495, shortly after the fall of the Medici, and was replaced by the *decima*, which remained in force through the eighteenth century. In contrast to the catasto, the decima was a tax on real estate only and, consequently, excluded stock in the Monte Comune and investments in trade and industry.[113] This change in policy was motivated by the desire to encourage trade which, it was stated, should not be allowed to decline because the livelihood of so many people depended upon the flourishing state of business.[114]

As Niccolò Machiavelli (1469–1527) points out in his *History of Florence*, the catasto of 1427 was a great improvement over existing taxes, which were generally regressive.[115] The catasto had at least one virtue: it was based on ability to pay. True, it was still far from perfect because generous exemptions favored the rich. Thus, the taxpayer's dwelling was exempt from tax, even if this dwelling was a palace containing priceless art treasures, as was the case of the Medici.

According to Machiavelli, the tax reform of 1427 pleased the lower classes, but was obnoxious to the rich and the wealthy. The most bitter criticism, however, came from the business men. Their objections were several. Some of them have a surprisingly modern ring. Of course, in the eyes of the merchant class, it was utterly wrong to lay taxes on movable property "which people possess today and lose tomorrow." Such a tax, it was charged, discouraged initiative, cut down the volume of business, and caused flight of capital.[116] It also encouraged evasion, since frauds were difficult to detect and movable property, unlike immovables, could easily be concealed. In fact, Florentine merchants falsified their books in order to evade the catasto. One silk merchant, Andrea di Francesco Banchi (1372–1462), tampered with his accounts in order to make his investments appear less than they actually were.[117] In a secret record, his junior partner states ironically that the figures were juggled around "for the love of the catasto" (per amore del catasto). Finally, the Florentine merchants and manufacturers objected to the inquisitive nature of the tax and to showing their books for inspection to tax commissioners who might be competitors.

The law of 1427 established a flat rate of one-half percent of the total value of the taxpayer's property after making certain allowable deductions. The catasto would thus be a property tax. The taxable value, however, was not determined by assessment or appraisal, but by capitalizing real or assumed income on the basis of seven percent return per annum. For instance, in Tuscany, rents on farm land were often paid in kind according to a sharecropper system (mezzadria). For purposes of taxation, the money income was determined by using prices set by the tax officials for various farm products: wheat, wine, oats, olives, and so forth. This assumed income was then capitalized on the basis of seven percent, so that an income of 7 florins corresponded to a property value of 100 florins, 14 florins to 200 florins in property, and so on. The value of urban property was determined simply by capitalizing the money rent received by the landlord. The value of stock in the Monte Comune, however, was set by the tax officials, who were guided by current market prices. The tax on business, at least in 1427, was based on invested capital plus accrued profits.[118]

The total value of the taxpayer's property, determined by the above rules, was called sostanze. From this figure, the taxpayer was then allowed certain deductions (detrazioni) for debts, charges (carichi), and 200 florins per mouth (bocca) for each member of his household, excluding servants and slaves.[119] The remainder represented the taxpayer's taxable wealth (sovrabbondante). In 1427 it was taxable at the uniform rate of one-half percent. In addition, there was a head tax (*testa*) varying from 2*s.* to 6*s. a oro* for each male between the ages of eighteen and sixty.[120]

Those who had no sovrabbondante were nevertheless taxed by agreement by the catasto officials. Such taxpayers were not among the wealthy or even the well-to-do and rarely paid more than one florin. People who owned no property at all, lived on their wages, and were afflicted with large families, were classified as paupers and paid no tax. About one third of the Florentine population was in this category. Incidentally, poor weavers had to report their looms because it was an investment in productive equipment.

The catasto law of 1427 with regard to rates and exemptions remained practically unchanged until 1480. It seems, however, that business investments were recorded separately in 1442 and 1446.

Table 1 is based on the return made out by Cosimo di Giovanni de' Medici for the seventh catasto of 1457. At that time, the household of Cosimo included his spouse (Madonna Contessina), his two sons (Piero

TABLE 1. TAX DUE FROM COSIMO DE' MEDICI AND PIERFRANCESCO, HIS NEPHEW, ACCORDING TO THEIR RETURN FOR THE CATASTO OF 1457

	f.	s.	d.
Total value of real estate excluding the two palaces in via Larga, the villas of Careggi, Cafaggiolo, and Trebbio, and the houses in Pisa and Milan.	59,741	18	8
Four slaves.	120	0	0
Stock in Monte Comune or in the public debt.	8,569	8	0
Business investments.	54,238	8	0
Total of assets (sostanze).	122,669	14	8

	f.	s.	d.		f.	s.	d.
Deductions (detrazioni):							
Five percent for administrative expense on value of real estate, viz. f. 59,700.	2,985	0	0				
120 pairs of oxen $\left(\dfrac{120 \times 100}{7}\right)$.	1,714	5	8*				
Fourteen mouths (bocche) at f. 200.	2,800	0	0		7,499	5	8
Taxable wealth (sovrabbondante).					115,170	9	0

	f.	s.	d.
Computation of tax:			
One-half percent on sovrabbondante.	575	17	1
Three heads (teste) — Piero, Giovanni, and Pierfrancesco.		18	0
Amount of tax.	576	15	1

* The catasto laws allowed a deduction of one florin annual income for each pair of oxen used to cultivate farmland. Canestrini, *L'arte di stato*, p. 172.

Source: ASF, Mediceo avanti il Principato, filza 82, fols. 559–597.

and Giovanni), his nephew (Pierfrancesco), and their wives and children, in all fourteen members of the family. Cosimo stated that counting retainers, servants, nurses, and tutors, he had about fifty mouths to feed every day, but he was allowed deductions for his immediate family only. As the table indicates, his taxable wealth amounted to 115,170 florins, on which he paid the flat rate of one-half percent. In addition he paid a tax per capita of 6s. *a oro* for the three males (Piero and Giovanni di Cosimo, and Pierfrancesco di Lorenzo) between the ages of eighteen and sixty. He himself, having reached the age of seventy, was exempt from this tax. Cosimo filed a joint return because the family estate was still partly undivided between himself and his nephew, the only surviving son of his brother Lorenzo.[121]

The catasto up to 1481 was a proportional tax to the extent that it was computed at a uniform rate. In any case, the reports of the Medici show that the tax rate in 1469–1470 for the eighth catasto was still one-half percent on the sovrabbondante, since Lorenzo the Magnificent, whose father had just died, was taxed f.332 5s. 4d. di suggello on 66,452 florins.[122] After several adjustments, his tax was finally reduced to f.253 15s. 2d. Lorenzo's cousin, Pierfrancesco, paid f.225 6s. 6d. di suggello on a *valsente* (taxable wealth) of 45,065 florins, also one-half percent.[123] Since this is a moderate rate, the catasto would not have been a heavy burden, if it had been collected only once a year. Unfortunately, it happened regularly that it was levied twice in the same year and sometimes more often in times of emergency.[124]

Prior to 1481, the principle of progressive taxation was not applied to the catasto, but it was not unknown. The Florentine authorities had tried it out in connection with two extraordinary levies: the *graziosa* of 1443 and the *dispiacente* of 1447.[125] In 1480, it was decided to extend progression to the catasto. After several changes, the progressive scale given in Table 2 was finally adopted in November, 1481. From the portata of Lorenzo the Magnificent for the catasto of 1480–1481 (Table 3), it appears that the tax was still based on the valsente, or the total amount of the taxpayer's assumed wealth. For tax purposes, annual income was computed by taking seven percent of this total. The progressive rate of 22 percent was then applied to the *whole* of this fictitious income and hence did not go up bracket by bracket as is true today of the income tax in the United States of America.[126]

Tax rates in fifteenth-century Florence were by no means low. According to the historian Giuseppe Canestrini, the graduated catasto was collected thrice between December, 1481 and August, 1482.[127] Since the rate was 22 percent in the highest bracket, the total levied in less than one year was 66 percent of taxable income. True, this taxable income was fictitious and much below real income. Nevertheless, the burden was

TABLE 2. Progressive Scale of the Catasto of 1481

Taxable Income	Rate in Percent
Below f. 50	7.0
From f. 50 up to f. 75	8.0
From f. 75 up to f. 100	11.5
From f. 100 up to f. 150	14.0
From f. 150 up to f. 200	16.0
From f. 200 up to f. 250	18.0
From f. 250 up to f. 300	20.0
From f. 300 up to f. 400	21.0
F. 400 and above	22.0

Source: Giuseppe Canestrini, *La scienza e l'arte di stato* (Florence, 1862), p. 235.

great and one can understand why the progressive catasto was even more hated by the well-to-do than the proportional tax in force before 1481. As a result, the catasto was abolished as soon as the Medici were expelled in 1494. Perhaps this experiment with progressive taxation was premature. It is remarkable anyhow that the Florentine catasto of the fifteenth century has so many traits in common with modern income taxes.

The catasto records shed an interesting light on the distribution of wealth and the financial and social status of different families who either had connections with the Medici or were their rivals in politics and in business. In 1427 the Medici were not yet the richest family in Florence. Giovanni di Bicci was only third on the list; he was surpassed by the two Panciatichi brothers, heirs of Messer Bartolomeo, and by Messer Palla di Nofri Strozzi (1372–1462), the banker and humanist who was later exiled by Cosimo.[128] Thirty years later, in 1457, the catasto records reveal, the Medici were far ahead of any rivals and paid the highest tax in the city of Florence. A comparison of different lists discloses also that some families were getting richer and richer while others were going downhill. As today, there was sometimes a great disparity in wealth between different branches of the same family or even between close relatives. The Medici family was no exception to the rule; it included branches which were well off — if not as rich as the descendants of Giovanni di Bicci — and others which possessed only moderate means or were even classified as paupers. This was the case of the children and grandchildren of Messer Vieri di Cambio de' Medici, who through ill-management were reduced to such poverty that they petitioned for remission of their catasto tax. The celebrated Florentine statesman, Niccolò di Giovanni da Uzzano, who was among the wealthiest citizens of Florence, supported, according to his catasto report, not only the

TABLE 3. Tax Paid by Lorenzo the Magnificent According to the
Catasto of 1481

	f	s	d
Total of valsente (property)................................	57,930	7	4
Less: five percent for administration........................	2,896	10	10
Net amount of valsente.........	55,033	16	6

	f.	s.	d.
Annual income: 7 percent on f. 55,033 16s. 6d.................	3,852	11	4
Deduct: extraordinary charges..............................	1,500	0	0
Taxable income...............	2,352	11	4

	f.	s.	d.
Tax: 22 percent according to scale (Table 2) on f. 2,352 11s. 4d...	517	11	8

Source: ASF, Catasto of 1481, No. 1,016, fol. 476ᵛ, Portata of Lorenzo de' Medici.

impoverished widow, but also the illegitimate daughter, of his brother Agnolo, apparently a ne'er-do-well who had squandered a fortune on wine, women, and song.[129]

Statistical analysis of the catasto data reveals that the distribution of

TABLE 4. Distribution of Taxpaying Households According to the
Florentine Catasto of 1457

	Unadjusted			Adjusted		
Amount of Tax	House-holds	Per-cent of Total	Cumu-lative Per-cent	House-holds	Per-cent of Total	Cumu-lative Per-cent
Paupers (*Miserabili*).............	.....	.....	.....	3,000	28.21	28.21
Below 5 *soldi*...................	3,753	49.15	49.15	3,753	35.29	63.50
From 5 *soldi* up to 10 *soldi*........	1,148	15.03	64.18	1,148	10.80	74.30
From 10 *soldi* up to 1 florin......	819	10.73	74.91	819	7.70	82.00
From 1 florin up to 2 florins......	661	8.66	83.57	661	6.21	88.21
From 2 florins up to 3 florins.....	330	4.32	87.89	330	3.10	91.31
From 3 florins up to 5 florins.....	381	4.99	92.88	381	3.58	94.89
From 5 florins up to 10 florins....	317	4.15	97.03	317	2.98	97.87
From 10 florins up to 20 florins...	165	2.16	99.19	165	1.55	99.42
From 20 florins up to 50 florins...	51	0.66	99.85	51	0.48	99.90
From 50 florins up to 100 florins..	8	0.11	99.96	8	0.07	99.97
One hundred florins and above...	3	0.04	100.00	3	0.03	100.00
Total........	7,636	100.00		10,636	100.00	

Source: ASF, Catasto Nos. 834–837, Sommario del 1457–1458.

wealth was very unequal and that the number of rich represented a small fraction of the total population. In 1457, the only year for which the summary lists are complete, there were 7,636 households. This figure naturally does not include the clergy, regular and secular, and the unknown number of paupers who did not contribute. This number may be set fairly safely at about 3,000 families, since we know from the 1427 catasto that it included a total of 10,171 returns, of which 2,924 were those of paupers.[130] If we consider as poor those who paid no tax or less than one florin, this category includes 82 percent of the households. The so-called "middle classes," paying from one up to ten florins, are themselves a small minority (less than 16 percent of the aggregate number of households). The rich, whose tax was 10 florins or more, number only 2.13 percent of the total population. If one rejects the above figure of 3,000 paupers, the percentages of the unadjusted data are different, but the general picture remains much the same. The rich still were only a tiny segment among the Florentine citizenry.

According to the sommario of 1457, only 227 households paid more than 10 florins (Table 4). In 1427, there were 200 households paying 25 florins or more.[131] This discrepancy is easily explained by the fact that assessments were generally higher in 1427 than in 1457, probably because of a change in the methods of valuation. At any rate, in 1457, there were only three households with a quota exceeding 100 florins (Tables 4 and 5). The Medici were far ahead of any others. Next came the heirs of Giovanni d'Amerigo Benci, who had been the Medici's general manager, and third, Giovanni di Paolo Rucellai, the banker, who employed Leo Battista degli Alberti (1404–1472) to build the famous palace and loggia in the via della Vigna Nuova and the façade of Santa Maria Novella.

There are only eight families in the next group paying from 50 florins up to 100 florins. It includes two Pazzi households, Jacopo di Messer Andrea and the sons of his brother Antonio. Their combined wealth exceeded perhaps that of any other family in Florence except the Medici. The Pazzi were thus the Medici's closest rivals. Perhaps it explains why one family would try to undo the other. The Strozzi do not appear on the list because they were living in exile. As for the Quaratesi, they were primarily large landowners and had little interest in business. Near the bottom of the list we find the name of Andrea Banchi, a silk manufacturer. In 1457, he was a very old man — he died a nonagenarian in 1462, without male heirs — and did not belong to a prominent family. Because of cunning and superior business ability, he had prospered and made a fortune. It is certain that he cheated the tax authorities and should have paid a much higher sum.[132] The Capponi were not very active in 1457;

TABLE 5.   List of the Taxpayers Who Paid More Than 50 Florins
According to the 1457 Catasto

	f.	s.	d.
1. Cosimo di Giovanni and Pierfrancesco de' Medici............	576	15	1
2. Heirs of Giovanni d'Amerigo Benci........................	132	10	8
3. Giovanni di Paolo Rucellai..............................	102	17	2
4. Castello di Piero Quaratesi.............................	98	12	0
5. Tanai di Francesco Nerli...............................	88	18	1
6. Jacopo di Messer Andrea dei Pazzi........................	84	3	7
7. Andrea di Lapo Guardi.................................	70	11	9
8. Gino di Neri di Gino di Neri Capponi....................	63	18	4
9. Jacopo di Piero Baroncelli	60	10	9
10. Andrea di Francesco Banchi.............................	54	4	8
11. Sons of Antonio di Messer Andrea dei Pazzi................	51	15	10
Total........	1,384	17	11

Source: Same as Table 4.

it was only after 1470 that their bank in Lyons became a dangerous
competitor of the Medici branch in the same city.[133]

However interesting a more exhaustive treatment of the catasto might
be, it lies beyond the scope of this study. Without going more deeply
into the matter, a few words needed to be said about the Florentine tax
system because there will be frequent occasion to refer to data taken from
catasto reports of the Medici, their partners, their factors, or their competitors.

4. Monetary Systems Used in the Medici Records

Another topic which calls for a few introductory remarks is money.
This is an intricate matter, but it can be greatly simplified by dealing
with only a few of the essential characteristics of the Florentine monetary
system and the foreign currencies frequently mentioned in the Medici
records.

In the fifteenth century, Florence was on a double standard: one based
on gold and the other on silver. The first was pegged onto the florin, a
gold coin so called because it bore on one side the emblem of the fleur-
de-lis. The silver currency (*moneta di piccioli*) was made up of small
pennies (*piccioli*) and later *quattrini,* pieces of four deniers *di piccioli.*
Complications arose from the fact that there was no fixed relation between the two systems because the rate of the florin was allowed to
fluctuate up and down in accordance with market conditions. In general,
the trend was upward so that the florin, first issued at one pound di
piccioli in 1252, was worth £7 di piccioli by 1500.[134] This rise was chiefly

due to the steady deterioration of the silver currency whereas the florin remained relatively stable in gold content.

According to law, only the international merchants of the Calimala Gild, the money-changers, the cloth and silk manufacturers, the grocers, and the furriers were allowed to transact their business and to keep their books in florins. All others, retailers and artificers, were expected to deal and to reckon in petty silver currency (moneta di piccioli).[135] Wages were paid in the same money: since employers controlled the government, it happened from time to time that they exerted pressure on the monetary authorities to debase the silver currency in order to lower real wages without touching nominal wages, a practice condemned by San Antonino, archbishop of Florence (1389–1459).[136] The existence of two rival currencies, of course, created a steady demand for the services of the money-changers, who, for a commission, exchanged florins for piccioli or vice versa. With the exception of Venice, this monetary system was without analogy in Europe.

When first issued in 1252, the florin weighed 3.53 grams or 72 grains, since 96 florins were coined out of a Florentine pound of 339 grams or 6,912 grains. The florin was 24 carats fine, although this fineness was never achieved in practice due to technical difficulties in completely removing impurities.

In order to prevent clipping and abrasion, it became customary to circulate the gold florins in small leather bags sealed by the mint, whence the name of *fiorini di suggello*. This practice is already mentioned in a regulation made in the year 1299 by the Money-changers Gild which threatened with heavy penalties any member who would fraudulently utter sealed bags containing light or counterfeit florins.[137] Despite these precautions, it proved impossible to maintain the standard set in 1252, presumably because the authorities failed to prevent the circulation of base florins issued by foreign mints. As a result, the fiorino di suggello ceased after 1321, if not earlier, to have its full weight of 72 grains. Not until 1433 did the Florentine government readopt the old standard by issuing the *fiorino largo* (large florin), which was 10 percent better than the current fiorini di suggello.[138] Within a few years, this premium rose to 20 percent, so that five *fiorini larghi* were equal to six fiorini di suggello.

On December 12, 1464, this exchange ratio was legalized, and it was decreed that all payments connected with dowries, real estate, bills of exchange, and bank deposits were to be made in *fiorini larghi* of just weight and fineness.[139] A subsequent law of October 22, 1471, abolished the fiorino di suggello altogether and prescribed henceforth the exclusive use of the fiorino largo as the monetary unit for all mercantile transactions customarily settled in gold and not in moneta di piccioli.[140]

In Florence, during the fourteenth century, a popular money of account was the pound *affiorino* or *a fiorini*. Like all moneys of account, this pound was not represented in circulation by any real coin, but was reckoned at twenty twenty-ninths of a florin. The pound affiorino, like the English pound, was divided into 20 *soldi*, shillings, or sous affiorino of 12 deniers affiorino each. The florin was consequently divided into 29 soldi affiorino or 348 deniers affiorino. This is the monetary system found in the libri segreti of the Medici Bank which extend from 1397 to 1450. Sometimes the florin was also divided into 20 *soldi a oro* or sous subdivided into 12 deniers *a oro*. This division became more and more popular after the introduction of the fiorino largo around 1450. The gold florin, of course, was a real coin, but its fractions, the sous and the deniers, were moneys of account, not existing in actual circulation. To put the matter even more succinctly, the Florentine monetary system can be reduced to the following set of equations:

GOLD

$$1 \text{ florin} = 20 \text{ soldi a oro} = 240 \text{ deniers a oro}$$
$$1 \text{ florin} = 29 \text{ soldi affiorino} = 348 \text{ deniers affiorino}$$
$$£1 \text{ affiorino} = 20 \text{ soldi affiorino} = 240 \text{ deniers affiorino}$$
$$20 \text{ florins} = £29 \text{ affiorino}$$

SILVER

$$£1 \text{ di piccioli} = 20 \text{ soldi di piccioli} = 240 \text{ deniers di piccioli}$$

As already pointed out, the two standards, gold and silver, were independent of each other and, as a result, gave rise to two different price systems. In general, wholesale prices were quoted in florins and fractions of the florin, but wages and retail prices were set in piccioli. Bankers, like the Medici, reckoned and kept their books in florins. They rarely used piccioli except in small transactions. In contrast to the bimetallic standard in use during the nineteenth century, there was in medieval and Renaissance Florence no fixed legal ratio between gold and silver. A florin was not always worth the same number of piccioli, because the rate went up and down — mostly up — and varied sometimes from month to month or from day to day.

In the Middle Ages, the pound system, which still survives today in Great Britain, was used nearly everywhere in Western Europe with the exception of Spain, Portugal, and Germany. Of course, the pounds differed in name as well as in value from country to country. One should not be mistaken for another. In the same way, one has to distinguish today between Belgian, French, and Swiss francs. Although they are all called francs, they are three different currencies which vary widely in value. Once upon a time, before 1914, they had the same value, but they have parted company since the outbreak of the first World War.

The English pound was, of course, the pound sterling which is still in use at the present time. In Flanders, the merchants favored the pound groat (Ital. *lira di grossi,* Fr. *livre de gros,* Flem.-Dutch *pond grooten Vlaamsch*) which was based on the groat (*grosso, gros, groot*), a small silver coin. This pound groat must not be confused with the Venetian pound groat (also called lira di grossi in the Medici account books) of ten ducats, which throughout the fifteenth century was worth twice as much as the Flemish pound. Moreover, it was anchored to the gold ducat instead of resting on a silver coin. In Milan there was the pound of 240 *imperiali* which was much smaller than any of the preceding pounds because of the steady depreciation of the silver imperiale to which it was pegged. A more complicated situation arose in Geneva where the monetary unit was not the pound, but the écu. The standard symbol representing this unit was an inverted triangle, thus ∇. Unfortunately, a matter which tends to create confusion, there were two kinds of écus, those of 64 and those of 66 to the gold mark. When the fairs of Geneva were moved to Lyons, the two écus went along. The Geneva branch of the Medici, transferred to Lyons in 1466, kept its books in écus of 64 to the mark. The Avignon branch reckoned in *fiorini pitetti* which were lighter than the fiorini di suggello and were worth 24 soldi of 12 deniers each, so that the florin of Avignon contained 288 deniers instead of the customary 240. The Medici branch at the Court of Rome kept accounts in cameral florins or *fiorini di camera* divided for convenience into 20 imaginary soldi of 12 deniers apiece. The Medici had no branches in Genoa or Barcelona, but the merchants in those two cities used the pound: the Genoese pound or *lira genovese* in Genoa and the Barcelonese pound or *lira di barcellonesi* in Barcelona. In Genoa, exchange rates were sometimes quoted on the basis of an imaginary florin of 25s. genovesi, or 25s. Genoese currency.

For the purposes of this study, there is no need to go deeper into this matter of currency, to deal with other complications, or to discuss monetary policy. To avoid confusion, it will suffice for the reader to be acquainted with the moneys of account and the monetary systems used in the records of the Medici and other merchants of the fifteenth century.

III

THE ANTECEDENTS AND THE EARLY YEARS OF THE MEDICI BANK UNDER THE MANAGEMENT OF GIOVANNI DI BICCI, 1397–1429

Until recently nothing was known about the antecedents of the Medici Bank. Historians were at a loss to explain its sudden appearance as a leading banking house in the early years of the fifteenth century, since none of the direct ancestors of Giovanni di Bicci (1360–1429), the founder of the Medici Bank, are recorded as bankers or as members of the Arte del Cambio. Their fortune was not conspicuously large and was chiefly invested in rural property in the Mugello (a region in the Apennines in the direction of Bologna) whence the Medici came.

When Giovanni's father, Averardo *detto* (known as) Bicci, died from the plague in 1363, he made a few small bequests and set aside £50 di piccioli (about $140) for restitution of ill-gotten gains.[1] After restoring his wife's dowry of 800 florins, he left all his remaining property to be divided equally among his five sons: Matteo, Francesco, Michele, Giovanni, and Paolo. On August 13, 1384, when his widow, Giacoma Spini, made her own testament, her principal heirs were also these five sons. There is nowhere any evidence that Averardo detto Bicci was a prominent or even a moderately successful business man.

Historians have failed to focus their attention on a distant cousin, Messer Vieri di Cambio (or Cambiozzo) de' Medici (1323–1395) who became, after 1370, one of the leading Florentine bankers. This man is important because there is no longer any doubt that the Medici Bank founded by Giovanni di Bicci was an offshoot of Messer Vieri's banking house.[2] Both Giovanni and his elder brother Francesco were employed by this firm and rose from apprentices to factors and then to partners.[3]

Messer Vieri di Cambio de' Medici did not, like his distant cousins, belong to the Cafaggiolo or Averardo branch of the family but to another line stemming from Lippo di Chiarissimo. Another representative of this line is Salvestro di Messer Alamanno, Vieri's first cousin, who played such a conspicuous rôle in the *Ciompi* revolt (1378). Vieri was one of the few Medici ever to accede to knighthood.[4]

In 1348 Vieri di Cambio was enrolled as a member of the Arte del Cambio.[5] He stayed in the banking business for over forty years, forming a succession of partnerships and gradually extending the scope of his business.[6] It comprised trade as well as banking, since in 1369 "Vieri di Cambio de' Medici & Co." is listed among the Florentine houses shipping goods through Pisan territory.[7] By 1385, the firm, Vieri de' Medici and Jacopo di Francesco Venturi, even had a Venetian branch, which dealt in foreign bills and had correspondents along the Dalmatian coast, in Zara where its representative was Paolo di Berto Grassini.[8]

According to the records of the Arte del Cambio, it was not until 1382 that Francesco di Bicci de' Medici (c. 1350–1412) was admitted as a junior partner.[9] Vieri's other partners were at this time: Niccolò di Riccardo Fagni or del Maestro Fagno, Giovanni di Arrigo Rinaldeschi da Prato, and Jacopo di Francesco Venturi.[10] Within eight years, Francesco di Bicci de' Medici rose to the rank of senior partner, since a bill of July 4, 1390, extant in the Datini archives, is made out in favor of "Messer Vieri e Francesco de' Medici" in Genoa, a suggestion that Vieri's bank had branches all over Italy.[11] In addition to those in Venice and Genoa, it had one in Rome. From 1385, the manager of this establishment was Giovanni di Bicci (1360–1429), Francesco's younger brother, the same person who later founded the Medici Bank and became the ancestor of the ruling Medici.[12]

Undoubtedly, the Rome branch was set up as a separate partnership in which Giovanni di Bicci participated as junior partner and branch manager, according to the pattern later adopted by his own bank. Perhaps he invested the dowry of 1,500 florins which his wife, Piccarda Bueri, brought him in October 1385.[13] From 1386 to 1393, that partnership was known under the style of "Vieri e Giovanni de' Medici in Roma." The evidence is conclusive, since this is the style used in signing five letters in 1392 to Francesco Datini's offices in Florence, Pisa, and Genoa.[14]

Giovanni di Bicci's association with Vieri di Cambio came to an end in 1393 at the latest. From then on, the letters extant in the Datini archives, which were dispatched by the Medici Bank in Rome, omit Vieri's name and bear the signature: "Giovanni de' Medici e compagni in Roma." It is probable that Vieri retired from business because of ill-health, since he was over seventy and died within two years (September 13, 1395). An entry in the first libro segreto, begun in 1397, confirms that Giovanni di Bicci, when establishing his own firm, was forced to take over all the assets and liabilities of "Messer Veri e compagni" (his partnership with Vieri) including a number of bad debts.[15] The new partnership in Giovanni's own name included as junior partner Benedetto di Lippaccio de' Bardi, later to become general manager of the Medici Bank.

Messer Vieri di Cambio's bank, upon its dissolution in 1391 or 1392, split into three independent units. The first was a firm established by

Vieri's nephew, Antonio di Giovanni di Cambio de' Medici (d. 1397) with Jacopo di Francesco Venturi and Giovanni di Salvestro as partners. It did not exist for long and the records of the Money-changers' Gild cease to mention it after 1395.[16] The second was the bank founded by Francesco di Bicci in the name of his son Averardo di Francesco (c. 1372–1434).[17] This firm, although not as powerful as Giovanni di Bicci's bank, lasted for quite a number of years and went out of existence only in 1443, long after Averardo's death. The third was located in Rome and operated by Giovanni di Bicci, Francesco's younger brother. It is this third bank which became so famous in the annals of history.

Although Vieri di Cambio de' Medici was old when he retired in 1393, his two sons, Niccola (1385–1454) and Cambiozzo or Cambio (1392–1463), were still boys and much too young to succeed him in the conduct of the business. This explains why Vieri, when he felt his health failing, was compelled to sell out to distant relatives instead of bringing in his own sons. Niccola and Cambio later went into partnership and established a banking house of their own with offices in Florence and Rome. Owing to their incompetence, this firm failed to thrive.[18] By 1433, the two brothers had sold most of their real estate in order to extinguish the liabilities of their bank.[19] They and their descendants were reduced to poverty and fell into oblivion. When, in 1438, the young Giovanni di Cosimo de' Medici (1421–1463) was serving his apprenticeship in Ferrara, in that year the temporary seat of the papal court, his tutor, ser Giovanni d'Ottaviano Caffarecci from Volterra, urged him to apply himself earnestly to his job and reminded him of the fate of Niccola and Cambio di Messer Vieri, who had lost their father's fortune because of their inexperience and ignorance in business matters.[20]

Historians — even Italians — often confuse the Medici Bank founded by Giovanni di Bicci with the rival institution managed by his nephew, Averardo di Francesco di Bicci. In fact, they were separate entities, although they cooperated closely from 1393 to 1397, when Giovanni di Bicci, by transferring his headquarters from Rome to Florence made himself entirely independent of his nephew's banking house. In order to avoid further confusion, it may be desirable to introduce a digression and to deal briefly with the history of Averardo's bank, which did not disappear until 1443, when the line descending from Francesco di Bicci died out.

Information about the activities of this firm is readily available because a fragment of its ledger covering the year 1395, Florentine style, that is, from March 25, 1395, through March 24, 1396, has survived by chance in the Florentine Archives.[21] Some have thought this fragment belongs to Giovanni's bank, but it really pertains to Averardo's.[22] Although the matter has been questioned, there is little doubt that the account book in question was kept according to all canons of double entry.[23] It reveals that the firm of Averardo di Francesco de' Medici was engaged in international as well as in local banking and dealt extensively in bills of exchange. It also traded in wool and other commodities and underwrote marine insurance, but exchange dealings predominated.[24]

At first, Averardo was represented in Rome by "Giovanni de' Medici e Co.," that is, by his uncle's firm. In the extant fragment of the ledger, there are even two accounts open to Giovanni di Bicci in Rome: an account *per noi* and an account *per loro*.[25] Since they are by far the most active as described in the surviving fragment, it is safe to conclude that the two Medici banks, the uncle's and the nephew's, worked hand in hand instead of being competitors. Of course, this relationship changed somewhat after Giovanni di Bicci established his own bank in Florence (1397) and no longer needed the services of his nephew's firm. Besides Rome, Averardo's company had, in 1395, correspondents located in most of the principal trading and banking centers of medieval Europe. All these correspondents were, of course, Florentine business houses with the possible exception of Paolo di ser Amato & Co. in Perugia.

Since the papal court was such an important source of funds, Averardo de' Medici decided to counter his uncle's move by opening a branch in Rome and diverting some of the deposits to his own bank. It is uncertain when this decision was taken, but such a branch existed in 1411 and was managed by Andrea di Lippaccio de' Bardi (d. 1433), who had been in the service of Averardo de' Medici since 1402 or earlier.[26] This Rome branch was not in Averardo's name but was styled "Andrea de' Bardi & Co." Perhaps it is worth mentioning that Andrea di Lippaccio was the brother of Benedetto and Ilarione di Lippaccio de' Bardi who, as we shall see later, were, in succession, general managers of Giovanni di Bicci's bank. From 1422 onward, Averardo's Rome branch was doing business under the name of "Francesco di Giachinotto Boscoli & Company." In managing his branch, Boscoli was assisted by two junior partners: Andrea di Guglielmino de' Pazzi and Averardo's own son, Giuliano de' Medici. Strange as it may be, no *corpo* (capital) was assigned to the Rome branch; perhaps this was deemed unnecessary, since the papal court was seeking to invest rather than to borrow. According to Averardo's report for the catasto of 1427, the Rome branch was not doing so well and was about breaking even. Perhaps this statement should be discounted, because its purpose was to evade taxation.[27]

Unlike Giovanni di Bicci's bank, Averardo di Francesco's never sought to expand beyond the Alps, but from 1420 onward it had an office in Pisa and branches in Spain — one in Barcelona and another in Valencia.[28] The latter were in the form of *accomandite* (limited partnerships) in which the investing partners, in this case Averardo de' Medici and

1. Giovanni di Bicci de' Medici, founder of the Medici Bank

2. Page of Libro segreto No. 3, 1435–1450, folio 97 (debit side), handwriting of Giovanni Benci, General Manager of the Bank

Bardo di Francesco di Messer Alessandro de' Bardi, assumed responsibility only up to the amount of their original investment.[29] During this period, both Medici banks chose their factors and partners as much as possible from among the Medici and Bardi families. For example, after 1426, Fantino di Fantino de' Medici, who had left the service of Giovanni di Bicci, was hired by Averardo to head his Barcelona office.[30]

In the political sphere, Averardo di Francesco de' Medici was a staunch supporter of his family's faction and was exiled in 1433 at the same time as his first cousins, Cosimo and Lorenzo di Giovanni de' Medici. He returned to Florence after their recall in October 1434, but he was so ill that he made his last will and testament on November 22 and died on December 5, 1434. His son Giuliano died on June 19, 1436, and his grandson Francesco, on February 20, 1443.[31] With the latter's death, the branch descending from Francesco di Bicci became extinct, and all its property in the Mugello, which was extensive and included the fortified villa of Cafaggiolo, reverted to Cosimo and his nephew, Pierfrancesco di Lorenzo.[32]

These paragraphs dealing with Averardo's bank and career may be less digressive than it appears. Besides clearing up the existing confusion, they show that, while the two rival Medici banks competed to a certain extent, they cooperated in other areas where their services did not overlap.

In 1393, as stated above, Giovanni di Bicci de' Medici (1360–1429) took over Messer Vieri's Rome branch, of which he had been manager for several years. For this purpose, he entered into partnership with Benedetto di Lippaccio de' Bardi (1373–1420), a young man of great promise and executive ability. Although Giovanni di Bicci thus became independent, he continued to operate in combination with his nephew, Averardo di Francesco, and to act as the latter's correspondent in Rome. This connection continued until October 1, 1397, when Giovanni transferred his headquarters to Florence, his home city. It is, therefore, reasonable to consider 1397, rather than 1393, as the founding date of the famous Medici Bank.

The gild records reveal that Giovanni di Bicci, upon moving from Rome to Florence, formed a partnership with Benedetto de' Bardi, who remained in charge of the branch at the Curia, and Gentile di Baldassare Buoni (1371–1427), who gave up a business in Pisa to join the new firm.[33] According to the libro segreto of the Medici Bank, the initial capital was 10,000 florins, of which over 50 percent (5,500 florins) was supplied by Giovanni di Bicci and the remainder, by his two partners (2,000 by Benedetto de' Bardi and 2,500 by Gentile Buoni).[34] This partnership did not last for more than a few months, either because Gentile failed to supply his share or because he and Giovanni were

TABLE 6. Correspondents of the Firm Averardo di Francesco de' Medici
in 1395

Place	Name of Correspondent
Avignon	Francesco Benini e Niccolao di Bonaccorso
Barcelona	Antonio di Guccio e Falduccio di Lombardo
Bologna	Filippo Guidotti
Bruges	Giovanni di Jacopo Orlandini e Piero Benizi & Co.
Gaëta	Agostino Bartolini
	Antonio di Jacopo e Doffo Spini & Co.
	Filippo di Michele & Co.
Genoa	Ruggiero di Messer Giovanni de' Ricci e Mainardo Bonciani & Co.
London	Bernardo di Giorgio de' Bardi
Montpellier	Deo Ambruogi e Giovanni Franceschi
Paris	Paolo Ramaglarti e Jacopo Ginocchi & Co.
Perugia	Paolo di ser Amato & Co., *cambiatori* (money-changers)
Pisa	Lorenzo di Cione del Buono e Gentile di Baldassare Buoni & Co.
Rome	Giovanni di Bicci de' Medici & Co.
Siena	Tommaso di Cecco & Co.
Venice	Antonio Dietifeci*
	Nanni e Bonifazio Gozzadini & Co.

* Giovanni d'Adoardo Portinari was with this firm from 1384 onward.
Source: ASF, MAP, filza 133, no. 1.

unable to get along together. Perhaps Giovanni de' Medici made a wise
decision in severing his connection with Gentile. The latter, as his subsequent career shows, did not have the making of a successful business
man. He died destitute in 1427 after having been imprisoned for debt at
the request of Messer Palla di Nofri Strozzi.[35] In any case, the gild
records disclose that, in 1398 and 1399, Benedetto de' Bardi was Giovanni
di Bicci's sole partner.[36]

Giovanni de' Medici was already a member of the Arte del Cambio,
having enrolled in 1386, but his partner, Benedetto di Lippaccio was not
matriculated, as is clearly stated in 1397 in the gild's Libro di compagnie.[37] In accordance with prevailing regulations, Benedetto was required
to join the gild because he was now a partner in Florence as well as in
Rome. Instead of appearing in person before the gild officials, he appointed Giovanni di Bicci as his proxy and was sworn in as a member on
February 25, 1398 (New style; henceforth N.S.)[38]

No record throws any light on the motives which prompted Giovanni
di Bicci to transfer his headquarters from Rome to Florence, but it is
not difficult to hazard a guess. Whereas Rome was a source of funds,

Florence, as the principal banking center of Europe, perhaps offered better investment opportunities. In all likelihood, Giovanni di Bicci sought employment for surplus funds of his Rome branch by operating in the Florentine money market. It is also possible that he wanted personally to control the granting of credit or that his nephew Averardo did not give him satisfactory service.

As a result of the withdrawal of Gentile Buoni, the capital of the bank in Florence was reduced from 10,000 to 8,000 florins of which 6,000 florins were invested by Giovanni di Bicci and 2,000 florins by his one remaining partner, Benedetto di Lippaccio de' Bardi.[39] Profits during the first eighteen months of operation, from October 1, 1397 to March 24, 1399, were satisfactory but not spectacular. They amounted to f. 1,728 25s. 3d. affiorino. After paying 160 florins for accrued salaries and setting aside 368 florins 25s. 3d. affiorino for unpaid rent and bad debts, the balance of 1,200 florins di suggello was divided between the partners in proportion to invested capital: three fourths went to Giovanni di Bicci and one fourth to Benedetto di Lippaccio.[40] This is a net return of exactly 10 percent a year, by no means excessive in a period when banks paid from 7 to 8 percent, and sometimes even more, on time deposits.

Shortly after the opening of an office in Florence, the Medici Bank also tried to gain a foothold in Venice. In both cases the purpose was probably the same: to find suitable investment for loanable funds. At any rate, in the beginning of 1398 the Rome office sent one of its factors, Neri di Cipriano Tornaquinci, to explore possibilities in Venice. His mission was apparently successful and he stayed for four years, from 1398 through 1401, doing business as a salaried agent of the Medici Bank. In remuneration for his services, he was awarded 1,600 florins as both salary and special bonus.[41]

When a branch was established on March 25, 1402, Neri Tornaquinci became the first manager.[42] Unfortunately, he did not live up to expectations and made the fateful mistake of granting credit to Germans in violation of the partnership agreement.[43] The Germans defaulted and Neri Tornaquinci, to cover up the loss, borrowed money at 8 percent and reported fictitious profits. When these irregularities were discovered by the senior partners, Neri Tornaquinci was recalled and replaced as branch manager by Giovanni di Francesco da Gagliano (April 25, 1406).[44]

At first the corpo of the Venetian branch was set at 8,000 florins, Florentine currency, or 7,716 ducats, Venetian currency.[45] After a few months, Neri Tornaquinci put up an additional 1,000 florins.[46] Although he contributed only one ninth of the capital, he received one fourth of the profits, in order to reward him for his services.[47] Instead of paying a salary to branch managers, the Medici Bank made it a policy to give them a larger share of the profits than their investment would warrant. The remainder of the profits, or three fourths, went to the Medici Bank and was then divided in the usual proportion between its two partners, Giovanni di Bicci and Benedetto di Lippaccio.[48]

The economic policy of the Venetian Republic was to keep control of the carrying trade with the Levant. As long as foreigners stayed out of this field, they were welcome to do business in Venice. Neither did the Venetians object if foreign banks established branches in Venice, since such institutions brought in capital and thus favored the expansion of trade.

Florence, in the fourteenth and fifteenth centuries, was the seat of an important and prosperous woolen industry in which most of the leading families had an interest. As early as April 1, 1402, the Medici Bank decided to follow suit and to extend activities to manufacturing by financing a *bottega* (workshop) for the production of woolen cloth. The new firm was in the name of Cosimo, Giovanni's elder son, then only thirteen years old. He was certainly too young and too immature to take any part in the management. Though it may seem odd, it was a common practice in Florence to have the names of minors appear in the style of business firms. In all probability this custom was a survival of the feudal cult of the family. In case of bankruptcy, liability rested presumably with the real partners named in the articles of association. According to another Florentine custom, the Medici Bank provided 3,000 florins, certainly the major part of the capital, but the management of the bottega was entrusted to a specialist well acquainted with the problems of the cloth industry. His name was Michele di Baldo di ser Michele. It is not known whether he supplied any additional capital. Since he was entitled to half the profits, it is probable that he contributed something, perhaps 1,000 florins.[49]

In 1408 another partnership was formed for the making of cloth. It was called "Lorenzo di Giovanni de' Medici e Co., lanaiuoli," after Giovanni's second son, then aged thirteen. The capital of 4,000 florins was furnished entirely by the Medici Bank, but the burden of the management was assumed by Taddeo di Filippo, a man with expert knowledge of the woolen industry.[50]

In the course of time, the second bottega turned out to be more profitable than the first, undoubtedly because of superior management. What else would have made any difference? Although the records give only hints, Taddeo di Filippo and later his son Antonio were men who knew their business thoroughly. They served the Medici faithfully for many years and became well-to-do. The other bottega failed to show profits and was discontinued in 1420 to be resumed ten years later with a new management.[51]

The creation of the second woolshop in 1408 marks the close of the first period of expansion of the Medici Bank. For many years — until 1426 — no new branches or subsidiaries were added to those in existence. Besides headquarters in Florence, the bank included two branches outside the city, one in Venice and one in Rome, and two industrial establishments inside the walls. The Rome branch also had under its control offices in Naples and Gaëta (opened in 1400). The nature of their legal status is unfortunately not clear from the records. However, the Naples subbranch in 1415 became an *accomanda* (limited partnership), in which the Medici were the silent or dormant partners; accordingly, they were liable only to the extent of their initial investment.[52]

In 1402, aggregate capital invested in banking by Giovanni di Bicci and his partner probably amounted to 20,000 florins: 8,000 florins in Florence and also in Venice and only 4,000 florins in Rome. This total, of course, does not include the additional 1,000 florins supplied by Neri Tornaquinci as his share of the capital in Venice. Later there were constant changes in the capital structure, as each renewal of partnership agreements usually involved some rearrangements. Thus the capital of the Venetian branch was set at 8,000 ducats, or £800 groat Venetian currency, when a new contract was made in 1406 with Giovanni di Francesco da Gagliano. As usual, the Medici Bank supplied the major part, or 7,000 ducats, and the junior partner the balance of 1,000 ducats. Nevertheless, Giovanni di Francesco was entitled to one fourth of the profits, as if his share had been 2,000 ducats and that of his principals only 6,000 ducats, instead of 7,000. Throughout the existence of the Medici Bank, investment in local industry played a subordinate role. In 1408, it amounted to 7,000 florins: 3,000 florins tied up in one woolshop and 4,000 florins in the other.

It would be a grievous mistake to have an exaggerated idea of the size of medieval banks and to picture them as giant institutions doing business in office buildings with marble lobbies and rows of windows behind which a crowd of employees operate machines and manipulate papers. In reality medieval bankers transacted their business in small offices adorned with a bank, or counter, a few desks, and, in the rear, the abacus on which the bookkeeper made his computations by casting his counters. It was exceptional for more than half-a-dozen clerks to be working in such a countingroom. According to the entries in the libro segreto, the payroll of the Medici Bank on March 24, 1402 did not include more than seventeen names. Only five clerks were employed at headquarters in Florence, and the staffs of the branches were even smaller: four factors in Rome and in Venice and the same number in Naples and Gaëta combined (Table 7).

As one would expect, the Medici were not overly generous in paying their clerical staff and did not outbid competitors. Only two factors were very well paid. One was Neri di Cipriano Tornaquinci, the manager of the Venetian branch, about to be admitted as a partner. The *maggiori* (senior partners) were so pleased with his services that they granted him 1,600 florins for four years, which was in excess of the salary agreed upon. The other was Ilarione de' Bardi, who received 100 florins, but he was the brother of Benedetto, Giovanni di Bicci's partner and right hand. Four more factors earned 50 florins or more. A cashier, like Geremia di Francesco, although placed in a position of trust, did not make more than 40 florins a year. It is true that his salary was raised to 50 florins in 1403.[53] Beginners, presumably office boys, started at 20 florins a year.

Increases in salary and promotions depended of course a great deal on performance and were more or less rapid according to circumstances. For example, the salary of Giuliano di Giovanni di ser Matteo, a clerk

TABLE 7. Staff of the Medici Bank on March 24, 1402 (N.S.)

Place	Name of Clerk or Factor	Salary per Year florins
Florence	1. Antonio d'Agnolo dal Canto...................	60
	2. Giuliano di Giovanni di ser Matteo.............	48
	3. Geremia di Francesco (cashier).................	40
	4. Antonio di Talento de' Medici.................	25
	5. Giovanni or Nanni di Nettolo Becchi............	20
	Subtotal for Florence...........................	*193*
Rome	1. Ilarione di Lippaccio de' Bardi..................	100
	2. Jacopo di Tommaso Tani.......................	40
	3. Giovanni or Nanni di Tommaso Bartoli..........	20
	4. Matteo d'Andrea Barucci......................	20
	Subtotal for Rome..............................	*180*
Naples and Gaëta	1. Francesco d'Andrea Barucci....................	No record*
	2. Accerrito d'Adoardo Portinari..................	60
	3. Adoardo di Cipriano Tornaquinci..............	40
	4. Andrea di Pierozzo Ghetti.....................	40
	Subtotal for Naples and Gaëta..................	*140*
Venice	1. Neri di Cipriano Tornaquinci (branch manager)..	400
	2. Andrea di Giovanni del Bellaccio (cashier).......	50
	3. Cristofano di Francesco da Gagliano............	50
	4. Zanobi di ser Paolo Riccoldi..................	40
	Subtotal for Venice............................	*540*
	Total payroll............................	1,053

* Francesco d'Andrea Barucci was certainly a factor of the Medici firm from 1398 onward, but we do not know the amount of his earnings per year, because it was not until 1403 that accrued salaries for several years were credited to his account in a lump sum. This item is entered on fol. 51 of the Libro segreto No. 1.

Source: ASF, MAP, filza 153, no. 1, fols. 12, 19, and 21.

in the Florentine office of the Medici Bank, was raised from 48 florins in 1401, to 65 in 1402, to 80 in 1403, and to 100 florins in 1406.[54] By that time, he was apparently in charge of the Tavola in Mercato Nuovo, since his salary increased suddenly, in 1407, from 100 florins to 200 florins because, the records state, he was being treated as a partner.[55] In 1408 he definitely ceased to be an employee and was awarded a share of one seventh in the profits made locally in the banking business.

This scale of salaries is more or less the same as Francesco Datini's, which also ranged from 15 or 20 florins for beginners to 100 florins or more for well-trained factors capable of running a branch office.[56] One hundred florins corresponds to less than 400 dollars today. This may not seem very impressive, but one has to consider that the purchasing power of money was much greater in the Middle Ages than it is at the present time. It is unlikely that business executives in those centuries were badly off. A man earning 150 or 200 florins per annum could live very comfortably according to the standards of his day and could afford a large house, one or two servants, and a horse or a mule in the stable.

Probably business ability, while important, was not the sole basis for advancement; connections also played a part. A good case is that of Ilarione di Lippaccio de' Bardi (c. 1379–1433). Although only twenty-one years of age, he was already getting 100 florins a year in 1400 and 1401 as assistant manager of the Rome branch.[57] For the next five years, 1402 to 1406 inclusive, he was granted for salary and bonus a total of 2,000 florins, or 400 florins per year.[58] It is likely that from 1402 onward Ilarione de' Bardi was taking charge of the Rome branch and acting as manager in place of his brother Benedetto, whose presence was probably needed in Florence at the side of Giovanni di Bicci. In 1407 Ilarione de' Bardi was admitted as a partner in Rome but not in Florence. He invested 1,000 florins out of a capital of 7,000 florins, the balance being supplied by the Medici Bank in which both his elder brother and Giovanni di Bicci were partners.[59] According to the articles of association, Ilarione was entitled to one fourth of the profits, despite the fact that his share in the capital amounted to only one seventh.[60] He remained until 1420 at the head of the Rome branch, or rather of the bank which followed the papal court in its peregrinations through Italy and even to the shores of the Swiss lakes. When Benedetto died in that year, it was Ilarione who succeeded him as general manager. Of course, such a successful career was not due solely to family connections; to retain for so long Giovanni di Bicci's confidence, and later Cosimo's, Ilarione de' Bardi must have been an exceedingly able administrator and shrewd financier.

The Medici Bank, in this period, to a certain extent favored members of the Medici and Bardi clans in recruiting clerical staff. Several who were hired did not stay for long, probably because their services proved to be unsatisfactory. Thus there is the record of Antonio di Talento de' Medici, who served for two years as a *giovane* (clerk) in the Florentine office and then was dismissed.[61] Another Medici, Cambio d'Antonio, who had been cashier for two years, was dismissed in 1420 when the partnership agreement came to an end.[62] The reason given for his dismissal was that he had left his job to flee from the plague. In the same year, a Bardi youth, Terrino di Giovanni, was fired for stealing a small sum. The same fate befell another office boy, perhaps an accomplice, also guilty of petty theft.[63]

As stated, three libri segreti belonging to the Medici Bank are still extant. Without any breach of continuity, they cover a period of more than half a century, from October 1, 1397 to March 24, 1451.[64] In the Florentine companies, the libro segreto was usually kept by one of the partners who put it away in a locked chest whenever he did not need it. A book of this kind contained information of a confidential character, such as data on capital investment and the allocation of profits among the partners, which it was thought advisable to conceal from the indiscreet eyes of the people working in the office. Sometimes the libro segreto also contained information regarding salaries of employees and deposits made by prominent customers, like cardinals, princes, or high officials, who wished to keep their investments secret for the same reason that rulers and politicians today have numbered accounts in Swiss banks.

In the Medici Bank, there was a libro segreto for the concern as a whole; in it were recorded the amounts of capital invested in the subsidiary partnerships and the profits or losses which the latter regularly reported to headquarters. Besides this general libro segreto, each branch kept a confidential record of its own. So much importance was attached to these secret ledgers that they were kept on parchment instead of on paper.

The three extant libri segreti are fortunately those kept at headquarters; hence they include all the business undertakings of the Medici. As a result, we have complete data on the financial structure and the operating results from 1397 to 1451 of the parent company and all its subsidiaries. Only the earliest of the three surviving manuscripts has many entries relating to salaries earned by branch managers and clerical staff. On the other hand, the first nine folios are missing: they contained transcripts of the partnership agreements of all the firms controlled by the Medici. The two later libri segreti are complete and have the text of the contracts in addition to the usual accounts found in a ledger of this type.

The first libro segreto gives the profits made by the various Medici enterprises from 1397 to 1420. These data are summarized in Tables

8 and 9. Of course, the profits listed are net profits accruing to the two partners, Giovanni di Bicci and Benedetto de' Bardi, after making provision for bad debts and unforeseen contingencies and after deducting in each case the share of the branch manager. As we have seen, local managers usually were not factors, or employees, but partners. Each manager, instead of receiving a salary, was remunerated by participating in the profits of his branch.

TABLE 8. PROFITS OF THE MEDICI BANK FROM 1397 TO 1420

| Office or Branch | Amount of Profits | | | | Percent of Total |
	f.	s.	d.	aff.	
Florence.................................	25,344	10	4		16.9
Court of Rome...........................	79,195	4	4		52.1
Venice..................................	22,705	9	7		14.9
Naples..................................	15,458	25	1		10.2
Customs of Gaëta........................	485	9	9		0.3
Miscellaneous...........................	159	22	3		0.1
Subtotal banking and foreign trade...............	*143,348*	*23*	*4*		*94.5*
Woolshop I (Cosimo de' Medici and Michele di Baldo).................................	1,634	20	9		1.1
Woolshop II (Lorenzo de' Medici and Taddeo di Filippo).................................	6,837	9	3		4.4
Subtotal manufacturing......................	*8,472*	*1*	*0*		*5.5*
Total..................................	151,820	24	4		100.0

Source: ASF, MAP, filza 153, no. 1: Libro segreto 1397–1420.

TABLE 9. PROFITS ASSIGNED TO THE PARTNERS OF THE MEDICI BANK, 1397–1420

| Names | Share | Amount | | | |
		f.	s.	d.	aff.
Giovanni di Bicci de' Medici............	Three fourths	113,865	18	5	
Benedetto di Lippaccio de' Bardi........	One fourth	37,955	5	11	
Total.......................................		151,820	24	4	

Source: Same as Table 8.

As Table 8 clearly shows, the branch following the Curia was the principal source of profits, producing more than half of the total during the period from 1397 to 1420. As depositary of the Camera Apostolica (Apostolic Chamber) the Medici not only handled funds for the papal treasury but attracted the financial business of cardinals and prelates residing at the "court of Rome," so called even when it was held in Bologna, Ferrara, or Florence itself. In the Middle Ages, the papacy was the only power which collected revenues in many countries and was thus forced to resort to international bankers who transferred the funds where needed. Moreover, the Curia was usually a lender, or a depositor, rather than a borrower. Under those circumstances, it is not surprising that the "Rome" branch of the Medici throve on *cambio* (exchange dealings). Not only did it bring in the bulk of the profits; it was also the most profitable of the branches in relation to invested capital. The yield exceeded 30 percent, which is high by any measure.

In contrast to Rome, the records show that Naples was losing ground and that profits were steadily falling off, especially after 1410.[65] It is therefore not surprising that the Medici were to discontinue this subsidiary within a few years (1425). Florence and Venice were holding their own but were far less important than Rome. Although headquarters were located in Florence, the Medici never made most of their money at home. According to Table 8, even combining banking and manufacturing did not bring local earnings up to 23 percent of the total. One of the two industrial establishments, as the table shows, was doing much better than the other, most probably because it was better managed.

It is impossible to give the profits or losses year by year for each of the branches, because the data are not available. Medieval bookkeepers are not consistent: sometimes they give the profits year by year and sometimes they lump those of several years together and give only an aggregate figure.

Some of the profits were plowed back into business and served to finance expansion. A considerable portion of them were, however, withdrawn and used to acquire real estate, both urban and rural. Giovanni di Bicci did not inherit a large estate from his father, but he greatly extended his holdings by purchasing farms and farmland in the vicinity of Florence and farther away in the Mugello, where his family hailed from. In any case, he was rapidly rising to the top.

Nothing shows his ascent better than the tax records. In 1396, he was assessed only 14 florins, whereas the heirs of Messer Vieri di Cambio de' Medici were put down for 220 florins.[66] In 1403, for another prestanza, Giovanni di Bicci for the first time paid more than his brother, Francesco di Bicci, their quotas being 150 and 132 florins, respectively. For the same levy, Francesco Datini was taxed 360 florins and the heirs of Vieri di Cambio, 748 florins.[67] Ten years later, in 1413, Giovanni di Bicci's assessment of 260 florins actually surpassed that of the sons of Vieri, which totaled 235 florins.[68] By 1427, when the catasto was introduced, Giovanni paid 397 florins, the second highest tax in Florence.[69] He was exceeded only by Messer Palla di Nofri Strozzi, who is listed for 507 florins. It is true that two Panciatichi brothers, Gabriello and Giovanni, would have paid more than anyone else, if their tax had not been split between the two. Both quotas together amounted to 636 florins.

When Benedetto de' Bardi, the general manager, died early in 1420,

he was succeeded by his younger brother Ilarione, who had been running
the branch at the Curia.[70] This change brought about a general reorganization of the Medici Bank. Apparently, Ilarione, when taking over,
asked to have a free hand. For example, all the giovani in the Florentine
office were dismissed.[71] A few were presumably rehired, in all likelihood
only those who stood in good stead with the new management. The
death of Benedetto had, of course, dissolved automatically all existing
partnership agreements. Since it was necessary to draw up new contracts,
advantage was taken of this opportunity to proceed with a thorough
house cleaning and to review all arrangements in operation. For example,
the partnership with Michele di Baldo, whose wool establishment was
losing money, was terminated forthwith.[72] New branch managers were
appointed and their powers carefully delineated. The same, of course,
happens in modern corporations when there is a change in management,
as for example, when in 1946 Henry Ford II succeeded his grandfather
as president of the Ford Motor Company.

To begin with, Giovanni di Bicci, now sixty years old, formally withdrew from business, though he may have continued to act informally as
an advisor. In any case, the new contract with Ilarione de' Bardi was
drafted in the name of Giovanni's sons, Cosimo and Lorenzo. The
capital was set at 24,000 florins of which 16,000 were to be provided by
the two Medici brothers and 8,000 by Ilarione. Profits were to be shared
in the same proportion. This capital was then allocated as follows to the
different subsidiaries: 10,500 florins to the Tavola of Florence, 7,500
florins di suggello (7,000 Venetian ducats) to the Venice branch, and
6,000 florins to the branch at the Roman Curia.

Important changes were made in two of the three branches. The new
local manager in Florence was Folco d'Adoardo Portinari (c. 1386–1431),
whose great-grandfather was a brother of Dante's Beatrice. In addition to
the 10,500 florins supplied by the Medici Bank, he put up 1,500 florins,
so that the total invested in the Tavola of Florence was 12,000 florins.
Although he furnished only one eighth of this sum, he was entitled to
one fifth of the profits. A similar agreement was made with Bartolomeo
d'Andrea di Bartolomeo de' Bardi (c. 1397–1429), who was placed at the
head of the Rome branch. According to his contract, he was to invest
1,000 florins in the capital and to receive one fourth of the profits. When
he left Florence to assume his new duties, the maggiori provided him
with detailed written instructions about the policy which he was expected
to follow in granting credit to cardinals, prelates, and local merchants.[73]
In Venice, no drastic changes were made, and the tenor of the new
contract did not much alter existing agreements. The manager, Giovanni
d'Adoardo Portinari (1363–1436), was retained upon the same terms,
namely, that he supply 1,000 ducats and the senior partners 7,000 of a

total capital amounting to 8,000 ducats. To reward him for his services, he was entitled to one fourth of the profits.[74]

As Table 10 shows, the total invested in the Medici Bank by both senior and junior partners was approximately 27,600 florins in 1420. This total is adjusted for the exchange difference between the heavier Venetian ducats and the lighter Florentine florins di suggello, a difference of about 7 percent. However, it does not include a sum of 3,800 florins invested in the woolshop managed by Taddeo di Filippo. Everything considered, aggregate capital amounted to approximately 31,500 florins. This is still far below that of the great Bardi and Peruzzi companies which went bankrupt toward the middle of the fourteenth century. The Medici Bank was in 1420 still a dwarf in comparison with these two giants.

The result of the reorganization of 1420 was to have two Portinari brothers as branch managers. Thus began the connection of the Medici with the Portinari family (see Genealogical Table), so momentous for the destiny of the Bank.

TABLE 10. CAPITAL OF THE MEDICI BANK IN 1420

| | | Amount Invested by | | |
| | | Senior Partners | Branch Manager | Total |
Place	Name of Branch Manager	florins	florins	florins
Florence	Folco Portinari...............	10,500	1,500	12,000
Rome	Bartolomeo de' Bardi..........	6,000	1,000	7,000
Venice	Giovanni Portinari............	7,500	1,070	8,570
	Total..................	24,000	3,570	27,570

Source: ASF, MAP, filza 153, no. 2.

Between 1420 and 1429, the year of the death of Giovanni di Bicci, there were no important changes in the structure of the Medici firm with the exception that one accomanda was ended and another was begun in a different city. On January 1, 1426, the accomanda of Naples with Rosso and Fantino de' Medici was terminated, probably because it was unprofitable.[75] On the other hand, in November, 1426, a new accomanda was started in Geneva, at that time the seat of famous fairs.[76] The latter were important as an international clearing center which regulated the distribution of specie all over Europe.[77] This first accomanda for Geneva was concluded with Michele di Ferro and Giovanni d'Amerigo Benci. The latter had been trained as a factor in the Rome branch; he was a man of outstanding ability and was destined to become general manager in 1435, after the return of Cosimo de' Medici from his year of exile in Venice.

Giovanni di Bicci de' Medici died on February 20, 1429. It is likely that, after 1420, with declining health and energy, he had gradually given more and more authority in the management of the Bank to Cosimo, the elder and abler of his two sons. This was a wise move, since it left Giovanni's successor fully informed about all business secrets and well prepared to assume supreme command. The chronicler Giovanni Cavalcanti reports that the expiring Giovanni di Bicci gave to his sons and the members of his family a death bed oration full of homely advice about the conduct of business and political affairs.[78] Historians have questioned the authenticity of this speech on the ground that a deathbed is not a pulpit from which to deliver homilies. On the other hand, Giovanni Cavalcanti must have been well informed, since he was related to the Medici, being a nephew of Ginevra Cavalcanti, Lorenzo di Giovanni's wife. Perhaps he embellished the speech a little for literary effect, but it rings true and it is plausible that Giovanni di Bicci, feeling his end near, mustered enough strength to give a last exhortation to his sons and to command them to live in harmony, a wish that was carried out. As we know from history, Cosimo and Lorenzo worked hand in hand, and the latter always followed his elder brother's lead. It is also likely that the dying Giovanni urged his sons to manage their business with wisdom and caution and warned them to avoid political entanglements and to shun the Palazzo Vecchio unless called for consultation.

From the little we know about the personality of Giovanni di Bicci, he was apparently a quiet man with a melancholic face, but this unassuming appearance concealed an astute and active mind.[79] Although not a good speaker, he always gave sound advice, had a dry humor, and sometimes made witty remarks.[80] He was first of all a business man who stayed aloof from politics. Nevertheless he was forced, because of the provisions of the Florentine constitution, to take public office when his name was drawn from the election bag. He was a prior several times and in 1421 he became Gonfalonier of Justice for the customary period of two months. But he had no political ambitions and these honors did not mean much to him. The success of his bank, of course, aroused the envy of the ruling clique, which included several competitors, but Giovanni di Bicci somehow managed to avoid an open breach.[81]

When Pope Martin V, in 1422, created him Count of Monteverde, he refused to assume this title and preferred to remain an ordinary citizen, perhaps because he was satisfied with this status, or perhaps because he did not want to antagonize the ruling class of Florence or to give them a chance to brand him as a magnate and an enemy of republican institutions.[82]

Machiavelli praises him for his charity and liberality.[83] This judgment seems to be true. The libro segreto discloses that Giovanni came to the aid of former business associates who were in need. Thus, in 1424 he sent a remittance of 36 florins to Neri Tornaquinci in Cracow upon hearing that the latter was living in poverty. This was the junior partner who had mismanaged the affairs of the Venice branch and had been responsible for heavy losses. "Although he had behaved badly" Giovanni felt that he should be generous toward a former partner.[84]

According to the *Ricordi* of Lorenzo the Magnificent, Giovanni di Bicci at his death left an estate appraised at nearly 180,000 florins.[85] This figure is plausible, if not entirely accurate. The *Ricordi* also state that Giovanni refused to make a testament. Why? Perhaps this decision has something to do with the Church's usury doctrine. By ordering extensive restitution in a testament, he would have denounced himself as a usurer and might have caused considerable trouble for his heirs. At any rate, it was preferable not to take chances.

The importance of family ties in business was on the wane, but their social importance was still undiminished. At the funeral of Giovanni di Bicci, the mourners included twenty-six males bearing the name of Medici, some of whom were only distantly related to the deceased banker, who as the oldest member of the entire clan was regarded as *capo della casa Medici*, or the head of the Medici house.[86]

IV

THE HEYDAY OF THE MEDICI BANK:
COSIMO AT THE HELM, 1429–1464

The death of Giovanni di Bicci did not necessitate any significant changes in the structure or policy of the Medici Bank. Because all contracts since the reorganization of 1420 were in the name of Giovanni's two sons, Cosimo (1389–1464) and Lorenzo (1395–1440), there was no legal or other need for any contractual adjustments. Ilarione di Lippaccio de' Bardi still enjoyed the confidence of his partners and was continued as general manager.

The senior partners were also pleased with the performance of Folco Portinari, the manager of the Tavola in Mercato Nuovo, who had succeeded in raising profits. Whereas, between 1410 and 1423, net earnings never reached 2,000 florins in any single year, they were much higher from 1423 onward, even above 3,000 florins in good years.[1]

When the local manager in Rome, Bartolomeo de' Bardi, died early in 1429, at about the same time as Giovanni di Bicci, the maggiori were lucky to find a suitable successor in Antonio di Messer Francesco Salutati da Pescia (1391–1443), who had served in Florence (1416–1418), Venice (1418–1419), and Rome (since 1420). In the new contract with Salutati, dated March 10, 1429, no corpo was assigned to the Roman branch.[2] According to entries in the second libro segreto (fol. 35), the capital had already been withdrawn in 1426. The practice of operating a bank without capital may seem strange, but the records of the Medici leave no doubt. Moreover, other Florentine companies, namely, the Pazzi and the bank of Averardo de' Medici, did likewise.[3] Since the papal court was a source of funds, it was not deemed necessary to have any capital in Rome, however odd it may appear. Under Salutati's able management, profits in Rome increased markedly. In 1430 they ran as high as 18,237 florins di camera, which was much above the average of previous years.[4]

In Venice profits remained more or less stationary up to 1430. Because the manager, Giovanni Portinari, was getting old, he was given as lieutenant a younger man, Lotto di Tanino Bozzi (1387–after 1450), who had been employed in Venice since 1414 and who was now raised to the rank of junior partner.[5] This promotion was followed by higher profits which increased 50 percent from 1430 to 1431.[6] It is possible that business conditions were especially favorable in 1430 and 1431.

The Geneva accomanda, started in 1426, also was giving satisfactory results, though earnings fluctuated more than elsewhere and conditions were more unsettled. Large reserves for bad debts were set up as a precautionary measure which later proved unnecessary.[7]

Death in the Middle Ages took a heavy toll. In 1429, it mowed down Taddeo di Filippo, the manager of the woolshop. This establishment was liquidated as a result, but a new start was made in 1431 with Giuntino di Guido Giuntini, another clothmaker, as managing partner.[8]

An even more grievous loss was that of Ilarione de' Bardi, the general manager, who died probably in late December 1432 or early January 1433. In any case, he is mentioned as deceased in a letter written in February, 1433 by Giovanni d'Amerigo Benci, then residing in Basel, to Ruggieri della Casa in Geneva.[9] The death of Ilarione de' Bardi came at a critical juncture when political events threatened to put in jeopardy the future of the Medici and their bank.

The unsuccessful attempt to conquer Lucca had failed (1429) and involved the Florentine Republic in hostilities with Milan. This protracted conflict was finally ended by a peace treaty concluded on May 10, 1433. It brought Florence no substantial gains, and the high cost of the war with nothing to show for it but humiliation created a great deal of discontent. The opposition looked to the Medici for leadership and the ruling oligarchy headed by Rinaldo degli Albizzi feared that Cosimo might be induced to seize power. In the spring of 1433 both parties were girding themselves for a contest and the problem was who would strike first.

The Medici records, in any case, give the impression that a coup was in the offing and that precautions were being taken to meet any emergency. On May 30, 1433, 3,000 Venetian ducats in coin were removed from the former residence of Ilarione de' Bardi and handed over for safekeeping to the Benedictine Hermits of San Miniato al Monte. Another 5,877 ducats were placed in custody at the Dominican friary of San Marco.[10] On the same day, 15,000 florins were transferred by the Tavola.of Florence to the credit of the Medici branch in Venice.[11] Cosimo and his brother Lorenzo sold stock in the Monte Comune, worth 10,000 florins, to their branch in Rome.[12] All these precautionary moves suggest that the Medici were mobilizing their resources and accumulating liquid reserves to ward off any run on their Tavola in Florence. At the same time, they were storing their specie in places where it would be safe from confiscation by a hostile Florentine government.

The deceased general manager, Ilarione de' Bardi, was replaced temporarily by his nephew, Lippaccio di Benedetto de' Bardi, who was already a partner in the Tavola in Florence. Because things were more or less in a flux during Cosimo's exile in Venice (October 3, 1433–

September 29, 1434), this makeshift arrangement lasted through the year 1434, Florentine style, that is, until March 25, 1435, when new contracts went into effect and Giovanni d'Amerigo Benci and Antonio di Messer Francesco Salutati became Cosimo's chief executives. This change in management marks the end of the period from 1420 to 1435 covered by the Libro segreto No. 2.

During this period of fifteen years, profits were larger than those recorded in the first libro segreto extending over the preceding twenty-two years. As previously, more than half the profits were made in Rome, but the proportion is even greater, nearly 63 instead of 52 percent, which proves that business at the Curia continued to grow both absolutely and relatively. On the other hand, the profits of the Tavola in Florence were falling off, as is ascertainable by comparing Tables 8 and 11. Venice improved its position. As for Geneva, earnings of this new accomanda must have been gratifying to the senior partners, and it is not surprising that they promoted the branch manager who made such a good record. In less than ten years, he had succeeded in earning four times the amount of invested capital. Whether this result was due to personal ability or to favorable conditions, it is impossible to tell. Probably it was attributable to both. Although the woolshop was not doing poorly, manufacturing continued to be of negligible importance as compared to banking.

TABLE 11. PROFITS OF THE MEDICI BANK FROM 1420 TO 1435

Office or Branch	Amount of Profits				Percent of Total
	f.	s.	d.	aff.	
Florence..............................	17,823	5	0		9.5
Rome.................................	117,037	21	8		62.8
Geneva...............................	20,605	3	11		11.1
Venice...............................	24,453	25	7		13.1
Naples...............................	684	24	2		0.4
Total profits from banking...............	180,604	22	4		96.9
Woolshop.............................	5,777	22	6		3.1
Total............................	186,382	15	10		100.0

Source: ASF, MAP, filza 153, no. 2.

TABLE 12. DIVISION OF PROFITS BETWEEN THE PARTNERS, 1420 TO 1435

Name	Share	Amount			
		f.	s.	d.	aff.
Cosimo and Lorenzo de' Medici...........	Two thirds	124,255	1	2	
Ilarione di Lippaccio de' Bardi...........	One third	62,127	14	8	
Total..		186,382	15	10	

Source: ASF, MAP, filza 153, no. 2.

In 1435 the Medici Bank had only one branch beyond the Alps, the one in Geneva. If other such establishments had existed, operating results, whether profits or losses, would have been recorded in the libro segreto. The absence of any entries of the kind militates against the existence of branches in Bruges or London at this stage.[13]

The reorganization of 1435 was scarcely less drastic than the one of 1420. First of all, it was the end of the close connection between the Medici and the Bardi, which had been tightened by the fact that, up to 1433, two general managers in succession belonged to the latter family. Why were these ties broken? Perhaps for political reasons. The richest of the Bardi, Bardo di Francesco di Messer Alessandro (1392–1443), was among those banished from Florence after the triumphal return of Cosimo. Perhaps Lippaccio di Benedetto de' Bardi wavered in his allegiance or failed in his duties during Cosimo's and Lorenzo's enforced absence from Florence. At all events, he and his brother Girolamo, a factor in Rome, were no longer in the service of the Medici in 1435.

With the Bardi out of the picture, the Medici called to Florence Antonio di Messer Francesco Salutati (1391–1443), manager in Rome, and Giovanni d'Amerigo Benci (1394–1455), manager in Geneva. New articles of association were drafted making them full partners of the Medici Bank as a whole and raising its capital from 24,000 to 32,000 florins.[14] The two Medici brothers supplied 24,000 florins, or three fourths of this total, and Benci and Salutati each 4,000 florins or one eighth. Profits, however, were not to be divided in the same proportion: two thirds were to go to the Medici and one sixth to each of the other two partners (Table 18). In 1439 the capital was further increased by 12,000 florins and brought up to a total of 44,000 florins by transferring accrued profits to capital.[15] As a result, the share of the Medici was fixed at 32,000 florins and that of their two partners at 6,000 florins each.

The reorganization undertaken in 1435 also affected the various branches. The capital of the Venetian branch was set at £800 groat, Venetian currency, or 8,000 ducats, of which 7,000 ducats were furnished by the Medici and their partners, Benci and Salutati.[16] Giovanni Portinari was so old and ill — he died in April 1436 — that he retired. The management in Venice was entrusted to Lotto di Tanino Bozzi, assisted by Antonio di Niccolò Martelli (1404–after 1473). Both invested 500 ducats, but Lotto, the manager, was entitled to one sixth of the profits and Antonio, the assistant manager, to only one eighth. In Rome, as we have seen, there was no longer any capital. The departure of Salutati left a vacancy that was filled by Antonio di ser Lodovico della Casa (1405–c. 1461), whose brother Ruggieri succeeded Giovanni Benci as manager of the Geneva accomanda.[17] This accomanda's capital was increased from 5,000 to 8,000 florins.[18] What happened to the Tavola in

Florence is not entirely clear. It certainly did not disappear, but no separate partnership was formed for this purpose. Working capital was apparently supplied by Venice, at least according to the books.[19] Perhaps this juggling of accounts was deliberate, since political conditions were still unsettled and Cosimo was not yet firmly in the saddle. As Fulco Portinari had died in 1431 and Lippaccio de' Bardi dropped out in 1434 or 1435, the post of manager was vacant; the surviving records suggest that it was given to Giovanni d'Amerigo Benci.

Not much is known about Antonio di Messer Francesco Salutati, but we are better informed about Giovanni d'Amerigo Benci, who played a more conspicuous rôle in the history of the Medici Bank. When Salutati passed away in 1443, he was not replaced and Benci alone assumed the task of general manager and became Cosimo's chief advisor in business matters.

Benci's career had started in Rome, where he had gone in 1409 at the age of fifteen to serve as an office boy.[20] Before 1420, he was the main bookkeeper, and, without any doubt, a very efficient one, thoroughly familiar with double entry.[21] In 1424 he was given a more responsible position when the firm sent him to Geneva to pave the way for the creation of a branch.[22] He was on a salary plus commission until the fall of 1426 when the accomanda was created. According to the catasto report for 1427, he was then earning 115 florins a year.[23] As already mentioned, Benci was quite successful in organizing the Geneva branch and in making it a profitable undertaking. He was responsible in 1433 for setting up a temporary office in Basel where the Council was in session.[24] Two years later, he was called to Florence to assist Cosimo as general manager and to take charge of the Tavola, which was not prospering as a result of the crisis of 1433–1434.

Thus began the second phase in the successful career of Giovanni Benci; it extended over twenty years, from 1435 until his death in 1455. The third libro segreto, which is entirely written in his very legible and neat, cursive hand, covers most of this period. Giovanni d'Amerigo Benci was perhaps the general manager whom Cosimo liked the best and trusted the most. This confidence was certainly deserved, and the Medici records decidedly give the impression that Benci was a very efficient business man with an orderly and systematic mind. It was during the years of Benci's management that the Medici Bank witnessed its greatest period of expansion and reached the peak of its earning capacity.

The private life of Giovanni Benci was not above reproach. Before marriage, in 1428 or 1429, he had an illegitimate son, Damiano, by a slave belonging to Lorenzo Barducci.[25] Benci married rather late, in 1431, when, being in Florence, he took as wife, Ginevra, the daughter

of Bartolomeo di Verano Peruzzi, who was much younger than her husband and bore him at least eight children before her premature death
(c. 1444).[26] Besides the illegitimate Damiano, Giovanni Benci had an
adulterine daughter by his own slave Maria.[27] Nonetheless, Giovanni was
a pious man: he donated and bequeathed large sums of money to the
Murate, a community of anchoresses, or secluded nuns, and was buried
in their church in front of the high altar.[28] Perhaps he thought of his
bequests as insurance premiums for safe arrival in paradise.

The conduct of Giovanni Benci followed a common pattern. In the
Middle Ages, Italian merchants, although they often resided abroad for
several years at a stretch, rarely married foreign women or even Italian
women from other cities. Of course, illicit relations with maids, slaves, or
local girls were quite common; indirect evidence is found in the sermons
of the friars who preached against the moral dangers to which merchants
exposed themselves by prolonged absences in foreign countries and long
separations from their wives.[29] Despite the fulminations of the Church,
laxity in private morals was regarded by the merchants with a great
deal of indulgence and did not meet with such strong social disapproval
that it was a handicap in making a career. Illegitimate children were
often brought up in the household along with the legitimate offspring.
In this respect, Cosimo himself is a good example of the prevailing
attitude: he had a son, Carlo, by a slave girl and had him reared in his
own house with his legitimate issue.

Giovanni Benci undoubtedly enriched himself through his association
with the Medici. According to his catasto report (1427), he came from a
family of moderate means who owned a house in town and a small farm
in the country.[30] Thirty years later, in 1457, the catasto report discloses
that he had left to his heirs a considerable estate including a palatial
home in Florence, urban property, several farms, stock in the Monte
Comune, and a deposit of 7,400 florins with the Medici Bank. The
property of the Benci family was assessed at 26,338 florins, which was
taxed 132 florins, a quota exceeded only by the Medici family (Table
5).[31]

After this biographical sketch of Giovanni Benci, let us retrace our
steps to 1435, the year in which he and Antonio Salutati became general
managers. How responsibility was divided between these two men is not
known. It is likely that Salutati kept an eye on Rome and possibly on
Venice, while Benci, having been in charge of the Geneva and Basel
offices, continued to take care of their affairs. Presumably Benci recom-
mended that the office in Basel, where the General Council of the Church
was still meeting, be kept in operation under the temporary management
of Roberto Martelli, released for this purpose from his duties in Rome.[32]
The financial business of the Council was probably important enough

to justify the existence of a branch office. Its legal status remains in doubt and it may have changed in the course of years. Profits made by the Basel office are duly entered in Libro segreto No. 3 from 1435 through 1440 and then vanish from the records. Yet the Basel office was still in existence in 1443, perhaps as a subbranch of Geneva.[33] It probably lasted as long as attendance at the Council made it worthwhile to keep a bank in Basel.

In the fifteenth century, Ancona was rather important for Florence as a seaport for shipping cloth to the Levant and for importing grain from Apulia along the Adriatic coast. Ostensibly in order to capture some of this transit business, the Medici decided in 1436 to enter into an accomanda, with other investors and two active partners, Bernardo d'Andrea di Messer Alamanno de' Medici and Bartolomeo di Niccolò Martelli.[34] According to Professor Frederic E. Gaupp, the Ancona accomanda was really formed to finance the campaigns of Francesco Sforza in the Marches.[35] This is plausible, since the total invested by all partners together was 20,000 ducats, a suspiciously large amount for a firm doing business in such a small trading center as Ancona. As a matter of fact, the partnership contract of 1436 expressly mentions the magnificent Count Sforza, and authorizes the managing partners to lend him up to 3,000 ducats, a limit which was probably exceeded with the consent of the Medici. Of course, the provisions of partnership agreements should not always be taken at face value. At this juncture and later, Cosimo was a staunch ally of Sforza and was backing him financially with subsidies from the Florentine government and loans from his bank. So politics were already dictating business decisions.

Since the Florentine republic had no vital interests in Flanders, political considerations did not carry much weight, if any, in making the decision to establish a branch in Bruges.[36] The records show that the Medici moved cautiously and did not take this step without appraising carefully all the risks involved in such a venture. From 1416, or earlier, they had been doing business in Flanders and England by means of correspondents, without having a branch of their own. Around 1430, their representatives were the Bardi and the Borromei firms, both in Bruges and in London. Because they failed to give satisfactory service, the Medici decided in 1436 to send to Bruges Bernardo di Giovanni d'Adoardo Portinari (1407–before 1457), the son of the manager of the Venice branch from 1417 to 1435. His mission was ostensibly to recover some outstanding claims and to settle other differences, but in reality he was to explore possibilities and investigate business prospects.[37] The results of this mission were presumably favorable, because Portinari, after making his report, returned to Flanders in 1438 as a simple agent of the Medici.[38] According to the entries in the libro segreto, the Bruges branch was not founded until March 24, 1439 (N.S.), under the form of an accomanda with Bernardo Portinari as active partner and with the Medici Bank as investing partner assuming only limited liability.[39] The accomanda was not transformed into a full-fledged partnership until 1455 when Angelo Tani (1415–1492) became junior partner and branch manager.[40]

In order to provide employment for the Florentine workers, the Medici expanded their interest in wool manufacturing. Since 1431, as explained above, they had money invested in a shop, with Giuntino Giuntini as manager and junior partner. Giuntino died before 1440, but his heirs left their investment in the firm and his brother Andrea took over the job of manager with the assistance of Fruosino da Panzano.[41] This shop was in the name of Giovanni di Cosimo de' Medici. On July 1, 1439, the Medici opened a second shop, and for this purpose went into partnership with Antonio di Taddeo (1417–after 1473), the son of Taddeo di Filippo, who had managed one of their woolshops successfully from 1408 to 1429.[42] The son proved to be as good a manager as the father and earned large profits for the Medici and himself. He prospered and was honored by becoming Gonfalonier of Justice in 1471 and podesta of Pisa in 1473.[43] This second shop was styled "Pierfrancesco de' Medici & Co." Its capital of 4,000 florins was made up as follows: 2,500 florins provided by the Medici Company and 1,500 by Antonio di Taddeo. Profits were shared half and half.

The Medici were also attracted by silk manufacturing, Florence's second industry. In 1438 they acquired a silkshop from Tumo Manetti at the price of 235 florins for *entratura* (good will).[44] As usual, the management was entrusted to a specialist, Francesco di Francesco Berlinghieri (1390–c. 1446), who had as assistant Jacopo di Biagio Tanaglia. The amount invested was 5,000 florins, of which Berlinghieri supplied 800 florins and the Medici the remaining 4,200. The profits, however, were to be divided as though the Medici had invested 3,000 florins, Berlinghieri 1,400, and Tanaglia 600.[45] Owing to Berlinghieri's managerial talents, the silkshop turned out to be a profitable undertaking.

All partnership contracts were automatically terminated when Lorenzo di Giovanni de' Medici, Cosimo's brother, died September 23, 1440, leaving a widow and a minor son, Pierfrancesco, who was still too young to step into his father's shoes. Nevertheless, Cosimo decided to continue operations on the basis of existing agreements until the end of the year according to Florentine style, that is, until March 24, 1441. At that date, all the branches were to balance their books and to determine their profits. After all the reports had been received, the Libro segreto No. 3 was balanced in order to determine the profits accruing jointly to the two Medici brothers and their partners, Giovanni Benci

TABLE 13.   BALANCE OF THE MEDICI BANK ON NOVEMBER 1, 1441

Assets

	f.	s.	d.	aff.
Nostri di Firenze (Tavola of Florence). working capital,,,,	11,707	24	6	
Rome: no corpo (capital)				
reserve 5,300 cameral florins.....................	4,960	0	0	

	f.	s.	d.	f.	s.	d.	
Venice: capital £700 groat, Venetian							
currency......................	7,560	0	0				
sopraccorpo (surplus)..............	6,587	10	5	14,147	10	5	
Geneva: corpo....................	10,000	0	0				
sopraccorpo,,...................	4,901	23	0	14,901	23	0	
Accomanda of Ancona: capital........	6,000	0	0				
undistributed profits..............	600	0	0	6,600	0	0	
Accomanda of Bruges: capital......................				6,420	0	0	
Woolshop with Andrea Giuntini: corpo	2,400	0	0				
sopraccorpo.....................	1,838	21	1	4,238	21	1	
Woolshop with Antonio di Taddeo:							
corpo...........................	2,500	0	0				
sopraccorpo.....................	925	0	0	3,425	0	0	
Silkshop with Francesco Berlinghieri:							
capital.........................	4,200	0	0				
surplus........................	3,120	0	0				
goodwill.......................	235	23	0	7,555	23	0	
Total........				73,956	15	0	

Liabilities

	f.	s.	d.	f.	s.	d.	aff.
Corpo (capital) of the Medici Bank as a whole:							
Cosimo de' Medici and heirs of Lorenzo, his brother..............	32,000	0	0				
Giovanni d'Amerigo Benci..........	6,000	0	0				
Antonio di Messer Francesco Salutati	6,000	0	0	44,000	0	0	
Sopraccorpo (surplus):							
Cosimo de' Medici and Lorenzo's heirs	19,562	9	10				
Giovanni d'Amerigo Benci..........	4,890	18	5				
Antonio Salutati.................	4,890	18	5	29,343	17	8	
Heirs of Giuntino di Guido Giuntini..................				612	26	4	
Total........				73,956	15	0	

Source: ASF, MAP, filza 153, no. 3: Libro segreto (1435–1450), fols. 56–63.

and Antonio Salutati. This balance is reproduced in Table 13 and does not raise any problems of interpretation for anyone who knows how to read financial statements. It shows that, on November 1, 1441 — because of delays in receiving the reports from the branches — total investment in the bank was 73,956 florins and 15s. affiorino, of which 44,000 florins represented the corpo and 29,956 florins and 15s. affiorino the *sopraccorpo* (accrued profits). How these resources were allocated to the different branches is indicated on the assets side of the balance. Of course, these items do not include any sums invested by branch managers or others, but only the share in the corpo and sopraccorpo of the Medici Bank. As these data show, the Medici Bank, in 1441, was made up of several partnerships combined in a larger unit similar to a modern holding company. This unit included the Tavola in Florence, the branches in Geneva, Rome, and Venice, the accomande of Ancona, and Bruges, and three industrial establishments, two woolshops and one silkshop. The branches in Avignon, London, Pisa, and Milan did not yet exist in 1441.

Expansion was resumed the next year with the foundation of a branch in Pisa. Giovanni di Bicci and Cosimo had used earlier the facilities offered by the Pisan office of their nephew and cousin, Averardo di Francesco de' Medici. In 1426, Cosimo even had paid small advances through this channel to Donatello for the purchase of Carrara marble and, in one case, for two pairs of hose.[46] Since Averardo died in 1434 and his grandson Francesco in 1443, the Pisan office of their bank was presumably closed between these two dates, which may have induced Cosimo to open his own branch.

An accomanda was formed to handle the Pisan business on December 26, 1442, for the duration of five years. It had a capital of 6,000 florins, 4,000 supplied by the Medici as silent partners and 1,000 by each of the two active partners, Ugolino di Niccolò Martelli and Matteo di Cristofano Masi.[47] Half of the profits were allotted to the Medici and one quarter to each of the other partners. Ugolino was to assume the management with the aid of Matteo Masi, who bound himself to stay in Pisa in order to attend to the accomanda's business. We do not know how this venture turned out because, after 1443, profits made in Pisa are no longer recorded in the libro segreto still extant in the Florentine archives; they were presumably entered in the books of the Tavola in Florence, which have not survived. In any case, the contract was extended in 1450 with some changes in the capital structure: the Medici reduced their participation from 4,000 to 2,000 florins, but the deficiency was made up by the famous humanist Messer Carlo di Gregorio dei Marsuppini of Arezzo.[48] According to the catasto report filed by Ugolino Martelli in 1457, the accomanda was still in existence at that time. Probably the Medici withdrew shortly thereafter, but Ugolino Martelli carried on the business until 1476 with the aid of his own relatives.[49]

The London branch was not established until 1446. There is no doubt that the Medici had been operating an office in London prior to that year, but it was financed and staffed by the Bruges branch.[50] By exception, the Medici took as manager an outsider, Gerozzo di Jacopo de' Pigli (1406–after 1469), who had been doing business in the City for many years.[51] The capital assigned to the new branch amounted to £2,500 sterling, of which the Medici supplied £2,166 13s. 4d. and Pigli the remainder or £333 6s. 8d.[52] Although the latter's share in the capital was only two fifteenths, the contract awarded him a fifth (or three fifteenths) of the profits to remunerate him for his services, the usual policy. From the start, this was a real partnership and not an accomanda.

In the same year that the Medici established a branch in London, they founded another in Avignon. Although this town had lost a great deal since the departure of the papal court, it was still the most important center in southern France, overshadowing Marseilles, Montpellier, or Toulouse. An accomanda was concluded with Giovanni di Benedetto Zampini (1405–c. 1479), who had been trained in Geneva and had been sent to Avignon as a factor in 1442. The bulk of the capital of 7,500 florins di camera was furnished by Geneva, but Zampini was expected to put up 500 florins for his share. The division of profits was: the Medici seven eighths and Zampini one eighth.[53] Within two years, the accomanda was changed into an ordinary partnership.

It is sometimes asserted that the Medici had a branch in Lübeck, but such a statement rests on misunderstanding.[54] In their records there is nowhere any trace of the existence of such a branch, but it is true that they had as correspondents in Lübeck, Gherardo Bueri and his partners. This Gherardo di Niccolò di Francesco di Jacopo Bueri (d. 1449) was related to the Medici, since he was a first cousin once removed of Giovanni di Bicci's wife, Piccarda Bueri, daughter of Odoardo di Jacopo.[55] In 1406 Gherardo Bueri was employed at a salary of twenty florins per annum by the Medici branch in Venice, but he quit this job, leaving a debt of 61½ florins, which was eventually written off and charged to bad debts.[56] His presence in Lübeck is recorded as early as 1413 when he was in business with a Lodovico Baglioni from Perugia, (Ludovicus de Ballionibus).[57] This partnership was engaged in money-changing and agreed to transmit funds to the Roman Curia on behalf of church dignitaries in Scandinavia.[58] Gherardo Bueri became a burgher of Lübeck without giving up his Florentine citizenship and continued to reside there until his death in 1449.[59] In the local records he is often described as "Gerardus de Boeris also called de Wale," which means simply "the Italian." [60] He was doing rather well according to local standards and married a German woman, Tybbeke, the daughter of Johann Bere, burgomaster of Lübeck from 1439 to 1449.[61] Bueri was a vestryman of the church of St. Egidius in Lübeck, another indication that he enjoyed standing in the community.[62]

In 1427 the Medici balance sheets reveal, Baglioni and Bueri owed 8,334 ducats to the Venice branch and 3,945 florins di camera to the Rome branch. On the other hand, there were 587 florins standing to their credit in Florence, but this amount was earmarked to settle part of their debt in Rome.[63] Relations with the Medici continued throughout the lifetime of Gherardo Bueri, but he seems to have experienced constant difficulties in settling debit balances in Italy. For this purpose, he sent consignments of amber, amber rosaries, and furs to Venice.[64] These shipments were usually entrusted to servants, but in 1446 Bueri himself made a trip to Italy, visited Venice and Florence, and returned to Lübeck by way of Geneva.[65] Three years later he died. In his will, he made adequate provision for his widow, left several bequests, and willed the residue to Cosimo in order to pay off his indebtedness to Italian banking houses, including the Medici. In order to settle the estate, Cosimo dispatched to Lübeck Benedetto di Stefano degli Obizi da Fucecchio, *in jure civili licentiatus,* who concluded an agreement by which all the goods in Venice and Italy were assigned to the Medici.[66] One interesting detail: Gherardo Bueri kept his books in Italian, so that nobody in Lübeck was able to read his records, except two compatriots, Niccolò di Bernardo Bonsi and Francesco Rucellai, who were appointed by the Lübeck authorities to settle the estate.[67]

As Bueri's story illustrates, transfers from Northern Europe to Italy were hampered by the lack of adequate banking facilities and regular currents of trade and, as a result, involved endless delays and difficulties. The Camera Apostolica experienced the same troubles with regard to transfers of revenues collected in the Baltic region, Scandinavia, or Poland.[68] To improve connections, the Italians made an attempt to gain a foothold in Hanseatic territory, and there existed, around 1420, a small Florentine colony in Lübeck. However, the Hanseatic League, fearful of competition, was on guard to prevent further penetration.[69] As a result, the colony was not allowed to grow. Moreover, the Italians were so few that they were unable to make any dent or to improve business methods and organization. It is not until the end of the sixteenth century that real progress was made and that Hamburg became a banking center.

Since Gherardo Bueri was only a correspondent, it is clear that the Medici Bank had no branches east of the Rhine. Neither is there any evidence that it had such establishments either in Spain or in the Levant. After 1450, the only branch which was added to those already in existence was the one in Milan, founded in 1452. The whole situation is very well summarized in the balance which Giovanni Benci drew up in closing Libro segreto No. 3 on March 24, 1451, or at the end of the year 1450, Florentine style.

Apparently a new partnership was being formed, starting the next day, March 25, 1451. Its capital amounted to 72,000 florins of which three fourths were supplied by the Medici family and one fourth by Giovanni d'Amerigo Benci, the general manager. Cosimo formally withdrew from business as his father had done thirty years earlier, in 1420. In Cosimo's case, however, this gesture was presumably more a legal fiction than a reality. The amount of 54,000 florins was divided equally between the two branches of the Medici family. Lorenzo di Giovanni's son, Pierfrancesco, now being of age, was admitted as a partner and given one half of the Medici share, so that he was credited with twice as much as each of Cosimo's sons, Piero and Giovanni. Besides the capital of 72,000 florins, a sum of 3,083 florins 24s. 10d. affiorino was still due to the heirs of Antonio Salutati, whose share was still in the process of liquidation. According to the balance, total resources amount to 75,083 florins 24s. 10d. affiorino (Table 14).

The assets side of the balance sheet shows how this total was distributed among the branches. The table is clear and raises no problems of interpretation, but the reader will notice that the Rome and the Pisa branches are not listed among the assets. The omission of Rome is easy to explain, since, as stated before, no capital was assigned to this branch from 1429 onward. The share of the Medici in the capital of the Pisa branch was 2,000 florins after November, 1450. This item is missing from Giovanni Benci's balance sheet. There are two possibilities: either this amount was invested by the Medici privately and not by their bank or it was provided by the Tavola in Florence. In the latter case, the 2,000 florins would be included in the item of 12,952 florins allotted as working capital to the Tavola. At any rate, the investment in the Pisan accomanda managed by Ugolino Martelli is included in a list of Cosimo's business investments prepared by the tax officials in connection with the sixth catasto, that of 1451.[70] Historians have usually given 1431 as the date of this record, but internal and external evidence prove clearly that this is wrong and should be 1451.[71]

Benci's balance sheet and supplementary data give a general picture of the bank's structure on March 25, 1451. At this date, the Medici Bank was composed of the Tavola in Florence, three branches in Italy (Pisa, Rome, and Venice), four branches outside (Avignon, Bruges, Geneva, and London), and three industrial establishments (two woolshops and one silkshop). With the possible exception of Pisa, all these subsidiaries were controlled and wholly or partly owned by the Medici Bank in much the same way as a holding company would today.

The Tavola in Florence was managed by Giovanni di Baldino Inghirami (d. 1454) who, although a partner with no share in the corpo, was entitled to one eighth of its profits.[72] In Rome, the manager was

TABLE 14. BALANCE OF THE MEDICI BANK ON MARCH 24, 1451

Assets

	f.	s.	d.	aff.
The Tavola in Florence in the name of the Venice branch: Giovanni di Baldino Inghirami, manager..............	12,952	1	10	
Venice branch with Alessandro Martelli as manager: capital £700 groat, Venetian currency......................	7,700	0	0	
Geneva branch with Francesco Sassetti: capital ▽ 10,500 of 64 to the mark......................................	11,807	6	10	
Avignon branch with Giovanni Zampini as partner: florins 14,000 of 12 groats, papal currency..................	8,400	0	0	
Accomanda of London with Simone d'Antonio Nori as manager: capital £800 sterling........................	4,800	0	0	
Accomanda of Bruges with Agnolo di Jacopo Tani as manager: £2,160 groat, Flemish currency..................	10,800	0	0	
Total invested in banking........	56,459	8	8	
Woolshop with Antonio di Taddeo as manager............	2,500	0	0	
Woolshop with Andrea Giuntini as manager..............	3,500	0	0	
Silkshop with Berlinghieri di Francesco Berlinghieri as manager...	4,800	0	0	
Silkshop: undivided profits...........................	7,824	16	2	
Total.......................	75,083	24	10	

Liabilities

	f.	s.	d.	f.	s.	d.	aff.
Capital							
Share of the Medici family:							
Piero di Cosimo di Giovanni......	13,500	0	0				
Giovanni di Cosimo di Giovanni..	13,500	0	0				
Pierfrancesco di Lorenzo di Giovanni.................	27,000	0	0	54,000	0	0	
Share of Giovanni d'Amerigo Benci................				18,000	0	0	
Total capital.................				72,000	0	0	
Balance due to the heirs of Antonio di Francesco Salutati, former partner, died in 1443....................				3,083	24	10	
Total......................				75,083	24	10	

Source: ASF, MAP, filza 153, no. 3, fols. 92–97.

Roberto di Niccolò Martelli (1408–1464) who had succeeded Antonio della Casa in 1439. At first he received one eighth of the profits, but this share was increased to one sixth in 1446.[73] He had no part in the capital, since there was none. In Venice, his brother Alessandro Martelli (1417–1465) was getting one eighth of the profits in remuneration for his services (Table 15).[74] The Pisa branch, as pointed out before, was an accomanda placed under the active leadership of Ugolino Martelli with the help

TABLE 15. CAPITAL STRUCTURE OF THE BRANCHES OF THE MEDICI BANK
ON MARCH 25, 1451

Branch	Name of Partners	Local Currency	Florentine Currency	Percent of Total
		Small florins	florins	
Avignon	Medici Bank...............	14,000	8,400	87.5
	Giovanni Zampini...........	1,000	600	6.25
	Verano di Bartolomeo Peruzzi	1,000	600	6.25
	Total.................	16,000	9,600	100.00
		pounds groat	florins	
Bruges	Medici Bank...............	2,160	10,800	72.0
	Gerozzo de' Pigli...........	540	2,700	18.0
	Agnolo di Jacopo Tani.......	300	1,500	10.0
	Total.................	3,000	15,000	100.0
		écus of 64	florins	
Geneva	Medici Bank...............	10,500	11,807	87.5
	Francesco di Tommaso Sassetti	1,500	1,687	12.5
	Total.................	12,000	13,494	100.0
		pounds sterling	florins	
London	Medici Bank...............	800	4,800	80.0
	Gerozzo de' Pigli...........	200	1,200	20.0
	Simone Nori................	.....	.....	....
	Total.................	1,000	6,000	100.0
			florins	
Pisa	Medici privately......................		2,000	33.3
	Carlo de' Marsuppini..................		2,000	33.3
	Ugolino Martelli......................		1,000	16.7
	Matteo Masi..........................		1,000	16.7
	Total..........................		6,000	100.0
		ducats	florins	
Venice	Medici Bank	7,000	7,700	100.0
	Alessandro Martelli..........	.....	.....	....
	Total.................	7,000	7,700	100.0
			florins	
Woolshop I	Medici Bank.........................		3,500	58.3
	Andrea Giuntini......................		2,500	41.7
	Total..........................		6,000	100.0
Woolshop II	Medici Bank.........................		2,500	62.5
	Antonio di Taddeo....................		1,500	37.5
	Total..........................		4,000	100.0
			florins	
Silkshop	Medici Bank.........................		4,800	66.7
	Berlinghieri Berlinghieri................		1,800	25.0
	Jacopo Tanaglia......................		600	8.3
	Total..........................		7,200	100.0

Source: ASF, MAP, filza 153, no. 3.

of Matteo Masi. In Geneva, the manager was Francesco di Tommaso Sassetti (1421–1490), who was slated to become the chief advisor of Lorenzo the Magnificent and the initiator of mistaken policies which brought about the disastrous decline of the Bank. He received one sixth of the profits, although his share in the capital was only one eighth.[75] In 1448 the accomanda in Avignon had become a regular partnership, with Giovanni Zampini still as managing partner. However, he was given as assistant manager the twenty-four-year-old Verano Peruzzi, who was a brother-in-law of Giovanni Benci. Both Zampini and Peruzzi, according to the articles of association, were to receive the same share of the profits, each one eighth.[76] Gerozzo de' Pigli was an investing partner in both the London and Bruges companies; the management was entrusted to Simone Nori (1417–before 1478) in London and to Angelo Tani (1415–1492) in Bruges. Although Pigli was not responsible for the conduct of the business, this conscientious man went in 1453 to Bruges and London on an inspection tour and perhaps to replace Tani who was dangerously ill and then absent to take a cure at the baths of Petriolo and to visit headquarters.[77]

There was no change in the management of the two woolshops. The silkshop, too, was making good under the lead of Berlinghieri di Francesco Berlinghieri (1426–1480), who had succeeded his father in 1447.

As Table 16 shows, more than 18,000 florins of capital were supplied by branch managers and outside investors. If this amount is added to the 72,000 florins supplied by the partners of the Medici Bank, one obtains a total capital investment of 90,000 florins. This is still less than the capital of the Peruzzi company which failed in 1343 and was the second

TABLE 16. Amounts Invested by Outsiders in the Capital
of the Medici Branches on March 25, 1451

Branch	Amount florins
Avignon	1,200
Bruges	4,200
Geneva	1,687
London	1,200
Pisa	4,000
Total	12,287
Woolshop I (with Andrea Giuntini)	2,500
Woolshop II (with Antonio Taddei)	1,500
Silkshop	2,400
Total	18,687

Source: Table 15.

largest at that time. The Bardi company, bankrupt in 1346, was still larger. It is extremely doubtful whether the Medici Bank ever reached the size of these two giants.[78] Of course, the amount of 90,000 florins is far from representing total resources. To obtain this aggregate, it would be necessary to add accrued earnings, deposits, and other sources of funds. No reliable data are available, and there is no point in making a wild guess.

An analysis of the Libro segreto No. 3 has made it possible to tabulate the earnings of the Medici Bank from 1435 to 1450 inclusive. These data are shown in Tables 17 and 18. Table 17 shows separately the profits made before and after March 24, 1441, because of the death of Lorenzo, Cosimo's brother, on September 23, 1440. Table 18 is arranged differently and has separate columns to show how another death, that of Antonio Salutati in 1443, affected the allocation of profits.

One startling fact is that the profits of the Rome branch declined both

TABLE 17. PROFITS OF THE MEDICI BANK FROM 1435 TO 1450

Branch	Profits for the Whole Period				Percent of Total	June 3, 1435 to March 24, 1441			March 25, 1441 to March 24, 1451		
	florins	s.	d.	aff.		f.	s.	d.	f.	s.	d.
Ancona.....	5,116	0	0		1.7	4,168	0	0	948	0	0
Avignon.....	8,948	14	6		3.1	.....	..	..	8,948	14	6
Basel........	5,065	0	6		1.6	5,065	0	6	.....	..	..
Bruges and London...	17,788	12	8		6.1	2,350	0	0	15,438	12	8
Florence.....	24,568	5	7		8.4	2,200	0	0	22,368	5	7
Geneva......	46,975	15	10		16.6	19,924	25	6	27,050	19	4
Pisa.........	1,000	0	0		0.3	.....	..	..	1,000	0	0
Rome.......	88,511	14	11		30.4	35,960	21	0	52,550	22	11
Venice......	63,319	16	11		21.8	27,740	1	10	35,579	15	1
Subtotal...	261,292	22	11		90.0	97,408	19	10	163,884	3	1
Woolshop I (with Antonio Taddei)...	4,917	3	6		1.7	925	0	0	3,992	3	6
Woolshop II (with Giuntini)..	5,455	15	7		1.8	1,225	23	9	4,229	20	10
Silkshop.....	19,125	17	10		6.5	4,810	23	0	14,314	23	10
Subtotal...	29,498	7	11		10.0	6,961	17	9	22,536	19	2
Total...	290,791	1	10		100.0	104,370	8	7	186,420	22	3

Source: ASF, MAP, filza 153, no. 3: Libro segreto, 1435–1450.

absolutely and relatively in comparison to the preceding period from
1420 to 1435. On the other hand, Geneva improved in its position both
in absolute numbers and in percentage of total profits. The Tavola of
Florence made a poor showing during the period from 1435 to 1441,
perhaps because recovery from the crisis of 1433–1434 was slow. In any

TABLE 18. PROFITS ASSIGNED TO THE PARTNERS OF THE MEDICI BANK
FROM 1435 TO 1450

	Total			From 1435 to 1443			From 1444 to 1450		
Name	f.	s.	d.	f.	s.	d.	f.	s.	d.
Medici or *maggiori*...	203,702	13	7	115,126	19	7	88,575	23	0
Antonio Salutati....	28,781	19	4	28,781	19	4	.....	..	..
Giovanni d'Amerigo Benci............	58,306	26	11	28,781	19	4	29,525	7	7
Total.........	290,791	1	10	172,690	0	3	118,101	1	7

Source: ASF, MAP, filza 153, no. 3: Libro segreto, 1435–1450.

case, as already stated, the Tavola never was a major source of profits for
the Medici Bank, probably because competition was fierce among the
Florentine tavole. Venice was next in importance to Rome. As earlier, by
far the major part of the profits — 90 percent — originated in trade and
banking.

As Table 18 shows, prior to 1443 the Medici received two thirds of the
profits and the two junior partners, Antonio Salutati and Giovanni
Benci, each one sixth. After the death of Salutati in 1443, this proportion
was altered: the share of the Medici was increased from two thirds to
three fourths and that of Benci from one sixth to one fourth. As no
appointment was made to replace Salutati, Benci alone became general
manager and retained this position until his own death in 1455.

Between 1450 and 1455, the only major event was the creation in
1452, or 1453 at the latest, of a branch in Milan.[79] It was to be the last,
since the transfer of the Geneva branch to Lyons in 1464 did not involve any increase in the number of establishments. From 1455 onward,
the Medici Bank ceased to grow and, as standing still is impossible in a
dynamic world, it soon entered into a period of decline, which began
with the death of Cosimo (1464), if not sooner.

The foundation of the Milan branch was perhaps more a move on the
chessboard of Italian politics than a decision prompted by economic
motives. There is no doubt that it was made at the behest of Francesco
Sforza (1401–1466), the condottiere who had married a natural daughter
of the last Visconti and gained the dukedom of Milan (February 26,

3a. Recto of a Protest with the text of the Bill of Exchange shown in lower corner. October 22, 1463

3b. Verso of the Protest (plate 3a), with verso of the Bill of Exchange shown at the top

1450), thanks to his own astuteness and the financial support of Cosimo. Sforza's accession to power was not at all to the taste of the Venetians, who had expected Milan, rent by internal dissensions, to fall into their lap like a ripe plum. To prevent a rupture of the balance of power, Cosimo forsook the old alliance with Venice and lined himself up with Milan, Florence's traditional enemy. The grateful Sforza in 1455 gave the Medici a building, which Cosimo remodelled for use of the Milan branch. It was not entirely ready for occupancy until 1459.[80]

The first manager of the Milan branch was Pigello Portinari (1421–1468), son of the Folco Portinari who had been manager in charge of the Tavola in Florence. Pigello had been trained in the Venetian branch. He was a very successful manager, who kept the favor of the Sforza court without compromising the solvency of the bank by granting credit indiscriminately.[81] Because of his efficiency and loyalty, he was very much liked by the Medici, who regretted his untimely death and continued to cherish his memory. He was succeeded as manager by his brother Accerrito (1427–c. 1503), who had neither a pleasing personality nor outstanding managerial ability. As a result, he involved the Milan branch in such grave financial difficulties that it had to be liquidated. The same happened to the Bruges branch because of the mismanagement of Tommaso Portinari, the third of the Portinari brothers.

Giovanni d'Amerigo Benci, Cosimo's favorite general manager, died in mid-July, 1455. It was not easy to find a suitable successor, since men of such high caliber are not met at every corner. As a matter of fact, Giovanni Benci was irreplaceable and was not replaced. Perhaps Cosimo thought that the duties of general manager could best be discharged by his own son Giovanni (1421–1463), now thirty-four years of age, who had been carefully trained for business, while Piero (1416–1469), the elder son, had been given a humanistic education more suitable for a ruler than for a banker.[82] Moreover, Giovanni impressed his father with his sound judgment in business matters and his executive abilities. In any case, he was to limit himself to the general problems raised by the management of the concern as a whole.

For the job of manager of the Tavola in Florence, the maggiori kept Francesco di Baldino di Giovanni Inghirami (c. 1414–1470), who had succeeded his brother Giovanni in 1454. Francesco may have received greater powers but he certainly was not suited to perform the functions of a general manager, since he lacked the experience to be gained from serving in one of the foreign branches. In his portata for the catasto of 1457, Inghirami states unambiguously that he is a partner only in the Medici Bank of Florence, that he manages this bank in person, and that he owns a share of 400 florins in its capital.[83] As assistant to Inghirami, there was Tommaso di Giovanni di Tommaso Lapi (1421–before 1486).[84]

Further confirmation is found in the Libro di compagnie of the Money-changers' Gild. From 1462 through 1469, this register lists regularly as partners in the Tavola: the Medici, Francesco di Baldino Inghirami, and Tommaso di Giovanni Lapi.[85] After 1469 the name of Lapi disappears from the gild records and is replaced by that of Francesco d'Antonio Nori, who was expelled from France in 1468 for incurring the displeasure of Louis XI.[86] Inghirami is no longer recorded since he died in 1470.

Probably Cosimo's scheme did not work out so well because Giovanni di Cosimo, a pleasure-loving man, was distracted from his main job by other pursuits. To lighten the burden, Francesco di Tommaso Sassetti was called from Geneva in 1458. He remained in Florence for the rest of his life with the exception of a few trips abroad; after Cosimo's death he became the trusted advisor of Piero the Gouty and Lorenzo the Magnificent. How these changes affected the structure of the Medici banking house is not altogether clear. There are serious gaps in the available sources. No libri segreti for this period are extant and only a few of the partnership agreements have survived. The correspondence, more abundant, sheds little light on this issue. It is certain that Sassetti continued to be a partner in Geneva (later Lyons) and to share in the profits of this branch. He was not admitted immediately as a partner of the Medici in Florence. In the Libro di compagnie of the Money-changers' Gild, his name is not mentioned until 1482, but the records of the preceding years are incomplete and badly kept.[87]

It is likely, if not certain, that, after Giovanni Benci's death in 1455, the structure of the Medici banking house was greatly altered and that it ceased to be a concern of the holding company type with a central partnership owning shares in several subsidiaries or branches. Instead the Medici family went directly into partnership with each of the branch managers; thus the intermediate layer of a parent company was eliminated.[88] Whether this type of organization was revived later is hard to tell. The records are so full of gaps that it would be unwise to venture any categorical statement.

For the seventh catasto, that of 1457 (Florentine style), Cosimo made out a statement about his business investments.[89] It confirms what has been said heretofore and lists eleven companies, or partnerships, in the capital of which the Medici had a share: (1) the bank in Florence managed by Francesco Inghirami (5,600 florins); (2) one woolshop managed by Andrea Giuntini (2,100 florins); (3) a second woolshop managed by Antonio di Taddeo (2,500 florins); (4) the silkshop managed jointly by Berlinghieri di Francesco Berlinghieri and Jacopo Tanaglia (3,300 florins); (5) the Rome branch managed by Roberto Martelli and an assistant, Leonardo Vernacci, who has not been mentioned previously; (6) the Venice branch managed by Alessandro Martelli, Roberto's brother

(6,000 florins); (7) the Milan branch managed by Pigello Portinari (3,000 florins); (8) the Geneva branch which was being operated under the style "Amerigo Benci and Francesco Sassetti & Co." and managed by Amerigo di Giovanni Benci (3,500 florins); (9) the Avignon branch, which was styled "Francesco Benci and Giovanni Zampini & Co.," managed by Zampini with Benci's assistance (2,400 florins); (10) the Bruges branch in which the partners were Gerozzo de' Pigli and Angelo Tani, but which was actually run by Tani under Pigli's distant supervision (3,500 florins); (11) the London branch, which also had Pigli as a partner, but was managed by Simone d'Antonio Nori (4,800 florins). In addition, Cosimo lists an investment of 5,500 florins in a company with Francesco di Nerone Neroni which was being liquidated. According to Francesco Neroni's portata for the catasto, this was a trading company with a branch in Pisa. It was doing well, since the two balance sheets (Florence and Pisa) reveal that aggregate profits exceeded 12,000 florins in the form of undistributed profits.[90] Why Cosimo was withdrawing from this venture is not known.

In his report Cosimo states again that the Medici have no capital in the Rome branch, but that this branch helps the business of the others (non abbiamo corpo nessuno, ma ci aiuta all'altre ragioni). Notice that not all the Medici branches operated under the Medici name; for example, in Avignon and Geneva it is omitted from the style of the partnership. By the way, Amerigo and Francesco Benci were sons of Giovanni d'Amerigo Benci, the deceased general manager.

According to Cosimo's report, the total investment amounts to 42,200 florins. This sum is certainly far below the actual amount. Although Cosimo claims to have prepared his report without malice or deceitful intent,[91] his correspondence with Alessandro Martelli, the manager in Venice, discloses that balance sheets were deliberately falsified by overrating losses due to bad debts, understating profits, and reducing the owners' equity to a minimum.[92] The first balance prepared for tax purposes by Martelli stated that the capital was 7,000 Venetian ducats or 7,700 florins, Florentine currency, but he received orders to redo the job and to make further adjustments in order to reduce this amount to 6,360 ducats or 7,000 florins, of which 6,000 florins supposedly represented the share of the Medici.[93] This is the figure recorded in Cosimo's report. Actually the capital of the Venice branch, according to the partnership agreement of January 20, 1455, was 14,000 ducats: 12,000 ducats for the Medici and 2,000 ducats for Martelli.[94] To make the fraudulent balance appear genuine, Martelli was even instructed to write a deceptive report that could be shown to the tax officials.[95] Cosimo must even have suggested that Martelli lay out a libro segreto, but the latter replied he did not think it necessary. He went on to point out that he kept the libro segreto himself and that his clerks were dependable and could be trusted not to divulge business secrets.[96]

The figures of Cosimo's tax report are no more reliable for the other branches than for Venice. According to the partnership agreement concluded on July 25, 1455, the Medici share in the capital of the Bruges branch was £1,900 groat, Flemish currency, which corresponded to more than 9,000 florins, but the report gives only 3,500 florins.[97] The same applies to Milan. In 1459 the Medici had an investment of £40,000 imperiali, equivalent to approximately 13,500 florins.[98] Yet the report states that they participated in the capital only to the extent of 3,000 florins. The unescapable conclusion is that, in order to evade the tax, Cosimo filed a return which grossly understated the magnitude of Medici business investments.[99]

As the case of Cosimo shows, tax evasion was a game that was not frowned upon by Florentine business men. The Medici, who should have set the example of civic spirit, were the first to conceal their wealth for the purpose of diminishing the tax burden. The story of Cosimo's catasto report teaches still another lesson: historians should be wary of data in tax records. Most of the time such data are absolutely worthless for certain statistical purposes, however valuable they may be for other purposes, even to give an idea of the scale and the distribution of incomes. In any case, they should be used with caution.

There is only scant information available on the history of the Medici Bank during the quiet years from 1458 to 1464, the year of Cosimo's death. An occurrence worth mentioning is the transfer of the Geneva branch to Lyons. This was a gradual process, because the Geneva branch had already maintained an office in Lyons for some time prior to 1460. One of its factors, Francesco di Antonio Nori, was already residing there in 1455. The process was certainly speeded up after the four fairs of Lyons were established by letters patent issued on March 8, 1463, by Louis XI, King of France.[100] As attendance at the fairs of Geneva declined rapidly, the Medici branch moved the center of its activities to Lyons, but the transfer was not made all at one time and was not completed until March 25, 1466, when new articles of association definitely stated that Lyons was henceforth to be the seat of the partnership.

Under the administration of Cosimo, the Medici Bank reached its zenith in size and prosperity. This success, there is no doubt, was largely due to his capacity for leadership aided by favorable trends in business conditions. After his death, the tide turned and his successors lacked either the strength or the ability to stem the flood and were carried off by the current.

What made Cosimo such an outstanding leader and administrator in business as well as in politics was, as one historian puts it, his ability to read character.[101] He had an uncanny flair for finding the right men and for fitting them into the right places. Thus he managed to rule Florence from behind the scenes while preserving the appearances of "liberty" and constitutional procedure. But no important decision was ever taken against his will or his advice. He inspired such awe that his power went unchallenged and no plots were hatched to overthrow his rule.

According to Pope Pius II (reigned 1458–1464), who was the humanist Aeneas Silvius Piccolomini, Cosimo had so much prestige that his political influence was not confined to Florence and his advice was actively sought by rulers and princes all over Italy. Even political conditions beyond the Alps were no secret to him, since he was kept posted on the course of foreign events by his business connections abroad.[102]

The same qualities which made for success in politics were responsible for his achievements in business. With Cosimo at the helm, the Medici Bank became the largest banking house of its time. Cosimo did not try to manage everything. On the contrary, instead of becoming submerged in detail, he understood how to delegate power while holding the reins of his team with a firm hand. Throughout his career, it was he who laid down the law, formulated policies, and saw to it that his instructions were obeyed to the letter. Woe to the branch manager who dared to exceed his powers or to override Cosimo's orders, as Angelo Tani, the manager in Bruges, learned at his expense when he involved his branch in losses by dealing with the lombards, or Italian pawnbrokers, and lending them excessive amounts.[103] The irate Cosimo threatened to terminate the partnership and would have done so, if his advisors had not interceded and dissuaded him from doing anything drastic.

Despite his involvement in politics, Cosimo did not relax his grip on business affairs and continued throughout his life to take an active part in the management of his bank. Because of the slowness of communication, it was unavoidable that the branch managers be given a great deal of leeway in making decisions. It was, therefore, very important to select efficient and honest men. As head of the firm, Cosimo knew how to pick them out. Next, he gave his managers firm guidance and was prompt in correcting any mistakes or in rebuking them for any failure. In this task he was ably assisted by Giovanni Benci, his general manager from 1435 to 1455, during twenty years of continuous expansion. Benci's death proved to be an irreparable loss for the Medici Bank.

Although a stern master, Cosimo was generous in sharing profits with his managers. Those who had a good record had no trouble in securing favorable contracts. Several families, especially the Benci, the Martelli, the Taddei, the Berlinghieri, enriched themselves in Cosimo's service.[104] Cosimo may have been a harsh man, but his heart had tender spots. When Folco Portinari, the manager of the *Tavola* in Florence, died in

1431 leaving several minor children, Cosimo took care of them and had them brought up in his household. As events turned out, the Medici were not repaid for their generosity as two of the Portinari brothers were to play a leading rôle in the downfall of the Medici Bank.

It may be that Cosimo's ability to judge men and to size up a situation weakened during the last years of his life when his health was impaired and he was tortured by gout. His decision to replace Benci by his son Giovanni was not altogether a happy one. Perhaps in trying to correct this mistake he made another by calling Francesco di Tommaso Sassetti from Geneva to Florence in order to assist Giovanni. In any case, it was the tragic fate of the Medici Bank that Cosimo's son Piero, crippled by gout, died so soon after his father and that his grandson Lorenzo, while a brilliant statesman, never acquired an aptitude for business.

When Cosimo realized that his end was near, he refused, like his father, to make a testament, but he expressed the wish to be buried simply, without pomp, as a private citizen. He expired on August 1, 1464, at the Medici villa of Careggi near Florence. His wish was respected and there was no state funeral. However, the Florentine republic paid him the highest tribute by proclaiming him *pater patriae,* the father of his country.

V

THE LEGAL STATUS AND ECONOMIC
STRUCTURE OF THE MEDICI BANK

1. The Central Administration

From a legal and structural point of view, it is possible to classify the Florentine banking and trading companies into two different types: those having a centralized form of organization and those constituted by a combination of autonomous partnerships controlled either by an individual or by another partnership topping the whole edifice. The first type was more popular in the thirteenth and fourteenth centuries and was adopted by the Bardi, the Peruzzi, and the Acciaiuoli companies. Their form of organization was rather rigid, a defect brought to the fore when all three companies failed around 1345. As a result, this type of organization declined in popularity after 1350 and gave way to the second and more flexible type. A good example is that of the merchant-banker Francesco Datini, who controlled a network of branches and, for this purpose, formed a separate partnership with each of his branch managers. A subspecies is typified by the Medici Bank where control, at least up to 1455, did not rest with an individual but with a partnership. There are consequently two layers: a controlling partnership — the parent — and several tributary partnerships — the subsidiaries. Only this subspecies prefigures the modern holding company.

As today, there were sometimes great structural differences from one company to another. It is dangerous, therefore, to make generalizations on the basis of one company without knowing to what an extent its organization is typical. Nevertheless, the Bardi and the Peruzzi companies, which have been studied with great care by Professor Armando Sapori, present some striking similarities. The same features, though to a lesser degree, are also present in the Alberti company. The essential characteristic of the Bardi and Peruzzi companies is that they formed single units or entities embracing the home office in Florence and all the branches abroad. Their capital was divided into shares and net profits were divided proportionately to the number of shares held by each partner. Thus, in 1331, the capital of the Bardi company was made up of fifty-eight shares: six members of the family were in possession of the majority of shares (36¾), while five outsiders owned the rest (21¼).[1] In 1312, the Peruzzi company had a capital of £116,000 affiorino, or 80,000 florins, distributed among eight members of the family and nine outsiders. It was only in 1331 that the family lost complete control, because more than half the capital belonged henceforth to outsiders.[2]

In theory, all the partners residing in Florence had a voice in the management. The number of partners was sometimes rather large: sixteen in 1324 and twenty-one in 1331 in the case of the Peruzzi company. Since it is impossible to run a business firm with a board, the partners in practice accepted the leadership of one of them, usually a strong personality, who was called "head of the company." (capo della compagnia).[3] He performed practically the same functions as the president of a modern corporation and stayed in office as long as he retained the confidence of his fellow partners. Their approval was needed only for major decisions. Usually the name of the capo della compagnia appeared in the style of the company. Thus, the Peruzzi company was officially called "Tommaso d'Arnoldo de' Peruzzi e compagni" from 1303 to 1333 while Tommaso d'Arnoldo was at the helm. The style did not change to "Giotto d'Arnoldo de' Peruzzi e compagni" until after Tommaso's death, when the partners voted to entrust the headship to his brother Giotto who had been treasurer for many years.[4] Incidentally, not only the company's head, but also the treasurer and chief accountant was usually a partner.[5] One of the drawbacks of this arrangement was that, in case of losses or difficulties, quarrels among the partners about policy and appropriate remedies were likely to make matters worse instead of better. Discord of this kind seems to have hastened the downfall of the great bank of Orlando Bonsignori, a Sienese company that failed in 1298, and may have played a part in causing the collapse of the Bardi and Peruzzi companies by alarming the depositors at a critical juncture.[6]

In contrast with these two companies, the Medici banking house was not a single unit but a combination of partnerships all controlled by a "parent" firm which included as partners the Medici and one or two outsiders (for example, from 1435 to 1443, Salutati and Benci). Each of the branches or manufacturing establishments was a separate legal entity (ragione) with its own style, its own capital, its own books, and its own management.[7] The several branches dealt with each other on the same basis as with outside customers. One branch charged commission to another branch as if both belonged to entirely different concerns.[8] When two branches joined in a deal, it was customary to determine in advance how the profits or losses were to be divided.

At the top, however, concentration of power was greater in the Medici firm than was the case with the Peruzzi or the Bardi companies. Cosimo, for example, did not have to report to a board or to ask its approval on this or that. He might consult Giovanni Benci, his general manager, and he undoubtedly always did before making any important decision.

Moreover, the two men fully trusted each other, were able to work hand in hand, and probably saw eye to eye on all major issues or problems. Whether such a concentration of power is good or bad is a matter of opinion. Different forms of business organization, like different forms of government, have their advantages and disadvantages. In the end much depends on the personality of the policy makers and the wisdom of their decisions. The best organization on paper will not work smoothly in practice if, because of conflict or incompatibility, the men at the top are unable or unwilling to cooperate or do not command the loyalty of their subordinates.

Lest there be confusion, it may be well, before proceeding, to straighten out some matters of terminology. First of all, the Italian business records use constantly the words *compagno* and *fattore*. What is their meaning and what is the difference between the two? Compagno was the medieval word for partner. Italian business firms of that time often called themselves companies, although they were really partnerships and not corporations or companies in the modern sense. A compagno was, of course, party to a partnership agreement and was entitled to a share in the profits in accordance with the provisions of this contract. He did not receive a salary but was sometimes granted an allowance to cover living and other expenses, especially if residing abroad.

In the parlance of the Middle Ages, the word fattore, or factor, did not refer to some kind of commission merchant or agent, but designated simply an employee of a trading or banking company, more specifically an employee serving in an establishment abroad.[9] Sometimes fattore was used as a synonym of giovane. In any case, a fattore or giovane was an employee who had more experience and was older than a *garzone* or a *discepolo,* terms reserved for office boys about twelve to fifteen years old. Fattori were sometimes bound to a company by a notarial contract which determined the terms of their employment.[10] It usually circumscribed their powers and defined their duties carefully without impairing the employers' rights in matters of promotion or dismissal. Factors received a salary "for the donation of their time," but they did not participate in the profits. However, they were sometimes awarded a bonus or a special stipend if their services had been outstanding.[11]

Branch managers could be either fattori or compagni. When they were factors, they were usually provided with a power of attorney which allowed them to represent and bind their employers.[12] For greater safety, partners were also supplied with a notarial procuration.[13] According to the Medici records, a branch manager was sometimes called *governatore* because the *governo* (management) of a branch was entrusted to him. Sometimes the word used was *ministro* (administrator) which was also applied to the general manager. Thus, Lorenzo the Magnificent in his

Ricordi called Francesco Sassetti *nostro ministro e compagno*.[14] In the correspondence and other records, the Medici were usually addressed or referred to as *maggiori,* that is, as seniors or senior partners.

In the case of the Peruzzi company, branch managers were either partners or factors. However, all branches of major importance were managed by partners (Table 19). Such partners, who went abroad to serve the company in the capacity of branch manager, received a regular salary for giving their time and efforts, irrespective of their right to a share in the profits. A good example is that of Donato di Giotto d'Arnoldo Peruzzi, who was in charge of the branch in Naples from December 9, 1332, until June 30, 1335.[15] It rarely happened that a factor rose to the rank of partner.[16]

In this respect, the Medici followed a different policy and selected their branch managers among their staff. These branch managers were, as a rule, junior partners who, instead of a salary, received a share in the profits plus an allowance for living expenses. While the Medici did not pay higher salaries than competitors, they were rather liberal in letting the junior partners share in the profits. This system had the advantage of encouraging endeavor and of providing a greater incentive

TABLE 19. STATUS OF THE BRANCH MANAGERS OF THE PERUZZI COMPANY
SHORTLY BEFORE JUNE 30, 1335

Branch	Name of Manager	Status
Avignon (Court of Rome)	Filippo Villani	Partner
Barletta (Apulia)	Passa di Bartolo Borghi	Factor
Bruges	Pacino di Guido di Filippo Peruzzi	Partner
Castello di Castro (Sardinia)	Michele Bottaccini	Factor
Cyprus	Gano Cambi	Factor
Genoa	Tommaso d'Arnolfo de'Bagnesi	Factor
London	Giovanni di Tano Baroncelli*	Son of partner
Majorca	Tommaso di Neri Perini	Factor
Naples	Donato di Giotto d'Arnoldo Peruzzi	Partner
Paris	Filippo di Pacino d'Arnoldo Peruzzi	Partner
Pisa	Francesco di Giamo Folchi	Factor
Rhodes	Simone Spigliati	Factor
Sicily	Francesco Forzetti	Partner
Tunis	Dato del Nero Albertini	Factor
Venice	Giovanni Bonducci Cambi	Factor

* Giovanni di Tano Baroncelli became a partner on July 1, 1335. His father did not die until April 17, 1337 (*Libri*, p. 354).

Source: Sapori, *I libri dei Peruzzi*, pp. 191–195.

to do well, because a satisfactory factor stood a fair chance of becoming a partner and of thereby greatly increasing his earnings. It also put pressure on the branch managers to make profits and to avoid losses. Junior partners, of course, could not be dismissed, but they could easily be removed because the Medici always reserved the right to denounce a partnership agreement at any time. Occasionally they made use of this privilege, but, it is true, only as a last resort and for serious reasons.

In studying the organization of the Medici Bank, one cannot fail to notice how closely it resembles that of a holding company.[17] This comparison is valid with the understanding that the Medici Bank was a combination of partnerships rather than of corporations or joint-stock companies, a form of organization unknown to the Middle Ages. In any case, as already pointed out, there were two layers: a "parent" company located in Florence and several subsidiaries. The parent company controlled the subsidiary partnerships, that is, the Tavola in Florence, the branches abroad, and the industrial establishments, by owning more than 50 percent of the capital. Besides, the articles of association clearly vested the maggiori with the power to lay down the law and to determine policy.

To give one example, the articles of association of the "company" formed in 1435 by Cosimo and Lorenzo di Giovanni de' Medici, Giovanni d'Amerigo Benci, and Antonio di Messer Francesco Salutati stipulate unambiguously that "all what is done by the Tavola in Florence, the branches in Geneva, in Venice, at the Curia and the Basel Council is and will be for [the benefit of] the said company from which these other ragioni issue" (tutto quello che ne' detti luoghi e conpagnie si fosse fatto o sia fatto . . . s'intenda essere e sia per questa conpagnia . . . e di questa [sono] uscite le sopradette ragioni).[18] The wording is clumsy, but the meaning is clear. The only possible interpretation is that the branches issue from the parent company and that their profits will accrue to the latter, of course after deduction of the share due to the junior partners. Another article stipulates that the Medici, Benci, and Salutati will exert themselves for the good of their company and visit, if need be, the other ragioni issuing from it.[19] In other words, the senior partners do not only intend to control the subsidiaries; they claim the right to inspect and supervise. The provisions of the partnership agreements did not remain a dead letter. As we know from the surviving libri segreti, net profits made by branches were credited first to the parent company and then reallocated to its partners (Tables 8 and 9, 11 and 12, 17 and 18). The evidence, it seems, is conclusive.

Although further proof is superfluous, let us nevertheless have a look at the contracts of one or two subsidiaries. Take, for example, the agreement concluded on October 16, 1420, with Folco d'Adoardo Portinari, the manager of the Tavola in Florence. The contract is not between the Medici and Portinari, but between, on the one hand, the company of Cosimo and Lorenzo de' Medici and Ilarione de' Bardi and, on the other hand, Folco Portinari, who is to be "companion" only in the "traffic" of Florence and nowhere else.[20] In other words, it is the holding company, not any individuals, that went into partnership with Portinari. The same procedure is followed when branches abroad are involved.

Thus, the partnership agreement of March 25, 1435, relating to the Venetian branch mentions three contracting parties: (1) the company of the Medici, Benci, and Salutati; (2) Lotto di Tanino Bozzi, the branch manager; (3) Antonio di Niccolò Martelli, the assistant manager.[21] It is the parent company as a unit which furnishes the major part of the capital, 7,000 out of 8,000 ducats, and receives a lesser share of the profits in order to reward the managing partners for their exertions. As a matter of fact, the division is as follows:

Medici, Benci, and Salutati together, seventeen twenty-fourths	17 shares
Lotto Bozzi, manager, one-sixth	4 shares
Antonio Martelli, assistant manager, one-eighth	3 shares
Total	24 shares

There are among the Medici papers a few later partnership contracts dating from the time of Piero di Cosimo and Lorenzo the Magnificent. In them the Medici appear as individuals and no longer in partnership with their general manager. It seems, therefore, that the Medici Bank, as mentioned above, ceased to be a combination resembling the holding company after Giovanni Benci's death in 1455.

Of course, owning the whole or the major part of the capital of each subsidiary was not the only means used by the Medici to keep control over branches or to discourage enterprising managers from breaking away and setting up competing firms, as did Antonio della Casa, who founded a rival bank in Rome. To prevent such defections, the Medici made it an absolute rule to stipulate in all articles of association that they retained the ownership of their merchant mark and the custody of books, papers, and archives after termination of the contract. The Medici name carried a great deal of good will, an advantage which would be lost if the senior partners chose to withdraw, as Tommaso Portinari found out after breaking with them. The same is true today; ownership of stock is not the only way of retaining control. There are trademarks, patent pools, limited voting rights, interlocking directorates, and other devices.

Since each one of the branches, as we have just seen, was a separate *ragione* (legal entity), one was not responsible for the actions of another. An issue on this point was raised in a lawsuit brought before the Bruges

INTERNAL ORGANIZATION OF THE MEDICI BANK (around 1455)

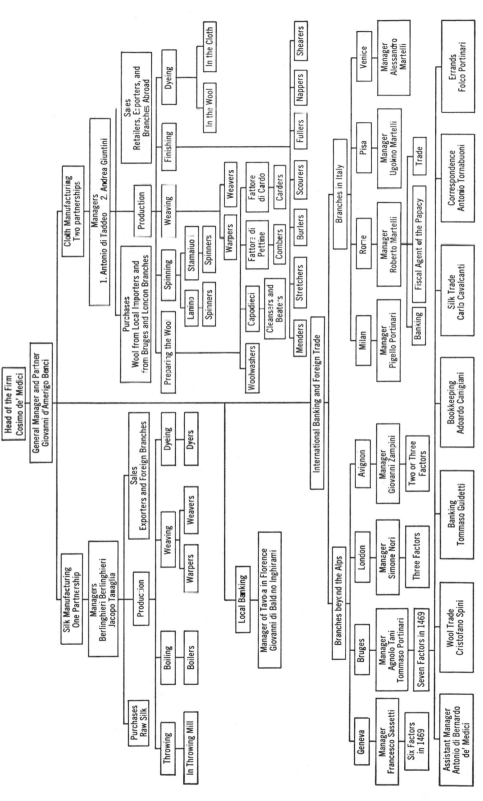

municipal court on July 30, 1455. A Milanese, Damiano Ruffini, sued the Bruges branch of the Medici Bank for damages because of defective packing of nine bales of wool bought by the plaintiff from Simone Nori, manager of the London branch. Tommaso Portinari, as acting manager of the Bruges branch, denied all responsibility because the bales had not been sold by the Medici of Bruges and pointed out that Ruffini, if he had any claims, should bring action against the Medici of London. To this argument the plaintiff replied that the two branches were part of the same company and had one master. Thereupon Tommaso Portinari declared under oath that, while it was true that both branches had the same master, they were nonetheless separate partnerships, that one was not answerable for the other, and that the wool had been sold to Ruffini for account of the Medici of London, not of Bruges. The court, in its sentence, found for the defendant and dismissed the plea of the plaintiff with the reservation that it upheld his right to sue Simone Nori and the Medici company in London.[22]

A similar issue would be raised if a person brought suit in an American court against the Standard Oil of New Jersey for defective merchandise received from the Standard Oil of Indiana and based his case upon the argument that all Standard Oil companies were controlled by the Rockefellers! Of course, such an action would be so absurd as to be inconceivable. But the Ruffini *vs.* Portinari case, one should not forget, dates back to the fifteenth century. At that time commercial law was still more or less in its infancy, especially in Northern Europe, and there were presumably no well-established precedents on the issue at stake. There is no doubt that the decision of the Bruges court is consonant with what was to become later accepted mercantile usage.[23]

For a long time the important position of the general manager in the organization of the Medici Bank was not fully realized.[24] He was not only the chief advisor of the Medici in all business matters, but he carried the administrative burden which they were unable to shoulder. It was, for example, the duty of the general manager to correspond with all the branch managers, to determine the policies which they were to follow, to give them instructions, to read their reports, and to discuss with the Medici at the top all problems that could not be solved without the latter's approval.

As a standard procedure, branch managers were expected to close their books once a year — usually on March 24 — and to send to headquarters a copy of the balance with a statement of profit and loss.[25] Since the accumulation of bad debts was a major threat to the solvency of banking companies like the Medici, it was one of the major functions of the general manager to audit the balances he received and to go over them item by item with a trained eye for aging and slow accounts and other irregularities.[26] Perhaps a shortcoming of the Medici was that, unlike the Fugger in the sixteenth century, they did not have traveling auditors and inspectors who would go from branch to branch to examine the books and to take inventories. Too much reliance was placed on confidence in the integrity and ability of the branch managers, with the result that serious disorders were not always discovered in time to apply remedies and prevent heavy losses.

When branch managers came to Florence to report or to negotiate the renewal of their contracts with the maggiori, it was the duty of the general manager to have conferences with them to discuss past performance and future plans. Usually advantage was taken of the opportunity to ask the branch manager for clarification of questionable items on the latest balance sheet.[27] Business prospects and current political events also came in for discussion. Next the terms of the new contract were debated and finally set after securing the approval of the maggiori. The general manager usually prepared at least one copy of the contract.[28] He also drafted the instructions with which branch managers, factors, and other emissaries were provided upon leaving Florence.

A minor duty of the general manager was to keep the libro segreto of the Medici Bank, that is, the parent company. The second of the extant libri segreti (1420–1435) is for the most part in Ilarione's hand and the third (1435–1450) entirely in that of Giovanni Benci.

Giovanni di Bicci took his general managers from the Bardi family and appointed in succession two brothers, Benedetto di Lippaccio (1402–1420) and Ilarione di Lippaccio (1420–1433). As already explained, Ilarione was not replaced immediately upon his death because of the looming political crisis leading to Cosimo's exile. Probably Lippaccio di Benedetto de' Bardi took care of affairs in Florence during this interim period. The Geneva and Rome branches probably received instructions directly from Cosimo in Venice. After Cosimo's return to Florence, a contract was made, in 1435, with Antonio di Francesco Salutati and Giovanni d'Amerigo Benci, who presumably worked as a team. This joint management lasted until 1443, when Salutati died and Benci alone assumed the burden. During his period of tenure (1443–1455), the Medici Bank reached its climax of power and prosperity.

After Benci's death in 1455, Cosimo entrusted the general management of his business interests to his own son Giovanni (1455–1463), but this arrangement did not work out well, and so Francesco di Tommaso Sassetti was called from Geneva in 1458 to help Giovanni in the discharge of his duties. After the deaths of Giovanni (1463) and Cosimo (1464), Sassetti became the trusted advisor of Piero the Gouty (1464–1469), and his power increased still further under the rule of Lorenzo the Magnificent (1469–1492). Nothing was done or decided against

Sassetti's will. This period (1463–1490) coincided with the decline of the Medici Bank because Sassetti was unable to avoid the disastrous liquidation of the Bruges, London, and Milan branches. He managed, however, to rescue the Lyons branch from sharing the same fate. In spite of all, Lorenzo the Magnificent could not bring himself to remove the inefficient Sassetti from office. After the latter had died from a stroke in March 1490, the last general manager, Giovambattista Bracci (1490–1494), tried hard to salvage the Medici Bank from impending doom. These efforts were not made easier by the constant and tempestuous interferences of Giovanni Tornabuoni (1428–c. 1497), the manager of the Rome branch and Lorenzo's uncle.

Three of the partnership agreements concluded by the Medici with their general managers are still extant.[29] They show that the capital of the Bank, that is, the holding company, was gradually raised from 24,000 florins in 1420 to 44,000 florins on March 25, 1441. A clause common to all the surviving contracts prescribed the creation of an adequate reserve for bad debts before proceeding to any distribution of profits. Another article forbade the granting of credit to any person who was not a reputable merchant, which would exclude, it seems, any loans to princes and noblemen. According to the contract of 1441 made after the death of Lorenzo di Giovanni, the general managers, Salutati and Benci, promised to exert themselves in behalf of the company and to go abroad, if Cosimo should decide to send them on an inspection tour. It is thus made clear who was really the "boss," to use a slang expression. The duration of the contracts was usually five years, but the Medici reserved for themselves the right to end the agreement at any time upon six months' notice. All contracts include an article listing the subsidiaries controlled by the Bank. Thus the agreement of 1441 mentions the Tavola in Florence, the branches in Bruges, Geneva, Rome, and Venice, the accomanda of the Marches, and the three "shops," or industrial establishments. An analysis of the three surviving contracts between the Medici and their general managers fully corroborates what we have said about the organization of the Medici Bank prior to 1455, namely, that it adumbrates the modern holding company.

2. Branch Management

The relations between the central administration and the branches had their legal basis in the partnership agreements concluded with the local managers. Quite a few of these contracts have come down to us. Since they all follow more or less the same pattern, it would be unnecessarily repetitious to discuss them one by one in detail. It is, therefore, preferable to confine the discussion to a typical contract. The best choice appears to be the articles of association of July 25, 1455, relating to the Bruges branch, because both the original text and an English translation are readily available in print.[30]

As the date indicates, this contract was signed a few days after the death of Giovanni Benci had put an end to the holding company. It is, therefore, not surprising that there is no reference to it in the contract. The contracting parties mentioned are three: (1) Piero di Cosimo, Giovanni di Cosimo, and Pierfrancesco di Lorenzo, members of the Medici family; (2) Gerozzo di Jacopo de' Pigli, former manager of the Bruges and London branches, investing partner; (3) Angelo di Jacopo Tani, active partner.[31] Cosimo is not listed, but this omission does not have any significance. As *pater familias,* he was still the real power behind the front of his two sons and his nephew.

After naming the partners, the preamble of the contract continues by defining the purpose of the company, which was "to deal in exchange and in merchandise in the city of Bruges in Flanders." The "government," or the burden of the management, was to be assumed by Angelo Tani, the junior partner, for the duration of four years beginning March 25, 1456, and ending March 24, 1460.

According to article one, the company was to be styled "Piero di Cosimo de' Medici, Gerozzo de' Pigli & Co." Next the capital was set at £3,000 groat, Flemish currency, to be supplied as follows: £1,900 — or more than half — by the senior partners, members of the Medici family; £600 by Pigli, and £500 by Tani. With this capital, the latter was to trade honorably in accordance with mercantile customs and the instructions of the Medici and Pigli. Further, he was supposed to engage only in licit contracts and exchanges, a clause which *ipso facto* excluded all usurious practices, in principle at least. Tani was expected to reside in Bruges and to devote himself body and soul to the welfare and interests of the company.

Profits were to be divided in the following way: 12s. in the pound or 60 percent to the Medici, 4s. in the pound or 20 percent to Gerozzo de' Pigli, and 4s. in the pound or 20 percent to Angelo Tani. The latter, who supplied only one sixth of the capital, received one fifth of the profits, the standard practice. No capital could be taken out for the duration of the contract, and approval of the Medici and Pigli was required to distribute any profits. Tani, however, was allowed £20 groat a year for living expenses. Losses, "may God forbid," were to be shared in the same proportion as profits (art. 3).

The purpose of the other provisions of the contract were mainly to circumscribe the powers of Tani, the manager, and to spell out what he could and could not do. They make it plain that he was scarcely more than a factor and that he was placed in a subordinate position in relation to his copartners who, instead of his equals, were his superiors.

First of all, he was not allowed to do any business for himself either directly or indirectly. If he did so, the profits would accrue to the partnership, but the losses would be his. In addition, he was liable to a penalty of £50 groat for any violation of this rule (art. 6). Further, he was not supposed to leave his post unless called to Florence to report on his management. However, he needed no special permission to attend the fairs of Antwerp and Bergen-op-Zoom, to go to Middelburg or the roadsteads of Zeeland, or to make trips to Calais or even London, if necessary (arts. 8 and 12).[32] Similar provisions are found in other partnership agreements: for example, according to the contract of 1446 relating to the London branch, the manager was expected to stay at his post, but he was authorized to visit Southampton (Antona) or to go into the Cotswolds to buy wool.[33]

Under no circumstances was Tani allowed to grant credit or to deliver money by exchange to any one who was not a bona fide merchant or a master manufacturer, such as a clothier, and then only with due consideration to this person's credit standing. Furthermore, he was permitted to issue letters of credit on Rome to lords temporal or spiritual, clergymen, or officials only if paid cash in advance. To issue such letters upon credit terms required the written consent of the Medici or Pigli. Any violation of this rule was subject to a penalty of £25 groat for each offense (art. 4). Consequently, loans to princes were ruled out, a point which should be kept in mind in view of later developments. Tani was also forbidden to stand surety for friends, or to send goods on consignment to business firms other than Medici companies, without express approval of the maggiori (art. 5).

Other provisions of the partnership agreement forbade Tani to gamble or to keep women at his quarters (art. 7), to accept bribes or gifts beyond the value of one pound groat (art. 16), to underwrite insurance or to make wagers (art. 15), to obligate the partnership in his own behalf or in behalf of friends or relatives (art. 17), or to violate local laws or statutes (art. 18).[34] Any goods sent by sea were to be fully insured except that Tani might venture up to £60 groat in one bottom when shipping goods aboard the Florentine or the Venetian galleys.[35] When sending goods overland, he was free to insure or not to insure, as he saw fit, but the value of each single shipment was not to exceed £300 groat (art. 14). In order to limit risks, Tani was not to purchase wool or cloth, either Flemish or English, for more than £600 in any one year, except by written permission of his partners (art. 13). As these provisions show, precautions were taken to confine the initiative of the junior partner within strict boundaries and to prevent him from making undue commitments.

According to article 10, Tani was not empowered to hire any factors or office boys without the consent of the maggiori. Other partnership agreements contained the same provision. As a matter of fact, the Medici made it a steadfast rule never to grant such permission and to do the hiring themselves, undoubtedly in order to prevent collusion between branch managers and staff, which would have opened the door to all kinds of abuses. Sometimes they made mistakes. Once the Bruges branch complained bitterly that an office boy sent from Florence was so dull that he was totally unfit for even the simplest jobs.[36] He was promptly recalled and replaced by a more intelligent and promising lad. However, the decision, it should be stressed, was made in Florence, at the central office, and not in Bruges.

Every year on March 24, or more often if so desired by the maggiori, the books were to be closed and balanced and a copy of the balance sheet was to be sent to Florence (art. 8). The correspondence shows that this provision was actually carried out.

Whenever the partnership agreement was not extended, Tani would have to serve without pay an extra six months in order to wind up the business. However, the contract could be denounced and ended at any time at the pleasure and discretion of the maggiori without Tani's having the right to present any objections (art. 11). After the liquidation had been completed, all books and papers were to remain in the Medici's custody but with the understanding that Tani would have access to them at any time (art. 9).

Any dispute arising from the partnership contract was to be settled by the Court of the Six of the Mercanzia in Florence. Tani, however, could also be sued for nonfulfillment of the contract before the *loya* (magistrates), of Bruges or the courts of London, Genoa, or Venice, and he recognized in advance their jurisdiction. Finally, the partners assumed joint and unlimited liability and pledged all their property, present and future, movables and immovables, in execution of the contract.

The Medici were not always willing to assume unlimited responsibility, especially during the first years after entering a new territory. Taking advantage of a Florentine law passed on November 30, 1408, they sometimes concluded a limited partnership (accomanda or società in accomandita), according to which they were not liable for any debts beyond their original contribution. When such was the case, the fact was always clearly stated in the articles of association. A good example is the contract concluded in 1422 between Cosimo and Lorenzo de' Medici and Ilarione de' Bardi & Co., on the one hand, and Rosso di Giovanni de' Medici and Fantino di Fantino de' Medici, on the other hand. First, it is declared that the contracting parties intend to form an accomanda with Rosso and Fantino as active partners in order to trade and to deal in exchange in Naples and Gaëta. Next, a stipulation exempts the Medici

Bank, that is, Cosimo, Lorenzo, and Ilarione, from all liability in excess of its initial investment of 3,200 florins.[37] Even in the accomanda contracts, including the ones for Pisa with Ugolino Martelli, the Medici were unwilling to give up their right to hire factors.

It would be a mistake to exaggerate the significance of partnership agreements. Today as well as in the Middle Ages most of their clauses are inoperative in the normal course of business and enter into play only when something has gone wrong and the partners do not live up to their commitments or disagree violently on the proper policy. Such an occurrence will then almost inevitably lead to the dissolution of the partnership.

Branch managers upon leaving Florence to join their posts were usually provided with instructions called *ricordi,* of which there are two interesting examples in the Medici archives. One is a set of rules and suggestions given to Bartolomeo de' Bardi when he went to Rome in 1420 to assume the management of the Medici branch in the Eternal City.[38] The other ricordo contains the instructions which Gerozzo de' Pigli received upon leaving Florence in 1446 to take charge of the London branch.[39]

The orders of Bartolomeo de' Bardi dwell especially upon the dangers of granting credit without discrimination. He was reminded of the fact that it was more profitable to do business with merchants than with the Curia. However, it would be advisable to distrust the Romans because they made great promises and had nothing to offer. Often it was better not to lend than to accommodate either churchmen or barons without having good security. The ricordo stressed the fact that a creditor who had to put pressure on his debtors in order to collect his claims ran the danger of losing friends as well as money. Bartolomeo's principal factor, Antonio di Lazzaro Bertini, was well informed about business conditions and the credit rating of customers, but he tended to be too lenient in making loans and needed to be watched from this point of view.

The instructions to Pigli are even more interesting.[40] Internal evidence shows that they were prepared by the general manager Giovanni Benci. The journey to London was all mapped out: Pigli was to travel by way of Milan and Geneva, then through Burgundy to Bruges, and thence to London. He was to proceed by moderate stages because of the youths, probably office boys, who were going with him. He was carrying a letter of introduction to Alessandro da Castagnolo in Milan, who would supply him with money if necessary and who would also give him information about the credit standing of various Milanese firms doing business with England. Stopping in Geneva, where the manager was absent, Pigli was expected to stir up the zeal of the clerks, to observe their behavior and to report on their doings. In Bruges, he would not find the manager, either, but he would meet the two principal factors, Simone Nori and Tommaso Portinari, who had received orders to help him and to give him any information that would be useful. Here, too, Pigli was urged to keep his eyes open and to report on what he saw. On arrival in London, he was to explain as delicately as possible to Angelo Tani, the oldest of the factors, why the latter had been denied promotion to the position of manager.

The instructions then outlined the policy which Pigli was expected to pursue. First of all, he was to cooperate closely with the Bruges branch. In places where the Medici had branches, he was to deal with them in preference to others and to send them goods on consignment. He was also to carry out their orders for wool or cloth without any limit being fixed, but for the Martelli in Pisa the ceiling was 1,500 florins. Where the Medici had no branches, he was to select his correspondents with care among reliable merchants and to favor those who gave him business.

Going over the map, Giovanni Benci thought that there was probably no one in Naples who was a safe credit risk. Coming to Rome, there were, besides the Medici branch, the Pazzi, to whom Pigli could grant unlimited credit, and the Cambini and Antonio della Casa, who were good up to 1,500 florins each. At Florence, Benci listed the Serristori, the Rucellai, the Cambini, and Filippo Rinieri, who could all be trusted up to 1,000 florins or even 1,500. With regard to Venice, Pigli was advised to ask the opinion of Lotto Tanini (Bozzi), the manager of the Medici branch. In Milan it was all right to deal with the da Castagniolo, the Ornati, and Guglielmo da Marliano. In Avignon and Montpellier, Benci named Zampini, the Medici agent, and the representatives of the Pazzi, Venturi, Nerli, and Carnesecchi as having good standing. He also thought that Francesco Neroni and the company of Giovanni Venturi and Riccardo Davanzati in Barcelona and Valencia were solvent houses, but he was mistaken as to the latter, since they failed the next year, in 1447, causing heavy losses to the Medici branches in Avignon, Bruges, and Venice.[41] Pigli did not need to be fully covered before assuming any obligations for Raimondo Mannelli and Piero Piaciti & Co., also in Barcelona and Valencia, a firm which Benci considered sound and well managed.[42] No permission was given to Pigli to buy bills of exchange from Genoese or Venetians or to accept their drafts without approval of the maggiori.[42] He was to have no business relations with either Brittany or Gascony, but he could accept consignments of good wine as long as it was a matter of no consequence and would not involve any risk or require advancing funds. He was warned to be extremely careful in

dealing with Catalans. With respect to the granting of credit to Englishmen, Benci relied on the experience of Pigli who had resided in England
for many years before joining the Medici firm.

It was hoped that Pigli would be able to settle some differences with
Giovanni Gherardini and Benedetto Borromei. Unfortunately, the extant
ricordo gives no detail, because the matter had been thoroughly discussed
di bocca (by word of mouth) during conferences prior to Pigli's departure. To obtain action, the help of influential friends at Court might
be required. In this connection, Benci cherished the hope that Pigli
would continue to enjoy the favor of the King and Queen (Henry VI
and Margaret of Anjou). If necessary, a letter of recommendation from
King René, Margaret's father, would be procured.

The ricordo for Pigli, like the one for Bartolomeo Bardi, shows plainly
that the Medici worried greatly about the unjudicious granting of
credit and feared above all the accumulation of losses through bad
debts. Pigli was, therefore, expected to follow a policy of caution in
making loans, selecting agents, and purchasing commodities. Diversification was not enough. Cosimo and his spokesman, Giovanni Benci, feared
the cumulative effect of small mistakes as much as the dangers arising
from an inadequate division of risks.

The ricordo deals not only with matters of credit policy; it also contains suggestions about the relations that Pigli should establish with
his staff. There were as factors in London at that time: Angelo Tani,
Gherardo Canigiani, and Alessandro Rinuccini.[43] Pigli was to distribute
the work so as to make the most of their aptitudes. There was no doubt
that Tani was qualified to act as assistant manager and to attend to the
correspondence. Canigiani, Benci thought, would best be suited as bookkeeper. As for Rinuccini, perhaps he could be used as cashier and, since
he had learned English, he would be able to do errands about the City.
The staff of the London branch was obviously small and included not
more than four persons, three factors and the branch manager. It is
doubtful that it was greatly increased later on. Perhaps one more factor
or an office boy was added, but certainly not more.

In the fifteenth century, Bruges was a more important trading and
banking center than London, and it should cause no surprise to find
that the staff of the Medici branch in Bruges was larger than that in
London. Owing to chance in the preservation of the records, there is
detailed and precise information available about the organization of the
counting house in Bruges and the personnel problems arising from time
to time. In 1466 the staff included Tommaso Portinari (the branch
manager), Antonio di Bernardo de' Medici (the assistant manager), and
six factors and office boys: Cristofano Spini, Carlo Cavalcanti, Tommaso
Guidetti, Adoardo di Simone Canigiani, Folco d'Adoardo Portinari, and

Antonio Tornabuoni, a relative of Piero de' Medici, who had married Lucrezia Tornabuoni.[44]

Tommaso di Folco Portinari (1428-1501) had just been admitted as a partner with the conclusion of a new contract on August 6, 1465. In official documents he called himself "governor and partner of the company of Piero de' Medici & Co." [45] Antonio di Bernardo de' Medici (b. 1440), a distant relative of the maggiori, was still a factor in 1466 and did not become a partner until the renewal of the partnership agreement in 1469. As assistant manager, his time was taken up by executive functions and in attending to important correspondence and supervising the other factors. He was certainly provided with a power of attorney which made him acting manager whenever Portinari was absent from Bruges and enabled him to represent the Medici Bank in deeds or in court and to issue or accept bills of exchange.

Next in rank to Antonio de' Medici came Cristofano Spini. He was in charge of the purchases of wool and cloth, which required the keeping of special records. Carlo Cavalcanti, because of his fluency in French, his attractive appearance, and his engaging manners, was entrusted with the sale of silk fabrics and brocades at the court.[46] French — not Flemish, the popular tongue — was the language of the Burgundian court and of fashionable society in medieval Bruges. It requires little imagination to picture Carlo Cavalcanti, dressed like a *damoiseau* in a handsome doublet, using his most persuasive charms to sell his silks to the fair ladies at the court of Burgundy. Adoardo Canigiani did not have such a pleasant assignment; he was the bookkeeper and spent his days bending over huge ledgers or casting counters on the exchequer or abacus. A surviving fragment of a ledger of the Bruges branch shows that the books were carefully kept according to all the rules of double entry.[47] No special information is available about the functions of Tommaso Guidetti; he had been released from the job of bookkeeper by the arrival of Adoardo Canigiani and had been given other duties previously performed by Antonio de' Medici. Antonio Tornabuoni, the garzone who had just arrived from Italy, was probably set to work on the letter book, in which all outgoing correspondence was copied before being dispatched.[48] No information is available about the job of Folco d'Adoardo di Giovanni Portinari (1448-1490). He was not a nephew of Tommaso di Folco, the present branch manager, but of Bernardo di Giovanni (1407-1455) who established the Bruges branch and was its first manager (1439-1448).[49] Later, in 1478, Folco Portinari was acting manager during a prolonged absence of Tommaso in Italy. He remained for a while in the service of his cousin after the latter took over the bank in Bruges from the Medici.

Since countinghouses were small, there was little specialization. Probably factors were shifted around so that they had a chance to become familiar with different types of work and could replace each other in case of illness.

Personnel problems were by no means unknown in the Middle Ages. As stated before, factors were hired by headquarters and sent out to the branches; the Medici did not brook any infringement of this rule. This policy no doubt had its advantages, but it also had its inconveniences when the central office made a mistake. We have already mentioned as an example of this the office boy who was sent by headquarters to Bruges so ill-trained that "when he arrived he did not even know how to hold a pen." [50] He was shipped back to Florence after a short trial. In 1467 Portinari, asking again for an office boy, pleaded with headquarters to send one who would be helpful and not one who still needed schooling.[51]

Antonio di Bernardo de' Medici, the assistant manager, was another source of trouble because he felt protected by his relationship, however distant, to the maggiori. Moreover, his father was one of the most active supporters of the Medici party. Because Antonio had a disagreeable disposition and a contemptuous attitude toward others, he was thoroughly disliked by the other members of the staff. Even Portinari held him in little esteem. Nevertheless, he groomed Antonio to be his successor. The other factors were greatly disappointed when they learned, in 1469, that Antonio had been raised above them to the rank of junior partner and prospective manager. After a quarrel between him and Cristofano Spini — they very nearly came to blows — all the factors threatened to resign if Antonio de' Medici remained in Bruges. Under those circumstances, Portinari saw no other alternative than to request Antonio's recall.[52] As a result, the partnership begun on March 25, 1470, was prematurely terminated.[53] A new agreement was drawn up on May 12, 1471, according to which Antonio was definitely dropped and replaced by Tommaso Guidetti as junior partner and assistant manager.[54]

These data about the size of the staff of the Bruges branch are fully confirmed by the chronicle of Benedetto Dei, which lists the Florentines residing in Flanders around the year 1470. It reports the following eight individuals as connected with the Medici Bank: Tommaso Portinari, Antonio di Bernardo de' Medici, Cristofano Spini, Tommaso Guidetti, Lorenzo Tanini, Folco d'Adoardo Portinari, Antonio Corsi, and Antonio Tornabuoni.[55] The handsome Cavalcanti had left the service of the Medici, but he was still in Bruges and presumably still selling silks to his fair customers at the court of Burgundy. The Bruges branch of the Pazzi bank, the principal competitor of the Medici, also had a staff of eight members.[56] According to the same chronicle, the staff of the Medici branch in Lyons was as large as that in Bruges and also composed of eight members. In Avignon, the staff of the Medici branch numbered only five, including the manager. The accuracy of Benedetto Dei's figures — confirmed by other sources — is beyond question.

According to reliable information, the Milan branch had a staff of six in 1460, to which one or two were added in the next few years.[57] In Venice the personnel included two managers and six factors in 1436.[58] In Rome the records give the figure of five staff members for the year 1438 when the pope was actually holding court in Ferrara.[59] In London, as we know, the staff was small, not more than four or five.[60] With respect to Florence, the only figures available are for the early years of the fifteenth century. At that time, the number of giovani did not exceed five. If we add to this figure the general manager and three secretaries employed in the central office, located in the Medici palace, the total is nine or ten at the most.

As Table 20 shows, the over-all figure for the staff of the Medici Bank around 1470 is fifty-seven. This total is based partly on reliable data and partly on reasonable guesses and may be too low rather than too high. In any case, it is extremely doubtful whether the Medici Bank, not including the industrial establishments, ever employed more than sixty-five persons in clerical and managerial capacities at any time. Although

TABLE 20.   Size of the Staff of the Medici Bank around 1470

Office or Branch	Number of Staff Members
Avignon	5
Bruges	8
Florence (Tavola and central office combined)	10
London	4
Lyons	8
Milan	8
Rome (Roman Curia)	6
Venice	8
Total	57

Source: ASF, Medici records.

the Medici Bank was the largest banking house of its epoch, it never reached the size of the Bardi or the Peruzzi companies of more than a century earlier. The Peruzzi company, the smaller of the two, in 1335 employed nearly ninety factors or clerks, but it had fifteen or sixteen branches, instead of the Medici's seven, besides the central office in Florence (Table 19).

3. Correspondence and Accounting Procedure

Correspondence was the only means by which the senior partners and the main office of the Medici Bank in Florence could keep in contact with the branches, since the slowness of transportation prevented frequent consultations with branch managers.[61] Only a small fraction of this voluminous correspondence has escaped destruction. Nevertheless, hundreds of letters have survived; all branches are represented, some by very few letters, others more adequately. The only portion of this correspondence available in print is a collection of some forty letters from the Bruges and London branches.

Among the papers of the Medici Bank there are two kinds of letters: the *lettere di compagnia* (business letters) and the *lettere private* (confidential private letters). The lettere di compagnia were addressed to the Tavola of Florence or were written by one branch to another; not many of them are still extant. They deal chiefly with routine matters: notices of remittances and drafts, bills collected and accepted or paid, information concerning shipments or the safe arrival of consignments, advices concerning debits and credits, and similar details. Such letters invariably give at the end the latest exchange rates quoted in the place of dispatch. Lettere di compagnia never contained any confidential material, since they were meant to circulate within the counting house so that the bookkeepers could make the necessary entries and the other clerks take care of matters falling within the compass of their duties.

The same is not true of the private letters. They were usually written by the branch managers and addressed to the maggiori in person or to their general manager. A number of the private letters belong in the category of social correspondence: congratulations for births or marriages, condolences, and the like. They are of little historical interest. However, this is not so of the majority of the private letters, which are really reports by the managers on business prospects, credit policy, managerial problems, and the financial condition of the branches. As the Medici were rulers as well as merchants, the private letters often contain comments on the course of political events and sometimes even secret intelligence about the designs of foreign princes. Furthermore, it should not be overlooked that men like Tommaso Portinari, who was councilor to the duke of Burgundy, moved in court circles and took part in important diplomatic negotiations. They had access to inside information and served the Medici not only as business managers but also as informants and diplomatic agents. In dealing with the Medici, one must remember that business decisions sometimes suffered from the dictates of political necessity. This is especially true of Medici policy regarding loans to sovereigns or princes.

In the private letters, the maggiori are usually addressed as *magnifico major mio* and the tone is that of a subordinate writing to his superior, not of a message exchanged between equals. This confirms what has been said about the junior partners ranking far below the seniors. As the Medici, after Cosimo's death, reach princely status, the tone becomes even more obsequious and Lorenzo di Piero is commonly addressed in the third person as *la Magnificenza Vostra*. This is how he came to be known as Lorenzo the Magnificent.

Since accountancy is an integral part of business organization and serves as a guide to management, it is desirable to say a few words about the efficiency with which the Medici kept their books and used balances and other data as a means of control. Within the compass of a few paragraphs, it is impossible to do more. Moreover, it would be going beyond the scope of this study to examine the Medici account books or surviving fragments from the point of view of accounting history.

By 1400, double-entry bookkeeping was well known in Italy. Whether it was practiced by the Medici Bank at this time is a moot question, since the necessary evidence is lacking. The ledger of 1395, presumably kept in double entry, does not belong to the Medici banking house founded by Giovanni di Bicci, but to the bank of his nephew, Averardo di Francesco di Bicci. It is not always possible to state categorically whether or not a given set of account books meets the requirements of double entry. Especially is it dangerous to draw sweeping conclusions from fragments or even entire ledgers, unless one knows how they were integrated into a system and the procedure used in closing the books.

In the case of the Medici, the balance sheets of the Tavola of Florence and the Rome and Venice branches attached to Giovanni di Bicci's catasto report of 1427 seem to indicate that the books were kept in double entry.[62] One should not, however, jump from there to the conclusion that the same necessarily applies to the libri segreti kept at headquarters by the general manager. It is somewhat doubtful whether the Libro segreto No. 1 (1397–1420) is or is not in double entry for the reasons just given, namely, that it is impossible to ascertain how it was linked to other account books, no longer in existence. By itself, the Libro segreto No. 1 does not balance, but this does not prove anything. Since the Medici used several ledgers, striking a balance could be accomplished by combining them. With regard to Libro segreto No. 2 (1420–1435), it probably measures up to the standards of double entry, though there is still a little bit of doubt. The answer is definitely yes in the case of Libro segreto No. 3, which balances both in 1441 and 1451 (Tables 13 and 14). Moreover, it seems that Giovanni Benci, undoubtedly an accountant of great competence, simplified and improved the accounting system of the Medici Bank.

This system had certainly reached a high level of technical proficiency even before Benci became general manager. It was far more complicated than Luca Pacioli's description of medieval bookkeeping would lead us to believe. The volume of business was already too large for the use of a single ledger to be practicable. It was necessary, therefore, to divide it up into sections, for example, into a *libro di creditori e debitori,* a libro segreto, and a cash book (*quaderno di cassa*). How these simultaneous ledgers were interconnected, with or without reciprocal accounts, matters very little provided the basic canons of double entry are not violated and each transaction gives rise to two entries: one on the debit side and one on the credit side. By following this rule throughout, books should balance, if correctly kept, whether only one ledger is used or several.

A good example is given by the balance of the *ragione di Corte,* or the Rome branch, on July 12, 1427 (Table 21). It shows that the ledger was divided into three sections or books: the quaderno di cassa; the *libro nero G* (black book); and the libro segreto. The credit balances of the cash book probably represent demand deposits, whereas those in the libro segreto are exclusively time deposits (*depositi a discrezione*) made by high churchmen and prominent laymen, among them, the Pope himself. The debit balances of the libro segreto are made up of only two items: an amount of 10,000 florins di suggello, or 9,400 florins di camera, on

TABLE 21. BALANCE SHEET OF THE RAGIONE DI CORTE, OR
THE MEDICI BRANCH AT THE CURIA, JULY 12, 1427

Assets

	fiorini di camera		
	f.	s.	d.
Debit balances in:			
Quaderno di cassa (cash book)............................	22,037	12	10
Libro nero segnato G (ledger).............................	116,639	16	10
Libro segreto (secret ledger)	19,765	18	0
Total........	158,443	7	8

Liabilities

	f.	s.	d.
Credit balances in:			
Quaderno di cassa..	36,609	0	3
Libro nero segnato G.....................................	55,409	8	1
Libro segreto..	66,219	18	6
Total........	158,238	6	10
Error in casting the balance..............................	205	0	10
Total........	158,443	7	8

Source: ASF, Catasto No. 51 (Gonf. Leon d'Oro, 1427), fols. 1191–1194.

deposit with the central office of the Medici Bank, and f. 10,365 18s. di camera in specie, probably locked in a chest. There is a discrepancy of about 200 florins between the totals of debit and credit. According to a note attached to the balance, this difference was due to the fact that there had been no time to recheck the books in order to trace the error. In any case, the reason why the books did not quite balance was human failure — errare humanum est — rather than ignorance of accounting principles.

It would be easy to give other examples, since several balance sheets are still extant.[63] But why belabor this point? One example is enough to refute the argument that the Medici presumably ignored double entry because the cash account seems to be missing from the ledger.[64] True, it is not there, but it is found in a complementary ledger, the quaderno di cassa, which, by the way, was more than just a record of receipts and expenditures.

Some will say that balance sheets attached to catasto reports are suspicious and cannot be used as evidence. It is true, as previously explained, that Cosimo prepared false statements for the catasto of 1457 and ordered his agents to alter certain figures in the balances to be submitted to tax officials. The same suspicions may apply to a certain extent to the first catasto, that of 1427. Attached to the report prepared by the Medici, there is a balance supposedly extracted from the libro segreto of the controlling partnership "Cosimo e Lorenzo de' Medici e Ilarione de' Bardi." [65] This libro segreto still exists, but neither the folio references nor the figures given in the balance sheet correspond to those of the extant ledger. One must conclude therefrom that there existed a fake libro segreto kept for tax purposes.

However, it is less likely that the balance sheets of the subsidiary partnerships (Florence, Rome, and Venice), also attached to the report, are similarly based on false records. To concoct a libro segreto, which summarizes data taken from more detailed books, is quite possible, but it would have been utterly impracticable to duplicate books of original entry recording thousands and thousands of transactions. In any case, it does not seem that the balance sheet of the Rome branch annexed to the report of 1427 was falsified, since it lists Pope Martin V among the depositors a discrezione. If the Medici were tampering with the figures anyhow, why didn't they suppress evidence which could be damaging for the reputation of His Holiness?

When the catasto was first introduced, in 1427, the business men were probably still cautious and trying to find out how far they could go in concealing assets. As time went on, they became bolder in cheating the tax officials, until the extent of the frauds led to the suppression of the catasto on business investments.

As already mentioned, the Medici insisted that branch managers send them every year the balance sheet, which was carefully scrutinized upon reaching headquarters. Medieval statements were not systematically arranged as are modern balance sheets; they listed separately debit and credit balances in the order in which the accounts appeared in the ledger, without any further attempt at classification. Some of the Medici balance sheets have two hundred items or more and are booklets of several pages. The audit consisted in going over the balance, item by item, to pick out any dubious or past due accounts. A thorough checking required the presence of the branch manager to answer questions. This is one of the reasons why branch managers were called to Florence once every year when residing in Italy and at least once every two years when residing beyond the Alps. Some of the balance sheets still extant in the Medici archives have check marks in the margin and comments on the prospects of recovery.

It was a constant policy of the Medici to make due provision for bad debts before proceeding with the distribution of profits. Reserve accounts were set up for this purpose exactly as is done today. A branch manager was severely reprimanded if it was discovered later that reserves were inadequate because of misleading reports about the solvency of debtors. It was also a standard practice of the Medici to open accounts for accrued salaries and wages.[66]

With the exception of a few pages at the beginning of Libro segreto No. 1, the Medici kept their books *alla veneziana,* or in bilateral form, the debit facing the credit on two opposite pages bearing the same number.[67] The adoption of the bilateral form does not necessarily mean that accounts are in double entry. However, this was usually the case with the accounts kept by the Medici Bank in Italy as well as abroad.

4. Time Deposits

The major part of the resources of the Medici Bank did not originate in the *corpo* (capital) but in the *sopraccorpo,* a phrase which is very inadequately translated by surplus. In fact, sopraccorpo had a more extensive meaning than the word "surplus" today. It included: (1) undistributed profits which were allowed to accumulate and thus to increase working capital; (2) money invested by the partners themselves *fuori del corpo della compagnia,* that is, above and beyond their shares in the corpo, (3) time deposits (depositi a discrezione), made by outsiders.[68]

The word sopraccorpo in the first of the three meanings given above is actually used in the text of an entry found on folio 56 of the Libro segreto No. 3, which refers to an amount of 43,225 florins available in the form of undivided profits.[69] Usually the Medici partnership agreements provided that profits could not be withdrawn, except by unanimous consent of the partners, before expiration of the contract. This policy was actually carried out, as is evidenced by the three libri segreti and the private account book of Francesco Sassetti.

According to the articles of association, each partner was bound to supply in full his share of the capital and was charged interest on the deficiency, if he failed to live up to his commitments. On the other hand, a partner was always welcome to invest additional funds fuori del corpo, or outside the capital. On such investments he was entitled to receive interest, which was payable prior to any division of profits among the partners. Thus, Francesco Sassetti had, in 1462, more than 6,000 écus of 64 on deposit with the Geneva branch in addition to his share of 2,300 écus in the capital.[70] According to the balance sheet of the Lyons branch at the end of the year 1466, his share in the capital had by then been reduced to 1,500 écus. His investment also included a deposit of 5,000 écus standing in the name of Amédée de Pesmes, burgher of Geneva, but the money was really Sassetti's.[71] Most probably this was done to evade the catasto. The Medici themselves placed money on deposit with the banco in Florence and with the branches outside. In 1430 Cosimo and his brother Lorenzo, according to their return for the catasto, had 10,000 ducats with the Venetian branch.[72] These two deposits yielded only 5 percent, which is low. It even happened that one branch had money standing out at interest with another branch. Thus the Medici branch in Venice, which apparently had affluent cash reserves and lacked investment opportunities, had on March 25, 1459, two time deposits with the Medici of Milan: one of £15,000 imperiali, renewable for periods of six months at a time, on which the return was 12 percent per annum; and another of 2,000 Venetian ducats or £7,800 imperiali, extensible year by year, on which the interest (discrezione) was only 10 percent.[73] Why this difference in the rate of return? Perhaps because one deposit was repayable in steadily depreciating Milanese silver currency and the other in stable gold ducats.

The Medici Bank and its subsidiaries also accepted deposits from outsiders, especially great nobles, church dignitaries, condottieri, and political figures, such as Philippe de Commines and Ymbert de Batarnay. Such deposits were not usually payable on demand but were either explicitly or implicitly time deposits on which interest, or rather discrezione, was paid.

This word discrezione was used with three different meanings in the Florentine records of the time. First, it meant that a deposit was irregular and that the borrower had the right to employ the funds in his business "at his discretion," or as he saw fit.[74] Second, discrezione referred to the return which was paid by the banker for this privilege.[75] In this meaning, the word dates back into the twelfth century and occurs in a notarial contract of 1190, according to which a Genoese banker named Rufus acknowledges receipt of £20, Genoese currency, placed on deposit with his bank and promises to repay the capital with profits to be determined "at his discretion" (*in mea discretione*).[76] Third, a deposito a discrezione, by a natural process of evolution, came to designate a time deposit with a banker.

The bankers professed that discrezione was a free gift and not a contractual obligation. In fact, it was not recoverable at law and did not give rise to a legal claim until it had been written to the credit of the depositor in the banker's books.[77] This rule may explain why Tommaso Portinari in 1464, at the end of a poor year, took the precaution of not adding any discrezione to depositors' accounts.[78]

It is true that the Church forbade the taking of interest as usury, but it did not forbid the bankers to make gifts and to be kind and generous toward depositors. Of course, a banker could not help offering the same discrezione, or yield, as his competitors, lest he lose his customers. This point, however, was not stressed. The medieval mind was legalistic: there was no compulsion as long as there was no formal or binding contract.

Nevertheless, the more rigorous theologians, among them San Antonino (1389–1459), archbishop of Florence, eager to plug this hole in the usury doctrine, condemned depositi a discrezione as usurious, because the lender *expected* to gain from a loan, even though there was no explicit agreement to pay interest.[79] Usury thus came to depend upon intention. Even to hope for a return on money lent was to be condemned by virtue of the well-known passage in Luke: "Lend, hoping for nothing thereby." [80] San Antonino, following the teaching of the rigorists, even went so far as to denounce the mere expectation of a recompense as mental usury, which he maintained to be as deadly a sin as contractual usury. The fear of committing this mortal sin, however, did not deter cardinals and other high churchmen from placing money openly or secretly on deposit with the Medici Bank.[81] Whatever uncompromising theologians had to say about the matter, depositi a discrezione were not regarded as reprehensible in everyday business practice. A Florentine statute of 1312 even declared that to treat interest as a gift was a laudable custom of the merchants. Therefore, the statute did not permit debtors to evade obligations which they spontaneously entered in their own books.[82]

If it were not dangerous to draw analogies, depositi a discrezione could perhaps be compared to modern income bonds on which interest is payable only when earned. A banker suffering heavy losses did not have to make his plight still worse by paying discrezione, or high interest charges, to depositors. This point may be illustrated by the story of Philippe de Commines' troubles with the Medici Bank.

Philippe de Commines, seigneur d'Argenton (1445–1509), a French diplomat of Flemish origin and the author of famous memoirs of the reign of Louis XI, had the considerable sum of nearly 25,000 écus *sans soleil* on deposit with the Lyons branch. A settlement of accounts took place in November, 1489 and the parties agreed on everything except one point: Francesco Sassetti, in the name of the Medici, refused to credit Commines with 5,000 écus which the latter claimed as discrezione for the last two years.[83] The parties agreed to submit the dispute to Lorenzo the Magnificent. It must be added that the Lyons branch was at that time in serious financial difficulties because of the mismanagement of Lionetto de' Rossi. As Commines felt that he had not received a square deal, he wrote to his dear friend "Seigneur Laurens" (Lorenzo the Magnificent). Seigneur Laurens replied that he was very sorry indeed, but that his losses in Lyons had been so great that they could not be concealed and that he was unable to do much for Commines.[84] The latter accepted Lorenzo's verdict, but not without complaining that it was harsh and unfavorable to him.[85] He was given to believe that if the Medici Bank recouped its losses, as expected, all would be made good.[86] As a matter of fact, a new settlement was concluded on March 4, 1491, which fixed the amount owed to Commines at 24,364 écus *sans soleil* and provided for the extinction of this debt in four yearly installments. This agreement was apparently carried out because only the last installment of 8,364 écus was still due to Commines when the Medici were expelled from Florence in 1494 and all their assets were seized by the new government.[87]

Commines tried to obtain payment from the Florentine republic of the balance that was still owing. For this purpose he sent emissary after emissary to Florence and wrote request upon request for the next fifteen years.[88] It was all in vain; he never collected the 8,000 écus, which represented about one third of his original deposit. It is, therefore, not true that Commines lost his entire deposit in the collapse of the Medici and their bank.[89]

Perhaps if Commines had insisted on withdrawing his deposit in 1489, he might have precipitated a crash. Fortunately, Lorenzo succeeded in appeasing him and in persuading him to have patience and to agree to a settlement providing for the gradual repayment of his claim. Nevertheless, it is clear from the records that he had lost confidence in the solvency of the Medici Bank. Bankers, of course, hesitated a great deal before taking the step of disallowing discrezione, because it would lay bare their difficulties and make their plight even worse by inducing depositors to withdraw their funds at a critical moment.

Customers who placed funds on deposit a discrezione were given a receipt or deposit certificate which was called *scritta* in Italian and *cédule* in French.[90] A few of such certificates are extant. One of them dates from March 12, 1434 (N.S.).[91] It certifies that Cosimo and Lorenzo de' Medici & Co. of Venice have received from Lady Jacopa, the wife of Malatesta de' Baglioni of Perugia, the sum of 2,000 fiorini larghi to be placed on deposit for one year. After this first year, the contract is automatically renewable from year to year, but with the understanding that principal and accrued interest, or rather discrezione, are repayable at any time at the request of the depositor. Of course, no rate of interest is stipulated. Apparently the depositor trusted the bank to provide a suitable return. The document is written entirely in the hand of Lotto di Tanino Bozzi, the manager of the Medici company in Venice, not merely signed by him. It bears the mark of the Medici company and states that the deposit has been written to the credit of Lady Jacopa on folio 237 of the company's ledger, marked with the letter O and bound in white leather.

Another certificate is written in French instead of in Italian; its purpose is the same, though its tenor is somewhat different.[92] Its date is April 21, 1478, and it states that Lorenzo de' Medici and Francesco Sassetti & Co. of Lyons acknowledge having received 10,000 écus au soleil from Ymbert de Batarnay, Seigneur du Bouchage (1438–1523), the King's councilor and chamberlain. This sum is to be placed in lawful trade of merchandise and the resulting profits or losses are to be shared equally between the contracting parties. This clause should not be taken literally, since it is unlikely that Batarnay really entered into partnership with the Medici. It meant that the depositor was not guaranteed a fixed rate of return, but would receive more, if the year had been good, and less, if it had been poor. If there were losses, instead of profits, the depositor might not receive any return at all. According to a statement of account attached to the contract, Batarnay was allowed 1,535 écus sans soleil for an unstated period ending February 12, 1491, and 1,640 écus sans soleil for the next two years ending in May, 1493. The rate of return was probably 7.5 percent in the first case and 8 percent in the second, but this is more or less a guess.[93] Batarnay's cédule — this is the terminology used in the contract itself — contains an unusual clause providing that the deposit is repayable either in Lyons or in any of the Medici branches in Italy at the choice of the depositor. As is the case with the previous certificate, this one is also in the hand of the local manager of the Medici Bank: "Lionnet de Roussi [Lionetto de' Rossi], gouverneur de la dite compagnie."

The Church's ban against usury was presumably taken more seriously in France than in Italy. Greater care was taken to conceal loans at interest under the color of licit transactions. Superficially the contract with Batarnay reads as if it were a partnership agreement involving participation in the profits or losses of a business venture, but the real purport is, of course, entirely different: it is a deposit certificate providing for the payment of interest. Because merchants were thus forced to disguise the true nature of their dealings, contracts were couched deliberately in obscure and ambiguous language that became a fertile breeding ground for expensive litigation.

According to the wording of the contracts, it was not even clear whether persons placing money on deposit with a bank should be regarded as creditors or as partners. In 1487 the heirs of Tommaso Soderini, a prominent Florentine and supporter of the Medici, brought suit against Tommaso Portinari, who had by that time broken his connection with the Medici and was doing business on his own account, for restitution of a sum of 4,204½ ducats which he had received in deposit and which was repayable after four months' advance notice.[94] Portinari refused to return this amount and contended that it had not been given to him on deposit, but that there existed a partnership because it had been agreed between the parties to employ the money in trade and to share the profits accruing therefrom. Why Portinari refused was probably that he was hard up for cash and desperately short of working capital. As a matter of fact, he was struggling to stave off bankruptcy and was harassed by other creditors. The court ordered Portinari to give bail for the sum in dispute but did not decide immediately upon the main issue of the suit. Unfortunately, we do not know how the case was eventually decided. We do not have the text of the contract between Portinari and Soderini, either, but its wording was probably misleading like that of Batarnay's deposit certificate.[95]

Besides churchmen, the depositors of the Medici Bank were often political figures who occupied prominent positions. We have already mentioned Commines and Batarnay, customers of the Lyons branch. The Medici company in Bruges had among its depositors the Count of Campo Basso, Charles the Bold's Italian condottiere, and Guillaume Bische, another outstanding member of the Burgundian court. Bische played a double game and eventually betrayed his master by running over to the French.

It was not without good reasons that such persons were eager to place funds in a secret account with international bankers. They wanted some investment that was safe from confiscation should they fall into disgrace and have to flee the country. Real estate could not be concealed, but accounts with an international banking house could be whisked out of the country with a stroke of the pen. A book transfer of two lines and a letter of advice was all that was necessary. The provision of Batarnay's contract, according to which his deposit was repayable abroad, was a precaution taken in the event of exile. Philippe de Commines drew on his deposit account with the Lyons branch to bribe his way out of the iron cage in which he was locked up for plotting against Anne de Beaujeu, regent of France, during the minority of Charles VIII.[96] Guillaume Bische was not as lucky as Commines. After Bische had betrayed Maximilian of Austria, in 1480, Tommaso Portinari was called to the court at Brussels. He was forced to take an oath on the Gospels and to reveal how much Bische had standing to his credit in two deposit accounts.[97] Maximilian confiscated a total balance of £4,666 13s. 4d. groat, Flemish currency.[98] Bische at first sued the Lyons branch, but without success because it disclaimed being answerable for Portinari's debts.[99] He recovered his funds fourteen years later by resorting to coercive and illegal methods. He took advantage of Charles VIII's campaign in Italy to extort an indemnity of 17,500 florins from the Florentine republic (1494–1495).

The entries in Sassetti's private account book show conclusively that the rate of return varied from 8 to 10 percent on different deposits.[100] The Milan branch sometimes paid up to 12 percent.[101] No clue explains why there were these variations; probably they depended upon profit opportunities, the condition of the money market, or the urgent need for credit of the borrower. In any case, deposits at 12 percent were hardly profitable, since it was difficult to find safe investments that would yield more and leave a profit for the banker. Angelo Tani, writing from London on May 9, 1468, complained to the maggiori that it was inept to be always begging "with one's mouth wide open" in order to borrow at 12 or 14 percent, because interest charges then devour most of the profits.[102] He went on to ask that £3,000 sterling, free of charge, be allocated to the London branch in order to buy wool so as to operate at a profit and to be able to extinguish past losses.

How important were deposits a discrezione as a source of funds? The Medici branch at the Curia, having no capital, derived, of course, the major part of its resources from deposits. According to the balance of 1427, total deposits amounted to 71,000 florins di camera, of which 58,000 florins were balances in the libro segreto and 13,000 florins in the ledger. In addition, the Rome branch held on deposit nearly 25,000 florins belonging to the Camera Apostolica (papal treasury).[103] This gives an aggregate of close to 100,000 florins, an amount almost four times the capital of the Medici Bank, all branches combined (Table 10). Deposits with the Medici company in Venice, also in 1427, were much less important, but reached, nonetheless, the figure of £800 groat or 8,000 ducats, an amount equal to the branch's capital. At the same date, the Tavola in Florence had a few deposits a discrezione made by outsiders, among them, Fantino de' Medici in Barcelona (4,400 florins), Pandolfo Contarini of Venice (2,000 florins), and Messer Ghirigoro de' Marsuppini of Arezzo (1,000 florins).[104] In addition, the Tavola was much indebted to the Rome and Venice branches. Unfortunately, the balance sheet does not clearly separate deposits from other accounts.

Later data are far less complete because the sources have so many gaps. At any rate, deposits made by outsiders with the Milan branch amounted in 1460 to £97,690 imperiali, more than double the capital of £43,000 imperiali. In addition, the Venice branch had a deposit of £41,600 imperiali, which is not included in the preceding total.[105] The Lyons branch, according to the balance sheet drawn up at the end of the year 1466, owed about 42,000 écus of 64 to depositors, both in the libro segreto and in the *libro grande* (ledger), while its capital did not amount at that time to more than 12,400 écus.[106]

As these figures show, the resources of the Medici Bank, thanks to the deposits of wealthy clients, were several times larger than its invested capital. Unfortunately, the data are too incomplete to give more precise information, especially for the period after 1460. How the resources were used in finance, trade, and manufacturing will be the topic of the next chapters.

VI

BANKING AND THE MONEY MARKET AT THE TIME OF THE MEDICI

During the Middle Ages, the Renaissance, and the Age of Mercantilism, merchants and merchant-bankers did not specialize in one line of business but in general diversified their activities and neglected no profit opportunities that happened to come along. A perusal of the extant balance sheets shows that the Medici Bank, without being an exception to the general rule, was more deeply engaged in banking than in trade and that lending in one form or another absorbed most of its resources. Manufacturing, as we have already seen, was of minor importance as a source of income.

The articles of association relating to the Tavola in Florence and the branches abroad invariably state that the partnership is concluded for the purpose of dealing in exchange and in merchandise, with the help of God and of good fortune.[1] Banking in the fifteenth century was to a large extent, if not exclusively, tied to exchange, and *fare il banco* (to run a bank) and *fare il cambio* (to deal in exchange) were synonymous expressions. Bankers like the Medici were chiefly exchange dealers. Dealing in exchange, of course, does not refer to manual exchange, which was the province of the money-changers, but to the negotiation of bills of exchange. Naturally, the purchase of commercial paper was not the only way of granting credit, but it was the more usual one among merchants operating in the money market. Loans to princes were on an entirely different basis, since the terms of such loans were not determined by the conditions of the money market, but depended largely upon the security offered by the borrower and the expectation of his being able to repay the debt when it fell due.

In discussing the medieval money market, one should not lose sight of the Church's usury doctrine. Merchants operating openly in the money market could not afford to disregard the teachings of the Church. Fortunately, the theologians, approaching the question from a legal point of view, made it possible for the bankers to invest their money profitably by switching from lending to exchange. As we have seen in Chapter Two, to discount bills of exchange, letters obligatory, or other credit instruments would have been outright lending at interest and, hence, usury.[2] To operate on the exchange, however, was not usury but a legitimate business transaction duly approved by the theologians. Since a *cambium* (exchange contract) was not a straight loan, so the theologians argued, there was no usury involved, provided it was genuine and not patently misused to cover up a usurious deal, as was the case with dry or fictitious exchange.

The practical result of this approach was to bind banking to exchange. This was still true of the Continent of Europe during the eighteenth century. England was an exception because the London goldsmiths, around 1620, developed the practice of discounting inland bills.[3]

A medieval bill of exchange was not simply a mandate to pay but, as the name suggests, always rested upon an exchange transaction. To be precise, the bill of exchange was the instrument commonly used to implement a cambium. Such a contract involved an advance of funds in one place and its repayment in another place and, usually, in another kind of currency.[4] By definition, a credit transaction was thus inseparably linked to an exchange transaction.[5] Because of the slowness of communications, even a sight draft was a credit instrument, since time elapsed while it was traveling from the place where it was issued to the place where it was payable. The theologians insisted a great deal upon the observance of the *distantia loci* (difference in place), but they tended to minimize the fact that the difference in place necessarily involved a difference in time (*dilatio temporis*). As the jurist Raphael de Turri, or Raffaele della Torre (c. 1578–1666), puts it neatly: *distantia localis in cambio involvit temporis dilationem* (distance in space also involves distance in time).[6] Although he could not deny that a cambium contract was a loan mixed with other elements, he wrote a ponderous treatise full of references to Aristotle, Aquinas, and a host of scholastic doctors in order to prove that exchange dealings were not tainted with any usury. In other words, the exchange transaction was used to justify profit on a credit transaction. This was the source of all the analytical difficulties and contradictions in which the scholastics found themselves trapped.

A cambium, in order to be complete, required the intervention of four parties, two of whom were instrumental in making the contract and two in carrying it out.[7] The first two parties were called the deliverer (It. *datore*, Sp. *dador*, Fr. *bailleur à change*) and the taker (It. *prenditore* or *pigliatore*, Sp. *tomador*, Fr. *preneur*).[8] The deliverer, also called remitter (It. *remittente* or *numerante*), usually gave value or consideration for a bill of exchange by buying it from the taker or drawer at the current price or prevailing rate of exchange. The other two parties were the payor or drawee, who was expected to accept the bill and to pay it at maturity, and the payee or beneficiary, who was supposed to collect the bill in the name of the deliverer. In most cases the payor was a correspondent of the taker and the payee or beneficiary was a correspondent of the deliverer. In the parlance of the fifteenth century, *mandare a rice-vere,* or *mandare credito,* meant to remit, that is, to send a bill of exchange for collection to a correspondent. *Mandare a pagare,* or *mandare debito,* was the opposite and consisted in drawing a bill of exchange on a cor-respondent abroad.

In the Middle Ages banking consisted in negotiating commercial paper, not in discounting.[9] Bills of exchange were neither discountable nor negotiable, but were bought and sold according to the prevailing rate of exchange. The deliverer who had money to invest and bought a bill acquired title to a balance in foreign currency; he was unable to determine his profit or his loss as long as he did not "make his returns" (*fare i suoi ritorni*), that is, as long as he did not reconvert the foreign currency into local currency. Of course, it was possible to make returns in wares, in specie, or in bills. However, bankers usually made their re-turns in bills. In other words, an exchange transaction to be complete involved at least two bills instead of one. In the case of triangular ex-change, three bills were needed: the first to transfer the funds from A to B, the second to transfer them from B to C, and the third to bring them back from C to A, the point of origin.

Medieval bills were payable at sight, at so many days after sight, at so many days from date, or sometimes at the conclusion of the fairs. Most bills, however, were payable at usance.[10] Usance was determined by merchant custom and varied more or less according to distance. Thus usance was ninety days in each direction between Florence and London and only sixty days between Florence and Bruges. The usance for bills of exchange going from Florence to Venice was five days' sight; since the trip usually took five days, bills matured ten days from date. From Venice to Florence, however, the usance was twice as long, or twenty days from date.[11] The round trip, exchange and rechange, thus took thirty days.[12] There existed also double usance and half usance. Exchange quotations, unless otherwise specified, always applied to usance bills. Contracting parties could make different terms, but they rarely did.

Although an exchange contract required the participation of four parties, it could, and did, happen that two of them were combined in the same individual. Such an anomaly did not invalidate the contract or alter its essence. Thus the deliverer was often the same as the payee in the case of the letter of credit which was oftentimes purchased by the person intending to collect it at destination. It frequently occurred that payee and payor were one and the same person. The bill then read *pagate a voi medesimi* (pay to yourself). This formula was used, for example, when both the deliverer and the taker had the same correspondent in another city. The payee who was also payor would then pay himself simply by making a transfer in his books, charging the amount of the bill to the taker, and crediting it to the deliverer. Another combination existed when taker and deliverer were the same person or company. This happened when a firm found it expedient to pay a creditor by drawing on a debtor living in the same city. The bill would then contain the formula *per la valuta ricevuta in noi medesimi* (for the value received from ourselves). Taker and payor could also be united, as in the case of a traveling merchant who was going to the fairs and sold a bill of exchange drawn on himself, probably to buy goods with the intention of selling them at destination and using the proceeds to pay off his debt. This case was quite common prior to 1300 when the traveling trade with the fairs of Champagne was still dominant but seldom presented itself in the fifteenth century.

Let us now see how a real bill of exchange fits the description just given. The following is a draft made out in Venice on July 20, 1463, and payable in London after three months:

† *YHS 1463 a dì 20 lujo in Vinexia*

[*Ducati*] *500*

Pagate per questa prima a uxo a Ser Girardo Chanixani ducati zinquezento a sterlini 47 per ducato per altretanti qui da ser Pierfrancesco di Medizi e compagni. Cristo vi guardi.

Bartolomeo Zorzi e Ieronimo Michiel

On the back:

Dominis Francesco Giorgio e Petro Morozino

Prima   *Londra*

The bill is typical and involves the usual four parties, two of whom were located in Venice and the other two in London:

In Venice

(1) the remitter or deliverer was the Medici company in Venice which supplied the value of the bill (500 ducats);
(2) the drawer or taker was the firm Bartolomeo Zorzi (or Giorgi) e Geronimo Michiel;

In London

(3) the payee or beneficiary was Gherardo Canigiani, factor and temporary manager of the Medici company, correspondent of the remitter;
(4) the payor or drawee was the Venetian firm, Francesco Giorgi e Piero Morosini, correspondent of the drawer.

Anyone acquainted with Italian will see immediately that the bill is written in Venetian dialect, which is natural since the drawer was a Venetian firm. The bill had a face value of 500 ducats and called for the payment of £97 18s. 4d. sterling, English currency, at the stated exchange rate of 47 sterlings, or pennies, per ducat. Since the bill was payable at usance, which was three months between Venice and London, it fell due on October 20, 1463, and was protested two days later by the notary, William Slade, because it was dishonored by the payor. Francesco Rapondi, a Lucchese billbroker active in London, testified in the protest that the Venetian ducat stood at 44 sterlings according to the latest quotation in Lombard Street.

According to merchant custom, when a bill was dishonored, the payee had the right to make out a redraft payable by the drawer, or taker, to the remitter of the first draft. In redrawing, the payee was allowed to add protest fees, commission, and other charges, and to reckon the exchange at the local rate according to the most recent quotation. In the case under discussion, protest charges and commission amounted to 4 shillings sterling which were added to the principal, so that the redraft was made out for the equivalent of £98 2s. 4d. sterling. By converting this amount into Venetian currency at 44d. st. per ducat, one obtains 535 ducats and 5 odd grossi, or groats. This figure is correct, since it corresponds to the sum which the drawee was actually called upon to repay according to an annotation on the rear of the protest.[13] The firm, Bartolomeo Giorgi and Geronimo Michiel, which had borrowed 500 ducats from the Medici Company in Venice, would thus be required to repay 535 ducats after six months, or two usances. The loss on the exchange was consequently 35 ducats, which correspond to a rate of 14 percent per annum, not an excessive rate in the fifteenth century.

In the Middle Ages, interest was always included in the price, or rate, of exchange, a fact which the scholastic doctors, both theologians and jurists, were reluctant to acknowledge, but which is undeniable, since it is a matter of simple arithmetic.[14] Perhaps it is fortunate that they were not more perceptive; otherwise all exchange dealings would have been condemned as usurious and the development of banking would have been greatly hampered, if not arrested.

Merchant-bankers like the Medici, who operated in the money market, had to observe the rules of the game. In order to understand how they operated, it is indispensable, therefore, to make an analysis of the forces that governed the money market in the Middle Ages.

First of all, it is essential to understand how the exchange rates were quoted. The rate could be expressed either in local currency (fixed exchange) or in foreign currency (movable exchange). Usually, between two places, one of them gave its currency to the other. Thus, Florence or Venice gave the florin or the ducat to London and Bruges. It means that the exchange rate both in Florence (or Venice) and in London was based on the florin (or ducat) and quoted in a variable amount of sterlings, or deniers sterling. Consequently, London quoted the exchange in local currency and Florence (or Venice) in foreign currency. A rising exchange was unfavorable to London and favorable to Florence or Venice, since a greater number of sterlings were then given for a florin or a ducat. The reverse was true of a falling exchange, since the florin or ducat was then worth less in English currency.

If no interest had been involved, the rate would have been the same in Florence (Venice) and London. This is the case today for cable rates, because any deviations are immediately adjusted by arbitragists who are kept informed by telegraph of the state of foreign markets. In the Middle Ages, however, there was no telegraph. Moreover, exchange quotations applied to time bills payable at usance. Between Italy and London, usance was three months in either direction. The money market, of course, took notice of this time interval. As a result, the exchange rate was lower in London and higher in Florence or Venice. Of course, a London banker offered fewer sterlings for having to wait three months before receiving a ducat in Venice or a florin in Florence. For the same reason, the banker in Italy was unwilling to part with a ducat or a florin unless he received in London a greater quantity of sterlings. In other words, economic equilibrium required that the exchange rate for usance bills be higher in Florence (or Venice) than in London.[15]

This rule can be made general. Between two places, the exchange rate tended to be higher in the place which gave its currency to the other. The organization of the money market was such that it favored the lender to the detriment of the borrower.

To illustrate this point further, it may be well to take a hypothetical case and to use a diagram similar to the one which, in the sixteenth century, was constructed for the same purpose by Bernardo Davanzati (1529–1606).[16] If historians and economists had studied it more carefully, they would have made fewer blunders in dealing with the history of banking.

In order to be as realistic as possible, the diagram is based in part on the bill of exchange discussed above. For purposes of demonstration, it is assumed, however, that it was paid, whereas it was actually dishonored. Consequently Canigiani, the representative of the Medici Bank in London, supposedly collects the bill at maturity and receives 23,500 sterlings or £97 18s. 4d. sterling from the payor. Next, it is assumed that Canigiani has received instructions from his principal to make returns by bill and to invest the proceeds of the first remittance in the purchase of a draft on Venice. These instructions, let us say, are carried out forthwith and Canigiani buys a bill of 534 ducats and 2 grossi which represent the exact equivalent of £97 18s. 4d. sterling at 44 sterlings per ducat, the actual rate of exchange in Lombard Street.[17] This second bill upon arriving in Venice is presumably accepted and collected when due at the end of three months. The Medici company has thus made a gross

DIAGRAM 1

REAL EXCHANGE TRANSACTION BETWEEN VENICE AND LONDON

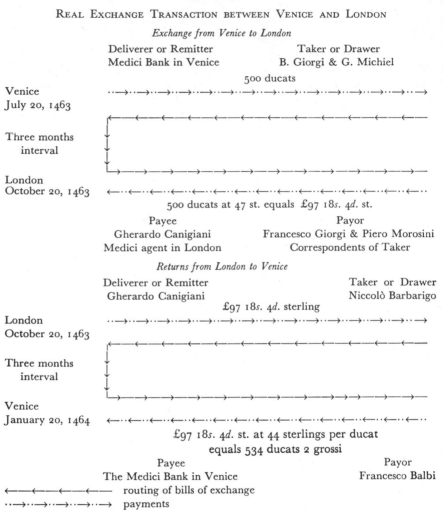

Exchange from Venice to London

Deliverer or Remitter | Taker or Drawer
Medici Bank in Venice | B. Giorgi & G. Michiel

500 ducats

Venice
July 20, 1463

Three months
  interval

London
October 20, 1463

500 ducats at 47 st. equals £97 18s. 4d. st.

Payee | Payor
Gherardo Canigiani | Francesco Giorgi & Piero Morosini
Medici agent in London | Correspondents of Taker

Returns from London to Venice

Deliverer or Remitter | Taker or Drawer
Gherardo Canigiani | Niccolò Barbarigo

£97 18s. 4d. sterling

London
October 20, 1463

Three months
  interval

Venice
January 20, 1464

£97 18s. 4d. st. at 44 sterlings per ducat
equals 534 ducats 2 grossi

Payee | Payor
The Medici Bank in Venice | Francesco Balbi

←——←——←——←——   routing of bills of exchange
··→··→··→··→··→   payments

profit of about thirty-four ducats in six months, not counting commission charges which have been disregarded to avoid complications. It is clear that this profit originates in the difference of three sterlings per ducat between the price of the first bill and the price of the second.

It would make no difference if we assumed the banker to reside in London. A banker in Lombard Street who bought a bill on Venice at 44 sterlings per ducat and made his returns at 47 sterlings would also realize a profit of 3 sterlings per ducat or £6 5s. 0d. sterling on 500 ducats. It would be like buying ducats at 44 sterlings and reselling them at 47 sterlings.

Of course, if the rate of the ducat were lowered in Venice to 46 sterlings and raised to 45 sterlings in London, the banker's profit would be reduced to one sterling. On the other hand, if the rate were raised in Venice to 48 sterlings and lowered in London to 43 sterlings, this widening of the spread between the two rates would increase the profits of the banker to five sterlings. Changes in the rate of interest, therefore, affected the exchange by widening or narrowing the gap between the rate of the ducat in Venice and the rate of the ducat in London.

As long as interest was the only factor affecting the exchange rates, the latter would stay at the same level and there would always be a profit for the banker; whether the profit were great or small would depend upon the scarcity or abundance of loanable funds. Interest, however, was not the only factor; on the contrary, more powerful forces were operating in the money market and tended to pull the level of the exchange rates up or down instead of acting like pincers upon the gap between the rate of the florin, the ducat, or the écu at home and the rate of these same currencies abroad. These forces were: (1) changes in the par itself due to monetary manipulations; (2) shifts in the position of the balance of trade; (3) speculation due to the forecasts, whether right or wrong, of the bankers; (4) maneuvers staged by ringleaders who sometimes tried to rig the market; and (5) disturbances resulting from clumsy attempts made by governments to interfere with the freedom of the money market.[18] The bankers, of course, did not have any command over these forces but had to operate by observing the rules of the game. The best they could do was to watch the trends of the market and to shape their policy accordingly. Although the presence of the interest factor favored the lender, the instability of the exchange rates made his profit uncertain and could even change this profit into a loss. It is precisely this "uncertainty" which justified exchange transactions in the eyes of the theologians.

To give an example, let us suppose for a moment that the Venetian ducat rose in the course of three months from 47 sterlings to 51 in Venice and from 44 sterlings to 48 sterlings in London. There is consequently no change in the spread between the rate of the ducat in Venice and the rate of the ducat in London, but the two rates have both gone up four points. This rise of the ducat would, of course, be very favorable to the banker in Lombard Street who had bought ducats at 44 sterlings and was now able to make his returns at 51. He would be making a profit of seven sterlings per ducat, of which only three sterlings represented interest and four sterlings, a speculative profit due to the rise of the ducat. On the other hand, the rise of the ducat or the fall of the sterling — which is the same — would be disastrous for the banker in Venice who had sent remittances to London. He would be forced to make his returns at a loss, because he had received 47 sterlings per ducat in London and was now forced to spend 48 sterlings for a remittance on Venice. This loss of one sterling is, however, a net loss obtained after deducting three sterlings for interest from a speculative loss of four sterlings on exchange.

If we assumed a fall of the ducat in both London and Venice, the results would be exactly the reverse. Such a falling exchange would benefit the banker in Venice who had bought English pounds, but would affect adversely the remitter in Lombard Street who had acquired balances in Venice. His profits were likely to be greatly reduced or even completely wiped out, depending upon the magnitude of the drop. Because of the dynamics of the market, it happened occasionally that the lender lost when equilibrium was momentarily disturbed and exchange rates were moving from one level to another. However, such a situation was not likely to last, since disequilibrium cannot be maintained.

It was altogether unnatural that lenders should continue for any length of time to pay a premium for the doubtful privilege of lending money. Unless the market was greatly upset, the lender made a profit at the expense of the borrower. Some of the scholastic doctors knew perfectly well that the chances were unequal and that the cards were stacked. Messer Lorenzo di Antonio Ridolfi (1360–1442), the decretalist, admits frankly that the banker may gain or lose, "although it happens more often that there is a profit" (licet ut plurimum contingat quod lucretur).[19] Notwithstanding this glaring fact, the later scholastic doctors continued to pass lightly over the presence of the interest factor and to justify the cambium contract on grounds altogether inconsistent with their basic premises. After all, the Church and the churchmen were among the best customers of international bankers such as the Medici and could not do without their services. If expediency was to be the criterion, there was no other way than to compromise with the stark facts and to bend the rigidity of the principles.

There are statistical data available in the Datini archives but this precious material is still untouched, though it would give detailed information on the behavior of the exchange rates in most of the banking centers during a period of twenty-five years, from about 1385 to 1410, the year of Francesco Datini's death. The Medici archives also contain data on exchange rates among the protests which are found in a separate collection of parchments. Unfortunately, this material is so full of gaps that it is unsuited for a time series, but it can be used for the purpose of sampling.

Such samples are given in Tables 22, 23, and 24, based on protests for nonpayment made at different dates in London, Bruges, and Venice. Tables 22 and 23 refer to exchange transactions initiated in Venice, but Table 24 refers to bills issued in Bruges and protested in Venice. Protests

TABLE 22. EXCHANGE AND RECHANGE BETWEEN VENICE AND LONDON
(Exchange rates were quoted in so many sterlings per Venetian ducat)

Date of Issue of Bill in Venice	Rate of Exchange	Date of Protest in London	Date of Rechange in Lombard Street	Rate of Rechange	Profit per Ducat	Percent of Profit per Year	Ref. No.
	Sterlings			Sterlings	Sterlings		
August 22, 1444	45	November 24, 1444	November 24, 1444	$40\frac{3}{4}$	$4\frac{1}{4}$	20.8	158
February 1, 1450	$45\frac{1}{2}$	May 4, 1450	May 4, 1450	43	$2\frac{1}{2}$	11.6	201
November 6, 1458	$47\frac{1}{4}$	February 14, 1459	February 7, 1459	44	$3\frac{1}{4}$	14.8	238
May 19, 1460	47	September 30, 1460	No record	43	4	18.6	268
November 8, 1460	47	February 9, 1461	February 9, 1461	$43\frac{3}{4}$	$3\frac{1}{4}$	14.9	279
November 14, 1460	46	April 13, 1461	February 16, 1461	$42\frac{1}{3}$	$3\frac{2}{3}$	17.3	288
May 15, 1461	$46\frac{3}{4}$	August 19, 1461	August 17, 1461	$43\frac{1}{2}$	$3\frac{1}{4}$	15.0	295
June 8, 1461	$46\frac{3}{4}$	September 9, 1461	September 9, 1461	$43\frac{3}{4}$	3	13.9	297
November 2, 1461	46	February 4, 1462	February 3, 1462	$44\frac{1}{4}$	$1\frac{3}{4}$	7.9	306
December 3, 1462	$46\frac{1}{3}$	April 4, 1463	March 4, 1463	43	$3\frac{1}{3}$	15.0	346
July 20, 1463	47	October 22, 1463	October 21, 1463	44	3	13.6	361

Source: Giulia Camerani Marri, *I documenti commerciali del fondo diplomatico mediceo nell'Archivio di Stato di Firenze (1230-1492).*

TABLE 23. EXCHANGE AND RECHANGE BETWEEN VENICE AND BRUGES

(In both places exchange rates were quoted in a variable amount of Flemish groats per Venetian ducat)

Date of Issue of Bill in Venice	Rate of Exchange	Date of Protest in Bruges	Date of Rechange on the Bourse	Rate of Rechange	Profit per Ducat	Percent of Profit per Year	Ref. No.
	Groats			Groats	Groats		
September 18, 1438	$49\frac{3}{4}$	November 28, 1438	November 18, 1438	$46\frac{3}{4}$	3	19.2	124
March 4, 1444	$52\frac{1}{2}$	July 4, 1444	July 4, 1444	50	$2\frac{1}{2}$	15.0	156
June 30, 1455	52	August 30, 1455	August 30, 1455	$50\frac{1}{2}$	$1\frac{1}{2}$	9.0	215
November 17, 1455	$52\frac{1}{2}$	January 21, 1455	January 19, 1455	$49\frac{1}{2}$	3	18.2	218
January 12, 1458	$55\frac{1}{2}$	March 14, 1458	March 13, 1458	$52\frac{1}{2}$	3	17.1	239
January 12, 1458	$55\frac{1}{3}$	March 14, 1458	March 13, 1458	$52\frac{1}{2}$	$2\frac{5}{6}$	16.0	240
February 1, 1458	$55\frac{1}{2}$	April 8, 1458	Not recorded	52	$3\frac{1}{2}$	20.2	241
May 16, 1458	$55\frac{1}{2}$	July 17, 1458	July 16, 1458	$54\frac{1}{3}$	$1\frac{1}{6}$	8.1	247
June 7, 1458	$55\frac{1}{2}$	August 10, 1458	August 8, 1458	$53\frac{1}{12}$	$1\frac{7}{12}$	9.0	248
July 26, 1458	56	September 22, 1458	September 22, 1458	54	2	11.0	250
July 24, 1458	56	October 4, 1458	Last day of September fair in Antwerp	54	2	11.0	251
July 12, 1459	57	August 31, 1459	Not recorded	....	....	....	261
June 4, 1460	$57\frac{1}{4}$	August 5, 1460	August 5, 1460	$54\frac{3}{4}$	$2\frac{1}{2}$	13.7	267
August 13, 1460	$58\frac{1}{4}$	October 15, 1460	October 15, 1460	54	$4\frac{1}{4}$	22.5	270
August 22, 1460	$58\frac{1}{2}$	October 23, 1460	October 23, 1460	$53\frac{1}{2}$	5	28.8	271
November 24, 1460	$57\frac{1}{4}$	January 26, 1461	January 26, 1461	$53\frac{3}{4}$	$3\frac{1}{2}$	19.5	275

November 29, 1460	$57\frac{1}{4}$	January 30, 1461	$54\frac{1}{4}$	3	16.5	276
December 10, 1460	$57\frac{1}{4}$	February 5, 1461	$54\frac{3}{8}$	$2\frac{11}{12}$	16.0	278
December 23, 1460	$57\frac{1}{4}$	February 23, 1461	$54\frac{7}{12}$	$2\frac{2}{3}$	14.5	282
February 12, 1461	57	Not recorded	…	…	…	283
January 16, 1461	$57\frac{1}{2}$	March 17, 1461	$54\frac{1}{3}$	$3\frac{1}{6}$	17.4	284
January 30, 1461	57	March 30, 1461	$54\frac{1}{2}$	$2\frac{1}{2}$	13.8	287
May 23, 1461	$56\frac{1}{2}$	July 24, 1461	55	$1\frac{1}{2}$	8.1	291
May 29, 1461	$56\frac{1}{2}$	July 31, 1461	$54\frac{2}{3}$	$1\frac{2}{3}$	9.6	292
January 28, 1462	$56\frac{1}{2}$	March 30, 1462	55	$1\frac{1}{2}$	8.1	320
September 16, 1462	$56\frac{3}{4}$	October 19, 1462	…	…	…	337
October 16, 1462	$56\frac{3}{4}$	December 17, 1462	54	$2\frac{3}{4}$	15.3	339
November 19, 1462	$56\frac{1}{2}$	January 21, 1463	$54\frac{1}{6}$	$2\frac{2}{3}$	13.0	340
January 11, 1463	$56\frac{1}{3}$	March 12, 1463	54	$2\frac{2}{3}$	12.9	344
January 21, 1463	$56\frac{1}{4}$	March 22, 1463	$54\frac{4}{5}$	$1\frac{3}{4}$	9.6	345
February 5, 1463	$56\frac{1}{3}$	April 5, 1463	$54\frac{7}{12}$	$1\frac{3}{4}$	9.6	349
March 18, 1463	56	May 20, 1463	$54\frac{1}{2}$	$1\frac{1}{2}$	8.2	351
June 17, 1463	56	August 18, 1463	$54\frac{3}{5}$	$1\frac{5}{8}$	8.8	353
August 13, 1463	57	October 4, 1463	$54\frac{1}{4}$	$2\frac{3}{4}$	15.2	356
October 4, 1463	$56\frac{1}{4}$	December 5, 1463	$54\frac{5}{6}$	$1\frac{5}{12}$	7.7	360
December 19, 1463	$56\frac{1}{4}$	February 20, 1464	54	$2\frac{3}{4}$	15.3	369

Source: Same as Table 22.

TABLE 24. EXCHANGE AND RECHANGE BETWEEN BRUGES AND VENICE

(Exchange rates in both places were quoted in Flemish groats for one Venetian ducat)

Date of Issue of Bill in Bruges	Rate of Exchange	Date of Rechange in Venice	Rate of Rechange	Profit or Loss	Percent Profit per Year	Ref. No.
	Groats		Groats	Groats		
March 5, 1437*	No record	May 16, 1437	$49\frac{1}{8}$	....	....	591
July 26, 1437	47	September 26, 1437	$50\frac{1}{2}$	$3\frac{1}{2}$	21.0	592
September 15, 1438	$46\frac{5}{8}$	November 16, 1438	$49\frac{1}{4}$	$2\frac{5}{12}$	14.4	628
November 8, 1438	47	January 8, 1439	$51\frac{1}{2}$	$4\frac{1}{2}$	26.1	627
June 7, 1439	48	August 7, 1439	$52\frac{1}{2}$	$4\frac{1}{2}$	25.8	593
October 24, 1439	$50\frac{3}{4}$	December 24, 1439	54	$3\frac{1}{4}$	18.0	629
May 27, 1441	$51\frac{1}{2}$	July 27, 1441	55	$3\frac{1}{2}$	19.0	595
March 14, 1443	52	May 14, 1443	$54\frac{1}{2}$	$2\frac{1}{2}$	13.8	597
July 27, 1443	49	September 27, 1443	$53\frac{3}{4}$	$4\frac{1}{4}$	24.0	598
March 3, 1465	55	May 4, 1465	$54\frac{1}{2}$	Loss	Loss	604

* This bill of exchange was payable 70 days from date instead of 60 days according to usance.

Source: ASF, MAP, Filza 93, nos. 591–629.

usually mention the date when the bill was issued, the rate of exchange at which it was issued, the maturity date, and the prevailing exchange rate at this time in order to figure out the rechange (*ricambio*). This is also the information given in the three tables. In order to interpret them correctly, one should remember that usance was three months between Venice and London and only two months between Venice and Bruges. Hence exchange and rechange took six months in the first case and only four in the second. In order to avoid confusion, it should perhaps be added that in exchange dealings between Venice and Bruges the Venetian ducat was rated in Flemish groats (Fr. gros, Flemish-Dutch grooten), whereas London expressed the rate in sterlings.

A glance at Tables 22, 23, and 24 reveals at once that the ducat was consistently worth more in Venice than in Bruges or London, with the consequence that the lender nearly always gained and the taker nearly always lost. For the persistence of this phenomenon, there can be only one explanation: the action of the interest rate. Among the fifty-seven cases recorded in the three tables, there is only one instance (Table 24) of a lender sustaining a loss. It involves a bill issued in Bruges at 55 groats and returned from Venice at 54½ groats, presumably because the exchange dropped several points during the two months which elapsed before maturity. As a result, the borrower made a slight profit of one-half groat per ducat in addition to having the free use of the borrowed funds during four months.

The three tables also show that profits varied greatly from one transaction to another and that the business of exchange was highly speculative. According to Table 23, yields ranged from 7.7 percent to 28.8 percent a year. The spread is even greater according to Table 24 and extends all the way from below zero to 26.1 percent, but these data are less reliable because some of the borrowers were not merchants. The result of the usury doctrine was thus to increase considerably the risks, already great, of doing business and of operating with borrowed funds. The median return on exchange transactions, according to both Tables 22 and 23, was in the neighborhood of 14 percent, which, in fact, was the commercial rate of interest in the fifteenth century. *Stare sui cambi* (to borrow by selling bills of exchange) was even more costly than *stare sugli interessi* (to raise money by borrowing at interest). The banker took the lion's share of the trader's profit.[20] It is not surprising that many merchants who operated with insufficient working capital went on the rocks. The practical effect of the usury doctrine was the opposite of that which was intended: the use of subterfuges, whether licit or illicit, increased risk and expense and kept the rate of interest high instead of lowering it.

Closer examination of the three tables discloses that the ducat some-times went down in Venice and up in Bruges, thus lessening the gap between the two rates. Such a phenomenon denotes that loanable funds were seeking investors. The reverse could also happen. Depending upon the state of the market, money was either tight or easy. These alternate periods of stringency (*strettezza*) and abundance (*larghezza*) even followed a seasonal pattern which is described in the merchant manuals, both in print and still in manuscript.[21] Giovanni da Uzzano even advises the bankers never to draw when money is tight or to remit when it is easy.[22] The bankers certainly were well acquainted with this seasonal pattern and undoubtedly tried to follow Uzzano's advice by borrowing where money was cheap and lending where it was dear. How successful they were in this endeavor is hard to tell. To play the game required great sagacity, because unforeseen events were likely to upset the best schemes. Lost opportunities never recurred, and the author of one manual even compares the exchange to a passing bird which, if not caught as it lights for a moment, will fly away and be gone for ever.[23]

The Medici had either their own branches or correspondents in all important banking centers of western Europe and were kept informed about the course of the exchange rates and the state of the money market. Other merchant-bankers, of course, did the same. They were so dependent upon regular reports from other places that the expression *stare sugli avisi* meant the same thing as to operate on the exchange.

Commercial letters always ended by giving the latest exchange rates. The Medici lettere di compagnia are no exception. Thus the London branch in a postscript dated October 4, 1453, reported to Florence that the exchange rates in Lombard Street were "Per costì 36⅔, Vinegia 40⅔, Bruggia 19⅔ in ¾, Genova 22¾." [24] This should be read as follows:

Florence: 36⅔ sterlings per florin.
Venice: 40⅔ sterlings per ducat.
Bruges: 19⅔ to 19¾ sterlings per écu of 24 groats,
           Flemish currency.
Genoa: 22¾ sterlings per florin of 25 soldi, Genoese
           currency.

A letter sent from Lyons on May 16, 1468, reporting on the conclusion of the Easter Fair, ends with the sentence: "Per chostì 73, Vinegia 60, Milano 63, Vignone 133, Bruggia 50⅔." [25] It means that the following rates were quoted for bills issued at the Easter Fair and payable a month later:

Florence: 73 florins di suggello per gold mark.
Venice: 60 Venetian ducats per gold mark.
Milan: 63 Milanese ducats per gold mark.
Avignon: 133 florins pitetti of 12 grossi each per gold mark.
Bruges: 50⅔ groats, Flemish currency, per écu of 66
           to the mark.

Unlike the Datini letters, the Medici correspondence is so fragmentary that it is impossible to give an account of developments in the money market over a period of time. What information is available does confirm the fact that the Medici followed the same policy as other merchant-bankers and tried to feel the pulse of the money market and to have a quick turnover of their funds. There were the usual disappointments and it was sometimes difficult to make transfers from Bruges to Venice and to Italy in general. Satisfactory *prenditori* (sellers of bills), could not always be found on the *bourse*. Thus, in May, 1441, Venice complained because the Bruges branch did not remit for want of reliable takers either in Bruges or in London.[26] There were apparently real transfer difficulties because the balance of trade was unfavorable to Flanders. As a result, the Bruges branch resorted to shipping specie and sent eighteen marks in gold via Geneva in January, 1441 and two shipments directly in April and May, 1441, all representing an aggregate value of £225 groat, Venetian currency, or 2,250 ducats.[27] Already in 1438, Bernardo Portinari proposed to send to Geneva as many as 500 English nobles at a time concealed in bales of cloth.[28] Unfortunately, the sources give no indication about the fate of this proposal. In any case, there is no doubt that Geneva, and later Lyons, played an important rôle in adjusting international balances, especially between Northern Europe and Italy. Italian exports to this region probably exceeded imports; the gap was presumably filled with the silver output of the German mines, though gold bullion was also shipped from Geneva to Florence and Venice in substantial quantities.[29]

London was having the same trouble as Bruges in finding ways of making settlements in Rome.[30] However, there was in Venice a market for wool, lead, and tin; the proceeds were used to pay debit balances at the Curia.[31] Rome thus had credits in Venice and used them to transmit funds to Florence rather than to remit directly. Another circuitous route was via Barcelona, where Bruges usually had credit balances on which Venice was eager to draw because rates were favorable and there were always on the Rialto *datori* (buyers) who had payments to make in Catalonia.[32] This situation, the Datini letters reveal, existed already around 1400 or half a century earlier.[33] While there was no longer a market for Flemish cloth in Italy, Catalonia continued to be a customer for says and other woolens.

Instead of stimulating business activity, war sometimes had a paralyzing effect. During the war of 1467–1468 between Florence and Venice, there was little fighting, only a few skirmishes, and the one battle, near Imola (May 10, 1467), was indecisive and quickly led to peace negotiations which dragged on for several months, until April 27, 1468. While the diplomats were dawdling around the conference table, business in

Venice came to a standstill. Giovanni Altoviti, the manager of the Medici branch in Venice, wrote to Milan on November 6, 1467, that business had fallen "asleep" and that there was little activity either in exchange or in the trade of merchandise. The money market was easy, but there were no takers or borrowers for any place (*non è prenditore per nessuna parte*).[34] Venice was in the trough of a depression and the banks had plenty of idle funds and were ready to lend, but the merchants did not take advantage of this opportunity because they were in a state of uncertainty and reluctant to start new ventures.

According to the merchant manuals, the following Italian cities were banking places: Bologna, Florence, Genoa, Milan, Naples, Palermo, Pisa, Rome or rather the Court of Rome, and Venice. Since the papal bankers followed the Curia in its peregrinations through Italy, Rome was a banking place only when the pope was in residence. At other times, wherever the pope went, the bankers went, too. In 1437 and 1438, they followed him to Bologna and Ferrara. The next year, Eugene IV moved to Florence to preside over the council which unsuccessfully attempted a unification with the Greek Orthodox Church. The Rome branch of the Medici Bank came along and rented a house in Piazza Santa Maria Novella, near the Dominican friary where the Pope was staying.[35] Two branches of the Medici Bank were thus for a while located in the same city but still kept separate offices. Papal bankers were often aptly designated as *mercatores Romanam Curiam sequentes,* that is, as merchants following the Roman Curia. The pope had the reputation of tightening the money market and of raising the cost of living wherever he settled down.

Outside Italy, business organization was less advanced. Since exchange was largely, though not exclusively, a monopoly of the Italians, only those cities were banking places where there existed Italian colonies of merchants. The commercial manuals list: Barcelona, Palma de Majorca, and Valencia in Spain; Avignon and Montpellier in France; Geneva in Savoy; Bruges in Flanders; and London in England. There were no banking places east of the Rhine and Italian efforts to establish one in Lübeck were checkmated by the Hanseatic League. Constantinople was a banking place for the Genoese and the Venetians until 1453 when the city was captured by the Turks. Paris had been an important banking place all through the fourteenth century, but it lost this position as a result of the civil strife and the English occupation which marked the last years of the infelicitous reign of Charles VI (1380–1422). As we have seen, Lyons, then located at the edge of the kingdom of France, did not become a banking place until after 1465.

A banking place presupposed the existence of an organized money market where exchange rates on other places were quoted regularly and where it was easy either to buy or to sell bills of exchange at the prevailing market price. Negotiations were usually conducted by means of bill-brokers, and the merchant manuals mention how much they were allowed to charge for commission.[36] Save on Sundays and feast days, the merchant-bankers and billbrokers met once a day in a public square (the Piazza del Rialto in Venice or the Place de la Bourse in Bruges), in the open street (la strada or Lombard Street in London), or in a loggia especially constructed for this purpose, such as the lonja of Barcelona, which is still the seat of the stock exchange today. Of course, bills of exchange were sometimes drawn on secondary centers, such as Zara, for instance, but such paper was difficult to negotiate and often the best way was to send it for collection to a correspondent at the nearest banking place.[37] Between the major banking places there was a regular service of couriers, called the scarsella, a service organized by the business community. Special couriers were used only by exception.

Not all places were in communication with each other. Thus Lombard Street quoted the exchange on Bruges, Florence, Genoa, and Venice, but it did not have direct connections with Palermo, for instance. A Londoner having money to collect in Sicily could do so by using the services of bankers in Genoa, because in London transactions with Palermo were so exceptional that there was no market for direct drafts.

As mentioned in the first chapter, Florence was the major banking center of Western Europe during the fifteenth century, and exchange rates on nearly all other places were quoted regularly. Table 25 shows how exchanges were quoted prior to November 1, 1471, when a law imposing the use of the fiorino largo instead of the fiorino di suggello went into effect. As a result, all exchange quotations were henceforth based on the large florin. Florence, as can be seen from Table 25, quoted for most places a movable exchange based on the florin, its own currency, and expressed in a variable amount of foreign currency, but there were a few exceptions. A fixed exchange was used in relations with Geneva, where the exchange was based on the gold mark, and with Venice, where it was based on the pound groat, Venetian currency, and quoted in pounds affiorino, worth twenty-twenty ninths of a florin. The Roman florin used by the Camera Apostolica was better than the florin di suggello; as the latter worsened, agio gradually rose from five and one-half percent in 1420, to 6 or 7 percent in 1440, the figure given by Uzzano, and gradually to 21 and 22 percent in 1461, according to the reports of the Medici branch in Rome.[38] It means that 100 cameral florins were the equivalent of 121 or 122 sealed florins. With Pisa, the exchange was quoted at par or slightly above or below par according to the conditions of supply and demand prevailing in the money market. Information on other banking places can be gathered from the merchant manuals.

TABLE 25. EXCHANGE QUOTATIONS IN FLORENCE AROUND 1450

Place	How Quoted	High	Low	Usance
Avignon	In so many florins di camera of 14½ grossi per one hundred florins di suggello	134	126	30 days from date
Barcelona	In so many s. and d., Barcelonese currency, per florin di suggello	15s.	14s.	60 days from date
Bologna	In so many florins di camera per hundred florins di suggello	107	103	3 days' sight (6 days from date)
Bruges	In so many groats, Flemish currency, per florin di suggello	54	46	60 days from date
Geneva	In so many florins di suggello per gold mark, Troy weight	78	..	next fair
Genoa	In so many s. and d., Genoese currency, per florin di suggello	44	42	eight days' sight
	Also in so many florins di suggello per hundred florins di camera in Genoa	108	104	eight days' sight
London	In so many sterlings, English currency, per florin di suggello	44	40	90 days from date
Naples	In so many ounces, Neapolitan currency, per 300 florins di suggello	48	44	10 days' sight
Palermo	In so many florins of 12 carlini per one hundred florins di suggello	114	104	30 days' sight
Pisa	Florins for florins at so much percent better (meglio) or worse (peggio)	..	..	3 days' sight
Rome	In florins di camera at so much percent meglio, or better than the florins di suggello	..	..	10 days' sight
Valencia	In so many s. and d., Barcelonese currency, per florin di suggello	18	16	60 days from date
Venice	In so many £, s., and d. affiorino per pound groat, Venetian currency, of 10 ducats	£16	..	5 days' sight (10 days from date)

Sources: El libro di mercatantie, ed. Franco Borlandi (Turin, 1936), pp. 9–11 and 169; Giovanni d'Antonio da Uzzano, Della mercatura in Pagnini, Della Decima (Lisbon-Lucca, 1766), IV, 100, 135–36.

The data they give are not always accurate, however, because medieval copyists were careless and made quite a few errors which editors failed to correct or even to notice.

Medieval bills of exchange were as a rule holograph documents.[39] Signatures did not have at that time the importance attached to them today. The validity of a bill of exchange depended upon its being written entirely in the hand of a person authorized to make out bills. Instances are known of a drawee refusing to accept a bill because he did not recognize the handwriting (*la mano*) of the drawer and thought it had been forged.[40] According to the Medici papers, only the top men, such as branch managers and assistant managers, were authorized to write out bills of exchange. A specimen of their handwriting was sent to correspondents and they were instructed not to honor bills by any other hand. Thus, in 1455, the Rome branch was notified that it was to honor (*dare compimento*) only the bills made out in the hand of Giovanni Benci, of Francesco Inghirami, or of Tommaso Lapi, that is, of the general manager and of the manager and assistant manager of the Tavola or bank in Florence. Likewise, Florence was not expected to pay any bills drawn by the Rome branch, unless they were written by Robert Martelli (the manager), Leonardo Vernacci (assistant manager), or Giovanni Tornabuoni (factor, brother-in-law of Piero de' Medici).[41]

In order to prevent mistakes, the Medici made out lists of their principal correspondents with the names of the persons empowered to make out bills for each of these firms. Two such lists are still extant: one for 1440 and one for 1455.[42] The latter is more nearly complete than the former and shows that the Medici were represented either by their own branches or by correspondents in all the banking places of Europe and even the Levant (Table 26). In Germany, the only Medici correspondent was Abel Kalthoff, a prominent merchant of Cologne.[43]

These lists gave rise to an amazing confusion created by one of the first historians who had the courage to dig into the papers of the Medici Bank. Misunderstanding the expression *per cui mano hanno a dare compimento* (whose hand they are expected to honor) he came to the conclusion that Giovanni Benci, the general manager of the Medici Bank, and his aids, Francesco Inghirami and Tommaso Lapi, were humble messengers who rode from city to city to deliver bills of exchange.[44] From there he proceeded to make learned comments upon the inadequacy of the postal service. This was half a century ago. One cannot help being amused. Nevertheless, it would be unfair to be critical and to forget that, in recent years, much progress has been made in the writing of economic history and in the handling of business records. Fifty years ago, historians were still groping their way and slowly learning how to deal with such material.

TABLE 26. CORRESPONDENTS OF THE MEDICI BANK IN VARIOUS PLACES WITH THE LIST OF THEIR AUTHORIZED AGENTS (1455)

Place	Correspondent	Names of Agents Empowered to Make Out Bills
Avignon	Francesco Sassetti and Giovanni Zampini & Co.	Giovanni Zampini
Barcelona	Filippo Pierozzi	Filippo Pierozzi
Bologna	Niccolaio da Meleto	Niccolaio da Meleto
	Antonio Bonafè & Co.	Antonio Bonafè *proprio*
Bruges	Piero de' Medici, Gerozzo de' Pigli & Co.	Gerozzo de' Pigli
		Tommaso Portinari
		Marco Bencivenni
		Agnolo Tani
Cologne	Michele Arnolfini	Michele Arnolfini
Ferrara	Abel Kalthoff	Abel Kalthoff
	Bandino da Meleto	Bandino da Meleto
	Taddeo Albregiani or Albresani	Taddeo Albregiani
	Baldassare di Giovanni Machiavelli	Baldassare Machiavelli
		Jacopo di Baldassare Machiavelli
Genoa	Filippo & Federigo Centurioni	Filippo Centurioni
		Federigo Centurioni
		Giovanni Batista di Filippo Centurioni
Geneva	Giovanni Benci, Francesco Sassetti & Co.	Francesco Sassetti *proprio*
Lyons	Francesco di Antonio Nori	Francesco Nori
London	Piero de' Medici, Gerozzo de' Pigli & Co.	Simone Nori
		Gherardo Canigiani
		Gaspare Vagliano
Milan	Commissària de' Castagnolo	Lorenzo di ser Lando
	Antonio da Castagnolo e Fratelli	Antonio da Castagnolo
		Rinieri da Castagnolo
	Piero de' Medici & Co.	Pigello Portinari
		Giovanni di Lazzaro Borromei

Montpellier	Antonio di Bernardo Canigiani	Antonio Canigiani *proprio*
Naples	Bartolomeo Buonconti	Bartolomeo Buonconti
		Carlo Buonconti
	Filippo Strozzi & Co.	Filippo Strozzi
		Bernardo Rondinelli
		Benedetto Guasconi
	Benedetto Guasconi	Ippolito di Bartolomeo
Perugia	Antonio da Pennino & Co.	Antonio da Pennino
	Eredi d'Alfano e Severi & Co.	Giovanni Batista d'Alfano
		Girolamo di Consolo
	Eredi d'Angelo e Ugolino Cespoldi	Ricco Petrozzi
		Nicolino Cespoldi
Pisa	Ugolino e Antonio Martelli & Co.	Matteo Masi
		Lodovico Masi*
		Jacopo da Colle
	Francesco di Nerone & Co.	Bernardo Salviati
Rhodes	Bernardo Salviati	Roberto Martelli, manager
Rome	Piero e Giovanni de' Medici & Co.	Lionardo Vernacci
		Giovanni Tornabuoni
Siena	Cosimo di Francio Berti	Cosimo di Francio Berti
		Francio Berti
Venice	Pierfrancesco de' Medici & Co.	Alessandro Martelli
	Filippo d'Agostino e Fratelli	Filippo d'Agostino
		Francesco d'Agostino
	Giovanni Rucellai e Giovanni di Francesco Strozzi	Giovanni di Francesco Strozzi
		Filippo d'Amerigo Rucellai

* Lodovico Masi was authorized to make out bills only up to the amount of 600 florins.
Source: ASF, MAP, filza 134, no. 3: Ricordi di cambi, Banco di Firenze (1455).

Today the profit of the banker is certain, in the sense that interest is computed on a percentage basis. In the Middle Ages, however, this profit was uncertain, since it depended upon the fickle behavior of the exchange rates. In any case, the accounts of the medieval merchant-bankers prove beyond doubt that earnings, instead of being derived from interest charges, originated in exchange differences. It would be useless to leaf through their ledgers looking for an account recording interest income derived from discounting commercial paper, because there is none.[45] What one finds is an account called *pro e danno di cambio,* or something equivalent, to which were posted profits and losses arising from exchange speculation. One also finds an account for commission earned in handling bills of exchange for foreign correspondents.

The fact that the Medici and other bankers operated with bills of exchange payable abroad in foreign currencies created some complications in bookkeeping. In order to solve the difficulty, they opened for most of their correspondents two accounts, a *Nostro* account and a *Vostro* (or *Loro*) account. This device is still used today by import-export firms, shipping companies, and other concerns doing a good deal of business in foreign currencies. Thus, a firm in New York may have two accounts with a correspondent in London, a sterling account and a dollar account. The sterling account corresponds to what was called in the Middle Ages a Nostro account, although this terminology is still in use today.

The characteristic feature of a Nostro account is that it is kept in both foreign and local currency, but the foreign currency is the regulator. If such an account balances in foreign currency but not in local currency, the difference represents either a profit or a loss originating in exchange disparities. Nostro accounts usually had, and still have, two extension columns on both the debit and the credit side, one for the foreign and one for the local currency. Unlike Nostro accounts, Vostro (or Loro) accounts have only one extension column on each side, for the local currency, and consequently do not differ from ordinary accounts. They do not require adjustments for exchange differences. In the books of merchant-bankers like the Medici, Vostro accounts frequently included charges for commission, brokerage, and consular fees.

How Nostro and Vostro accounts were used is rather difficult to grasp without some technical knowledge of accounting.[46] First of all, one must find out who is principal or who is agent in a given exchange transaction. The words "principal" and "agent" have here a strictly technical meaning. The principal was the person who initiated an exchange transaction and who received any profit accruing therefrom or assumed the responsibility for any loss. The agent simply carried out the principal's instructions and might receive a commission for his services, but he was entitled to no other rewards since he did not run any risks resulting from adverse exchange fluctuations. There were in all four possibilities: (1) a bill could be drawn by a principal on his agent, or (2) the reverse, by an agent on his principal; (3) bills could be remitted by a principal to his agent or (4) the reverse. Thus, the Tavola of the Medici Bank in Florence could act either as principal or as agent of one of the branches. The same was true of the relation between branches. The Venetian branch, for instance, would be acting as principal if it decided to remit to the Bruges branch or to draw on the Bruges branch, or ordered the Bruges branch either to remit or to draw. On the other hand, the Venice branch would be acting as agent if it remitted, drew, collected, or paid a bill of exchange for account of the Bruges branch.

To simplify matters, let us assume, for example, that the Venice branch buys a bill of exchange of 100 ducats at 48 sterlings, remits it to the London branch for collection, and orders this branch to make returns by bill at the best possible rate. Then the Venice branch would be principal and would charge this remittance to the Nostro account of the London branch, 100 ducats in one column and £20 sterling in the other. Suppose now that returns are made at the rate of 45 sterlings. Then the London branch would be able, by spending £20 st., to buy a bill on Venice of 106 ducats and 16 grossi. Upon acceptance of this draft by the payor, the Venice branch would credit the London branch with £20 sterling or 106 ducats and 16 grossi. Now the Nostro account would balance in sterling, but there would be left a credit of 6 ducats and 16 grossi representing the profit on this exchange transaction and arising from the disparity in the exchange rates between going and coming back. This profit, of course, would be transferred to Profit and Loss on Exchange to make the Nostro account balance in ducats as well as in sterling.

The London branch would be acting as agent of the Venice branch. After collecting the remittance of 100 ducats, it would credit the Vostro account of the Venice branch with £20 sterling, the equivalent in English currency. When buying the draft on Venice, it would charge £20 sterling to the same account, which would thus cancel out. Perhaps the London branch might charge a commission of 2 per mille, or ten sterlings, for its trouble. This small charge would then be settled eventually by the Venice branch.

Of course in practice exchange transactions rarely matched as perfectly as in this simplified model. However, complications, while they do not alter fundamental principles, make it more difficult to understand the mechanism. Nostro and Vostro accounts appear in all the surviving fragments of Medici ledgers, namely, in the ledger of the Tavola in Florence (1460), the ledger of the Milan branch (1459), and the ledger of the Bruges branch (1441).[47] The same system was adopted by other Florentine bankers. One finds many examples in the Datini ledgers, in the ledger of Averardo de' Medici's bank (1395), and in the ledger kept in London by the Milanese firm of Filippo Borromei & Co. (1436–1439). Nostro and Vostro accounts can therefore be considered as a bookkeeping device which was in general use among the Italian banking and mercantile companies from the late Middle Ages onward. Only the Venetians followed a somewhat different procedure in handling foreign exchange accounts.

Although the Medici professed to confine their activity to licit exchange dealings, their records prove that they sometimes granted credit under the form of dry exchange, a practice reproved by the theologians because they claimed it to be a concealed loan or a contract *in fraudem usurarum*. What was dry exchange? It was a product of the usury doctrine; therefore it is without analogy in modern business. It can best be described as a transaction involving *cambium et recambium,* or exchange and rechange, but without any final settlement taking place abroad. In fact, it mattered little whether or not the contracting parties took the trouble of actually making out and dispatching bills of exchange.

Several examples of dry exchange between Bruges and Venice are found in the ledger of the Bruges branch for the year 1441. One of the accounts, that of Antonio di Niccolò del Conte, even refers to three such transactions.[48] The first relates to a disguised loan made by the Medici branch in Venice on or about March 15, 1441. As Antonio del Conte had no correspondents in Flanders, he was told by the deliverers to draw on the Medici in Bruges and to make the bill also payable to the same. Consequently, the bill — which has not been preserved — probably read "pagate a voi medesimi," which meant that the Medici of Bruges were both payor and payee. The value of the bill was 533 Venetian ducats, at 51½ groats per ducat, which corresponded to £114 10s. groat, Flemish currency (Diagram 2).[49]

When this bill of exchange matured in Bruges on May 13, 1441, the Medici branch in this city charged the amount of £114 10s. groat to Antonio del Conte and posted the same sum to the credit of the Vostro (or Loro) account of the Venice branch with the additional annotation that this transfer was made *sopra di loro,* that is, upon the responsibility of the Medici of Venice.[50] It is thus abundantly clear that the Bruges branch of the Medici Bank was acting as agent and carrying out the orders of the Venice branch. Antonio del Conte's account was also charged with 5s. 6d. groat for commission at 2 per mille and consular fees at the rate of 2 mites per pound groat, or about one-third per mille.

Two days later, or on May 15, the Medici branch in Bruges then reversed its entry of May 13 and charged the account of the Venice branch with £114 15s. 6d. groat, or 534 ducats and 21 grossi, and credited Antonio del Conte with the same amount. This transfer, it is specifically stated, was also *sopra di loro*, or at the behest of the Medici branch of Venice. Probably the Bruges branch made out a bill *pro forma* payable by Antonio del Conte to the Medici bank in Venice for the value of 534 ducats and 21 grossi "received from ourselves." The formulas *pagate a voi medesimi* and *valuta da noi medesimi*, "pay to yourselves," and "value from ourselves," were apparently always used in cases involv-

DIAGRAM 2

EXAMPLE OF DRY EXCHANGE BETWEEN VENICE AND BRUGES BASED ON A
REAL CASE TAKEN FROM THE MEDICI RECORDS

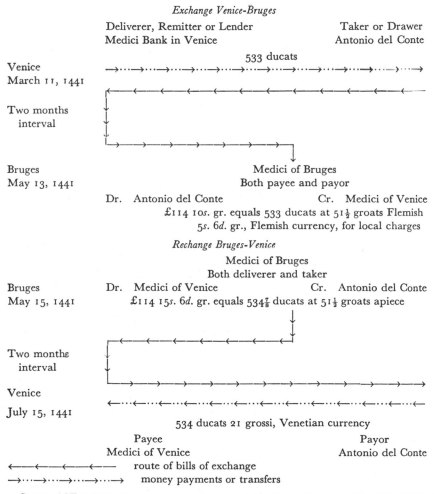

Exchange Venice-Bruges

	Deliverer, Remitter or Lender	Taker or Drawer
	Medici Bank in Venice	Antonio del Conte

533 ducats

Venice
March 11, 1441

Two months
interval

Bruges   Medici of Bruges
May 13, 1441   Both payee and payor

Dr.   Antonio del Conte   Cr.   Medici of Venice
£114 10s. gr. equals 533 ducats at 51¼ groats Flemish
5s. 6d. gr., Flemish currency, for local charges

Rechange Bruges-Venice

Medici of Bruges
Both deliverer and taker

Bruges   Dr.   Medici of Venice   Cr.   Antonio del Conte
May 15, 1441   £114 15s. 6d. gr. equals 534⅞ ducats at 51½ groats apiece

Two months
interval

Venice

July 15, 1441

534 ducats 21 grossi, Venetian currency

	Payee	Payor
	Medici of Venice	Antonio del Conte

←——←——←——←—— route of bills of exchange
→···→···→···→···→ money payments or transfers

Source: ASF, MAP, filza 134, no. 2: Ledger of the Bruges branch of the Medici Bank (1441), fol. 231; R. de Roover, *The Medici Bank* (New York, 1948), pp. 82–85.

ing dry exchange. But some bills containing these formulas are based on real transfers. Therefore, their presence in the text of a bill is not a sure indication of dry exchange.

Professor Giulio Mandich, an Italian expert on monetary history, believes that this transaction of *cambium et recambium* bears great resemblance to the *cambio con la ricorsa* in use during the sixteenth and seventeenth centuries with the difference that the earlier form retained its speculative character, because the rate of the rechange was not determined in advance. This is correct, since a Venetian banker who sold ducats at 50 Flemish groats and promised to repurchase them later at 48 Flemish groats, for example, would make a profit of two groats per ducat, whether the rate of the ducat went up or down in the meanwhile. If, however, the repurchase price were not set beforehand, there could be either a profit or a loss depending upon the unpredictable swing of the exchange rates.

In the case under discussion, the Medici branch in Venice neither gained nor lost, because it drew a bill on Bruges at $51\frac{1}{2}$ groats and made returns at the same rate. It is true that Antonio del Conte borrowed 533 ducats and repaid 534 ducats and 21 grossi after four months, but this small difference of one ducat and a fraction represented local charges in Bruges and by no means originated in exchange fluctuations, since the ducat was computed at the same rate in figuring out both the exchange and the rechange. This was a matter of pure chance which rarely occurred.

In the two other cases recorded in the account book of 1441, the rate is not the same; otherwise they are identical with the first and involve the same parties. The second case relates to a bill of 377 ducats and 17 grossi at $54\frac{1}{2}$ groats, Flemish currency, per ducat, which was returned from Bruges to Venice at $51\frac{1}{2}$ groats, so that the lenders, that is, the Venice branch of the Medici Bank, made a profit of 3 groats per ducat, or the difference between the two rates, at the expense of Antonio del Conte.[51] In Venetian currency, total profit amounted to 21 ducats and 20 grossi. The third case concerns an amount of $441\frac{1}{4}$ ducats which were converted into Flemish currency at $53\frac{1}{4}$ groats and reconverted from Flemish currency into Venetian ducats at 51 groats, so that the lenders earned $2\frac{1}{4}$ groats per ducat.[52]

The Venice branch of the Medici company just broke even in the first case; their return corresponded to 17.5 percent a year in the second case, and to 13.2 percent a year in the third. Dry exchange, consequently, yielded an uncertain profit and retained a speculative character. Nevertheless it was regarded as usurious by the theologians as early as the fifteenth century, although it was not formally condemned until Pius V promulgated the decretal *In eam* on January 28, 1571.[53] The reason usually given was that in the case of dry exchange the *distantia loci* was no longer observed, because there was really no transfer of funds and the transaction was completed in the place where it had originated. This reasoning is fallacious, however, because simple commercial arithmetic shows that the lender's profit would have been *exactly the same* if the exchange had been real instead of dry. It is, therefore, not clear why one form of exchange should be licit and the other illicit.

There were other varieties of dry exchange. Sometimes the first bill of exchange was protested at destination, presumably to give the lender an unquestionable right to claim the full amount of the recambium from the borrower. This is the procedure adopted in the case of several bills drawn in 1462, 1463, and 1464 on the Geneva branch by the Milan branch of the Medici Bank, apparently in connection with loans to Angelo Simonetta, councilor and secretary to the Duke of Milan. The bills are protested under the pretext that Simonetta could not be located in Geneva and had no funds standing to his credit with which to pay the draft.[54] Of course, the Medici branch in Geneva knew very well who Simonetta was: it was a farce to look for him on the shores of Lake Leman.[55] The purpose of putting on this little show was presumably to circumvent a Milanese law of 1439 which invalidated bills of exchange not based on a real transfer but on a concealed loan.[56]

Fictitious exchange, in the eyes of the theologians, was even more pernicious than dry exchange. It consisted in using fictitious names, fictitious rates, fictitious bills, or no bills at all. The Medici records refer from time to time to *cambium sine litteris* (exchange without bills).[57] In reality, it differed little from dry exchange, as long as the profit of the lender was still determined by the rates prevailing in the money market.[58] This speculative element could be eliminated by stipulating in advance the rate of the recambium. By so doing, fictitious exchange became undistinguishable from a straight loan at interest, and it is not surprising that it was censured by the theologians.

Although the merchants, in contrast to the theologians, were inclined to regard as licit any exchange transaction which retained its speculative character, a Florentine law was passed in 1429 to outlaw cambium sine litteris, "commonly called dry exchange," allegedly because so many people were ruined by resorting to this expedient in order to raise funds. Presumably the law did more harm than good, because it was suspended for two years by a vote of 137 ayes and 64 nays in 1435, soon after the Medici came to power.[59] There is no indication that it was ever revived, the reason being that it clashed with the interests of the leading bankers, among whom the Medici were the most prominent.

As an adjunct to the exchange business, the Medici Bank sold letters of credit to pilgrims, travelers, students, diplomats, and churchmen, either going to Italy or residing there. This activity did not elicit any opposition on the part of the theologians. Letters of credit were usually paid for in advance like travelers' checks today. They differed from the bill of exchange in that they sometimes took the form of a letter by which one branch of the Medici Bank instructed another to pay up to a certain sum against a receipt signed by the beneficiary. The following is such a letter by which the Medici branch in Bruges requests the Medici branch in Milan to pay up to 200 ducats to Paul, son of Baptist, a Flemish student at the University of Pavia.[60]

† *IHS, a dì 8 di giungnio 1474*
Per questa solo vi diremo che richiegiendovi Paholo di Batist, studiante a Pavia, per fino alla somma di ducati dugiento, cioè duc. 200 di camera, glie li paghiate, prendete quitanza e ponete a nnostro conto, che ssono per la valuta n'abiamo avuto da Stefano Van der Gheyst. Paghate glieli a ssuo piaciere. Idio vi guardi.

*Lorenzo de' Medici e Tommaso Portinari
et compagni di Bruggia, inn Anversa*

pagati

On the back:

*Lorenzo e Giuliano de' Medici et compagni
in Milano*

Prima

The letter was presumably issued while a representative of the Bruges branch attended the fairs in Antwerp where he received the value of the letter from Stephen Van der Gheyst, probably a relative of the beneficiary. The latter was entitled to collect the amount of 200 ducats at one time or in several installments upon giving a receipt for each payment. As *pagati* (paid) is written at the bottom of the letter in another hand, and the text is crossed out by diagonal strokes, Paul probably received the entire amount in one payment.

Letters of credit were also issued in favor of ecclesiastics who had benefices north of the Alps but resided temporarily or permanently at the Roman Curia. An example is that of Master Anselm de Smit, or Fabri (d. 1449), *doctor decretorum,* deacon of the Church of Our Lady in Antwerp and *abbreviator litterarum* at the Roman Curia.[61] In June 1441, the Bruges branch issued in his favor two letters of credit for a total of 500 cameral ducats, one of 400 ducats and the other of 100 ducats, at the price of 51 groats, Flemish currency, per ducat.[62] The smaller amount was paid in Rome to Anselm Fabri's servant, Gualtiere da Ghalda (Wouter van Gouda?), presumably a Fleming or a Dutchman, because his name does not sound Italian. He gave a receipt which was apparently forwarded from Rome to Bruges. The larger amount was still unclaimed when the books were closed on March 24, 1442. At least, the Bruges branch had not been notified of any payment to either Anselm Fabri himself or his representative. The entries in the ledger of the Bruges branch show that letters of credit were handled in a different way from bills of exchange. It would, therefore, be a mistake not to differentiate between these two instruments.

Not infrequently, letters of credit were payable to a beneficiary or to his order.[63] Thus the Tavola of Florence issued one on October 1, 1455, to be paid to Astorre Manfredi, lord of Faenza, himself or "to whom he will order" (*o chi lui ordinassi*).[64] It would, however, be a mistake to jump from there to the conclusion that credit instruments in the Middle Ages were fully negotiable so that the bearer could have a better title than the original creditor or a previous holder. Medieval order clauses did not have such a wide scope, and the doctrine of negotiability did not gain general acceptance until the seventeenth century. It rested on the practice of endorsement and altered so completely the fundamental characteristics of the cambium contract involving four parties that the bill of exchange, losing all connection with this contract, eventually was transformed into a mere mandate to pay and became a form of currency. In the seventeenth and eighteenth centuries, it is not rare to encounter bills of exchange with two or more endorsements on the back.

Although endorsement did not become general practice until after 1600, it is possible to find transfer orders written on the back or on the front of bills of exchange, checks, and other instruments at a much earlier date. A few years ago, Professor Federigo Melis discovered a bill of exchange, dated 1519, bearing on the back a transfer order by which a payee named another person as beneficiary, an order which was actually carried out according to an entry in the journal of the payor.[65] Other entries in the same account book indicated that the practice of giving such transfer orders either on the instrument itself or by separate letter might even be older. Professor Melis did not expect it to be much older, until he himself discovered in the Datini Archives an "endorsed" draft dated 1410 and a letter dated 1394 by which the payee of a bill of exchange ordered it to be paid to a third person, a request with which the payor complied.[66] Two remarks need to be made in this connection. First, endorsement was still far from being common, since Professor Melis found only one example of it among thousands of bills in the Datini archives. Second, the transfer order was not always written on the instrument itself, but sometimes on a separate sheet of paper.

To date, the earliest known example of this procedure goes back to 1386.[67] It involves a bill drawn on April 11, 1386, in Florence by Jacopo Ardinghelli & Co. on Antonio di Messer Luca in Zara. Since the deliverer (*datore*), the firm Guido Fagni & Co., did not have correspondents in Zara, the payor was ordered to pay to Nannino Pellacane of Venice or to whomever the latter would designate in writing (*o chui vi scrivesse*). Accordingly, on June 4, 1386, Nannino Pellacane wrote a separate note ordering the payor to pay to Paolo di Berto Grassini and attached it to the bill. On June 28, 1386, the bill was protested because the payee insisted on being paid in Hungarian florins current in Zara and refused to accept Florentine florins with the fleur-de-lys offered in payment by the payor. It is interesting that Paolo Grassini, according to the text of the protest, took recourse against Nannino Pellacane who made out the complementary transfer order and not against the drawer of the original bill. The case was certainly exceptional, because Zara was not a regular banking place. Nevertheless, it shows that the roots of endorsement go back farther than is commonly suspected: whether the transfer order is written on the instrument itself or on a separate strip of paper affixed to it makes, in the author's opinion, very little difference; it is just a matter of form or custom.

Another early example of a transfer order, this time written on the back of a bill, is found in 1430. This case relates to a bill of exchange drawn on Alphonse V, King of Aragon, by his confessor Antonio da Fano, then on a mission in Rome, for an amount of 500 cameral ducats, which he had received from Francesco Boscoli, formerly a factor of Giovanni di Bicci, but now the Rome manager of the competing Medici bank of Averardo di Francesco. The bill was sent for collection to Barcelona to the firm Antonio Pazzi and Francesco Tosinghi. Since the King had left town to go to Valencia, the payees wrote on the back that they would be satisfied (*siamo contenti*) if the draft were paid to their proxy, Bartolomeo Benci.[68] Of course, this was not a real transfer but simply a request to pay to a representative of the payee.

By a stroke of luck, another "endorsed" bill was found recently in the Florentine archives. It is of a little later date (1438), but it has the merit of being actually endorsed by the Medici Bank. The original has not been preserved, but the text is given verbatim in a protest for nonpayment and reads as follows:[69]

Al nome di Dio a dì 5 di maggio 1438

Pagate per questa prima a dì LX fatta, a Cosimo et Lorenzo de' Medici et compagni, fiorini trecento, cioè f. 300, per la valuta a s. 14 d. 9 da Filippo Borromei et compagni et ponete per voi. Christo vi guardi.

Francesco Tosinghi et Vanni Rucellai
et compagni in Barzalona

In two different hands:

Acceptata a dì 6 di giugno 1438

Noi Cosimo et Lorenzo de' Medici e compagni vogliamo che al tempo gli pagate per noi a 'Douardo Giachinotti et compagni.

On the back:

*Pierantonio et Jachopo Pierozi e compagni
in Firenze*

Prima

Except for its being endorsed, this is the usual four-party bill involving:
(1) Francesco Tosinghi and Vanni Rucellai, in Barcelona (drawer); (2)
Filippo Borromei & Co., also in Barcelona (remitter); (3) the Medici Bank
in Florence (payee); and (4) Pierantonio and Jacopo Pierozzi & Co., in the
same city (payor). The bill issued in Barcelona on May 5, 1438, was
accepted in Florence on June 6 following. The assignment is written
on the front rather than on the back of the bill and says: "We, Cosimo
and Lorenzo de' Medici & Co., order you, at maturity, to pay *for us* to
Adoardo Giachinotti & Co." Whether this assignment constitutes the
equivalent of a modern endorsement is questionable. It certainly enabled
the drawee to pay validly to Adoardo Giachinotti & Co., but it apparently did not confer to the assignees the power to sue upon the bill
in their own name or as holders in due course. The use of the words "for
us" in the text of the assignment strongly suggests that the Medici Bank
regarded itself as principal. This interpretation receives further confirmation from the fact that the assignees did not protest the unpaid bill,
but that this step was taken by Cambio di Antonio de' Medici, factor of
the Medici Bank, acting, it is stated, in this capacity and secondarily, as
if (*tanquam*) he also were factor of Adoardo Giachinotti & Co. It is
thus clear from the text of the protest itself that the new holder, the
firm Adoardo Giachinotti & Co., did not act *ex proprio jure* (in its own
right), but only as an *adjectus solutionis* (collecting agent).

Incidentally, the bill remained unpaid and was protested, because the
drawees, Pierantonio and Jacopo Pierozzi, who had fled from the city on
account of the plague, could not be located. Although the bill became
due sixty days from date, or on July 4, 1460, it was not protested until
July 24. A bill broker, Andrea di ser Bartolomeo, called Astrolago, as
usual testified that, on July 24, the exchange rate with Barcelona stood
at 15s. 3d. Barcelonese, per Florentine florin. In other words, there was
a difference of only six points between the rate of exchange (14s. 9d.)
and the rate of re-exchange (15s. 3d.). This corresponds to a return of
3.4 percent in four months, or 10.2 percent a year.

A more complicated case is raised by a bill, dated April 18, 1494, issued
in Rome, and payable in Naples in favor of a Milanese merchant named
Bernardino de Carnago.[70] The payee endorsed the bill and declared himself willing to accept credit in the Tornabuoni bank in Naples, a
subsidiary of the Medici branch in Rome.[71] This bill gave rise to an
involved lawsuit which centered around two points: (1) whether a transfer

in bank was final payment and completely discharged the debtor and (2) whether the Medici branches in Rome and Naples were one legal person or separate entities not liable for each other. To complicate matters, the Tornabuoni bank failed in March 1495 while the French were occupying Naples.[72] After they had evacuated the city, the lawsuit was resumed, but never decided, because one of the litigants, the payee Bernardino de Carnago, had chosen to decamp with the French army.

As to the issues raised by the lawsuit, two observations need to be made. One, the payee's endorsement was clearly a permission to pay in bank. According to medieval merchant custom, a transfer or assignment in bank, if accepted by the creditor, was regarded as a final settlement.[73] If the bank were to fail afterwards, the creditor had no claim against the debtor. Two, the Tornabuoni bank in Naples was almost wholly owned by the Tornabuoni bank in Rome which was, consequently, responsible for all the liabilities of its subsidiary.[74] As a matter of fact, the Neapolitan courts also reached the decision that the two Tornabuoni banks were a single concern. Hence, the case is not similar to the one, discussed above, of the Bruges and London branches.

Despite the discoveries made in recent years, it would be rash to jump to the conclusion that endorsing bills was a common practice in the fifteenth century or that bills of exchange were fully negotiable. First of all, endorsed bills were the exception, perhaps one in a hundred or a thousand, and remained so throughout the sixteenth century. It is only shortly after 1600 that the practice of endorsement spread like wildfire.[75] Among bills of exchange of this period, it is not even difficult to find examples of multiple endorsements, sometimes as many as four or five.[76] The jurists were slow to evolve the principle of negotiability and only reluctantly, under the pressure of merchant custom, came to recognize the holder in due course as principal, to grant him the right of recourse against previous holders, and to admit that his title might even be better than that of the original beneficiary or of subsequent endorsers.[77]

In the fifteenth century, legal doctrine had not reached this stage of sophistication: the status of the bearer was still uncertain at law. At best, he was regarded as the agent of the payee named in the instrument. However, in medieval practice, the payee had action against the acceptor only, and not against the drawer. The right to bring suit against the drawer of a dishonored bill belonged to the deliverer or remitter who had given consideration by furnishing the value which formed the basis of the cambium contract.[78]

With regard to loans to princes or rulers, it is extremely difficult to make any generalizations, since the terms varied from contract to contract, according to the circumstances and the type of security which the borrower was able to offer. In lending to princes, bankers were not bound by the usages and customs of the money market which regulated dealings in exchange. In general, loans to princes were secured either by pledges of crown jewels or other valuables or more often by assignment of tax revenues, the proceeds of which were turned over to the lender, unless he was granted the right to do the collecting himself. Thus lending to princes often involved tax-farming in one form or another. Interest was rarely openly stipulated but was usually called by various euphemisms and concealed more or less successfully by a number of devices which often led to difficulties and disagreements when it came to rendering accounts. One favorite device was to foist overpriced commodities upon the borrower. Another was to make excessive charges for commission or other services. Often such charges were later disallowed by auditors or comptrollers appointed to scrutinize the lender's accounts, a practice conducive to justified or trumped up accusations of embezzlement. This is the familiar story of many financiers from the Frescobaldi in the fourteenth century to Jacques Cœur in the time of the Medici.

Loans to princes entailed serious dangers. First of all, the amounts involved were usually large and thus precluded an adequate division of risks. If they were allowed, as frequently happened, to grow disproportionately, they absorbed a greater and greater percentage of available resources until scarcely anything was left for other purposes. For example, when Francesco Sforza died on March 8, 1466, he owed the Medici of Milan more than 115,000 ducats, for which the latter managed to secure assignments on the salt gabelle and other imposts from the Duke's successor, but some of the income was not due until 1469. In addition, the Duke had borrowed a sizable sum by pawning some of his jewels, but they proved difficult to sell except to other potentates whose credit was not much better, if not worse.[79] As this example shows, amortization was often slow and, what is even more disastrous, was rarely carried out on schedule, because war, civil strife, or other events were likely to upset the most careful plans. Instead of being repaid, the lender was willy-nilly forced to lend more and to throw good money after bad in the hope of saving what he had already lent. Once engaged in making advances to princes, it was impossible to pull out and to retrench without courting disaster. Inevitably the lender was sucked deeper and deeper into the whirlpool, as the Medici found out to their detriment. And a banker who had been pressed dry was mercilessly dropped like an orange whose juice has been squeezed out. He became an importunate solicitor whose plight was scarcely pitied, as turned out to be the fate of the Portinari brothers in Bruges and Milan. The Medici themselves barely succeeded in retrieving their political fortune, and did so only because a unique set of circumstances favored their return to power as ruling princes, after they had been driven out in 1494.

VII

THE MEDICI AS MERCHANTS AND AS DEALERS IN ALUM AND IRON

1. THE VENTURE TRADE

The organization of international trade in the days of the Medici differed as much from that of the present day as did the banking system. The two main characteristics of medieval trade were venturing and diversification.[1] Both were the outcome of conditions which prevailed in the Middle Ages and persisted for a long time thereafter, and in colonial trade until the end of the eighteenth century. As a rule, medieval merchants were merchant adventurers who sought protection from high risks in distributing their investments among many ventures. This policy is well expressed by Antonio in Shakespeare's *Merchant of Venice* (Act I, Scene 1):

> Believe me no, I thank my fortune for it,
> My ventures are not in one bottom trusted,
> Nor to one place: nor is my whole estate
> Upon the fortune of this present year:
> Therefore my merchandise makes me not sad.

The Medici were no exception to the general rule. They also diversified their risks by dealing in a great many commodities, but the mainstay of their business was trade in certain staple products and luxury articles for which there was a steady demand in the principal commercial centers. Leading staples were wool, alum, cloth, spices, olive oil, and citrus fruits. Since their clientele was aristocratic, the Medici also dealt extensively in luxury articles, such as silk stuffs, brocades, jewelry, and silver plate. Risks were further spread by entering into joint ventures or temporary partnerships with other merchants.[2] In many cases, the Medici refused to take any risks at all and confined themselves to selling consignments on a commission basis. In some instances commodities were bought for others "on their account" and at their risk. Relations between branches were on much the same basis as with outsiders. For example, in 1441 the Medici branch in Venice bought common ginger for the Medici branch in Bruges and charged the purchase to the latter's Loro (or Vostro) account, an entry which shows plainly that, in this particular transaction, Venice was only carrying out instructions and acting as agent. The Bruges branch did the opposite and wrote the cost of the ginger to the credit of the Venice branch's Nostro account kept in Venetian ducats.[3] So the Venetian branch ran no risk at all, not even that of adverse exchange fluctuations.

The extent to which diversification was carried is sometimes astounding. The Medici branch in Bruges, for example, participated in the recruitment of choir boys with high-pitched voices for the choir of St. John in Lateran.[4] A tenor, after a disappointing visit to Lyons, came all the way to Bruges for this purpose and, with the assistance of Tommaso Portinari, found what he wanted in the region of Douai and Cambray, where apparently boys with soprano voices were plentiful. Several were hired and the Medici branch in Bruges provided them with the necessary money for the long trip to Rome. Medici agents all over Europe also took part in the hunt for lost classics and were instructed to buy interesting manuscripts from monks who, not realizing their value, would sell them cheaply. Gherardo Bueri, Cosimo's agent in Lübeck, received orders to search for a lost work of Livy supposed to be in a Cistercian monastery near Röskilde, but he was unable to locate it.[5] However, luck served him better on another occasion when he managed to buy a Pliny from the Dominicans in Lübeck.[6] Pigello Portinari in Milan on April 9, 1456, reported to Giovanni di Cosimo that he had an expert examine a manuscript of Suetonius but it was not very good and not worth the price asked for it.[7]

Today, in the overseas trade, the buyer usually seeks out the seller and goods are not shipped without being sold. This is especially true of heavy equipment and manufactured goods which are made to order according to the specifications of foreign buyers. In the Middle Ages, however, the consignment trade was dominant because buyers wanted to inspect personally the quality of the goods offered for sale and did not usually place orders in foreign countries. Because of the prevalence of this practice, it was up to the seller to find an outlet for his wares. Most medieval merchants were adventurers in the sense that they sent their goods on consignment without knowing whether or not they would sell. It was the job of the consignee to sell the consignor's merchandise at the best price obtainable. Of course, merchants did not act blindly, since they regularly received reports from their correspondents about market conditions abroad. Even so, "adventuring" involved many risks: because communications were slow, information was never up to date so that decisions were made upon expectations which might or might not materialize. Scarcity and high prices often attracted excessive supplies, so that the market, after being understocked, became glutted. If a merchant, following the advice of his correspondents, shipped goods to a place where they were reputedly in brisk demand, he would frequently discover that others had been doing the same and had spoiled the market by the time his shipment reached its destination.

Although the consignment trade predominated, there were a few exceptions to the general rule. The tapestry trade was one of them. The Low Countries were the production center of tapestries, the famous *arazzi,* which during the fifteenth century became fashionable not only as wall hangings but also as seat covers and backs, cushions, bed spreads, and canopies. There were apparently two kinds of tapestries which differed both in kind and in quality. Those of the cheaper sort were called *verdure* (greenery), because they were covered with foliage of a simple design. Since the same pattern was repeated over and over again, these tapestries could be cut to fit the shape of any room, like wallpaper today. They were a staple article of export and were consigned to foreign dealers in the usual way. The same was not true of the more expensive tapestries à *personnages* of special design which were always made to order, often according to cartoons prepared by Italian artists.[8] The tapestry makers were also given the dimensions of the room for which the tapestries were intended.[9] The Medici accepted such special orders and had them executed by the best tapestry makers in the Low Countries.[10] According to Gerozzo de' Pigli, the manager in Bruges, the most skillful among them was someone in Lille who, being well off, cared more about his reputation than about making profits.[11] He was entrusted with the weaving of a set of tapestries representing the Triumphs of Petrarch for Giovanni di Cosimo and still another set for his brother Piero.[12] The Medici branch in Bruges placed other orders for the bank's customers, such as Gaspare, Count of Vimercato, a courtier in Milan.[13] Probably the Medici earned only a commission on such orders.

Besides tapestries, the Medici branch in Bruges supplied horses to Giovanni and Piero di Cosimo and their cousin, Pierfrancesco di Lorenzo.[14] It purchased at the fairs of Antwerp painted panels, probably for the adornment of the palace in the via Larga.[15] Once a brass chandelier ordered by the maggiori was completely taken apart and sent to Italy overland, packed in a barrel with all the pieces carefully numbered so that they could be easily reassembled.[16]

Sometimes bargains came unexpectedly on the market. Thus, Francesco Sassetti, manager of the Geneva branch, was offered in 1450 a beautiful set for one of those Renaissance monumental beds, in red serge embroidered with silk, including canopy, hangings, and spread, all at the bargain price of 56 ducats. He could not resist the temptation of buying this outfit and sent it on to Giovanni di Cosimo. If the latter did not want it, Sassetti was sure that Giovanni Inghirami, the manager of the Tavola, could sell it at a profit in either Florence or Rome. Sassetti was a trifle uneasy, because the set was made to fit French beds which, it seems, were a bit shorter than their Italian counterparts.[17]

Special orders for tapestries and other luxury products were exceptional. Volume was provided by the venture trade. A good example of venturing is afforded by an account in the ledger of the Bruges branch for the year 1441.[18] The account relates to one hundred bales of almonds bought by the firm of Piero del Fede and Co. in Valencia. The partners in this joint venture were four: the Medici branch in Bruges; Piero del Fede & Co. of Valencia; Riccardo Davanzati & Co. of Barcelona; and Bosco di Giovanni of Valencia. The first two were interested for one third each and the last two, for one sixth each. Later on, Piero del Fede & Co. sold its share to the Medici for £79 7s. 6d. groat, Flemish currency, so that the latter's share was brought up to two thirds. The gross proceeds amounted to £313 13s. 5d. groat, Flemish currency.

The account is very well kept and gives an itemized list of all the charges paid by the Medici in Bruges. The biggest item is a payment of £52 groat to the scribe of the Florentine galleys for freight from Valencia to Sluys, the seaport of Bruges, and for pilotage in the harbor of Sluys, after deducting £3 groat because eleven bales had been damaged by water. This item of £52 groat alone amounts to 16.6 percent of gross proceeds. In Sluys the one hundred bales of almonds were transhipped into small boats, and then conveyed by canal from Sluys to Bruges. In this connection, the Medici paid £1 13s. 4d. groat, including the toll of Damme, plus 8s. 4d. to have the bales unloaded and carried to the cellar or warehouse. This item was less than one percent of gross proceeds (Table 27). As eleven bales had been soaked, the contents were spread out on the floor of an attic to dry at the negligible cost of 2s. 11d. groat. Eleven bales were reshipped to be sold at the Easter Fair of Bergen-op-Zoom and twenty bales were sent for the same purpose to the summer fair of Antwerp. This transhipment increased charges only slightly, by less than one percent. The Catalan customs, the tolls of Damme and Antwerp on the bales reshipped to Brabant, and the Florentine consular fees, all together did not exceed £6 0s. 6d. groat or 2 percent of sales. Protectionism certainly was not yet born. Although we hear a great deal about the crushing burden of tolls in the Middle Ages, charges in Flanders and Brabant were far from excessive, if this case is typical. The largest item was £5 3s. 4d. groat for Catalan customs at 4 groats per pound ad valorem. on a declared value of £310 groat. The rate of the Florentine consular fees was only one sterling, Flemish currency, per pound groat, which corresponds to less than 1.5 per mille.[19] Brokerage was 4 groats per bale and the Medici branch of Bruges charged commission at the rate of 1.5 percent, or £4 18s. 11d. groat. Storage and weighing

TABLE 27. ACCOUNT OF ONE HUNDRED BALES OF ALMONDS SOLD
BY THE MEDICI BRANCH OF BRUGES

Explanation	Amount			Percent of Total
	Flemish groats			
	£	s.	d.	
Freight charges from Valencia to Bruges on the Florentine galleys...............................	52	0	0	16.6
Charges in Spain to put the almonds on board.......	5	8	0	1.7
Local charges for unloading and transhipment in Sluys and Bruges..................................	2	1	8	0.6
Damage by water................................		2	11	0.1
Charges on 31 bales sent to Antwerp and Bergen-op-Zoom..	2	6	0	0.7
Customs, tolls, and consular fees..................	6	0	6	1.9
Storage and weighing............................	2	3	3	0.7
Brokerage......................................	1	13	0	0.5
Commission....................................	4	18	11	1.6
Total charges...........	76	14	3	24.4
Net proceeds............	236	19	2	75.6
Gross proceeds..........	313	13	5	100.0

Source: ASF, MAP, filza 134, no. 2, fol. 246; R. de Roover, *The Medici Bank* (New York, 1948), pp. 87–90.

in Bruges, Bergen-op-Zoom, and Antwerp did not cost much, only £2 3s. 3d. groat or less than one percent of the sales value. All in all, charges paid by the Bruges branch on this shipment of almonds amounted to £76 14s. 3d. groat, or 24.4 percent of gross proceeds. After deducting 18.3 percent for freight and expenses in Spain, local charges in Bruges were only 6.1 percent of sales, which is far from excessive, in my estimation.

How were the hundred bales sold? As already stated, 31 bales were sold at the fairs of Brabant and the remaining 69 bales in Bruges. Of these 69 bales, 44 were sold to local grocers in Bruges, 17 to an Englishman named Thomas, 7 to Nicholas van Drijl, a merchant in Brussels, and one bale was kept by the Medici for their own consumption. This Nicholas van Drijl — he is called Niccolò de Deril in the ledger — also bought the 11 bales sent to the Easter Fair of Bergen-op-Zoom; he was an important customer who had frequent dealings with the Medici.[20] The prices obtained varied from £3 to £3 10s. groat, Flemish currency, per *carica* of 400 pounds avoirdupois, Flemish weight.[21] The net proceeds, £236 19s. 2d. groat, were divided among the partners in this joint venture: one sixth or £39 9s. 11d. each to Riccardo Davanzati & Co. of Barcelona and to Bosco di Giovanni of Valencia and two thirds or £157

19s. 4d. to the Medici. The records are unfortunately incomplete. As there are no data available for the purchase cost of the almonds in Spain, it is impossible to know whether the Medici made any profit on this venture.

The extant fragment of the Bruges ledger also contains the account of a consignment of eight bales of grains of paradise, or cardamom, sold by the Bruges branch for Bartolomeo di Niccolò Martelli in Florence.[22] This account also gives the same impression that local charges were moderate: they did not exceed 2.6 percent of proceeds, including brokerage and commission (Table 28). Three of the eight bales were sold at the fairs of Antwerp and Bergen-op-Zoom, one to a merchant from Cologne. The five remaining bales were all sold to local grocers in Bruges.

TABLE 28. ACCOUNT OF EIGHT BALES OF CARDAMOM SOLD BY THE BRUGES BRANCH OF THE MEDICI BANK

Explanation	Amount			Percent of Total
	Flemish groats			
	£	s.	d.	
Freight paid to the scribe of the galleys and pilotage in Sluys....................................	21	2	1	13.0
Local transfer charges and tolls....................		17	6	0.5
Brokerage...	1	1	10	0.7
Consular fees.....................................		4	6	0.1
Commission of the consignees: 1½ percent...........	2	8	8	1.5
Total charges...........	25	14	7	15.8
Net proceeds...........	136	17	10	84.2
Gross proceeds..........	162	12	5	100.0

Source: ASF, MAP, filza 134, no. 2, fol. 242.

If these two cases are representative, the main outlet for spices and nuts was among the local grocers of Bruges. This agrees with the thesis of Professor J. A. van Houtte, who insists that Bruges was a regional trading center rather than an international market or meeting place for merchants from all over Europe; it imported goods for local consumption and exported manufactured products, chiefly cloth, from the surrounding district.[23] It is disappointing that the surviving fragment of the Medici ledger is not more extensive, because a few more samples would yield conclusive evidence and settle the point at issue once and for all. In any case, there is thus far no proof that the Medici branch in Bruges did much business with the Hanseatic merchants, but it dealt with Englishmen. London grocers and mercers, it is well known, visited Bruges regularly to lay in supplies. This fact, however, is fully acknowledged by Professor van Houtte and is not irreconcilable with his thesis, since London in the fifteenth century was a satellite moving in the orbit of Bruges.

It was the custom of merchants, including the Medici, to open a separate account for each venture or lot of merchandise. Such accounts were charged with all outlays, costs, and expenses and credited with proceeds from sales. The difference remaining after conclusion of the venture represented either a profit or a loss and was usually transferred to an account, "Profit and Loss on Merchandise" (*Avanzi e disavanzi di mercatantie*). Thus profits from trade and from exchange were kept separate. This system of opening a separate account to each venture has been called "venture accounting" by accountants and students of the history of accounting. Venture accounting eliminated the necessity of inventory valuation. Since records were generally kept according to this system, it is not surprising that Luca Pacioli and other early authors on bookkeeping are silent on the subject of inventory valuation. Neither is it surprising that there are no examples of it in the Medici records.[24]

As the example of the one hundred bales of almonds shows, each consignment required considerable attention: shipping arrangements had to be made, warehouses hired, customs and transit charges paid, and prospective buyers approached. It was doubtless the job of the factors to attend to all these details. The rôle of the manager was probably to approve the bargains made by his subordinates and to see to it that the merchandise was sold as quickly as possible: the quicker the turnover, the greater were the returns on invested capital.

Venture trading rested on confidence, because the principal had little control over his agents. At best he could check whether they were cheating him by selling under the market price or by keeping part of the proceeds.[25] Since the Medici companies dealt preferably with one another, they probably had less trouble with unreliable or unsatisfactory agents than smaller merchants. Nevertheless, the problem was not eliminated altogether, and the Medici correspondence is full of recriminations of one branch manager against another because goods sent on consignment were sold more slowly than anticipated or did not fetch as much as expected. Consignors, not being on the spot, did not always realize the difficulties resulting from the fact that shortage of money was an acute problem in the Middle Ages. As a result, it was difficult to find buyers able to pay cash instead of asking for easy credit terms.

According to the Medici correspondence, either the consignor or the consignee was at fault. The first sometimes sent goods of poor quality which were hard to sell. Thus in 1458 the Milan branch complained because of the inferior wool received on consignment from the Venice branch.[26] On the other hand, consignors were often dissatisfied because they thought, rightly or wrongly, that consignees gave them poor service.

As early as 1441 the Medici of Venice wrote Bernardo Portinari in Bruges to protest against his slowness in selling consignments of ginger and pepper.[27] Even Tommaso Portinari, in charge of the Bruges branch, put pressure on his brother Accerrito, in charge of the Milan branch, to quicken the sale of English wool.[28] Headquarters in Florence were not spared criticism; in 1455 the London branch grumbled because the main office sold English wool at such a low price and on such long terms that there was little or no profit. Florence, so London claimed, was also too liberal in granting credit to buyers of English says.[29] In 1467 Giovanni Altoviti, the manager in Venice, inquired whether there would be any sale for cotton in Bruges. After being urged by Tommaso Portinari to send a lot, Altoviti found that it did not sell because the Genoese had glutted the market with Turkish cotton and no buyer was willing to make a reasonable offer even on easy terms.[30]

Because of the limited use of substitutes, shortage of money was a universal evil in the Middle Ages. Oftentimes it was impossible to find a buyer without accepting other goods in exchange. As a result, barter was a common practice. Thus the London branch, after bartering alum for 200 pokes of wool, sent the wool to Florence where it could only be disposed of by taking silks and brocades in exchange.[31] Then there arose the problem of finding buyers for these luxury articles at the Court and among the English nobles. The whole process took several months during which funds were tied up. In an age of dollar shortage (1957) such difficulties have reappeared: an official of the Standard Oil Company (New Jersey) told me an amazing story of his company dealing in Dutch cheese and Greek raisins acquired in payment for oil. After a circuitous process, the cheese and the raisins eventually helped to finance the construction of a tanker in an Italian shipyard.

Mention has already been made of transfer difficulties. Of course no statistics are available, but it is significant that Giovanni Tornabuoni, the branch manager in Rome, constantly complained because the branches beyond the Alps were draining away his cash reserves by not remitting promptly the proceeds of the sale of alum or the funds received for the papal treasury.[32] The latter were unilateral payments which, far from alleviating the problem, made it worse by increasing the imbalance. As late as the first half of the fourteenth century, there was an extensive market in Italy for Flemish cloth, but this market no longer existed after 1400. English wool was about the only product that Florence bought in Northern Europe, and the volume of this trade was steadily shrinking because licenses were increasingly hard to get and the expanding woolen industry left less and less wool available for export.

The best evidence is perhaps afforded by the cargo lists of the Florentine galleys, several of which are available. One of them, dating from

1466, enumerates 2,253 pokes of wool, 84 bales of cloth, tin and lead blocks, all commodities which certainly were loaded in England. The only cargo coming from Flanders consisted of 30 bales of mercery and 26 bales of feathers.[33] There were also on board 40,000 ducats in gold bullion, but it is impossible to ascertain whether this gold came from Flanders or from Spain, where the galleys usually called at one or two ports. The following year, the cargo list does not include any merchandise that could possibly have been loaded at Bruges.[34] In 1468 the Florentine galleys carried 1,273 pokes of wool, 67 bales of cloth, 416 blocks of lead, all cargo coming from England.[35] And from Flanders? Nothing, but seven bales of feathers.[36]

The cargo list of the Burgundian galley, captured in the spring of 1473 by a Danzig corsair off Dunkirk while crossing from Zeeland to England, tells an even more eloquent story. Tommaso Portinari, in the name of the Medici company as operator of the galley, filed a claim for damages. The estimates of the cargo aboard vary, but this matters little for our purpose. The bulk of the cargo was made up of alum destined for England.[37] According to one estimate, it represented a value of 30,000 florins. In addition there were aboard 7,000 or 8,000 florins' worth of silks, satins, brocades, and gold thread, presumably coming from Italy and going to England.[38] As goods taken aboard in Zeeland, the estimate mentions two chests of bonnets, linens and canvas, two bales of cloth from Bruges and Armentières, feathers, a parcel of furs, one lot of tapestries, and two altarpieces, having an aggregate value of 2,470 florins.[39] In other words, the Flemish cargo bound for Italy was almost negligible. The galley, we know, was heading for Southampton to unload the alum and the silkstuffs and to take on a cargo of wool with some tin and lead as ballast.

It is true that trade relations between the Low Countries and northern Italy were less lopsided because some Flemish cloth was still reaching Milan overland and the Venetian galleys were carrying, besides some cloth, Dutch linens and other products. Nevertheless, everything seems to indicate that the situation grew from bad to worse as the fifteenth century drew to a close and as wool exports from England kept falling off. It is not surprising that the Florentine galleys, lacking a return cargo, were the first to be discontinued.[40] Another significant fact is that ships bringing alum from Civitavecchia to Flanders had to return in ballast unless a shipload of wool could be procured.[41] The crisis of the Italian trade also sealed the doom of the port of Southampton, which declined rapidly, as the Genoese carracks disappeared soon after the Florentine galleys.[42] These remarks, of course, do not impair the pertinence of Professor van Houtte's thesis; on the contrary, they give it more weight, since the galleys were dependent upon Flemish and English

exports and apparently carried very few products from the Baltic or
other regions.[43]

The dwindling of the Italian trade certainly had an adverse effect on
the position of the Medici Bank. It increased the bickerings between
Tornabuoni, the manager of the Rome branch, and Portinari, the manager of the Bruges branch. More important, it pulled away the props
which gave a solid foundation to the Bank and increased the pressure
for seeking employment of idle funds in the dangerous field of government finance.

The Medici were not very active as underwriters. The partnership
agreements relating to Bruges and London expressly forbade the manager to underwrite any insurance but imposed upon him the obligation
to fully insure all cargoes unless shipped aboard the Florentine or Venetian galleys. Some underwriting was done in these two cities, as is evidenced by insurance policies taken out by Bernardo Portinari, the first
manager of the Bruges branch, in 1444 on a shipment of English wool
and in 1445 on a cargo of general merchandise, including tapestries,
linens, furs, caps, and other merceries from Sluys in Flanders to Porto
Pisano, aboard the Florentine galleys.[44] However, if the cargo was valuable, it was not always possible to find in Bruges or London enough
underwriters to cover the risk. The big insurance center was Venice,
even for ships or cargoes which never touched at that port. It is therefore not surprising that the Venice branch took out insurance for other
branches. Thus, in 1455, it negotiated a policy of £120 groat, Venetian
currency, or 1,200 ducats, covering a cargo of wool going from Southampton to Venice by the Venetian state galleys. The premium was only
3 percent, since accidents with the galleys were rare occurrences.[45]

The rate was much higher on other ships, even when the distance was
shorter. For example, according to another policy of the same year, the
premium amounted to 6 and 7 percent on a cargo of cloth, wool, and
lead from London to Porto Pisano on board a sailing ship commanded
by Apollonio Massari. The insured value was 1,600 Venetian ducats
subscribed by fifteen different underwriters. As previously, insurance was
secured by the Venice branch for the London branch managed by Simone
Nori.[46] This difference in rates between galleys and other types of vessels
was quite normal.[47]

Although branch managers were not supposed to engage in underwriting, Gherardo Canigiani, the Medici representative in London, underwrote insurance, lost or not lost, on a cargo of alum aboard a ship
that was overdue on the short trip from Zeeland to London. The premium was 50 percent.[48] When the loss of the ship was confirmed, Canigiani refused to pay on the ground that the insured, Francesco Zorzi and
Piero Morosini, two Venetians residing in London, had taken out insur-

ance after having received secret intelligence of the shipwreck, a fact which they themselves acknowledged as being true. Although the insured would have no case according to modern law, they sued Canigiani in the Venetian courts and seized goods belonging to the Medici aboard the Venetian galleys. The records unfortunately do not reveal how the case was finally settled.[49]

Slavery, as has been pointed out, was prevalent in Italy and Spain during this period, but it was not tolerated either in the Low Countries or in France save in the Mediterranean provinces of Provence, Languedoc, and Roussillon.[50] The Medici branch in Venice, one of the main slave markets in Renaissance Europe, occasionally participated in this disreputable trade. Cino di Filippo di Cino Rinuccini reports in his diary that in 1466 he bought from this branch a Russian female slave of about twenty-six years at the price of 74½ florins.[51] Cosimo de' Medici himself, according to his catasto report for 1457, owned four slaves, all females of different ages.[52]

2. The Alum Monopoly

In the fifteenth century, one of the principal articles of trade was alum. It was extensively used in glassmaking, in tanning, and in the textile industry as a cleanser to remove grease and impurities from the wool and as a mordant to fix the dyes so the fabrics would not discolor. Today chemicals are used for these purposes, but in the fifteenth century there was no satisfactory substitute for alum.

It was, therefore, indispensable; a situation conducive to monopoly, since alum deposits of superior quality were concentrated in only a few locations. Rock alum, the finest quality, was found near the town of Karahissar in Asia Minor, not far from Trebizond, but the output was apparently small and this commodity was scarce.[53] By far the richest deposits of alum were found at Phocea, on the coast of Asia Minor, in the immediate vicinity of Smyrna. This alum was the second best in quality. The mines at Phocea remained under the control of the Genoese from 1275 until 1455, when they were driven out by the Turks.[54] All other kinds of alum, whether from the Barbary Coast or from other sources, were of inferior quality and their use was often forbidden by gild regulations.[55] In Christendom, there were small deposits on the Lipari Islands, off the coast of Sicily, and on Ischia, a small island in the Gulf of Naples. By 1460, however, these mines were nearly exhausted, and anyhow their output was not considered of high grade.[56]

As long as the Genoese were in control of the mines at Phocea, they knew how to maintain the price of alum by keeping the market short in supply. Their monopoly was somewhat tempered by the existence of competing kinds of alum, albeit of a less desirable quality.[57] The situation, however, grew steadily worse as the Turks became more and more menacing and used threats to exact higher and higher tributes from the Genoese.[58] The West could not get along without alum and, in order to get it, was thus forced to finance indirectly the Turkish campaigns.

Such was the situation when in 1460 rich deposits of alum were discovered at Tolfa, near Civitavecchia, by Giovanni da Castro (d. 1470 or before), a Paduan, who had resided for some time in the Levant.[59] This discovery, after being confirmed by experts, caused general elation at the Roman Curia, since it would free Christendom from being dependent upon the Turks for the supply of an essential commodity. The Tolfa alum, when tested, was also found to be of good, if not superior, quality. No time was lost by the Curia in concluding an agreement (July 6, 1462) for the exploitation of the new mines with the prospector Giovanni da Castro and his financial backers, two Roman residents, a Genoese (Bartolomeo da Framura), and a Pisan (Carlo Gaetani). These three men formed a partnership which became known as the Societas Aluminum. The terms are not known but they were ratified by Pius II on September 3, 1462, and went into effect on the following first of November.[60] This first agreement with the Societas Aluminum was renewed for nine years on March 20, 1465, with some new provisions.[61] The Camera Apostolica (papal treasury) was to receive a minimum of 30,000 cantars a year at the price of three-fourths ducat per cantar. This arrangement left to the papal treasury the task of finding a market for the alum and of regulating the supply so as to prevent a catastrophic fall in price. Presumably the scheme did not work so well, because the agreement lasted less than a year and a new contract was concluded in which the powerful Medici Bank took the place of Bartolomeo da Framura.

This agreement of April 1, 1466, modified the earlier contract on several important points. Although it was concluded for nine years, it could be denounced by the Curia upon giving thirty months' notice in advance.[62] The Societas Aluminum undertook not only to mine the alum and to deliver it to the papal warehouses in Civitavecchia but also to organize the sale of it abroad. The Medici Bank, of course, with its network of branches had a sales organization ready made. Moreover, the principal markets were England and Flanders, where the Medici had not only branches but connections with the courts. Instead of paying for the alum delivered by the mines, the pope now received a royalty of two ducats for each cantar taken from the papal warehouses in Civitavecchia.[63] From the point of view of the papacy this arrangement was no doubt more satisfactory than the first: it placed upon the operators of the mines the entire responsibility of adjusting output to demand and relieved the Camera Apostolica from the burden of peddling alum. Its rôle was greatly simplified and reduced to collecting a severance tax of two ducats on each cantar extracted from the mines.

It has been said that the alum works employed 8,000 men, but this figure is probably grossly exaggerated.[64] Perhaps 800 would be closer to the truth.[65] There is a settlement still called Allumiere on the road between Tolfa and Civitavecchia, but it is a hamlet today and there is no evidence that it ever was a town of any size.[66]

From the outset, the papacy strove to establish a monopoly in favor of the papal alum mines. The first step was to get rid of the competition of Turkish alum. To achieve this aim, the Pope did not hesitate to make full use of his spiritual powers. The income which the Camera Apostolica derived from the Tolfa alum mines was set aside and earmarked for the crusade against the Turks and the Hussite heretics of Bohemia, a project dear to Pius II (1458–1464) and his immediate successor, Paul II (1464–1471).[67] The latter appointed a special commission of three cardinals to administer the funds of the crociata (crusade) which, under his pontificate, were undoubtedly used to pay subsidies to princes, such as the King of Hungary, whose dominions were threatened by the Turks.[68] As a logical consequence, to trade in Turkish alum was unquestionably to abet the infidel and to deprive the crusade of financial support. Supplying Saracens with weapons or navy and army stores, such as ships, timber, and horses, had been outlawed for centuries by the canons of the Church.[69] Paul II went further and issued a decree which renewed these prohibitions and specifically forbade the importation of alum from Moslem countries into any part of Christendom. Cargoes of Turkish alum were declared contraband and were seizable by anyone either in port or on the high seas, but the lessees of the Tolfa mines and the papal treasury claimed a share of the prizes.[70]

To get rid of the competition of alum produced in Christian countries was not so easy, since this trade could not be suppressed by the convenient device of using ecclesiastical censures. The most dangerous competition came from the Ischia mines owned by the King of Naples but farmed by a Neapolitan merchant, Angelo Perotto. In order to do away with this rival, the Rome branch of the Medici in 1470 entered into a twenty-five year cartel agreement with the operator of the Ischia mines.[71] The deal was ratified by the King of Naples on June 1, 1470, and by the Pope on June 11 as owners of the Ischia and Tolfa mines, respectively. The purpose of the agreement was avowedly to suppress ruinous competition because an oversupply of alum had caused a decline in prices, and as a consequence, it was claimed, the revenues of the crociata and of the kingdom of Naples had been greatly reduced. This was a laudable aim, but the purpose of the contract was not so innocuous

as it appears on the surface. In reality, the contracting parties intended
to tighten an existing monopoly or quasi monopoly, to restrict output,
to keep up prices, and to regulate the sale of alum according to a quota
system. Because the output of the Ischia mines was of low grade, the
agreement was certainly detrimental to the consumer as an attempt to
foist upon him an inferior product.

The contract stipulated that the exploitation of the mines should
remain in the hands of the two lessees, but it forbade them to sell inde-
pendently without each other's knowledge. The proceeds of all sales
were to be divided equally between the two members of the cartel, unless
one of them was unable to supply his full quota (it was expected that the
operator of the Ischia mines would be unable to do so). In that case,
profits were to be shared proportionately to the quota actually supplied
by each member.

The two contracting parties agreed to sell only at the price fixed by
the cartel. If one of them sold below that price, he had to make good the
loss in revenue suffered by the other party.

The cartel agreement became effective immediately, but certain exceptions were made with respect to the stores of alum which the lessees of
the papal mines had accumulated in Flanders and Venice. The agreement did not apply to these two markets until the existing stocks had
been sold. In the meantime, the Ischia lessees were to receive one sixth
of the profits as compensation.

Any violation of these provisions entailed a penalty of fifty thousand
ducats. The payment of this enormous fine did not relieve the offender
from his obligation to comply with the terms of the contract.

The agreement of 1470 was much more than an attempt to rig the
market. The contracting parties, it is clearly stated, intended to conclude
a permanent alliance and to form one body (*maona*) — these are the
terms used in the text of the compact.[72] Although some economists will
maintain that cartels are a modern phenomenon and do not antedate
the end of the nineteenth century, it is possible to find earlier examples,
and there is little doubt that the purpose of the alum contract was to
maintain prices by limiting output and to eliminate competition by
establishing a quota system.

According to scholastic doctrine, monopoly was regarded as an evil
practice that embraced any conspiracy in restraint of commerce or attempt to manipulate prices.[73] In canon law, monopoly profits were
classified as *turpe lucrum* and, like usury, were subject to restitution.[74]
Gauged by these criteria, the alum cartel was inconsistent with the
teachings of the theologians. The papacy was well aware of the discrepancy between its policy and the Church's doctrine in the matter of

social ethics, but it tried to vindicate its action by invoking the questionable principle that the end justifies the means, because profits were being used for a righteous cause, the struggle against the infidel.

Although the cartel agreement was concluded for twenty-five years, it did not remain in effect very long; it was dissolved in 1471, probably because the Medici discovered that their partner was not as formidable a competitor as they had anticipated and that they had paid too high a price for his cooperation.[75] It is also possible that the poor quality of the Ischia alum caused general dissatisfaction among users. In any case, experience revealed the conclusion of the cartel agreement to have been a wrong move.

An even worse blunder somehow connected with the alum monopoly was the ghastly episode of the sack of Volterra. In 1470 alum was discovered in a cave near this little Tuscan town subject to Florentine rule.[76] A group of Florentine promoters having Medici support managed to obtain a lease in opposition to local interests.[77] The resulting discontent combined with other incidents caused the people of Volterra to revolt against Florentine domination (February, 1472). Florence sent an army under the command of the "virtuous" condottiere, Federigo of Montefeltro, duke of Urbino, to subdue the rebellious town, which surrendered on June 16, 1472, after a siege of twenty-five days. Although respect for life and property had been promised, the victors, once inside the town, sacked it nonetheless (June 18); Montefeltro's lawless soldiery did not stop at looting but committed the usual atrocities (rape, torture, and murder).[78]

In how far Lorenzo the Magnificent was responsible for these cruelties remains a debatable question. He was not present at the siege or the surrender and he did not order the sack, but from the start he had been one of the main advocates of a punitive expedition. To what extent his decisions were influenced by his interests in alum is even more debatable. Certainly possession of the alum mine near Volterra was not the only reason for repressing the revolt. Perhaps Lorenzo feared unduly to lose control of an important source of alum. The tragic part of the story is that both sides had great illusions about the richness of the deposits in the region of Volterra and thought that another Tolfa of inexhaustible wealth had been discovered. This expectation failed to materialize and turned out to be a bitter disappointment. After being worked for a few months, the mine ceased to yield satisfactory returns and production was halted in 1473 because output was so small and quality so poor. Mining was resumed for a while in 1479 after the Pazzi conspiracy, probably because Florence, being at war with the Pope, was cut off from other sources of supply. In any case, the mine was permanently abandoned in 1483 because income failed to cover cost of operation.[79]

The principal markets for alum were in Venice, England, and Flanders.[80] To secure exclusive privileges for the sale of the papal product proved no less difficult than the elimination of rival producers. From the start, the papacy ran into the opposition of organized consumer groups. Moreover, its policy clashed with national interests, so that the local governments were reluctant to lend the Pope a helping hand in bolstering up his monopoly.

The Venetians, who had obtained from the Turks the farm of the old Phocea mines, were certainly not willing to listen to the Pope's entreaties until war broke out with the Sultan in 1463 and they were expelled. As a matter of fact, Bartolomeo Zorzi (or Giorgi), the farmer of the mines, barely escaped with his life.[81] The war lasted until 1479. Taking advantage of this opportunity, the Pope in 1469 concluded an agreement with the firm of Bartolomeo Zorzi and Geronimo Michiel, the former farmers of the Turkish mines, who bound themselves to take yearly 6,000 cantars of papal alum during a period of at least three years.[82] In exchange, they were granted the exclusive right to sell papal alum in Venetian territory, Lombardy, Romagna, Austria, and Germany. On the other hand, they were not permitted to re-export any alum to Flanders or England.[83] By using pressure, the papacy had this agreement confirmed by the Venetian republic.[84] Probably these arrangements did not outlast the restoration of peace with the Turks. By 1481, it seems, Bartolomeo Zorzi and his associates had been reinstated as farmers of the Phocea mines in defiance of the papal decrees.[85]

In 1467 Paul II dispatched Stefano Trenta, bishop of Lucca, to England with instructions to secure from the King a ban against Turkish alum and exclusive privileges for the rival papal product.[86] This mission was a failure, probably because Edward IV (1461–1483), whose throne was by no means secure, could not afford to antagonize the English merchants and clothiers, who were violently opposed to the alum monopoly. Subsequent attempts did not meet with greater success.

In Flanders, the papal nuntius was Luke de Tolentis (1428–1491), archdeacon of Curzola, who was elevated in 1469 to the dignity of bishop of Sebenico in Dalmatia.[87] As long as Philip the Good (1419–1467) was alive, the papal envoy made little headway, but he was more successful after Charles the Bold (1467–1477) had succeeded his father as ruler of the Low Countries and Burgundy. Since Tommaso Portinari, the Bruges manager of the Medici Bank, was a member of the Council, the new Duke was persuaded to conclude the treaty of May 5, 1468, for a duration of twenty-five years: it banned all non-Roman alum from his dominions

and named the Medici Bank or any other papal agents as the sole dis-
tributors of this commodity.[88] In compensation, the Duke was to share
in the profits and to receive six shillings groat, Flemish currency, for
each carica of papal alum imported into the Low Countries.[89] A maximum price of £4 10s. groat, Flemish money, or about eighteen ducats
per carica was stipulated. However, to prevent discrimination against
the Duke's subjects, the treaty provided that this price should never
exceed what alum fetched in neighboring states. Despite the presence of
this clause which protected the consumer somewhat, the treaty raised
such an outcry that its going into effect was postponed twice and delayed
for several months. In the meanwhile, the Pope, losing patience, sent
another envoy, Tommaso di Vincenzio de' Zaccherelli da Fano with
Carlo Martelli, a Medici factor of the Rome branch, to investigate
conditions in Bruges and to demand that Charles the Bold carry out
the treaty.[90] This mission, too, was a dead failure: as opposition did
not abate, the treaty, instead of being observed, was shelved within a
few months. Under pressure of the Estates General, Charles the Bold was
forced to issue the ordinance of June 7, 1473, allowing the importation
of all Christian alum in competition with the papal product.[91] Although
Luke de Tolentis, in the name of the Pope, protested vigorously, he did
not succeed in obtaining the repeal of this ordinance, and the treaty of
1468 was never revived.[92]

From the point of view of the Camera Apostolica, the results were rather
disappointing. It was not the fault of Luke de Tolentis, a diplomat of
rare ability, who claimed in one of his reports that "he had bestirred
himself more to promote the papal alum than he would have done to
save his own life." [93] Probably this is scarcely an overstatement. Despite
all his exertions, he achieved little, because the Roman Curia followed
an unrealistic policy and assumed that it could fleece the consumer without inviting resistance. Moreover, its doctrinal position was weak and its
foes did not hesitate to point out that the alum monopoly was unjusti-
fiable, since accruing income was being diverted "from the defense of
the faith to the pockets of private persons." [94]

There are indications that the papal monopoly was never complete
in the Low Countries and that alum from other sources, even from the
Barbary Coast, continued to be imported without being seized by the
customs officials at the seaports.[95] After 1473, the Ferrandine, or Neapolitan, galleys also brought alum from Ischia to the roads of Zeeland,
whence it was reshipped to Bruges, Antwerp, or Bergen-op-Zoom.[96]

The difficulties encountered by the Medici Bank in its attempts to
dominate the alum market are best illustrated by its business correspondence. The letters reveal that as early as 1463 strenuous efforts were
made to monopolize this trade. From the start, Angelo Tani, the man-

ager of the Bruges branch, and Tommaso Portinari, his assistant manager, called the attention of the Rome branch to the stumbling blocks which stood in the way of such an undertaking, but their advice was not readily accepted. The managers in Rome, Roberto Martelli until his death early in 1464 and then his successor, Giovanni Tornabuoni, never fully realized these difficulties. Tornabuoni, especially, was so bent on making profits that he deluded himself by taking his desires for realities. His attitude became a source of friction between the two branches, because he blamed Bruges whenever things did not work out according to his wishes and expectations.

The wrangle began while Roberto Martelli was still alive. To the great dissatisfaction of the Bruges branch, either he or the Camera Apostolica sent to Bruges a Sienese by the name of Niccolò Spannocchi, a nephew of Ambrogio Spannocchi who acted as depositary general of the papacy during the pontificate of his compatriot, Pius II.[97] Why Niccolò Spannocchi was sent to Bruges is not altogether clear from the records. At any rate, he boasted upon his arrival that the Rome branch intended to put him in charge of the sale of alum. As all the available stocks had been sold, there was nothing for him to do but to make a study of market conditions while waiting for the next shipment. He probably disappeared from the scene shortly after the death of Pius II, which occurred on August 15, 1464. As a result of this event, the Sienese lost most of their power at the Curia.

In the meantime, the Bruges branch complained to headquarters that Spannocchi, whom they regarded as a spy, had little experience and that his interference was annoying. If he had been in charge of the sale of alum, Portinari claimed, prices would have fallen to one third of those actually obtained by the Bruges branch.[98] Portinari further pointed out that the alum business needed to be well managed (à bisogno di buon governo) and that the Apostolic Chamber should let the Medici handle all the sales without competitors interfering, lest there be a sag in prices so drastic that they would never recover. The Pope should not produce more than the market could absorb and should follow the precedent set by the Genoese who, while in control of the mines of Asia Minor, had known how to adjust supply to demand.

In the next letter (March 28, 1464), the Bruges branch reported the safe arrival of two Florentine galleys bringing cargoes of alum, but the third carrying a shipment of about 820 cantars, the smallest of the three lots, had been lost, mouse and man, "God have mercy upon the souls of the mariners!" Tani and Portinari were happy to discover that all the alum was consigned to them and not to Niccolò Spannocchi, as Roberto Martelli had announced shortly before he died.[99] They expected to sell it quickly without reducing the price, provided none came to

Bruges from other sources. Instead of simply selling on commission, the Bruges branch hoped that Cosimo de' Medici would allow it to participate in the profits of the alum business.[100] In another letter, Tommaso Portinari — Angelo Tani was in Florence — again stressed that Rome's dissatisfaction with the Bruges branch was without foundation and rested only on malicious reports written by Spannocchi, whose recall was requested once more "because his presence was a nuisance in more respects than one." [101]

After hearing that the Rome branch had contracted in the spring of 1464 to buy another lot of 20,000 cantars of alum,[102] Portinari penned a report which dwelt extensively upon the pitfalls confronting this business.[103] He warned headquarters that a middle course between two extremes would be the most expedient: on the one hand, it was imperative not to glut the market because once the price was allowed to fall it would never recover; on the other hand, it would be equally unwise to withhold supplies and to drive prices up so high as to lose the customers' good will. The best policy, in Portinari's opinion, was not to arouse any discontent but to keep prices stable at a reasonable level (a un pregio ragionevole). As a Venetian was selling rock alum from Trebizond at £5 groat per carica or less, one could not expect Tolfa alum, which was not as good, to fetch more than £4 groat, Flemish currency. The cost in Civitavecchia being three ducats per cantar, there would still be a handsome profit; furthermore, it would be inadvisable "to pull on the rope until it breaks." [104]

Today, monopolists or oligopolists who feel insecure in their position often adopt a policy of "administered" prices which are below monopoly level but are kept stable over long periods of time because this is the line of least resistance. Such a policy is usually associated with modern business practices; it is, therefore, rather interesting to find it clearly formulated five hundred years ago.

Apparently the buyers of alum were an organized group of wholesalers who, according to Portinari, were substantial men and knew their business. There was no danger in granting them credit, but it was better to make deliveries according to their needs than to force them to lay up stocks. Moreover, these buyers were also in some sort of cartel agreement and did not undercut each other. It was, therefore, necessary to watch and not to overstock the market, because the buyers would take advantage of the situation to press prices down and it would be extremely difficult to raise them again without great murmurs and protests. Fortunately, no alum was coming from the Levant because of the war between Venice and the Sultan. Portinari expected this state of affairs to continue for some time. Therefore, he had persuaded the Flemish wholesalers that they could safely sign a contract with the Medici Bank and that they need not fear a fall in price within the near future.[105]

On November 3, 1464, Portinari received word that the vessel bringing alum from Civitavecchia had been wrecked near Boulogne on the eve of All Saints. Some of the crew escaped with their lives, including the skipper, but all the cargo was lost because it was stowed in bulk instead of being packed in barrels. However, the loss was covered by insurance, and the market was still well supplied because the Genoese were also bringing alum to Bruges, so that the Medici were no longer in control. As a matter of fact, the price might have dropped if it had not been for the shipwreck.[106] Writing from Bergen-op-Zoom where he had gone to attend the fairs, Portinari reported on November 27 that the Flemish alum dealers were willing to take all that the Florentine galleys would bring. So he asked headquarters to send as much as possible with the ships that were about to leave Pisa.[107] After much bargaining, the alum dealers finally agreed to take 3,000 or 4,000 cariche (from 540 to 720 metric tons), presumably at the price of £4 groat per carica, but only upon condition that they could pay their debt in several installments extending over a period of three years. Portinari also had to promise that no more alum would be sent by the Medici to Flanders or England for a full year.[108]

In accordance with Portinari's request, the Florentine galleys took on a cargo of alum, but Giovanni Tornabuoni, the manager of the Rome branch, complained that he experienced difficulties in collecting enough barrels.[109] In the next letter of February 16, 1465, he expressed his satisfaction over the deal successfully concluded by Portinari, while insisting that the slowness of the Bruges branch in making remittances caused great inconvenience because the Apostolic Chamber required prompt payment from the Rome branch.[110] Perhaps he did not understand that, the balance of trade being unfavorable to Flanders, the Bruges branch was constantly struggling with transfer difficulties and even sought to pay with English wool. In April 1465, there were still 5,200 cantars unsold of the 20,000 cantars purchased the previous year, so that Tornabuoni was glad to get rid of this remaining stock by selling it to the Lucchese merchant Giovanni Guidiccioni, especially as no alum could be sent to either Flanders or England.[111]

Shortly thereafter, on May 3, 1465, Portinari wrote sadly that the market for alum was upset and that the price was dropping because of the news that a Genoese ship, as well as the Florentine galleys, was bringing alum.[112] As a result, he reported, the group of Flemish wholesalers would like to get out of their agreement, because they might be able to buy at £3 groat, Flemish currency, per carica, whereas they were bound to pay £4 by the terms of the contract.

The Florentine galleys expected in the spring did not reach Sluys until October, 1465. As stocks were depleted, the Flemish wholesalers were glad to take the entire shipment of alum and pay the price agreed upon several months before. Portinari was puzzled by the disconcerting news that the Venetian galleys had passed at La Coruña a Venetian sailing vessel loaded with alum and apparently chartered by the Rome branch of the Medici Bank. He asked himself how he would be able to dispose of this alum, too.[113] However, the Venetian ship went to London instead of Sluys, but the alum had a poor market there. To make matters worse, several ships, both Genoese and Venetian, had arrived in Flanders and England with cargoes of alum, so that there was enough to last three years and prices were sure to drop steeply.[114] To halt somewhat the decline, Portinari counted on the Flemish wholesalers. He had offered them some of the alum sent to London, but to no avail.[115]

On April 2, 1466, Giovanni Tornabuoni gleefully reported to Piero de' Medici the conclusion, on the preceding day, of the agreement by which the Medici Bank became the exclusive seller of papal alum. Since, henceforth, all sales would pass through the hands of the Medici agents in Bruges and London, Tornabuoni expected confidently that he would be able to raise the price of alum in Bruges to £6 groat per carica of 400 pounds and in London to £1 15s. sterling per cantar.[116] This was being overly optimistic, since such high prices would encourage the importation of Turkish alum and cause a concert of protests to which the rulers of England and the Low Countries could not remain indifferent. As we know, papal embassies sent to England achieved nothing. In Bruges, Portinari got together with Messer Luke de Tolentis, the papal envoy, and initiated negotiations which, after great difficulties, led to the conclusion of the ill-fated treaty of May 5, 1468.

On November 28, 1469, the Bruges and the Rome branches concluded an agreement for the purpose of regulating the sale of alum in the Low Countries and of eliminating further sources of friction.[117] First of all, the Rome branch promised to procure another papal bull demanding that the Duke of Burgundy ban all Turkish alum from his dominions and threatening interlopers with excommunication and seizure of any contraband. Although the contract does not say so, Tommaso Portinari was apparently expected to use this document for the purpose of putting pressure on the Duke, so that he would promulgate the treaty of 1468. As a reward, the Bruges branch was to get the exclusive selling agency of all papal alum imported into Flanders with the understanding, however, that the price would not be below £3 2s. groat, Flemish currency, per carica of 400 pounds, Flemish weight. Profits were to be shared equally by the two Medici branches.

The duration of the contract was three years beginning March 1, 1470.

It was further provided that, from November 1, 1470 onward, the Bruges branch would remit each month 1,250 ducats either to Rome or to Florence and continue these payments for three years.[118] If sales were higher or lower than this amount, adjustments were to be made later. The purpose of this provision was undoubtedly to prevent the Bruges branch from retaining the proceeds of the alum sales. As pointed out, it was a standing complaint of Giovanni Tornabuoni that the Bruges branch was depleting his resources by its tardiness in making remittances. While this complaint was undoubtedly justified, he overlooked the fact that the Bruges branch was probably experiencing difficulties in purchasing bills and was reluctant to ship specie.

Contrary to expectations, the contract of 1469 failed to settle the conflict between the two branches of the Medici Bank. Irked by the Duke of Burgundy's failure to execute the treaty of 1468, Pope Paul II and Giovanni Tornabuoni blamed Tommaso Portinari for this setback and accused him of mismanaging the alum business. To straighten out the difficulties, it was decided to send to Flanders Messer Tommaso de' Zaccherelli da Fano, as the Pope's special envoy, flanked by Carlo Martelli, Tornabuoni's representative.[119] As mentioned before, it is doubtful whether these emissaries accomplished much, if anything. They certainly did not succeed in overcoming local opposition to the alum monopoly. Perhaps Zaccherelli induced the Roman Curia to moderate its demands. As for Tornabuoni, the Medici correspondence shows that he continued to indulge in wishful thinking, saw only his own interests, and continued to ignore all other aspects of the problem.

The news that Charles the Bold had repudiated the treaty of 1468 and restored freedom of trade for all alum from Christian sources reached Rome by the end of June 1473 and came to Giovanni Tornabuoni as a shattering blow. Dispiritedly he wrote his nephew, Lorenzo the Magnificent, that he expected prices to collapse and to drop in Bruges below £3 groat per carica.[120] As a matter of fact, the year 1474 witnessed a glut of the alum market, and the drop in prices was so sharp that the Medici persuaded Sixtus IV (reigned 1471–1484) to reduce his royalty from two ducats to one.[121] In a letter of March 18, 1475, Tornabuoni wrote Lorenzo that the alum business showed a loss and went on to complain, whether rightly or wrongly, that Tommaso Portinari and Carlo Martelli, his own man, were cheating the Rome branch.[122] Such complaints were nothing new and, already in 1473, had caused Lorenzo to interfere in order to appease the quarrels between the two branches. Apparently, Carlo Martelli, after reaching Bruges, had been won over by Portinari's persuasive charms and had ceased long since to promote Tornabuoni's policy.[123]

The following July, Tornabuoni reluctantly agreed to a decision taken by Lorenzo the Magnificent with reference to Portinari's and Martelli's conduct of the alum affairs. However, he continued to complain, probably with reason, that the delays of Bruges in settling accounts were depriving him of liquid funds and forcing him to borrow heavily at interest.[124] Disagreement between the two branches did not disappear and Tornabuoni was glad to hear in October 1477 that Carlo Martelli was coming to Rome to adjust differences connected with the alum business.[125]

After 1470, there are unfortunately great gaps in the surviving correspondence, with the consequence that it is impossible from then on to give a detailed account of the policy followed by the Medici Bank with respect to the alum monopoly. As relations between Sixtus IV and Lorenzo the Magnificent became more and more strained, the Apostolic Chamber gradually withdrew its account from the Medici Bank. By July, 1474, the latter had ceased to function as Depositary General of the Holy See and was replaced by a Genoese merchant, Meliaduce Cigala.[126] In June, 1476, the alum contract was given to the Pazzi, whom Sixtus IV showered with favors.[127] Consequently, alum shipments sent to Bruges were no longer consigned to the Medici but to Guglielmo and Giovanni de' Pazzi.[128] After the Pazzi conspiracy (1478) had brought about a war between the Pope and the Florentine republic, the alum stocks still in possession of the Medici were seized.[129] Even after the war was over, the Medici did not regain control of the alum trade, although some of their claims on the Camera Apostolica were later paid by assignment on the output of the Tolfa mines.[130]

The story illustrates that even a monopolist cannot always do what he wants. It is true that the Medici enjoyed no absolute control over the alum trade, but monopolies, in practice, are rarely so complete that the interests of the consumers can be entirely overlooked, not to mention those of other groups, such as producers who would be unemployed if output were curtailed. Under those circumstances, the monopolist will not try to maximize profits, but may set his price at a level which will not cause widespread discontent with his policies. The case of the Medici shows the difficulties involved in achieving such an aim and the tensions created by the existence of conflicting interests within the firm and without.

3. THE IRON ORE OF ELBA

The Medici were interested also in another monopoly, that of iron ore. In Italy the only iron ore deposits were, and still are, located on the island of Elba, off the coast of Tuscany. This concentration was conducive to monopolistic exploitation, since Elba iron had no competition as long as its price remained below that of imported Spanish iron, the only alternative source of supply. In the fifteenth century, the island of Elba belonged to the princes or lords of Piombino, for whom the iron mines were the main source of income. These rulers knew how to take advantage of their monopoly and, in order to facilitate the collection of their royalties, they sold the entire output of their mines to a group of merchants organized in what may be described as a territorial cartel. Each member of the group was granted exclusive rights in a certain territory where he resold the ore to local ironmasters, who operated furnaces in wooded areas of the Apennines since there was no fuel to smelt iron ore on the island of Elba itself.

From 1455 to 1477, the *Magona del Ferro* (the Iron Ore Cartel) was in the hands of a group of Genoese merchants.[131] It was not until 1477 or 1478 that Lorenzo the Magnificent, in search of new sources of profit, cast longing eyes upon the lucrative deals in iron ore and secured a contract from the lord of Piombino, who was in no position to thwart the designs of his more powerful neighbor. The agreement, concluded by Piero Filippo Pandolfini, was to last five years during which Lorenzo secured control of the entire output of Elba for a lump sum of 15,000 ducats.[132] This contract apparently never went into effect or was not renewed because, in 1489, Lorenzo the Magnificent made another out-and-out effort to gain control of the Elba iron ore. This time negotiations were conducted in his name by Giovanni di Bernardo Cambi and brought to a successful conclusion, with the result that the Pisa branch of the Medici Bank acquired a controlling interest in the *magone* of Pisa and Pietrasanta.[133]

Such a magona was a contract by which a grantee promised to pay royalties in exchange for monopoly privileges. The magona of Pietrasanta, near Carrara where the famous marble quarries are located, covered a mountainous area close to the sea and abounding in timber. The ironmasters bought the ore from the magona and paid for it, not in cash, but in cast iron or in such manufactured products as horseshoes and nails. The customers of the magona of Pisa were ironmasters from the neighborhood of Pistoia or even from the faraway Casentino, a wooded and hilly region near Arezzo. They paid either in cash or in iron staves, more rarely in manufactured products. According to an extant account book, the iron which the Medici thus acquired was either sold locally to other business firms or sent to agents in Rome, Naples, or Palermo. Such consignments involved many risks and did not always fetch the expected price. Despite occasional disappointments, this iron venture, the records show, proved to be successful and yielded handsome profits which the Medici sorely needed to recoup their losses elsewhere. Unfortunately the surviving records do not extend beyond March 24, 1492, two years before the final crash which engulfed the Medici Bank.

In all probability, the contract concerning the magone of Pisa and Pietrasanta was then cancelled and went to the Lucchese firm of the Buonvisi, who took over all receivables and the iron ore stocked in warehouses.[134]

Cartel agreements are usually regarded as modern phenomena, but the study of economic history reveals that they have roots deep in the past. It is true that permanent monopolies, such as the alum cartel, were still exceptional in the fifteenth century. This trend, however, gained momentum during the next century with the mining cartels sponsored by the Fuggers and reached a climax in the seventeenth century with the development of the first joint-stock companies and the monopolistic organization of colonial trade.[135] Adam Smith was not entirely wrong: the age of mercantilism was also the age of monopolies.

VIII

THE MEDICI AS INDUSTRIAL ENTREPRENEURS

For many years, the Medici controlled three industrial establishments: two woolshops (*botteghe di lana*) and one silkshop (*bottega di seta*). In the fifteenth century, the making of woolen cloth and the production of silk fabrics, including taffeta, velvets, and brocades, were the two major industries of Florence. It was an old tradition among Florentine families, even when they owned extensive landed estates, either to control or to manage a wool or silkshop in order to provide work for the "poor." True to this tradition, Giovanni di Bicci, as early as 1402, invested some of his accumulated earnings in the woolen industry and went into partnership with Michele di Baldo di ser Michele who, because of his experience, was entrusted with the management of the new establishment.[1] As has been already mentioned in Chapter Three, a second woolshop was started in 1408 with Taddeo di Filippo as managing partner.[2] As it turned out, this second shop was more profitable than the first, which was apparently poorly managed. Since it was losing money, it was discontinued in 1420.

For a few years, the Medici had only one woolshop, the one managed by Taddeo di Filippo. He died in 1429, but work in the shop was resumed after a few months' interval with Giuntino di Guido di Giuntino as managing partner. After his premature death, probably in 1433, he was replaced by his brother Andrea.[3] A second shop was opened in 1439; as manager, the Medici selected Antonio Taddei (b. 1417), the son of Taddeo di Filippo, although he was only twenty-two years of age.[4] This proved to be an excellent choice. The two woolshops continued to operate side by side for several years. The one headed by Andrea Giuntini went out of existence sometime between 1458 and 1469, probably because of the manager's death.[5] The other was still in existence in 1480 according to Antonio Taddei's catasto report, but it was doing badly and being liquidated.[6] At that time, the Florentine woolen industry was in decline; however, some firms were still making profits, for example, the shop owned by Giuliano di Giovenco de' Medici, who belonged to an elder branch of the family. Perhaps ill-health and failing energy explain why Antonio Taddei ceased to be successful. If so, there remains the question of why the Medici did not persuade him to retire and replace him by a younger and more efficient manager.

In 1491 Lorenzo the Magnificent was apparently still optimistic about the prospects of the Florentine woolen industry, since he was induced to invest f.2216 13s. 4d. in a company managed by Paolo Benci.[7] The other investing partners were Filippo da Gagliano and Lanfredino Lanfredini. Aggregate capital amounted to 5,000 florins. This venture was profitable, because the Medici share in the capital and accrued earnings was seized in 1495 by the syndics who administered the property of the exiled Medici.

We do not know the exact date when the Medici became interested in the silk industry. Their catasto report of 1433 mentions the woolshop with Giuntino di Guido but contains no reference to another industrial establishment. The libro segreto, however, reveals that within the next few months the Medici joined a partnership existing between two silk manufacturers, Piero di Domenico Corsi and Francesco di Francesco Berlinghieri. The terms of this agreement are unknown, but the partnership was of short duration.[8] In 1438 Piero Corsi dropped out, and the Medici made a new contract with Francesco Berlinghieri as manager and Jacopo di Biagio Tanaglia as assistant manager of the silkshop. As mentioned in Chapter Four, the capital was set at 5,000 florins, of which the Medici supplied 4,200 florins and Francesco Berlinghieri the rest. Tanaglia invested nothing; nevertheless, he was awarded a share in the profits to remunerate him for his services.[9] This partnership was periodically renewed until Francesco's death in 1446 or 1447. The terms, however, were somewhat changed in 1444 when the capital was raised to 7,200 florins: 4,800 florins were furnished by the Medici Bank, 1,900 by Francesco Berlinghieri, and 500 by Jacopo Tanaglia (Table 15). Profits were divided in the following proportions: one half to the Medici Bank (Cosimo and Giovanni Benci), one third to Francesco Berlinghieri, and one sixth to Jacopo Tanaglia.[10]

Francesco Berlinghieri was succeeded by his son, Berlinghieri di Francesco Berlinghieri (1426–1480). A new partnership agreement was drawn up on March 25, 1447, on terms slightly modified in favor of Jacopo Tanaglia, whose share in the capital was raised to 600 florins and in the profits to one fourth, at the expense of the new partner, probably because of the latter's youth and inexperience.[11] It seems logical to assume that Tanaglia was promoted to manager and given the task of initiating the young Berlinghieri. This partnership was still existing in 1469, according to the catasto report filed by Piero di Cosimo de' Medici shortly before his death.[12] Apparently it continued after 1469 and was repeatedly extended, without drafting new articles and without changing the distribution of the profits, until Berlinghieri's death in 1480. During all these years, Jacopo Tanaglia continued to play an active part in the management, since he still styled himself in 1477 *socius* (partner) in the company of Lorenzo and Giuliano de' Medici, *setaiuoli* (silk manu-

facturers).[13] In the beginning of the next year, Berlinghieri served as
gonfaloniere di giustizia (titular head of the Florentine state).[14] He was
still alive on January 11, 1480, when he addressed a letter to Lorenzo the
Magnificent, who had gone to Naples to wean Ferdinand of Aragon away
from the Pope.[15]

Berlinghieri must have died rather unexpectedly within the next few
months. The liquidation of the partnership gave rise to difficulties, because Lorenzo the Magnificent, in 1486, sued Berlinghieri's sons for the
amount of 769 fiorini larghi which allegedly were owed by their father,
presumably because his share in accumulated losses exceeded his equity.[16]
Lorenzo obtained a judgment assigning to him several pieces of property
despite the protestations of Berlinghieri's heirs, who disclaimed any liability and complained of being illegally and arbitrarily dispossessed.

When the Medici were expelled from Florence in 1494 they still had a
capital of 7,500 florins invested in a silkshop which was sequestered by
the new government and taken over by Lorenzo di Giovanni Tornabuoni
(1466–1497).[17] They also owned a share in a partnership of goldbeaters,
a trade subject to the jurisdiction of the Arte di Por Santa Maria.[18]

Several partnership agreements relating to the wool and silkshops controlled by the Medici Bank are still extant. They follow the usual pattern
described in connection with other subsidiaries. Ultimate control was
vested with the maggiori who usually provided half or more of the capital
and reserved for themselves the right to terminate the partnership at
any time should they become dissatisfied with the performance of the
junior partners. As a rule, the latter were chosen among specialists or
experts well acquainted with the problems, technical and managerial, of
the silk or woolen industry. The junior partners assumed the entire
burden of management and were expected to give unstintedly their
time and their services. As a reward, they received no salary but were
granted a larger share of the profits than was warranted by their participation in the capital. On the other hand, losses were shared in the same
proportion as profits, so that inefficient managers were penalized and
ran the risk of losing whatever property they had, if losses should exceed
the small amount invested as capital.

Junior partners usually continued to hold their posts as long as they
retained the confidence of the maggiori. I know of no instance in which
the Medici ever refused to renew the contract with a manager who had
given them satisfactory service.

There is one major difference between the partnership agreements relating to the textile industry and those relating to foreign trade and
banking. In the latter field, as we have seen, the Medici followed a steadfast policy of doing all the hiring themselves and of not permitting their
branch managers to take any initiative in this matter. Such a rule would

have seriously interfered with the efficient operation of the industrial establishments. The articles of association, therefore, either implicitly or explicitly left the manager of each shop entirely free to do all the hiring and firing and to engage the services of industrial factors or subcontractors, dyers, weavers, and other artificers, whether pieceworkers or journeymen. For one thing, there was such a rapid turnover among the textile workers that it would have been impractical to refer each decision to the central office: the maggiori would have had no time left for more important matters. In the second place, the manager of a bottega, having the requisite technical knowledge, was best able to judge who qualified for a certain job and should be given materials on which to work. As a matter of fact, it was one of the manager's main functions to organize production and to see to it that there were no hitches while the material went through the successive stages of the manufacturing process.

In banking, of course, recruiting the clerical staff raised entirely different problems. To let branch managers select their own staffs would have opened the door to fraud and collusion. What the central administration sought to avoid was to have employees loyal to the local manager rather than to the company or the maggiori.

In industry as well as in banking, the managing partner occupied a key position, and success or failure depended to a large extent upon his integrity and efficiency. Sometimes, the Medici picked the wrong man as, for example, in the case of Michele di Baldo. For a number of years he was successful as a manager and his shop was a profitable undertaking. Then he must have made a mistake which made a dent in his working capital. To cover up the loss, he borrowed money a discrezione from outsiders, presumably without the maggiori's knowledge. According to the ledger of Lazzaro di Giovanni Bracci, Michele di Baldo borrowed from him 300 florins at 8 percent a year.[19] This loan, first made in 1415, was still outstanding in 1420.[20] As these funds did not suffice, Michele di Baldo began in May, 1417 to borrow from the same source by taking up money on exchange with Venice, a much more expensive form of short-term borrowing. This loan also was renewed several times.

It is likely that the maggiori, when they discovered these dealings, lost confidence in Michele and either refused to renew the partnership agreement or denounced it prematurely. In any case it was dissolved in 1420. The books, when closed, revealed a loss of 1,736 florins 15s. 5d. affiorino during the last months of operation.[21] Profits and losses being divided equally, the share of each partner was 868 florins 7s. 9d. aff. Since the Medici had an investment of 3,000 florins, this figure represented a loss of nearly 30 percent. For Michele however, whose equity probably did not exceed 1,000 florins, this loss was much more serious and corresponded to 87 percent of his share in the capital. Thus he suffered the brunt of his own blunders. As it turned out after the liquidation got under way, losses were much larger than expected and an additional amount of 1,887 florins 28s. 5d. aff. was charged to the Medici Bank, presumably because many claims considered as good proved to be uncollectible.[22]

The disastrous liquidation of the woolshop managed by Michele di Baldo must have been due to poor management, because the second shop, managed by Taddeo di Filippo, was prospering and yielding satisfactory profits throughout the period from 1408 to 1420.

A common provision in the partnership agreements relating to the textile industry required the manager, if the contract was not renewed, to stay on for six months in order to wind up the business and to have all the goods still in process made into finished products. After paying off the creditors, the assets were then to be divided among the partners, each taking his share, first in liquid funds and afterwards in outstanding claims and inventories.[23] Differences arising from this allotment were to be settled by arbitrators. The contracts of the silkshop contain a curious provision: if the plague visited the city, the managing partners, after settling all matters in abeyance, were allowed to flee and to take refuge in the country until the danger had subsided.[24]

The Medici wool and silkshops were not, of course, factories in the modern sense of the word. Both the Florentine wool and silk industries were organized on the basis of the domestic, or putting-out, system (Fr. *manufacture à domicile,* Ger. *Verlagssystem*). Most of the materials to be processed were given out and the work to a large extent was done in the homes of the artisans. In the woolen industry, only beating the wool, carding, and combing were probably done on the premises of the *lanaiuolo* (clothier).[25] All the other work, including wool washing, spinning, warping, weaving, fulling, finishing, and dyeing, were done outside. In the silk industry, none of the work was done in the shop of the *setaiuolo* (silk manufacturer). This shop was not a large establishment but consisted ordinarily of one or two rooms used to keep the raw silk until it was issued to reelers, to shelve the unfinished materials between two successive steps of the manufacturing process, and to store the finished fabrics awaiting sale or shipment. One of the main tasks of the lanaiuolo or setaiuolo was to keep track of the materials given out to home workers or artisans and returned by them after completion of the assigned job.

The organization of the Florentine woolen industry has been studied by the German historian, Alfred Doren (1869–1934), whose book on the subject is a pioneering work, admirable in many respects and unsurpassed up to the present day.[26] Nevertheless, it has two major shortcomings which distort the picture: first, Doren used mainly the gild statutes to the neglect of other sources, such as business records and account books, and second, under the influence of Marxian ideology, he greatly exaggerated the size of the typical industrial establishment, and the extent to which the textile workers were the victims of exploitation and oppression.[27] On the other hand, because of his concern with class antagonism, he did not always give due emphasis to managerial problems and was inclined to attribute to the grasping covetousness of the master measures which were simply designed to maintain high standards of workmanship or to prevent "cabbaging," that is, the pilfering by workers of materials entrusted to their care.[28] This is, of course, a perennial problem in any industry where the work is largely done at home and not in a central workshop under the direct supervision of the employer or his overseers.

According to Alfred Doren, the Florentine woolshops were "gigantic plants" (Riesenateliers), "establishments similar to modern factories," or "large-scale enterprises" (Grossunternehmungen). The lanaiuoli are described as "industrial magnates" or "supercapitalists" who had achieved "a tremendous accumulation of capital in the hands of a few." [29] These epithets would apply to Andrew Carnegie or Henry Ford, but it is permissible to be a bit sceptical about the existence of such industrial tycoons in the Middle Ages or the Renaissance. While the organization of the Florentine textile industry was capitalistic in many respects, one should not exaggerate and lose one's sense of proportion.[30] The great Florentine fortunes were made in banking and foreign trade, not in manufacturing. The Medici were no exception to this rule, and their industrial investments were far from equaling those in banking or from being a major source of profits.[31] The statistical evidence presented in Tables 8, 11, 15, and 17 is conclusive in this respect. It is also significant that the Medici for a long time financed two woolshops rather than one larger unit. It would be hard to explain such a policy if there had been economies of large-scale production.

According to Doren's own data, the average output of a Florentine woolshop in the year 1381–1382 was seventy bolts of cloth per annum and the maximum attained by any producer did not exceed 220 pieces.[32] These are the figures for all four districts (conventi). The average of the convento di San Martino alone, where the most important shops were located, is somewhat higher than the general average and amounts to 91 bolts of cloth. How these figures are reconcilable with Doren's view that the woolshops were "large" establishments is not clarified.

Although the Medici records do not always give the desired information — medieval bookkeepers did not think of satisfying the curiosity of modern historians or statisticians — data on output can be gathered from entries in the Libri segreti, Nos. 1 and 2. In a period of thirty-two months, from January 1, 1405, to September 6, 1407, the shop managed by Michele di Baldo produced 242 pieces or bolts of cloth, which corresponds

TABLE 29. DATA ON OUTPUT AND PROFITS AND LOSSES OF THE WOOLSHOP STYLED "COSIMO DE' MEDICI E MICHELE DI BALDO & CO." 1402–1420

Ragione or Period	Beginning	Ending	Duration Months	Output Bolts of Cloth	Profits or Losses f.	s.	d.
A	April 1, 1402	December 31, 1404	33	No record	1,150	11	0
B	January 1, 1405	September 6, 1407	32	242	1,854	6	0
C	September 6, 1407	May, 1408 (?)	9 (?)	162	1,11?	9	6
D	May, 1408 (?)	No record	No record	No record	864	0	8
E	No record	March 25, 1415	No record	No record	1,933	26	8
F	March 25, 1415	No record	No record	No record	1,862	2	0
			Total profits.........		8,784	26	10
			Adjustment (losses)......		−1,735	15	6
			Net profits of period.......		7,045	11	4*

* The share of the Medici Bank was half, or 3,522 florins and 20s. 2d. aff. which, after deducting the additional loss of 1,887 florins 28s. 5d. aff., gives 1,634 florins and 20s. 9d. aff., the total given in Table 8.
Source: ASF, MAP, filza 153, no. 1.

to an output of 91 pieces per annum (Table 29). The second shop managed by Taddeo di Filippo turned out 554 bolts of cloth in a period of exactly six years, from 1408 to 1414 (Table 30). This figure gives a yearly average of 92 bolts. In the next seventeen months, this rate of output was maintained, but it fell to seventy bolts of cloth during the period from September 1, 1415, to May 29, 1420. Presumably these were lean years, since profits, too, sank from around 900 florins to about 550 florins a year. In the next few months, business apparently recovered. Output climbed again to its former level and reached an average of 90 pieces per year during the sixty-six months extending from March 9, 1424 to September 15, 1429. At the same time profits recuperated and went up to 1,160 florins per annum. One may conclude from these figures that in good times the yearly output of the woolshop was in the neighborhood of 90 bolts of cloth. This corresponds exactly to the average given by Doren for the convento di San Martino, where the Medici shops were located. It is therefore safe to conclude that these shops were of average size, but their relatively small output does not support the thesis that the Florentine woolen industry was an early example of large-scale production.

In 1420 the woolshop of the Medici with Taddeo di Filippo as partner had a capital of 4,000 florins, which was increased to 4,500 florins in the next few years.[33] The woolshop with Michele di Baldo as manager probably had an initial capital of 4,000 florins in 1402. This amount was presumably average for the convento di San Martino, where only fine English wool of superior quality was used, since the same figure recurs with reference to a woolshop established in 1434 by Bernardo and Giovenco d'Antonio de' Medici.[34] (These two men belong to the elder branch whose records are now at Harvard University.) This partnership was renewed several times without changing the total amount of capital. In 1441 Bernardo d'Antonio established a subsidiary to make cloth in Oltrarno, but with a total capital of only 1,550 florins.[35] The shops in this district used only cheaper and coarser Spanish or native wool. In 1451 the Medici Bank controlled two woolshops, both in San Martino: one had a capital of 4,000 florins and the other of 6,000 florins (Table 15). Probably the latter was above average size, but data on output are unfortunately not available. In any case, 6,000 florins corresponds to less than $24,000. Even if one takes into consideration that the purchasing power of money was much greater than it is today, such an amount did not suffice to finance a sizable industrial plant or establishment.

Besides the modest proportions of output and invested capital, the smallness of the managerial staff is another indication that the typical Florentine shop was not a large business unit. According to the Medici records at Harvard, the staff of a typical woolshop reduced itself to a

TABLE 30. DATA ON OUTPUT AND PROFITS OF THE WOOLSHOP STYLED
"LORENZO DE' MEDICI E TADDEO DI FILIPPO & CO."
1408–1429

Ragione or Period	Beginning	Ending	Duration Months	Production Bolts of Cloth	Total Profits f. s. d.			Medici Share of Profits £ s. d. aff.			
A and B	March 25, 1408	No record	} 72	{ 432	4,100	0	0	2,581	14	0	
C	No record	March 24, 1414		122	1,500	0	0	1,000	0	0	
D	March 25, 1414	August 31, 1415	17	130	1,354	0	0	903	3	2	
E	September 1, 1415	No record	} 57	{ 212	1,740	18	4	967	0	9	
F	No record	May 29, 1420		129	1,350	0	0	750	8	3	
					10,044	18	4	6,201	26	2	
								635	12	1[a]	
								6,837	9	3[b]	
G	May 30, 1420	March 9, 1424	45	No record	4,000	0	0	2,522	6	5	
H and I	March 10, 1424	September 15, 1429	66	494	6,400	0	0	3,555	16	1	
					20,444	18	4	12,615	2	9[c]	

[a] This item represents later adjustments.
[b] This figure agrees with the total given in Table 8.
[c] Profits were divided as follows: Ragioni A and B, seven twenty-fourths to Taddeo and of the remainder, one ninth to Piero di Michele di Baldo and eight ninths to the Medici Bank. C and D, one third to Taddeo di Filippo and two thirds to the Medici Bank. E and F, one sixth to Lionardo d'Agnolo de' Baglioni and of the remainder, one third to Taddeo and two thirds to the Medici Bank.
Source: ASF, MAP, filza 153, nos. 1 and 2.

manager, an assistant manager, sometimes a bookkeeper and one or two apprentices who ran errands and did routine office work. Since the manufacturing process in the woolen industry involved a great many steps, it required much planning and supervision with the result that there was a definite limit to the volume of business that this small staff could handle efficiently. The duties which burdened the management were manifold and included purchasing and selling, pricing, hiring and firing, bookkeeping and control, maintenance of quality, and checking the materials that were steadily going out to home workers and being returned after a while. This was enough to keep the manager and his helpers fully occupied, even though the scale of operations was small if gauged by modern standards.

Of course, Alfred Doren is quite right when he insists on the capitalistic character of the Florentine woolen industry. It had an elaborate organization and depended to a large extent on a steady stream of capital. It was circulating capital, however, and not fixed capital. The amount invested in equipment or in means of production, to use Marxian terminology, was negligible and depreciation did not even enter into consideration as an element of cost. In accordance with the description still found in Adam Smith's *Wealth of Nations,* the stock or capital of a woolshop was a revolving fund which was employed "in setting to work industrious people" and in supplying them with materials which, when finished, were sold to replenish the fund.[36] Only simple tools were used and, as a rule, belonged to the workers. Although they thus owned the "means of production," they nevertheless depended upon wages which were advanced by the employer who furnished the materials and assumed the risk of finding a market for the finished product. As the division of labor was far reaching, production needed to be organized. This function was assumed by the manager who, as the Medici records show, was not necessarily the owner or part owner of the shop: he might not have any capital invested in it at all. Thus management was already a special function, sometimes entirely divorced from ownership.

In Florence, clothmaking involved at least twenty-six different steps; hence, it was a complicated process which raised many technical and managerial problems.[37] These steps can be grouped together conveniently in five major processes: preparing the wool, spinning, warping and weaving, dyeing, and finishing.

The preparatory process itself can be subdivided into several subsidiary steps: willeying or beating of the fleeces, sorting, washing, cleansing, beating, and combing or carding, depending on the kind of wool. With the exception of washing, these were the only operations performed in the shop of the industrial entrepreneur.[38] Woolsorters, being expert wool graders, often acted as brokers and advised the *lanaiuoli* in purchasing.[39] Because of their technical skill, they were rather highly regarded and relatively well paid. Moreover, since their services were not needed all year around, they did not depend upon a single employer; usually they had a clientele of several clothiers and went from one to the other.

After being willeyed and sorted, the wool was sent to be washed. This was done outside the shop by woolwashers who, in Florence, were small masters established along the Gora Canal, since they used great quantities of water. According to the Medici records in the Selfridge Collection at Harvard University, the woolwashers were paid a flat rate per 100 pounds of washed wool returned to the lanaiuolo, plus something per pound of alum which was used to remove the grease.[40] In the course of the washing, there was a considerable loss in weight, which amounted to 20 percent or more and varied considerably from one lot to another depending upon the quality, origin, and condition of the raw wool. Of course, the clothier knew by experience the amount of impurity. Nevertheless, here appears one of the chief weaknesses of the putting-out system: since most of the work was done outside shop, the lanaiuolo had no effective means of controlling spoilage and waste, a situation leading to filching and carelessness.[41]

The wool, after being washed, was returned to the shop to be cleansed with the use of scissors, beaten, and then carded if short staple or combed if long staple. In Florence these were some of the few operations performed in the shop itself under the watchful eye of a foreman called *capodieci*.[42] The beating, combing, and carding were menial and monotonous jobs which required more muscular effort than real skill. Among the workers in the woolen industry, the beaters, carders, and combers were the roughest, the most irresponsible, the most despised, and the most poorly paid.[43] Even San Antonino, archbishop of Florence, describes them as a rowdy lot, vile in language and loose in morals, if not addicted to filthy vices.[44] Part of the blame is squarely placed by him upon the masters who do not restrain their workers and who acknowledge no responsibility beyond paying the wages agreed upon, and some of whom even cheat by paying in truck or in clipped coin. As a matter of fact, the lanaiuolo dealt only with the capodieci, or foreman, and let him hire his helpers.[45] In view of these social conditions, it is not astonishing that the woolbeaters and carders took the lead in the Ciompi revolt of 1378 and in all the riots which broke out in Florence when the masses were driven to despair by famine or widespread and prolonged unemployment.[46]

The capodieci is the first of a series of industrial factors or subcontractors who were called *fattori sopra i lavoranti* and whose importance has not been fully recognized by students of the Florentine woolen industry.[47] These factors stood between the cloth manufacturer and the workmen. Factors were responsible to the employer for the completion of the work which they undertook to perform. They were paid according to output on a piece-rate basis. It was up to the factor to hire the necessary assistants or workers, to distribute the work among them, to supervise it, and to pay their wages out of his own remuneration. The master manufacturer, dealt only with his factors, or subcontractors, and had nothing to do with the rank and file of the workers, whose names do not even appear on the pay roll or in the cash book. The entries record only the sums received by the factors.

Spinning, the second major step in cloth manufacturing, was a time-consuming process until the invention of the spinning jenny in the eighteenth century. Although requiring a considerable degree of skill, spinning was not very tiresome and could be combined, if necessary, with cradling the baby. In Florence it was mainly a by-occupation for country women who lived in the surrounding district. Because it would have been utterly impractical for the lanaiuoli to deal with each one of the women spinners, this task also was entrusted to industrial factors, or subcontractors, who went into the country with a mule or a donkey to deliver the wool and to collect the yarn after it was spun.[48] There were two different factors: the *stamaiuolo* who took care of the combed wool, which was spun from the distaff, and the *lanino* who was in charge of the carded wool, which was made into thread with the aid of a spinning wheel.[49] These factors had to pay the spinner out of what they received from the lanaiuolo and were responsible to him for any loss of material.[50]

Although the women were poorly paid, output was so small that spinning was an expensive process. According to reliable data taken from account books, it exceeded the cost of warping and weaving.[51]

The next step after spinning was weaving, the most important in the manufacture of cloth.[52] Before the weaver could start, the warp had to be prepared, an operation usually entrusted to women who were paid on a piece-rate basis.[53] In the Middle Ages, cloth contained a weft of carded yarn and a warp of combed yarn to give it strength. The weft usually required twice as much material as the warp.[54]

In Florence it was probably the weaver himself who sized the warp, placed it on the warp beam, and fastened it to the cloth roll after drawing the threads through the eyes of the heddles. The weavers worked in their homes, and some of them were even small masters who owned two or three looms and used apprentices to weave the coarser fabrics. Since the flying shuttle had not yet been invented, it took two persons to operate the wider looms: the weaver who raised and lowered the harnesses and a helper who threw the shuttle.[55]

In articles of association relating to the woolen industry, it is sometimes stipulated that one of the main duties of the manager was to supervise

the work of the weavers, literally "to go to the looms." [56] Apparently
the employer had the right to go into the weaver's home in order to
ascertain that the work was done properly and proceeding according to
schedule. This practice was not actuated by the desire to oppress the
poor weavers, but by the legitimate concern of maintaining quality.
Looms, although relatively expensive pieces of equipment, usually belonged to the weavers. The Medici records at Harvard University do not
substantiate Alfred Doren's statement that the masters often made advances secured by looms, either to tie the weavers to their service or to
exploit them more easily.[57] What these records show is that the manufacturers helped the weavers by buying looms for them and by allowing
them to pay for this purchase in weekly installments deducted from their
wages. In 1534, according to the Medici records at Harvard, a loom cost
£42 piccioli, or six florins, which corresponded approximately to six
weeks' wages.[58] If these records may be considered as reliable guides,
there was a great deal of mobility among the weavers who, instead of
working for the same employer, shifted from one to the other in quest
of job opportunities.[59] All weavers were not equally good or reliable.
The better ones probably had the least trouble in finding jobs; those
who were the least efficient were presumably the first victims of unemployment when business was slack and the clothiers were retrenching
because their stocks did not move and tied up their funds.

Weavers were paid piece rates which varied considerably according to
the length and the type of cloth, for example, whether it was a plain
weave or a twill. The setting of proper rates was not such a simple problem and often became a source of friction between employers and
workers.[60]

How many looms were maintained by a typical firm is hard to tell
because output was irregular and depended a great deal upon the turnover of stock. Even under the most favorable circumstances, this turnover
was slow, less than twice a year, since the manufacturing process normally
extended over about six months.[61] A typical firm having a capital of 4,000
florins probably kept from four to eight looms in operation, depending
upon business conditions and the scheduling of production. It is doubtful whether many firms in the Florentine woolen industry had more
than ten looms going for any length of time.

Unlike silk, woolen cloth was not finished when it came from the
loom. It still had to be fulled and tentered and to go through several
other steps before it could be offered for sale. In Florence, on account of
the far-reaching division of labor within the industry, a different artisan
specialized in each step of the finishing process.

Fulling, for example, was done by small masters who operated fulling
mills in the country along streams which supplied both water and power

to operate the hammers. In the fifteenth century, they were the property of rich landowners who rented them out to the fullers.[62] The Wool Gild, or Arte dela Lana, also owned fulling mills.

Stretching, or tentering, was an operation performed in large establishments called tiratoi, which, in the fifteenth century were owned by the Wool Gild. These tiratoi were huge structures covered with pointed roofs, the only buildings in Florence which in any way prefigured modern factories. Like the churches and other major edifices, the tiratoi stand out on old city plans, for example, the plan designed by Dom Stefano Bonsignori in 1584.[63] In 1498 there were seven or eight tiratoi owned by the Wool Gild but the four largest were: the Tiratoio all'Uccello located Oltrarno near the Gate of San Frediano, the Tiratoio delle Grazie next to the bridge of the same name, the Tiratoio degli Angeli situated in the present via degli Alfani behind the Hospital of the Innocents, and the Tiratoio della Pergola which stood on the site of the present theatre still bearing this name.[64] Two of these massive structures still existed in the beginning of the nineteenth century: the Tiratoio all'Uccello was destroyed by fire and the Tiratoio delle Grazie, the largest of the four, was demolished to make way for the present Palazzo della Borsa, which houses the stock exchange and the Chamber of Commerce. The tiratoi were equipped with frames and other apparatus which were rented by the tenterers from the gild authorities.

With the exception of the fullers and the tenterers, most of the other finishers — burlers, nappers or teaselers, shearmen, and menders — apparently worked at home or in their own workshops. Like most of the other workers employed by the Florentine lanaiuolo, the cloth finishers were remunerated by the piece, usually at a flat rate per full-length cloth. None of the cloth finishers worked for only one employer but always for several. The reason was technical: as the steps in the finishing process were all of short duration, there was not one manufacturer whose output was large enough to keep a fuller, a tenterer, or any of the other finishers steadily employed.[65] This is further evidence that there were in Florence no fully integrated woolen mills.

Dyeing had no assigned place in the manufacturing process, since cloth could be dyed in the wool, in the thread, or in the cloth. Accordingly, dyeing came after any of the three following steps: washing, spinning, or stretching. In Florence dyeing was in the hands of small firms — single proprietorships or partnerships — which possessed some capital and employed several laborers.[66] Their status was higher than that of any other category of woolworkers.[67] The Medici themselves did not disdain entering into partnership with master dyers. Of course, the capital of such firms was even smaller than that invested in a typical woolshop.[68] Dyers did not work for one employer only, but usually had a clientele of several clothiers.[69]

There were in Florence two main groups of dyers: the *tintori di guado* and the *tintori d'arte maggiore*. The former used woad and indigo as basic dyestuffs, while the latter dyed with kermes, madder, brazil wood, or other substances to give cloth all shades of red, purple, brown, or yellow.[70] A third group of dyers, called *tintori d'arte minore,* dyed only cheap cloth not destined for the export trade. Like the other artisans in the woolen industry, the dyers were paid by the piece. Rates varied according to the dyestuffs used in the process. These were often supplied by the lanaiuolo, apparently in order to make sure that they were of good quality. The bookkeeping of the Medici does not confirm Doren's assumption that either the gild or the manufacturer made an extra profit by selling supplies to dyers.[71] In fact, no sale took place, because the entries show that the value of the dyestuffs was charged directly to cost. Unlike the wage earners, the dyers did not receive weekly advances, but payments to them were made in fairly large amounts or sometimes in kind, a practice which aroused many protests.

No account books belonging to the industrial establishments controlled by the ruling Medici have come down to us, but Harvard University has a collection of such records pertaining to another branch of the family.[72] It can safely be assumed that methods of bookkeeping would vary little, if at all, from one branch to the other. As a matter of fact, they were probably more or less uniform throughout the industry, because all the firms would be confronted with the same problems.[73]

Because of the complex organization of the woolen industry, it was necessary to keep quite an elaborate set of records. Besides the ledger (*libro dei debitori e creditori*), which was standard in all Florentine business firms, the woolshops had to have an array of subsidiary books in order to keep track of the materials given out at various stages of the manufacturing process. These books were the *libro dei filatori* which contained the accounts with the industrial factors or subcontractors who distributed the wool among the spinners, the *libro dei tessitori* in which were recorded the dealings with warpers and weavers, the *libro dei tintori* which harbored the accounts with dyers and finishers, and the *libro dei lavoranti* in which were written down materials received and the wages earned by the other subcontractors or workers with whom the clothier came in contact. Details in accounting procedure might vary slightly from firm to firm. Often the libri dei filatori e dei tessitori were bound together in one volume and the libri dei tintori e dei lavoranti, in another. Then there was the quaderno di cassa which in some firms was a sort of wage ledger containing accounts to which were posted, on the debit side, the weekly advances paid to each worker and, on the credit side, his earnings. Most of the firms had also a cash book in which were recorded receipts and expenditures excluding wages, which were entered only periodically in a lump sum.

A serious complication arose from the fact that the clothier dealt with two currencies. He reckoned with subcontractors and wage earners in *lire di piccioli* (silver currency), but accounts with dyers, customers, and wool dealers were kept in gold florins. The lack of a fixed ratio between the two currencies interfered seriously with orderly bookkeeping and prevented the adoption of double entry. Profits were determined at irregular intervals by deducting liabilities and initial investment from total assets.

Some firms went further and kept records enabling them to figure out the cost of each piece of cloth with great accuracy.[74] A beginning was thus made with cost accounting, although the purpose was still primarily to keep track of the goods in process and to prevent waste and "cabbaging." Nevertheless, the information thus collected was already used to determine cost, and the Datini records even show that a system of ratios was used to allocate overhead to each piece of cloth, a rational procedure which betrays a high level of technical proficiency and managerial skill. Thus far there is no evidence that this system was adopted by other firms, but all the extant records have not been explored, even superficially.

Annexed to the report of the Medici for the catasto of 1427, one finds a statement of assets and liabilities relating to the woolshop controlled by their bank (Table 31). This statement is not really a balance sheet, since assets exceed liabilities plus net worth — decisive evidence that books were not kept in double entry. Moreover it is incomplete, since it does not give the value of the goods in process or of raw materials and finished products in stock. Despite these gaps, the statement is revealing in many respects.

The woolshop had a capital of 4,500 florins, of which the Medici had supplied 3,800 florins and the manager, Taddeo di Filippo, 700 florins. In addition, there were 1,500 florins of accumulated profits which the partners had left in the business, so that total equity amounted to 6,000 florins plus an unspecified sum of current profits which were still undivided. The assistant manager was Lionardo d'Agnolo Baglioni, who had no share in the capital but was nonetheless treated as a third partner and entitled to one sixth of the profits. The remaining five sixths were then allocated as follows: two thirds to the Medici Bank and one third to Taddeo di Filippo.

Most of the cloth was apparently sold locally to exporters, either individual merchants or companies of merchant-bankers, the bulk of it

TABLE 31. STATEMENT OF ASSETS AND LIABILITIES OF THE WOOLSHOP MANAGED
BY TADDEO DI FILIPPO ACCORDING TO THE CATASTO REPORT OF 1427

Assets

	f	s	d	aff
Accounts Receivable According to the Libro Nero				
Cosimo and Lorenzo de' Medici in Florence (6 items)...	2,411	22	8	
The Medici branch in Rome	1,529	5	4	
Sundry debtors (11 items)	443	5	9	
Florentine mercantile and banking companies (6 items)...	635	1	6	
Drapers and other retailers (5 items)	376	26	11	
Customers in Pisa and Perugia (2 items)	151	0	6	
Private customers (5 items)	203	14	3	
Filippo di Lionardo da Bisticci, *stamaiuolo* (subcontractor)	86	17	0	
Total	5,837	6	11	
Accounts Receivable According to Quaderno di Cassa				
Advances to workers	8	4	0	
Medici Bank in Florence (3 items)	680	22	7	
Medici Bank in Rome (3 items)	632	20	4	
Florentine banking companies (9 items)	1,388	27	4	
Sundry debtors (18 items)	935	17	9	
Draper (one item)	92	0	0	
Customers in Prato, Cortona, Viterbo	392	10	6	
Total	9,967	22	5	
Advances to wage earners	£68	17s.	6d. picc.	
Raw materials and supplies on hand, goods in process, and finished goods in stock	Not recorded			

Liabilities

	f.	s.	d.	aff.
Accounts payable (13 items)	477	17	7	
Cosimo and Lorenzo de' Medici, Florence	1,707	26	0	
Banking companies in Florence (2 items)	509	4	0	
Accrued wages (4 items)	70	0	0	
Grain venture	94	17	6	
Total liabilities	2,859	7	1	

	florins	s.	d.			
Capital						
Medici Bank	3,800	0	0			
Taddeo di Filippo di Taddeo	700	0	0	4,500	0	0
Surplus						
Lionardo d'Agnolo Baglioni	640	6	7			
Taddeo di Filippo	62	24	9			
Medici Bank	830	25	4	1,533	27	8
Total liabilities and net worth				8,893	5	9
Excess of assets over liabilities and net worth				1,074	16	8
Total				9,967	22	5

Source: ASF, Catasto No. 51 (Gonf. Leon d'Oro, 1427), fols. 1170–1171.

going to the Florentine bank of the Medici. The papal court must have been an important outlet, since the Rome branch owed the wool-shop a substantial sum of money, presumably for cloth sent on consignment. Drapers in Florence and neighboring towns were not customers of any consequence. Some cloth, but very little, was sold directly to consumers, all belonging to the Medici circle. One of them was donna Ginevra, the wife of Lorenzo di Giovanni de' Medici. In any case, the financial statement does not confirm the view that a Florentine lanaiuolo had an elaborate sales organization and agents scattered all over Europe. His attention was focused on manufacturing, and the export trade was largely in the hands of the great trading companies.[75] They distributed Florentine cloth all over Italy, their main market. Among their best customers were the Venetians who bought it for re-export to the Balkans and the Levant.[76] In Spain conditions were not so favorable because of the keen competition of Flemish piece goods, especially says from Wervicq (Vervi), which were holding their own in this market. In Northern Europe, there was a demand for Italian silks but apparently none for Florentine cloth.

The extent to which exploitation prevailed in the Florentine woolen industry has been for a long time a controversial subject. In any case, it should be stressed that not exploitation but low productivity was the basic cause of the wretched condition of the workers. Even if there had been no exploitation at all, their standard of living would not have been much higher, since it is axiomatic that a society, whatever its organization, whether planned or unplanned, cannot possibly consume what is not first produced. Exploitation arose from the fact that the clothiers were in a much better bargaining position than the wool workers and used the power of the gild to prevent the latter from creating any combinations even under the disguise of religious fraternities. In accordance with scholastic doctrine, such associations were branded as monopolies and conspiracies in restraint of liberty.

The statutes of the Wool Gild (Arte della Lana) explicitly outlawed all "conventicles" or "congregations" formed by artisans or workers in defiance of its authority and required them to swear that they would not join such organizations.[77] It would not be anachronistic to say that the workers were required to enter into some sort of "yellow-dog contract" as a preliminary condition of employment. Attempts to violate the rule might entail severe penalties. In 1345 a wool carder named Ciuto Brandini was actually condemned to death and executed for having tried to form a "brotherhood," or labor union.[78] The indictment, which is still extant, accuses him of being a man "moved by a diabolic spirit" to introduce harmful "innovations," to imperil property, and to disturb peace and order. There are several other cases on record to show that the gild did not hesitate to resort to drastic action against any agitators who threatened to stir up unrest among the laborers.[79]

Although well acquainted with social conditions obtaining in the Florentine woolen industry, San Antonino is no more favorable to seditious labor movements than other medieval moralists. Nevertheless he reproves the employer who, taking advantage of the worker's need and poverty, pays less than the wage set by common estimation, which means the current rate determined by supply and demand in the labor market.[80] He even more strongly condemns employers who, driven by greed rather than by necessity, do not pay wages when due or who force the worker to accept payment in truck or in clipped coin.[81] It is not clear from San Antonino's text whether this is a reference to the behavior of employers as individuals or as a group, because the Wool and Silk Gilds dominated by the master manufacturers sometimes put pressure on the Florentine government to debase the silver currency (moneta di piccioli) in order to lower real wages without touching nominal wages.[82] The truck system existed both in the woolen and the silk industries. Probably it was more prevalent in times of depression than of prosperity, because the employer who paid in truck ran the risk of spoiling the market for his own products.

The greatest hazard facing the worker was probably prolonged unemployment, since the woolen industry was subject to violent ups and downs owing to its dependence on foreign markets and its sensitivity to such disturbances as war, famine, and pestilence. In 1378, at the time of the *Ciompi* revolt, one of the major popular demands was that the clothiers be required to produce an aggregate of 2,000 pieces a month in order to keep the labor force more steadily employed.[83] This full-employment scheme miscarried because the clothiers failed to cooperate. Whether it would have been at all feasible, even if the employers had offered no opposition, is debatable: in a severe slump, how long could they keep people on their pay roll after income from sales had fallen off? The volume of production, it should be clear, depended upon demand, and the producers, whether employers or employees, had no command over consumers.

Even in normal times, Florentine artisans and laborers were not overworked: because of the Sundays and the numerous holidays when rest was prescribed by the gild statutes, there were scarcely 275 workdays in a year.[84] Work hours were from sunrise to sunset with one interruption for the noonmeal in winter and two in summer.[85] These rules, of course, applied only to the few workers, such as wool beaters or carders, who were hired by the day. Those who were paid by the piece and worked at home could schedule their time as they saw fit, but nightwork, of course, was prohibited by the gild statutes. Naturally, the workers had not much opportunity to loaf during regular workdays if they wanted to earn a living enabling them to raise a family at even a bare subsistence level. Conditions in the silk industry were perhaps a little better than in the woolen industry, especially for the weavers of brocades and figured velvets, who were relatively well remunerated because they were highly skilled.

The organization of the silk industry was based on the same principles as that of the woolen industry, but there existed significant differences between the two. For one thing, unlike wool, raw silk is already a thread obtained by twisting together several filaments or strands as they come off the cocoons. In the second place, silk weaves do not require finishing after leaving the loom. As a result, the making of silk fabrics involved fewer steps than the making of woolen cloth.[86] Moreover, the manufacturing process in the fourteenth century was already so highly mechanized that little or no progress was made before the nineteenth century when power-driven machinery was introduced.

The major steps in silk manufacturing were and still are: (1) reeling from the cocoons, (2) throwing, (3) boiling, (4) dyeing, (5) warping and weaving. The first of these steps does not need to detain us, since unwinding the cocoons was seldom if ever done in Florence, but nearly always in the regions where the silkworms were raised. In the fifteenth century, raw silk of the highest grade came from Modigliana near Faenza.[87] Other Italian centers of sericulture were located near Pistoia, in the Marches of Ancona, in the Abruzzi, in Calabria, and in Sicily.[88] Although the Italian raw silk found a ready market among the Florentine silk manufacturers, demand exceeded the available supply and had to be filled by imports from abroad, chiefly from Spain, but also from Asia Minor, Georgia, and even China. Chinese silk reached Europe by way of the Genoese colonies of Caffa and Tana on the Black Sea. However, this source of supply finally dried up, as wars and anarchy repeatedly closed the silk route across the steppes of Asia.

Even before the fifteenth century, the throwing of silk had become a mechanized process which was performed by an elaborate machine called a *torcitoio* or *filatoio*.[89] Such a machine was composed of two circular frames, an outer frame which was stationary and an inner frame which rotated around a vertical axis in much the same way as a revolving door. Each frame was divided by uprights into the same number of compartments, usually ten or twelve. The outer frame was generally provided with several rows or stories of reels. In each row, there was one reel per compartment and several spindles to each reel. The inner frame, when in motion, caused the reels to turn slowly and the spindles to rotate much more rapidly in their glass sockets. The silk was twisted into a strong thread by being drawn through the eyes of an S-shaped wire from the fast-rotating spindles onto the slow-moving reels. Since throwing was largely automatic, the operation of a torcitoio required only one or two attendants whose principal task was to rejoin broken threads. The torcitoio was, therefore, a laborsaving device which replaced several hundred throwsters doing the work by hand. In 1385 one Lucchese torcitoio was described as having five rows of 96 spindles or 480 spindles in all.[90] As the detailed description in Diderot's *Encyclopédie* shows, such machines continued in use until the eighteenth century without being appreciably changed or improved.

Apparently the throwing mills used in Florence had fewer spindles than those of Lucca, perhaps because the irregular flow of the Arno did not permit the application of water power, which was used in Lucca. In Florence some of the torcitoi were located, far from the river or from any stream, on the outskirts of town near the Gate of San Gallo in the street of the same name.[91] In all likelihood, silk throwsters were small masters who worked with one or two assistants and enjoyed a certain degree of independence because they were not at the mercy of one employer but accepted orders from several manufacturers. In any case, the throwing mill, although it was a complicated machine, did not give rise to factories in the modern sense.[92]

The object of boiling, the third major step in silk manufacturing, was to remove the natural gum which had been an advantage up to this stage but would prevent the silk from taking the dye. In Lucca the boiling was done by a *cocitore* (silk boiler), whereas in Florence it was combined with dyeing.[93] The boiling left the silk lustrous and soft, pearly white in color.[94] To obtain pure white, it was bleached by being exposed to sulphur fumes.[95] Other colors, of course, were obtained by dyeing the silk skeins.

Dyeing was a delicate process, and a fifteenth-century treatise on the Florentine silk industry describes in great detail the methods in use: they varied more or less for different dyestuffs.[96] As in the woolen industry, dyers were small masters who were not tied to one employer and were paid on a piece-rate basis. In general, dyestuffs were supplied by the manufacturer, presumably in order to prevent waste or damage.[97]

Before weaving, it was necessary to prepare the warp, a job which in Florence was entrusted to both men and women. The most important step was weaving, especially in the case of figure weaving, which required elaborate drawlooms and great technical skill.[98] Such looms were rather expensive pieces of equipment, and it happened often that a weaver borrowed the necessary funds from a silk manufacturer and paid off the loan gradually by weekly or monthly deductions from his earnings. This system entailed the serious inconvenience of forcing the worker to remain with the same employer until the complete repayment of his debt, a situation conducive to abuse and exploitation.[99]

Weavers were paid piece rates which varied greatly depending upon the time and skill required for a given job. According to the fifteenth-century treatise previously mentioned, these rates ranged from 6s. piccioli per *braccio* for plain taffeta to £18 piccioli per braccio for heavy gold brocade.[100] It is true that it took only one month to weave fifty braccia of taffeta and over six months to produce the same quantity of brocade. Nevertheless, there was a wide difference in the pay. A weaver of brocades, around 1460, could earn over £700 di piccioli, or about 130 florins, per annum, a figure which corresponds to more than twice the salary of a cashier of the Medici Bank. On the other hand, a woman weaving taffeta barely made £145 di piccioli, or about twenty-seven florins, in a whole year. Despite the inducement of good wages, highly skilled weavers of brocades were apparently scarce and did not have to compete for jobs, because their services were sought after by the silk manufacturers.[101]

As a rule, weavers worked at home and not in the employer's workshop. An amendment to the gild statutes, enacted in 1429, explicitly enjoined the silk manufacturers, even if they owned the looms, to treat weavers as masters (*maestri*) and not as workers (*lavoranti*). The purpose of this provision was evidently to restrain employers from setting up looms on their own premises; instead, they were required to give out the work in the usual way and not to pay less than the minimum piece rates fixed by the gild.[102] This regulation was motivated less by a concern for the workers' welfare than by the fear that weavers and other skilled craftsmen, resenting the loss of their independence, might emigrate and settle in towns eager to establish rival silk manufactures. The Silk Gild was completely dominated by the master silk manufacturers; although the artisans were not matriculated and not eligible to any office in the Gild, they were nevertheless placed under its jurisdiction and discipline and required to swear that they would observe its statutes as a necessary condition for employment.[103]

Not only was silk more expensive than wool, but the silk industry made great use of such precious materials as gold and silver thread; as a result, "cabbaging," or filching, was a perennial problem, far more serious than in the woolen industry, and it is not surprising that the gild took stringent measures to stamp out this evil.[104] No one was allowed to buy silk stuffs from a suspicious source, that is, from a person who was not a regular dealer, either a merchant or a manufacturer. Receivers were bound to restore stolen goods to their rightful owners and, in addition, were liable to heavy penalties.[105] Without express consent of the gild

officials, licensed pawnbrokers and unlicensed moneylenders were prohibited from granting loans secured by a pledge of any materials pertaining to the silk industry.[106] Artificers, apprentices, or factors convicted of
pilfering were put on the blacklist, and thereafter no gild member was
supposed to hire them.[107] Since many offenders were so poor that it was
futile to fine them, the gild officials secured authority to inflict other
forms of punishment, such as the whip, the stocks, or the pillory. They
were even allowed to apply torture to persons suspected of stealing or
sabotage.[108]

Manufacturers, of course, took the precaution of weighing all materials
when they were given out and of weighing them again when they were
brought back by the workers. The difficulty was that steps in the manufacturing process involved some unavoidable wastage for which it was
necessary to make an allowance. To prevent fraud, such allowances were
cut down to a minimum by the gild statutes: weavers, for example, were
held responsible for any shortage exceeding one sixth of an ounce per
pound in the case of plain weaves and one third of an ounce per pound
in the case of figured velvets, brocades, and baldachins.[109] Workers also
were accountable for any damage resulting from defective workmanship,
whether due to carelessness or to malice. According to the statutes, if a
worker failed to fulfill his obligations, the employer had the right to
recover the debt from his immediate family or even from his "girl friend"
(l'amica). In the same way, husbands or sons of women employed in the
silk industry were answerable for their wives or mothers.[110]

As a rule, the gild did not favor the truck system, and repeated
statutory provisions required that wages be paid in coin and not in
kind.[111] The reasons behind this policy were probably two: first, it was
realized that payments in truck tended to spoil the market for all, because the workers, in order to raise money, were likely to sell the goods
at greatly reduced prices; secondly, toleration of this practice interfered
with the prevention of "cabbaging" and, furthermore, was actually in con-
tradiction with the guiding principle that the trade in silk fabrics was
exclusively reserved to manufacturers, merchants, and retailers affiliated
with the gild. In 1420 an amendment to the statutes made two exceptions
to the rule by allowing the silk manufacturers to sell dyestuffs to the
dyers and to pay part — up to one fourth — of the wages of other workers
in victuals, such as grain, wine, oil, or meat.[112]

The account books of the setaiuolo Andrea Banchi show that he
bought such commodities as wine and oil in large quantities and resold
them to his workers in smaller lots, probably below the retail price.[113]
There is no evidence that the workers were being exploited or coerced.
Andrea Banchi was a shrewd business man who must have realized that

there was little to gain by creating discontent. His purpose was almost certainly to cultivate good will among his weavers by enabling them to buy wine and oil at bargain prices.

In accordance with the business policy followed by the Medici, the burden of organizing and supervising production rested entirely upon the shoulders of the junior, or managing, partner. The senior partners could not be bothered with technical details. For example, whether to make plain weaves or patterned silks, whether to select this or that design, whether to choose one color scheme rather than another were matters with which they did not concern themselves but which were left for the manager to decide. He was expected to produce only goods that would sell and have a quick turnover, because otherwise funds would be tied up and profits impaired.

Because silk fabrics were luxury products, the market for them was restricted to the upper classes, chiefly the Church, the courts, and the nobility. As a result, the Florentine silk industry to an even larger extent than the native woolen industry depended upon foreign markets. Most of the silk fabrics were undoubtedly sold locally to international merchants who resold them abroad, but the more important setaiuoli, such as Banchi, were sometimes exporters as well as manufacturers and were represented in distant places by their own agents to whom they sent their products on consignment.[114] This method of distribution, of course, involved greater risk and a slower turnover of invested capital. The Medici silkshop enjoyed the privilege of being part of a concern which had branches and correspondents scattered all over Italy and Western Europe. They were expected to push the products of the Medici shop in foreign markets, although they were not always able to do so because consumer tastes varied and often favored the products of rival silk-producing centers, such as Lucca or Venice.

One of the main outlets was the Rome branch, which had close connections with the papal court, a steady buyer of figured velvets and brocades used extensively in liturgical vestments. The Milan branch of the Medici Bank took advantage of its financial dealings with the Sforza court, one of the most magnificent in Europe, to capture its orders for silk fabrics. However, most of these were imported from Venice, because the Milanese preferred Venetian to Florentine silks.[115] In Bruges, the situation was for a long time the same, if not worse, because of the entrenched position of the Lucchese silks strongly promoted by Dino Rapondi, Giovanni Arnolfini, and other merchants from Lucca who wielded their influence at the Burgundian court to defend the interests of their home city.[116] It was not until 1464, after Giovanni Arnolfini had entered the service of Louis XI, that Tommaso Portinari, the manager of the Bruges branch, succeeded in securing from the Court an order for Florentine silks.[117]

The first really large sale did not take place until 1468 on occasion of the wedding of Charles the Bold and Margaret of York, Edward IV's sister.[118] By the way, this marriage proved to be a boon also for the London branch, because Edward IV bought from it all the silk for the trousseau of his sister and her suite.[119] As a matter of fact, throughout the fifteenth century, London was a better outlet for Florentine silks than Bruges.[120] Geneva, and later Lyons, was another important market because of the proximity of the court of Savoy and the concourse of German merchants who came to the fairs to buy spices and merceries.

The Medici also supplied the Aragonese court of Naples. A *legaggio* (invoice) relating to two chests of velvets shipped in 1477 by the Medici from Florence to Naples discloses that not a single piece came out of their own shop but that the entire lot was purchased from several other setaiuoli.[121] So the Medici Bank itself dealt in silks produced by competitors of one of its subsidiaries. There is nothing strange in such a policy: in order to retain customers, the Medici Bank had to offer an assortment more varied than was produced by one establishment of average size.

Since the making of silk fabrics involved fewer steps than the transformation of wool into cloth, the bookkeeping of the setaiuoli was also less elaborate than that of the lanaiuoli, but it served the same purpose of keeping track of the amounts to be collected or to be paid and of the materials given out and returned at each stage of the manufacturing process. In addition to a ledger and a journal, silk manufacturers kept a libro dei tessitori and other subsidiary books in which the materials entrusted to home workers and their earnings were recorded. The fact that the setaiuoli use one standard, the florin, in their relations with customers and another standard, the moneta di piccioli, in their relations with wage earners, stood in the way of the adoption of double entry. A number of account books belonging to setaiuoli have come down to us, but none from the ruling Medici.[122]

The only accounting record still extant is a statement of assets and liabilities — I deliberately avoid using the word "balance sheet" — dated 1497 and pertaining to the firm, Piero di Lorenzo de' Medici & Co., ragione D (fiscal period D) begun in 1493 [123] (Table 32). When the Medici were expelled from Florence in 1494, this firm was apparently taken over by Lorenzo di Giovanni Tornabuoni for an amount of 11,500 fiorini larghi. Although this financial statement bears the date of 1497, it probably refers to 1494, when the Medici were expelled and all their property was confiscated.[124] If so, the silkshop was one of their few still prosperous ventures: according to the statement, net worth amounted to 18,616 fiorini larghi, of which only 7,500 florins represent capital and all the rest undistributed profits. Besides, assets exceed liabilities and net worth to the extent of 522 florins, presumably another addition to undivided profits. However, there is on the assets side an offsetting item of 3,067 florins which refers most likely to funds withdrawn from the business by the heirs of Lorenzo the Magnificent. The amount of 844 florins standing to the debit of Cardinal Giovanni de' Medici (1475–1521), later Pope Leo X, may be of the same nature and relate to a loan instead of a debt arising from purchases of silk. If this interpretation is correct, net worth would be reduced from 16,670 to 12,758 florins, which brings us nearer to the amount of 11,500 florins paid by Lorenzo Tornabuoni. The plausibility of this interpretation is further enhanced by the fact that the Medici were having financial troubles even before the crash of 1494 and were drawing on all available resources in order to meet the crisis.

TABLE 32.   STATEMENT OF ASSETS AND LIABILITIES OF THE MEDICI SILKSHOP
1497 (?)

Assets

	f.	s.	d.	a oro
The heirs of Lorenzo de' Medici & Co. in Rome........	3,425	0	10	
Heirs of Lorenzo de' Medici, private account..........	3,067	12	8	
Medici Bank in Florence for account of the Camera Apostolica or papal treasury............................	2,743	16	2	
Piero de' Medici and Lorenzo Tornabuoni & Co. in Lyons	997	11	3	
Cardinal Giovanni de' Medici.......................	844	6	0	
Piero de' Medici & Co., goldbeaters..................	535	9	8	
Bad debts and past due accounts.....................	258	4	6	
Advances to weavers................................	187	11	2	
Subtotal..........	12,059	12	3	
Sundry accounts receivable (99 items).................	7,078	16	9*	
Total.............	19,138	9	0	

Liabilities

	f.	s.	d.	a oro
Accounts payable (7 items).........................	2,468	8	3	
Capital account....................................	7,500	0	0	
Avanzi (undistributed profits)......................	8,647	19	1	
Subtotal..........	18,616	7	4	
Excess of assets over liabilities......................	522	1	8	
Total.............	19,138	9	0	

* This amount includes only personal accounts, since there is no record of any goods in stock or in process.

Source: ASF, MAP, filza 136a, fols. 79ᵛ–81ʳ.

Closer inspection of the statement discloses that the Rome branch and the papal court were still the most important buyers of the fabrics made by the Medici silkshop. Sundry accounts receivable include 99 items, most of them small, the largest being an amount of 662 florins charged to Giuliano d'Antonio Borghi of Mantua, probably a supplier of the Gonzaga court. Lyons is still mentioned as an outlet abroad, but no reference is made to Bruges, London, or Milan, where the Medici no longer maintained branches in 1494. Advances to weavers (*tessitori*) amount to 187 florins 11s. 2d. a oro, which shows that such loans were fairly common, but which does not prove that they were extensively used to oppress workers. On the credit side, there are only seven items of accounts payable; the two highest amounts are debts to Florentine bankers: 1,386 florins to the Tavola of the Medici and 457 florins to Bartolomeo Bartolini & Co.

As the records show, the Medici did not center their activity in the textile industry, which absorbed only a minor portion of their capital (Tables 14, 15, and 16). Moreover, the three industrial establishments never yielded more than a small fraction of the total profits derived from business ventures (Tables 8, 11, and 17).[125] Throughout the history of the Bank, manufacturing remained a sideline far less important than the combination of banking and international trade. On this point the statistical and other data presented in this study leave no room for doubt.

THE MEDICI AND THE FINANCIAL BUSINESS
OF THE PAPACY: THE ROME BRANCH
OF THE MEDICI BANK

To talk about the "Rome" branch of the Medici Bank may be using a convenient abbreviation, but it is properly speaking incorrect. In the Medici records the Rome branch is often referred to as "ours who follow the Court of Rome" (*i nostri che seguono la Corte di Roma*) or "the branch which follows the Roman court" (*la ragione che segue la Corte*). In reality, the Rome branch was located in Rome only when the pope was in residence. At other times it followed the papal court in its peregrinations through Italy and even beyond the Alps. Thus the Rome branch had its office in Florence itself while Martin V resided at Santa Maria Novella from February, 1419, to September, 1420. His successor, Eugene IV, stayed away from Rome for nine years, and the Medici *di Corte* followed him while he moved about holding court and presiding over ecumenical councils in one city after another: Florence (1434–1437), Bologna (1437), Ferrara (1438), and Florence again (1439–1443). While Eugene IV took his lodgings in the famous Dominican friary of Santa Maria Novella, the Medici rented a house on the square of the same name for the use of their "Rome" branch.[1] For a time the Medici Bank had three offices in Florence: the general office in the via Larga, the Tavola in Mercato Nuovo, and "ours of Rome" doing business in Piazza Santa Maria Novella. Even while the latter were in Florence, they kept their books in cameral florins or fiorini di camera used by the papal treasury or Camera Apostolica (Apostolic Chamber), not in fiorini di suggello, the Florentine currency.

The pope had the enviable reputation of causing monetary stringency, creating a housing shortage, raising prices, and increasing the cost of living wherever he went, obviously because the demands of his numerous suite of cardinals, protonotaries, ambassadors, and officeholders of all ranks put a strain on local resources, on means of payment as well as food supplies.[2] All medieval merchant manuals insist on this fact: why should there be any doubts?

Among medieval rulers, the pope was the only one who had revenue flowing into his treasury from all corners of Europe, even from Scandinavia, Iceland, and Greenland.[3] The cardinals, prelates, and clerics residing at the Roman Curia likewise had revenues coming to them from benefices beyond the Alps and wanted to dispose of this income in Rome or in some other Italian city. Besides, there was the constant shuttle of pilgrims, suitors, and emissaries of all kinds who had business at the Curia and who preferred to provide themselves with letters of credit instead of carrying money in belts or saddle bags. As a result, there arose an international transfer problem. Under those circumstances, the popes, whether they wished it or not, depended upon the services of bankers, such as the Medici, who had correspondents in all banking places of Western Europe and could transfer funds with celerity from one place to another where the papacy needed them the most. In outposts, such as Scandinavia or Poland, or even in relatively backward countries, such as Germany where there were no banking facilities, papal transfers suffered long delays and were attended with great risks and difficulties. Often papal agents would have to rely on casual means such as traveling merchants, pilgrims, or students who would undertake to carry money or goods to the nearest banking center.[4] Transfers from Poland sometimes took six months or more, whereas funds received in Bruges or London were made available in Rome within a month or less by a simple letter of advice.[5] The bankers provided expeditious and efficient service. The smooth operation of this system depended, of course, on the existence of a regular money market, and this was found only in a few trading centers where the volume of business was large enough to make it worth while for the Italian banking houses to maintain branch offices.

Councils attracted ecclesiastical dignitaries and delegates from all over Europe. The financial transactions to which such gatherings gave rise were so numerous and so important that the Medici and other Italian bankers were induced to open a temporary office in any town where an ecumenical council was being held. Examples are the banks which the Medici operated in Constance (1414–1418) and Basel (1431–1443) while a council was meeting there. Neither one of these two towns remained a banking center after the council had disbanded. In 1456 there was still in Basel only a single Florentine money-changer who would sell drafts or letters of credit on Rome.[6]

Papal remittances were unilateral payments which disturbed the equilibrium of international trade relations by making it more difficult for Northern Europe to settle Italian claims, since English wool was about the only commodity which the Italians would accept in exchange for alum, spices, silks, and other luxuries and which could be used in last resort to pay tributes to Rome. As the fifteenth century progressed, less and less wool became available for export until there emerged a real crisis due to the disruption of the equilibrium in the trade between

Northern and Southern Europe. To put the matter succinctly, the Italians were eager to sell but were not willing to buy, and the papal tributes only aggravated the situation. It is doubtful whether the silver output of the German and Bohemian mines was large enough to fill the gap and to provide the specie necessary to restore the balance. A minor difficulty arose from the fact that Rome, at least before the discovery of the Tolfa mines, was not a trading center but the residence of a court that was a consumer of all kinds of luxuries, from heavy brocades for vestments to silver plate for the table of cardinals and prelates, and had practically nothing to offer in exchange. At any rate, Rome had no textile industry worth mentioning. The Tuscan bankers, however, knew their business, and this problem was easily solved by means of triangular exchange and by using Barcelona, Florence, or Venice as intermediate banking places. As a matter of fact, the settlement of international balances raised more intricate problems: already in the fifteenth century, all banking places in Western Europe were interdependent and any disequilibrium was reflected immediately in the exchange rates and was speedily adjusted by means of arbitrage, a transaction which the Italian bankers understood perfectly well, since it is described in merchant manuals and in treatises on commercial arithmetic.

Although the absence of banks east of the Rhine hampered the speedy settlement of international debts, this inconvenience was partly mitigated by routing transfers by way of banking places located near the periphery of this region and assiduously frequented by German merchants. Those hailing from South Germany visited Venice or the fairs of Geneva (later of Lyons). The Hanseatic merchants traded extensively with Bruges, and their connections extended all over Scandinavia and the Baltic region from Bergen in Norway to Novgorod in Russia. How transfers were made is illustrated by the following case: in 1416 Filippo Rapondi, a well-known Lucchese merchant-banker residing in Bruges, acknowledged in the name of Giovanni de' Medici & Co. having received the sum of 2,350 Rhenish florins which the factors of the latter in Constance had loaned to the ambassadors of Lübeck and the Hanseatic League attending the ecumenical council.[7] The receipt stipulates that payment was received from the City of Lübeck through the medium of Rudolph Comhaer and other merchants of the said city residing temporarily in Bruges. The procedure followed was clumsy, even though secure, since the acquittance took the form of a public instrument requiring the intervention of the burgomaster and aldermen of Bruges. However, business methods in Northern Germany were backward in comparison with those of the Italian merchant-bankers; this was perhaps the main reason why the latter failed to develop Lübeck into a banking center.

To understand the relations between the Medici Bank and the Apostolic Chamber, it is necessary to say a few words about the organization, the functions, and the traditions of this administrative body. In a general way, the Chamber administered the pope's temporalities and, as such, its powers were broad and diversified. It performed, however, two main functions: it was the department responsible for the government of the papal states and it managed the pope's finances both as a spiritual and as a temporal ruler.[8] At the head of the Chamber stood the Chamberlain, who was always a bishop and often an archbishop if not a cardinal; he was one of the two or three greatest and most powerful personages of the Roman court.[9] Beneath him came the Apostolic Treasurer, whose function it was to receive and disburse the monies of the Holy See and to take care of its finances.[10] The Treasurer was not necessarily a bishop, but he was usually at least an abbot or a dignitary of high rank.[11]

By the fifteenth century the Treasurer no longer kept the pope's monies stored in a chest in his own custody. Funds were deposited with an official who was called Depositary General of the Apostolic Chamber and who was as a rule a representative of one of the papal bankers.[12] In practice it meant that the bank with which the depositary was connected acted, so to speak, as fiscal agent of the papacy. In the Medici books, the Camera Apostolica's account is, curiously enough, in the depositary's name, but there is no doubt that it would correspond to what is today the United States Treasury's account with one of the Federal Reserve banks.

All the funds which the depositary received for the papal treasury were written to the credit of this account. On the other hand, this account was charged with all sums disbursed by the depositary upon a warrant issued by the pope himself, the chamberlain, the treasurer, or any other authorized official of the Apostolic Chamber. This was, of course, the procedure followed in the books of the bank. To comply with the regulations of the Apostolic Chamber, the depositary kept a special book recording all his receipts and disbursements listed separately and in chronological order. Two authenticated copies of this record, translated from the Italian into Latin, were then made by a notary: one for the Camera and one for the treasurer.[13] These account books are called *Introitus et Exitus;* a few Italian originals and an almost complete series of the Latin copies are still extant in the Vatican archives.[14] The *Introitus et Exitus* were checked and approved each month by a clerk of the Chamber. For the purpose of this audit, a balance was struck at the end of each month and carried over to the next. If disbursements of a given month — plus or minus the balance of the preceding month — exceeded receipts, it meant that the Chamber had overdrawn its account and owed the difference to the depositary, instead of having a credit in its favor.

During the fifteenth century the pope favored as a rule the Medici Bank and usually appointed the manager of its Rome branch as Depositary General. During the pontificate of John XXIII (Balthasar Cossa), this office was held by Matteo Barucci.[15] The latter was succeeded by Bartolomeo de' Bardi (1420–1429), Antonio di Messer Francesco Salutati da Pescia (1429–1435), Antonio della Casa (1435–1438), and Roberto Martelli (1438–1443).[16] This period from 1420 to 1443 covers the pontificate of Martin V and part of that of Eugene IV. During his last years, Pope Eugene IV, angered by the Medici's support of Francesco Sforza in the Marches, appointed as depositary another Florentine banker, Tommaso Spinelli. Nicholas V (1447–1455), upon his accession to the papal throne, reinstated Robert Martelli, who retained the office until 1458, through the pontificate of Calixtus III (1455–1458). Pius II (1458–1464), being Sienese, conferred the office of depositary upon a compatriot of his, the banker Ambrogio Spannocchi. After the election of Paul II (1464–1471), a Venetian, Spannocchi was supplanted by Giovanni Tornabuoni, the Medici representative in Rome, who kept the office of depositary until August 1465, when it was given to the Pope's relative, Giovanni Condolmer.[17] In 1471 it was restored to the Medici by Sixtus IV (1471–1484).

Giovanni Tornabuoni was not at all enthusiastic about resuming the functions of Depositary General. He wrote to Lorenzo, after the latter had approved this appointment, that the office involved more trouble and risk than profit, because Pope Sixtus IV was living beyond his means and expected the depositary to advance the funds necessary to fill the deficit between *introitus* (income) and *exitus* (outgo).[18] So Giovanni Tornabuoni was probably relieved when, within four or five years, the post of depositary was taken away from him because of the fast-developing rift between Sixtus IV and the Medici.[19] The office went to a succession of Genoese bankers — Meliaduce Cigala, Gerardo Usumari — with the Medici making no effort to recover it, presumably because it was a drain on their resources; they were at this time short of funds and in no position to expand their loans.

In all likelihood, the post of depositary was less of a burden in earlier years, when there was either a surplus or a deficit of manageable proportions. During the pontificates of Martin V and Eugene IV, the Camera Apostolica managed somehow to balance its accounts with the depositary general. In any case, small deficits in some months were compensated by surpluses in other months. The next pope, Nicholas V, was not as careful as his two predecessors. By the time of his death, in March, 1455, the deficit had run up to the sum of 70,432 cameral florins, an amount which Calixtus III found so high that he ordered a special audit of the depositary's accounts and applied himself to reducing the Camera's

4. Piero di Cosimo de' Medici

5. Francesco Sassetti, General Manager of the Medici Bank, 1463–1490, with his eldest son, Teodoro

indebtedness.[20] Pius II and Paul II, as we have seen, withdrew the papal account from the Medici, but spendthrift Sixtus IV restored it to them during the early years of his pontificate. Soon the deficit soared to 107,000 cameral florins, at which figure it stood in July 1472.[21] During the following months, Tornabuoni succeeded in getting assignments on customs (*dogane*) and on the salt pits in the Marches, so that the debt was reduced to 62,918 cameral florins, according to a settlement ratified by the Pope in March 1473.[22] After Sixtus' rift and later reconciliation with the Medici, the repayment of the Camera's debt proved slow and arduous and was effected by turning over to the Medici stocks of alum instead of cash.

Because of the usury doctrine, the depositary was not allowed to charge any interest on the Apostolic Chamber's overdraft, or debit balance. To recoup this loss, the Medici overcharged the pope on the silks and brocades, the jewels, and other commodities they supplied. This practice, however, gave rise to difficulties because the auditors objected and refused to approve the accounts submitted by the depositary unless prices were scaled down.[23] The position of depositary had a prestige value and, by inspiring confidence, attracted the lucrative deposits of cardinals and other courtiers who had money to invest and who did not wish to purchase real estate; such real property was likely to be seized, should a new pope, as often happened, force the favorites of his predecessor to disgorge the wealth acquired by alienation of Church property. Not even the pope had the right to give away Church land. As pointed out, the Medici promised their customers to keep secret the amount of deposits made with them.

Besides the depositary general, the papacy employed other papal bankers to act as special depositaries or to transmit funds collected abroad. The papacy, for example, never used the services of the Medici in Spain, since they had no branches in this country. They were papal agents in England, but they had no monopoly, since it was the policy of the Camera to give business to competitors also, such as the Pazzi, the Baroncelli, the Spinelli, Antonio da Rabatta and Bernardo Cambi & Co.[24]

Perhaps it should be stressed at this point that the papal bankers did not actually collect the Church's revenues, especially not the proceeds from indulgences or jubilees. This task was entrusted to papal collectors who were usually ecclesiastics of high rank. They organized each campaign to collect special funds in conjunction with the local ecclesiastical authorities in much the same way as a charity drive today. After having been collected, the indulgences or jubilee funds were turned over by the collector to the papal banker, who delivered a receipt in duplicate in which he promised to transfer the sum received to Rome. Such a receipt was called an *instrumentum cambii:* one copy was kept as a voucher by the collector and the duplicate was sent to the Apostolic Chamber, which saw to it that it received due credit from the papal bankers. The chamber then sent a discharge to the papal collector, who usually surrendered the voucher for which he had no longer any use.[25]

As an example of a receipt delivered by a papal banker to a papal collector, one may cite a document dated January 21, 1468, by which Christopher Spini, acting as proxy for Tommaso Portinari, the manager of the Medici Bank in Bruges, acknowledges having received an amount of £1773 10s. 3d. groat, Flemish currency, from Luke de Tolentis, archdeacon of Curzola, nuncius and papal collector in the dominions of the Duke of Burgundy.[26] This personage, whom we have met in connection with the alum trade, was in charge of a jubilee by which the pope granted plenary indulgence to the faithful who worshipped in the churches of Ghent, took communion after confessing their sins, and made an oblation for the prosecution of the crusade against the Turks.[27] The above amount of £1773 groat, by no means a negligible sum of money, represents the total coin found in the boxes which had been emptied in the presence of Luke de Tolentis and other witnesses. The receipt given by Spini lists in great detail the different coins actually received, how many of each, and the corresponding value in groats, the Flemish money of account. It contains the specific promise to remit the equivalent to the Curia. The receipt is in the form of a deed, or public instrument, drafted by an apostolic and imperial notary. All precautions were consequently taken to prevent any misuse of papal funds, and the procedure followed, if somewhat cumbersome, insured maximum safety from the point of view of the Apostolic Chamber.

A different procedure was followed in the collection of taxes and other revenue within the Papal States. In each district or major city, there resided a provincial treasurer, who disbursed local receipts as directed by the rector (provincial governor) or the Apostolic Chamber.[28] If there was any surplus, he was often ordered to consign it to the Depositary General in Rome or to pay the assignments issued by the Chamber for the payment of mercenary troops.[29]

Important sources of income for the papacy were the annates and the common and petty services. By the mid-fifteenth century, the word "annates" was used loosely to designate both of these sources, although, strictly speaking, it referred only to benefices, such as canonries, the collation of which was implemented by papal provision only. The term "common and petty services" correctly applied to benefices of higher status, such as archbishoprics, bishoprics, and abbeys, which were granted by the pope in consistory.[30] From a financial point of view, the distinction was that the pope had to share the income of common services with the college of cardinals but did not share the annates with anyone. This distinction, however, is not very important for our purpose. Annates and common services were supposed to equal the first year's fruits of a benefice, although in practice they were much less. They had to be paid by the nominee before he could take possession of his office. The collection of these dues was not often entrusted to papal collectors, but was handled by the papal bankers to whom the bulls of nomination were usually sent and who did not release them unless they received payment or a pledge backed by serious guarantees.[31] In the fifteenth century, the practice prevailed of charging the papal bankers as soon as they were handed over the bulls, but of giving them the option of "regress," that is, the privilege of returning the sealed bulls within an appointed time with the understanding that the debit would be cancelled.[32] Moreover, an ecclesiastic who did not live up to his obligations in connection with annates or common services exposed himself to the serious penalty of excommunication which was inflicted automatically whenever a papal banker complained of being unable to collect.[33]

Like all papal bankers, the Medici were very active in the collection of annates and common services, and they used their influence at the Curia to promote the suits of their clients. They did not hesitate to bribe: it was common and accepted practice. According to a reliable study, the collation of Scottish benefices passed mostly through their hands.[34] The payment of these dues must have been quite a burden for as poor a country as Scotland, which had nothing to export except a little wool, and not the best. Transfers, of course, went via London, since there was no banking place in Scotland.

How the Medici operated in this matter is best shown by a letter which their Bruges branch wrote in December 1448, to John Kemp, cardinal and archbishop of York. They informed him that their partners in Rome, by their "exertions," had secured the appointment of his nephew, Thomas Kemp, to the bishopric of London in preference to a rival candidate sponsored by Henry VI and William de la Pole, first duke of Suffolk.[35] At the same time, they told the Cardinal to pay his nephew's dues within a month to Gerozzo de' Pigli, the manager of the London branch; otherwise, to their great regret, they would have to return the sealed bulls to Rome. If necessary, the Medici did not hesitate to take drastic action with defaulting churchmen; in 1441 they warned the papal collector that they would have the Bishop of Nevers excommunicated if he tarried any longer in fulfilling his commitments.[36]

The Medici were instrumental not only in collecting papal revenues abroad but also in paying out subsidies to foreign princes who had trouble with the Turks or with heretics, such as the Hussites of Bohemia. Papal subsidies to Mathias Corvinus, King of Hungary (1458–1490), whose dominions were threatened by the Turks, were paid in bills of exchange on the Medici branch in Venice.[37] Since there was no banking center in Hungary, the bills were presumably paid either directly to the king's agents in Venice or indirectly to merchants who traded in Hungary.

Because of the international character of its business, the interests of the papacy were best served by companies controlling a more or less extensive network of branches in Italy and beyond the Alps. Only the Tuscan companies provided such a service. Neither the Venetians nor the Genoese built up such an organization, probably because traditions and customs born in the trade with the Levant were unfavorable to the formation of large units, such as the Florentine banking houses.

As Giovanni di Bicci set out to capture the papal business, it is no wonder that he was soon forced to branch out and to open offices in Florence, Naples, and Venice. Although headquarters were transferred to Florence, the Rome branch continued to be of pivotal importance. Up to 1435, it produced more than 50 percent of the Medici Bank's aggregate earnings. During the twenty-three years extending from October 1, 1397, to December 20, 1420, the share accruing to Giovanni de' Medici and his partner Benedetto de' Bardi amounted to a total of 79,195 florins 4s. 4d. affiorino, or to an average of nearly 3,500 florins per annum (Table 8). Of course, this figure was obtained only after deducting the remuneration of the managing partners, Ilarione de' Bardi and Matteo d'Andrea Barucci.

Ilarione was in all likelihood an extremely able business man, since he was slated to become general manager upon his brother's death. Although Matteo Barucci was not treated as a partner until 1416, he had been in the service of the Medici since 1400 (Table 7). According to the partnership agreement of March 25, 1416, which is still extant, it is doubtful whether he invested anything in the capital.[38] Apparently, he contributed only his "person" and was on this account entitled to one eighth of the profits. The contract required that Barucci go and stay wherever the Curia might be. He was allowed to withdraw 100 florins per year to meet expenses. If he exceeded this amount, interest was chargeable at the rate of 12 percent per annum.

Barucci's being made a partner at this juncture is certainly in some way connected with the convocation of the ecumenical council of Constance. It seems that part of the clerical staff, with Ilarione de' Bardi as head, followed the Pope, John XXIII (Balthasar Cossa), when he went thither to meet his destiny — abdication and imprisonment. The others, with Barucci, presumably were left in Italy to wind up affairs and to transact whatever business there was. At any rate, Ilarione's presence in Constance is attested by a notarial contract of March 23, 1415.[39] After the end of the Great Schism and the election of Martin V (November 11, 1417), the "Rome" branch probably followed the new Pope as he made his way back to the Eternal City, where he did not arrive until September 28, 1420, after sojourning in Florence for more than a year, from February 1419 to September 1420.

Evidence that the Rome branch followed in the train of the Pope is found in an entry of Libro segreto I, which relates to the profits made by the "Rome" branch during the four years (1416, 1417, 1418, and 1419) while it was residing in Constance and "keeping bank" at Santa Maria Novella in Florence, temporary residence of the Pope.[40] On the same page, there is another entry covering about the same period, from March 25, 1417, to December 20, 1420, and also relating to the profits made by "ours of the Court in Florence" (nostri di Corte di Firenze). The two entries obviously overlap. The most plausible explanation of this riddle is that the "Rome" branch was split into two subbranches: one at the Council and the other continuing to attend to the business of John XXIII (Cossa), who, although deposed by the Assembly at Constance on May 29, 1415, did not make his formal submission to Martin V until June 23, 1419. As is well known, Pope John was a staunch friend and faithful customer of the Medici who, as the executors of his will, built for him the beautiful tomb by Donatello and Michelozzo in the baptistry of San Giovanni.[41]

According to the Memoirs of Vespasiano da Bisticci, Cosimo de' Medici went to Constance to gain business experience by working in the branch office of the Bank and took advantage of this opportunity to make a tour into France and Germany in search of rare manuscripts.[42] Whether this trip actually took place is questionable, since no reference to it has been found in the Medici records.

In 1420, as stated in Chapter Three, Ilarione, upon becoming general manager, undertook to reorganize the Medici Bank. In Rome, the new manager was Bartolomeo d'Andrea de' Bardi. The articles of association, still preserved among the Medici papers, contain nothing that deviates from the usual pattern and put all the burdens and responsibilities upon the managing partner while subjecting all his actions to the ultimate approval of the maggiori.[43] The contract, however, clarifies one point by stating that the purpose of the partnership is "to traffic and deal in exchange at the Court of Rome as it may please God and as is customary in this kind of banking business, above all staying within the bounds of fair and licit contracts." The emphasis is consequently on banking and exchange with the understanding that heed be paid to the usury doctrine of the Church by making only permissible contracts and no patently usurious loans.[44]

More interesting than the articles of association is the ricordo with which Bartolomeo de' Bardi was provided when leaving Florence to assume his post.[45] Reference was made to this in Chapter Five, but it seems profitable to discuss it here in more detail, even at the risk of some repetition. The reason is that the ricordo contains a formulation of the policy which Bartolomeo was expected to follow. His main problem was to know to whom he could safely lend and how much. First of all, he was instructed to consult his main assistant, Antonio di Lazzaro Bertini, who was experienced in dealing with skippers (marinai).[46] In the second place, he should beware of wine dealers because they were likely to cause more trouble than would be worth while. He should also avoid extending credit to any Roman traders or small merchants because they were unreliable and had little to offer by way of security. In dealing with courtiers, Bartolomeo de' Bardi should be on his guard: he was allowed to lend up to 300 florins to each cardinal upon the assignment of his "hat," presumably upon assignment of the revenues which the cardinal derived from the camera cardinalium. To courtiers other than cardinals, the limit was reduced to 200 florins, and only upon good security. As for the Pope, Martin V, it was hoped that he would not ask for more, as he had already borrowed enough. On the contrary, he was expected to pay off some of his indebtedness, unless war broke out with the Kingdom of Naples. At any rate, Bartolomeo might lend the Pope up to 2,000 florins, but the maggiori would be more pleased if he did not. To Roman barons, no loans were to be made even on pledges, since they were a law unto themselves and did not keep to the terms of any contracts, so that the lender lost his money as well as the friendship of debtors and sureties.

In case of necessity, Bartolomeo de' Bardi could always count on the protection and counsel of Cardinal Rinaldo Brancaccio (d. 1427); of Alamanno Adimari, cardinal of Pisa (d. 1422); of Branda da Castiglione, cardinal of Piacenza (d. 1443); of Antonio Casini, bishop of Siena and papal treasurer, and of Messer Paolo da Giovinazzo, a protonotary and a clerk in the Apostolic Chamber. They were all very influential personages at the court of Martin V and among the most faithful customers of the Medici Bank. Bartolomeo was allowed to grant them credit in the usual way: up to 1,000 florins to the cardinal of Pisa and up to 3,000 florins to Cardinal Rinaldo Brancaccio. The maggiori considered that the cardinal of Piacenza had run up such a large debt that Bartolomeo de' Bardi was urged to discourage further borrowing. He was allowed, if requested, to accommodate Messer Louis Aléman (d. 1450), a Frenchman, bishop of Maguelonne in Languedoc, who, in 1420, was vice-chamberlain of the Apostolic Chamber and who was to become cardinal in 1426.[47] Although the representatives in Rome of Niccòla and Cambio di Messer Vieri de' Medici had sometimes been incorrect in dealing with Giovanni di Bicci's bank, Bartolomeo de' Bardi was instructed to treat them well and to oblige them as much as possible. In general, it was impressed upon him that it was better to grant credit gingerly than to be too liberal, lest bad debts swallow everything, capital as well as profits.

Bartolomeo's task was made easier by the fact that he could rely on an able clerical staff. His assistant, Antonio di Lazzaro Bertini, was soon to be sent to the Geneva fairs to carry on business for the Rome branch and to see whether it would pay eventually to establish another Medici subsidiary. His place in Rome was taken by Antonio di Francesco Salutati, also called Antonio da Pescia. This newcomer was transferred from the Venice branch. Once in Rome, he was promoted rapidly and, by 1428, was treated as a partner, getting one tenth of the profits in reward for his services.[48] The books were kept by Giovanni d'Amerigo Benci, who was excellent at this job, which he performed with the assistance of Bartolomeo di Tommaso Spinelli.[49] As office boy, there was Antonio della Casa, destined to become manager of the Rome branch in 1435.[50]

In the fifteenth century the Medici, when residing in Rome, held their bank in the street which was called then Canale di Ponte and is now the via del Banco di Santo Spirito. It is located on the left bank of the Tiber across from Castel San Angelo and near the present church of San Giovanni dei Fiorentini. This quarter of town, called rione di Ponte, was the business and banking district of medieval and renaissance Rome.[51]

The balance sheet attached to the catasto report of 1427 belongs to the period during which Bartolomeo de' Bardi was manager of the Rome branch (Tables 21 and 33). It is a revealing document in many respects, and its analysis confirms entirely what has been said before about the nature of the business conducted by the Rome branch. Mercantile transactions, according to the balance sheet, were of subordinate importance and absorbed only a small fraction of the working capital. Of course, it is not certain whether the merchandise accounts represent the value of inventories. It is possible that some of the items refer to expenses incurred on goods received on consignment. The presence among the assets of silver plate for an amount of more than 4,000 florins reveals at any rate that the Rome branch dealt more or less extensively in this luxury product for which there was a demand among the high churchmen of the Curia who did a great deal of entertaining and liked to display their magnificence. Cash on hand amounts to more than 10,000 florins, a substantial sum which certainly does not consist of till money but must represent the reserve kept in the money chest which is mentioned in Bartolomeo de' Bardi's ricordo. Neither the cashier nor any visitor was allowed to sleep in the room where this chest stood.[52]

The Rome branch, it was stated before, supplied the other Medici companies with working capital. The balance sheet of 1427 bears out this point and shows that Florence and Venice owed more than 40,000 florins to the Rome branch (Table 34). In addition, the parent company,

TABLE 33. BALANCE SHEET OF THE ROME BRANCH OF THE MEDICI BANK
JULY 12, 1427

Assets

	f.	s.	d. di cam.
Debit balances in the quaderno di cassa (cash book):			
Past due accounts of last year (75 items)............	9,683	8	2
Sundry accounts receivable of present year (73 items)	10,480	2	2
Gift to Antonio Colonna, prince of Salerno..........	87	0	0
Merchandising expense............................	136	7	0
Three petty services..............................	173	0	0
Household expenses (spcse di casa).................	149	6	6
Executors of the will of Cardinal Brancaccio.........	1,328	9	0
Subtotal..........	*22,037*	*12*	*10*
Debit balances in ledger G (libro nero segnato G):			
Sundry accounts receivable with balances below 1,000 florins (80 items).............................	16,381	10	6
Six accounts with balances exceeding 1,000 florins (see Table 35).....................................	13,929	12	3
Merchandise accounts............................	6,003	15	5
Silver plate......................................	4,934	14	1
Correspondents abroad (see Table 38).............	33,233	15	11
Other Medici companies (see Table 34).............	42,156	8	8
Subtotal..........	*116,639*	*16*	*10*
Debit balances in the libro segreto of the Rome branch:			
Deposit with the company of Cosimo and Lorenzo de' Medici and Ilarione de' Bardi, 10,000 florins di suggello......................................	9,400	0	0
Cash on hand...................................	10,356	18	0
Subtotal..........	*19,765*	*18*	*0*
Total............	158,443	7	8

Source: ASF, Catasto No. 51 (Gonf. Leon d'oro, 1427), fols. 1191ᵛ–1200ʳ.

Cosimo and Lorenzo de' Medici & Ilarione de' Bardi, had received an advance of 10,000 fiorini di suggello, Florentine currency. As a matter of fact, this item reappears as a liability in the Libro segreto No. 2 of the parent company: consequently, there can be no doubt about its accuracy.[53] Another significant fact brought out by an analysis of the balance sheet is that more than 33,000 florins were due from foreign correspondents (Table 38). Those in London alone had in their hands a balance of nearly 15,500 florins which had not been remitted to Rome. Because Ubertino de' Bardi was a brother of Bartolomeo, it is possible that the latter favored him by allowing him to retain funds belonging to the Rome branch, instead of insisting on prompt remittance. While this practice may account for the debit balance of Ubertino de' Bardi and

TABLE 33 (Continued)

BALANCE SHEET OF THE ROME BRANCH OF THE MEDICI BANK

JULY 12, 1427

Liabilities

	f.	s.	d. di cam.
Creditors in quaderno di cassa (cash book):			
Sundry accounts payable with balances below 1,000 florins (239 items)....................	26,792	0	0
Three creditors with balances above 1,000 florins.....	5,434	0	0
Three petty services.............................	1,488	7	3
Merchandise accounts............................	2,894	13	0
Subtotal........	36,609	0	3
Credit balances in ledger G (libro nero segnato G):			
Sundry accounts payable with balances below 1,000 florins (56 items)............................	11,822	19	5
Seven creditors with balances above 1,000 florins (see Table 37).....................................	18,240	6	10
Account of Bartolomeo de' Bardi as depositary of the Apostolic Chamber......................	24,497	0	8
Undistributed profits...........................	658	0	6
Retention of monies paid for the Apostolic Chamber..	191	0	8
Subtotal.........	55,409	8	1
Credit balances in the libro segreto of the Rome branch:			
Twelve deposits (depositi a discrezione) listed in Table 36.....................................	55,480	0	0
Pope Martin V, special account (conto a parte)......	1,185	1	3
Undistributed profits............................	7,471	8	2
Accrued salaries.................................	100	0	0
Reserves.......................................	1,500	0	0
Bartolomeo de' Bardi, personal account.............	483	9	1
Subtotal.........	66,219	18	6
Total of liabilities.............	158,238	6	10
Error in casting the balance.....	205	0	10
Total......................	158,443	7	8

his partners, it does not explain why all the correspondents north of the Alps were indebted to the Rome branch. It does seem, therefore, that there were transfer difficulties. Because papal remittances were not compensated by purchases of goods in Northern Europe, Rome was naturally in a creditor's position and the problem arose how to settle its claim on Bruges, Geneva, London, or Lübeck. The result was that debit balances with correspondents beyond the Alps tended to accumulate, as the balance sheet of 1427 reveals.

The only other item of interest on the assets side of the balance sheet relates to six accounts above 1,000 florins. What each one of these debit

TABLE 34. Investment of the Rome Branch in Other Medici Companies

	f.	s.	d. di cam.
Florence..	29,436	10	4
Venice..	12,719	18	4
Total............	42,156	8	8

Source: Same as Table 33.

TABLE 35. Debit Balances Exceeding 1,000 Cameral Florins According to the Balance Sheet of the Rome Branch

	f.	s.	d. di cam.
Matteo de' Bardi & Co. in Rome....................	4,601	3	11
Averardo di Francesco de' Medici & Co., Florence.....	3,291	10	0
Cardinal Alfonso de Carillo........................	2,805	6	8
Bartolomeo de' Bardi, *proprio* (private account)........	1,201	1	10
Lodovico de Verme, commander of papal troops.......	1,030	9	10
Messer Filippo, archbishop.........................	1,000	0	0
Total............	13,929	12	3

Source: Same as Table 33.

TABLE 36. Deposits a Discrezione Listed in the Balance Sheet of the Rome Branch

	Cameral florins
1. Antonio Colonna, prince of Salerno, and his brothers Odoardo and Prospero (*il principe e fratelli*).....................................	15,000
2. Antonio Colonna (*il principe solo*)...............................	5,000
3. Articino della Porta, cardinal of Novara..........................	4,000
4. Hermann Dwerg (Duverche), German, protonotary.................	4,000
5. Giovanni degli Annibaldi, protonotary............................	4,000
6. Albato Scienche (?), German.....................................	4,000
7. Giovanni d'Orlando da Genazzano................................	3,580
8. Branda da Castiglione, cardinal of Piacenza......................	3,500
9. Oddo Poccia de Varris da Genazzano, Apostolic Treasurer..........	3,400
10. Paolo da Sulmona..	3,400
11. Agnolo Massi da Genazzano......................................	3,000
12. Master Johannes Tronar...	2,600
Total........	55,480

Source: Same as Table 33.

TABLE 37. CREDIT BALANCES EXCEEDING 1,000 FLORINS IN THE LEDGER
OF THE ROME BRANCH ON JULY 12, 1427

	f.	s.	d. di cam.
1. Cardinal Francesco Lando as *camerlingo* (chamberlain) of the College of cardinals...........	4,795	8	6
2. Henry Beaufort, cardinal of Winchester (*Messer Arigho, cardinale di Vinicheri*).............	4,000	0	0
3. Branda da Castiglione, cardinal of Piacenza.........	3,074	19	0
4. Alessandro Tagliamilo of Naples.................	2,199	14	0
5. Messer Tomaso Ciopen (?), Englishman...........	1,986	0	0
6. Executors of the will of Cardinal Brancaccio........	1,116	0	0
7. Articino della Porta, cardinal of Novara...........	1,068	5	4
Total........	18,240	6	10

Source: Same as Table 33.

TABLE 38. BALANCES DUE FROM CORRESPONDENTS ABROAD ACCORDING TO THE
BALANCE SHEET OF THE ROME BRANCH

Place	Correspondent	Amount		
		f.	s.	d. di cam.
London	Ubertino de' Bardi, per noi.............	5,700	0	0
	Ubertino de' Bardi, per lui.............	4,223	14	4
	Totto Machiavelli e Ubertino de' Bardi, per loro..........................	4,031	17	3
	Totto Machiavelli e Ubertino de' Bardi, per noi...........................	1,452	0	0
	Subtotal for London...........	*15,407*	*11*	*7*
Bruges	Gualterotto de' Bardi.................	5,400	0	0
	Galeazzo Borromei & Co...............	1,143	0	0
	Subtotal for Bruges...........	*6,543*	*0*	*0*
Geneva	Michele di Ferro.....................	4,085	0	0
Lübeck	Lodovico Baglioni e Gerardo Bueri.......	3,945	0	0
Avignon	Niccola e Cambio di Vieri de' Medici....	2,279	3	0
Nuremberg	Guglielmo e Arrigo Rumoli (Rommel?)...	704	0	0
Valencia	Vieri de' Bardi & Co.................	251	13	4
Cologne	Simone Colin........................	18	8	0
	Total.....................	33,233	15	11

Source: Same as Table 33.

balances really represents is hard to tell. The amount of 1,200 florins
standing to the debit of Bartolomeo de' Bardi probably means that he
withdrew funds in anticipation of his share in the next distribution of
profits. It is also interesting to note that the Medici made an advance

to Lodovico, or Aloisi, de Verme, a condottiere in the service of the Pope. Condottieri, at that time, were business entrepreneurs as well as army commanders.[54]

On the liabilities side of the balance sheet of 1427, the absence of a capital account is perhaps the startling feature, but it should not cause any surprise, since we know that no capital was assigned to the Rome branch after 1426. An important item of nearly 24,500 florins is Bartolomeo de' Bardi's account as depositary of the Apostolic Chamber. This is in reality the current account of the papal treasury. Inasmuch as it had a credit balance, the papacy was not borrowing at this time to meet current expenditures. In the ledger there were only seven accounts payable with balances over 1,000 florins (Table 35). Three of the creditors were cardinals. One of them was Henry Beaufort (d. 1447), a natural brother of Henry IV, King of England.

Of greater significance is the list of the depositi a discrezione (Table 36). All the depositors, the balance discloses, had a deposit certificate (ha scritta), which entitled them to interest, if earned by the banker, but bound them, on the other hand, to leave their money on deposit for a certain time. This list is headed by the Pope's nephews (Martin V belonged to the famous Colonna family). Since deposits a discrezione were denounced as usurious by many of the leading theologians, it is edifying to find two cardinals on the list. The other depositors are without exception prelates who occupied important functions at the Curia or were clerks of the Apostolic Chamber. One of the most influential was the German, Hermann Dwerg, who, it is said, enjoyed the confidence of Martin V and always had access to the Pope, even when he was ill in bed. When Dwerg died on December 14, 1430, he was reputed to have been one of the wealthiest men in Rome. "But," according to Ludwig von Pastor, "amidst all his riches he retained a spirit of evangelic poverty" — presumably by placing his money at interest with the Medici! [55] Another personage who had the ear of Martin V was Oddo Poccia de Varris, Apostolic Treasurer after 1426, a position usually held by a bishop. After the Pope's death in 1431, he was thrown into jail by Eugene IV, who wanted to discover the whereabouts of his predecessor's secret funds and, of course, to lay his hands on any hidden treasures he could find.[56]

Some of the secret funds were entrusted to the Medici, since the balance sheet of 1427 discloses that Martin V had nearly 1,200 florins standing to his credit in a special account (conto a parte). This money came from his private purse; but the purpose of having a special account is not indicated. Since the Pope had no scritta, there is no evidence that he received interest, or a so-called share in the profits. Several of the depositors, the reader will note, hailed from Genazzano; this is a village near Palestrina where the Colonnas had their ancestral stronghold. Apparently

Martin V used as much as possible his family's retainers, whom he could trust: feudalism was far from being entirely dead.

Bartolomeo de' Bardi, having died rather unexpectedly in January or February, 1429, was replaced by Antonio di Messer Francesco Salutati da Pescia (near Pistoia). In the Vatican records he is often called Antonius de Piscia without reference to his connection with the Medici Bank, so that historians have not identified him.[57] In the contract concluded on March 10, 1429, his share in the profits was raised from one tenth to one eighth.[58] Neither the maggiori (Cosimo and Lorenzo de' Medici and Ilarione de' Bardi) nor Antonio Salutati were bound to invest any capital. According to the articles of association, the first contributed only the good will of depositors and creditors and the latter was expected to dedicate his person to the conduct of the business.[59] This statement is repeated in later contracts and confirms once more what is known from other sources, namely that the Rome branch operated without capital.

Antonio Salutati did not remain for many years at the head of the Rome branch. In 1435, after Cosimo's return from exile, he was called to Florence to assume the functions of general manager. Management of the Rome branch was transferred to Antonio di ser Lodovico della Casa (1405–1459) on much the same terms, save that his share in the profits was one sixth and that of the maggiori five sixths.[60] This partnership was to last three years, from March 25, 1435 to March 25, 1438. When it expired, it was not extended, because Antonio della Casa left the service of the Medici to set up his own firm with Jacopo Donati as a partner. This undertaking was quite successful and the account books of the firm founded by Antonio della Casa are still preserved in the Archivio dello Spedale degli Innocenti.

The next manager of the "Rome" branch was Roberto Martelli (1408–1464). In the partnership agreement concluded on March 25, 1439, the manager's share in the profits was again reduced to one eighth.[61] Otherwise the provisions remained unchanged. As usual, he was expected to devote himself entirely to the partnership's affairs and to grant credit only to merchants and courtiers in good repute. Roberto Martelli continued to be in charge of the Rome branch until his death in 1464 and was succeeded by Giovanni di Francesco Tornabuoni, Piero de' Medici's brother-in-law.

Before going into the history of the Rome branch after 1464, it may be well to pause for a moment and to consider some of the major developments between 1429 and 1464, that is, from the death of Bartolomeo de' Bardi to that of Roberto Martelli. These are also the years during which Cosimo de' Medici was guiding the destinies of the Medici Bank. The first fifteen years of this period were a time of great tribulations for the papacy. Since the Curia was the *raison d'être* of the Rome branch, the latter was necessarily affected by the course of events which shook the foundations of the papacy's temporal and spiritual power. Either by dint of circumstances or by want of character, Eugene IV put his predecessor's work into jeopardy.[62] Driven from Rome by a republican uprising, he wandered through Italy for nine years (June 4, 1434–September 28, 1443). At the same time that the temporal power crumbled, the conciliar movement challenged papal supremacy in spiritual matters. It culminated in the attempted deposition of Eugene IV by the Council of Basel (June 25, 1439) and the election on November 5, 1439 of the anti-Pope Felix V (Amadeus of Savoy). The Rome branch, of course, followed Eugene IV in his travels.

In 1433, at the request of Cardinal Giuliano Cesarini (d. 1444), the Medici opened an office in Basel and sent Giovanni d'Amerigo Benci from Geneva to organize this new establishment.[63] Once it had a good start, Roberto Martelli, a factor of the Rome branch since 1424, was put in charge. His presence in Basel is recorded from December 1433 up to 1438, when he went to Ferrara where the council was convened by Pope Eugene IV.[64] Since not all members of the Council obeyed the Pope's summons to meet in Ferrara, the office in Basel was continued by Giovenco di Lorenzo della Stufa (1413–after 1469), also a factor of the Rome branch.[65] He left in 1441 to go to sea and eventually became commander of the Florentine galleys.[66] As the Council was moribund by that time, a relative, Lorenzo di Giovanni della Stufa, was given the task of winding up the business and closing the temporary office which the Medici maintained in Basel from 1433 to 1443.[67]

The legal status of this office is in doubt; it is not even certain whether it was a direct subsidiary of the Medici Bank or one layer below, a dependence of the Geneva or the Rome branch. As long as Roberto Martelli was in charge of the Basel office, he was always called factor of Cosimo and Lorenzo de' Medici & Co. and never partner.[68] The same applies to Giovenco della Stufa who, in one notarial contract, is described as *eorum factor,* "their factor." [69] The Basel office, therefore, was merely an agency managed by a factor provided with a power of attorney but not ranking as a partner.

The business of the Basel office resembled that of the Rome branch and consisted mainly in handling the financial business of the Council or in transferring funds for attending ecclesiastics. Often such transfers involved a loan. To give one example, on June 10, 1435, the Basel branch of the Medici Bank, moved "by mere friendship," lent 1,100 cameral florins to Hugues de Lusignan, cardinal of Cyprus and brother of the titular king of Jerusalem, and received from him an assignment on the revenues of one of his benefices, the abbey of Montevergine near Avellino in the realm of Naples.[70] The recognizance of debt is in the form of a solemn notarial deed written on parchment instead of paper. Not all loans involved large sums. On January 30, 1435, for example, Francesco Bosso, doctor in civil and canon law, soon to become bishop of Como, acknowledged to have received a loan of forty cameral florins from Roberto Martelli, factor of Cosimo and Lorenzo de' Medici in Basel, and promised to repay his debt within eight months.[71] The deed is witnessed by one cardinal and two bishops, so that further guarantees were deemed unnecessary.

Apparently, ecclesiastics were more reliable debtors than laymen, because there was always the weapon of excommunication, and the Medici had little hesitation about using it against defaulters.[72] However dreadful, it sometimes failed to impress, especially laymen who were impervious to the frightening prospects of damnation and did not have to fear the loss of their benefices. According to an illuminating comment made on the balance sheet of the Basel branch (1442), a claim of nineteen florins was regarded as irrecoverable because the principal debtor had been dead for many years and his surety, a layman, although excommunicated, was unmoved. "Perhaps," a melancholic commentator adds, "there would be some hope, if he were a priest." [73]

The Basel agency, the third of the extant libri segreti reveals, yielded a profit of 5,499 florins 15s. aff. from 1433 to 1437, but sustained losses of 434 florins 14s. 6d. from then on, presumably because of an accumulation of bad debts not written off in previous years and because of a steady decline in the volume of business as attendance at the Council slowly dwindled away.[74] Over-all profits amounted to 5,065 florins 0s. 6d. aff. (Table 17), not such a bad result, if one considers that the Medici assigned no capital to their office in Basel but "banked" exclusively on their reputation.

There is a balance sheet in the Florentine archives, dated March 24, 1442 (N.S.), of Giovanni Benci & Co. in Basel.[75] This was the style under which the Geneva branch of the Medici Bank was operating at this time, which suggests that Basel had become dependent upon Geneva. This balance is of special interest because it throws a great deal of light on the procedure followed in auditing and checking financial statements. Each item is accompanied by a comment on the prospects of obtaining payment in the case of receivables and on the likelihood of having to repay in the case of deposits. A typical comment, for instance, is the following: "This customer has such great difficulty in making a living that he is unable to pay us, and selling the contents of his shop will involve much trouble and not bring in enough to cover his debt." There also was little hope of being paid by Messer Roberto degli Adimari, formerly bishop of Volterra, because "he had barely enough to subsist" (ha fatica di vivere). In other cases, the comments strike a more cheerful note and state that the claim will surely be collected. Many of the ecclesiastics attending the Council had deposit accounts on which they drew to meet living expenses. A frequent comment is: "he withdraws his funds little by little." On the basis of the annotations made on the balance sheet, one comes to the conclusion that at least twenty-two items appearing as assets and totalling 575 florins represent overdue accounts which should have been written off.

A summary of the balance of the Basel branch as of March 24, 1442, is given in Table 39. Although the Medici were merchant-bankers, this balance shows again that banking rather than trade was the core of their business. Nevertheless, they dealt in woolen cloth, silk fabrics, and silver plate, three commodities for which there was a demand among the ecclesiastics attending the Council.

The debt of 574 cameral florins due from the delegates of the Greek Orthodox Church is offset by another item of like amount on the credit side. Apparently the funds received by them were provided by Cosimo de' Medici, who probably intervened on behalf of the Pope. The item of 200 cameral florins for expenses would not appear today among the assets but in the profit and loss statement. Other Medici companies owed the Basel branch nearly 3,100 cameral florins: the bulk of this sum (2,248 florins 17s. 2d. di camera) was due from the Geneva branch and an additional amount of 777 florins 10s. from the Venice branch. The debit of the "Rome" branch was only sixty-four florins 5s. and was dwarfed by a credit of 1,660 florins 7s. 3d. As usual, the "Rome" branch was in a creditor position, doubtless because of remittances to the Curia. A detailed record of the different species held in the money chest shows that nearly half of it consisted in Rhenish florins and a few *clinkaerts* of Gelderland, but no Florentine florins or Venetian ducats. Besides gold, the cash reserve included local silver currency for an amount of 308 Rhenish florins and unredeemed pledges, all jewelry, to the value of 132 Rhenish florins. It seems, therefore, that the Medici were also lending on pledges, a business usually left to licensed and unlicensed pawnbrokers. Notice that office furniture appears in the balance for the negligible amount of eleven florins 11s. di camera.

On the liabilities side, the balance sheet omits any reference to a capital account, because there was none. The principal creditor was apparently Bernard de la Plaigne, bishop of Dax, one of the leaders of the conciliar movement, whom Felix V created a cardinal. He was withdrawing funds at the rate of thirty or forty ducats a month. Since he had a balance of 2,000 cameral florins, it would have taken him five or six years to clear his account. The item of 889 florins for profits in 1440 and 1441 would have been nearly eliminated if all bad debts had been written off.

TABLE 39. BALANCE SHEET OF THE BASEL BRANCH OF THE MEDICI BANK
MARCH 24, 1442

Assets

Explanation	Number of Items	Cameral florins	s.	d.
Cash on hand: 1,170 Rhenish florins 5s. 10d........	8	936	4	0
Debit balances in *quaderno di cassa* (cash book):				
Sundry accounts receivable.....................	29	779	14	8
Debit balances in *libro* (ledger):				
Greek delegates.............................	1	574	8	0
Expenses (*spese di banco*).......................	1	200	12	0
Other Medici branches.......................	3	3,090	12	2
Giovenco della Stufa, private account...........	1	141	14	1
Lorenzo di Giovanni della Stufa, private account..	1	47	18	0
Goods in stock (woolens, silks).................	1	478	14	0
Silver plate.................................	1	285	2	6
Office furniture.................................	1	11	10	0
Sundry accounts receivable....................	6	74	12	4
Total........................	53	6,621	1	9
Error in casting the balance........	..	10	11	10
Total.......................	53	6,631	13	7

Liabilities

	Number of Items	florins	s.	d.
Credit balances in *quaderno di cassa* (cash book):				
Sundry accounts payable.....................	26	1,339	14	0
Credit balances in *libro* (ledger):				
Sundry accounts payable.....................	7	127	16	8
Medici of the Court of Rome..................	1	1,660	7	3
Cosimo de' Medici, special account.............	1	574	8	0
Undistributed Profits for 1440 and 1441..........	2	889	1	8
Bernard de la Plaigne, bishop of Dax, cardinal Aquensis...................................	1	2,040	6	0
Total........................	38	6,631	13	7

Source: ASF, MAP, filza 104, No. 60, fols. 598–603.

One must not forget that the balance sheet belongs to the period during which the Council of Basel was being deserted by all but the schismatic adherents of Felix V. The volume of business was certainly much greater while the Council was in full swing.

Because of the many gaps in the records, not much is known about the business of the Rome branch during the years from 1435 to 1439 in which it followed Pope Eugene IV from one temporary residence to another.[76] The constant breaking up of camp did not interfere with the

Rome branch's showing satisfactory profits, since they increased from 5,510 cameral florins in 1435 and 5,816 cameral florins in 1436 to 8,066 cameral florins in 1437 and 8,585 cameral florins in 1438. All these profits, however, were not distributed among the partners, because substantial reserves were set up for bad debts and accrued salaries. All in all, the partners received only 8,304 cameral florins for the period of three years from the beginning of 1435 to the end of 1437, Florentine style. In accordance with the articles of association, the share of the Medici amounted to 6,920 cameral florins and that of Antonio della Casa, the manager, to 1,384 cameral florins. When the latter broke his connection with the Medici at the end of 1437 (Florentine style) that is, March 24, 1438, he received an additional 1,370 florins in final settlement; his partners assumed all responsibility for any losses on bad debts and the payment of any unforeseen contingencies.

There are hints in the correspondence that Antonio della Casa was not quite satisfied with this settlement and complained that he had received an unfair deal because too much had been deducted for all kinds of provisions.[77] As he had given a complete discharge, the matter was probably not brought to court, but it seems that the charges were not entirely unfounded according to rules of equity. As Antonio della Casa was a clever business man, he probably tried to obtain more, but he was careful to avoid a breach of friendship. Although he founded a competing firm, he continued to cultivate good relations with the Medici and he was repaid by retaining their confidence. In later years, they instructed their agents to consider della Casa's bank as a trustworthy firm with which they were allowed to deal.[78]

Some of the undistributed profits of the Rome branch were used to finance expansion. An amount of 5,500 écus of 64, or 5,690 cameral florins, was invested in the Geneva branch and another sum of 6,000 cameral florins was used to provide the necessary capital with which to start the Bruges branch on March 25, 1439.[79] As the entries in the libro segreto show, expansion was financed mainly by plowing back earnings rather than by the partners making new investments. The funds which they withdrew from business went either into the purchase of extensive estates or the display of munificence in the form of art treasures, book collections, gifts to monasteries, or the re-building of churches, such as San Lorenzo.

On March 24, 1439, the Rome branch had a yearly payroll of 300 ducats, or cameral florins, and a staff of five factors: Roberto Martelli, about to become managing partner, Andrea Bartolini, Giovanni di Baldino Inghirami, soon to become manager of the Florentine Tavola, Leonardo Vernacci, and Bartolomeo di Nanni di Nettolo Becchi.[80] While the Rome branch was in Ferrara (1438), Giovanni, Cosimo's son, then a lad of seventeen, worked for a while in the office to get business training. His mother wrote him on June 6, 1438, that he ought to be glad "to stay in the bank and to learn something." [81] Ser Giovanni Caffarecci, a former tutor, also wrote him about the same time and in the same vein, adding that nothing would be more pleasing to Cosimo than to have a son who was well acquainted with the practices of the counting house.[82] Furthermore, Giovanni was admonished not to envy his brother Piero because the latter was not put to work behind a desk. As is well known, Cosimo groomed his younger son for business while preparing his elder son for political leadership. The premature death of Giovanni (1463) interfered, however, with the realization of this scheme; after Cosimo's death (1464), Piero was forced to assume the responsibility of his family's interests both in business and in politics.

Because of gaps in the surviving records, there is not much that can be said about the Rome branch during the period from 1439 to 1464, when both Roberto Martelli and Cosimo de' Medici passed away. It is likely that the Rome branch continued to prosper, since there is nowhere any hint of difficulties. During the first twelve years, at least, from 1439 to 1450, profits were gratifying and averaged about 6,200 cameral florins a year (Table 40). The peak was 1439, when they soared to nearly 14,400 cameral florins. This spectacular result was due less to the talents of Robert Martelli than to the fact that business at the Curia was brisker than usual. This is the year when the ecumenical council met in Florence to bring about the ephemeral union of the Latin and Greek churches. Among the distinguished visitors were the patriarch of Constantinople and the Byzantine emperor, John VIII (Palaeologus). The latter's purpose was mainly to enlist in the West military support against the Turks who threatened to swallow the last remnants of the Roman (Greek) Empire and to lay siege to Constantinople. This affluence of visitors, prelates, and dignitaries, of course, favored the Rome branch, which throve on the exchange business. Net profits, after provision for bad debts and other contingencies, dropped to a more normal level in subsequent years, but they never fell below the level of 3,000 florins. The maggiori were so pleased with the results that, from 1446 onward, Martelli's share in the profits was increased from one eighth to one sixth.

In 1455, according to Table 26, the staff of the Rome branch included three persons who were empowered to make out bills of exchange and whose hand was to be honored by foreign correspondents: Roberto Martelli, the manager; Leonardo Vernacci, his chief assistant; and Giovanni Tornabuoni, the bookkeeper. However, it was not until 1458, as a result of a reshuffle in the organization of the Rome office, that the latter was called upon to take charge of what would be called today the banking department.

TABLE 40.   Net Profits of the Rome Branch (1439–1450)
(All amounts are in cameral florins)

Years	Number of Years	Total			Share of Roberto Martelli			Share of Maggiori		
		f.	s.	d.	f.	s.	d.	f.	s.	d.
1439	1	9,098	16	6	1,137	7	0	7,961	9	6
		5,300	0	0ª	662	10	0	4,637	10	0
1440	1	3,700	0	10	462	10	1	3,237	10	9
1441	1	3,471	4	6	433	19	0	3,037	5	6
		4,000	0	0ª	500	0	0	3,500	0	0
1442	1	7,230	15	10	903	17	0	6,326	18	10
1443	1	3,021	8	5	377	13	5	2,643	15	0
1444–1445	2	14,297	13	0	1,787	3	5	12,510	9	7
		50,119	*19*	*1*	*6,264*	*19*	*11*	*43,854*	*19*	*2*
1446–1448	3	12,000	0	0	2,000	0	0ᵇ	10,000	0	0
1449–1450	2	12,447	12	3	2,074	12	0	10,373	0	3
		24,447	*12*	*3*	*4,074*	*12*	*0*	*20,373*	*0*	*3*
	12	74,567	11	4	10,339	11	11	64,227	19	5

ª These amounts represent later adjustments made after it was ascertained that reserves set aside had been excessive.
ᵇ After 1446, Martelli's share in the profits was increased from one eighth to one sixth.
Source: ASF, MAP, filza 153, no. 3: Libro segreto, fols. 35, 42, 44, 60, 66, 73, 81, 88,
and 92.

During the late 1450's Roberto Martelli was absent from Rome most
of the time, because he was called away by official duties. In 1457 and
1458 he was podesta of Prato (Tuscany).[83] During his absence, the Rome
branch was managed by his main assistant, Leonardo d'Angelo Vernacci
(1418–c. 1476), son of a Florentine lanaiuolo, who had been in the Rome
branch since 1435 or thereabouts. In accordance with the usual policy,
Vernacci upon becoming acting manager was treated as a partner and
awarded a share of one tenth of the profits.[84]

At this time, the factors in Rome were: Giovanni Tornabuoni, who
was keeping the ledger; Filippo Masi, who was in charge of the quaderno
di cassa, a complementary ledger, and took care of some of the correspondence; Filippo d'Ugolino Martelli, who was keeping the cash book,
or *entrata e uscita;* and Zanobi Macinghi who, together with Carlo
d'Ugolino Martelli, was active in the *fondaco,* which means probably
the merchandise department. At the beginning of March 1458, Roberto
Martelli thought that, with the beginning of the new year (March 25)
changes should be made in the tasks assigned to the different factors:
Filippo Martelli was to be made cashier, Filippo Masi was to be given
the ledger, and Giovanni Tornabuoni was to handle the bills of exchange
and the routine correspondence, not done by the manager himself.[85]

Vernacci, who either disliked or distrusted Tornabuoni, did not approve the latter's promotion. The friction between the two men was nothing new. Tornabuoni did not enter the service of the Medici until 1443, at the age of fifteen, the year that his sister Lucrezia married Piero di Cosimo de' Medici.[86] Vernacci was consequently his elder in age and in seniority. Already in 1449, Tornabuoni complained of being nagged and ill-treated by Vernacci, who, besides, accused him to Giovanni Benci of being intractable and neglecting his job as cashier. Benci wrote Tornabuoni a scolding letter, which the latter promptly sent to Piero di Cosimo, his brother-in-law, denying the charges and maintaining that he was diligent in doing his job. Tornabuoni was sure that his devotion to duty would be vouchsafed for by Roberto Martelli, who happened to be in Florence.[87]

Vernacci gave vent again to his antipathy for Tornabuoni in a letter dated June 21, 1453, and addressed this time to Giovanni di Cosimo. In it Vernacci complained because one of the factors, Alessandro di Bernardo de' Bardi, a very capable and well-behaved lad, who had been for eight years in the service of the Rome branch, resigned because he had been denied promotion and had not received due recognition for his services. Vernacci, with a sly reference to Tornabuoni, pointed out that such unfair treatment was contrary to the policy of the Medici company which used "to advance anyone doing well without regard to family connections."[88] "While advancement was based entirely on merit," Vernacci went on, "everyone was satisfied."

In the spring of 1458, while Martelli was absent, Vernacci was in charge of the Rome branch. Tornabuoni complained to Piero that Vernacci, resenting his promotion, was interfering and preventing him from performing his new duties. Piero apparently wrote Vernacci, who replied that he treated Tornabuoni with the utmost kindness.[89] In a letter to Cosimo, Vernacci even enlarged upon this statement and asserted that Tornabuoni and he were like two brothers. Of course, Tornabuoni denied this and wrote that relations were strained instead of cordial, and that Vernacci was more antagonistic than ever.[90] What was really at stake was the eventual succession to Roberto Martelli. Such clashes between personalities often exist in modern corporations and not infrequently interfere with the efficient conduct of business, because people who should cooperate are more interested in plotting each other's downfall. The conflict between Vernacci and Tornabuoni shows that the problem is not new and that human nature has been much the same over the centuries.

When Martelli died early in 1464, the maggiori did not provide immediately for his replacement and left matters in abeyance for several months.[91] The death of Cosimo on August 1, 1464, led to further post-

ponement of a decision. In the meantime, Vernacci became acting manager again and the conflict with Tornabuoni grew more acute than ever.
On March 23, 1465, Tornabuoni wrote bluntly to Piero de' Medici that
the situation was impossible, that Vernacci was trying to read all his
mail, and had a character incompatible with his own, and that he,
Tornabuoni, would rather resign than continue to serve under Vernacci.[92]
This argument was decisive: Piero could not very well abandon his
brother-in-law and Vernacci was sacrificed.

According to his catasto report for 1470, Vernacci joined the firm of
Rinaldo della Luna e Fratelli, bankers in Florence and Rome.[93] When
it went bankrupt, Vernacci lost most of his money and was left in a
rather precarious financial condition. As he had friends among the
papal courtiers, he was able to start his own bank in May 1469. It had
no capital, but rested exclusively on the confidence of Vernacci's friends
who were willing to place their money on deposit. He was still in business
in 1474 and had Benedetto Salutati as a partner.[94]

The new contract between Piero di Cosimo and Giovanni Tornabuoni
was not actually signed until October 1465, although it was retroactive
and went into effect on the preceding 25th of March.[95] It was to last five
years. As usual, it put all the burden of the management on the shoulders
of Tornabuoni, who was given authority to trade, to deal in exchange,
and to serve the Apostolic Chamber in the expedition of bulls and other
matters. Since there was no invested capital, Tornabuoni was expected
to do business only with the credit of the Medici (*godendosi il credito
nostro*) and was granted a share of one sixth in the profits. His duties
were carefully defined: he was not allowed to hire or dismiss any factors
and was to carry out Piero's will and instructions, that is, Piero's policy.
In short, while the wording may be different from the other partnership
agreements, the substance is the same. It is probable that this contract
was extended again and again, since Giovanni Tornabuoni remained at
the head of the Rome branch for thirty years until 1494 when the Medici
were driven out of Florence. During this long period, he managed to
retain the trust of Piero, his brother-in-law, and later of Lorenzo, his
nephew.

From 1465 onward, no accounting records have survived, and we have,
therefore, to rely on the extant letters addressed by Tornabuoni to the
maggiori. The material is unfortunately incomplete. Besides, medieval
business letters are wordy and somewhat obscure, so that their interpretation is not always easy. One little detail may not be entirely devoid of
importance: in writing to Lorenzo de' Medici, Giovanni Tornabuoni,
who was his maternal uncle, uses the familiar *tu* (thou) to 1481 and then
shifts to the more formal *voi* (you). Of course, Lorenzo is always addressed
as Your Magnificence (*La Magnificenza Vostra*), but this form of address

was already in use in Piero's time and during Cosimo's last years. Do these changes reflect the gradual ascent of the Medici from the status of simple citizens and merchants to that of sovereign princes? And did even Giovanni Tornabuoni see fit to recognize their eminence and to observe the new rules of etiquette?

In contrast to the earlier period during which the Rome branch was the main pillar supporting the Medici Bank, the period from 1464 to 1494 is one characterized by increasing difficulties, especially after 1478, the year of the Pazzi conspiracy, which threatened to topple the Medici Bank. Not only did the irate Pope (Sixtus IV) sequestrate all the property of the Medici in Rome, but he took advantage of the crisis to repudiate the debt of the Apostolic Chamber to their bank and to cancel the alum contract. When the Medici returned to Rome in December 1481, one of the first tasks of Giovanni Tornabuoni was to reach an agreement with the Apostolic Chamber about past indebtedness.[96] His claims were recognized, but their repayment was slow and painful, as the pressing needs of the papal treasury prevented the Chamber from being punctual about meeting maturities or carrying out promises.[97] Since there was no money, Giovanni Tornabuoni was offered stocks of alum, which were difficult to sell now that this trade was again in the hands of the Genoese and the Medici branches in Bruges and London had been liquidated.[98]

To appeal to the Pope was of little use, since he was unwilling to overrule his advisors. In a mood of disillusionment, Giovanni Tornabuoni wrote to Lorenzo the Magnificent: "His Holiness is more prone to ask favors than to fulfill obligations." [99] In another letter he makes the rather shocking statement that the Pope (Innocent VIII) "instead of being liberal and magnanimous is as rigid as a corpse." [100]

It is not that Innocent VIII was unfavorably disposed toward the Medici, since Lorenzo's daughter, Maddalena, married the Pope's son, Francesco Cibò, and the Pope made Giovanni de' Medici (later Leo X) a cardinal at the age of fourteen. But the renaissance popes — Martin V is said to have been the last medieval pope — were spendthrift and nepotic and found themselves involved in incessant and costly wars as a result of their tortuous foreign policy. In the spring of 1487, however, Innocent VIII was trying to economize by disbanding mercenaries and curtailing sumptuary expenses. Giovanni Tornabuoni was already rubbing his hands and wrote to Lorenzo with unjustified optimism: "If the Pope is well off, we are, too." [101] Rather the reverse was true, for the papacy was living beyond its means and the days of surpluses and comfortable reserves belonged definitely to the past. So it was with the Medici Bank. Gone were the days of easy profits.

When he sent the balance sheet of the year 1476, Florentine style, to the maggiori, Giovanni Tornabuoni reported that profits had been few because of interest charges and losses on bad debts.[102] The next year, he proposed to write off all dubious claims and to set aside generous reserves in order to have no unrealistic dreams about the magnitude of the profits.[103] After the Pazzi conspiracy (1478), things went from bad to worse. It is a marvel that the Medici were able to survive this blow and to retain the confidence of depositors and creditors.[104] The crisis past, Tornabuoni noted with satisfaction that there had been no alarm, but he urged that measures be taken to clear the balance of doubtful assets and to reduce the burden of interest charges.[105] In 1483 he congratulated himself because, thank God, there had been no loss during the previous year; he expressed the hope that the Rome branch would be profitable henceforth and that a settlement with the Apostolic Chamber would be reached, but thus far he had only received encouraging words and no deeds.[106] If only the alum problem were solved, everything would be fine and the Rome branch would prosper again.[107]

Alas! Giovanni Tornabuoni was entertaining illusions and his hopes were soon dashed to pieces. In April 1488, he had to admit that results of the preceding year were again unfavorable, because of excessive charges and interest payments incurred in connection with the papal treasury in the Marches and advances to Francesco Cibò.[108] The following year, Tornabuoni struck a more hopeful note, but he advised taking precautions against the impending bankruptcies of Carlo Martelli and of the Spannocchi, so that the Medici, "after escaping so many perils, would not be drowned in a glass of water." [109]

The partnership agreement concluded at this time between Lorenzo the Magnificent and Giovanni Tornabuoni suggests that the latter was still hopeful about keeping the Rome office afloat but was much less sanguine about the prospects of the Lyons branch. At any rate, the contract shows that he was eager to abandon that sinking ship. Although it is dated July 22, 1487, the contract really went into effect the preceding 25th of March, the first of the year according to Florentine style.[110]

As usual, no capital is given, but it is stated that the old partnership, just terminated, owed 18,783 cameral ducats to the new. Shall we conclude therefrom that liabilities already exceeded assets by this amount? If so, even the Rome branch was virtually bankrupt. In any case it was hoped that, because assets were underestimated, the liquidation of the old partnership would not leave a deficit. Any surplus, after paying off the debit of 18,783 ducats, was to be divided as follows: three fourths to Lorenzo de' Medici and one fourth to Giovanni Tornabuoni. The surplus, however, was not to be paid out to the partners but was to remain invested in the new partnership, in order to make it more affluent (per tenerla più grassa), that is, to increase its working capital. Profits of the new partnership were to be shared in the same proportion.

The Rome branch would receive all the profits, if any, of the accomanda of Naples. It was understood that Giovanni Tornabuoni would assume the burden of the management upon the usual terms.

What is significant about the contract of 1487 is not so much the agreement regarding Rome as two unusual clauses regarding Florence and Lyons. Apparently Giovanni had become a partner both in the Florentine Tavola and in the Lyons bank a few years before. He was now so anxious to pull out, if possible without damage to himself, that a special clause was inserted in the partnership agreement of 1487. According to it, Lorenzo the Magnificent allowed his uncle to withdraw as a partner in Florence and in Lyons, released him from any further liability, and promised him to repay, without deduction for losses, both his share in the capital of the Florentine Tavola and the 3,000 écus which he had invested in the Lyons branch. The latter, especially, was at this time in very bad shape because of the mismanagement of Lionetto de' Rossi. Giovanni Tornabuoni had always distrusted him and had never approved Sassetti's policy with regard to the Lyons branch; it is likely that he became a partner reluctantly to please Lorenzo. Now Tornabuoni was unwilling to bear the consequences of policies which he had opposed. Whether his agreement with Lorenzo was legal is a question which specialists on the history of commercial law will have to decide. Today a partner would not be able to evade so easily his liability.

After 1487 Giovanni Tornabuoni spent most of his time in Florence and left the management of the Rome branch to his nephew, Onofrio, or Nofri, di Niccolò Tornabuoni. In 1492 correspondents were expected to honor bills of exchange made out by these two and by Leonardo Bertolini and Donato Tornabuoni.[111]

The Rome branch was still alive in 1494, but it was gasping for breath. How much is Giovanni Tornabuoni responsible for letting the state of affairs come to such a pass? This is a difficult question to answer. It is certain that he was to a degree the victim of circumstances and that the maggiori did not always take his advice or involved him in unsound credit transactions for political or family reasons. Such were, for example, the loans to the Orsini and to Francesco Cibò.[112] It is also certain that Giovanni Tornabuoni was not a man of outstanding abilities or of great vision. His horizon was limited by the narrow confines of the counting-house and he could not see the broader aspects of economic problems. Moreover, he was impulsive and inclined to overlook difficulties, as in the case of the alum monopoly, where he did not foresee the impact and ramifications of his policies. He complained, for example, about the failure of Bruges or London to remit but overlooked entirely transfer difficulties. He failed to see that the alum contracts made him more and more dependent upon the Apostolic Chamber and the state of papal finance.

Giovanni Tornabuoni did not always cooperate. Yet, he complained easily about others, such as Tommaso Portinari, whom he found difficult to deal with.[113] His quarrels and outbursts lowered, undoubtedly, his prestige with the maggiori. On the other hand, there is no question about his honesty. After 1478 he tried to retrench but was dragged willy-nilly into new ventures. His devotion to the Medici is unquestionable. In a letter dated November 29, 1487, about the renewal of the partnership contract, he writes Lorenzo: "I have God in heaven and Your Magnificence on earth." [114] This was probably not abject flattery.

In 1494, when the Medici lost power, Giovanni Tornabuoni went into partnership with his son Lorenzo to take over the Rome branch and concluded an arrangement with the new government about the equity in the business of the exiled family. As it turned out, the Medici were debtors rather than creditors and the new regime was glad to let the Tornabuoni settle the matter.[115] In 1497 Lorenzo Tornabuoni was tried and beheaded for participating in a plot to restore Medici rule, but his father, Giovanni, fortunately did not live to witness this tragedy.

There is no sign that Giovanni Tornabuoni had any part in the intellectual movement of the Renaissance, that he was a collector of books or antiques, or that he was a connoisseur in painting or sculpture. Nevertheless, he followed the example set by the Medici, by Francesco Sassetti, and other managers of the Medici Bank and commissioned Ghirlandaio to paint frescoes: first, on the wall of the chapel in the church of Santa Maria sopra Minerva in Rome, where Giovanni's wife, Francesca di Luca Pitti, was buried in 1477, and later, in the Tornabuoni chapel behind the main altar of Santa Maria Novella in Florence. The latter are regarded as the artist's masterpiece. In two of the panels, the donor, Giovanni Tornabuoni, and his deceased wife are portrayed kneeling in adoration, as was customary in this period.[116] Giovanni's portrait does not convey the impression of a forceful personality but of a man who conformed to conventions and was a follower rather than a leader. This was the great shortcoming of Giovanni Tornabuoni as a business man.

X

MEDICI ESTABLISHMENTS IN ITALY: THE TAVOLA IN FLORENCE AND THE FONDACO IN VENICE

1. FLORENCE

As we have seen in Chapter Two, a distinction should be made between the central office of the Medici Bank as a whole and its Florentine establishment, or Tavola. The first was situated in the *scrittoio,* or counting room of the Medici palace, and its staff included the general manager, with a small number of assistants and secretaries; the second was located in via Porta Rossa, in the heart of the business district, two steps from the public square which today still bears the name of Mercato Nuovo. It is because of the Tavola that the Medici are called *tavolieri in Mercato Nuovo* in contemporary records.[1] It is also because of the Tavola, which was a local bank, that the Medici were required to enroll as members of the Arte del Cambio.

The Tavola, in other words, was the Florentine subsidiary of the Medici Bank. As such, it was a separate legal and economic entity, whose status the entries in the libri segreti make absolutely clear. An example will illustrate this point: in 1408, Florentine style, profits amounted to 1,779 florins 13s. 11d. affiorino. After setting aside 279 florins 13s. 11d. aff. as a reserve for bad debts, the remaining 1,400 florins were allotted as follows: one seventh, or 200 florins, to Giuliano di Giovanni di ser Matteo, manager of the Tavola, and six sevenths, or 1,200 florins, to Giovanni de' Medici and Benedetto de' Bardi jointly, that is, to the two partners who controlled the concern as a whole with all its branches and subsidiaries. Giuliano, the libro segreto states explicitly, was nostro compagno, or "our partner," but he was partner only in the Tavola and, unlike Giovanni di Bicci or Benedetto de' Bardi, he did not share in the profits of any other Medici enterprise.[2]

Since the Tavola was a local bank, it engaged in money-changing, accepted demand deposits, and undertook to make payments by transfer for its customers. Thus Rosso di Giovanni di Niccolò de' Medici, a distant relative, had an account with the Tavola and drew on it to satisfy his creditors.[3] The Tavola, however, did not confine its activities to local banking; it also engaged in the import and export business and dealt extensively in bills of exchange. Thus, on November 8, 1415, the Tavola sold a bill of 200 florins, payable in Barcelona, to Lazzaro Bracci, an importer of Spanish wool. Since he had no account with the Tavola, he paid for the bill through his own bankers, Massaiozzo di Giglio e Fratelli.[4] Unfortunately, the extant records do not cast any light on the procedure followed in making settlements between a debtor and a creditor who were customers of two different banks. There are also no documents indicating to what extent polizze (checks) were displacing the transfer order given by word of mouth.[5] Most probably this innovation met with resistance, and polizze were used only as substitutes whenever a depositor, for one reason or another, was unable to go in person to the bank.

Only fragments of the records of the Tavola have survived the destructive action of time: a few folios, stained black by fire, of the ledger for the year 1460; three *ricordanze di cambi,* recording bills receivable and payable, and covering the years 1440, 1455, and 1477; and two complete balance sheets attached to the Medici reports for the first (1427) and the

TABLE 41. STATEMENT OF ASSETS AND LIABILITIES OF
THE MEDICI'S FLORENTINE TAVOLA, JULY 12, 1427

Assets

Explanation	Number of Items	Amount f.	s.	d.	aff.
Debit balances in the quaderno di cassa (cash book):					
Cash on hand..........................	1	4,223	0	0	
Other Medici companies.................	3	11,087	21	4	
Partners' drawing and private accounts......	3	2,891	0	1	
Goods in stock.........................	2	12	16	7	
Sundry accounts receivable...............	60	4,055	19	7	
Subtotal of quaderno di cassa.........	*69*	*22,269*	*28*	*7*	
Debit balances in general ledger (*libro rosso* G):					
Goods in stock.........................	4	3,509	18	4	
Other Medici companies.................	7	6,102	25	3	
Correspondents in other places, excluding Medici subsidiaries.......................	13	4,913	10	4	
Loans to government agencies..............	2	3,689	1	10	
Partners' drawing and private accounts......	8	8,424	8	8	
Sundry accounts receivable...............	90	35,804	8	7	
Subtotal of general ledger...........	*124*	*62,443*	*15*	*0*	
Debit balances in *libri di ricordanze* F and G:					
Debts arising from sales of silk and wool.....	19	4,910	6	2	
Debit balances in libro segreto:					
Folco d'Adoardo Portinari................	1	423	17	11	
Rome branch (*i nostri di Roma*).............	1	10,000	0	0	
Total........................	214	100,047	9	8	

Source: ASF, Catasto No. 51 (Leon d'Oro, 1427), fols. 1162–1168ᵛ.

third (1433) catasto. Perhaps the latter are the most satisfactory for giving an over-all picture of the Tavola's business. They have their shortcomings, however. A major stumbling block is that medieval bookkeepers did not classify and condense their data when drawing up balance sheets. Hence, such statements do not give the information which a modern accountant would expect.

Each balance sheet is a lengthy document covering several folios tied together to form a booklet. The earlier balance, of 1427, lists 214 items on the debit, or assets, side and 155 items on the credit, or liabilities, side.[6] Since it is not practical to publish this material *in extenso,* the data have been condensed and are presented in summary form in Table 41.

TABLE 41 (Continued)
STATEMENT OF ASSETS AND LIABILITIES OF
THE MEDICI'S FLORENTINE TAVOLA, JULY 12, 1427

Liabilities

Explanation	Number of Items	f.	s.	d.	aff.
Credit balances in the cash book (quaderno di cassa):					
Sundry accounts payable....................	47	3,880	26	0	
Credit balances in the general ledger (*libro rosso* G):					
Partners' private accounts..................	7	3,790	1	5	
Other Medici companies..................	12	47,411	17	2	
Correspondents in other places, excluding Medici subsidiaries......................	6	6,717	23	1	
Sundry accounts payable..................	57	13,489	3	2	
Subtotal of general ledger............	*82*	*71,408*	*15*	*10*	
Credit balances in *libro di ricordanze* F and *libro delle mandate* G:					
Credits arising from purchases of woolen cloth and silk fabrics.........................	20	2,355	25	7	
Credit balances in the libro segreto:					
Corpo (capital):					
Giovanni de' Medici e Ilarione de' Bardi...	1	10,500	0	0	
Folco d'Adoardo Portinari..............	1	1,500	0	0	
Sopraccorpo (undistributed profits)...........	1	2,938	4	7	
Accrued salaries.........................	1	280	0	0	
Reserve for bad debts....................	1	630	4	9	
Venice branch (*i nostri di Venegia*)..........	1	4,000	0	0	
Subtotal of libro segreto...............	*6*	*19,848*	*9*	*4*	
Total liabilities and net worth........	..	97,493	18	9	
Excess of assets over liabilities........	..	2,553	19	11	
Total........................	155	100,047	9	8	

Notice that this so-called balance sheet does not really balance and that there is an excess of assets over liabilities of more than 2,500 florins, because the bookkeeper either made errors or, more likely, did not adhere strictly to the principles of double entry. In any case, this excess probably represents undivided profits.

A superficial analysis of the figures presented in Table 41 discloses three major facts. First of all, the Tavola emphasized banking rather than trade, since goods in stock were only a small fraction of total assets. As was to be expected, it imported into Florence wool and silk and exported woolen cloth and silk fabrics bought from local lanaiuoli and setaiuoli. Second, the Tavola tapped the resources of other Medici companies, chiefly the Rome and Venice branches which, together, were creditors for nearly 35,000 florins (Table 42). If this situation is representative, and it probably is, one must conclude that Florentine banking relied heavily on outside capital, which was then reinvested in local trade and industry. Third, cash on hand barely exceeded 4,000 florins against liabilities, mostly short term, amounting to approximately 80,000 florins. This is not more than 5 percent. Although one might be tempted to consider such a cash reserve as inadequate, one should not forget that, in an emergency, the Tavola would have the support of the vast private resources, including liquid funds, of the Medici family. The puzzling fact is that it was quite common among Florentine bankers and merchant-bankers to operate with slender cash reserves.[7] This policy made such firms vulnerable and may explain the collapse of Florentine banking during the severe business depression which crippled the Italian economy during the last two or three decades of the fifteenth century.

Thorough analysis of medieval balance sheets is hampered by the fact that they are arrays of figures and names, usually without any meaningful description of the items listed as assets or liabilities. The balance of the Florentine Tavola is no exception to the general rule. Nevertheless, it is possible to make a few comments. First of all, there is no question about the correctness of the figure of 12,000 florins representing the capital of the Tavola.[8] In addition, net worth included undistributed profits. The balance sheet also shows that provision was made for accrued wages and expected losses on bad debts. Whether these reserves were adequate, it is impossible to decide.

Goods in stock included chiefly Spanish and Italian raw silk with the exception of one odd item described as "a unicorn's horn" (*un chorno di liochorno*) and appraised at the respectable sum of eighty-four florins. It was undoubtedly either the tusk of a narwhal or the horn of a rhinoceros. The Medici presumably hoped to sell this museum piece to a despot collecting curiosities or charms against being poisoned. Silk was not the

TABLE 42. BALANCES OF OTHER MEDICI COMPANIES WITH THE TAVOLA OF
FLORENCE, JULY 12, 1427

	f.	s.	d.	aff.
Credit balances:				
Venice branch....................................	9,313	22	7	
Rome branch....................................	24,735	9	8	
Woolshop with Taddeo di Filippo..................	698	2	5	
Florence, *ragione vecchia* (preceding partnership).......	1,544	8	11	
Total................	36,291	14	7	

	florins	s.	d.				
Deduct debit balances:							
Geneva branch: Michele di Ferro e							
Giovanni d'Amerigo Benci........	484	13	9				
Cosimo e Lorenzo de' Medici e							
Ilarione de' Bardi..............	1,586	1	3				
Shipment of specie for account of							
Rome branch...................	10,000	0	0	12,070	15	0	
Total................				24,220	28	7	

Source: Same as Table 41.

only commodity in which the Medici dealt. Most of the wool imported
by the Tavola was presumably for the account of foreign correspondents.
Such items, of course, would not appear in the balance sheet until the
goods received on consignment were sold, when proceeds would be credited to the consignor's personal account. This is probably why the largest
item standing to the credit of a foreign correspondent is an amount of
over 3,600 florins due to the firm, Totto Machiavelli e Ubertino de' Bardi
& Co. of London, which sent large consignments of wool to be sold in
Florence.

The heading "partners' drawing and private accounts" covers, as the
title suggests, money withdrawn by members of the Medici family and
other partners for their own use. The two brothers, Cosimo and Lorenzo,
have several accounts in their private name. Only once is the purpose
indicated: *per il muramento di San Lorenzo* (for the building of San
Lorenzo), obviously an account to which were charged all expenses connected with the rebuilding of the Medici's parish church and burial place.

Why certain accounts appear in the general ledger and others in the
so-called quaderno di cassa is not quite clear. Apparently only temporary
accounts found shelter in the quaderno di cassa. A good example is the
account opened to Michelozzo and Donatello, sculptors, for the tomb of
Cardinal Rinaldo Brancaccio.[9] The debit balance of this account, it is
certain, does not represent money owed to the Tavola by these two

famous sculptors but advances paid to them for the completion of the Cardinal's funeral monument and eventually chargeable to the estate, as the Medici were the executors of Brancaccio's will.

The second balance sheet bears the date of May 31, 1433, a few months before the two Medici brothers, Cosimo and Lorenzo, were sent into exile by the ruling oligarchic clique.[10] It was a time of crisis and turmoil. Although peace had ended the disastrous and prolonged Lucchese war (May 10, 1433), there was little rejoicing: the mounting burden of debt was straining public finances to the breaking point, business was suffering from a slump, and political factions were preparing themselves for a showdown. Cosimo, in his report for the third catasto (May 1433), draws a gloomy picture of the financial condition of the Florentine Tavola which, he claims, had lost 10,000 florins in 1431 and 1432, because of aid given to the hard-pressed Commune and because of adjustments occasioned by the death of Ilarione de' Bardi, the general manager, who had been associated with the Medici for nearly forty years (1397–1433).[11] As a result, Cosimo points out, the Tavola had been running into debt and borrowing "by exchange" up to 40,000 florins. The poor man concludes his statement with the plea that the tax officials consider his plight and grant him relief commensurate with his losses and sacrifices.

Of course, in order to reduce his assessment Cosimo was apt to exaggerate the wretched condition of the Tavola and the extent of his losses. It would be wrong, however, to conclude therefrom that there was no truth in his statements. The balance sheet attached to his catasto report corroborates his contentions and shows that there existed indeed a liability of 32,720 florins 17s. 10d. aff. "for money taken up by exchange" (danari tolti a chambio), that is, for funds raised by selling bills of exchange on Venice and Rome, presumably. In addition, the Tavola owed 1,281 florins to Costantino and Antonio di Branca and 1,616 florins to Andrea de' Pazzi for cambium ad Venetias sine literis, an expensive form of borrowing.[12] One may object that the figures in the balance sheet of 1433 were perhaps manipulated. But this argument lacks cogency, since the entries in the second libro segreto (1420–1434), a source above suspicion, prove that the Tavola suffered serious losses in 1432 and 1433.[13] Furthermore, in the next libro segreto (1435–1450) there is no record until 1440 of any distribution of profits among the partners, which suggests that it took several years for the Tavola to recover from the blow.[14]

The balance sheet of 1433 confirms that the Tavola relied on the Rome and Venice branches to supply it with part of its capital. Folco d'Adoardo Portinari, the manager, died in May 1431 and was replaced by Lippaccio di Benedetto de' Bardi, the son of Giovanni di Bicci's first partner. Bardi contributed 2,000 florins for his share in the capital, which

6. Giovanni Tornabuoni, manager of the Rome branch, 1465–1494, first from the left, with other members of the Tornabuoni family

7. Portinari Chapel, Church of Sant'Eustorgio, Milan

was thus increased from 12,000 to 12,500 florins. On the other hand, the heirs of Folco Portinari did not receive his share of 1,500 florins, which was retained to take care of possible losses for which he was responsible as a partner with unlimited liability.

Unlike the financial statement of 1427, the balance of 1433 has assets nearly equal to liabilities: there is a small discrepancy of f.52 3s. 1d. on a total of more than 150,000 florins, but this is certainly due to an error in casting the balance rather than to lack of understanding of elementary principles of double-entry bookkeeping.[15] One small item is an amount of 15 florins charged to the sculptor Michelozzo Michelozzi (c. 1396–1472) and accompanied by the annotation *sono perduti,* which means that the debt was uncollectible. It is not explained why.

No financial statements for the Tavola of a date later than 1433 have been located thus far in the Florentine archives. It is, therefore, impossible to give precise information on the financial condition of the Tavola during the remaining sixty years of its existence.

The first manager of the Tavola, or banco di Firenze, was Giuliano di Giovanni, who had entered the service of the Medici on December 20, 1400, as a simple clerk, at a salary of 48 florins per annum. Because of his outstanding ability, he was rapidly advanced and his salary was gradually raised to reach 100 florins in 1406.[16] The next year, it is stated in the libro segreto, Giuliano, although still a factor, was being treated as if he were a partner and he received a salary — or should it be called a stipend? — of 200 florins.[17] In 1408 he was admitted as a full-fledged partner entitled to one seventh of the profits made by the Tavola.[18] What happened to him in 1409? His name suddenly vanishes from the records, so he must either have died or left the service of the Medici.

No suitable successor was found immediately, but some of the responsibilities of manager were apparently delegated to Niccolò di Baldassare Buoni, a younger brother of Gentile, who for a very short time had been one of the maggiori of the Medici Bank. In any case, Niccolò Buoni was better paid than any of the other clerks and drew a salary of 100 florins.[19] Whether he was not very capable or not very good at bargaining, it was only in 1417 that he was promoted to the rank of partner and granted a share of one seventh in the profits of the Tavola.[20] Within three years, he severed his connection with Giovanni di Bicci's company to join the rival firm of Niccòla and Cambio de' Medici, Messer Vieri's sons, a move which he probably regretted later.[21]

During the period from 1398 to 1420 covered by the first of the extant libri segreti, the profits of the Tavola never rose to impressive figures but hovered around an average of 1,150 florins for the share of the senior partners (Table 8). Between 1410 and 1416, while Niccolò Buoni was in charge of the Tavola, profits dropped far below this average in certain years. Thus, in 1410 they fell to 671 florins and in 1415 they went down to 588 florins.[22] Of course, the manager is not necessarily to blame, and the decline in profits may have been due to slack business or other circumstances beyond his control.

In 1414 the clerical staff of the Tavola numbered eight (Table 43). There would not have been room for many more in the narrow quarters on via Porta Rossa.

The place of Niccolò di Baldassare Buoni was taken by Folco d'Adoardo Portinari (c. 1386–1431), mentioned earlier, who was a brother of Giovanni Portinari, the manager of the Venice branch. The partnership agreement, concluded on October 16, 1420, is still extant.[23] Perhaps it should be stressed that this is a contract distinct from the one concluded between the maggiori, Cosimo and Lorenzo de' Medici, on the one hand, and Ilarione de' Bardi on the other hand. This latter contract is also extant but it bears a different date: September 1, 1420.[24] Moreover, it states that the partnership's purpose is to engage in banking and trade both in and outside Florence (*in Firenze e fuori di Firenze*), while the agreement with Folco Portinari is strictly confined to the activities of the bank located in the city of Florence (*alla ragione e traffico di Firenze*). This is further evidence that the two contracts involved separate entities, but one of them was dependent upon the other. As a junior partner, Folco Portinari occupied a subordinate position in relation to the maggiori and was subject to the usual restrictions. He was expected to dedicate himself entirely to the management of the common venture and to carry out the decisions made by the senior partners. In reward for his services, he was entitled to one fifth of the profits, although he had supplied only one eighth, or 1,500 florins, of an aggregate capital of 12,000 florins. The remaining 10,500 florins represented, of course, the

TABLE 43. CLERICAL STAFF OF THE TAVOLA IN FLORENCE, 1414

Name of Clerk	Salary per Year			
	f.	s.	d.	aff.
1. Niccolo di Baldassare Buoni	100	0	0	
2. Agnolo di Zanobi de' Bardi, cashier	50	0	0	
3. Vieri di Bartolo de' Bardi	40	0	0	
4. Giovanni di Nettolo Becchi	40	0	0	
5. Bonsignore di Niccolo Spinelli	24	0	0	
6. Carlo di Marco degli Strozzi	20	0	0	
7. Gherardino d'Antonio Gherardini	20	0	0	
8. Giovanni d'Antonio de' Medici, garzone (office boy)	15	0	0	
Total of payroll	309	0	0	

Source: ASF, MAP, filza 153, no. 1, fols. 76 and 93.

contribution of the parent company consisting of the two Medici brothers and Ilarione de' Bardi, their partner and general manager.

The partnership contract with Folco Portinari remained in force through 1427 without any substantial change. From 1428 onward, a new partner was added: Lippaccio di Benedetto de' Bardi, who presumably became assistant manager. He was to receive one sixth of the profits and Folco's quota was reduced at the same time from one fifth to one sixth.[25] This was hardly fair to Folco, but Lippaccio de' Bardi, being a nephew of Ilarione, the general manager, was probably a protégé of the maggiori.

Under the leadership of Folco Portinari, the Tavola flourished and profits increased markedly. From October 21, 1420, to March 24, 1425, that is, during a period of four years and five months, gross profits amounted to f.8,590 4s. 4d. aff., which corresponds to an average of nearly 2,000 florins a year.[26] After making provision for accrued wages, unpaid interest on deposits, and bad debts, an amount of 6,800 florins was made available for distribution among the partners. In accordance with the articles of association, one fifth, or 1,360 florins, went to Folco Portinari and the remainder, 5,440 florins, to the Medici and Ilarione de' Bardi. In the next two years, gross profits went up to an average of about 3,200 florins per year or an aggregate of f.6,393 12s. 5d. aff. After reserving 900 florins for accrued wages and bad debts, there remained f.5,493 12s. 5d. to be distributed among the partners.[27] Folco received f.1,098 19s. 10d. for his share, so that he was making over 500 florins a year. The peak was reached in 1428, when f.3,652 7s. 3d. aff. were divided as follows: Folco Portinari and Lippaccio de' Bardi each f.608 20s. 6d. aff., and the maggiori f.2,434 24s. 3d. aff.[28] Profits declined greatly in the next three years.[29] In 1432, there was a loss, but Folco Portinari was already dead, leaving Lippaccio de' Bardi to steer the boat through the gathering storm.[30]

Folco Portinari, according to the catasto records, belonged to an impoverished branch of an ancient and distinguished family that traced descent from another Folco, the father of Beatrice, immortalized by Dante. Folco d'Adoardo was manager of the Tavola for so few years that he did not have an opportunity to build up a fortune. When he died on May 28, 1431, at the age of forty-five, he left several minor children, among them three sons: Pigello aged ten, Accerrito four, and Tommaso three.[31] Since Folco was well liked by the Medici, it is said that Cosimo took care of the orphans and had the sons brought up in his own household. All three followed in the footsteps of their father and eventually entered the service of the Medici Bank. All three were destined to become branch managers: Pigello and Accerrito in Milan and Tommaso in Bruges. This association with the Portinari brothers was to have disastrous consequences for the Medici because Accerrito's and Tommaso's reckless management of their branches involved the Bank in staggering losses which were a major factor in its downfall.

As a result of the events of 1433 and 1434 — Cosimo's exile, recall, and assumption of power — some major changes were made in the management of the Tavola. Lippaccio de' Bardi, the protégé of the maggiori, was dropped, perhaps because they held him responsible for the losses of the Tavola, but much more likely because he played a dubious rôle during Cosimo's and Lorenzo's enforced absence. This was the end of the long-standing and close association between the Medici and the Bardi, a connection that was not confined to business, since Cosimo's wife, Contessina, belonged to a branch of this famous Florentine family. It is true that her father was only a very distant cousin of her husband's business associates, and that he was not a merchant but a landlord who bore the title of Count of Vernio, from a village in the Apennines between Prato and Bologna.

Who took Lippaccio's place and what happened to the Tavola is rather difficult to figure out, because the records are confused and full of gaps. In any case, no new partnership was set up for some time. It is likely that the Tavola was in such a bad shape that no one was willing to run the risk of assuming its management on a profit-sharing basis. The Medici, therefore, were forced to supply the necessary operating capital to keep the Tavola afloat. For a reason which is far from clear, the funds were supplied through mysterious channels by way of the Venice branch. For several years to come, the Tavola thus became an annex of that branch. This was still true in 1451 (Table 14). Why these arrangements were made is another puzzle. Perhaps it was a precautionary move to forestall sequestration in case the Medici should again be driven out, not a remote possibility, as the numerous plots to overthrow them prove.

For the time being, the management of the Tavola was entrusted to Giovanni d'Amerigo Benci, one of the two men selected by Cosimo to succeed Ilarione de' Bardi. At any rate, a *ricordanze di rimesse e tratte,* a book recording remittances and drafts, has an entry mentioning that, up to 1440, only Giovanni Benci had the power to commit the Tavola and to make out bills of exchange in its name.[32] Correspondents were instructed to honor no drafts if they were written in a hand other than his. On October 15, 1440, and not sooner, the same power was granted also to Giovanni di Baldino Inghirami (c. 1412–1454), who became Benci's assistant in the management of the Tavola. This Giovanni Inghirami had been a factor in the Rome office at least from 1435 onward. He had followed the papal court to Bologna and Ferrara in 1437 and 1438.[33] In 1439, before being called to Florence, he was earning 80 ducats per annum.[34] After his transfer, Giovanni Inghirami remained on a fixed salary until 1445, when he was given a share of one eighth in the profits of the Tavola.[35] He continued to serve the Medici Bank until his death in the spring of 1454.[36]

There is no record of the Tavola making any profits from 1434 to 1440. According to the entries in the libro segreto, the first profitable year was 1440, when an amount of 2,200 florins was written to the credit of the maggiori.[37] In the next two years further progress was made, but the Tavola again showed a loss in 1443, because money was borrowed at interest in order to relend it to the Florentine government, presumably at a lower rate.[38] In 1444 the situation improved again, and the Tavola continued to yield a profit through 1448. Since there is no record of any distribution of profits during 1449 and 1450, when the libro segreto stops, one must assume that there were no net earnings available after making due allowance for bad debts and other unforeseen contingencies.[39] The data are presented in summary form in Table 44, which shows that, during the eleven years from 1440 to 1450, inclusive, distributed profits amounted in the aggregate to f.26,277 19s. 9d. aff., or an average of close to 2,400 florins a year. This is not a bad record, since no profits were available for distribution in three out of the eleven years.

When Giovanni di Baldino Inghirami died in 1454, he was succeeded as manager by his brother, Francesco (1414–1470), about whose background nothing is known except that around 1447 he was employed by the Tavola as bookkeeper.[40] Probably, Francesco became a partner at the same time. In any case, the quaderno di ricordanze di cambi in 1455 lists the following as having the power to obligate the Tavola and to issue bills of exchange: Giovanni d'Amerigo Benci, Francesco di Bal-

TABLE 44.   NET PROFITS OF THE FLORENTINE TAVOLA FROM 1440 TO 1450

Year	Total			Share of the Medici			Share of Giov. Inghirami			Remarks
	f.	s.	d.	f.	s.	d.	f.	s.	d.	
1440	2,200	0	0	2,200	0	0	.....	..	..	Inghirami did not
1441	3,449	22	3	3,449	22	3	.....	..	..	share in the profits
1442	3,957	12	7	3,957	12	7	.....	..	..	until 1445.
1443	.....	..	..	.....	..	..	.....	..	..	Loss.
1444	2,994	16	6	2,994	16	6	.....	..	..	
1445	3,275	26	5	2,866	12	3	409	14	2	Inghirami's share
1446–47	8,000	0	0	7,000	0	0	1,000	0	0	was one eighth.
1448	2,400	0	0	2,100	0	0	300	0	0	
1449–50	.....	..	..	.....	..	..	.....	..	..	No record.
Total....	26,277	19	9	24,568	5	7*	1,709	14	2	

* This total corresponds to the figure given in Table 17.
Source: ASF, MAP, filza 153, no. 3.

dino Inghirami, and Tommaso di Giovanni di Tommaso Lapi (1421–c. 1486).[41] The latter was still a factor in 1460 but is mentioned as a partner by 1462 in the records of the Arte del Cambio.[42]

In his report for the catasto of 1457–58, Francesco Inghirami makes it clear that he is a partner of the Medici, but only in their Florentine partnership of the Bank, or Tavola.[43] He claims his share in the capital to be 400 florins. As Cosimo in his report declares that his investment in the corpo is 5,600 florins, one must conclude that the total capital of the Tavola was not more than 6,000 florins in February, 1458.[44] This figure seems low; it is probable that Cosimo scaled down the amount of his business investments. If so, his partners had to do the same and to report figures agreeing with his; otherwise the fraud would have been detected immediately by the tax officials.

There is extant a fragment of ninety-seven folios of the Tavola's ledger for the year 1460, Florentine style.[45] It confirms what we know from other sources. Officially Cosimo was no longer a partner and the Tavola was supposedly directed by his sons, Piero and Giovanni, and his nephew Pierfrancesco with the effective assistance of Francesco Inghirami. It will cause no surprise that the ledger entries show the interests of the Tavola to be very diversified. The Tavola did not confine its activities to money-changing and local banking; it also dealt in bills of exchange and traded extensively in commodities, either on its own account or for that of correspondents who gave commission to buy or sell goods. These correspondents were outsiders as well as Medici branches in other places. As might be expected, the Medici silk and woolshops had current accounts with the Tavola, which handled all the remittances they received from abroad and all the payments they made for imports of wool or raw silk. Thus the Tavola charged the Medici Bank in Milan with 2,445 florins which were credited to Piero de' Medici & Co., setaiuoli, undoubtedly in payment of a consignment of silk fabrics.[46] Besides business firms, the Tavola had as customers persons in all walks of life from cardinals and princes to ordinary Florentine citizens who were not always among the well-to-do.[47] In the Middle Ages, having a bank account was far more common than economic historians have been willing to admit.

One line of activity perhaps deserves special mention: the Tavola dealt extensively in shares of the Monte Comune (public debt). On March 25, 1460, it held such shares for a nominal value of 105,950 florins and a market value of only 18,358 florins. The shares were greatly depreciated and were worth only 21 percent of their nominal value, because interest payments were so irregular and depended so much upon contingencies of war and peace. As the Commune decided to pay the interest due in May, 1460, the shares in the Monte improved somewhat in value and the price went up in the next few months from below 21 percent to 24 percent and even higher. This rise apparently induced the Tavola to take advantage of the opportunity and to sell half of its holdings at a slight profit.[48]

On time deposits, the Tavola paid either 6 or 7 percent interest. Some of these funds were reinvested at 12 percent with the Milan branch.[49] Another source of profits was exchange dealings with the fairs of Geneva. These transactions took the form of dry exchange and adumbrated what later came to be called cambio con la ricorsa. They consisted in buying gold marks payable in Geneva at one of the fairs and reconverting these marks into florins at the fair's end. A profit resulted because the reconversion rate was usually higher than the purchase rate. Thus the Tavola in March, 1460, bought bills payable at the August fair at 69 florins per mark and made its returns at 73¾ per mark, thereby making a profit of 4¾ florins per mark in six months. As the fair approached, the rate usually went up: by July 1460, the rate of exchange for the August fair had risen from 69 to 70½ florins per mark.[50] What else is necessary to prove the presence of the rate of interest? The fair of All Saints in 1460 also turned out to be profitable because of a wide margin between exchange and re-exchange.[51]

The ledger entries confirm that Bruges had trouble in settling debts in Italy. Remittances to Florence by the Bruges branch of the Medici Bank were rarely made directly but were routed either via London or via Geneva.[52] Lucca, it seems, had ceased to be a banking place because the Tavola sent specie by special courier to transmit to Girolamo Guinigi in Lucca the proceeds of remittances sent by the Lucchese firm, Michele Arnolfini & Co. in Bruges.[53]

One should not assume that the *commenda* and the *societas maris,* so popular in the twelfth and thirteenth centuries, had fallen into disuse by 1460. Contracts of this type concluded for the duration of a single voyage survived within the framework of more permanent relationships, such as the terminal partnership. The Tavola's ledger gives us the example of an *incetta di Barberia* (a venture with Barbery) which was entrusted to Bongianni Gianfigliazzi, who carried with him on the galleys a shipment consisting of silver (both ingots and coin), cheese, and oil and brought back gold and Spanish raw silk.[54] Part of the goods were entrusted to Gianfigliazzi in the form of a commenda which entitled him to only one fourth of net proceeds. For the rest, he had a share of one half, typical of the societas maris. The capital invested in the commenda alone amounted to about 6,053 florins di suggello. In addition, Gianfigliazzi delivered to his partners their half of 3,000 florins in gold bullion and raw silk worth another 1,500 florins.

Such ventures were by no means an exception. In 1477, a year of dearth, Lorenzo and Giuliano de' Medici, in order to do their duty

toward the public (*per fare il debito nostro verso il pubrico*), sent
Schiatta di Francesco Bagnesi to Tunis for the purpose of purchasing
grain, if possible, in barter of Florentine and English cloth.[55] Un-
fortunately, we do not know how this venture turned out or even whether
Bagnesi was able to secure an export license from the Hafsid ruler of
Tunis.

The ledger of 1460 reveals that, in addition to Francesco Inghirami,
there were at least four clerks on the staff of the Florentine Tavola: Francesco di Bartolomeo Baldovini and Tommaso di Giovanni Lapi, who
both received a salary of 66⅔ florins per year, Guidetto di Francesco
Guidetti who earned 55 florins, and Giuliano di ser Simone whose salary
is unknown but who was apparently the cashier.[56]

Since money-changing was one of the major functions of the Tavola,
the cash showed regularly a surplus which was counted about every two
months. Profits from this source totaled 916 florins 12s. 8d. a oro during
the year 1460, Florentine style, but were less important than commissions
(*provvigione*) and earnings on exchange by bills, which came to the sum
of 1,982 florins 1s. 3d. a oro.[57] Expenses (*spese di banco*) during the same
period amounted to 156 florins 12s. 10d. a oro. After taking into account
a few other small adjustments due to errors and the like, banking yielded
a profit of 2,746 florins 9s. 1d. a oro during 1460. Although the extant
fragment does not disclose the total of trading profits, it gives the impression that the Tavola was still in a prosperous state.

From 1460 onward, there is a great gap in the extant records of the
Medici Bank; no accounts and no business correspondence relating to the
Florentine Tavola are available. One therefore has to rely mainly on
the records of the gild, which give factual information but shed no light
on business problems. Unlike the writer of fiction, the historian needs
documentary evidence to depend on. If it is lacking, he has no story to
tell.

According to the libro di compagnie of the Money-changers' Gild, the
Tavola continued to be operated through 1469 by Francesco Inghirami
as manager and Tommaso Lapi as assistant manager.[58] Whether Inghirami ever assumed part of the duties of general manager seems rather
doubtful. Not having been abroad, he was ill-acquainted with the problems of foreign branches. However, it is possible that he helped with
some auditing and other jobs of a more or less routine character. A
major change was made in 1470 when Tommaso Lapi withdrew as
partner and was replaced by Francesco d'Antonio Nori and Lodovico
d'Antonio di ser Tommaso Masi. Inghirami died soon thereafter; his post
was undoubtedly filled by Francesco Nori (1430–1478), who was a trained
administrator, inasmuch as he had been at the head of the Lyons branch

before being expelled from France.[59] Masi came to the Medici after having been for several years with Ugolino and Antonio Martelli, their representatives in Pisa (Table 26).

As is well known, Francesco Nori was a victim of the Pazzi conspiracy. He was slain on April 26, 1478, in the Cathedral of Santa Maria del Fiore while covering the escape of Lorenzo the Magnificent from the assassins. Even the gild records are incomplete for this period, but there is no doubt that Masi filled the void left by Nori's untimely death. In 1482 Masi declared to the gild authorities that the Tavola of the Medici had as partners: Lorenzo the Magnificent, Francesco di Tommaso Sassetti, Masi himself, and Giovanni d'Orsino Lanfredini. Membership did not change the next year, but there was a complete turnover in 1484. According to the gild records, the new partners were: Lorenzo the Magnificent, his uncle, Giovanni di Francesco Tornabuoni, manager of the Rome branch, and Agostino di Sandro Biliotti.[60] The latter, who had been a factor for the Medici in Naples, was probably the managing partner in lieu of Lodovico Masi, who was either dead or had chosen to retire. Why Sassetti dropped out is hard to guess. Certainly not because he was demoted, since he continued to be general manager. In fact, Lorenzo de' Medici wrote to Lionetto de' Rossi in Lyons, on July 3, 1484, that Francesco Sassetti retained the same "reputation" and authority as ever, notwithstanding his no longer being a partner in the banco of Florence.[61]

By 1487 conditions had changed for the worse: the only partners of the Tavola were Lorenzo the Magnificent and Giovambattista Bracci. The latter had no capital invested in the business but was awarded one tenth of the profits "by way of salary to compensate him for his exertions." [62] The end was near, anyhow. Bracci was to be the last manager of the Tavola. He was still in charge when, in 1494, the Medici lost power and went into exile. All their property, including the Tavola, was sequestrated.

The end of the Medici Bank was also the end of the famous Arte del Cambio. One bank after another had disappeared. By 1495 membership had dwindled to the point that it was no longer possible to fill the gild's offices. The records ceased to be kept. This crisis was not confined to Florence but extended to banking all over Europe. In Bruges the money-changers' tables, which had grown into deposit banks, were strangled by a hostile monetary policy and driven out of business.[63] The story was repeated in Venice where, in 1499, all the *giro* (transfer) banks save one were engulfed in a wave of bankruptcies.[64] Only in Spain did the medieval transfer and deposit banks weather the storm.[65] What caused this general crisis remains a mystery. It is probably one aspect of the

disruption of European trade at the end of the fifteenth century. Florentine banking reflourished after 1500, but on a new basis, under a new
form, and with new names.

2. VENICE

In 1398, shortly after setting up headquarters in Florence, Giovanni di
Bicci de' Medici and his partner, Benedetto di Lippaccio de' Bardi, decided to open an office in Venice. As related in an earlier chapter, this
was only an experiment and no separate partnership was formed at
first, but the new office was a subbranch of Rome managed by a factor,
Neri di Cipriano Tornaquinci.[66] The profits made by Venice during the
first three years (1398, 1399, and 1400) are included in those made by
Rome and do not appear as a separate item in the libro segreto of the
Medici Bank.[67]

On March 25, 1402, a real branch was created and a capital of 5,000
ducats, Venetian currency, or 5,225 florins, Florentine currency, was
assigned to it. Within a few months, this capital was increased to 9,000
florins, as the Medici provided another 2,775 florins and Neri Tornaquinci put up 1,000 for his share.[68] According to the latter's reports, net
profits for 1401 — the last year before the partnership — amounted to
1,720 florins, which were written to the credit of Giovanni di Bicci and
Benedetto de' Bardi.[69] The next year (1402), after making the usual deductions for accrued salaries and bad debts, it was estimated that net
profits amounted to an even 3,000 florins, of which Neri received one
fourth, or 750 florins, for his share. The remaining 2,250 florins were
duly divided between Giovanni di Bicci and Benedetto de' Bardi.[70]
These last entries were later cancelled when it was discovered that Neri
had been reporting fictitious profits and that there actually was a loss.[71]
He also reported profits for the next three years (1403–1405), but these
were never credited to the partners' accounts.[72]

As Neri's doings aroused suspicion, an investigation was made, and
all sorts of frauds were uncovered. Among other things, as was mentioned in Chapter Three, Tornaquinci had extended credit to South Germans and Poles without securing approval of the senior partners and
had been unable to collect what was due. To replenish his depleted
working capital, he had then borrowed at 8 percent and, finally, he had
deceived his partners by reporting nonexistent profits and concealing the
losses on bad debts.[73] It goes without saying that Neri's contract was
terminated forthwith. An audit of the books disclosed that bad debts
amounted to the sizable sum of 13,403 florins. In addition, salaries were
in arrears to the extent of 683 florins, so that the aggregate loss exceeded
14,000 florins. After deducting the profits made in 1403, 1404, and 1405,
there still remained a net loss of 5,356 florins.[74] The Medici sued Torna-

quinci before the *Sei di Mercanzia* (the mercantile court), and obtained judgment against him.[75] The sale of his property, a house in town and a share in a farm at Careggi, brought about 1,000 florins, a sum which did not suffice by far to indemnify the senior partners for the losses sustained. Neri Tornaquinci went to Cracow and was able to collect some of the outstanding claims, but he neglected to remit any of the proceeds to his former partners.[76] His dishonesty did not bring him luck: he failed to earn a living in Poland and fell into such poverty that Giovanni di Bicci, hearing about his plight, had the decency to send him a few florins.[77]

Despite this disheartening experience, the Medici did not withdraw from Venice, but formed a new partnership on April 25, 1406, with Giovanni di Francesco da Gagliano as manager. The capital was set at 8,000 ducats, of which he supplied 1,000 ducats. The style remained as before, "Giovanni de' Medici & Co.," and the manager was granted one fourth of the profits.[78] The Venice branch prospered under the new management: profits amounted to 1,670 florins in 1406, 2,100 in 1407, 2,200 in 1408, and 2,594 19s. 10d. aff. in 1409, so that the senior partners received 6,423 florins 21s. 9d. aff. for their share and Giovanni da Gagliano, 2,140 27s. 1d. aff. (Table 45).[79]

When the contract expired in 1410, at the end of three years, it was renewed for four years with some slight changes on three points: (1) Giovanni was allowed to come to Florence once a year without asking for permission from the senior partners; (2) he was given a free hand in deciding how much to invest in trade and how much to invest in banking; (3) he was given a yearly allowance of 100 Venetian ducats prior to any distribution of profits.[80] At that time, there were only five factors employed in the Venice branch: Andrea di Lancelotto, Checho (Francesco) d'Antonio de' Medici, Francesco Bueri, a brother of Gherardo who settled in Lübeck, Antonio di Lazzaro Bertini, Giovanni Bruscolini.[81] Returns continued to be more or less satisfactory: during the six years extending from March 25, 1410, to March 24, 1416, net profits available for distribution amounted to an aggregate of 8,533 florins, or an average of approximately 1,400 florins per annum (Table 45). Of course, some years were better than others; profits went up and down, and there may even have been losses in one or two years between 1410 and 1413, which might explain why the profits of four years have been lumped together. On the average, profits were less during the later period (from 1410 to 1416) than during the earlier years (from 1406 to 1410) of Giovanni da Gagliano's management.

On May 30, 1416, the capital of the Venice branch was increased by £300 groat or 3,000 ducats, Venetian currency, by transferring undistributed profits to the credit of the capital account.[82] Giovanni da

Gagliano must have died soon thereafter, and rather unexpectedly, because before the year was over the Medici appointed Giovanni d'Adoardo di Giovanni di Manetto Portinari (1363–1436) to be manager of the Venice branch at an annual salary of 150 florins.[83] This is one of the rare instances in which the maggiori did not promote one from the ranks but selected an outsider. Perhaps none of the factors in the service of the Venice branch had enough experience or the necessary qualifications for

TABLE 45.   NET PROFITS OF THE VENICE BRANCH FROM THE BEGINNING OF 1406
TO THE END OF 1415 (FLORENTINE STYLE)
(All amounts are in florins di suggello of 29s. aff.)

Year	Number of Years	Total			Share of Giovanni da Gagliano			Share of the Senior Partners		
		f.	s.	d.	f.	s.	d.	f.	s.	d.
1406	1	1,670	0	0	417	14	6	1,252	14	6
1407	1	2,100	0	0	525	0	0	1,575	0	0
1408	1	2,200	0	0	550	0	0	1,650	0	0
1409	1	2,594	19	10	648	12	7	1,946	7	3
1410–1413	4	3,400	0	0	1,150	0	0*	2,250	0	0
1414	1	2,500	0	0	700	0	0	1,800	0	0
1415	1	2,633	6	8	733	6	8	1,900	0	0
Total	10	17,097	26	6	4,724	4	9	12,373	21	9

* From 1410 onward, Giovanni da Gagliano was entitled to an allowance of 100 florins prior to his share of one fourth in the remaining profits.
Source: MAP, filza 153, no. 1, fols. 55, 56, 57, 67, 68, 88, and 91.

the job of manager. Giovanni Portinari was no longer a young man, since he was fifty-three years old. He had been a resident of Venice for many years and had been in business there since 1384, at first with Niccolò Diotifeci and later, after 1406, with Matteo di Bartolo Tanaglia.[84] Giovanni remained a manager pro tempore until March 25, 1419, when the maggiori decided to regularize his status by making him a partner.[85] In the meantime, returns continued to be satisfactory. After setting aside something for unpaid salaries and bad debts, profits credited to the maggiori amount to 1,400 florins in 1416, 2,000 in 1417 and 1418 combined, and 1,200 in 1419.[86]

As a result of the death of Benedetto de' Bardi and the withdrawal of Giovanni di Bicci from active leadership, the agreement concluded with Giovanni d'Adoardo Portinari in 1419 did not remain in effect for more than a year. It was replaced by a new contract signed on October 23, 1420, but retroactive to March 25, 1420. This agreement probably did not alter the articles already in effect: capital was kept at the reduced figure of £800 groat, or 8,000 ducats, Venetian currency, of which 7,000 ducats were furnished by the maggiori and the balance, or 1,000 ducats, by

Giovanni Portinari. To reward him for his services, the latter was granted a share of one fourth in the profits. The only major change was that the partnership was henceforth styled "Cosimo e Lorenzo de' Medici & Co." instead of "Giovanni de' Medici & Co." [87]

During the period from 1420 to the end of 1434, the Venice branch continued to yield an adequate return and the maggiori had every reason to be satisfied with financial results. As Table 46 indicates, in fifteen years they received an aggregate amount of 24,453 florins for their share in the profits after deducting reserves and the share of the junior partners. This total corresponds to an average of 1,630 florins. Since the capital invested by the maggiori amounted to 7,000 ducats, or slightly less than 8,000 florins in Florentine currency, this average represents a return of more than 20 percent, which is good but not spectacular for a time in which the commercial rate of interest fluctuated between 12 and 15 percent.

Up to 1428 Giovanni Portinari was the only junior partner. Since he was close to sixty-five years, it is probable that he delegated more and more authority to his assistant and confined himself more and more to supervisory activities and to what is called today policy-making, that is, the formulation of general rules to be followed in the conduct of business. Under those circumstances, the maggiori probably considered it advisable to give more incentive to Giovanni's assistant by admitting him as a partner and giving him a share of one eighth in the profits, after deducting the usual reserves for bad debts and accruals. The remaining balance was then divided between the maggiori and Giovanni Portinari in the proportion of three to one. [88]

The new partner was Lotto di Tanino Bozzi from La Scarperia (1387–c. 1457) who changed his name from Bozzi to Tanini. He had been in the service of the Venice branch since 1414 or 1415 and had given evidence of executive ability. Lotto had to mark time and to wait before becoming branch manager until 1435, when illness forced Giovanni Portinari to retire at the age of seventy-two. [89] He was still at the head of the Venice branch when the Serene Republic offered asylum to Cosimo de' Medici.

According to the one surviving balance sheet, prepared for the catasto of 1427, the Venice branch emphasized trade a great deal more than the other Medici establishments (Table 47). To keep track of its commodity transactions, it kept a separate ledger called *libro di mercatantie*. As usual, the consignment trade was very important: the Medici in Venice sold saffron for a correspondent in Aquila (Abruzzi); furs, amber, linen, and tin vessels for Gherardo Bueri in Lübeck; says from Wervicq (*panni di Vervi*) for an Italian resident in Bruges; and English cloth for the Tornabuoni of London. [90] They traded in Spanish wool from Valencia

TABLE 46. PROFITS OF THE VENETIAN BRANCH FROM 1420 TO 1434 (FLORENTINE STYLE)

(All amounts are in Venetian pounds groat except the last column which is in florins di suggello of 29s.)

Year	Total (£ s. d.)	Reserves (£ s. d.)	Net Profits (£ s. d.)	Share of Lotto Tanini (£ s. d.)	Share of Giovanni Portinari (£ s. d.)	Share of Maggiori: Venetian Currency (£ s. d.)	Share of Maggiori: Florentine Currency (f. s. d.)
1420	172 3 8	...	...	...	...	...	...
1421	154 2 3	...	...	...	...	...	...
1422	154 14 3	...	...	...	...	...	...
1423	129 18 0	...	...	...	...	...	...
1424	189 10 11	...	...	...	...	...	...
1425	800 9 1	210 9 1	590 0 0	...	147 10 0	442 10 0	4,678 14 6
1426	191 3 10	43 0 0	227 11 4	...	56 17 10	170 13 6	1,825 0 0
	79 7 6						
1427	195 18 7	20 0 0	175 18 7	...	43 19 8	131 18 11	1,432 13 0
1428	210 9 4	64 14 11	155 14 5	...	38 18 2	116 16 3	1,254 21 0
1429	215 14 0	40 0 0	175 14 0	21 19 3	38 8 8	115 6 1	1,244 13 10
1430	259 0 0	29 0 0	230 0 0	28 15 0	50 6 3	150 18 9	1,624 21 8
1431–1432	775 15 11	94 13 9	681 2 2	85 2 9	148 19 10	446 19 7	4,850 0 0
1433–1434	No record	No record	No record	No record	No record	No record	7,870 0 0
	2,727 18 3	501 17 9	2,236 0 6	135 17 0	525 0 5	1,575 3 1	24,779 26 0
Deduct: later adjustments.........							326 0 5
Total......							24,453 25 7*

* This total corresponds to the figure given in Table 11.

Source: ASF, MAP, filza 153, no. 2, fols. 38, 43, 46, 52, 59, 67, 77, and 83.

and in malmsey from Crete. Foreigners being excluded from any participation in the trade with the Levant, the Medici branch in Venice purchased spices, above all pepper, and cotton from Venetian importers.

As pointed out before, dealing with Germans was avoided ever since the discouraging experiences of Neri Tornaquinci; the Medici were cautious and preferred to deal with Florentine merchants whose credit standing they knew or with Venetians who had the reputation of being reliable. To lend to Germans who were not permanent residents in Venice but stayed from time to time at the *Casa dei Tedeschi* (German House) was too dangerous a game, for one never knew whether they would come back to pay their bills. To pursue debtors in Germany involved great trouble and expense for meager results, since it was impossible to obtain speedy justice from local courts.[91]

Since the Medici dealt extensively in bills of exchange, it is not surprising that accounts with correspondents abroad were major items both on the assets and on the liabilities side of the balance sheet. The firm Ubertino de' Bardi of London owed as much as £500 groat, or 5,000 ducats, to the Medici branch in Venice. Another sizable item was an amount of £229 groat, or 2,290 ducats, due from the firm Galeazzo Borromei & Co. of Bruges. The size of these balances again seem to indicate that credits tended to pile up in Bruges and London because of transfer difficulties, since it was not always possible to arrange wool shipments to Italy. In 1427 the Medici did not yet have branches in Bruges and London and were represented there by correspondents.

The Medici branch had relations with the local *banchi di scritta* (transfer and deposit banks), but they did not maintain sizable balances with these institutions. Neither did the Medici branch overdraw to any great extent.

Deposits made by outsiders were less important in Venice than in Rome but still represented a fair amount, equal to invested capital if not larger. It is possible that the item of £109 groat, or 1,090 ducats, standing to the credit of the Magnificent Lord Lorenzo degli Attendoli should be regarded as a time deposit. One of the depositors was Monna Bartolomea di Gherardo from Bologna: she had 4,000 ducats, a small fortune, placed on deposit a discrezione. Another was Giovanni Bianchi dalla Magna (from Germany), who had only 1,050 ducats put out at interest. All in all, the total of deposits on which discrezione was paid exceeded perhaps £930 groat, or 9,300 ducats. The owners' equity, capital plus undivided profits and reserves, amounted to approximately 13,500 ducats. Permanent resources, equity plus long-term liabilities combined, thus reached the total of nearly 23,000 ducats, or well over 50 percent of recorded assets. This percentage would indicate a rather sound financial condition if these assets were really liquid, which we do not know.

TABLE 47. BALANCE SHEET OF THE MEDICI BANK IN VENICE, 1427
(All amounts are in Venetian pounds groat)

Assets

	£	s.	d.	p.
Debit balances in the ledger (*libro rosso G*):				
Correspondents abroad (19 items)	2,246	12	9	4
Other Medici companies	599	7	6	6
Advances to members of the staff (6 items)	218	10	8	23
Deposits with other Medici branches	184	5	9	10
Bad debts (8 items)	127	6	0	4
Sundry accounts receivable	92	11	8	29
Merchandise accounts	45	5	0	24
Household and office furniture	42	13	6	16
Expenses during the year 1426 (*spese di casa*)	31	6	5	20
An error in the preceding ledger	2	5	2	9
Transfer banks (*banchi di scritta*)	40	13	6	1
Subtotal	*3,630*	*18*	*3*	*18*
Debit balances in libro di mercatantie:				
Sundry accounts receivable (12 items)	476	15	3	3
Debit balances in the quaderno di cassa:				
Sundry accounts receivable	93	18	6	6
Petty expense	2	19	3	0
A horse for the bank's use	1	8	6	0
Cash on hand	0	16	0	0
Subtotal	*99*	*2*	*3*	*6*
Total	4,206	15	9	27
Error in casting the balance	7	17	1	26
Total	4,214	12	11	21

Source: ASF, MAP, Catasto No. 51 (Leon d'Oro, 1427), fols. 1187–1190.

There were no fixed assets except household furniture and a saddle horse, representing in all £44 groat (440 ducats). Of course, one wonders why the Medici branch needed a saddle horse in Venice; one would think a gondola to be of greater use. It is likely that the horse was kept in a stable in Padua and used for trips on the mainland.

As a rule, the Medici forbade their branch managers to underwrite insurance, but this policy did not apply to the Venice branch, probably because the Rialto was a center of the underwriting business — the other was Genoa. In fact, the Venice branch did some underwriting but was never very active in this line of business, which was still confused with gambling and gave rise to many frauds. At any rate, insurance was an unimportant source of profits, as the balance sheet of 1427 reveals.

The clerical staff was very small. According to the balance sheet, it included only four factors in addition to the branch manager: Lotto di

TABLE 47 (Continued)
BALANCE SHEET OF THE MEDICI BANK IN VENICE, 1427
(All amounts are in Venetian pounds groat)

Liabilities

	£	s.	d.	p.
Credit balances in the ledger (*libro rosso G*):				
Correspondents abroad (15 items).....................	1,062	3	1	23
Time deposits (4 items)...............................	722	7	11	8
Lorenzo degli Attendoli (time deposit?).................	109	6	11	0
Creditors for merchandise sent on consignment...........	61	4	1	24
Sundry accounts payable (7 items)....................	30	11	11	0
Banking profits (*avanzi di banco*)......................	28	14	11	13
Credit balance of a wool account......................	8	1	6	20
Insurance (premiums collected?)......................	7	7	6	0
Overdrafts with transfer banks (3 items)................	6	9	5	11
Commission on exchange and insurance.................	1	7	5	0
Florentine consulate for consular fees...................		5	11	6
Subtotal....................	*2,038*	*0*	*10*	*9*
Credit balances in the libro di mercatantie:				
Sundry accounts payable (13 items)....................	556	15	1	25
Credit balances in the quaderno di cassa:				
Sundry accounts payable (27 items)...................	172	9	6	8
Credit balances in libro segreto:				
Cosimo and Lorenzo de' Medici, capital account.........	700	0	0	0
Giovanni d'Adoardo Portinari, capital account...........	100	0	0	0
Giovanni Bianchi, German, deposit a discrezione.........	105	0	0	0
Undistributed profits 1425 and 1426....................	320	7	15	25
Reserves for bad debts...............................	221	19	1	18
Subtotal of libro segreto.......	*1,447*	*7*	*5*	*11*
Total..................	4,214	12	11	21

Tanino Bozzi (he is still called giovane although he was forty years old), Antonio di Niccolò Martelli, Francesco d'Antonio de' Medici, a distant relative, and Paolo di Domenico Guasconi. The Medici in Venice also used the service of a female slave, Maria Rossa. As stated in a preceding chapter, slavery was quite prevalent in all the seaports along the Mediterranean. Venice, in particular, was a regular slave market.

After Cosimo's return from exile (September, 1434), there was a complete review of all existing contracts. In Venice, Giovanni Portinari retired and a new agreement was made with Lotto Tanini (Bozzi) and Antonio di Niccolò Martelli, manager and assistant manager, respectively. The senior partners supplied 7,000 ducats and the two managing partners each 500 ducats, making a total of 8,000 ducats.[92] Although these two contributed the same amount, Lotto Tanini, because he had the more responsible position, received one sixth of the profits and Antonio

Martelli, only one eighth. The remainder, seventeen twenty-fourths, went to the maggiori. The contract was to last five years, from March 25, 1435, to March 24, 1440. The other clauses are those customary in Medici contracts. Both Lotto Tanini and Antonio Martelli were bound to reside in Venice and to attend *al governo di detto traffico,* "to the government of the said traffic."

During this period, from 1435 to 1440, the Venice branch was a nursery of future branch managers.[93] There was, first of all, Bernardo Portinari (1407–1455), the son of Giovanni, who was recalled from Venice in 1436 and sent to Bruges to establish there a branch of the Medici Bank. Next was Francesco Davizi, who in 1440 was paid £30 groat for five years of service, which means that his annual salary was sixty ducats. He was still employed by the Venice branch in 1448 but seems to have left shortly thereafter to go into business for himself. Perhaps he was discontented because he was not promoted to a post of greater responsibility. Third was Alessandro Martelli (1417–1465), who, despite his age — he was only twenty-three in 1440 — was already earning fifty ducats a year. He was destined in later life to become manager of the Venice branch. The fourth was Pigello Portinari (1421–1468), who served in Venice until 1452 when Cosimo entrusted him with the task of establishing a new branch in Milan. The fifth was Angelo Tani (1415–1492), who was getting forty ducats in 1440 and within the next two or three years left Venice to join Bernardo Portinari in Bruges. After serving as factor in London for some time, he eventually became manager of the Bruges branch. The records also mention a servant, about whom we know nothing more than his first name, Cristofano.

At this time, around 1438, the Medici branch in Venice sold cloth which was sent on consignment by the firm Bernardo d'Antonio de' Medici, cloth manufacturers. This Bernardo d'Antonio was only a distant relative of Cosimo's but a close friend, being a strong supporter of the Medici party. In a letter dated August 9, 1438, the Venice branch expressed regret that the cloth sent on consignment was selling so slowly although no efforts were spared to find buyers.[94] A later letter dated June 27, 1442, contains an account relating to the sale of five pieces of cloth which brought an amount of £22 9s. 10d. groat, Venetian currency. After deducting expenses (carriage charges, brokerage, customs, and commission), net proceeds were £21 13s. 9d. groat, or about 42 ducats per bolt of cloth, which is a rather good price.

During the next six years, from March 25, 1435 to March 24, 1441, the Venice branch continued to yield handsome profits, which reached a peak in 1439 when they surpassed 8,000 ducats and equaled the amount of capital, a truly spectacular result. Even after making the customary deductions and paying off the share of the junior partners, the maggiori divided among themselves a total f.27,740 1s. 10d. aff., which on an investment of 7,000 ducats, Venetian currency, or 7,560 florins,

TABLE 48.   PROFITS OF THE VENICE BRANCH FROM 1435 TO 1440
(FLORENTINE STYLE)

Year	Amount in Venetian Currency (Pounds Groat)			Amount in Florentine Currency (Florins di Suggello)		
	£	s.	d.	f.	s.	d.
1435	398	8	9	4,304	0	0
1436	601	12	0	6,497	0	0
1437	685	15	4	7,406	0	0
1438	590	1	1	6,370	0	0
1439	801	0	3	8,650	0	0
1440	767	14	6	8,320	0	0
Total	3,844	11	11	41,547	0	0
Deduct: later adjustments	−225	5	0	−2,394	0	0
	3,619	6	11	39,153	0	0
Deduct: share of Lotto di Tanino, one sixth	−603	14	4	−6,521	23	8
Deduct: share of Antonio Martelli, one eighth	−452	9	11	−4,891	3	6
Share of the maggiori	2,563	2	8	27,740	1	10*

* This amount corresponds to the figure given in Table 17.
Source: ASF, MAP, filza 153, no. 3, fols. 17, 22, 23, and 44.

Florentine currency, represents a return of about 60 percent per annum (Tables 17 and 48). In the next decade, this level was maintained more or less through 1445, but this period of high earnings came to an abrupt end the next year (Table 49). Instead of profits, there were heavy losses in 1446 and 1447 because, a note in the libro segreto explains, an accumulation of bad debts wiped out the existing reserves, absorbed all the profits, and even made a dent in capital.[95] One of the contributing causes of this setback was the failure of the firm Giovanni Venturi e Riccardo Davanzati & Co. in Barcelona. During the last fortnight of July, 1447, bills of exchange amounting to 2,973 ducats were dishonored by this firm and protested by the payees, so that the remitters could take recourse against the drawer, who was in this case the Medici branch in Venice. The flow of unpaid bills continued to pour in through August and September. All in all, the total of protested bills amounted to 8,100 ducats.[96] Drawing on Barcelona was quite normal because the Medici Bank had credit balances there and was able to sell drafts to Venetian importers of saffron and Spanish wool. At that time, Venice had presumably an unfavorable balance of trade with the Aragonese Kingdom, but equilibrium was achieved by means of the triangle, Venice–Bruges–Barcelona, since Bruges had payments to make in Venice and used claims on Barcelona for this purpose.

TABLE 49. PROFITS OF THE VENICE BRANCH FROM 1441 TO 1450
(FLORENTINE STYLE)
(All amounts are in Venetian pounds groat except the last column
which is in florins di suggello)

Year	Total			Share of Lotto di Tanino			Share of Antonio Martelli			Share of Maggiori Venetian Currency			Florentine Currency		
	£	s.	d.	£	s.	d.	£	s.	d.	£	s.	d.	f.	s.	d.
1441	728	1	9	121	6	11	91	0	3	515	14	7	5,633	0	0
1442	840	17	5	140	2	10	105	2	1	595	12	6	6,500	0	0
1443	781	7	9	130	4	7	97	13	6	553	9	8	6,100	0	0
1444–1445	1,281	18	10	213	13	2	160	4	10	908	0	10	10,004	6	0
1446–1447[a]	....	..	..	....	..	..	....	..	..	...	..	..	...	..	..
1448	229	17	8	....	..	..	28	14	8[b]	201	3	0	2,212	0	0
1449–1450	527	11	9	....	..	..	65	19	0[b]	461	12	9	5,130	9	1
	4,389	15	2	605	7	6	548	14	4	3,235	13	4	35,579	15	1[c]

[a] In 1446 and 1447 there were losses and no profits were distributed.
[b] From 1448 onward, this is the share of Alessandro Martelli instead of his brother, Antonio.
[c] This amount corresponds to the figure given in Table 17.
Source: ASF, MAP, filza 153, no. 3, fols. 63, 65, 73, 79, 88, and 90.

Lotto di Tanino Bozzi was apparently away from Venice because of ill-health and the maggiori put all the blame for these occurrences on Antonio Martelli, who was acting manager.[97] As a result, he was "eased out" and "persuaded" to join the firm of his brother Ugolino Martelli in Pisa. A new contract was concluded which made Alessandro Martelli (1417–1465) manager of the Venice branch.[98] He was the youngest brother of Antonio and Ugolino, now partners in the accomanda of Pisa, and of Roberto Martelli, the manager in Rome. The maggiori supplied all the capital (7,000 ducats) of the new partnership; although Martelli invested nothing, his services were estimated as the equivalent of an investment of 1,000 ducats and entitled him to receive one eighth of the profits.

Alessandro Martelli lived up to expectations and was able to put the Venice branch on its feet again. There was a modest profit of 2,300 ducats in 1448 and slightly more in the next two years (Table 49).

Although there is no evidence in the Medici records, it may be taken for granted that the succeeding years were far less profitable. Most probably the Venice branch was unable to operate, not because of any fault of Alessandro's, but because of the war in which Florence and Milan were pitted against Venice and Naples (1451–1454). Even before hostilities really began, the Venetian republic ordered all Florentine merchants to evacuate its territory and seized their goods (May 1451).[99] Cosimo, it may be safely assumed, was not taken by surprise. Books, records, and goods were probably carried to safety before the Venetians had a chance to get hold of them.

After the peace of Lodi (April 1454), activities were resumed with Alessandro Martelli as manager. The maggiori must have been satisfied with his services, because they were willing to renew his contract in 1455, a few months before the death of Giovanni Benci.[100] Capital was raised to 14,000 ducats, of which 2,000 ducats were furnished by Alessandro. His share in the profits also was raised from one eighth to one fifth. A minor innovation was a change in the style which now read: "Pierfrancesco di Lorenzo de' Medici & Co." In trading either with the Levant or with the Ponent, Martelli was allowed to ship in one bottom up to the value of 2,000 ducats on the larger galleys and of 1,000 ducats on the smaller galleys without taking out insurance. Galleys were considered so safe that their cargoes were rarely insured to their full value. Of course, medieval merchants were venturers who were used to taking risks but sought safety in diversification as has been pointed out.

After five years, the contract of 1455 was renewed with practically no changes save that the capital was increased to 15,000 ducats, of which Alessandro promised to supply 3,000 ducats.[101] His share in future profits was set at one fourth. Returns continued to be rewarding. According to a report sent by Martelli to Cosimo, a few weeks before the latter's death, profits amounted to an aggregate of 17,878 ducats in the last three years:[102]

1461	7,082 ducats
1462	5,761 ducats
1463	5,035 ducats

Alessandro Martelli did not outlive Cosimo very long, since he died in the summer of 1465. The existing contract was continued with his heirs for the remaining months of the year or until March 24, 1466, when it expired anyhow.[103]

Venice at this time was able to help other branches: it had a deposit of 4,861½ ducats in Milan which, at the request of the maggiori, was transferred to the Tavola in Florence. Martelli also claimed in a letter addressed to headquarters that he had saved the Geneva branch when its solvency was threatened by a wave of bankruptcies among its customers.[104]

The contract becoming effective on March 25, 1466, was made with Giovanni d'Oddo Altoviti (b. 1422) on the same terms as that with his predecessor.[105] Altoviti inherited a rather difficult situation because of several debtors who owed excessively large amounts. Most of them were merchants belonging to prominent Venetian families, such as the Corner and the Dandolo.[106] Nevertheless, the size of their loans so worried Piero de' Medici that he ordered Giovanni Altoviti to retrench.[107] Following these instructions, the latter also sought to reduce the discrezíone paid to depositors and was not willing to pay more than 5 percent if Alessandro Martelli's heirs wished to leave some of their money on deposit.[108] Whether such a policy was wise or unwise at this juncture is a difficult matter to decide without more information than is available. In any case, there seems little doubt that Giovanni Altoviti lacked Alessandro Martelli's business ability. Nevertheless, one should not forget that the short and inconclusive war between Venice and Florence (1467–1468) caused trade to slacken and the money market to slumber, so that there were no profit opportunities (see Chapter Six). Even so, Altoviti must have lacked initiative and did not impress the maggiori with his resourcefulness. On January 16, 1468, Giovanni Tornabuoni advised Piero to provide "better management" (*buon governo*) for the Venice branch and approved highly of Sassetti's going thither on an inspection tour to see what was wrong and what should be done.[109] Because Sassetti, then general manager, was not the man to take the bull by the horns, he chose the easiest way out and persuaded Piero de' Medici to liquidate rather than to dismiss Altoviti and replace him by a more efficient branch manager. By 1469 the Venice branch was in the process of liquidation. Piero di Cosimo in his report for the catasto of 1470 states that he has no longer any business in Venice.[110]

The liquidation dragged on for some time because of contingent claims and obdurate debtors. The settlement of accounts regarding alum sales with Piero Guidiccioni, among other things, gave rise to all sorts of complications and delays. The Dandolo also caused trouble and were extremely slow in paying off their loans.[111] Then there were difficulties with the heirs of Alessandro Martelli, who were represented by their uncle, Antonio, former manager of the Venice branch.[112] They claimed repayment of Alessandro's share in the capital plus one fourth of all undistributed profits for the years 1464 and 1465 without any deduction being made for assets, such as bad debts, which were worth less than book value.[113] The Medici offered to pay the heirs 7,000 ducats, or even more than the amount claimed, but only after deduction of one fourth on specific uncollectible claims dating back to Alessandro's administration. The Martelli family considered this proposal unfair and bitterly complained of being cheated because they received 1,650 ducats less than expected. After 1494 the Martelli succeeded in making good their claim by petitioning the curators of sequestrated Medici property and thus received some of the spoils against all rules of equity.

The liquidation of the Venice branch was apparently a mistake, because it was re-established in 1471 with Giovanni d'Orsino Lanfredini (1437–1490) as manager.[114] Because of the great gaps in the surviving records, not much is known about the fate of this new venture.[115] It was founded at an unpropitious time when trade was in decay. In any case, it lasted only a few years and a new liquidation took place between 1479 and 1481.[116] In September 1480 Giovanni Lanfredini was recalled to Florence and replaced for a while by Giovambattista Ridolfi, who had been Lanfredini's assistant and was informed about business conditions in Venice.[117] He was probably relieved by Piero d'Antonio di Taddeo, whom Lorenzo sent to Venice in April 1481 "to wind up our affairs" (*per finire quelle nostre cose*), a task which he probably performed by reducing losses as much as possible and by trying to solve all matters remaining in abeyance.[118] History does not record to what extent his mission achieved its purpose.

XI

MEDICI ESTABLISHMENTS IN ITALY:
THE BRANCHES IN NAPLES, MILAN, AND PISA

1. NAPLES

The Naples branch was one of the first established by the Medici Bank. It was founded almost as early as the fondaco in Venice. Already in 1400, Giovanni di Bicci de' Medici and Benedetto di Lippaccio de' Bardi were represented in Naples by Castellano di Tommaso Frescobaldi, "our factor" who died from the plague the same year.[1] As assistant he probably had Adoardo di Cipriano Tornaquinci, who was a brother of Neri Tornaquinci, the first managing partner of the Venice branch from 1402 to 1406.[2] We do not know exactly who was placed in charge of the Naples office after Frescobaldi's premature death. Perhaps it was Accerrito di Adoardo Portinari (b. c. 1362), because his salary of 60 florins exceeded that of any of the other factors.[3] Francesco d'Andrea Barucci was stationed, apparently, in Gaëta where the Medici, at this time, were farming the customs and needed a permanent representative to look after their interests.[4] In any case, on March 24, 1402 (N.S.), the Medici had four factors in Naples and Gaëta: the three already mentioned and Andrea di Pierozzo Ghetti (Table 7).

According to an entry in the first of the libri segreti, Giovanni di Bicci was doing business in Naples not under his own name but under that of his partner; the style of the branch was Benedetto de' Bardi & Co.[5] In the course of 1402, two brothers were sent down from Rome: Jacopo di Tommaso Bartoli, who joined the staff in Naples and received a yearly salary of 60 florins in 1402 and 80 florins in 1403 and 1404, and his brother Giovanni, or Nanni, who was assigned to Gaëta and earned 30 florins in 1402 and 40 florins in 1403 and 1404.[6] Jacopo, who "stays for us in the Kingdom" (*che sta per noi nel Regno*), soon worked his way up to branch manager and in 1405 was given a share of one sixth in the profits;[7] whether the partnership was formalized remains doubtful.

The personnel was rather rapidly increased; at the end of 1404 the payroll includes the following names with indication of yearly salary:

1. Jacopo di Tommaso Bartoli (Naples) .... 80 florins
2. Francesco d'Andrea Barucci (Gaëta) .... no record
3. Adoardo di Cipriano Tornaquinci (cashier in Naples) 60 florins
4. Rosso di Giovanni di Niccolò de' Medici (Gaëta) ... 50 florins
5. Giovanni di Tommaso Bartoli (Gaëta) .... 40 florins

6. Francesco di Giachinotto Boscoli (Naples) .... 35 florins
7. Niccolò di Francesco Cambini (Naples) .... 25 florins.[8]

Boscoli did not stay in Naples very long and returned to Rome where he possibly remained until he participated in 1411 in a syndicate to finance Pope John XXIII (Baldassare Cossa), a syndicate which included the two Medici banks (Giovanni di Bicci and Averardo di Francesco di Bicci), Filippo and Bartolomeo di Giovanni Carducci, and Jacopo del Bene. Later Boscoli became the manager in Rome of Averardo's bank.[9]

During the period from 1397 to 1420 covered by the first of the libri segreti, Naples with Gaëta was the least important of the Medici branch offices, far less important than Rome and even behind Florence and Venice. Aggregate profits of Naples and Gaëta, combined, amounted to 15,944 florins 5s. 10d. aff., or only 10.5 percent of the over-all total of the Medici Bank (Table 8). It is true that Naples always had a hard struggle for existence and that, between 1400 and 1420 there were presumably losses in several years, namely in 1407, 1408, 1410, and 1420. The reason is probably that the volume of trade was not very large because Naples as a trading center had more frequent contacts with Genoa than with Florence. Another factor, which one should perhaps not overlook, is that business conditions were repeatedly upset because of internal strife fomented by rival pretenders to the Neapolitan throne.

The most prosperous year was 1405, when Naples reported gross income amounting to 2,845 florins.[10] After setting aside 445 florins as a reserve and giving Jacopo Bartoli 400 florins for his share, there remained an even 2,000 florins to be divided among the maggiori (Table 50). The following year, net earnings were slightly less: an amount of 1,833 florins 9s. 8d. aff. was allocated to them after the usual deductions.[11] Profits vanished in 1407 and 1408: an entry crediting the maggiori with 3,528 florins of supposed earnings was cancelled later because a check of the books revealed that there were none.[12] On the average, profits barely exceeded 760 florins per annum over a period of approximately twenty-one years extending from 1400 to September 1, 1420. The branch in Naples was relatively prosperous, but the one in Gaëta had losses in most years: it is a wonder that it was not closed sooner.

One item among the profits perhaps calls for brief comment. It concerns the restitution of 142 florins which apparently had been stolen by Niccolò Cambini, cashier of the Naples branch until April 1410. He pretended to have collected this sum from a customer, Martino Iscatono in Naples, but inquiries revealed that this man knew nothing about a debt of 142 florins.[13] The Medici took no further action, since the money was restored voluntarily, probably to relieve a guilty conscience or to obtain absolution.

TABLE 50. Profits of the Medici Bank in Naples and Gaëta
from circa 1400 to September 1420
(All amounts are in Florentine florins of 29s.)

	f.	s.	d.	aff.
1400 to January 1, 1403	1,600	0	0	
1403–1404, Florentine style	2,519	0	0	
1405	2,000	0	0	
1406	1,833	9	8	
1407–1408	Losses			
1409	833	9	8	
1410	No record			
1411–1414	2,467	14	2	
1415–1416	1,300	0	0	
1417–1419	2,400	0	0	
1420	No record			
Restitution of stolen money	142	0	0	
Indemnity for stolen goods	226	20	7	
Later adjustment	137	0	0	
Subtotal	15,458	25	1*	
Farming of customs of Gaëta	485	9	9*	
Total	15,944	5	10*	

* These figures correspond with the data given in Table 8.
Source: ASF, MAP, filza 153, no. 1, fols. 32, 33, 43, 54, 64, 77, 79, 80, 84, 95, 96, and 112.

In 1407 the share of the maggiori in the capital of the Naples branch was 1,000 ounces, Neapolitan currency, equal to 6,426 florins di suggello.[14] When the partnership was dissolved in 1415, this sum was refunded through the Tavola in Florence. At the same time the maggiori put 3,000 florins into an accomanda; the active partners, fully liable, were Jacopo Bartoli and Rosso di Giovanni de' Medici (1377–1429).[15] The latter had been a factor in Naples since 1403; his beginning salary was 50 florins a year, which was increased to 60 florins in 1408.[16] The terms of this contract with Jacopo and Rosso di Giovanni are unfortunately unknown, but it continued until January 1, 1423, when it either expired or ended because of the death of Jacopo Bartoli.

A new accomanda was then concluded with Rosso di Giovanni de' Medici and Fantino di Fantino de' Medici, two distant relatives, as active partners. This contract still exists.[17] According to its stipulations, the Medici brothers, Cosimo and Lorenzo, with their partner, Ilarione de' Bardi, invested 3,200 florins *in accomanda,* beyond which sum they ceased to be liable, in conformity with the rules of the Florentine Mercanzia. The active partners invested together 800 florins: Rosso 300 florins and Fantino 500 florins. Profits were divided half and half between investing and active partners. The latter then shared equally in their half, so that Rosso and Fantino each received one fourth. The other provisions do not deviate from the customary rules.

This contract was to last three years, from January 1, 1423, to January 1, 1426. When it expired, the maggiori decided not to renew it and to liquidate the Naples branch.[18] The liquidation was far from disastrous. The maggiori recovered their initial investment and, in addition, received 684 florins 24s. 2d. aff. for their share in the profits of three years (Table 11). This was a return of about 7 percent on invested capital, which was below the normal return on commercial investments. The maggiori probably decided to discontinue the Naples branch because returns failed to compensate them for rather heavy risks, in view of the disturbed conditions prevailing in the Kingdom of Naples.

What became of Rosso and Fantino de' Medici? The former died within four years (July 31, 1429), according to the chronicle of Buonaccorso Pitti, his father-in-law.[19] As for Fantino de' Medici, he settled in Barcelona as an agent of Averardo's bank and died there in 1429.[20]

From 1426 to 1471 the Medici Bank had no branch in Naples. It was represented, however, by correspondents who handled its business on a commission basis. In 1455 the Medici correspondents in Naples were Filippo Strozzi & Co., Benedetto Guasconi, and Bartolomeo Buonconti (Table 26).

What induced Lorenzo the Magnificent to reopen an office in Naples in 1471 can only be guessed. Perhaps political reasons were not alien to this decision. Lorenzo's manager was Agostino di Sandro Biliotti.[21] No partnership agreement has survived, but it is likely that the bank in Naples was a subsidiary placed under the control of the Rome branch. In any case, it is clear from the Tornabuoni correspondence that the manager in Naples reported to Rome rather than directly to headquarters in Florence.

Biliotti proved to be a poor choice. He was not a good administrator because he was much too lenient in granting credit and allowed customers to borrow beyond the safety limit.[22] After he left Naples in April, 1475, the branch was saddled with frozen credits which absorbed the available resources and thus impaired earning capacity. Also chances of collecting many of the claims were slight, while other claims were likely to involve expensive litigation (the rapacity of Neapolitan lawyers and the venality of judges were notorious).[23]

Biliotti's successor was Francesco Nasi, or Nazi, who had been connected with the Pazzi company as a factor in Geneva and Bruges.[24] He was a man of no mean ability who did his best to reorganize the Naples branch. His task was made more complicated by the financial difficulties which plagued another Medici venture, the accomanda of Apulia, of which Angelo di Piero Serragli was the manager with headquarters at Trani near Barletta.[25]

In the fifteenth century this region of Apulia was one of the granaries of Italy; it also exported all kinds of fruits and foodstuffs to the north and center of the peninsula, especially to Venice. Most of this coastwise trade was presumably in the hands of Venetians and small local merchants who enjoyed a well-entrenched position. The Medici certainly were not successful in ousting them or even in competing with them effectively.[26] By 1477 the accomanda was in bad shape. Perhaps it was set up on too grandiose a scale, since it had factors located in different regional centers: Antonio Scarazzi at Bitanto near Bari, Bernardino Spina at Gallipoli on the Gulf of Taranto, Piero Velluti at Monopoli, Berto Belfradelli at Ostuni, and Niccòla Doitera at Terlizzi near Bari. Coordinating the activities of these men must have been quite a challenge, and Angelo Serragli was probably not equal to the task. According to a balance sheet of February 28, 1478 (N.S.), the accomanda's resources were depleted and the problem was how to stave off a crash.[27] As usual, it was thought that a shot in the arm would save the situation, and appeals were sent out to Florence and Rome. They fell on deaf ears. The Rome branch had already strained its resources to relieve Lyons and Naples. In a letter dated April 19, 1477, Giovanni Tornabuoni had notified his nephew that he would be henceforth unwilling and unable to rush to the rescue of other branches in distress.[28]

At this critical juncture, the Pazzi conspiracy struck another blow at the tottering Medici branches in the Kingdom of Naples. King Ferdinand I (1458–1494) allied himself with the Pope to make war against Florence. Without wasting time, he promulgated, on June 14, 1478, a decree which ordered the sequestration of all Medici property and claims within his dominions.[29] Royal officials impounded the goods stored in Trani and Ostuni (Apulia), occupied the bank building in Naples, and seized the quaderno di cassa; they did not, however, get hold of the other records, so that they were unable to make much headway with the collection of receivables. After the conclusion of peace (March 17, 1479), all the confiscated property was restored; however, it was of little use: the battered Naples branch was in such a plight that it scarcely managed to keep afloat.

Salvage operations were again entrusted to Francesco Nasi, and he performed miracles to save the sinking ship. One of the problems was to effect a settlement with the Court about the balance which was due to the Medici Bank. In this connection, Nasi received support from Antonio di Bernardo de' Medici, the Florentine envoy, who had received instructions from Lorenzo the Magnificent to press this matter and to reach an agreement about the amount of the debt, even though there was no chance of being repaid as long as the Ferrarese war (1481–1484) was raging.[30]

Unpaid creditors caused as much trouble as defaulting debtors. The Venice branch sent one of its factors, Giambattista Ridolfi, to the South, in order to claim payment of 5,600 ducats due from the Naples branch and 3,700 ducats due from Angelo Serragli and the accomanda of Apulia.[31] Branches in distress, by draining the resources of branches that were still prosperous, thus involved all of them in financial difficulties. It is likely that Giambattista Ridolfi's mission was a failure, because neither the Naples branch nor the accomanda in Apulia were in a position to pay off their indebtedness.

The Naples branch was even more indebted to the Rome branch than to the Venice branch. Prospects of repayment to the Rome branch were so poor that Giovanni Tornabuoni was near despair in December 1481, because he had 10,000 ducats of the Rome branch and 7,000 ducats of his own money sunk in the Naples venture.[32]

In the spring of 1483 Francesco Nasi was summoned to Rome for a conference: after his arrival, on March 29, Tornabuoni made the gloomy announcement to Lorenzo de' Medici that, despite all endeavors, there would be a big loss in Naples.[33] A few days later, the second of April, he reported that Nasi and he had gone over the balance sheet very carefully and that the loss was likely to exceed the staggering amount of 30,000 ducats.[34] He proposed to pay the foreign creditors first. For the partners the liquidation was bound to be disastrous, especially for Biliotti, who would be owing a fortune, but it was only fair that he should bear the consequences of his mismanagement.[35] The impulsive Tornabuoni did not ask himself whether Biliotti would be in a position to discharge his obligations and would not try to shift the burden of ultimate liability to the Medici.

In the end, the liquidation of the Naples branch turned out to be much less disastrous than expected at first. The Medici were so satisfied with Francesco Nasi that, beginning with the year 1486, Florentine style, they decided to set up a new company under the style of Francesco Nasi & Co.[36] It did very well, no doubt owing to the talents of its manager. An audit of the first balance sheet, dated March 25, 1487, disclosed that there was no insolvent debtor of any consequence and that no money was borrowed at interest. According to Tornabuoni, Francesco Nasi had every intention of doing even better in the future than he had done in the past. He was given the hope that the Medici might eventually allow him to use their name in the style of the partnership, but this permission was never given.[37]

Nasi died in 1489 shortly after making a trip to Florence. For a few months his company continued to operate under the name of "Heirs of

Francesco Nasi & Co," with Bernardo di Francesco Carnesecchi, apparently a son-in-law of the deceased, as temporary manager.[38]

This provisional arrangement was regularized on March 25, 1490, when a formal partnership contract was drawn up.[39] Bernardo Carnesecchi was retained as manager, but the style was changed to Lorenzo di Giovanni Tornabuoni & Co. The duration of the new company was three years and its capital was fixed at 9,500 ducats, Neapolitan currency, of which Lorenzo de' Medici & Co. in Rome was expected to contribute 9,000 ducats, 3,000 ducats in the form of the bank building located in the City of Naples and 6,000 ducats in ready cash and in collectible claims of the firm "Heirs of Francesco Nasi & Co." Bernardo Carnesecchi was to furnish the remaining 500 ducats. This provision makes it clear that the Naples branch was a subsidiary of Rome placed under the direct control and supervision of Giovanni Tornabuoni. After deducting 3 percent for charities (per l'amor di Dio), profits were to be divided thus: 17s. in the pound to Lorenzo de' Medici & Co. of Rome and 3s. in the pound to Bernardo Carnesecchi. As usual, the latter bound himself to live in Naples and to attend to "the government" of the company in accordance with the instructions given by Lorenzo de' Medici or Giovanni Tornabuoni.

Bernardo was expressly authorized to take up money at interest or "at exchange and rechange" to the extent of any balance which the preceding partnership owed to the new. Should this be interpreted to mean that, after all, the preceding partnership had not been in such a flourishing state? Another unusual provision forbade Bernardo to lend beyond 6,000 ducats to the royal court or beyond 2,000 ducats to any noble without special permission of the senior partners. The Medici branch in Naples, consequently, was dealing more and more exclusively with the Court and the aristocracy; in Cosimo's time, it had been a rule that such loans were to be avoided and that credit was to be granted only to merchants and "artificers" (industrial entrepreneurs) in good standing. Was the reversal of this policy not a dangerous course? Despite the dangers, of which Lorenzo the Magnificent must have been well aware, this new policy may have been motivated by his desire to be on good terms with Ferdinand of Aragon, King of Naples.

The firm "Lorenzo Tornabuoni & Co." was still in business when the Medici regime collapsed in 1494.[40] Being a subsidiary of the Rome branch, it shared the same fate and was taken over by Giovanni Tornabuoni. In any case, the Medici had lost so much that, far from owing any equity, they were heavily in debt to their Rome branch. What happened to the firm "Lorenzo Tornabuoni & Co." after the disappearance of the Medici from the stage is a rather obscure story. The French invasion of Naples (1495) caused the firm to fail, but apparently it did

not remain in a state of bankruptcy because the firm Giovanni Tornabuoni & Co. was forced to give aid to avoid being declared bankrupt
itself.[41] After hearing the testimonies of several Florentine merchants,
the Neapolitan courts held that the two Tornabuoni banks in Rome
and Naples were but one entity (*fuerant et erant unum corpus*) and that
one obligated the other (*et unum obligavit alterum*).[42] There is no doubt
that the Tornabuoni Company of Rome almost entirely owned its Naples
subsidiary and was fully liable for all its debts. Presumably Lorenzo
Tornabuoni & Co. resumed business for a few months with Giuliano di
Giorgio Ridolfi as manager. Then came the final catastrophe: Giovanni
Tornabuoni died in 1497 and his son Lorenzo was executed a few months
later. Their firm was certainly liquidated, since it had lost whatever
credit it still enjoyed. One may, however, raise the question whether
Lorenzo Tornabuoni's participation in the plot to restore the Medici was
inspired entirely by loyalty or whether it was a desperate move to avert
impending bankruptcy.

2. MILAN

There is no mention of a branch in Milan in the Libro segreto No. 3,
which closes at the end of 1450, Florentine style, or on March 24, 1451,
New Style. One must, therefore, conclude that such a branch did not
yet exist at this date, Apparently, it was founded in 1452, at the request
of Francesco degli Attendoli, called Sforza, the condottiere who made
himself duke of Milan (reigned 1450–1466). Until the end of his life, he
remained a staunch ally of the Medici because they had actively supported his claims to the dukedom of Milan and, of course, because the
alliance with Florence continued to serve his interests.

The foundation of the new branch was, therefore, not actuated solely
by business considerations; political motives probably played a decisive
part. Milan, in the fifteenth century, was only a banking and trading
center of secondary importance. According to the merchant manuals,
Milan quoted the exchange with Avignon, Genoa, Venice, and the fairs
of Geneva, a sure indication that its relations with other places were not
active enough to give rise to a regular bill market.[43] With Florence there
existed probably no sizable current of traffic, since the route over
the Apennines involved high transportation costs, and the economies of
the two cities were competitive rather than complementary. Ties with
Genoa and Venice were undoubtedly closer because these cities were
nearer to Milan and were its natural ports, one on the Tyrrhenian Sea
and one on the Adriatic. Another factor favoring Venice and Genoa
was Milan's geographic position in the center of the Po valley and at
the head of several important roads over the Alpine passes.

From the start the Milanese branch of the Medici Bank catered, therefore, to the Sforza court, supplying it with jewelry and luxuries and granting it credit accommodation secured by assignment of future revenues.[44] This was setting a course which Cosimo thus far had managed to avoid, but now political dictates got the best of sound business judgment.

As manager of the new branch, Cosimo de' Medici appointed Pigello di Folco Portinari, who, because his services were appreciated by the maggiori, retained this post until his untimely death in October, 1468, at the age of forty-seven. He had entered the service of the Medici in 1434 as a simple office boy "to help out in raising his brothers and sisters." [45] After being a short while with the Rome branch, he was transferred to the Venice office and remained on its staff for many years until he was called to assume the management of the newly founded establishment in Milan.[46] Because of his acquaintance with business conditions in northern Italy, he was well qualified for this new job.

The selection of Pigello Portinari as manager proved to be an excellent choice, at least in the beginning. He had a pleasing personality coupled with great administrative efficiency, so that he ingratiated himself with Francesco Sforza to the extent of becoming his financial advisor.[47] In gaining the favor of the Duke, Pigello Portinari also gained that of Cosimo, whose foreign policy was geared to the alliance with Milan in order to prevent Venice from disturbing the balance of power in Italy. Moreover, Pigello succeeded in showing profits, the touchstone by which the maggiori judged the performance of their branch managers. Achieving this objective was made easier because of the financial policy pursued by Sforza during the earlier years of his reign. Upon acceding to the ducal throne, he had announced his intention of ruling as a prince and not as a tyrant, a promise he endeavored to keep. Accordingly, he did not overburden his subjects with taxes or overstrain his resources. Although a soldier, he strove to maintain peace and refrained from aggressive wars. Everything went well with the Milan branch for a few years, during which loans to the Sforza court were kept within bounds. Nonetheless, the policy adopted by Pigello Portinari with Cosimo's approval led to a slippery path skirting an abyss which had engulfed many bankers unable to resist the temptation of seeking easy profits by lending money to princes. Besides, this new policy set a bad precedent for other branches to follow.

In order to bind the Medici Bank more tightly to his service, Francesco Sforza donated to Cosimo a site with buildings and appurtenances located in via Bossi, in the parish of Saint Thomas near the gate of Como. In the deed dated August 20, 1455, Francesco Sforza pays Cosimo the compliment of calling him a man "of singular virtue" who has always been his devoted friend and deserves to be honored and loved as his own father.[48] Responding in a fitting way to so much munificence, Cosimo renovated completely the existing structures and transformed them into a palace for the use of his bank.[49] For this purpose he enlisted the services of his architect, Michelozzo Michelozzi, who designed the façade and prepared the general plan which provided ample space for offices and storage rooms, in addition to living quarters for the manager, his family, and his entire clerical staff.[50] Of this magnificent building, one of the sights of Milan in the fifteenth century, nothing remains except the main or center portal, which is now in the Archeological Museum of Milan. It has finely carved bas-reliefs: two medallions, one on each side, representing Francesco Sforza and his spouse, Bianca Maria Visconti, with, in the center of the lintel, their coat of arms in which the eagle of Sforza is quartered with the serpent vorant an infant of the Visconti dukes.[51]

The courtyard and some of the rooms were decorated with frescoes by Vincenzo Foppa, a painter of no mean repute in his day. In the scrittoio, the walls were covered with Cosimo's emblem, a falcon holding a diamond and scrolls bearing the motto "Semper." According to the architect, Filarete, the interior decoration was directed by Pigello Portinari, whom he describes as a worthy man who manages and guides all the business of the Medici in Milan.[52]

The remodeling of the building took much longer and was more costly than expected. The palace was not ready for occupancy until 1459 and not completely furnished until 1461. According to the ledger of 1459, the Medici were buying tapestries for one of the halls, beds for the guest room, equipment for the kitchen, and a walnut chest with several locks in which to keep the libro segreto and other important records, such as deeds, contracts, reports, and balance sheets.[53] In 1461 Pigello Portinari urged Giovanni di Cosimo to come to Milan in order to view the bank building in all its splendor.[54] Although the expense had been great, Pigello thought that the money was well spent because of the resulting prestige and good will. On the other hand, this lavish display may have given the Duke and the people of Milan the false impression that the Medici controlled inexhaustible wealth and that their profits were fantastically high.[55]

It should perhaps be pointed out that the building remained the private property of Cosimo and that the Milan branch paid rent for the use of the premises. It was a steadfast policy of the Medici not to relinquish title to any real estate placed at the disposal of one of their branches or establishments. In 1459, according to a profit and loss statement, rent on the palatial residence of the Milan branch amounted to £200 imperiali, or about 50 ducats a year, a charge corresponding to less than 1 percent of current earnings (Table 52).

TABLE 51. BALANCE SHEET OF THE MILAN BRANCH, MARCH 24, 1460
(All amounts are in Milanese pounds or lire imperiali)

Assets

	£	s.	d.
Debit balances in the ledger:			
Cash on hand.	25,776	5	7
Cash in bank (accounts with tavolieri)	8,516	18	4
Goods in stock (*merci di nostra ragione*).	42,114	4	1
Furniture and equipment (*masserizie*).	2,000	0	0
Sundry receivables.	76,033	6	3
Bad debts.	351	16	9
Officials of the Sforza court.	19,013	5	4
Correspondents abroad.	21,000	10	6
Claims to be collected for correspondents	106,396	5	5
Loans to rulers:			

	£	s.	d.			
Duke and Duchess of Milan.	218,072	8	10			
Lodovico Gonzaga of Mantua.	14,664	0	0			
Giacomo Antonio della Torre, bishop of						
Modena.	157	10	0	232,893	18	10

	£	s.	d.
Pigello Portinari (drawing account).	7,603	13	7
Salaries paid.	2,438	0	6
Living expenses (*spese di casa*)	1,760	7	9
Debit balance in the libro segreto:			
Piero, Giovanni and Pierfrancesco de' Medici.	42,485	3	1
Total.	588,383	16	0
Error in addition.		1	3
Error in casting the balance.	914	16	5
	589,298	13	8

Source: ASF, MAP, filza 83, no. 9.

As already explained, Medici partnership agreements required branch managers to close their books every year and to dispatch a copy of the balance sheet and other pertinent documents to headquarters in Florence. In compliance with this rule, Pigello Portinari sent in his report on April 12, 1460, and attached to it the following documents: (1) a copy of the balance sheet, called *conti saldi,* as of March 24, 1460; (2) a profit and loss statement covering the year 1459, Florentine style (March 25, 1459–March 24, 1460); (3) an itemized record of all the specie in the hands of the cashier (*rivedimento della cassa*); and (4) a list of all debtors and creditors recorded in the libro segreto of the Milan branch.[56] This is the only complete set of such documents which is still available. It is, therefore, of great importance. What does an analysis reveal about the activities and the financial condition of the Milan branch?

TABLE 51 (Continued)

BALANCE SHEET OF THE MILAN BRANCH, MARCH 24, 1460

(All amounts are in Milanese pounds or lire imperiali)

Liabilities

	£	s.	d.
Credit balances in the ledger:			
Overdraft with Paolo da Lampugnano, tavoliere...........	200	0	0
Sundry accounts payable..............................	45,563	17	8
Duke of Milan, balance of an old account................	311	4	6
Correspondents abroad................................	69,291	17	4
Officials of the Sforza court...........................	2,380	8	4
Proceeds of cloth and caps for account of Angelo Tani			
in Bruges...	997	19	6
Sundry creditors, long term (*a conto di tempo*).............	99,917	9	6
Time deposits a discrezione............................	66,183	17	1
Subtotal..................	*284,846*	*13*	*11*

	£	s.	d.		£	s.	d.
Credit balances in libro segreto:							
Capital (corpo)							
Maggiori (senior partners).............	40,000	0	0				
Pigello Portinari.....................	3,000	0	0		43,000	0	0
Undivided profits							
1457..........................	30,206	2	10				
1458..........................	28,410	3	8				
1459..........................	27,785	3	3		86,401	9	9
Time deposits a discrezione............................					174,810	10	0
Gentile d'Angelo Simonetta............................					240	0	0
Subtotal..................					*304,451*	*19*	*9*
					589,298	13	8

It should be noted first of all that all the statements enclosed in Portinari's report were carefully prepared and exhibit a high degree of technical proficiency in the art of bookkeeping. There is no doubt that double entry was in use. It is true there is a discrepancy of £914 16s. 5d. imperiali between debit and credit (Table 51), but this is due to error and not to the lack of knowledge of elementary principles of accounting. As a matter of fact, a note clarifies that the books will be rechecked to trace the difference and expresses the pious hope that "God will guard us in the future against greater errors." [57]

Of course, medieval bookkeepers sometimes did puzzling things. Thus, the balance sheet of the Milan branch of March 24, 1460 (Table 51), includes among the assets an item of £1,760 7s. 9d. imp. for living expenses (*spese di casa*). One would think that this is an error, but it is not. Entries in the ledger indicate that this item properly appears where it does, because it represents stores of food and other supplies that were not consumed in 1459 (Florentine style) but carried over to

TABLE 52. Profit and Loss Statement of the Milan Branch,
Year 1459 (Florentine Style)
(All amounts are in Milanese pounds or lire imperiali)

Explanation	Amount			Percent of Total
	£	s.	d.	
Mercantile profits:				
Sales of silks and brocades.....................	7,104	17	3	23.3
Sales of English wool........................	1,527	0	0	5.0
Sales of jewelry and belts.....................	3,025	18	3	9.8
Credit balance of *spese di mercatantie* or merchandise expense........................	1,207	11	9	3.9
Subtotal..................	*12,865*	*7*	*3*	*42.0*
Commission (*provedigione*) on exchange and merchandise..............................	1,482	18	9	5.0
Banking profits:				
Cash surplus.................................	1,648	10	10	5.5
Exchange with Rome.........................	160	0	0	0.5
Exchange with Geneva fairs...................	3,043	13	4	10.0
Fifty percent of profits of treasury of Pavia........	603	8	0	2.0
Interest (discrezione) on loans to the Duke of Milan	10,711	19	11	35.0
Subtotal..................	*16,167*	*12*	*1*	*53.0*
Total gross profits..........	30,515	18	1	100.0

Deduct expenses:	£	s.	d.				
Depreciation furniture..........	169	3	6				−0.5
Rent bank building.............	200	0	0				−0.7
Living expenses (spese di casa)...	1,200	10	1				−3.9
General expense (spese di banco)..	1,161	1	3				−3.8
				2,730	14	10	
Net profits.................				27,785	3	3*	91.1

* This amount corresponds to the figure given in Table 51.
Source: Same as Table 51.

the next year.[58] In other words, this item was what we would call today
"a deferred or prepaid expense" in technical terminology.

The capital of the Milan branch in 1460 was £43,000 imperiali, or
about 10,500 Venetian ducats, at the prevailing exchange rate of 82s. imp.
per ducat. Of this amount, £40,000 were furnished by the Medici and
only £3,000 by Pigello Portinari (Table 51). Aggregate resources, as the
balance sheet shows, were nearly fourteen times as great and amounted
to £589,000 imperiali, or 144,000 ducats, a staggering sum in the fifteenth
century. The Milan branch, therefore, operated to a large extent with
borrowed funds, mainly time deposits on which discrezione was paid at
rather high rates. According to the statements attached to Portinari's

TABLE 53.   List of the Amounts Borrowed a Discrezione by the
Milan Branch, March 24, 1460
(All amounts are in Milanese pounds unless otherwise indicated)

Name of Depositor	£	s.	d.
	Amount		
Deposits recorded in the libro segreto of the Milan branch:			
Cosimo de' Medici & Co. of Venice (12,600 florins)	41,600	0	0
Giovanni Benci & Co. of Geneva *per conto vecchio*	27,210	0	0
Angelo Simonetta, the Duke's councillor	23,500	0	0
Castello di Piero Quaratesi (5,000 florins di sug.)	17,414	0	0
Francesco di Tommaso Sassetti	16,895	0	0
Count Gaspare da Vimercato (4,000 florins)	16,400	0	0
Anonymous (*un amico della compagnia*)	6,700	0	0
Giuliano da Vimercato	6,000	0	0
Anonymous (1,500 florins)	5,000	0	0
Anonymous (1,400 florins)	4,690	0	0
Antonio di Paolo of Florence (920 florins)	3,082	0	0
Giovanni di Rinieri Bonafè (900 florins)	3,015	0	0
Giovanni degli Angiolelli of Bologna (600 ducats)	2,310	0	0
Bernardo di Jacopo di Ciacco (300 florins)	994	10	0
Subtotal	*174,810*	*10*	*0**
Deposits recorded in the ledger:			
Pierfrancesco de' Medici & Co. of Venice (3,000 ducats)	12,000	0	0
Pandolfo Contarini of Venice	11,600	0	0
Giovanni and Pierfrancesco de' Medici & Co. of Florence (3,000 florins di suggello)	10,050	0	0
Leonardo Vernacci (1,610¼ florins)	5,394	17	0
Giovanni d'Adoardo di Giovanni Portinari (1,448 florins 12s. 6d. a oro)	5,230	12	0
Giovanni d'Antonio of Pavia for account of a friend	5,099	6	4
Leonardo da Pietrasanta, chancellor of Messer Perino da Campofregoso	4,000	0	0
Amerigo di Giovanni Benci (1,080 florins)	3,593	6	6
Torniello di Salvestro di Bettino	2,761	12	0
Giovanni Varesino, chancellor of Messer Tiberto Brandolini, condottiere	2,608	14	6
Fazzino de' Tanzi	2,079	10	0
Anonymous (*la Crociata di Lombardia*)	1,765	18	9
Subtotal	*66,183*	*17*	*1**
Total	240,994	7	1

* These two subtotals correspond to the figures given in Table 51.
Source: ASF, MAP, filza 83, no. 9.

report, close to £241,000 imperiali, or 59,000 ducats, were raised in this way (Table 53).

As Pigello Portinari himself admits in a letter to the maggiori, high interest charges were cutting down earnings.[59] In 1460 the profits were falling rather than increasing but were still gratifying and represented a return of 65 percent on the invested capital.[60] This high rate of return was made possible by trading on the equity: in other words, by borrowing from friends at 10 or 12 percent and relending the same money at 15 percent or more, the Medici company in Milan was earning the difference between these interest rates on a sum much larger than its capital. The result was to swell profits but also to increase the chances of a breakdown in the event that bad debts should wipe out the partners' rather slender equity.

This danger was greatly increased by an inadequate division of risks. As the balance sheet reveals, loans to the Duke and Duchess of Milan alone absorbed 36 percent of aggregate financial resources. The life of the Milan branch depended therefore to a great extent upon the ability of Sforza to meet his obligations.[61] In the report accompanying the balance sheet of March 24, 1460, Pigello points out already that the Court has nearly exhausted its credit and is approaching the safety limit set by Cosimo. He suggests curtailing further advances.[62] Very well, but one may ask whether it was at all feasible to turn off the faucet without courting disaster.

Like the other Medici branches, the one in Milan combined trade and banking. According to the profit and loss statement for the year 1459 (Florentine style), 42 percent of earnings originated in mercantile activities, chiefly the sale of silks, brocades, and jewelry to the Sforza court, most probably at inflated prices (Table 52). One source of profits is the credit balance of the account "Merchandise Expense." It may seem strange that "Merchandise Expense" has a credit instead of a debit balance, but this anomaly is easily explained by the fact that charges to customers for brokerage, warehousing, cartage, and other items of this sort exceeded actual disbursements.[63] The Milan branch also acted as commission agent for foreign correspondents in selling their wares or handling their bills of exchange. Commissions earned in this way were a minor source of profits, only 5 percent of the total.

Banking profits arose either from exchange or from interest charged to borrowers. One puzzling item may be the cash surplus of £1,648 10s. 10d. imp. (Table 52). It appears clear from the rivedimento della cassa that this surplus came from profits on money-changing. According to a check made on March 24, 1460, the different species in the hands of the cashier were worth £25,776 5s. 7d. imp. at current rates, but the balance of the Cash Account was only £25,083 9s. 10d., hence a profit of £692

15s. 9d. obtained by writing up the book value to correspond to market value. Such checks of the Cash Account took place every three or four months.[64] The next two items listed in Table 52 refer to profits made on exchange dealings by means of bills. Notice the importance of the fairs of Geneva which had very active relations with Milan. Not all exchange dealings were real, and some of the profits undoubtedly originated in fictitious, dry exchange transactions, since the Milan branch sometimes resorted to this form of credit.[65] By far the major source of profits — 35 percent of the total — consisted in interest on loans to rulers. The amount of £10,711 19s. 11d. imp. appearing in the Profit and Loss statement represents the *net* return on these loans after paying discrezione to depositors.[66] The margin between the rate which the Milan branch paid to depositors and the rate which it charged to borrowers was probably around 5 percent. Apparently no effort was made to conceal interest, except that it was given euphemistically the name of discrezione. This seems to have been a general rule in Milan, perhaps because the secular courts, while claiming the exclusive cognizance of usury cases, were lenient toward merchants and failed to enforce the canon law in all its rigor.[67]

Operating expenses were not high, less than 9 percent of gross profits. Depreciation and even rent were both negligible. The clerks, or factors, received room and board in addition to their salaries, a practice which explains the presence of an item for living expenses (spese di casa) in the balance sheet.

It is not clear why some of the deposits a discrezione were recorded in the libro segreto and others in the ledger (Table 53). The number of such deposits was not great: twenty-six in all, fourteen in the libro segreto and twelve in the ledger. In general, they were for large amounts, ranging all the way from 300 to 12,600 florins or from about £1,000 to £41,600 imperiali. Some of the depositors, it will be noted, preferred to remain anonymous. The Medici company in Venice had apparently excess funds to invest and leads the list of depositors with more than 13,000 ducats standing to its credit.

By a stroke of luck, there still exists in the Florentine archives an extensive fragment (113 folios) of the ledger of the Milan branch for the year 1459, Florentine style. It consequently covers the same period as the surviving balance sheet and Profit and Loss statement.[68] The data given in this fragment fully confirm the above analysis and give some additional information. The interest rate, (discrezione), paid on time deposits varied from 8 to 12 percent.[69] Thus, the Medici company of Venice received a return of 12 percent on a deposit of £15,000 imp. and only 10 percent on another of 2,000 ducats, or £7,800 imp.[70] Giovanni Portinari was entitled to 10 percent according to his contract.[71] As for

Pandolfo Contarini of Venice, no set rate was stipulated, but he was awarded a fair share in the profits for the time that his money was invested with the Milan branch.[72] Perhaps this depositor was a little bit squeamish about accepting interest, so it was dished up as gain on invested capital: another name, and the devil was transmuted into an angel.

The surviving fragment of the ledger shows that the Milan branch had frequent business relations with the ducal treasurers in the provincial towns of Pavia, Novara, Como, and Parma. This is not surprising, since the proceeds of the gabelle (local tolls) and other taxes were assigned to the Medici and were remitted to them by the collectors instead of flowing directly into the ducal treasury.[73] Instead of being civil servants, these tax collectors were usually money-changers, or local bankers, who farmed out taxes as a sideline. The Milan branch was even in partnership with Amaretto di Raimondo Mannelli, treasurer of Pavia (the favorite residence of the ducal court), and received a share of 50 percent in the profits of tax farming (Table 52).

Most of the dealings in bills of exchange were with the fairs of Geneva. Among the buyers or sellers of commercial paper payable at the fairs, there were quite a few South German and Swiss merchants from Constance, Saint Gall, Ravensburg, and other towns which communicated with Italy through the St. Gotthard and the central passes over the Alps.[74] Some of these merchants, among them Lienhart Frei (Lionardo Franco), the factor of Jos Humpis and the Great Company of Ravensburg, paid tolls due at Como through the Medici company in Milan.[75]

By far the most important line of mercantile business of the Milan branch was the sale of silks, and its best customer was the Sforza court.[76] It bought all kinds: light taffeta and satins, as well as velvets, damasks, and heavy brocades. Most of these fabrics were imported from Venice, although the Milan branch tried to push the sale of Florentine products which were consigned to it either by the Medici silkshop or other manufacturers.[77] Next to silk came jewelry and belts. Again the major buyer of such luxuries was the Court. For account of the Medici in Venice, the Milan branch sold to the Duke a large bejeweled shoulder-clasp and a necklace set with rubies, pearls, and diamonds, all for the trifle of £8,664 imperiali, or 2,166 ducats at £4 per ducat.[78] Tapestries also were bought exclusively by the Duke or his entourage. Thus Count Gaspare da Vimercato, one of Sforza's favorites, purchased ten pieces of Flemish tapestry, six of which were interwoven with silk, made to order in Bruges. The cost of the whole set amounted to £2,234 10s. imp., or 545 ducats at 82s. each.[79] The Medici branch in Milan did not confine its activities to trading in luxuries but also handled wool, cloth, and caps sent on consignment by the London and Bruges branches.[80] These commodities usually came overland, carried by mules across the Alps. The best wool was Cotswold which sold for £80 imp., or 20 ducats, a centner, whereas the lesser qualities sold for £70 or even £60 (middling wool). Buyers were predominantly local hatters and clothiers, or *lanari* as they were called in Milan. The market for English and Flemish cloth was rather restricted because it sold in competition with cheaper Florentine and local weaves.[81]

Although a money market of second rank only, Milan was nonetheless an important link in the network of banking centers extending over Western Europe. It was the principal funnel through which specie poured into Italy to settle the unfavorable balance of the countries north of the Alps. The correspondence of the Milan branch is full of references to gold shipped to Venice or Florence, sometimes 300 or 400 ducats in one lot.[82] This gold was usually sent by courier or concealed in bales of cloth. Our knowledge about specie flows in the Middle Ages, their direction and intensity, is admittedly very scant, but this is no reason to shun this obscure subject. Any information that projects a small ray of light into the darkness may help to solve the riddle of the apparent disequilibrium of the European economy in the fifteenth century.

Around 1459, the date of the one surviving balance sheet, the staff of the Milan branch included four factors, in addition to the manager: Giovanni di Lazzaro Borromei, Jacopo Giannotti (cashier), Antonio di Dino dal Canto, Andrea di ser Giovanni.[83] The records also mention a maid servant named Maria. In 1459 Giovanni Borromei received the highest salary, about 80 ducats a year, and was presumably Pigello's right hand; however, he lacked the necessary qualifications to become a partner.[84] He was still with the Medici company in 1461, but the records do not tell what happened to him after this date.[85] Jacopo Giannotti, the cashier, apparently was not endowed with great ability, either. By January 15, 1464, his job of cashier had been given to Andrea di Piero Petrini.[86] Giannotti was sent to Pavia to help Amaretto Mannelli, the treasurer, who was in partnership with the Medici (Table 52). Giannotti was dismissed in 1470 because of an indiscretion he committed out of "simplicity."[87] Although his blunder was prejudicial to the Medici company, it was decided in 1473 to give him 300 florins, probably as recompense for past services.[88] The new cashier, Andrea Petrini, came from a family of setaiuoli.[89] In the course of years he worked his way up to assistant manager, a position he still held in 1477 when he fell ill and Antonio di Bernardo de' Medici took his place. This Antonio is the same one who had been recalled from Bruges because he had made himself objectionable to the entire staff.[90] He did not stay in Milan very long: in 1479 he was sent by Lorenzo the Magnificent as ambassador to Constantinople to demand from Sultan Mohammed II the extradition of Bernardo Bandini, one of the murderers of Giuliano de' Medici.[91] As for Antonio di Dino dal Canto, he was still with the Milan branch in 1473 when he was advised to look around for another job because the volume of business had shrunk so much that his services were no longer needed.[92] This is another indication that the Milan branch was not doing so well and that the Medici, to reduce expenses, were trying to get rid of superfluous employees.

From the very beginning, the whole trouble with the Milan branch was too much reliance on one customer: the ducal Court. More than half a century ago, the German historian Heinrich Sieveking diagnosed the situation correctly by stating that the Medici company in Milan was mainly *Hoflieferant* and *Hofbankier,* that is, the Court's purveyor and banker.[93] Pigello Portinari was well aware of the limitations which the absence of alternatives placed upon his freedom of action: he had to do the best he could since, as he wrote to the maggiori, "what little business there is here depends entirely upon the Lord Duke." [94] He went on to add: "and if there will be no profits, there may be no expense, at least we hope so." [95] But this hope was nothing more than wishful thinking.

Outside the Court and the Court's circle, there was little, if any, demand for many of the luxury articles in which the Milan branch was dealing. When the maggiori, for example, inquired about the possibility of selling richly brocaded silk cloth, Pigello Portinari replied that this merchandise would find no buyers in Milan with the exception of Madama (the duchess), who, however, was very particular and bought only what appealed to her taste.[96] Furthermore, the brocades in question were not what she liked and, consequently, would be a drug on the market.

In the field of finance, conditions were even worse because of limited opportunities for productive investment either in the money market or through other channels. As a result, the Milan branch was thrown back on making loans to the Court. Instead of financing business ventures, such loans encouraged conspicuous consumption or helped to finance the exploits of condottieri. From the point of view of the banker, they involved dangerous immobilization of funds because rulers tended to pay off maturing obligations by contracting new loans without ever extinguishing the debt. On the contrary, it was usually allowed to grow: the lender, to save what he had already lent, was induced to continue his advances until he had exhausted his credit and reached the end of the rope.

As we have seen, Pigello Portinari used all his diplomacy to dissuade Francesco Sforza from exceeding the maximum set by Cosimo. Nevertheless, he was unsuccessful in this attempt. By 1467 Sforza's debt had increased from about 53,000 ducats, the figure given in the balance sheet of March 24, 1460, to the fantastic amount of 179,000 ducats, of which 94,000 ducats were guaranteed by assignments of revenues collectible in 1467 and 1468, 64,000 ducats were secured by jewels held in pledge by the Venice branch, and 21,000 ducats were not yet covered by any assignments of specific revenues.[97] In his report Pigello explains that, if the Medici were so deeply involved, this was not due to any new loans but to a general moratorium following the death of Francesco Sforza (March 8, 1466). If it had not been for this untoward event, Pigello thought, matters would have been straightened out to his entire satisfaction. However, no progress was made within the next few months. On April 11, 1468, Pigello, in his annual report to headquarters, had to admit that the Milan branch was doing "as usual," that is, losing money instead of making any gains.[98] In spite of this, he expected large profits after "reducing things to order in accordance with our aims," a reference to the policy of retrenchment which Piero de' Medici, now the head of the firm, was pursuing at this time.

Pigello did not live to discover that his expectations were a delusion; he died on October 11, 1468, and was succeeded as manager by his younger brother, Accerrito Portinari. Until the expiration of the contract, the Medici remained in partnership with Pigello's heirs, that is, with Pigello's minor children and their guardian, Accerrito.[99]

Accerrito Portinari (1427–c. 1503) had been a factor in Venice from 1454 onward and did not join the staff of the Milan branch until 1463 or perhaps 1464.[100] In any case, he was in Milan during Pigello's illness, which occurred in July 1464 and gave rise to unjustified anxiety.[101] In view of later events, one may question whether it was wise on the part of the Medici to allow the Milan branch to develop into a fief of the Portinari family. When Pigello died in 1468, it proved impossible to prevent Accerrito from succeeding his brother, although he was wanting in both character and personality. It is true that the Milan branch was already stuck in a muddy rut, but Accerrito was not the man who had the strength or the authority to pull the wagon out of the mire. Where Pigello might have succeeded, Accerrito with less ability was bound to fail. Moreover, he knew that the maggiori did not think as highly of him as of his brother and it made him feel suspicious and insecure.

A struggle developed right away about Pigello's succession. Apparently, Piero de' Medici ordered Francesco Nori, who happened to be in Milan on his way from Lyons to Florence, to examine the books of the Milan branch and to report on its financial condition.[102] This action aroused the suspicion of Accerrito, who feared that the maggiori might select Nori instead of himself as Pigello's successor. As a result, he refused to cooperate or to let Nori see the books. The latter complained to the maggiori that Accerrito Portinari was getting more and more puffed up every day, denying him access to the records, and giving vent to all kinds of inventions (*novelluzze*) without the slightest foundation. Nori asked the maggiori to issue strict instructions enabling him to carry out his mission.[103] In the meantime, Tommaso Portinari rushed to the support of his brother and wrote indignantly from faraway Bruges that the services of the beloved Pigello should not be forgotten so soon and that it was an imposition to require Accerrito to show the books when he intended to go to Florence and to report in person to the maggiori.[104] It is quite possible that Piero de' Medici hesitated about appointing Accerrito; he was finally prevailed upon to do so, perhaps much against his better judgment. As for Nori, who was without a job after being expelled from France by Louis XI, he was made assistant manager of the Tavola in Florence, as we have already seen. The story illustrates one point: unlike the Fuggers in the next century, the Medici did not use traveling auditors who went from branch to branch to inspect the books.

After Accerrito Portinari took charge, the financial condition of the Milan branch, instead of improving, went from bad to worse. Because of frozen assets, there were soon difficulties in repaying the principal when a depositor wanted to withdraw his funds. As early as March 24, 1470, Accerrito had to confess that, if Braccio Baglioni of Perugia insisted on having back his deposit, money would have to be taken up by exchange, since there were no liquid funds available.[105] It even became difficult to meet interest payments and the Milan branch was reluctant to write discrezione to the credit of depositors' accounts. In 1471 it was necessary to notify Antonio Giacomo Venier (1420–1479), the grasping and wealthy bishop of Cuenca, destined to receive the cardinal's hat in 1473, that the discrezione on his deposit was reduced to 400 ducats because the failure of the Duke of Milan to repay large sums borrowed by him had greatly lowered profits. As erstwhile opportunities for investment were lacking, the Milan branch offered to refund the principal, if the bishop did not wish to renew the contract (scritta), on terms less favorable to him.[106]

By 1478 losses and dead assets had accumulated to such an extent that Lorenzo the Magnificent, after the Pazzi conspiracy, decided to lay down the burden and to liquidate the Milan branch. He wrote to Girolamo Morelli, the Florentine ambassador, that he was losing many thousands of florins through the mismanagement of both Portinari brothers, Accerrito in Milan and Tommaso in Bruges, and was determined to break off his association with them.[107] What kind of settlement took place is not clear from the surviving records. In any case, Accerrito complained bitterly that it was unfair to him, and Tommaso accused Lorenzo of never having liked his brother, which may very well be true.[108] Nevertheless, Lorenzo did not dismiss Accerrito but kept him as the head of the Milan branch, despite increasingly disappointing results. Cosimo, in his time, did not have so much patience with branch managers whose achievement fell short of expectations.

It is likely that Accerrito was discontented because he was forced to take over some of the doubtful claims as live assets. In any case, after severing his ties with the Medici he continued to do business in Milan and found financial backers willing to enter into partnership with him: they were Matteo Ghini, Giovanni d'Adoardo Portinari, and Michele Bonsi, a Florentine settled in Rome.[109] Perhaps the injection of new capital and a thorough reorganization gave this company a fresh start and enabled it to keep alive. Whatever evidence there is does not suggest that it did a thriving business.

In the years immediately following the Pazzi conspiracy, Lorenzo the Magnificent was in such dire need of cash that, on January 1st, 1481, he borrowed 2,000 ducats, interest free, from Accerrito Portinari but with the understanding that the latter would have the use of the bank building until repayment of the loan.[110] In 1486, at the expiration of this five-year term, Lorenzo commissioned Folco di Pigello Portinari to sell to Lodovico il Moro, Francesco Sforza's son, the palace which his father had given to the Medici.[111] After some haggling, Lodovico met the price asked by Lorenzo: 4,000 ducats, not including furnishings and tapestries.[112] Later, on May 22, 1492, shortly after Lorenzo's death, Lodovico il Moro restored the palace to the Medici, who kept it for some years.[113] After many vicissitudes, too long to tell, it was reacquired by the Medici grand dukes in the sixteenth century; their successors of the House of Lorraine, however, let it fall into decay until nothing remained of its former splendor.[114]

3. Pisa

Florence conquered Pisa in 1406 and at the same time acquired the harbor of Porto Pisano, the gateway of Tuscany to the sea. It was conveniently located a few miles southwest of Pisa, in a sheltered inlet, near, but not at, the mouth of the Arno River, where shoals made navigation unsafe. Although the Arno was so capricious a river as to be unnavigable during most of the year, its broad valley provided a level and easy route from Florence to the coast. Leghorn, in the immediate vicinity of Porto Pisano, was a fortress — in possession of the Genoese up to 1421 — but not a harbor for seagoing vessels of any size. The port of Leghorn was built much later by the Medici grand duke, Ferdinand I (1587–1609), precisely to replace Porto Pisano, which had silted up and become unusable after 1540, if not earlier.[115]

Despite the economic importance of Pisa and its harbor at Porto Pisano, the Medici Bank did not have a branch there until 1442. Prior to that year it used the services of the firm founded by Averardo di Francesco di Bicci de' Medici and continued by his son, Giuliano, and his grandson, Francesco (1415–1443). This concern had a fondaco in Pisa and establishments in Spain.[116] It imported from Spain large quantities of wool and other commodities, such as mercury.[117] Because such shipments usually went through Porto Pisano, its Pisa fondaco handled all the business connected with the unloading of the goods in the harbor and their conveyance to Florence by pack animals or river craft (as far as Signa). Of course, Averardo's office in Pisa did not limit its activity to its own business but also acted as forwarding agent in dispatching goods in transit for other Florentine firms, including the bank directed by Giovanni di Bicci and later by Cosimo. Although the two Medici banks, Averardo's and Cosimo's, were competitors to a certain extent, they cooperated and favored each other in territories where their network of branches did not overlap.

As mentioned earlier, Cosimo de' Medici waited until 1442 to establish in Pisa a branch of his own bank. As he was wary of becoming involved to the hilt, he set up an accomanda in which the Tavola of Florence — not the Medici Bank as a whole — participated to the extent of 4,000 florins with liability limited to this figure. Full liability was assumed by the active partners, Ugolino di Niccolò Martelli (1400–c. 1476) and Matteo di Cristofano Masi (b. 1425), who contributed 1,000 florins each. Although they together supplied only one third of the capital, they were entitled to one half of the profits in order to compensate them for carrying the burden of management and assuming most of the risk. The weight of management rested chiefly upon the shoulders of Matteo Masi, who was bound by the articles of association to reside in Pisa and to devote himself entirely to the welfare of the accomanda. The partnership was to be known as "Ugolino Martelli and Matteo Masi & Co." Its purpose was all embracing and included trade as well as exchange (banking), the familiar combination. Cosimo, although his name does not appear in the style of the partnership, was not exactly a sleeping partner, content with pocketing his share of the profits; on the contrary, he retained the right to interfere and to veto any policies he disapproved of. The accomanda was to last five years, from November 18, 1442, to November 18, 1447, and was renewable for another three years by tacit agreement.[118]

The Medici share in the profits of the first year amounted to 1,000 florins, not a bad result (Table 17). No information is available for later years, since earnings were presumably recorded in the books of the Tavola which are lost. In any case, results must have been satisfactory, since the accomanda was renewed on November 28, 1450, for another period of five years.[119] However, some changes were made in the distribution of the shares. The Medici reduced their participation from 4,000 florins to 2,000 florins. The other 2,000 florins were supplied by Messer Carlo di Gregorio de' Marsuppini (1398–1453), the famous humanist and chancellor of the Florentine Republic, who was accepted as an investing partner. At the same time, Antonio Martelli, Ugolino's brother, who had been relieved from his post as manager of the Venice branch, was taken in as an active partner. The style of the accomanda was changed to "Ugolino e Antonio Martelli & Co." [120] According to the report filed by Ugolino and Bartolomeo Martelli for the catasto of 1457, the capital of the Pisa accomanda had been raised by that time from 6,000 to 8,000 florins: 4,000 florins placed in accomanda by the Medici and the heirs of Carlo Marsuppini and 4,000 florins supplied by four of the Martelli brothers (each 750 florins) and Matteo Masi (1,000 florins).[121] Although all of the Martelli brothers were fully liable, only two were active in the Pisa branch, Ugolino and Antonio. Bartolomeo, who had served the Medici in the Ancona accomanda, was now a commander of the Florentine galleys and made trips both to the North Sea and to the Levant, and Roberto was manager of the Medici branch in Rome.

Probably in the early 1460's the Medici decided to withdraw from the accomanda, for reasons which are not disclosed in the extant papers. Ugolino Martelli continued in business with the support of his own relatives and acted as agent for the Medici.

For more than twenty years, the Medici had no branch in Pisa. Then suddenly, in 1486, a lone balance sheet shows Lorenzo the Magnificent to be in partnership with Ilarione di Bartolomeo, the son of one of the Martelli brothers.[122] This venture, apparently, was not prospering any more than other Medici companies in this period. The balance sheet shows that the firm was loaded with past due accounts and other dubious assets without adequate reserves to counterbalance these items (Table 54). In all likelihood, this partnership was discontinued within the next two years, since it seems that by 1489 Lorenzo had associated himself with Giovanni di Bernardo Cambi for the purpose of wrestling exclusive privileges from the lords of Piombino, owners of the iron mines on the island of Elba, as explained at the end of Chapter Seven.[123]

Although this venture was profitable, its resources were soon depleted because the Medici, instead of pouring money into the business, were pumping it out. On March 24, 1494, the youthful cardinal, Giovanni de' Medici, alone owed more than 1,260 fiorini larghi.[124] Giovanni Cambi was beheaded in 1497 with Lorenzo Tornabuoni and others who took part in a plot to overthrow the government and restore the Medici to power.

It is fair to assume that Cambi's participation in this conspiracy was

TABLE 54. BALANCE OF THE PISA BRANCH, 1486
(All amounts are in fiorini larghi or large florins)

Debit

	f.	s.	d. a oro
Furniture and equipment..........................	300	0	0
Sundry receivables (*debitori diversi*).....................	2,592	14	4
Overdue and slow accounts (*debitori lunghi e dubbiosi*).......	2,192	16	2
Bad debts (*debitori cattivi*)...........................	116	8	0
Losses on exchange, living expenses, and salaries.........	627	12	6
Depreciation of furniture...........................	102	13	5
Merchandise expense.................................	211	12	10
Total.........	6,143	17	3
Error in striking the balance........................	10	18	8
	6,154	15	11

Credit

	f.	s.	d. a oro
Sundry payables..................................	1,188	9	8
Lorenzo de' Medici................................	1,171	2	9
Ilarione di Bartolomeo Martelli.....................	972	5	5
Gross profits (*avanzi*)............................	2,822	18	1
	6,154	15	11

Source: ASF, MAP, filza 83, no. 7, fols. 26–31.

prompted by the same motives as Tornabuoni's, since only a restoration might have enabled the Medici to live up to their commitments and to save their former partners from impending bankruptcy.[125]

XII

BRANCHES OF THE MEDICI BANK
OUTSIDE ITALY: GENEVA, LYONS, AND AVIGNON

1. GENEVA

In the opening years of the fifteenth century, according to Francesco Datini's business records, Paris was still an important banking center, but it declined soon thereafter, undoubtedly because of the calamities (foreign invasion, civil strife, famine, and plague) which marked the unpropitious reign (1380-1422) of Charles VI and reduced to shambles the kingdom of France. As roving bands of soldiers laid waste the countryside and halted all traffic of merchandise, trade routes were moved east, outside the king's dominions, to Lorraine and the two Burgundies, where the ruling princes, not being at war with England, maintained peace and order.

While the Italian banking houses deserted Paris, a new trade and financial center grew up at Geneva, an episcopal city under the suzerainty of the dukes of Savoy. It had an eminently favorable geographical location at the intersection of important routes running from Italy to Flanders through Burgundy and Lorraine and from South Germany and the Swiss cantons to Spain through Lyons, Montpellier, and Perpignan. Because of the rising Swabian and Swiss fustian industry, this east-west axis was steadily gaining in importance.[1]

The characteristic of Geneva was that business was concentrated at its four fairs: Epiphany (January 6); Easter or Quasimodo; Saint Peter in Chains (August 1); and All Saints (November 1).[2] The fairs not only attracted merchants from all parts of Europe but soon developed into a clearing center for international settlements; this was a function which the fairs of Lyons and, much later, of Besançon inherited from those of Geneva and continued to perform until well into the seventeenth century.[3] International balances were settled as far as possible by means of bills of exchange; inasmuch as specie shipments were cumbersome, risky, and expensive, the bankers resorted to this means of settlement only when bills of exchange were not available on more advantageous terms. Thus a bullion market arose beside the bill market. Although historians are still groping in the dark about the direction and intensity of specie flows in the Middle Ages, there is no doubt that the fairs of Geneva played a cardinal role as a redistribution center of gold and silver.[4] The

Medici records contain evidence of gold being shipped from Flanders to Geneva and from Geneva to Italy.[5] Other sources reveal that the fairs of Geneva, and later Lyons, were the funnel through which poured the output of the German silver mines.[6]

To facilitate transactions, the merchants frequenting the fairs of Geneva devised an inalterable standard of value: the gold mark, troy weight. For the sake of convenience it was divided into either 64 or 66 écus.[7] The Medici reckoned in écus of 64. Unless otherwise specified, all écus mentioned in this chapter will, therefore, be écus of 64. As explained before, the common symbol of the écu was an inverted triangle, thus ∇. In conformity with this usage, the same sign will be adopted here.

The merchant manual of Giovanni da Uzzano, compiled probably around 1425, does not yet mention the fairs of Geneva as an international clearing center; however, this is not true of the *Libro di mercatantie,* falsely attributed to Giorgio Chiarini and published in 1481 but based on data which were collected by an unknown compiler around 1450.[8] This manual shows that the fairs of Geneva were in direct contact with most of the banking centers of Europe. Bills of exchange drawn on Geneva were usually payable at the end of an approaching fair, although it sometimes happened that the next fair was skipped and that a bill matured at the second fair after the date of issue.[9] This practice, however, aroused the suspicions of the theologians. As a rule, bills of exchange issued at the fairs and payable in other parts were due thirty days from date, but the contracting parties could always make their own terms and choose another maturity date (Table 55). Exchange rates between the fairs and other banking places, regardless of whether the bills were being sent to or from the fairs, always had as a yardstick the gold mark or one of its fractions, either the old écus of 64 or the new écus of 66. As a rule, the rate for bills of exchange payable at the fairs of Geneva and issued in another banking center tended to rise with the fair's approach. With bills issued at Geneva and payable elsewhere, it was exactly the opposite: the exchange rate tended to be higher the more remote the maturity date. This fact alone suffices to uncover the presence of interest.

All the leading Italian banking houses maintained either permanent or temporary representatives at Geneva.[10] The Medici Bank, of course, could not afford to stay aloof while the business went to competitors. During the early 1420's, perhaps even sooner, they used the services of Michele di Ferro, who was apparently a commission agent rather than a factor receiving a fixed salary.[11] After 1420 the Rome branch sent its factor, Antonio di Lazzaro Bertini, who had been a factor in Venice and lately in Rome.[12] Why he was sent to Geneva is not told in the extant records. Perhaps the purpose of his mission was to assist Michele

TABLE 55.   EXCHANGE QUOTATIONS AT THE FAIRS OF GENEVA AROUND 1450

Place	How Quoted	High	Low	Usance
Avignon	In so many florins of 12 groats (grossi) per gold mark troy.......	122	118	As per agreement between parties
Barcelona	In so many s. and d., Barcelonese currency, per écu of 64 to the mark	18s.	15s.	As per agreement between parties
Bruges	In so many groats (gros), Flemish currency, per new écu of 66......	50	47	30 days from date
Florence	In so many florins di suggello per gold mark....................	78½*	...	30 days from date
Genoa	In so many florins of 25s., Genoese currency, per gold mark........	128	120	As per agreement between parties
London	In so many sterlings or pennies, English currency, per écu of 66...	48	44	30 days from date
Milan	In so many pounds imperiali per gold mark....................	£216	£208	15 days from sight
	Also in so many s. and d. imperiali per écu of 64..................	67s.	63s.	same
Venice	In so many ducats of 24 groats (grossi) per gold mark..........	67	66	30 days from date

* This figure is an actual quotation found in a Medici letter dated September 3, 1455 (MAP, filza 138, no. 446).
Source: El libro di mercatantie, ed. Franco Borlandi (Turin, 1936), pp. 8–17.

di Ferro during the busy days of the fairs or to study the prospects of eventually establishing a branch office on the shores of Lake Leman. At any rate, while in Geneva Bertini stayed at Michele's house, where he left his belongings (money and clothes) when he went away on trips.[13] Records kept by himself disclose that he traveled a great deal.[14] In 1422 he left Geneva on May 1 to go to Florence and did not return until the fourteenth of June. When the plague broke out in Geneva, Bertini fled to Fribourg, where he remained from August 8 until September 15. On October 3 he was in the saddle again to go to Milan, whence he returned to Geneva October 23. In November he made a short trip to Chambéry and in December to Bourg-en-Bresse. The following year, he was absent twice: in February on a brief visit to Milan, and from the end of April to the middle of June on an extended journey to Florence. These comings and goings seem to suggest that something was afoot, but what? The most plausible guess is that Bertini was sent to Geneva to set up a branch and was making a careful survey of its prospective territory.

Michele di Ferro's activity was not confined to banking but included a lively trade in textiles of all sorts: Venetian velvets, Milanese fustians, and Florentine piece goods, both silk and wool. The firm of Gualterotto Gualterotti & Co., in Bruges, sent Michele a consignment of says of Wervicq (panni di Vervi) — of the same quality as was commonly shipped to Catalonia and Pisa — and cloth from Courtrai, Malines, Lierre, and Herenthals (panni rintalzi).[15] Besides the Gualterotti in Bruges, Michele had as correspondents the Pazzi in Avignon, the Vitali in Milan, and the Rommels in Nuremberg. He was also doing business with the duke of Savoy, Amédée VIII, later Pope Felix V, who bought from him silks, cloth, and merceries, and eventually appointed him treasurer general.[16] Apparently Michele was remunerated on a commission basis for his services to the Medici.[17]

Antonio Bertini suddenly vanishes from the records in 1424; it is not known whether he died or left the employ of the Medici. In any case, his mission had been successful and he had laid the foundations for a new branch. Profits "for the time that Antonio di Lazzaro Bertini stayed in Geneva" amounted to the considerable sum of 2,120 Florentine florins, or 2,000 cameral florins, and were written to the credit of the Rome branch, further evidence that the new establishment was at first an emanation of this branch.[18]

In Bertini's place, the Rome branch sent to Geneva another of its factors, Giovanni d'Amerigo Benci, who, as we have seen, later became Cosimo's right hand. Exactly what his status was is not altogether plain. An entry in the Libro segreto No. 2 states that he did business "in the name of Michele di Ferro and in his own." [19] Did the pair form a partnership with Medici backing? Probably so. At any rate, it is certain that the Medici were reluctant to commit themselves to the full and preferred to stand off. As was to be expected, the Geneva venture continued to prosper under Benci's able management. By November 1426, profits reaching a total of 8,760 cameral florins, or 9,200 Florentine florins, accrued to the Rome branch (Table 56).

Apparently an accomanda was formed beginning in October or November, 1426. Nothing is known about the tenor of this agreement or about the extent of the Medici Bank's participation.[20] Probably the Tavola of Florence and the Rome branch each supplied some of the capital. The division of profits was rather complicated: after setting apart the usual reserves and paying a fixed salary to Michele di Ferro, Giovanni Benci was allotted one fourth of the profits, and the remainder was then divided equally between the Rome branch and the Tavola of Florence (not the parent company).[21]

This arrangement remained in effect for two years and a few months. Commencing on March 25, 1429, a new accomanda was set up, in which the maggiori invested 5,000 florins with liability limited to this amount.[22] It is probable that an equal sum was provided on similar terms by the

Tavola of Florence. As for Giovanni Benci, it appears from his catasto report that he contributed his services only and no money.[23] Together with the capital structure, the system of profit allocation was changed: the Rome branch dropped out and the maggiori, that is, the Medici and Ilarione de' Bardi, stepped into its place. Thus, in 1429, profits amounting to ▽2,880 were divided as follows: after deducting one fourth, or ▽720, for the share of Giovanni Benci, the remaining ▽2,160, or 2,400 florins, were divided equally between the maggiori and the Flor-

TABLE 56. ALLOCATION OF THE PROFITS OF THE GENEVA BRANCH
FROM 1424 TO 1432
(All amounts are in florins di suggello and in soldi and denari affiorino)

Explanation	Total Net Profits			Share of the Rome Branch			Junior Partners			Maggiori		
	f.	s.	d.	f.	s.	d.	f.	s.	d.	f.	s.	d.
1424 1426	9,200	0	0	....	..	..	2,300	0	0[a]	6,900	0	0
1427	4,812	0	0	2,406	0	0	481	5	9[b]	1,924	23	3
1428	2,800	0	0	1,400	0	0	466	19	4[c]	933	9	8
1429	2,400	0	0	....	..	..	400	0	0[c]	2,000	0	0
1430	1,500	0	0	....	..	..	250	0	0[c]	1,250	0	0
1431–1432	4,357	0	0	....	..	..	....	..	..	4,357	0	0
Excess reserves	3,240	0	0	....	..	..	540	0	0[c]	2,700	0	0
Later adjustment	1,080	0	0	....	..	..	540	0	0[d]	540	0	0
Total	29,389	0	0	3,806	0	0	4,977	25	1	20,605	3	11[e]

[a] One fourth to Bartolomeo de' Bardi, manager of the Rome branch.
[b] One tenth to Folco Portinari, manager of the Tavola in Florence.
[c] One sixth to Folco Portinari and Lippaccio di Benedetto de' Bardi, managers of the Tavola in Florence.
[d] One half to the heirs of Folco Portinari and the heirs of Benedetto de' Bardi.
[e] This total corresponds to the figure given in Table 11.
Source: ASF, MAP, filza 153, Libro segreto No. 2, fols. 40, 41, 51, 52, 67, 71, and 76.

entine Tavola. As the maggiori were entitled to two thirds of the profits of the Tavola, they received another 800 florins, which brought their total share to 2,000 florins (1,200 florins plus 800 florins). The other third, or 400 florins, went to the junior partners of the Tavola, at that time Folco Portinari and Lippaccio di Benedetto de' Bardi (Table 56).[24]

As was to be expected, profits of the Geneva branch during the period from 1424 to 1432 varied greatly from year to year, but they were on the whole highly satisfactory and amounted on the average to 3,265 florins a year, not including the share of Giovanni Benci, the junior partner (Table 56). This is a return of over 30 percent on a probable investment of 10,000 florins. Some confusion arises from the fact that Ilarione de'

Bardi, who certainly kept Libro segreto No. 2, did not follow a consistent procedure in handling operating results. As a consequence, an amount of 3,806 florins, which should be included in the profits of the Geneva branch, appears among those of the Rome branch. Table 56, in any case, gives the data as recorded in Libro segreto No. 2. It reveals that the Medici followed an overly cautious policy by building up reserves that were more than adequate and later were distributed as profits.[25] Earnings in 1433 and 1434 amounted to 3,000 florins; instead of being distributed among the partners, they were plowed back into the business and used to raise the maggiori's capital investment.[26] Ilarione de' Bardi having died prior to March 24, 1433, his heirs had no claim to a share in these earnings, with which the Medici could do as they pleased.

During all these years, at least from 1424 onward, the Geneva branch did business under the style of "Giovanni Benci e Compagni." The Medici name was left out: otherwise the maggiori would have been fully liable. However, they were not mere investors, since they retained control of business policy and of the managing personnel.

In 1435, a few months after Cosimo's triumphal return from exile, there was a radical reorganization which affected all departments of the Medici Bank. Giovanni Benci had been so successful in running the Geneva branch that he was recalled to Florence to assume new duties and become one of the maggiori. In his stead, the Medici appointed Ruggieri di ser Lodovico della Casa (1408–c. 1456). The new manager was a brother of Antonio della Casa, who had just been placed at the head of the Rome branch. Ruggieri had already been acting manager while Giovanni Benci was absent from Geneva in 1433 to organize the Basel office. Apparently no change was made either in the style, which continued to be "Giovanni Benci & Co.," or in the legal status of the branch, which remained an accomanda. However, the maggiori increased their investment from 5,000 to 10,000 florins.[27] It is not clear from the surviving records whether Ruggieri della Casa contributed any money of his own; if so, not more than 1,000 florins. He was entitled nonetheless to one sixth of the profits.

It is not until June 23, 1439, that the Geneva accomanda was transformed into a full-fledged partnership, endowed with a capital of 11,000 florins, of which 10,000 florins were supplied jointly by the maggiori and 1,000 florins by Ruggieri della Casa.[28] The style and the division of profits remained the same. The contract was expected to last five years, until June 22, 1444, unless the maggiori chose to terminate it sooner, in which case they were to notify Ruggieri three months in advance. Apart from the usual clauses designed to define the duties of the junior partner and to circumscribe his powers, the agreement contains one exceptional provision: in shipping specie from Geneva to Venice, Ruggieri della Casa was expected to use his best judgment and to select the safest way, but he was to be mindful of the risk involved in sending too large a sum at any one time. Apparently such shipments were a common occurrence, which proves that specie was flowing into Italy by way of the fairs of Geneva, perhaps to pay the unfavorable balance of Northern Europe.

When the contract expired in 1444, it was extended for another two years. Ruggieri della Casa was retained as branch manager, but his assistant, Giovanni Zampini, was promoted to junior partner and given one tenth of the net profits prior to distribution to the other partners.[29] At the end of two years, he left Geneva to assume the management of the newly founded branch at Avignon and his job was taken over by Francesco Sassetti (1421–1490), who was barely twenty-five and had been a factor for only five or six years.[30]

Ruggieri della Casa withdrew rather suddenly and for reasons unknown toward the end of 1447, without waiting for the expiration of his contract, and returned to Florence, where he established himself as a silk manufacturer.[31] He was succeeded by his assistant, Francesco Sassetti, whose rapid advancement — he was not yet thirty — must have been due to outstanding abilities plus a knack for gaining the favor of the maggiori by rather abject flattery. Examples of this abound at this early stage of his career as well as later. For instance, shortly before becoming branch manager, Sassetti wrote to Giovanni di Cosimo whom he "thoued" familiarly (they were of the same age): "please let me know what thy intentions are so that we can carry them into effect with that pure devotion and love which a disciple ought to have for his master." [32]

In 1437 and 1438 the Geneva branch had only three factors: Giovanni Zampini, Domenico Salvestri, and Pietro Malzi. As business was expanding, the number was increased to four the next year by adding Attaviano Altoviti to the staff. The total payroll in 1439 amounted to $\nabla 177$ with salaries ranging from $\nabla 25$, the earnings of Altoviti, to $\nabla 75$, the stipend of Giovanni Zampini, the senior factor.[33] The Medici, as already stated, were not overly generous in remunerating their clerical staff, but they paid competitive wages and salaries. Around 1440 Francesco Sassetti, then a youth of nineteen, was sent from Florence to acquire business experience in Geneva, which he proceeded to do with such alacrity that he rose to the top within a few years.[34] Another factor, who appears on the scene in the late 1440's, is Amerigo di Giovanni d'Amerigo Benci (1432–1468), the son of the general manager, who apparently did not inherit his father's managerial talents. Thanks to his connections, he nonetheless took Sassetti's place when the latter left Geneva in 1459 to become the assistant of his friend, Giovanni di Cosimo.[35]

As Table 57 shows, the Medici continued to reap handsome profits from the Geneva branch during the entire period covered by Libro

Year (Florentine Style)	Total Net Profits écus of 64			Share of Assistant Manager écus of 64			Share of Branch Manager écus of 64			Share of Maggiori or Senior Partners écus of 64			Florins di suggello		
	▽	s.	d.	▽	s.	d.	▽	s.	d.	▽	s.	d.	f.	s.	d.
1435	3,657	13	3	. . .	. .	. .	. . .	. .	. .	3,657	13	3	4,023	0	0
1436–June 23, 1437 . . .	3,139	13	9	. . .	. .	. .	. . .	. .	. .	3,139	13	9	3,453	20	0
June 24, 1437–1439 . . .	11,194	12	5	. . .	. .	. .	1,865	15	4[a]	9,328	17	1	10,355	5	6
1440	2,260	13	0	. . .	. .	. .	376	15	4	1,883	17	8	2,093	0	0
1441	4,088	5	1	. . .	. .	. .	681	7	6	3,406	17	7	3,780	0	0
1442	4,895	0	10	. . .	. .	. .	815	16	10	4,079	4	0	4,532	0	0
1443	3,636	17	10	. . .	. .	. .	606	2	9	3,030	15	1	3,383	0	0
1444–1445	4,903	3	10	490	6	5[b]	735	9	7	3,677	7	10	4,118	19	4
1446–1447	2,820	0	0	282	8	0[c]	423	0	0	2,115	0	0	2,327	0	0
1447 (supplement)	1,274	3	11	127	8	0[c]	191	15	11	955	0	0	1,060	0	0
1448	2,400	0	0	. . .	. .	. .	400	0	0[d]	2,000	0	0	2,200	0	0
1449–1450	6,088	15	3	. . .	. .	. .	1,014	15	10	5,073	19	5	5,650	0	0
	50,358	19	2	899	14	5	7,110	19	1	42,348	5	8	46,975	15	10[e]

[a] From 1435 to 1447 (incl.), the branch manager was Ruggieri della Casa. He was entitled to one sixth of the profits, that is, net profits minus the share of the assistant manager.

[b] During these two years, the assistant manager was Giovanni Zampini. He received one tenth of net profits.

[c] During these two years, the assistant manager was Francesco Sassetti. Like Zampini, he received one tenth of net profits.

[d] From 1448 onward, the branch manager was Francesco Sassetti. He was entitled to one sixth of net profits.

[e] This total corresponds to the figure given in Table 17.

Source: ASF, MAP, filza 153, Libro segreto No. 3.

segreto No. 3, from 1435 to 1450. On the average, earnings amounted to ∇3,147 a year, after making the usual adjustments for accrued salaries and bad debts. This is even slightly higher than the previous average for the period from 1426 to 1432 (Table 56). Of course, operating results were better in some years than in others; business fluctuations are nothing new, and the Middle Ages had their periods of prosperity and depression, of ups and downs. Businessmen accepted this as a matter of course. More unusual is the fact that, according to the entries in the libro segreto, the maggiori's share in the profits was remitted to Florence either by assigning balances available in Venice or by sending specie directly.[36] This confirms once more the important fact that Northern Europe had an unfavorable balance with Italy, which ultimately was settled in specie. Second, Geneva was trading actively with Venice and Milan, but there was no current connecting it with Florence, and, consequently, there was no market for bills, either. As a matter of fact, the merchant manuals do not give the exchange quotations between Florence and Geneva, an indication that exchange dealings between these two banking centers were infrequent.

About Sassetti's management of the Geneva branch during the eleven years extending from 1448 to 1459 there is no information available because of a gap in the extant Medici records. All we know is that the capital of the Geneva branch was set at ∇12,000 on March 24, 1451 (Table 15). Sassetti's share was one eighth, or ∇1,500, but he was entitled to one sixth of the profits in order to reward him for his labors. Scattered references in other sources reveal that the Geneva branch was engaged in diversified activities which embraced both merchandise and finance. In 1450 Sassetti is mentioned as a member of a syndicate of "exchangers" (changeurs) who had lent 10,000 florins to the town of Fribourg. As usual, repayment of the loan was attended with so many delays and difficulties that Sassetti threatened to lay Fribourg under interdict, a threat which apparently was carried out, since Pope Nicholas V, on March 10, 1453, issued a bull authorizing the bishop of Lausanne to lift the ban.[37] Sassetti belonged to the group of money dealers who are indiscriminately called bancherii and campsores in the municipal records of Geneva.[38] At the urgent request of the city fathers, the Geneva branch lent 500 florins to buy a present for the coronation of the Duke of Savoy's son, who had become king of Cyprus.[39] In order to keep on good terms with the local authorities, the Medici could not avoid becoming entangled in public finance.

After Sassetti became branch manager, business was conducted under the style of "Giovanni Benci, Francesco Sassetti & Co."[40] This style remained in use until Giovanni Benci's death, which occurred in mid-July, 1455. Within two months of this event, Amerigo Benci was admitted as a partner in his father's stead and the style was changed to read: "Amerigo Benci, Francesco Sassetti & Co." [41] Because of his youth, Amerigo remained assistant manager; it was only after Sassetti's departure in 1459 that the management of the branch was entrusted to him. His term of office was rather brief: by 1461 he had either resigned or was forced to quit.[42] The fact that his brother Francesco, who was connected with the Avignon branch, also gave up his job at about the same time strongly suggests the existence of disagreement between Cosimo and the two brothers, perhaps over the liquidation of Giovanni Benci's share in the business. At any rate, the rift so embittered Amerigo that in 1466 he participated in a plot to overthrow the Medici and spent some time in prison.[43]

Since Sassetti was retained in Florence by his new duties as the factotum of Giovanni di Cosimo, Amerigo's place was taken by Giuliano di Giovanni del Zaccheria (1431–1470) as branch manager and Francesco d'Antonio Nori (1430–1478) as assistant manager.[44] The latter is the same who was later slain on the fateful day of the Pazzi conspiracy and whose brother Simone was employed by the Medici in Bruges and London. Like Giuliano del Zaccheria, he had been a factor for some time.[45] The Medici were thus following a consistent policy of promoting from the ranks. New articles of association were drafted and the name of Amerigo Benci was dropped from the style of the partnership, which became "Francesco Sassetti & Co." with no reference to either the Medici or other partners.[46] Profits were apportioned as follows: one half to the Medici, one fourth to Sassetti, and the remaining fourth jointly to Giuliano del Zaccheria and Francesco Nori. Francesco Sassetti, in his private account book, states that his own share in the capital was ∇2,300, but he does not tell how much was invested by his copartners. Probably the total was ∇12,000, of which ∇8,200 were furnished by the Medici and ∇1,500 by the junior partners (Zaccheria and Nori). However, this is only a plausible guess which rests on no documentary evidence of any sort. In addition to his share in the corpo Francesco Sassetti had ∇6,000 standing to his credit in a deposito a discrezione, on which he received interest at the rate of 8 percent, or ∇480 per annum.[47]

During the period from 1461 through 1465, the Geneva branch was more profitable than ever. Earnings in these five years reached the total of ∇44,831 10s., or an average of ∇8,966 per annum, more than double the previous mean covering the period from 1435 to 1450 (Table 58). Unfortunately, no figures are available for the intervening years. As Table 58 shows, not all the profits were distributed to the partners, but it was thought advisable to put aside a substantial reserve of ∇4,831½ to meet any unforeseeable losses or contingencies. At least once, in March 1464, Sassetti's share in the profits, a sum of ∇1,500, was paid out to him in coin which was sent from Geneva to Florence in several shipments. This unusual procedure establishes the persistent fact that, between these two places, it was difficult to remit funds by any other method.[48]

The days of the fairs of Geneva were, however, drawing to a close. As appears from Table 58, profits in 1465 were already much below those of previous years, a sign that the volume of business was shrinking. As a matter of fact, it was shrinking so fast that the Medici moved their Geneva branch to Lyons, where a new ragione (partnership) was launched on March 25, 1466. For some time, they still kept a factor in Geneva to transact whatever business there was.[49] He was withdrawn when attendance at the fairs dwindled to the point that his presence became superfluous.

TABLE 58. NET PROFITS OF THE GENEVA BRANCH FROM 1461 TO 1465
(FLORENTINE STYLE)
All amounts are in écus of 64

Year	Amount		
	∇	s.	d.
1461	8,423	4	6
1462	9,435	13	2
1463	9,876	18	9
1464	9,703	14	0
1465	6,565	3	8
Reserve transferred to profits	826	15	11
Total	44,831	10	0
Distributed among the partners	40,000	0	0
Reserve for contingencies	4,831	10	0

Source: ASF, Carte Strozziane, Series II, No. 20, Francesco Sassetti, Libro segreto fol. 17. Cf. F. E. de Roover, "Francesco Sassetti and the Downfall of the Medici Banking House," Bulletin of the Business Historical Society, 17:74 (1943).

2. LYONS

The fairs of Lyons were rapidly gaining what those of Geneva were losing. This development was the result of a "cold war" which Lyons waged against its rival with the full support of King Louis XI (reigned 1461–1483).[50] Lyons had the advantage of being located on the border, but within the kingdom of France. Already in the reign (1422–1461) of Charles VII, the city of Lyons had tried to woo the merchants away from Geneva, but with scant success, despite the fact that Lyons in 1444 obtained a royal grant establishing three fairs and forbidding French merchants from visiting those located in foreign territory.[51] The ordinance did not produce tangible results because the franchises granted were not sufficiently liberal.

The struggle reached a climax when Louis XI issued the famous ordinance of March 8, 1463, which conceded the most sweeping privileges designed to attract the merchants and created four fairs on dates coinciding with those of Geneva.[52] With the exception of Englishmen, "our old enemies," merchants visiting the fairs were exempt from all tolls and customs duties and free from reprisals and arrest.[53] The King renounced his *droit d'aubaine* according to which the goods of a deceased foreigner escheated to the Crown. More important, visitors to the fairs of Lyons were granted the same privileges as those enjoyed once upon a time by the merchants frequenting the fairs of Champagne. It is true that the latter had been defunct for over a century, but the memory of these great international gatherings was still lingering on. To be sure, the venerable customs of the fairs of Champagne were completely out of tune with current business practices; however, there was one important exception to this rule: they allowed interest up to 15 percent in any deals among merchants.[54] This was a major concession in view of the fact that the taking of interest, in theory at least, remained illegal in France until the French Revolution, more precisely, until October 12, 1789.[55]

With respect to finance, the charter of Louis XI was surprisingly liberal, more so even than in matters pertaining to "the train of merchandise." No restrictions were placed on either money-changing or on exchange and re-exchange by means of bills. Everyone was free to remit funds abroad or to lend money at interest "from fair to fair" (*de foire en foire*).[56] All coins, foreign as well as French, were allowed to circulate at their just value, meaning "market value," and specie could be freely imported or exported.[57] This was tantamount to suspending the monetary ordinances during the fairs and to letting the merchants fix the rates at which the different coins would be current. In fact, the bankers brought over from Geneva the écus of 64 and 66 and thus introduced a monetary standard which was independent from government regulation and solidly anchored to a fixed weight of gold. This standard was to remain in use until 1575.

When Geneva foolishly supported a revolt (October 1462) against the duke of Savoy — who happened to be the father-in-law of Louis XI — the King took advantage of the situation to take economic sanctions against the rebellious town. A decree of October 21, 1462, forbade any Frenchman to visit the fairs of Geneva and made liable to confiscation the wares of any foreigner who crossed French territory while going there or returning.[58] Unlike the previous ordinance of 1444, this one was enforced and guards were placed at strategic spots along the major trade routes leading to Geneva. Louis XI's ordinances were a severe blow. Geneva sought to mitigate it by negotiating a compromise, but this attempt, halfheartedly supported by the duke of Savoy, was a dismal failure.[59]

The Medici records confirm that the fairs of Geneva suffered a precipitous decline after 1464. As already seen (Chapter Four), the transfer from Lyons to Geneva was made gradually, and for a time the Medici Bank had an office in each town. Instead of proceeding with haste, its policy, consequently, was to follow trends rather than to take the lead.

The Lyons branch, when first organized, had a capital of ∇ 12,400 and was styled "Francesco Sassetti & Co." Capital and profits were divided as shown in Table 59. Although the Medici had an investment exceeding

TABLE 59. DIVISION OF CAPITAL AND PROFITS OF THE LYONS BRANCH ON MARCH 25, 1466

Name of Partner	Share in Capital	Percent of Total	Share in Profits*	Percent of Total
The Medici............	∇ 8,200	66.1	8s. 0d.	40.0
Francesco Sassetti.....	1,500	12.1	4s. 4d.	21.7
Francesco Nori.......	1,500	12.1	4s. 4d.	21.7
Giuliano Zaccheria....	1,200	9.7	3s. 4d.	16.6
Total..........	∇ 12,400	100.0	£1 0s. 0d.	100.0

* So many shillings and pence in each écu of profits.
Source: ASF, MAP, filza 83, no. 49, fol. 304ᵛ; ASF, Carte Strozziane, Series II, No. 20, Francesco Sassetti, Libro segreto, fol. 24.

60 percent of total capital, they shared in the profits only to the extent of 40 percent in order to compensate the two managing partners and Francesco Sassetti, whom Piero di Cosimo employed as chief advisor or general manager without paying him a regular salary. It seems that Francesco Nori was in charge of the office in Lyons and that Giuliano del Zaccheria was stationed in Geneva, at least part of the time.

There is extant among the Medici papers a balance sheet of the Lyons branch, dated April 2, 1467, and a Profit and Loss statement covering the year 1466, Florentine style, that is, as has been explained, a fiscal period extending from March 25, 1466, to March 24, 1467.[60] Since no similar documents for later years have come down to us, it may be worth while to examine them with scrutiny.

Like other Medici balance sheets, this one is a booklet of several pages in which are listed 172 items on the assets' side and 96 items on the liabilities' side (72 taken from the libro grande and 24 from the libro segreto). For the convenience of the auditor, items relating to receivables are accompanied by brief comments on the prospects of collecting each claim: such as *debbe pagare ora* (he will pay presently), *pagherà di qui a san Giovanni* (he will pay between now and St. John's Day), or *sianno*

TABLE 60. Balance Sheet of the Lyons Branch
April 2, 1467
(All amounts are in écus of 64)

Assets

Explanation	▽	s.	d.	Percent of Total
Fixed Assets				
Furniture..............................	572	12	10	0.5
Horses................................	418	4	8	0.4
Subtotal............	*990*	*17*	*6*	*0.9*
Current Assets				
Cash (quaderno di cassa)...................	2,248	1	0	2.1
Goods in stock (silver, cloth, etc.)............	8,134	7	1	7.5
Sundry accounts receivable.................	36,827	13	9	34.0
Bad debts..............................	683	13	6	0.6
Lords, temporal and spiritual...............	18,580	12	6	17.2
Correspondents abroad......................	8,161	3	11	7.5
Deposits with other Medici companies.........	14,575	0	0	13.5
Officials...............................	2,011	9	9	1.9
Subtotal............	*91,222*	*1*	*6*	*84.3*
Special Accounts				
Francesco del Tovaglia.....................	9,991	13	6	9.3
Accomanda dei drappi (silks)..................	4,428	9	0	4.1
Prepaid salaries...........................	307	4	0	0.3
Miscellaneous accounts.....................	1,049	19	9	1.0
Subtotal............	*15,777*	*6*	*3*	*14.7*
Total............	107,990	5	3	99.9
Error in casting the balance.................	60	8	6	0.1
	108,050	13	9	100.0

Source: MAP, Filza 83, no. 49, fol. 301–306.

sichuri e di già si è ne avuto la più partte (we are sure to collect and we have already received the greater part). Sometimes the comments about the chances of prompt repayment are less optimistic, as, for example, *paghera con tempo* (he will pay in the course of time). Such items, however, are not numerous, and the impression is that the Lyons branch in 1467 was a sound business and was not overburdened with slow or dubious accounts.

Although the Medici professed to be traders as well as bankers, a perusal of the assets' side shows that the emphasis was on banking rather than on trade, since goods in stock were a minor item representing less than 10 percent of the total. Fixed assets, which include only furniture and riding horses, are even more negligible and do not add up to one percent. The modern mind is more baffled by the fact that the Lyons branch operated with a tenuous cash reserve of about 2,000 écus, barely

TABLE 60 (Continued)
BALANCE SHEET OF THE LYONS BRANCH
APRIL 2, 1467
(All amounts are in écus of 64)

Liabilities

Explanation	∇	s.	d.	Percent of Total
Payables				
Sundry creditors..........................	6,235	8	7	5.8
Letters of credit paid in advance.............	2,143	14	0	2.0
Exchange with Venice for customers..........	2,544	16	1	2.4
Acceptances..............................	2,762	8	8	2.6
Correspondents abroad.....................	20,453	1	4	19.0
Proceeds of spices sold for consignors.........	63	7	6	0.0
Subtotal............	*34,202*	*16*	*2*	*31.8*
Deposits				
As listed in Table 62......................	*41,931*	*7*	*9*	*38.7*
Accruals, Reserves, and Miscellaneous Accounts				
Francesco Sassetti, personal account..........	3,068	7	4	2.8
Accrued salaries..........................	1,602	17	9	1.5
Reserve for bad debts and unpaid salaries.....	719	8	6	0.7
"The poor" (*Annosi a distribuire per Dio*)........	7	13	3	0.0
Subtotal............	*5,398*	*6*	*10*	*5.0*
Old Account of Lyons Branch................	*49*	*10*	*6*	*0.0*
Owners' Equity				
Corpo (capital)..........................	12,400	0	0	11.5
Undistributed profits left over from preceding years.................................	5,575	5	0	5.2
Profits of current year.....................	8,493	7	6	7.8
Subtotal............	*26,468*	*12*	*6*	*24.5*
	108,050	13	9	100.0

2 percent of total assets. However puzzling it may be, this situation was rather common, and other examples are found among contemporary business firms, for example, the Borromei of Milan.[61]

The largest figure on the assets' side of the balance sheet is represented by sundry accounts receivable, 113 items in all aggregating nearly ∇37,000. Very few items exceed ∇1,000 and only two are much above ∇2,000. Most of the debtors are local customers, but some are from places as distant as Limoges, Paris, Poitiers, Reims, or Rennes. The Medici also dealt with lords, temporal and spiritual, including the King of France, the Duke of Savoy, the Duke of Bourbon, and several prelates (Table 61). The total indebtedness of this group amounts to ∇18,600 approximately distributed among 14 items, of which the largest, a debt owed by the Duke of Savoy, remains below ∇5,000. The amount chargeable to thc King of France is a trifle, merely ∇350 which, it is explained, are collectible in Languedoc and well secured. In one or two cases at least, the lending to prelates stems from their inability to pay for bulls of investiture immediately upon delivery. Such loans were not hazardous, since a defaulting debtor would be liable to excommunication, an effective deterrent for ecclesiastics of all ranks, as has been said. As this survey

TABLE 61. LOANS TO LORDS, TEMPORAL AND SPIRITUAL, ACCORDING TO THE
LYONS BALANCE SHEET OF APRIL 2, 1467

		∇	s.	d.
1.	Amadeus IX, Duke of Savoy	4,824	17	4
2.	John II, Duke of Bourbon	2,473	12	0
3.	Godefroy de Pompadour, Bishop of Angoulême	2,320	7	0
4.	Urbain Bonivard, Abbot of Pinerolo in Piedmont	1,648	2	0
5.	William III, Marquis of Montferrat	1,360	5	2
6.	Charles of Bourbon, Archbishop-elect of Lyons	1,247	0	0
7.	Jacques de Comborne, Bishop of Clermont-Ferrand	1,238	2	0
8.	Galeazzo Maria, Duke of Milan	1,201	9	0
9.	Raynaud de Chauvigny de Blot, 34th Abbot of La Chaise-Dieu in Auvergne	701	14	0
10.	Toussaint de Villeneuve, Bishop of Cavaillon	465	8	0
11.	The Duchess of Bourbon	443	2	0
12.	The King of France (to be paid in Languedoc)	352	8	0
13.	Luigi, eldest son of the Marquis of Saluzzo	197	12	0
14.	Jacques d'Armagnac, Duke of Nemours	106	14	0
	Total	18,580	12	6*

* This total corresponds to the figure given in Table 60.
Source: Same as Table 60.

reveals, the Medici branch in Lyons was not, at this time, lending to princes or great lords on such a grandiose scale that its solvency would be endangered.

In view of the fact that the Lyons branch dealt extensively in exchange, it is not surprising that correspondents abroad, chiefly Simone Nori in London and Giovanni Altoviti in Venice, owed large amounts of money. Both, we know, were agents of the Medici Bank. The bulk of the funds on deposit with other Medici companies was in the hands of the Milan branch (∇13,440) and the remainder (∇1,135) in the hands of Angelo Tani in Bruges. It is a fair guess that these deposits were interest-bearing. As explained in the preceding chapter, the Milan branch, in order to minister to the demands of the Sforza court, was borrowing right and left and outbidding competitors by offering depositors a higher return than any other of the Medici branches.

The balance sheet shows that more than ∇14,000, a rather sizable sum of money, were in the hands of Francesco del Tovaglia, who was in charge of the sale of silks and, apparently, ran this business as a separate department; on what basis exactly, the extant records do not disclose. The Lyons fairs, there is no question, were an important market for Italian silks of all provenance.[62]

On the liabilities side of the balance sheet of April 2, 1467, the most striking feature is that the owners' equity was only a minor source of funds and that the Lyons branch derived most of its working capital from time deposits, on which interest was paid .This item amounts to nearly ∇42,000, corresponding to 38.7 percent of total resources (Table 60). In

TABLE 62. TIME DEPOSITS (DEPOSITI A DISCREZIONE) ACCORDING TO THE
BALANCE SHEET OF APRIL 2, 1467

		∇	s.	d.
In the libro grande (general ledger):				
1. Francesco di Berto (Roberto) Peruzzi		12,428	0	0
2. Georges, lord of Hauterives (Dauphiné)		1,177	3	0
3. Jean de Mareuil, Bishop of Uzès		946	13	0
4. Boniface of Challans (?), gentleman of Savoy		871	7	3
5. Galeotto Corbinelli, broker in Florence		800	0	0
6. Jean de Cambray, brother of the Archbishop of Bourges, Guillaume de Cambray		467	15	0
7. Claude Viennois, notary and clerk of the châtelain of Geneva		108	1	2
8. Antoine Jacquet, servant of the priory of Saint-Victor		101	1	3
Subtotal		*16,900*	*0*	*8*
In the libro segreto (private ledger):				
9. La ragione vecchia di Ginevra (in reality Francesco Sassetti)		5,000	0	0
10. Amédée de Pesmes, citizen of Geneva (in reality Francesco Sassetti)		5,000	0	0
11. Giuliano del Zaccheria		3,300	0	0
12. Françoise de Rossillon, lady of Thorens		2,285	4	1
13. Simone di Giovanni Folchi		2,050	0	0
14. Guillaume Majeur (?), physician in Roanne		2,040	4	5
15. A friend from Florence (un amico da Firenze)		1,857	15	0
16. Urbain Bonivard, abbot of St. Mary's in Pinerolo		1,502	13	7
17. A friend from Florence (un amico da Firenze)		1,198	0	0
18. Jean André, canon of Lausanne		416	10	0
19. Claude Bergerolles (?), barber-surgeon in Lyons		381	0	0
Subtotal		*25,031*	*7*	*1*
Total		*41,931*	*7*	*9*

Source: Same as Table 60.

all there are only nineteen depositors, so that the Medici Bank did not need to be in fear of a run, but the defection of one or two "friends" might cause serious embarrassment, since assets were not very liquid

(Table 62). The solution was then to raise funds by selling bills of exchange, but this form of credit was much more expensive and more uncertain, because it made the borrower dependent upon the vagaries of the money market and the willingness of foreign correspondents to honor his drafts.

As appears from Table 62, the largest deposit is that of Francesco di Berto (Roberto) Peruzzi, listed by Benedetto Dei as one of the wealthier citizens of Florence.[63] Deposits, as noted before, were not always in the depositor's true name. For one reason or another, a customer might wish to conceal his identity under the cloak of anonymity or under the name of another party. Thus, the books of the Lyons branch mention a deposit of ▽5,000 supposedly belonging to Amédée de Pesmes, prominent citizen of Geneva, and a like amount owing to *La ragione vecchia di Ginevra,* or the old Geneva partnership.[64] However, Sassetti records in his libro segreto that this money was actually his and that neither Amédée de Pesmes nor la ragione vecchia had a single écu on deposit with the Lyons branch.[65] This is not an isolated case. The same Sassetti had nearly 16,250 petty florins on deposit with the Avignon branch; instead of being in his name, these funds were standing to the credit of the local monastery of the Celestines.[66] Two depositors, according to Table 62, are listed as "friends from Florence." There is no assurance that they were not actually Frenchmen who wanted to play safe and to keep an emergency fund out of the clutches of Louis XI. The latter had no compunction about confiscating the property of courtiers fallen in disgrace and ordered his officers to proceed with the utmost rigor in hunting for the hidden assets of such unfortunates. After the arrest of Cardinal Jean de la Balue (1469), Louis XI had the books of the Medici and the Pazzi searched in order to discover whether the Cardinal had any deposits or had transmitted funds to Rome in defiance of a royal ban on such transfers.[67] A similar episode led eventually to the expulsion from France of Francesco Nori, who was accused of providing the funds which helped Antoine de Châteauneuf, baron du Lau, to escape from the Castle of Usson (Forez) where he was detained.[68] The story of Commines, in a like predicament, has already been told.

Next to the deposits a discrezione, the principal liability of the Lyons branch was toward correspondents in other places. About ▽7,000 were held for the Bruges branch of the Medici Bank and another ▽3,000 for the Rome branch. In addition, liabilities under this heading include amounts due to other branches in the vicinity: ▽3,000 to the suboffice in Geneva, ▽5,000 to Avignon, and ▽1,400 to Rosso da Sommaia, who was apparently in charge of a Medici agency in Montpellier.

On the whole, this analysis of the balance sheet of April 2, 1467, shows that the Lyons branch was still at this date a thriving business. Working

balances held for other branches were not so large as to justify the statement that the Lyons branch was draining their resources by failing to
remit. On the contrary, this item was compensated in part by claims on
London and Venice. Besides, the Lyons branch was supplying funds to
the one in Milan. On balance, it was in a creditor's rather than a debtor's
position. The financial condition of the Lyons branch was undoubtedly
sounder than that of the Milan branch, since it did not depend too much
on one customer, the Court, but risks were fairly well spread out, with
loans to princes or great nobles reduced to a minimum.

This impression of soundness and profitability finds further support
in a perusal of the Profit and Loss statement attached to the balance sheet
of April 2, 1467. This illuminating statement confirms, if confirmation
were needed, that 70 percent of the profits came from finance, with exchange dealings looming large and accounting for 36 percent of gross
earnings (Table 63). Next in importance as a source of revenue is the
expedition of papal bulls of nomination or indulgence.

The Lyons branch apparently followed the same practice as Milan and
proceeded four times a year to a rivedimento della cassa. Usually there
was a surplus originating, no doubt, in money-changing. In 1466 the
resulting gain, as the statement shows, came to over 5 percent of gross
earnings, by no means to be brushed aside as negligible.

Trade did not bring much income except for the silk fabrics which
were in steady demand among the French courtiers and clerics. Francesco del Tovaglia's accomanda apparently was doing very well. Commission and brokerage were a source of earnings, albeit a minor one, rather
than a charge. As for the suboffice in Geneva, it yielded a profit of ∇700,
which proves that the fairs there were moribund but not yet dead.
Among the operating expenses, the major item is living expenses, which
covered the cost of feeding and lodging the staff. Apparently managers
and factors all lived in the same house and ate at the same table at the
expense of the employer, as they did in Medici branches in other cities.
The reader will notice that depreciation on furniture, although negligible, is not overlooked. "Loss by robbery" refers to pewter which had
been sent overland from London and looted by "those of Liège," then in
revolt against the benevolent rule of their prince-bishop, Louis de Bourbon, the brother of Charles, Archbishop of Lyons, and John II, Duke of
Bourbon, both customers of the Lyons branch.[69] Among operating expenses there appears an item of ∇188 18s. for rent. The Medici never
owned any real estate in Lyons but did business in a rented house, or
hôtel, conveniently located on the right bank of the Saône River in the
Rue de la Juiverie, near the Place de la Draperie, later called Place du
Change, the favorite meeting-place of the exchange-dealers.[70]

According to the Profit and Loss statement for the year 1466, the staff

TABLE 63. PROFIT AND LOSS STATEMENT OF THE LYONS BRANCH
YEAR 1466 (FLORENTINE STYLE)
(All amounts are in écus of 64)

Explanation	Amount			Percent of Total
	∇	s.	d.	
Cash surplus...................................	728	10	6	5.6
Profits on exchange dealings (*Pro di cambio*)				
	∇	s.	d.	
with Florence.................. 2,682	8	0		
Rome...................... 1,300	0	0		
Avignon.................. 365	12	5		
Montpellier.............. 250	0	0		
Milan.................. 63	3	4	4,661	3	9	36.0
Interest (*discrezione*) and expedition of papal bulls	3,630	13	0	28.0
Profits on trade (*Pro di mercanzie*)...............	111	18	0	0.9
Two thirds of ∇ 3,900 earned by the accomanda of silks with Francesco Tovaglia.................	2,600	0	0	20.0
Earnings of the Geneva suboffice (*ragioniamo si sia avanzato a Ginevra*).........................	700	0	0	5.5
Commission and brokerage.....................	523	10	10	4.0
Total gross profits.........	12,955	16	1	100.0
Deduct operating expenses:				
	∇	s.	d.	
Office supplies............... 17	13	0		
Shipping specie............... 21	0	0		
Couriers.................... 46	12	0		
Living expenses.............. 1,096	16	6		
Rent....................... 188	18	0		
Wages of domestic servants..... 49	11	0		
Presents.................... 77	0	8		
Depreciation furniture......... 40	0	0		
Discrezione................. 352	0	3		
Charities................... 15	0	0		
Loss by robbery............. 25	10	0	−1,930	1	5	−14.9
	11,025	14	8	85.1
Deduct interest on deposits.....................	−2,532	7	2	−19.5
Net profits..............	8,493	7	6*	65.6

* This total corresponds to the figure given in Table 60.
Source: ASF, MAP, filza 83, no. 49, fol. 305.

of the Lyons branch was composed of the two managers (Francesco Nori
and Giuliano del Zaccheria), four factors (Lionetto de' Rossi, Terrino
Manovellozzi, Tommaso di Federigo Sassetti — nephew of Francesco
Sassetti — and Gianetto Ballerini), and two domestic servants (Ormanno

Clavello and Giovanni Carelli, probably both Swiss).[71] Perhaps one should also include Francesco del Tovaglia, who is difficult to classify because he sold his silks either on commission or on a profit-sharing basis. This list differs somewhat from the one given in Benedetto Dei's Chronicle. However, the latter dates from the year 1469 instead of 1466 and, consequently, omits the name of Francesco Nori, who was expelled from France during this time interval. It also fails to mention Gianetto Ballerini, who served as cashier in 1466 and was still with the Medici ten years later when he was sent to negotiate some business at the French court.[72] On the other hand, Benedetto Dei, usually well informed and reliable, mentions Alamanno Giugni, Piero di Niccolò Bonaccorsi, and Lapo del Tovaglia, whose names do not appear in the Profit and Loss statement of 1466 as being in Lyons in Medici employ.[73] Of course, it is quite possible that additional clerks were hired between 1466 and 1469 to take care of a growing volume of business. If so, the Lyons branch employed in 1469 as many as eight factors and two servants, a number not exceeded by any other of the Medici branches.

According to Sassetti's libro segreto, the year 1467, Florentine style, was still a profitable year, although less so than the preceding one, but 1468 ended up with catastrophic results and losses amounted to nearly ▽3,450 (Table 64). This may have been due in part to a business slump, but the major cause was political. Louis XI was highly displeased because of the financial support which the Medici Bank was giving to his foes.

TABLE 64.   PROFITS OF THE LYONS BRANCH FROM 1466 TO 1472
(FLORENTINE STYLE)

	▽	s.	d.
Partnership with Francesco d'Antonio Nori:			
from March 25, 1466 to March 24, 1467	8,493	17	6
from March 25, 1467 to March 24, 1468	4,855	17	5
Remainder of reserve for contingencies (Table 58)	719	8	6
Total	14,069	3	5
Deduct: losses up to December 1, 1468	−3,442	9	1
Available for distribution	10,626	14	4
Actually distributed among the partners	−8,493	17	6
Transferred to new partnership as a reserve for contingencies	2,132	16	10

	▽	s.	d.
New partnership with Lionetto de' Rossi:			
from March 25, 1470 to March 24, 1471	7,200	0	0
from March 25, 1471 to March 24, 1472	5,400	0	0
Total	12,600	0	0
Distributed among the partners	−1,200	0	0
Undistributed profits	11,400	0	0

Source: Francesco Sassetti, Libro segreto, fols. 24 and 33.

He resented the fact that Tommaso Portinari, the manager in Bruges, was the financial prop and the influential advisor of his archenemy, Charles the Bold, duke of Burgundy.[74] The King was even more irritated at the Lyons branch which, he contended, abused his hospitality by aiding Antoine de Châteauneuf and, above all, Philip of Savoy, count of Bresse, who, despite close bonds of kinship, was fighting the King's attempts to get hold of Savoy.[75] Finally, the irate Lous XI expelled "Francequin Nori" from France (August 1468) and wrote a stern letter to the duke of Milan asking him to warn his ally, Piero di Cosimo, and demanding that the Medici Bank change its policy and cease helping his opponents.[76] There was nothing to do but to comply and to appease the King's wrath. The existing partnership with Francesco Nori was dissolved and a new contract was made with Giuliano del Zaccheria.

As a result of this change in management, the Lyons branch came to be styled: "Giuliano del Zaccheria & Co." The new regime lasted but a few months, since Giuliano — he was called in Lyons Julien de la Jacquerie — died on May 12, 1470, and was buried in the Dominican church of Notre Dame de Confort where the Florentine colony had its chapel.[77] During the short time that he was solely in charge of the Lyons branch, Giuliano probably tried to mend matters and repair the damage. According to a settlement made between the Medici and his heirs — he was a bachelor — profits during a period of fifteen and one-half months, from December 1, 1468, to March 24, 1470, did not surpass ▽2,892 11s. 9d.[78] However, there is no mention of any profits in Sassetti's private ledger, which leads one to suspect that the entire amount, after paying the share of Zaccheria's heirs, was set aside as a reserve and not distributed.

From March 25, 1470, onward, a new ragione was begun with the fateful Lionetto di Benedetto d'Antonio de' Rossi (1433–after 1495) in the driver's seat. He did not belong to one of Florence's prominent families. So far as can be made out, he had been in the service of the Medici at least since 1453, first in Geneva and after 1457 in Lyons.[79] It is probable that he married Maria de' Medici, natural daughter of Piero di Cosimo, when he went to Florence in 1470 to discuss the terms of the new contract. This marriage was a clever move on the chessboard, since it made Lionetto the brother-in-law of Lorenzo the Magnificent. Unfortunately Maria did not live long, since she died in March 1479 and was buried in the same chapel as Giuliano del Zaccheria.[80]

When Lionetto de' Rossi took over, the style was changed to "Lorenzo de' Medici, Francesco Sassetti & Co." Apparently the partners were required to put up the capital in ready money. Sassetti supplied ▽1,800, or about 2,000 Florentine florins, for his share.[81] No data are given about the share of the other partners, nor about the total amount of the capital.

At first, things went relatively well and there were handsome profits in 1470 and 1471 (Table 64). Unfortunately, the entries in Sassetti's account book stop in 1472. From then on, no numerical data are available and the story has to be based entirely upon the surviving correspondence, which is far from complete. Perhaps it is all to the good, since letters give better insight than accounting records into managerial problems and policy matters.

The first inkling of something amiss appears in letters dating from 1476. Apparently Francesco Nori and headquarters in Florence were unhappy about the latest balance sheet submitted by Lionetto de' Rossi because "it was too full of slow debtors and stocks of merchandise." [82] Contrary to instructions, Lionetto had been unwilling to curtail operations and to turn down any business which would involve an immobilization of funds. He even accused Sassetti, the general manager of the Medici Bank, of destroying the "reputation" of the Lyons branch.[83] The intervention of Lorenzo the Magnificent was necessary to exact from Lionetto the promise that he would mend his ways and not stray from the path that he was expected to follow.[84] He may have kept his word for a while, but not for long, since the balance sheet for 1480 showed a loss.[85] Overruling his objections, the maggiori decided to send to Lyons Lorenzo Spinelli, Medici agent in Montpellier, to investigate matters. He reported that Lionetto, after some resistance, declared himself ready to cooperate and to retrench, up to a certain point at least. Lionetto, however, was not eager to have Spinelli stay in Lyons and urged him to return to Montpellier, where his presence was allegedly needed. It is clear that Lionetto de' Rossi did not want anyone around who would be "spying" on him and reporting his doings to Sassetti. As an eventual successor, he favored Filippo d'Antonio Lorini instead of Lorenzo Spinelli who, Lionetto asserted, was more likely to promote his own interests than those of the Medici Bank.[86]

In the spring of 1482, Lionetto de' Rossi, for reasons of his own, did something very strange and sent two balance sheets: one to Francesco Sassetti in the usual form, full of puzzling details, and another to Lorenzo with everything explained in the most plausible way.[87] What Lionetto expected to achieve is in itself a riddle, since at headquarters the two documents would certainly be compared. Unfortunately, we have only the letters sent in one direction and not the replies, so that it is impossible to find out how headquarters reacted to his underhanded trick. Doubtless, not favorably.

During the year 1482, Florentine style, earnings seem to have picked up, at least if Lionetto may be trusted. In sending the balance sheet on June 23, 1483, he drew a glowing picture of the state of the Lyons branch and its future prospects.[88] Among other things, he claimed that he had been able in two years to amortize ▽22,000 in bad debts and to set up a reserve of ▽12,000. As earnings were on the increase, he expected to straighten everything out, so that the Lyons branch was likely to become the most prosperous venture which the Medici ever had. In addition to creating a reserve of ▽12,000, Lionetto boasted of possessing nearly as much in jewels and commodities, which were "neither in Pera nor in Brusa, but right here." What he did not state was that high-priced jewels were hard to sell and then only to great lords who were not the best payors. Moreover, one may question the wisdom of acquiring dead stock when operating with borrowed funds. The letter accompanying the balance sheet ends with a diatribe against Francesco Sassetti, who according to Lionetto was constantly dinning into Lorenzo's ears that the Lyons branch was an "inferno." Such an accumulation of raving passion was more apt to arouse suspicion than to inspire confidence. One wonders why the maggiori did not take the drastic step of getting rid of Lionetto de' Rossi right away, despite his family relationship to the Medici. Cosimo, in his time, would not have hesitated one moment to do so.

Slow accounts was only one of the troubles that plagued the Lyons branch. The clerical staff was rent with jealousy. Much to Lionetto's annoyance, the maggiori had sent to Lyons Sassetti's own son, Cosimo di Francesco (1463–1527).[89] He was, of course, suspected of being planted there as a sort of informer who was supposed to report anything irregular to his father. This may very well have been in Francesco Sassetti's mind. Lionetto, in order to show that he had nothing to conceal, put Cosimo to work as a bookkeeper, but confidential matter was still handled by Antonio Mellini.[90] The two giovani did not get along, of course.[91] Moreover, Cosimo was conceited and took advantage of his colleagues. He was also disliked by Filippo Lorini, who labelled him contemptuously "a pretentious nobody": the epithet was not entirely undeserved, as will be shown presently.[92]

Far more serious than dissension among the staff was the sharp conflict which developed between the Rome and Lyons branches as a result of the policy initiated by Lionetto. One source of trouble was the Lyons branch's failure to remit promptly to Rome the proceeds from the expedition of papal bulls and the collation of benefices.[93] Another difficulty was that the Lyons branch fell into the habit of drawing on Rome to cover its growing debit balance at the four fairs.[94] Although Tornabuoni had agreed to support Lyons to the extent of five or six thousand ducats, he protested strongly to Lorenzo as the balance gradually increased and, in 1483, reached 8,000 ducats or more.[95] Still Lionetto de' Rossi kept on draining Rome of its resources while complaining at the same time that Tornabuoni begrudged him any help. Finally Lionetto, to settle part of his balance, sent to Rome some of his jewels and tapestries, but these commodities were hard to sell because the Pope was cutting down expenses and was not buying such luxuries.[96] But Lionetto was so befogged and so suspicious that Giovanni Tornabuoni despaired of making him understand that the Rome branch did not have inexhaustible resources and was doing the best it could.[97]

Matters came to such a pass that in May, 1485, the Rome branch dishonored a draft of Jules Thierry of Rennes at the risk of undermining forever the confidence of the French in the solvency of the Medici Bank.[98] Lionetto, upon learning this, nearly exploded with anger and charged that the managers of the Rome branch — Tornabuoni's nephews — considered only their own narrow interests and disregarded those of the Medici Bank as a whole. Perhaps he was right in this particular instance, but he forgot that he had been remiss in supplying funds with which to pay drafts.

The crisis of the Lyons branch was rapidly coming to a head and Lorenzo's confidence in Lionetto de' Rossi was badly shaken.[99] In July, 1484, in order to make a better impression, Cosimo Sassetti was sent to Florence with the balance sheet as of March 25 preceding.[100] Lionetto claimed that it was entirely free of bad debts, that profits amounted to $\nabla 8,000$, and that he had used $\nabla 4,000$ of them to write off irrecoverable claims of Francesco del Tovaglia and other insolvent debtors. However, Lionetto, to his great regret, had not been able to reduce liabilities, because the capital had been supplied chiefly in bad debts and because, unbelievably, he was supporting the maggiori and other Medici companies to the tune of fifteen or twenty thousand écus! Cosimo, Lionetto added brazenly, was well informed about the state of things and would be able to answer any queries. Whether or not the youth was a dupe is anybody's guess. In truth, Lionetto's balance sheet was a fraud and figures had been juggled around to conceal huge losses. The maggiori were not so easily deceived and, by August 4, Lionetto had to admit that the financial condition of the branch was not quite as favorable as pictured and that his aim henceforth would be to remain in business, recoup losses, and, if possible, make a profit.[101]

Rumors, probably spread by competitors, that the Lyons branch was in difficulties were going the rounds. Finally Lorenzo the Magnificent was persuaded to send Lorenzo Spinelli, who had been on a similar mission before, to investigate matters on the spot. Spinelli arrived in Lyons early in February, 1485. In the first interview with Lionetto de' Rossi, the latter gave the impression of being out of his senses.[102] As usual, he accused Francesco Sassetti of being the source of all evil. If it were not for the love of Lorenzo, Lionetto shouted, he would give Sassetti such a beating as to cripple him for life. While making these threats, Lionetto grew so ebullient that Spinelli had to calm him down.

It also transpired that Lionetto was about thirty-five marks (about
▽2,240) short for the current fair of Epiphany and did not know how
to cover the deficit.

Despite Lorenzo's reluctance to reach a decision, Francesco Sassetti
became quite insistent about the urgency of recalling Lionetto, if necessary by sending to Lyons someone in authority to have Lionetto
arrested and, perhaps, brought to Florence as a prisoner. But this proved
to be unnecessary and ill-advised.[103] Instead, Lorenzo, by friendly letters,
coaxed Lionetto to come to Florence for a conference.[104] The latter, however, took his time about setting out on this trip and did not leave Lyons
until mid-June, 1485.[105] No sooner had he arrived in Florence than he
was arrested and incarcerated in the Stinche, the debtors' jail, undoubtedly on the petition of his senior partners, Lorenzo de' Medici and
Francesco Sassetti.[106] He stayed in prison for at least four months and
was released on bail early in November.[107] Two years later, on June 27,
1487, he was rearrested, again at the request of his former partners, who
claimed he owed them 30,000 florins — a fortune which he certainly did
not have — and he was not set free until October 20, 1487, then probably
because there was no use in keeping him in jail any longer.[108]

Lionetto's first arrest created more stir than was anticipated because
it brought home the fact that something was amiss and that the Medici
Bank was in serious trouble.[109] In Lyons the news caused general con-
sternation. The municipal council of Lyons and several prominent
citizens petitioned Lorenzo the Magnificent for Lionetto's release.[110] At
the French court the dismay was as great as in Lyons. As a matter of fact,
the alarm was such that Agostino Biliotti, who had been sent to Lyons
as a "trouble shooter," feared a run on the bank by panicky depositors.[111]
Uncertainty upset the August fair: the settlements by clearing required
more time than usual, but the Medici Bank somehow managed to honor
all its acceptances and to save its "reputation," that is, to preserve its
credit, as we would say today.[112]

Biliotti, soon after his arrival in Lyons, proceeded to make an audit of
the books; it did not take him long to discover that they had been
tampered with and that the bookkeeping was in a muddle (infuscato).
After straightening out the mess, he warned Lorenzo on October 1, 1485,
that the balance sheet was going to be quite different from the one sent
months earlier by Lionetto de' Rossi. A few days later, he reported that
he had nearly finished the job and that he was disturbed and frightened
by the size of the loss.[113] It was as bad as, if not worse than, the disastrous
liquidation of the Bruges branch, with similar mismanagement and
fraudulent practices.[114] No exact or even approximate figure is quoted
in the extant records, but it is plausible to estimate that the deficit

exceeded ▽50,000 or 780 gold marks, which corresponds roughly to $220,000 at the present (1962) price of $35 an ounce.[115] However, the purchasing power of gold was several times what it is today.

At first, Lorenzo the Magnificent wanted to liquidate, but he was prevailed upon by his advisors to stay in business and to revitalize the Lyons branch with an infusion of fresh capital. A new ragione was formed for this purpose.[116] It was named "Francesco Sassetti and Giovanni Tornabuoni & Co.," a style which remained in use until Sassetti's death in March, 1490.

At Biliotti's suggestion, the position of manager was offered to Lorenzo Spinelli, since Francesco Sassetti's sons (Galeazzo and Cosimo) were still too young and too inexperienced to carry such a heavy load (a portare tanto peso).[117] Spinelli, however, had his own commitments and was not eager at all to assume command of a ship that was more likely to founder than to stay afloat.[118] After much prodding, he finally was induced to accept. Only Francesco Sassetti, who did not care much for Spinelli, felt unhappy about this appointment. His dislike became a new source of friction.

Although Spinelli perhaps lacked vigor and initiative, he was the best man available. When, in May, 1486, he returned to Lyons from a trip to Florence, presumably to settle the terms of the new ragione, he found business in a rather satisfactory state with credit restored, but the task awaiting him was still formidable. The maggiori were slow in supplying the new ragione with fresh capital and still slower in providing funds to pay off the liabilities of the old ragione, whose liquidation thus continued to be a steady strain on resources. As a result, the new ragione was forced to borrow at interest or to take up money by exchange, and these charges were eating up all the profits.[119] Moreover, the maggiori wanted Spinelli to retrench and to concentrate on collecting old claims and on paying off past liabilities, but it was impossible to make profits without being ready to undertake new ventures.[120] How to solve this dilemma was a perennial source of conflict between Florence and Lyons. Coordination was lacking in still other respects: the Lyons branch protested vigorously to the maggiori because the Tavola in Florence sent silk stuffs on consignment to competitors instead of favoring its own people. Such a procedure created the unfavorable impression that one branch of the Medici Bank no longer trusted another branch.[121]

To make matters worse, there was the usual trouble with the staff. Snobbish Cosimo Sassetti, for example, pretended to consider Spinelli as an equal and had to be reminded of the fact that the latter was his superior and intended to be treated with deference.[122] It is likely that Cosimo, in revenge, wrote derogatory reports to his father behind

Spinelli's back. These reports, it is a fair guess, added oil to the fire and caused Francesco Sassetti to be more and more critical of Spinelli's management.

Rightly or wrongly, Francesco Sassetti blamed Spinelli for not making better headway with the liquidation of the old ragione, for not pursuing with more vigor the collection of outstanding claims, and for not having greater authority over his staff. Sassetti even went so far as to intimate that Spinelli's management was not much better than that of Lionetto de' Rossi. These criticisms were galling to Spinelli, who expected to be commended rather than condemned for his management.[123]

Inasmuch as Sassetti did not want a repetition of the Rossi scandal, he made the heroic decision, despite his age and his rheumatism, to go to Lyons and see for himself. He arrived in May, 1488, and wrote that he felt twenty years younger because, to his great surprise, he found so many old acquaintances still alive and glad to welcome him. After visiting his friends, he settled down to business and was at first appalled by the state of things. Spinelli, he discovered, had taken ∇3,000 out of the business as his share in the profits, notwithstanding the fact that the ragione needed to fatten and not to reduce. He also had removed jewelry from the counting house to put it in safety somewhere else. Sassetti objected further to Spinelli's lending company funds in his own name. It looks as if Spinelli lacked confidence in the solidity of his own bank. He may not always have done the right thing; but, while Sassetti found proof of inefficiency and laxity, there was no evidence of dishonesty. When it came to the conduct of the staff, there was one thing Sassetti disapproved of: Guglielmo di Niccolò and Pellegrino Lorini, who were stationed at the French court, spent freely, did nothing, and cost more than ambassadors.[124]

To be sure, there were many things to set right, and Sassetti announced to Lorenzo the Magnificent that he planned to stay until everything had been straightened out to his satisfaction. Relations with Lorenzo Spinelli improved markedly after Sassetti had reassured him that he would be retained as partner and manager.[125] Spinelli, whatever his faults, was hard to replace and he was willing to cooperate. Sassetti congratulated himself on the success of his trip. Perhaps he should have undertaken it sooner. His presence had done much to restore confidence and his prestige had made it possible to push the settlement of outstanding claims and to make agreements providing for the gradual extinction of overdue accounts. These were chiefly with members of the nobility or the higher clergy who were by no means easy to deal with and even more difficult to coerce by going to court.[126] Some were quite obdurate and thought it beneath their dignity to pay debts.[127] Sassetti, who knew the ways of the world, succeeded in making them amenable to reason and equity.[128] It is doubtful whether Spinelli with less experience and prestige would have done half as well.[129]

Sassetti seized the opportunity of his being in Lyons to draft new articles of association in which he, Lorenzo, and Giovanni Tornabuoni, jointly, were the senior partners and Lorenzo Spinelli, the junior partner. After some discussion, he secured the approval of all concerned.[130] In February, 1489, he announced to Lorenzo the Magnificent that, since everything was settled, he was about to leave.[131] However, he was detained by one thing after another and did not return until October, 1489. One untoward event was that Philippe de Commines, after his liberation from prison, needed funds to pay a heavy fine and asked for some of the money which he had on deposit with the Medici Bank. The request came at a bad moment.[132] But what to do? It was impossible not to help an old friend, especially someone of the quality of Monseigneur d'Argenton.

When Sassetti finally reached Florence after an absence of seventeen months, he was fairly satisfied with the results of his mission, for he had accomplished what he had set out to do: he had succeeded in speeding up the collection of receivables pertaining to the old ragione, now in the process of liquidation, and in reducing the loss as much as possible; furthermore, he had placed the new ragione on a firm footing and made sure that it was well managed according to the wishes of the maggiori. The Medici Bank in Lyons, though battered by the storm, was under sail again. But would the weakened hulk withstand another gale which was already gathering at the horizon?

The Medici correspondence is very informative about managerial problems but much less so about general business conditions, which are rarely alluded to. It thus happens that there is no reference to the crisis which the fairs of Lyons were going through during the period from 1484 to 1494. As a matter of fact, they had been formally abolished by a decree of March 8, 1484, because the Italian bankers, it was alleged, carried specie out of the realm and brought in silk fabrics and other superfluous luxuries or, what is still worse, flooded the country with debased coins.[133] In order to prevent these abuses, the fairs were transferred from Lyons to Bourges, that is, from the periphery to the center of France. Behind the scheme were the maneuvers of the cities of Languedoc (Montpellier and Aigues Mortes), whose carrying trade with the Levant was in full decadence because the Italians, using better techniques and superior business methods, were able to undersell French merchants by bringing spices over the Alpine passes from Venice to Lyons.[134] To obtain government support, the foes of the Lyons fairs used, it will be noted, arguments that might be branded as mercantilistic, if it were not too early to speak of mercantilism.

As Bourges was remote from any trade routes, its fairs failed to attract merchants and proved to be a complete fiasco.[135] The Medici letters give the impression that the fairs of Lyons continued to be held as usual because the local authorities winked at the evasion of the decree of suppression. Only the Duke of Savoy took advantage of the situation to attempt a revival of the fairs of Geneva by stopping goods whose destination was Lyons.

In 1484 Lionetto de' Rossi reported to headquarters that the Easter fair had been exceptionally good and that silk fabrics were sold in large quantities, but no brocades.[136] In April, 1486 the same fair was well attended and would have been successful if the goods coming from Italy had not been seized by the Duke of Savoy and sent to Geneva.[137] Money, a letter reveals, was unusually tight during the August fair in 1487.[138] Attendance at the Epiphany fair in 1489 was poor save for a few Italians, and the Medici had to cover a debit balance of 130 marks at the final clearing.[139] The Easter fair, on the contrary, attracted a crowd, and the money market was easy (larghezza).[140] In 1491 business conditions were adversely affected by the war of Brittany. The Epiphany fair was in a turmoil because of several bankruptcies and the fear that others would follow.[141] Business was at a standstill and stringency prevailed in the money market, but the credit of the Medici Bank was still so great that it paid half a ducat and even up to one ducat per mark less than the current rate of exchange.

After 1483 one of the main concerns of the Lyons branch was the hunt for benefices in favor of Giovanni de' Medici (1475–1521), Lorenzo's son, who was tonsured at the age of eight, became a cardinal at thirteen, and a pope at thirty-seven. Since the Medici had lost so much in their business ventures, they were determined to retrieve their wealth and prestige, if necessary at the expense of the Church. Everything, consequently, was set in motion to secure benefices for Messer Giovanni, and the spiritual interests of the Church were gladly sacrificed to the most barefaced and shocking rapacity. French benefices seemed to be an easy prey and the Lyons branch was instructed to be on the lookout for "vacancies."

Messer Giovanni had scarcely been tonsured when the Lyons branch secured for him the abbey of Fontdouce in Saintonge (1483).[142] To their dismay, the Medici discovered that there was competition and that the Pope had conferred the same benefice on Antoine Balue, Bishop of Saint-Pons de Tomières, the brother of Jean Balue (1421–1491), Cardinal of Angers and prime minister of Louis XI.[143] It took a lot of diplomacy to eliminate this serious contender, but in the end Messer Giovanni remained in secure possession of his abbacy. Next Louis XI announced his intention of making the lad archbishop of Aix in Provence. Immediately Giovanni Tornabuoni went into action and had made good progress when he received from Lionetto de' Rossi the disconcerting news that the supposedly deceased incumbent was still very much alive. When he actually died a few months later (January 28, 1484), Louis XI had expired and the regent, Anne de Beaujeu, favored another candidate.[144] After this lost opportunity, the Medici cast longing eyes on the Benedictine abbey of La Chaise-Dieu in Auvergne — but this plum never fell into their lap. However, as a sop, Messer Giovanni received the priory of Saint Gemme near Chartres.[145] The Medici had no better luck with the Cistercian abbey of Le Pin near Poitiers. Here the monks stood their ground, elected their own abbot, and barricaded the church when Cosimo Sassetti came to take possession.[146] The contest ended with a Medici defeat.

Lorenzo the Magnificent succeeded much better in Italy than in France and was able to secure for his son a plurality of benefices which, after the collapse of the Bank, provided the financial foundation on which the Medici again rose to power.

Sometimes the Medici factors were given unusual errands. Thus, Lionetto de' Rossi, on December 4, 1482, insisted that Lorenzo the Magnificent grant the request of the dying Louis XI, who had asked for the ring of Saint Zenobius, a relic which reputedly performed miracles. And the letter added: "The King can be trusted to return it promptly." [147] On another occasion, Cosimo Sassetti was very much embarrassed because a giraffe which was being sent to the duchess of Bourbon died on the way.[148]

After Francesco Sassetti's departure in 1489, the affairs of the Lyons branch went rather smoothly for a while. The liquidation of the old ragione continued, however, to drag on because Lorenzo the Magnificent failed to provide funds to pay off loans on which interest was steadily accumulating.[149] As a result, the deficit was still growing. Since it was impossible to undo past mistakes and to negate the existence of a deficit, Spinelli thought that the issue should be faced squarely and that the necessary sacrifices should be made to get rid of the burden.[150] In this he was undoubtedly right, but Lorenzo was probably unwilling to diminish his prestige by putting up for sale some of his villas or landed property.

After the death of Francesco Sassetti, which occurred in the last days of March 1490, the style of the Lyons branch was changed to "Heirs of Francesco Sassetti & Giovanni Tornabuoni & Co." [151] But Spinelli was of the opinion that it would have been better to include Lorenzo de' Medici's name, because the French did not have confidence in anyone else. Francesco's son, Cosimo Sassetti, did not have his father's qualities. He was a supercilious and tactless young man.[152] When sent to the French court, he offended the nobles by his presumptuous manners. On the other hand, he was so impressed by nobility that he felt it beneath his own dignity to remind them that their accounts were overdue. Cosimo did not get along well either with his chief, Lorenzo Spinelli, as has been pointed out, or with Francesco (Franceschino) di Francesco Nori, a younger member of the staff, whom he tried to dominate and refused to train for positions of responsibility.[153] Guglielmo di Niccolò, another factor, was finally sent back to Florence because of his inefficiency and Spinelli asked that he be replaced by someone with greater ability. Besides Spinelli and the two sons of Francesco Sassetti (Cosimo and Galeazzo), the staff of the Lyons branch included at this time: Giuliano d'Agostino Biliotti, two grandsons of Matteo di ser Giovanni da Gagliano, and a Frenchman, Pierre Fossier, who spent most of his time in Geneva or other parts of Savoy; in all there were eight persons, which corresponds to the figure given before.[154]

Prior to 1478, the main competitor of the Medici in Lyons had been the Pazzi bank. Its manager was Francesco Capponi and he is said to have had six factors in his service.[155] After the Pazzi had been wiped out, the more important rivals of the Medici were the Mannelli and the Capponi. In 1470 the former had as manager Bartolomeo Buondelmonti and employed three factors only. After 1480 Neri di Gino Capponi, a very able man, developed his bank into a leading concern. Lorenzo Spinelli suspected him of duplicity, of rejoicing in any setback suffered by the Medici, and of spreading false alarms.[156]

The death of Lorenzo the Magnificent, on April 8, 1492, was a severe blow for the Lyons branch, since his son Piero, interested only in wrestling and other sports, lacked either political or business ability. Within less than two years, clouds were gathering on the horizon, as Charles VIII prepared himself to invade Italy and to revive the Angevin claims to the Neapolitan throne. Because Piero di Lorenzo refused permission for the French army to cross Florentine territory, the King in June, 1494 ordered the expulsion from France of Piero's ambassadors and the entire personnel of the Medici Bank in Lyons.[157] They moved to Chambéry in Savoy, but the Bank's credit was nearly gone. It received another blow when Piero was driven out of Florence and all his property was confiscated. By agreement with the custodians of the Medici estate the Lyons branch was taken over by a partnership composed of Lorenzo di Giovanni Tornabuoni, Cosimo Sassetti, and Lorenzo Spinelli. From the start, it was handicapped by lack of working capital and squeezed between creditors clamoring for payment and debtors using all legal technicalities to evade their obligations. According to a provisional list, bad debts amounted to over ∇ 19,500, not including sundry accounts owed by Piero di Lorenzo and his brother, the Cardinal, whose combined debit balances by far exceeded their equity. Spinelli wrote to

Lorenzo Tornabuoni: "As one knows, people will crush completely a fellow who is already down." Things were bad and they were getting worse.[158]

After the failure of Charles VIII's expedition, Spinelli and Sassetti returned to Lyons and tried to carry on, but their firm, without operating capital, was unable to engage in profitable business. The death of Lorenzo Tornabuoni, in August 1497, struck the final blow. The only thing to do was to liquidate, and many creditors, including Philippe de Commines, were never paid. Thus the Lyons branch shared the fate of the other Medici branches and came to an inglorious end.

3. Avignon

Although Avignon, in the fifteenth century, had ceased to be the residence of a pope or an antipope, she remained for at least half a century the commercial metropolis and banking center of Provence and, to a certain extent, of Languedoc.[159] Montpellier was at best only a satellite which throve on the neighboring fairs of Pézenas and Montagnac. With Marseilles, relations were less active than might be supposed.[160] As a connection with the sea, Port-de-Bouc, today an unimportant village on the Bay of Fos, was much preferred to Marseilles by the Italian merchants settled in Avignon.[161] One of the reasons for this state of affairs was probably that Marseilles failed to adopt progressive business methods and, for example, made only a limited use of the bill of exchange. Another is that she was sacked in 1423 by the Catalans, one of the episodes in the contest between the houses of Anjou and Aragon for the crown of Naples, and did not recover from this major disaster for several years.[162] Merchants of Marseilles, to the extent that they had bills of exchange to negotiate, used the services of the Italian bankers in Avignon. The trade of Marseilles with the Levant was fettered by lack of capital, initiative, and efficient organization.

It was not until June 1, 1446, that the Medici established a branch in Avignon by entering into an accomanda with Giovanni di Benedetto Zampini (1405–c. 1479), who had been a clerk in Geneva since 1437, if not earlier.[163] According to the account books of the bank founded by Antonio della Casa, Zampini was already in Avignon in 1442, and it is likely that he had been sent there from Geneva to operate a suboffice and to lay the foundations for the erection of a new branch.[164] It is not known whether, at first, he was given a salary or remunerated on a commission basis. In 1444 and 1445, at any rate, as we saw in the beginning of this chapter, Zampini participated to the extent of 10 percent in the total profits of the Geneva branch wherever they were made (Table 57).

The accomanda founded on June 1, 1446, had a capital of 8,000 cameral florins, of which 7,500 florins were contributed by the Medici

Bank (holding company) and the remainder by Giovanni Zampini.[165] Results were highly satisfactory and profits amounted to nearly 7,000 petty florins of Avignon after the first twenty-two months of operation (June 1, 1446–March 24, 1448). Seven eighths of these profits, or 3,556 florins 14s. 6d. aff., went to the Medici Bank, a return of about 23.7 percent per annum on an investment of 8,175 florins di suggello.[166]

The accomanda was terminated on March 24, 1448, and replaced by an ordinary partnership which included the Medici Bank (holding company), Giovanni Zampini, and a newcomer, Verano di Bartolomeo Peruzzi.[167] The latter was the brother-in-law of Giovanni d'Amerigo Benci, the general manager. The capital was set at 16,000 petty florins or 9,600 florins di suggello, as indicated in Table 15. Each of the junior partners was entitled to one eighth of the profits, so that the parent company received three fourths. Its share amounted to 1,972 Florentine florins in 1448 and 3,420 florins in 1449 and 1450 combined.[168] These figures give an average return of 21.4 percent on an investment of 8,400 florins during a period of three years. From its foundation on June 1, 1446, to the end of 1450, Florentine style, the Avignon branch yielded an aggregate of 8,948 florins 14s. 6d. aff. in profits accruing to the Medici Bank (Table 17).[169]

Verano Peruzzi probably died or withdrew from the partnership in 1456 because by 1457 he had been replaced by his nephew, Francesco Benci, Giovanni's second son, and by Francesco Baldovini.[170] At the same time, Giovanni Zampini increased his contribution to capital from 600 to 800 florins, while Francesco Benci invested another 800 florins and Francesco Baldovini, 400.[171] Thus the non-Medici partners had a total investment of 2,000 florins. Cosimo de' Medici, in his report for the catasto of 1457, claims that the Medici share in the corpo of the Avignon branch amounts to 2,400 florins, but this figure is certainly much below reality and should perhaps be trebled.[172]

After 1457 the Avignon branch was called "Francesco Benci, Giovanni Zampini & Co." This style was shortened to Giovanni Zampini & Co." when Francesco Benci resigned on March 24, 1461, for reasons unknown.[173] In his stead, Francesco Sassetti joined the partnership. According to his libro segreto, he supplied 5,000 petty florins of Avignon, or 2,628 florins di suggello, for his share in the corpo, but there is no entry giving a clue concerning the amounts invested by the other partners. The allocation of profits, at any rate, was as follows: the Medici, one half; Zampini and Sassetti, each one fourth (Table 66).

On December 10, 1468, a strange thing happened: according to Sassetti's secret account book, the Medici drew out all their capital and their share in accrued profits, leaving Sassetti and Zampini as the only partners.[174] It is not at all clear why. Perhaps it was a way of evading the catasto, since Piero di Cosimo, in 1469, when filing his report with the tax officials, made no reference to Avignon in listing his business investments.[175] In any case, in June, 1470, the Medici re-entered the partnership on the old basis.[176]

During the eleven years covered by Sassetti's private ledger, the Avignon branch was fairly lucrative. Profits reached a total of 58,436 petty florins of Avignon, or about 5,312 petty florins per year on the average (Tables 65 and 66). This average was never attained after 1468, and therefore it seems that business was contracting. The cause is not far to seek, since Avignon rapidly lost its rank of banking center during the last quarter of the fifteenth century. The Avignon branch had relations with the court of René of Anjou, titular king of Naples, who was count of Provence, but his death in 1480, followed by the annexation of Provence to France, may have had a bad repercussion on the volume of

TABLE 65.   PROFITS OF THE AVIGNON BRANCH FROM 1461 TO 1471
(FLORENTINE STYLE)

Date	Currency of Avignon			Florentine Currency		
	f.	s.	d.	f.	s.	d.
Ragione begun on March 25, 1461						
March 25, 1461–March 24, 1462.........	3,082	19	8	1,600	0	0
March 25, 1462–March 24, 1463.........	7,045	13	7	3,676	0	0
March 25, 1463–March 24, 1464.........	5,680	9	4	3,044	0	0
March 25, 1464–March 24, 1465.........	5,365	14	0	2,912	0	0
March 25, 1465–March 24, 1466.........	6,680	11	11	3,644	0	0
March 25, 1466–March 24, 1467.........	6,088	15	9	3,070	0	0
March 25, 1467–March 24, 1468.........	7,500	20	6	4,045	0	0
March 25, 1468–December 10, 1468......	5,133	12	8	2,749	0	0
Reserves retransferred to profits..........	1,977	22	4	1,080	0	0
Subtotal............	48,555	19	9	25,820	0	0
New Ragione begun in December 1468						
December 10, 1468–March 24, 1469......	1,012	0	0	552	0	0
March 25, 1469–March 24, 1470.........	1,332	10	3	702	0	0
March 25, 1470–March 24, 1471.........	3,184	4	1	1,612	0	0
March 25, 1471–March 24, 1472.........	4,118	20	3	2,149	0	0
Subtotal............	9,647	10	7	5,015	0	0
Adjustment or error......................	233	6	8	130	0	0
Total.............	58,436	13	0	30,965	0	0
Deduct: profits distributed among the partners at various dates................	51,133	12	8	27,478	0	0
Put aside as a reserve for contingencies.....	7,303	0	4	3,487	0	0

Source: ASF, Carte Strozziane, Series II, No. 20, Libro segreto of Francesco Sassetti, fols. 15, 16, 25, 26, and 35.

TABLE 66. PROFITS ALLOCATED TO THE PARTNERS BY THE AVIGNON BRANCH, 1461–1471

Date	Total Florentine Currency			Total Currency of Avignon			The Medici Currency of Avignon			F. Sassetti Currency of Avignon			G. Zampini Currency of Avignon		
	f.	s.	d.	f.	s.	d.	f.	s.	d.	f.	s.	d.	f.	s.	d.
March 25, 1465..........	10,608	0	0	20,000	0	0	10,000	0	0	5,000	0	0	5,000	0	0
March 26, 1467..........	8,488	0	0	16,000	0	0	8,000	0	0	4,000	0	0	4,000	0	0
December 24, 1468.......	3,184	0	0	6,000	0	0	3,000	0	0	1,500	0	0	1,500	0	0
November 28, 1470.......	3,106	0	0	5,133	12	8	2,566	18	4	1,283	9	2	1,283	9	2
March 26, 1471..........	2,092	0	0	4,000	0	0	2,000	0	0	1,000	0	0	1,000	0	0
Total..........	27,478	0	0	51,133	12	8	25,566	18	4	12,783	9	2	12,783	9	2

Source: Same as Table 65.

business, since royal courts were important consumers of the luxury products in which the Medici were dealing.[177]

Giovanni Zampini withdrew as managing partner in 1476, presumably because of ill health: in the catasto of 1481, he is mentioned as deceased.[178] His position was given to Michele Dini, who had served the Medici as a factor for seventeen years. Henceforth, the Avignon branch operated under the style: "Michele Dini & Co." Dini did not hold his new job for long, since Francesco Sassetti, in his catasto report for 1481, states that the Avignon partnership is no longer in existence.[179] The only indication about decaying trade is found in a letter of Michele Dini, dated October 23, 1476, in which he complains about the difficulty of making profits in an honest way, so that many are turning to illicit contracts, which undoubtedly means usury.[180] As pointed out before, the Medici did not allow their agents to enter into overtly usurious deals. Although the Avignon branch had ceased to exist in 1480, the correspondence with Dini continued after this date, perhaps because it took some time to wind up the partnership or because the Medici continued to have relations with Dini who was now in business for himself.[181] In 1491 he was having trouble and Lorenzo Spinelli offered to pull him out, but the offer was refused either because it was not needed or because it would do no good.[182] It seems that Dini was a straightforward person who, unlike many poor swimmers, did not grab any straw in order to keep afloat.

According to the chronicle of Benedetto Dei, there were not more than five persons on the staff of the Avignon branch in 1470: Giovanni Zampini, Francesco Folchi, Guglielmo da Sommaia, Francesco di Giovanni del Zaccheria, and Michele Dini.[183] The other Florentine firms of note were the Mannelli, the Pazzi, and the Peruzzi banks.[184] The Pazzi also had a branch in upcoming Marseilles which employed four people.

About the activities of the Avignon branch little is known, but the business letters reveal that it combined trade and banking, as usual. One letter, for example, refers to linens from Verdun and Bordeaux which were shipped from Aigues Mortes to Majorca and Barcelona on board the Venetian galleys.[185] Avignon was apparently still a stopping place for ecclesiastics going to Rome, and the Medici branch provided them with letters of credit payable at various places along the road. The Avignon branch also accepted deposits: one of the main depositors was Dominique Panisse, a rich, local man, who on July 21, 1485, wrote Lorenzo the Magnificent to obtain the release of Lionetto de' Rossi.[186]

Throughout the 1460's and 1470's the Medici maintained a subbranch in Montpellier, which operated under the same style as the Avignon partnership: "Giovanni Zampini e compagni." From before 1466 this office in Montpellier was under the management of Rosso di Gentile da Sommaia, a nephew of Giovanni Zampini.[187] In 1471 he had as assistant,

Simone di Giovanni Folchi.[188] Lorenzo Spinelli, later manager of the Lyons branch, also got his training in Montpellier. In 1481 his brothers declared in their catasto report that Lorenzo was attending to the winding up of the Montpellier office subsequent to Zampini's death.[189]

The Avignon branch probably did not end with a calamitous deficit, but it was not prospering. According to a letter of Michele Dini written on January 12, 1483, the principal debtor of the Avignon branch was Rinaldo Altoviti, a Florentine residing in Avignon and Marseilles, who was either recalcitrant or insolvent. Next in importance came a claim of 7,000 florins on the late King René, whose heir, the king of France, raised all kinds of difficulties. The king of Naples, that is, Ferdinand of Aragon, also owed a substantial amount which was hard to collect.[190]

Giovanni Zampini left all his property to his nephew, Rosso da Sommaia.[191] In making his report for the catasto of 1481, the latter declared that his uncle's inheritance was so encumbered with debts that nothing remained. As long as the Medici Bank was thriving, branch managers usually made a fortune. The fact that Zampini died poor is further evidence that losses in the last years of his career swallowed up the profits made earlier and that the Avignon branch had become a losing business.

XIII

MEDICI BRANCHES OUTSIDE ITALY:
BRUGES AND LONDON

1. The Medici Bank in Bruges and London prior to 1451

In the fifteenth century, London was not yet the world metropolis it later became. On the contrary, it was a banking place of only secondary importance, a satellite that moved in the orbit of Bruges. The two places were, of course, closely connected, and any disturbance in one had a repercussion on the other. As already explained, the Low Countries depended upon England to settle their unfavorable balance of trade with the Italian city-states, Florence in particular. With the exception of Flemish tapestries and Dutch linens which were coming into vogue, the Low Countries had little to offer in exchange for the alum, spices, silks, and other luxuries which the Italians were importing. True, some Flemish cloth was still finding a market in Northern Italy, but probably not in quantities large enough to fill the deficit. Wool was the only commodity which the Italians were always eager to buy and which could be used to restore the balance. But English wool was needed at home to feed an expanding cloth industry; and export licenses, for various reasons, were increasingly hard to get.

How to settle Italian claims on the Low Countries created a real problem that grew more acute as the century progressed. It eventually engendered a crisis which not only brought about a shrinkage in the volume of international trade, but also had an adverse effect upon the prosperity of the Italian banking houses. It was undoubtedly a potent factor in causing the downfall of the Medici branches operating in Bruges and London.

The economies of the Low Countries and England were thus linked by a common interest in the wool trade and were interrelated in still other respects, because Bruges needed credits in England in order to buy wool with which to pay Italian claims. The task of adjusting international balances fell upon the Italian banking houses, and it is no wonder that there were active relations between the *bourse* in Bruges and Lombard Street in London. The Medici Bank maintained branches in both places. Since these two branches had to work hand in hand and to cooperate closely, it would be inadvisable to deal with them separately.

By the early years of the fifteenth century, the Medici Bank was doing business in Bruges and London. Although it had no branches in either place, it was represented in both by correspondents. In 1416 the Medici representative in Bruges was presumably Filippo Rapondi, who collected funds for his principals.[1] Filippo Rapondi was a merchant-banker of Lucchese origin, high in favor with John the Fearless, Duke of Burgundy and Count of Flanders (ruled 1404–1419).[2] In the 1420's and 1430's, the Medici Bank was represented in Bruges by Galeazzo Borromei & Co., a Milanese firm, and by Gualterotto de' Bardi & Co., or Gualterotto Gualterotti & Co., a Florentine banking house (Table 38).[3] In London the Medici correspondents were Totto Machiavelli and Ubertino de' Bardi & Co. Ubertino was a brother of Bartolomeo d'Andrea who, from 1420 to 1429, the year of his premature death, was branch manager in Rome. Gualterotto Gualterotti was also acting as agent for the rival bank of Averardo de' Medici, Giovanni di Bicci's nephew, although Averardo's firm used in addition the services of the firm Giovanni Orlandini & Co. (failed in 1422).[4]

These correspondents, it is likely, sold spices and silk stuffs which were sent to them on consignment by the Tavola of Florence and the Venice branch. They also attended to the dispatch of papal business, since Ubertino de' Bardi owed up to 15,400 cameral florins and Gualterotto Gualterotti 5,400 cameral florins to the Rome branch, according to the balance sheet of 1427 (Table 38).[5] In addition, the correspondents in Bruges and London handled remittances and drafts for the Medici establishments in Italy. In short, there is no doubt that the Medici bank had extensive business interests in the Low Countries and England before 1427, even though it had no real branch offices located there.[6]

The growing debit balances of their correspondents in these two countries must have worried the maggiori, especially Ilarione de' Bardi, the general manager, because he availed himself of Marco Spinellini's going to Bruges and London (1430) to convey a special message to the Borromei and to Giovanni di Zanobi da Pino, a Florentine merchant residing in Flanders.[7] Spinellini, apparently a factor or a partner of Ubertino de' Bardi, was instructed to put pressure on them and to urge them to speed up the settlement of a loan made in Rome to Scottish ambassadors, which was being repaid piecemeal and much too slowly, in Ilarione's estimation. Perhaps this slowness was not due entirely to ill will; there may have been transfer difficulties, since there were no banking places in Scotland at that time and this poor country had nothing to sell except some wool of inferior and coarse grade.[8] Spinellini also was to impress upon the Bruges and London correspondents that they were not supposed to issue letters of credit on other terms than for ready cash.

It is doubtful whether Spinellini was successful, because extant letters reveal that the maggiori were quite disappointed with his ineffectiveness,

especially his failure to collect 2,500 ducats from Giovanni di Zanobi da
Pino.[9] They also continued to complain because goods sent on consignment did not move as rapidly as expected, their correspondents were slow
in remitting, and kept excessive working balances. Of course, the trouble
in dealing with agents is always that the principal is more or less at their
mercy and does not have as much control over them as over his own
factors or branches.

Losing patience, the maggiori decided in 1436 to send to Bruges one
of their most trusted and able factors, Bernardo Portinari (1407–1455),
the son of Giovanni d'Adoardo who had been manager of the Venice
branch from 1417 to 1435. Bernardo himself had been a factor in the
service of Niccolò degli Strozzi and later of the Medici.[10] He was earning
one hundred ducats per annum in 1435.[11] The purpose of Bernardo's
mission was ostensibly to settle outstanding differences and to adjust
accounts with the Medici correspondents in Bruges, but in reality it was
much broader: Bernardo was instructed to conduct an investigation of
local conditions and business prospects in order to determine whether
conditions were favorable to the establishment of a branch office in Bruges
and later in London. The matter is not in doubt, since the text of his
instructions — and they are very detailed — is still extant among the
Medici papers.[12]

Bernardo Portinari, although free to choose his itinerary, was urged to
take the safest route and to find traveling companions, rather than run
the risk of unpleasant encounters by riding alone except for his attendant.
If possible, he was to journey by way of Geneva and Basel, where the
Medici had branches and where he might collect useful information before going on his way. Once in Bruges, he was to stay at the house of
Ubertino de' Bardi, where he would be welcomed by Marco Spinellini,
who had been informed of his coming. Portinari's most urgent assignment
was to expedite the sale of the silks and brocades which had been consigned to Ubertino de' Bardi & Co. If necessary, Bernardo was empowered
to sell them at reduced prices, but he was not allowed to grant long terms
of credit without approval. However, if market conditions improved, he
could ask the branches of Basel and Geneva, which also had slow-moving
stocks, to send some of their unsold silks to Bruges. Should spices be in
demand, Bernardo was to ask the Venice branch to send a consignment
by the first sailing of the Flanders galleys.

Bernardo Portinari was expected to follow the same policy in London
as in Bruges and to accelerate the sale of goods and the remittance of
funds which were in the hands of correspondents. It was hoped that he
would be able to reach an understanding with respect to a dispute between the Borromei and the Rome branch.

Portinari was to consider himself as representing not only the maggiori but all the Medici branches and companies, including those of Geneva and Basel. In order to press the claim of the Medici on Giovanni di Zanobi da Pino, Portinari was provided with a special power of attorney enabling him to prosecute the matter in court and even to secure a writ of *capias,* if he had to go to such an extreme in order to be paid.[13]

Keeping the eventual creation of a branch office in mind, Bernardo was urged to look around, to inquire about local customs with respect to trade as well as to bills of exchange, and to find out the strength and the credit standing of the principal foreign merchants residing in Bruges, especially of the exchange dealers. How were the Florentines doing? And how did they feel about future business prospects? The maggiori were anxious to know whether the Bruges court was still living up to its reputation of meting out prompt and impartial justice when foreign merchants were concerned. The maggiori's only worry was that the revival of the Hundred Years' War, by dragging the Duke of Burgundy into the conflict (on the side of France), might invite reprisals and seriously disturb trade relations between England and Flanders.[14]

It is likely that, upon his return to Florence, Bernardo Portinari was able to make a favorable report, for he was sent back to the Low Countries in 1438. Although he took up residence in Bruges, he visited the fairs of Antwerp in March and August of the same year.[15] Among other things, he looked after the delivery of papal bulls of nomination, one concerning the see of London and another concerning the see of Ely.[16] These transactions involved the considerable sum of £2,347 18s. 4d. groat to be collected from the Borromei in London. Portinari was also busy negotiating bills of exchange and wrote Antonio Salutati in Ferrara that he would send to Basel or Geneva a shipment of English nobles (gold coins) concealed in bales of cloth.[17] He was still a simple factor,[18] because entries in the libro segreto of the Medici Bank reveal that the Bruges branch was not set up as a separate entity until March 24, 1439 (N. S.).[19] An accomanda was then formed, in which the Medici invested 6,000 cameral florins supplied in entirety by the Rome branch and, in accordance with the Florentine law of 1408, limited their liability to their initial investment and no more. How much Portinari contributed is not known. Perhaps not a penny. Nevertheless, he was entitled to one sixth of the profits and the maggiori jointly to the remainder.

In the first two years of its existence, 1439 and 1440, Florentine style, the Bruges branch did rather well, the net earnings amounting to £670 1s. 5d. groat. After deduction of a reserve of £100 gr., Portinari received £95 3d. groat for his share and the Medici bank, £475 1s. 2d. groat.[20] Modest profits were also entered in the following three years, 1441–1443 (Table 67), but there is no trace of any earnings being recorded in the libro segreto of the Medici Bank from 1444 through 1449 (Florentine style), which means that none were distributed among the partners. In 1450 there were again some profits, but they were lumped together with those of the London branch, with the result that there is no way of telling how much or how little was earned in Bruges (Table 68). Why the Bruges branch made such a poor showing during six years, from 1444 to 1450, is nowhere clarified. In all likelihood, losses were caused by defaulting debtors, and we know for certain that the Bruges branch took a beating because of the failure of their Barcelonese correspondents, Giovanni Venturi and Riccardo Davanzati & Co., which occurred in 1447.[21] It is likely that this loss was large enough to wipe out existing reserves in addition to the undistributed profits of preceding years.

Barcelona at that time was still an important outlet for Flemish cloth, especially for such lighter fabrics as the says of Wervicq. The Bruges branch sent one of its factors, Attaviano Altoviti, to Barcelona in an effort to retrieve some of the goods held in consignment by Venturi and Davanzati. Whether he accomplished anything is another matter: probably the trip only served to add expense to the loss.

It is probable that Bernardo Portinari opened a suboffice in London and put in charge Angelo Tani with whom he was well acquainted because they had worked side by side as factors in Venice.[22] Since Tani knew no English he was not promoted, much to his disappointment, when in 1446 the maggiori made up their minds to detach the London office from the Bruges branch and to form a new partnership for this purpose.[23] Contrary to their usual policy, they did not select the managing partner from the ranks of their own factors but chose an outsider, as they had done once before when they appointed Giovanni Portinari manager of the Venice branch in 1416. Their choice for London fell upon Gerozzo de' Pigli (1406–after 1469), who knew English and the City very well, since he had been doing business for some years in Lombard Street.

The capital of the new partnership was set at £2,500 sterling, of which Cosimo de' Medici and Giovanni Benci jointly were to supply £2,166 13s. 4d., equivalent to 13,184 florins 1s. 10d. affiorino, and Gerozzo de' Pigli the remainder, or £333 6s. 8d.[24] In addition to an allowance of 100 nobles (£33 6s. 8d. st.) a year to cover expenses, Pigli was entitled to one fifth of the profits in order to remunerate him for his work. As usual in similar agreements, Pigli was expected to stay at his post in London but he needed no special permission to go on business to Southampton or to ride into the Cotswolds or other English counties to buy wool. The contract went into effect on June 1, 1446, and was to last four years, until June 1, 1450, a date to remember. Actually the terms regarding the division of profits were never carried out because they were amended within a short time. To pacify Angelo Tani, who was displeased

TABLE 67. NET PROFITS OF THE BRUGES BRANCH FROM 1439 THROUGH 1443 (FLORENTINE STYLE)
(All amounts are in pounds groat, Flemish currency, except the last column)

Year	Total			Reserve for Bad Debts			Share of Bernardo Portinari			Share of the Maggiori Flemish Currency			Florentine florins			
	£	s.	d.	£	s.	d.	£	s.	d.	£	s.	d.	f.	s.	d.	aff.
1439–1440.........	670	1	5	100	0	0	95	0	3	475	1	2	2,350	0	0	0
1441.............	498	16	4	100	0	0	66	9	4	332	7	0	1,661	21	9	9
1442.............	302	0	0	...	..	..	50	6	8	251	13	4	1,312	0	0	0
1443.............	538	7	6	124	0	0	69	1	3	345	6	3	1,860	0	0	0
	2,009	5	3	324	0	0	280	17	6	1,404	7	9	7,183	21	9	

Source: MAP, filza 153, no. 3, fols. 46, 63, 64, 65, 66, and 73.

TABLE 68. NET PROFITS OF THE LONDON AND BRUGES BRANCHES FROM 1447 THROUGH 1450 (FLORENTINE STYLE)

(All amounts are in pounds sterling, English currency, except the last column)

Year	Total			Reserve for Bad Debts			Share of Junior Partners			Share of the Maggiori						
										English Currency			Florentine florins			
	£	s.	d.	£	s.	d.	£	s.	d.	£	s.	d.	f.	s.	d.	aff.
1447–1448	875	0	0	75	0	0	240	0	0[a]	560	0	0	3,300	0	0	0
1449	899	8	1	100	0	0	239	16	5[a]	559	11	8	3,357	0	0	0
1450	1,031	17	10	..	..	..	371	1	10[b]	660	16	0	4,000	0	0	0
	2,806	5	11	175	0	0	850	18	3	1,780	7	8	10,657	0	0	0
Deduct adjustment........													52	9	1	
													10,604	19	11[c]	

[a] The junior partners were Gerozzo de' Pigli, entitled to one fifth of net profits, and Angelo Tani, entitled to one tenth of net profits.

[b] The share of the junior partners was allocated as follows:

	£	s.	d. st.
Simone Nori..............	87	18	1
Angelo Tani..............	117	19	9
Gerozzo de' Pigli.........	165	4	0
Total.................	371	1	10

[c] This total plus f. 7, 183 21s. 9d. aff., the total of Table 67, gives an aggregate of 17,788 florins 12s. 8d. aff., which corresponds to the figure given in Table 17.

Source: MAP, filza 153. no. 3, fols. 85–86 and 88–90.

by not being made manager, he was given a share of one tenth in the net profits; that of the maggiori was accordingly reduced from four fifths to seven tenths.[25]

When leaving Florence for his new post, Pigli was provided with detailed instructions, in which the maggiori laid down the law and told him to whom it was safe to lend or to whom it was risky to grant credit. Since the tenor of these instructions has been discussed above in Chapter Five, there is no need to dwell here on the same subject.[26]

The London branch under the management of the experienced Gerozzo de' Pigli was successful from the very start and produced encouraging results in the first three years of operation (Table 68). In the third year, the maggiori received a return of approximately 25 percent on invested capital. By contrast, the Bruges branch was doing so poorly that Bernardo Portinari was recalled to Florence in the course of 1448 and the maggiori prematurely denounced their agreement with him, as they had the unquestionable right to do.[27] Reversing the situation which had existed before 1446, they now placed the Bruges branch under the authority of the London branch. Accordingly, on December 21, 1448, a new partnership was formed between "Piero di Cosimo de' Medici e Gerozzo de' Pigli & Co." of London on the one hand, and Simone d'Antonio Nori, on the other hand, for the purpose of trading and carrying on banking in Bruges.[28] The entire capital of £2,000 groat, or £1,691 3s. 4d. sterling, was furnished by the London branch, but the actual management was entrusted to Simone Nori under the aegis of Angelo Tani.[29] Profits were to be allotted in the following proportion: 2s. 6d. in the pound (one eighth) to Simone Nori and 17s. 6d. to the London branch. This partnership, a temporary expedient, was scheduled to expire after a short period of eighteen months, or on June 1, 1450.

It should perhaps be pointed out that we have here a pyramid composed of three layers of superimposed partnerships: at the top, the Medici Bank, which had as partners Cosimo de' Medici and Giovanni Benci; in the middle, the London branch whose partners were the Medici Bank, Gerozzo de' Pigli, and Angelo Tani; at the bottom, the Bruges branch controlled by the London branch and managed by Simone Nori. The same was true of profits: Cosimo de' Medici participated for three fourths in the profits of the Medici Bank and Giovanni Benci for one fourth; the Medici Bank in turn received seven tenths of the profits of the London branch; and, finally, the London branch was entitled to seven eighths of the earnings of the Bruges branch.

When, on June 1, 1450, both existing contracts for Bruges and London came to an end, they were not extended and another reversal of policy took place. The Bruges branch regained its independence from the London branch. Two separate accomandite were formed. At the same time,

Angelo Tani and Simone Nori exchanged jobs, since the former was transferred from London to Bruges and the latter, who was in Bruges, was sent to London to take Tani's place. The capital of the Bruges branch was set at £3,000 groat, Flemish currency, of which the Medici Bank supplied £2,160, Gerozzo de' Pigli £540, and Angelo Tani £300 (Table 15).[30] The capital of the London branch was much less: it amounted to only £1,000 sterling, of which £800 were contributed by the maggiori (Cosimo and Giovanni Benci, jointly) and the balance by Gerozzo de' Pigli. Simone Nori, although a partner, invested nothing "but his person" and received a share in the profits in remuneration for his services as manager: a common practice of the Medici Bank, as has been shown.

According to surviving examples, business letters sent by the accomanda of London are signed: "Simone Nori e compagni di Londra."[31] Following the same pattern, the accomanda of Bruges called itself "Agnolo Tani e compagni di Bruggia."[32] The Medici name, consequently, disappeared from the style used heretofore by their Bruges and London branches, a sign, it seems, that the Medici were uncertain about the future and perhaps contemplated withdrawing altogether from the Low Countries and England.[33] The business community apparently thought so, too; this move of the Medici did not enhance their credit and caused adverse comments by envious competitors. According to Nori, some malicious Italians "were croaking about it" like ravens.[34]

2. THE LONDON BRANCH FROM 1451 TO 1480

After March 25, 1451, the London branch and the Bruges branch parted company and for a few years their paths did not cross. Therefore, it seems advisable to follow for a while the destiny of the London branch. Gerozzo de' Pigli, it is true, was still a partner in both branches, but according to the rules of law on accomandite he left the actual management to the junior partners, Tani and Nori. Inasmuch as the articles of association exempted him from any residence requirement, he returned to Florence, although he did not exactly go into retirement; being a conscientious man, he returned to Flanders and England on an inspection tour and stayed for over a year, from October 29, 1453, date of his arrival in Bruges, to November or December, 1454.[35] From then on, he resided permanently in Florence, and it is probable that age and infirmities prevented him from undertaking another tiresome trip on horseback. It is also likely that he continued to advise the maggiori on their English and Flemish business affairs and to recommend caution, but one wonders, in the light of subsequent events, to what an extent they heeded his advice.

One purpose of Pigli's visit to Bruges was apparently to reconvert the accomanda into an ordinary partnership which would reassume the Medici name and merchant's mark. Nori would have liked the maggiori to form the same kind of partnership to protect their honor and reputation in London, but if they did not care enough to do so he resigned himself to wait till the termination of his contract. After all, Nori claimed, he enjoyed credit and, "though an Italian," he was well liked in the City.[36] "Tolerated" would perhaps be a better word, because the English of the time had strong anti-alien prejudices and the "Lombards" were hated by the merchants of the City, who regarded them as unwelcome intruders and sought by all means, fair and foul, to exclude them from control of the carrying trade.[37] Popular feeling finds its expression in the Libelle of Englyshe Polycye (1436), in which the poet waxes indignant against Venetians and Florentines, who in their galleys bring in apes and jades, nifles and trifles, and all manner of chaffer, and carry away the lifeblood of England, her precious wool.[38]

Wool, indeed, was still England's main article of export, although the quantity was steadily declining and the exports of cloth were going up at an increasing tempo. But the Florentines were hungry for wool and were interested to a much lesser extent in lead, tin, brass chandeliers, and a few other articles. They bought little cloth; however, the Medici correspondence refers occasionally to suantoni (cloth from Southampton) and charisea (kerseys).[39] In principle, the Merchants of the Staple, a regulated company, had a monopoly on the export of wool, and the wool Staple was located at Calais. There were two exceptions to this rule: one, coarse wool from Scotland and the North Country could be sent directly from Berwick and Newcastle-on-Tyne to Bruges and Middelburg without passing through the Staple of Calais; two, it was possible to export wool to the Straits of Marrock and beyond under a special license of the King.[40] The Italians undoubtedly bought some wool, but not much, at the Staple of Calais and then sent it overland to Lombardy; the bulk of their purchases, however, was shipped aboard the galleys from Sandwich or Southampton with the King's license.[41] This trade, of course, aroused the strenuous opposition of the Merchants of the Staple who resented it as an infringement of their monopoly. It was one of the main reasons why the Italians were so unpopular in the City and why there were periodic anti-Italian riots.[42] In the process of time, licenses became increasingly hard to get and could be obtained only by granting favors to the King. The favors which the King appreciated most were loans, and his demands never ceased. They became even more pressing as the War of the Roses, which broke out in May 1455 and lasted intermittently until 1485, played havoc with royal finances.[43] Thus the stage was set for the tragedy of the London branch of the Medici Bank.

It was well-nigh impossible to refuse the King's requests because the Florentine galleys depended almost entirely on wool as return cargo, and

8. Courtyard of the Medici Bank in Bruges (now a convent). Above the archway, medallion representing Clarice Orsini, wife of Lorenzo the Magnificent

9. Angelo Tani, manager of the Bruges branch, 1449–1464, and his wife, Caterina Tanagli. From the wings of the triptych "The Last Judgment," by Hans Memling

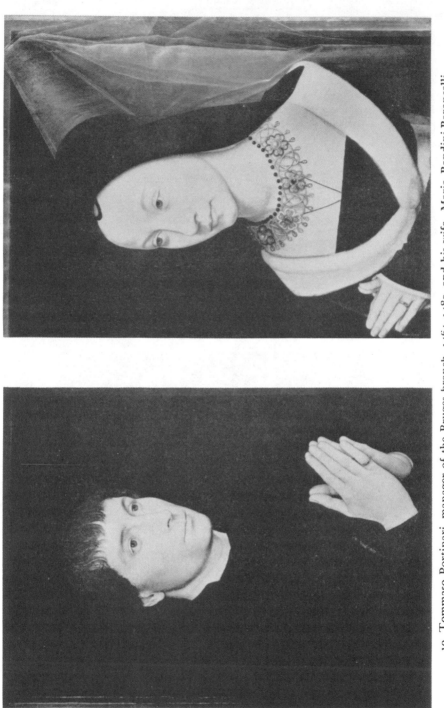

10. Tommaso Portinari, manager of the Bruges branch, 1464–1480, and his wife, Maria Bandini-Baroncelli

Flanders, as explained, had a very unfavorable balance with Italy and had practically no return cargo to offer. The galleys went to Sluys or the roadstead of Zeeland chiefly to unload their outbound cargo and then to Southampton to unload the rest and to take a full shipment of wool with some tin or lead as ballast.[44] If it had been otherwise, the galleys would have called at Southampton first and then gone on to Flanders. The reason is obvious: in order to load or reload a ship, it must first be empty.

The available evidence leaves little room for doubt. Several of the itineraries followed by the Florentine galleys have been preserved. They all mention Southampton as terminal and list Sluys as a port of call on the outbound voyage.[45] The fact that Southampton is much nearer than Sluys when coming from Cape Finisterre and going up the Channel is of no importance whatsoever. Even today, according to maritime custom, the homeward limb of a voyage begins where a ship takes on board its inbound cargo, and not sooner: it is not a matter of distance but of loading and unloading. If this evidence does not suffice, there are also the cargo lists of the Florentine and Burgundian galleys, discussed in Chapter Seven. Before 1464 the Florentine galleys, in contrast to the Genoese carracks, had difficulty filling their holds even on the outward voyage because the spices and luxury products, while representing a great value, took little space.[46] After 1464 the situation changed completely: papal alum was the main cargo outbound from Italy and wool, inbound. When one of the Burgundian galleys was captured while crossing the North Sea from Walcheren to England, it carried very little that was going to Italy, but the bulk of the cargo was papal alum bound for Southampton, with some luxuries, such as brocades and gold thread, having the same destination.[47]

What constantly worried the branch managers in London and Bruges was how to settle debit balances in Italy. Bruges usually had credits in Spain but not enough to cover the deficit. In a letter of October 4, 1453, Simone Nori revealed what was on his mind when he wrote: "As you know, we are always in need of funds over there," meaning in Italy.[48] And Tommaso Portinari, manager in Bruges, writing on November 9, 1464, congratulated himself because he hoped to have a stock of wool ready to exchange for the alum which the galleys were bringing.[49] Although the Medici managers were quite aware of the necessity of making returns in one way or another, it is doubtful whether they grasped all the implications of this problem and fully realized that a persistent disequilibrium in international balances created an economic problem of first magnitude which business men, however able, could not solve within the compass of a single firm.

Unfortunately, the Medici branch managers in London after Gerozzo de' Pigli were far from possessing outstanding ability. Perhaps Simone Nori was the best, but he was too easygoing and lacked an essential quality: that of being a tough negotiator bent upon driving hard bargains. At first, things went rather well, since funds were not yet tied up in loans to the King. Business was good. Late in the summer of 1453 Nori rode into the Cotswolds to buy wool.[50] He intended to buy only sixty sacks, but as the clip was unusually fine and prices low, eleven marks (£7 6s. 8d. st.) the sack, he could not resist the temptation of buying a hundred.[51] Silks from Florence found a ready market and were selling better in London than in Bruges, perhaps because of preparations for the christening of Prince Edward, the son of Henry VI and Margaret of Anjou. Royal births and marriages were always an occasion for festivities and lavish display.

Nori got along fairly well with Gerozzo de' Pigli, his immediate superior. He was supposed to cooperate closely with Bruges but relations in fact were not very cordial. According to Nori, "ours" of Bruges did not pay enough attention to his commissions and gave him poor service.[52] Angelo Tani, Nori complained, was never willing to admit that he might be wrong and "always had scissors hanging from his belt" to slash any criticism. His acolyte, Tommaso Portinari, was equally prompt to take offense and "sniff up immediately any fumes." [53] Nori also claimed that Bruges constantly had a debit balance of about £2,000 st. because of drafts and purchases of English wool.[54] One might safely assume that these purchases of wool were made to settle accounts in Italy.

Much to Nori's delight, the accomanda was changed into an ordinary partnership on March 25, 1454, while Gerozzo de' Pigli was still in Bruges.[55] No alteration was made either in invested capital or in the allocation of profits. The duration of the contract was for four years ending March 24, 1458. The only change was in the style of the company, which took the name of "Piero de' Medici, Gerozzo de' Pigli e compagni di Londra." It is probable that the London branch was still making profits at this juncture, but they soon vanished after the War of the Roses got under way: it had an adverse effect upon business conditions and decimated the Medici Bank's customers in both camps.

Edward IV, being a usurper, could not afford to antagonize public opinion or to disregard the mercantile interests so powerful in the City and in Parliament. To placate the English merchants and the clothiers, he had to give his assent to the statute of 1463 which, under the pretext of combatting "idleness," forbade aliens to buy up wool and any person, alien or denizen, to ship it to any place other than the staple town of Calais, thus abolishing the license system.[56] But Edward IV needed all the money he could scrape together. Without repealing this legislation, he managed the next year to insert in another statute a little clause which exempted wools from staple regulations, if they were "to pass out of this Realm by the Straits of Marrock," and thus restored the license system as it had existed before.[57] In actual fact, Edward IV continued to grant licenses, but perhaps more sparingly than before.[58]

To obtain these precious permits, Simone Nori and even more his successor, Gherardo di Bernardo Canigiani (1424–1484), were induced to lend more and more. Losses soon were piling up and working capital became impounded in frozen credits which impaired earning capacity still further.

By 1457, if we may believe Gerozzo de' Pigli's return for the catasto, losses had already devoured all the capital.[59] The liquidation of the partnership of March 24, 1458, however, turned out to be less disastrous than expected because assets just covered liabilities.[60] The difficulties became very serious only after Edward IV's accession in 1461. An aggravating factor, of course, was that the Medici were unable to make good their claims on any supporters of the House of Lancaster, such as Robert, Lord Hungerford, who owed a sizable sum of money which had been paid by the Medici Bank for his ransom after he had been captured by the French at the battle of Castillon and imprisoned from 1453 to 1459.[61]

During the early 1460's, Simone Nori spent a great deal of time in Italy, perhaps because the English climate did not agree with him and his lungs were giving him trouble. He was away from London during most of 1461; he made another trip to Florence in March, 1464, and did not return to his post until more than a year later, in May, 1465.[62] After being back in London a few months, he fell dangerously ill (December, 1466) and it is doubtful that he was able to attend to business.[63] As soon as he was able to undertake the trip, he set out for Florence and never returned to England again. He was still alive in 1469, since he made out a return for the officials of the catasto, but he must have died soon thereafter. Because he shared in the losses of the London branch as well as in the profits, his half-brother, Francesco Nori, inherited only a huge debt.[64]

While Simone Nori was absent from London, the burden of the management fell upon the shoulders of his assistant, Gherardo Canigiani. It was then that the mischief was done, because Canigiani was more intent upon ingratiating himself with Edward IV than upon giving faithful service to his masters. Unable or unwilling to resist pressure, he granted the King loan after loan. It is true that Canigiani was in a quandary, since new licenses could be obtained only by making new loans. A common procedure was to repay loans by granting permission to export a certain number of wool sacks free from all customs and subsidies. Thus, on April 26, 1464, Edward IV, in return for a loan of 800 marks, or £533 6s. 8d. st., gave Canigiani the right to ship 200 sacks of wool from London or Sandwich to the Staple of Calais and thence beyond the mountains without paying customs and subsidies.[65] As the duty for aliens was four marks per sack, such a loan would automatically be extinguished by shipping the sacks allowed in the license.[66] Loans in this form, if moderate in amount, were not particularly dangerous, but it was unsafe to lend large sums if not fully and tightly secured by pledges or assignments.

By 1465 the plight of the London branch was so bad that Piero di Cosimo de' Medici refused to renew the existing partnership agreement when it expired, but he was persuaded, probably by Tommaso Portinari, to join him in forming an accomanda with Giovanni de' Bardi and Gherardo Canigiani as active partners. This accomanda was to last three years, beginning March 25, 1466, and ending March 24, 1469; it was to transact business under the name of Gherardo Canigiani and Giovanni de' Bardi without mentioning any other partner or using any merchant's mark.[67] The capital was set at £2,000 sterling, of which £900 were supplied by Piero de' Medici, £500 by Tommaso Portinari, and £300 by each of the active partners. After giving 10 percent of the profits to charities or pious works, the remainder was to be allocated in the following way: Piero de' Medici 8s. 4d. in the pound, Portinari 5s. in the pound, and Canigiani and Bardi each 3s. 4d. in the pound.[68] The articles of association, which are still extant, contain the usual clauses defining the duties of the active partners and limiting their powers, but they significantly do not put a ceiling on loans to the King. Of course, since the partnership was an accomanda, Piero de' Medici's and Tommaso Portinari's liability was limited to their initial investment plus undistributed profits.

Gerozzo de' Pigli, who had been a partner since the very beginning, that is, for the last twenty years, was still alive; he decided wisely to withdraw with as little damage to himself as possible. In consequence, he made an agreement with Piero de' Medici which provided for the payment to Pigli of 1,500 florins in final settlement of all claims and counterclaims and exonerated him from any further liability in connection with either London or Bruges: a clever exit, especially since his advice was no longer sought or was entirely disregarded.[69]

Whether or not the accomanda formed on August 2, 1465, went into effect as scheduled on March 25, 1466, is uncertain because of gaps in the extant records; if so, it is doubtful whether it lasted the full three years stipulated by the articles of association. According to the interpretation offered by the Belgian historian, Armand Grunzweig, Giovanni d'Agnolo di Zanobi di Messer Andrea de' Bardi (c. 1433–1488), when sizing up the risks involved in this venture, shrank away from such heavy responsibility and left Gherardo Canigiani as sole manager.[70] It is even more likely that the two managers, once they began working together, did not see eye to eye and could not agree on the policy to be pursued. In any case, there is a letter from Giovanni de' Bardi, written from Bruges on February 27, 1470, which shows that he was still concerned on that date with the Medici interests in England.[71] During the restoration of Henry VI, on February 22, 1471 he secured for himself and his three clerks a royal patent of protection and a guarantee that the duty on wool would remain at four marks (£2 13s. 4d. st.) per sack.[72] Giovanni de' Bardi was still doing business in Lombard Street in 1482 when, upon one occasion, Edward IV granted to "John de Barde," in repayment of a debt of £200 st., or 300 marks, the right to export seventy-five sacks of wool, quit of duty at four marks per sack, and to take them to foreign parts by the Straits of Marrock.[73] When Giovanni de' Bardi died at Florence on January 11, 1488, Galeazzo di Francesco Sassetti described him as "a great merchant and, in private, a man of honor and worth." [74] There is no evidence that Giovanni de' Bardi was in any way responsible for the plight of the London branch of the Medici Bank. Perhaps serious trouble might have been avoided had Piero di Cosimo listened to Bardi's advice instead of staking his fortunes on Canigiani.

According to the Chronicle of Benedetto Dei, the staff of the London branch around 1470 did not include more than four persons: Gherardo Canigiani, Lorenzo Barducci, Lorenzo Ottavanti, and Jacopo del Zaccheria.[75] After Canigiani, the best known of this group in England is probably Lorenzo Barducci, whom the English called Laurence Bardoce.[76] After being a factor in Bruges from at least 1455 to 1461 or later, he was transferred to London and went into the service of Canigiani when the latter broke off his connection with the Medici.[77] In 1468 he took part in the negotiations for the dowry of Margaret of York, Edward IV's sister, betrothed to Charles the Bold, Duke of Burgundy.[78] In 1480 he was arrested for debt, as Canigiani's partner, but he was released because he was able to prove that he was a simple factor on a salary.[79]

In 1467 the London branch of the Medici Bank was already in such bad shape that Piero di Cosimo, upon Sassetti's advice, decided to send Angelo Tani to London with instructions to straighten out the muddle and to proceed to an audit of the books. He arrived early in January, 1468, and discovered that Edward IV owed the fantastic amount of £8,500 st. for which Canigiani had already secured assignments on the moiety of several sources of revenue and permission to export wool with the understanding that the duty at the rate of four marks per sack be deductible from the debt until its complete extinction.[80] This agreement thus provided for the gradual amortization of the debt, but very slowly; as a matter of fact, much too slowly in Tani's opinion.[81] Besides, the King owed another £2,000 st., which was secured by divers pledges and not by assignments. On the whole, the financial condition of the London branch was far from rosy, and Tani intimated that it was on the brink of bankruptcy unless speedy help from headquarters and the other branches was forthcoming. "I understand very well," he wrote tartly to Piero di Cosimo, on February 12, 1468, "that my assignment is to resurrect a corpse; nonetheless, I hope to succeed if you and Tommaso (Portinari) do as I say."

Assets, in Tani's estimation, covered liabilities. In addition to the King's debt aggregating £10,500 st., they included £1,000 st. due from Englishmen, mainly lords, and £7,000 st. in merchandise (wool and cloth) sent in consignment to the Tavola of Florence and the branches in Bruges and Milan. Of the King's debt, Tani did not expect to collect more than £2,500 st. in the first year. The claims on Englishmen were supposedly good, but Tani thought that they would be difficult and slow to collect. On the liabilities' side, there was a goodly sum owing to the Rome branch — the transfer problem again — but most of the resources consisted in funds borrowed at high interest rates of 12 or 14 percent a year. Such was the general picture. While assets, for the most part, were slow and unproductive, the branch depended for its survival on borrowed funds, and interest charges "were consuming its substance." [82] To get out of this quagmire, Tani saw no other alternative than to accelerate the settlement of the King's debt and to step up the shipment of wool and cloth to the continent, especially to Italy.

With regard to the first part of this program, Tani hoped that he would be able to get some of the subsidies to be granted by Parliament and expressed willingness to accept wool and cloth in payment of the debt.[83] Actually, Edward IV, despite his worrying about the disaffection of Warwick, made a serious effort to liquidate his indebtedness to the Medici. He turned over to them some of the proceeds of the parliamentary subsidies and made deliveries of wool and cloth. Tani hoped to reduce the debt secured by assignment on the customs to £2,500.[84] This was being too optimistic. To retain Edward IV's favor, the Medici were moved to make new loans, the largest being one of £2,600 st. in November, 1468.[85] Moreover, they had been unable to resist the temptation of granting credit to Edward IV in order to sell him £1,000 st. worth of silks in connection with the wedding of the King's sister to Charles the Bold, which was celebrated with great pomp at Damme, near Bruges, on Sunday, July 3, 1468.[86] Nevertheless, some progress was made and amortization of the old debt exceeded the amount of the new loans. Apparently, a settlement of accounts took place in December, 1468, by which the unamortized balance of the old debt was set at £3,225 6s. 8d. st., the figure given in a patent issued on January 8, 1469.[87]

The second part of Tani's rescue operation surprisingly was more difficult to carry out than the first. He appealed to Francesco Sassetti for an advance of £3,000 st. on the goods sent on consignment and actually in the hands of other Medici branches.[88] Tani's appeals, however, fell on deaf ears, and Sassetti, a compromising politician rather than a business leader, failed to act beyond generously dispensing his advice. With some exaggeration, Tani complained testily to Lorenzo de' Medici: "What we need is help and not advice; we can get plenty of advice here, since lawyers form *one fourth* of the population of this realm." And he pursued: "When I was about to leave [Italy], every one promised me to do miracles, but now all are mute." [89] The most favorable response came from Pigello Portinari in Milan, who declared himself willing to take more wool and cloth and promised to make quick sales and prompt returns. His brother Tommaso also cooperated, although he could have done more. However, if it had not been for his help, the London branch would have succumbed. Francesco Nori in Lyons did not raise a finger, and Giovanni Tornabuoni in Rome, as usual, could see only his own problems and his own immediate interests. He refused to accept cloth in payment of London's debit balance.[90] Then, in 1469, he suddenly took alarm, because the debit reached the sum of 40,213 florins, or £6,702 st., with no settlement in sight. He rushed to Florence and, with Sassetti's lame acquiescence, he took possession of wool and cloth which Tani had sent on consignment by the Burgundian galleys and which really belonged to the Bruges branch.[91] This precipitate and illegal action became a source of further difficulties. In short, there was no coordination of efforts and the team did not pull together; it is a wonder that the wagon did not bog down in the mire.

His mission accomplished, Angelo Tani, accompanied by Tommaso Portinari, returned to Italy in the spring of 1469.[92] Most probably he had a feeling of satisfaction because he had been able to salvage the London branch and to put it back on its feet. However, the unreliable Canigiani was still in charge. Furthermore, the success of Tani's mission depended upon the preservation of peaceful conditions in strife-torn England. And this is precisely what did not occur, because the War of the Roses flared up again and broke out with new fury. Warwick, the kingmaker, rebelled and drove Edward IV from the throne and into exile, while Henry VI regained the crown for a few months (October 1470–March 1471). During this brief restoration, the Medici agents were not molested, because Henry took under his protection Gherardo Canigiani, Lorenzo Barducci, "and all other of the Fellowship of Medici." [93] But, naturally, he repudiated the usurper's debt. Canigiani, therefore, must have hailed Edward IV with relief, when the latter, after the rout of his opponents, reascended the throne of England. However, the Medici reaped little benefit from the victory of their client. Most of their customers, Lancastrians and Yorkists alike, had been slain on the battlefields of Barnet and Tewkesbury. The King himself had sunk deeper into debt and was less able to pay than ever before. On August 30, 1471, he acknowledged owing Canigiani the sum of £6,600 st. and granted him the usual license to export wool to foreign parts by the Straits of Marrock without paying customs or subsidies, the duty to be deducted from the debt.[94] Perhaps some wool was shipped under this license, but the feats of Angelo Tani were not to be repeated. Conditions in England seemed so hopeless and so unstable that the Medici, in 1472, decided to withdraw and to break off their ties with Gherardo Canigiani.

To please Francesco Sassetti, Tommaso Portinari agreed that the Bruges branch would take over the assets and liabilities of the *ragione di Londra,* including the doubtful claims on Edward IV. The latter acknowledged on June 6, 1475, that he still owed £5,000 st. to Lorenzo and Giuliano de' Medici, Tommaso Portinari, and their agents, and granted them the usual patent authorizing them to export wool and to apply the customs duties (at four marks per sack) toward amortization of this debt.[95] The deal between Sassetti and Portinari was certainly made behind the back of Angelo Tani, who was a partner of the Bruges branch but not of the London branch. When he learned about it, he penned a vigorous protest in which he emphasized over and over again that the London branch and the Bruges branch were separate legal entities (*La ragione di Londra . . . era ragione da parte e ciascuna faceva per se*), and that he was in no way responsible for the losses of the London branch. He was undoubtedly right in this contention, but it was not to the liking of Francesco Sassetti, who was fond of expedients that postponed the making of unpleasant decisions — an approach which, instead of solving a problem, made it worse in the end.[96] As Tani rightly remonstrated, the Bruges branch, by assuming the liabilities of the London branch, also assumed interest charges which became a permanent burden and seriously impaired earning capacity. As a matter of fact, it was a contributing cause leading to the downfall of the Bruges branch in 1478. It was not until then that the losses of the London branch, amounting to 51,533 florins, were finally written off.[97]

What happened to Gherardo Canigiani, or Gerard Caniziani as he came to be known in England? Soon after severing his connection with the Medici, he secured from his good friend, Edward IV, letters of denization for himself and the heirs of his body (November 3, 1473).[98] Within the next few days he married a wealthy English woman, Dame Elizabeth Stokton, and became a country squire, because the King, in satisfaction of a sum of £360, granted him the manor of Great Lynford, Buckinghamshire, with the advowson of the parish church.[99] Apparently he joined the Mercers' Gild and, henceforth called himself "merchant, citizen and mercer of London, sometime of the fellowship of the Medicis of Florence and factor and attorney of the same." [100] By the way, he disclaimed ever having been their partner.

When Tommaso Portinari heard that Canigiani was so prosperous and had made such a brilliant match, it was decided that the latter should make good some of the losses caused by his mismanagement. To achieve this aim, a scheme was devised which fell little short of being a swindle. Cristoforo, or Cristofano, Spini, Tommaso's henchman, was sent to London and, with many entreating and soft words, persuaded Canigiani to help him organize a large venture in wool (incetta di lane) under the license of £6,600 granted by Edward IV on August 30, 1471.[101] As Canigiani enjoyed the trust of the wool dealers, he was induced to stand surety for the wool purchased from them, in all 711 sacks and 20 nails, enough to fill the holds of a galley. Spini made the down payment. No sooner was the wool shipped from Southampton than Spini threw off the mask of friendship and refused to make any further payments, alleging that the remainder would be deducted from what Canigiani owed the Medici company. The latter, now realizing that he had been a dupe, petitioned the Chancery for a writ to arrest Spini or to prevent his leaving the country. Apparently this request was granted and the writ executed, but Canigiani, for fear of reprisals against his own relatives in Florence, was impelled to set Spini free and let him go back to Bruges.

On January 13, 1475, Canigiani received from Edward IV a five-year protection for himself, his servants, and his property against "Christopher Spyne" and other Florentine merchants of the society of the Medici.[102] They, the King understood, intended to annoy Canigiani "without cause" on account of his services to the Crown and his English marriage, a slight misrepresentation of the facts. Canigiani also took the matter to court, where a judgment rendered on February 25, 1475, decided that the society of the Medici should pay £2,000 st. still due to the English wool dealers and Canigiani the rest, presumably £952 of incidentals. The King's debt to the Medici, at any rate, was reduced from £6,600 to £5,000 st., the figure given in the grant of June 6, 1475, since the duties on 711 sacks amounted to more than £1,600.[103] Canigiani wrote a letter of complaint to Lorenzo the Magnificent charging that Spini was "less trustworthy than a Turk." [104] On reading this, Lorenzo must have smiled wryly and shrugged his shoulders.

Although the London branch was discontinued as an independent entity after the dissolution of the partnership with Gherardo Canigiani, there is no doubt that the Medici in 1473 reopened an office in the City because they could not very well get along without one as long as they were dealing in wool. This new ragione, as opposed to the old ragione in the process of liquidation, was a subsidiary of the Bruges branch and was placed under the management of Tommaso Guidetti. Conclusive evidence is afforded by a balance sheet, dated November 12, 1477, among the Medici papers (Table 69).[105] It shows that the resources of this new

TABLE 69. BALANCE SHEET OF THE MEDICI BANK'S LONDON OFFICE,
NOVEMBER 12, 1477
(All amounts are in pounds sterling, English currency)

Assets

	£	s.	d.
Cash on hand and balances in cash book (quaderno di cassa).....	471	18	2
English merchants..	107	5	7
English clergymen..	226	6	0
Medici factors...	128	16	5
Correspondents abroad....................................	1,747	16	6
Sundry debtors..	88	13	5
Tommaso and Giovanni Portinari..........................	579	10	8
Incidentals paid for the King's nef.......................	32	7	4
Furniture...	112	6	4
Living expenses...	168	15	0
Bank expenses..	87	5	5
Total.............	3,751	0	10

Liabilities

	£	s.	d.
Deposits payable on request...............................	169	5	10
Payable to English merchants..............................	1,111	6	9
Letters of credit paid in advance..........................	86	15	7
Italian merchants in Lombard Street.......................	457	18	8
Captain of the ship of Naples..............................	17	7	6
Consular fees..	5	12	10
Due to brokers for fees...................................	22	19	8
Correspondents abroad....................................	920	19	1
Due on consignments of silkstuffs..........................	9	12	1
Medici of Bruges in connection with the royal patent of £5,000*..	666	13	4
Accrued profits..	278	12	8
	3,747	4	0
Error in balance sheet....................................	3	16	10
Total.............	3,751	0	10

* This is certainly the patent of June 5, 1475 (Rymer's *Foedera*).
Source: MAP, filza 99, no. 3, fols. 4 and 5.

ragione were rather considerable and amounted to about £3,750 st., a large sum in the fifteenth century.

On both sides of the balance sheet, a conspicuous item is represented by accounts with foreign correspondents, a standard feature in all financial statements of the Medici Bank and of other Italian merchant-bankers of the period. On the debit side, the highest amount due from any correspondent is an item of £554 17s. 1d. st. charged to a special account of the Medici and Portinari firm in Bruges for supplies of wool. There are two other accounts with the same firm, one Nostro account with a balance of £171 15s. 1d. and one Loro account with a balance of £303 2s. 6d., so that its total debit reached the sum of nearly £1,030 st. "Ours" of Florence (i nostri di Firenze) owed another £520, almost certainly for wool shipped to Pisa by the galleys. The only other balance of importance in the hands of a correspondent abroad is an item of £118 st., approximately, charged to Giovanni Frescobaldi and Filippo Nerli of Venice. It may also be worth noting that the London office was in active business relation with Bartolomeo Marchionni of Lisbon, who sent consignments of sugar and wine.

On the credit side, the highest amount payable to a correspondent abroad is an amount of nearly £333 st. in connection with bills of exchange drawn on Federigo de' Prioli & Co. of Venice. Was the London office short of operating capital and raising funds by selling bills of exchange? The next highest item is a sum of £287 st. representing probably the proceeds of a shipment of currants sent on consignment by the Medici Company in Venice. Then there is a balance of £82 17s. 6d. st. standing to the credit of Frescobaldi and Nerli and nearly offsetting their debit balance. The Rome branch has only about £60 to its credit, a negligible sum, perhaps because it preferred to keep its account with a firm not affiliated with the Medici Bank: Giovanni Tornabuoni was not always cooperative. The only other item of importance is an amount of £116 which relates to a consignment of sugar belonging to Bartolomeo Marchionni of Lisbon.

The liabilities, according to the balance sheet, include £1,111 st. payable to English merchants. Several of them, it will cause no surprise, were woolmen who combed their districts to collect the wool and resold it either to Italian exporters or to merchants of the staple of Calais. The Medici did not have a deposit bank in London but nonetheless they accepted deposits payable at the customer's pleasure (sono or stanno a suo piacere). There is among the liabilities an item of £666 (1,000 marks exactly), probably representing custom duties deductible from the King's debt. The other items are self-explanatory, such as fees due to brokers or to the Florentine consulate and money received in advance for letters of credit payable in Italy. In London, as in Bruges, the Florentine consul levied a tax on all merchandise imported or exported and on all remittances or drafts. No capital account appears on the liabilities' side, unless one considers the item "accrued profits" as an equity account taking its place.

On the assets' side, there are one or two puzzling items. The amount due from English clergy relates, of course, to the delivery of bulls and other ecclesiastical matters. The account of Tommaso di Folco and Giovanni d'Adoardo Portinari certainly refers to a transaction in wool in which each of them had an interest of 50 percent. Since Tommaso Portinari, as a Medici partner, according to standard practice was not supposed to do business on his own account, one wonders whether he was not cheating his masters by excluding them from certain lucrative deals and pocketing the profits himself.

The London office was managed by Tommaso Guidetti, because he is called *Tommaso Guidetti nostro* and has a drawing account charged with £121 13s. 9d., possibly down payments on his accrued salary. Apparently he was running the London office with the help of only one assistant, Alessandro d'Adoardo Portinari, mentioned along with his brother Folco and with Guidetti in Edward IV's patent of June 6, 1475. It looks as though Tommaso Portinari was surrounding himself as much as possible with his own relatives, who were loyal to him instead of to the Medici Company, a practice which Cosimo, in his time, had always unbendingly opposed as a matter of principle and which was consistently ruled out by the partnership contracts.

In 1477 the London office of the Medici Bank was on its last legs. A few months later, Lorenzo the Magnificent took the irrevocable decision to end his association with Tommaso Portinari and forced him to take over the Medici Company in Bruges and its subsidiary in London. Thus the London office became part of a new firm no longer under Medici control.

3. The Bruges Branch from 1451 to 1473

As we have seen earlier in this chapter, the Bruges branch in 1450 was placed under the management of Angelo di Jacopo Tani (1415–1492), first as an accomanda and, after a few months, as a full-fledged partnership. The contract concluded on this occasion has not come down to us, but we have the one of July 25, 1455, which embodies certain amendments made necessary by the death of Giovanni Benci. The provisions of this contract having been discussed at great length in Chapter Five, there is no need for repetition here. The contract of 1455 went into force March 25, 1456, and expired four years later, on March 24, 1460. It is likely that it was extended for five years with little or no change and with Angelo Tani still at the head of the Bruges branch.[106]

Tani's assistant was the ambitious Tommaso Portinari (1428–1501), the son of Folco, once manager of the Tavola of Florence, and the brother of Pigello and Accerrito, who were successive managers in Milan. In 1465, when the time came to renew the contract of the Bruges branch, Tommaso, by now thirty-seven years of age, had been in the service of the Medici Bank in Bruges for nearly two decades and was fretting because Cosimo, being a connoisseur of men, had denied promotion to this self-confident egotist who aspired to play a rôle in international diplomacy.[107] After so many years in Bruges, Portinari was fluent in French, the language of the court and of fashionable society, and perhaps had picked up a smattering of Flemish, the popular tongue. He was very much at home at the Burgundian court and acted already as advisor to the Count of Charolais, later Charles the Bold (ruled 1467–1477), for whom he had an unbounded admiration.[108] Portinari belonged to the latter's entourage and, although a foreigner, was appointed to the Duke's council even before Charles the Bold succeeded his father and took in hand the reins of government.[109] Already in 1464, while Tommaso Portinari was still a factor, it was reported to headquarters that he spent too much time at court instead of attending to the Bank's business. He cleared himself in a letter to Piero by saying that he did not know who spread such false rumors, but that it was the "last" thing for which he expected to be blamed.[110] His excuse was that he had finally secured an order for silk-stuffs from the Court which had heretofore favored exclusively the Lucchese.[111] In order to promote this new business, he even asked for permission to hire on the spot a factor who spoke French, but it is likely that his request was turned down.

Tani, having left Bruges on April 24, 1464, was at this time in Florence and, in his absence, Portinari was acting manager.[112] For quite a while he had been eyeing Tani's job and had been doing his best to discredit his chief with the maggiori. Tani, although no longer young, was by no means eager to retire and was quite willing to continue as manager of the Bruges branch. Cosimo, who was still alive in the spring of 1464, hesitated about appointing Tommaso Portinari as Tani's successor. In order to force the issue, Tommaso Portinari wrote his brother Pigello that he, Tommaso, would leave the service of the Medici if Tani returned to Bruges.[113] Although his letter was full of false imputations and disparaging remarks describing Tani as a "Turk" who made himself obnoxious to many of the Bank's customers, Pigello sent it on to headquarters with a few words in support of his brother.[114] Whether it created a good impression may be doubted. As Cosimo died on August 1, 1464, the matter of Portinari's appointment was tabled for several months; apparently Piero hesitated as much as his father, and a decision in Tommaso Portinari's favor was not reached until April 1465.[115]

The contract bears the date of August 6, 1465. It went into effect retroactively on March 25, 1465, and was valid for a period of three years, that is, until March 25, 1468.[116] The capital was set at £3,000 groat, Flemish currency, of which £2,000 were supplied by Piero di Cosimo de' Medici, £600 by Angelo Tani, and £400 by Tommaso Portinari. Profits, however, were to be shared in the following way: Piero di Cosimo 12s. 6d. in the pound, Angelo Tani 2s. 6d. in the pound, and Tommaso Portinari

5s. in the pound. Apparently, Tommaso drove a hard bargain; although his share in the capital was only two fifteenths, his share in the profits was one fourth. Tani, on the other hand, did not fare well: he furnished one fifth of the capital and received only one eighth of the earnings. Tommaso Portinari, the managing partner, was, of course, required to reside in Bruges and to devote all his time to the common business, which was to be conducted under the style of "Piero di Cosimo de' Medici e compagni." Otherwise, the clauses did not vary much from those found in other Medici partnership agreements, including the well-known contract of 1455.

Portinari did not lack initiative, but he liked impressive ventures and big undertakings without first figuring out whether risks were not greater than the chances of making a profit. As soon as he became manager, he set out to do things on a grand scale. In order to impress the court and the good people of Bruges with the wealth and prestige of the Medici Bank, Portinari in 1466 persuaded Piero de' Medici to let him acquire for 7,000 Rhenish florins the Hotel Bladelin, one of the finest residences in Bruges.[117] It was a brick building in gothic style with two graceful turrets, and on the ground floor it had a large hall for receptions, a "countingroom," and other facilities. In the courtyard, above the arch over the driveway, Portinari eventually installed two medallions with the busts of Lorenzo the Magnificent and his wife, Clara Orsini, in high relief.[118] The building, it should perhaps be pointed out, became and remained the private property of the Medici family and not of the Medici Bank, which always paid rent for occupancy of the premises.

In Italy, merchant-princes living in palaces and owning villas were already a common sight, but in the more barbarous North, such a spectacle must have shocked the public as well as the court. While he was purchasing a palace, Portinari had the effrontery to write the maggiori that, contrary to reports reaching Florence, he was not living in pomp and ostentation.[119] At the very moment, he was setting out for Saint-Omer to participate in the conference at which the Earl of Warwick met Anthony, the Great Bastard of Burgundy.[120] Portinari's reason was that others "should not catch the hare which he had been chasing." [121] It is not made clear, however, what benefit the Medici would derive from the chase.

While Portinari was trying his hand at diplomacy and meddling with affairs of state, he also was toying with two hazardous projects. One was the farming of the toll of Gravelines, at the boundary of the Low Countries and the English enclave of Calais, which he was trying to take away from the Lucchese merchant, Giovanni Arnolfini.[122] Portinari hoped to get the farm of this important toll on all the wool imported into the Low Countries for the same price that Arnolfini had been paying, that is ▽10,800 at 48 groats per écu, or £2,160 gr., Flemish currency.[123] In Portinari's eyes, this was a marvelous opportunity which promised fat returns without any risk, so to speak. Because the Duke of Burgundy had banned all English cloth from his dominions, Portinari even expected wool imports to increase, as a result.[124] He failed to consider that the Duke's ban was likely to invite English reprisals and to affect adversely economic and political relations between England and the Low Countries.[125] He argued further "that once the farm got into the hands of others, it would never be possible to snatch it away."

In the end, Portinari had his way and secured the charter of May 28, 1465, which granted him and the *compagnie des Médicis* the toll of Gravelines for five years beginning on St. John's Day, or June 24, 1465. The yearly rent was set at 16,000 francs of 32 groats, or £2,133 6s. 8d. gr., payable in four installments, a little less than the price paid by Arnolfini.[126] Portinari kept the farm of the toll of Gravelines for many years and even remained in possession of it after breaking off relations with the Medici.[127] When the contract was renewed in 1470, during the reign of Charles the Bold, the price of the farm was increased to £2,700 groat, or £16,200 Artois of 40 groats.[128] In 1472 Folco d'Adoardo Portinari (1448–1490), in the name of his cousin, secured a refund of £4,000 Artois, or £666 13s. 4d. gr., because from Christmas, 1470, to August 31, 1471, receipts had fallen to nearly nothing on account of the civil strife in England.[129] There is no question that the toll of Gravelines was the first step which led Tommaso Portinari and the Medici with him on the road to greater and greater involvement in loans to the Duke of Burgundy, the uncrowned king of the Low Countries.

While Portinari succeeded in securing Piero di Cosimo's reluctant agreement to the farm of the toll of Gravelines, it was more difficult for him to get support for another of his undertakings: the ill-starred venture of the Burgundian galleys. Two in number, they had been built at Porto Pisano by order of Philip the Good, who, responding to the appeal of Pius II, had planned to lead a crusade against the Turks.[130] When the plans for this campaign were abandoned after the Pope's death (August 15, 1464), the galleys were already completely rigged out and ready to put out to sea, but the Duke no longer had any use for them.[131] Since the Medici Bank had made all the arrangements and received an advance of ▽7,000 to pay the shipbuilders, Philip the Good's minister, Antoine de Croy, approached Portinari again and asked him to put the galleys up for sale.[132] But galleys were not a commodity in current demand and, although the Duke was quite willing to take a loss, no buyer could be found. In order to please the court, Portinari then hit upon the idea of chartering or buying the galleys and of operating them with Florentine crews but under the flag with the St. Andrew's cross raguly of the house of Burgundy, hence the name of Burgundian galleys. This proposal had the double advantage of eluding the regulations of the Florentine Consuls of the Sea and of flattering the Duke of Burgundy, eager to see his flag displayed in Mediterranean waters and to emulate the King of France and the King of Naples, who also were operating galley fleets.[133] At first, Portinari secured Piero's consent to the operation of the galleys by the Medici Bank, perhaps as a temporary solution until a buyer was found.

At any rate, the Burgundian galleys were in operation from 1467 onward and made regular voyages from the Low Countries to Pisa and occasional trips from Pisa to Constantinople.[134] It is not clear from the records exactly under what terms the Medici operated the galleys, but they apparently came to own them outright. The correspondence reveals that Piero di Cosimo, after relenting in his opposition to Portinari's proposal, changed his mind again and in 1469 became quite insistent about the urgency of liquidating this venture, which he regarded as excessively risky and unprofitable.[135] Portinari promised to comply, but he was no more able to find a buyer than before; the galleys were still being operated by the Medici and sailing under the Burgundian flag in June, 1469.[136]

In the summer of 1469, Portinari went to Florence to report and to negotiate the terms of a new contract. It was signed on October 14, 1469, but it never went into effect, since it was voided by the death of Piero di Cosimo which occurred on December 2, 1469.[137] Another agreement was made on December 15, 1469.[138] Its terms were the same except that the names of Lorenzo and Giuliano de' Medici were substituted for Piero's. The capital was set at £3,000 groat, Flemish currency, supplied as follows: £2,000 by Piero de' Medici's two sons, £400 by Tani, £400 by Portinari, and £200 by Antonio di Bernardo de' Medici. As usual, profits were not to be shared in the same proportion: Lorenzo and Giuliano were to receive 10s. in the pound, Tani 2s. 6d., Portinari 5s. 6d., and Antonio de' Medici 2s. in the pound. Portinari was not quite pleased with the share allotted to him, because he had expected to receive one third of the profits instead of 27.5 percent.[139] This was being rather greedy, but Portinari was that way and considered only his own interest. The duration of the agreement was five years beginning March 25, 1470, and ending March 24, 1475. The partnership was to do business under the name "Lorenzo de' Medici, Tommaso Portinari & Co." This style remained in use until Lorenzo the Magnificent withdrew in 1480.

As in other contracts, the burden of the management was laid upon the shoulders of the junior partners, Tommaso Portinari and Antonio de' Medici, whose duties were strictly defined. They were supposed to reside in Bruges, to devote all their time to the welfare of the partnership, and to follow the policy prescribed by the senior partners. To meet current needs, Tommaso Portinari was allowed to draw out £30 groat per annum and Antonio de' Medici, £10. All this is typical of Medici articles of association; what is more unusual is a special clause which urged Portinari "to deal as little as possible with the court of the Duke of Burgundy and of other princes and lords, especially in granting credit and accommodating them with money, because it involves more risk than profit." The text goes on to point out that "many merchants in this way fared badly" and that "our fathers have always been wary of such involvements and stayed aloof, unless it was a matter of a small sum lent to make or to keep friends." The junior partners were further admonished to shun "great" undertakings and were reminded of the fact that the policy of the senior partners was "to preserve their wealth and credit rather than enrich themselves by risky ventures." This was, of course, aimed at Tommaso Portinari. In accordance with Piero di Cosimo's policy, the contract clearly intended to apply the brakes and to curb Portinari's penchant for venturesome and spectacular schemes which often turned sour instead of fulfilling expectations. Another clause ordered the sale of the galleys and the liquidation of this venture, if necessary at a loss; it also forbade in the future any other investments in shipping.[140] This was fettering Tommaso Portinari and putting him in a strait jacket.

Portinari returned to Bruges early in December, 1469. Unaware of Piero's death on December 2, he wrote to his master, with many apologies for keeping secret his intentions, that he had decided to carry out a marriage project which had matured during his recent visit to Florence.[141] Arrangements were made to send the bride, still a child, all the way from Florence to Bruges where the marriage was celebrated with great pomp. Portinari was forty and his wife, Maria di Francesco Bandini-Baroncelli, only fifteen. In the triptych of Hugo van der Goes, painted shortly after the marriage, the unhappy girl looks very uncomfortable wearing the monumental *hennin* (headdress) then in fashion among noble ladies at the courts of France and Burgundy.[142] Although Portinari pretended not to be given to ostentation, he bedecked his wife as if she were a lady of high station.

It is understandable that Portinari was not altogether pleased with the terms of his contract. Nevertheless, he did comply to a certain extent. Whether he spent less time at court is doubtful, but, willy-nilly, he, or rather the Bruges branch, sold seven eighths of its property rights in the two Burgundian galleys to a group of speculators headed by Giovanni d'Adoardo Portinari.[143] The selling price amounted to £2,171 13s. 4d. groat, Flemish currency, including 2,901 florins 4s. a oro, which the group had advanced for repairs, victuals, and other provisions, when the two galleys were last in Porto Pisano. The sale had retroactive effect from the time that the galleys had sailed from that port. After reaching their destination, they had been requisitioned by the Duke of Burgundy and were actually serving in a fleet which he had collected to fight the French. The result of this contract was, of course, that the Medici still participated for one eighth in the ownership of the galleys and continued to assume the responsibility and the burden of operating them for the new society of owners.

The partnership contract of 1469 remained in effect for only twelve months because, as explained in Chapter Five, Antonio de' Medici, the new assistant manager, made himself so obnoxious to the entire staff that all the giovani threatened to walk out if he stayed. Perhaps with relief, Portinari was forced to ask for Antonio's recall.[144]

With Sassetti's connivance, Tommaso Portinari secured a new contract which, because Piero was now dead and no longer there to raise objections, considerably enlarged his powers and gave him a free hand.[145] In Antonio's place, Tommaso di Jacopo Guidetti was assumed into the partnership, though as an inferior (compagno et inferiore). Tommaso Portinari himself got a much better deal and was raised to the status of senior partner, ranking immediately after the two Medici brothers, Lorenzo and Giuliano. Instead of being required to reside in Bruges, he was relieved from any such obligation and was at liberty to repatriate himself and to settle down in Florence with wife and children, leaving Guidetti in charge of the actual management. Although Tommaso Portinari from now on shuttled back and forth between Florence and Bruges, he was not yet able to make his abode in Italy, because he was detained in the Low Countries most of the time by business or diplomatic affairs.

The capital remained as before at £3,000 groat, but its allocation was slightly changed as follows: £2,075, Lorenzo and Giuliano de' Medici; £400, Tommaso Portinari; £375, Angelo Tani; and £150, Tommaso Guidetti. The division of profits, on the other hand, was not altered and remained the same as in the contract of 1469:

	In the pound		Percent of total
Lorenzo e Giuliano de' Medici	10s.	0d.	50.0
Tommaso Portinari	5s.	6d.	27.5
Angelo Tani	2s.	6d.	12.5
Tommaso Guidetti	2s.	0d.	10.0
Total	20s.	0d.	100.0

With regard to loans to princes, it was again impressed upon Portinari that the risks involved were so great that it was better to avoid such business as much as possible.[146] The contract reaffirmed the principle that it was the Medici's traditional policy not to become embroiled in government finance and to keep the family fortune intact by avoiding questionable investments. Nonetheless, because of the many virtues and the great benevolence of His Highness, Charles the Bold, Portinari was allowed, if need be, to lend him up to £6,000 groat, but not more, lest "it happens to us as of late to Gherardo Canigiani of London and in the past to many merchants of our nation whose example we should have constantly before our eyes." Apparently the Medici were thinking of the disastrous failures of the Bardi and the Peruzzi who lost "a treasure worth a kingdom" in making loans to Edward III of England and Robert of Anjou. This being the case, one wonders why the Medici gave Portinari the green light and did not ask themselves whether it would be possible, once involved, to keep the loans below the ceiling of £6,000 groat. Portinari had his way in two other matters: he was allowed to keep the farm of the toll of Gravelines and to settle in the best possible way the problem of the Burgundian galleys.

Tommaso Guidetti came to Florence for the signing of the new partnership agreement. When he left to return to Bruges, he was provided with a ricordo dictated by Lorenzo the Magnificent himself.[147] First of all, Guidetti was to secure Tommaso Portinari's approval of the new articles and for this purpose carried with him a copy of the contract to be signed by his chief and returned to headquarters. The ricordo then dwelt on the existing differences between the Bruges branch and the Rome branch concerning a contract of 11,000 cantars of alum and the seizure by Giovanni Tornabuoni of a consignment of wool and cloth in payment of the balance due from Gherardo Canigiani. Lorenzo promised somehow to adjust the matter (how exactly, he did not explain). In the meantime, however, the two branches should work hand in hand instead of being at each other's throats. Therefore, Portinari was urged to cooperate graciously with Carlo Martelli, whom Tornabuoni had sent to Bruges to promote the alum sales. Guidetti was reminded of the fact that the Medici Bank had established new branches: one in Naples with Agostino Biliotti as manager and another in Venice with Giovanni d'Orsino Lanfredini as manager. The Bruges branch was expected to favor them if opportunity arose. The instructions further stressed that Guidetti's duty was to serve the Medici Bank devotedly and honestly and to be deferent and faithful toward Tommaso Portinari, so that diligence might repair the harm done in years past.

This contract became effective March 25, 1471, and was expected to last three years. However, it was prematurely terminated after two years, or on March 26, 1473, and superseded by new articles of association according to which Cristofano Spini took the place of Tommaso Guidetti, who was sent to London as manager of a newly reorganized subsidiary.[148] The major provisions were much the same as before: Tommaso Portinari retained his position as senior partner with even fewer restrictions than in the contract of 1471. The surviving text contains no reference to any ceiling on loans to Charles the Bold or to the fate of the Burgundian galleys. Everything is left to Portinari's discretion and good judgment. The new contract was to be valid for five years, or until March 26, 1478.

Like Guidetti, Cristofano Spini, upon leaving Florence for Bruges (May 1472), was given a ricordo.[149] However, instead of containing instructions as to future policy, this document dwells chiefly on the liquidation of the London branch and the difficulties with Canigiani who, Lorenzo complains, has "accommodated His Majesty the King from our money and not from his with the result that we and not he are made to sustain the full impact of the losses." How to get out of this impasse was for Portinari to figure out, and he was given to understand that whatever he did would be approved and ratified; in order to succeed he would have needed a magic touch for changing lead into gold! In any case, any agreement with Canigiani about the liquidation of the old ragione was to be phrased so clearly as to leave no possibility of cavil or escape. Also everything should be done to send with the first sailing of the galleys the two hundred bales of wool which Canigiani had promised to deliver. With regard to the alum contract with Rome, Lorenzo the Magnificent reminded Spini of the importance of this matter because any mismanagement was likely to bring about an uproar (scompiglio). Lorenzo apparently had trouble keeping in line his impatient and irascible uncle, Giovanni Tornabuoni.

4. The Difficulties with Tommaso Portinari (1473–1481) and the Disastrous Liquidation of the Bruges and London Branches

The conclusion of the contract of 1473 marks the beginning of the serious difficulties which within a short time beset the Bruges branch because of the advances to Charles the Bold and the assumption of the deficit left by the London branch. Although Angelo Tani is still named as one of the partners, the articles of association concluded in 1473 with Portinari and Spini were never submitted to his approval or signed by him: a highly irregular and suspicious procedure. Later on, with good reason, Tani refused to be liable for any losses suffered by the Bruges branch after 1473. The fact is that, without Tani's knowledge, Portinari and Sassetti agreed that the Bruges branch would assume the debts left by the liquidation of the London branch.[150] This solution, if it can be called a solution, simply postponed the amortization of these debts and saddled the Bruges branch with interest charges too heavy to carry without running up a deficit. To make matters worse, a distinct ragione from which Tani was excluded, was formed for the wool trade, which was still yielding handsome profits, with the result that the Bruges branch was left with heavy charges and little revenue. No contract of this separate partnership has survived, but its existence is revealed by Tani's report and by a memorandum Lorenzo the Magnificent himself dictated.[151]

The first venture to go wrong was that of the Burgundian galleys. On April 27, 1473, the two vessels heading for Southampton were attacked off Gravelines by Danzig privateers under the command of Paul Beneke, regardless of the fact that they were flying the neutral flag of Burgundy.[151] One of the two galleys, the *San Matteo,* escaped by outsailing its pursuers, but the other, the *San Giorgio,* commanded by Francesco di ser Matteo Tedaldi, was boarded and captured.[152] Thirteen Florentine crewmen perished miserably in the fray.[153] The captured galley carried a valuable cargo of alum and silks bound for Southampton and some dry goods and two altarpieces which were going to Italy.[154] One of them was the "Last Judgment" of Memling, commissioned by Angelo Tani and destined for a Florentine church. Instead, it was brought to Danzig where it still is today, although it was carried off to the Louvre in 1807 and barely escaped destruction in World War II. The second galley safely reached Porto Pisano on October 27, 1473, but it was wrecked in a storm within a year.[155]

The value of the prize, ship and cargo, amounted to £6,540 groat, according to one estimate, and to 40,000 écus of 48 groats, or £8,000 groat, according to another.[156] Whatever figure is correct, the loss was substantial and Tommaso Portinari immediately lodged claims against the privateers with the delegates of the Hanseatic League meeting at Utrecht (1473).[157] Charles the Bold also protested vigorously because the assailants had hauled down his flag and trampled it under their feet.[158] Even the Pope came to Portinari's support and excommunicated Paul Beneke and his henchmen as pirates who robbed papal alum on the high seas.[159] It was all to no avail. Danzig, secretly supported by Hamburg and Lübeck, did not yield an inch.[160] Furthermore, the Flemish cities under the leadership of Bruges were very much opposed to a breach with the Hansa for the sake of an alum cargo belonging to Italians; they exerted a restraining influence on Charles the Bold, who cared more for the interests of his subjects than for those of Portinari.[161] Anyway, the Duke had his hands full already and did not wish to pick up another quarrel.

As diplomacy failed, Portinari went to law and, in reprisal, laid arrest upon the goods and possessions of Hanseatic merchants in Bruges and at the fairs of Antwerp, but the town authorities forced him to desist.[162] Finally, in 1496, he secured from the Grand Council of Malines, the supreme court of the Low Countries, a judgment which was entirely in his favor.[163] Hanseatic merchants in the Low Countries were molested again.[164] In order to keep the good will of the Hanseatic League, the city of Bruges, which was not involved in the conflict at all, finally agreed in

1499 to pay 16,000 florins to Folco and Benedetto di Pigello Portinari, if they renounced all rights arising from the decision of 1496.[165] The last installment on this sum had not been paid by 1512.[166] Nearly forty years had then elapsed since the capture of the *San Giorgio* by Paul Beneke and his privateers.

To what extent the disastrous end of the Burgundian galleys entailed losses for the Medici Bank is anybody's guess. No extant records give any clue. It is certain, however, that hull and cargo were at least partly insured, since the ledger of Bernardo Cambi contains entries relating to the receipt of premiums and the paying out of insurance on goods aboard the captured galley.[167]

Despite the dismal failure of this venture with the Burgundian galleys, Portinari retained the confidence of his masters until 1476. What undermined their trust was most probably the military defeats and the financial plight of Charles the Bold. His reckless campaigns had ruined his finances and by 1476 he was scraping the bottom of the barrel.[168] Even Tommaso Portinari, having exhausted his resources, was unable to lend more. Then came the disaster of Morat (June 22, 1476), in which Charles the Bold's army was utterly routed by the Swiss and lost all its baggage and artillery. It was a frightful slaughter. Lorenzo the Magnificent, well informed by his agents, drew his conclusions and began to worry about Portinari's loans.[169] The final blow came when Charles the Bold, after escaping from the field at Morat, was killed in another desperate battle before Nancy on January 5, 1477.

His death very nearly caused the collapse of the Burgundian monarchy. And, as far as the Medici Bank was concerned, it brought to light the fact that Portinari had by far exceeded the limit of £6,000 groat set by the partnership contract of 1471, but omitted in that of 1473. According to one source, Charles the Bold at the time of his death owed the Medici Bank £57,000 Artois, or £9,500 groat.[170] Portinari, in order to save what he had already lent, was induced to provide another £20,000 Artois, or £3,333 6s. 8d. groat, to Charles' successors, Mary of Burgundy and her impecunious husband, Archduke Maximilian of Austria. Total advances thus amounted to approximately £13,000 groat, but Lorenzo's own memorandum puts the figure at £16,150 groat.[171] It does not matter very much which total is correct. Perhaps both are, because we do not know how these aggregates were computed and what items were included or excluded. In any case, one thing is certain: Portinari had disobeyed orders and sacrificed the interests of the Medici Bank to satisfy his ego. As Lorenzo the Magnificent bitterly remarks in his memorandum, Portinari, "in order to court the Duke's favor and make himself important, did not care whether it was at our expense." [172]

Portinari violated the articles of association in yet another respect. Although he was expected to stay out of risky ventures overseas, he invested a large sum in an expedition of the Portuguese to the coast of Guinea, which, Lorenzo points out in his memorandum, he should not have done, inasmuch as the Bruges branch was short of funds and borrowing at interest.

Not much is known about this profitless venture, but it was certainly one of the voyages along the African coast organized in 1474 or 1475 under the auspices of Prince John, afterwards King John II of Portugal.[173] Portinari, in one of his letters, mentions Giovanni Rodrigo who advises "the Prince" in matters of commerce.[174] This is almost certainly the cosmographer, Master Rodrigo, who is known to have acted frequently in such an advisory capacity.[175] Other papers mention Bartolomeo Marchionni, who is reputed to have been the richest Italian banker in Lisbon and who undoubtedly financed some of the exploration and trade voyages sponsored by Prince John.[176]

Finally, Lorenzo the Magnificent reproves Portinari sharply for having inveigled him into approving the formation of a separate partnership for the still profitable wool business.[177] In this venture Portinari shared in the profits to the extent of nine shillings in the pound (45 percent), whereas his share in the profits or losses of the Bruges branch was only 5s. 6d. in the pound (27.5 percent).[178] He had thus found the means of giving himself a lion's share in the profits while shifting the losses to his master, a trick which Lorenzo had not understood at first; only later did it dawn upon him that he was being victimized.

Lorenzo's memorandum certainly dates from 1479 and was undoubtedly dictated by the Magnificent himself, since it is prefaced with the words: "Lorenzo de' Medici speaking" (Parlla Lorenzo de' Medici). It includes a statement which shows that the losses of the Bruges bank amounted to £982 5s. 10d. groat (Table 70). If those, much higher, of the London branch are added, the total attains the fantastic figure of £18,982 5s. 10d. groat, or about 70,000 ducats. "These," Lorenzo adds with bitter irony, "are the great profits which are accruing to us through the management of Tommaso Portinari." [179] Besides, Lorenzo complains, Portinari wasted 8,000 ducats in the purchase and remodelling of a house (the Hotel Bladelin). In all, the Medici Bank supplied the Bruges branch with about 88,084 ducats in deposits, alum, and advances in current account and received in exchange only 62,500 lbs. of wool to the value of 12,500 ducats. And these funds did not suffice, because the Bruges branch continued to draw — on Medici branches in Italy evidently — without remitting much, if anything.

The losses of the Bruges branch were undoubtedly greater than £952 5s. 10d. gr. For one thing, the memorandum makes a grave error by deducting from net losses the comprehensive profits of the wool business,

TABLE 70. Statement of the Profits and Losses of the Bruges and London Branches According to a Memorandum of Lorenzo the Magnificent, 1479[a]
(All amounts are in pounds groat, Flemish currency)

	£	s.	d.
Losses for the year 1469 as appears from the balance.........	313	15	7
And for the years 1476 and 1477.........................	5,565	10	3
Total losses of three years..............................	5,879	5	10

	£	s.	d.
Profits for the year 1471 as appears from statement...........	994	0	0
Idem for the year 1472.................................	801	0	0
Idem for the year 1473.................................	2,004	0	0
Idem for the years 1474 and 1475.......................	30	0	0
Total profits..............	+3,829	0	0
Deduct the above losses.................................	−5,879	5	10
Excess of losses over profits.............................	−2,050	5	10
Add estimated losses for 1478...........................	−2,500	0	0
Net losses (will probably be larger).......................	−4,550	5	10
Profit in the wool business...............................	+3,568	0	0[b]
Net losses of the Bruges branch...........................	−982	5	10
Add losses of the London branch estimated at...............	−18,000	0	0
Total losses of Bruges and London branches combined........	−18,982	5	10

[a] The presentation of this table is somewhat unusual, but it follows closely the original.
[b] This amount includes the share of Lorenzo de' Medici, £1,605, or 45 percent, and that of Tommaso Portinari and Cristofano Spini, £1,963, or 55 percent.
Source: ASF, MAP, filza 84, no. 21, fol. 46.

whereas only the share therein of Lorenzo, amounting to £1,605 gr., should have been subtracted. This correction would have raised actual losses to £2,945 5s. 10d. groat, corresponding to about 12,000 ducats, a respectable sum in the fifteenth century, when people still reckoned in thousands instead of in millions, and billions were entirely unthinkable.[180] Even this large figure grossly understates the extent of the loss, since it rests on the assumption that most of the assets were worth their book value, which is certainly optimistic considering the high proportion of dead claims and slow accounts.

Tommaso Portinari, not being required by the articles of association to reside in Bruges, arrived in Milan on April 10, 1478, and, after a brief visit to Florence, spent several months in the capital of Lombardy, perhaps to be near his brother Accerrito.[181] In October, his entire family, escorted by Giovanni d'Adoardo Portinari, came down from Bruges to live in Milan.[182] It is during these months that Lorenzo made up his mind to discontinue his association with both of the Portinari brothers, whom he reproached for having neglected his interests in order to promote their own. They had caused him to lose from seventy to eighty thousand florins; while acquiring considerable wealth, they had never let him use any of it, even when he was in a pinch, an allusion, no doubt, to the crisis which followed the Pazzi conspiracy.[183]

This decision was not to the taste of Tommaso Portinari, who objected that it could not be implemented without losing face and impairing the credit that the Medici Bank still enjoyed.[184] It was imperative, according to Portinari, to keep the business going in order to collect outstanding claims and to pay off the balance owing to the Rome branch for shipments of papal alum. In order to relieve the Bruges branch from the burden of interest charges, Portinari added, it would also be necessary to amortize the debt left by the defunct London branch. Precisely, but who was the man who, together with Sassetti, chose to temporize instead of facing the issue squarely? With regard to voyages to the coast of Guinea, Portinari regretted that the first of these miscarried, but he thought it would be a mistake to withdraw, since future expeditions were likely to yield more favorable results. As for taking over the Bruges branch, Portinari contended that the load was too heavy for him to carry and that, moreover, this solution would not suit the interests of the Medici.

However, Lorenzo was determined to liquidate and to force Portinari to take over the Bruges branch and thus suffer the consequences of his own mistakes. Portinari, sensing the danger, proved to be intractable. He even enlisted the support of Bona of Savoy, regent of Milan, and of Cecco Simonetta, the all-powerful ducal secretary. This interference by outsiders disturbed Lorenzo to such a degree that he wrote angrily to his ambassador, Girolamo Morelli, accusing Portinari of turning "business into a matter of state" and of divulging private affairs of no concern to other people.[185]

While Tommaso Portinari was still lingering in Milan, Lorenzo de' Medici decided to take the bull by the horns and to force the issue by sending to Bruges Rinieri da Ricasoli in order to investigate the state of the ragione and to make recommendations for a settlement (September, 1479). Rinieri da Ricasoli was an older man of experience who had been in Bruges for many years as partner in the firm Antonio da Rabatta and Bernardo Cambi.[186] To give him the necessary authority to act in Lorenzo's name, he was provided with a power of attorney which enabled him to collect all outstanding claims, to renew or to wind up any partnership either in Bruges with Tommaso Portinari and Cristofano Spini or in London with Tommaso Guidetti, and to make any necessary settlements or compromises in this connection.[187] Rinieri was also given full authority over Folco d'Adoardo Portinari and Bernardo Masi, the two factors who were in charge of the Bruges branch during Tommaso Portinari's absence. The power of attorney interestingly enumerates the principal debtors of the Medici company in Bruges. This list is topped by the late Duke Charles of Burgundy, his heirs and successors (for the amount due at the time of his death), Archduke Maximilian of Austria (for the new loans), and Charles' widow, Margaret of York. It also mentions one cardinal (George Hessler, Bishop of Würzburg), a former factor of the Medici (Carlo Cavalcanti), a Genoese firm (Giovanni and Agostino Doria), and several nobles, among them "Loysium dominum della Gratturgia," who is certainly Louis de Bruges, seigneur de la Gruuthuse (Earl of Winchester), whose beautiful hotel is today a famous museum. The list ends with the names of Benedetto Portinari (presumably a cousin of Tommaso) and Bartolomeo Marchionni, both of Lisbon, who were without any doubt implicated in the Guinea venture of which Lorenzo the Magnificent so strongly disapproved.

As usual, Rinieri da Ricasoli was provided with a ricordo which spelled out the purpose of his mission and made various suggestions for carrying it out.[188] In Lorenzo de' Medici's opinion, the Bruges branch had been badly managed, and it was Rinieri da Ricasoli's main task to make recommendations about the proper course of action: to reorganize or to liquidate. Perhaps the damage was beyond repair. The main source of the trouble, Lorenzo now recognized, was that the Bruges branch had been burdened with the debts of the London branch. As a result, it was paying interest or exchange on borrowed funds without receiving a corresponding income from investments. The most urgent task, as Lorenzo saw it, was to get the Bruges branch out of debt in order to reduce the crushing load of interest charges. For this purpose, Rinieri was supplied with a small sum in coin and with about 20,000 ducats in bills of exchange on Bruges and Lyons. However, he was not to make any use of them unless strictly necessary.

After reaching his destination, Rinieri da Ricasoli's first duty was to make a general audit of the books, especially the libro segreto, in order to ascertain the financial condition of the Bruges branch. To insure the cooperation of Folco d'Adoardo Portinari and Bernardo Masi, the two giovani who were in charge of the Bruges office during Portinari's absence in Milan, strict orders were issued that they must obey Ricasoli as if he were Lorenzo the Magnificent in person. Another matter to be given prompt attention was to diminish the balances which Bruges owed to other Medici branches, especially Venice and Lyons, by remitting to them instead of drawing. Of late, the Lyons branch had even allowed drafts of the Bruges branch to be protested. Upon hearing of this incident, Lorenzo had been greatly displeased "as he valued his honor more than all the gold in the world." Perhaps there was one thing which Lorenzo overlooked or did not fully grasp. On account of Flanders' unfavorable balance of trade with Italy, bills of exchange on Venice were short in supply on the *bourse*. There was, therefore, a tendency for the bankers in Bruges to accumulate debit balances in Italy.

Because of gaps in the surviving correspondence, we do not know exactly what occurred in the next few months. It may safely be assumed that Tommaso Portinari left Milan in a hurry as soon as he heard that Ricasoli had taken command of the countinghouse in Bruges, was prying into his papers, and going through his files. Negotiations about terminating the partnership with the Medici were started at once by Ricasoli, but Portinari was obdurate and claimed that Ricasoli underrated the value of the assets and that the financial condition of the Bruges branch was not as bad as pictured. As Portinari was persuasive, he even got Ricasoli to propose that the partnership with the Medici be renewed, but Lorenzo the Magnificent was unwilling to listen to any suggestion of this kind. By letter of July 29, 1480, Ricasoli received peremptory orders to conclude a settlement which would dissolve the existing bonds between the Medici and Portinari.[189]

Reluctantly, the latter had to submit, since Lorenzo de' Medici, in accordance with the articles of association, had given him due notice in advance. Portinari, by claiming that he was not guilty of mismanagement and that most of the investments were sound, had undermined his own bargaining position. Now he was taken at his word and forced to take over many doubtful assets at book value. Nevertheless, the agreement concluded on August 7, 1480, was not as favorable as Ricasoli had hoped, because the financial condition of the Bruges branch had further deteriorated on account of bad news from Portugal about the Guinea venture and trouble with the toll of Gravelines, which had been wrested from Portinari by a government in desperate need of revenue. Details about the settlement of August 7, 1480, cannot be given because no copy of the contract itself is extant.[190]

A later adjustment took place on February 15, 1481, and was approved by Lorenzo the Magnificent and Accerrito Portinari in his brother's behalf. According to this settlement of accounts, Tommaso Portinari owed Lorenzo a balance of 16,616 ducats, which remained due on a contract of alum amounting to 56,000 ducats (Table 71).[191] On the other hand, Lorenzo owed Portinari 17,716 ducats for the principal of several deposits which the latter undertook to pay off. The net result was that Lorenzo the Magnificent remained a debtor to the extent of 1,100 ducats. What this balance really represents is uncertain, since it relates to a partial settlement involving only the alum and wool accounts. To draw from this figure of 1,100 ducats any conclusions regarding the liquidation of the Bruges branch would be extremely dangerous, since the available data are manifestly incomplete. Probably the settlement was relatively favorable to Portinari. Among the concessions which he wrung from Ricasoli was the free use of the Hotel Bladelin for four years.

While Ricasoli was negotiating a settlement with Portinari, Angelo Tani also appeared on the scene; he had come all the way from Florence to Bruges for the purpose of coming to an agreement about the liquidation of his share in the Bruges branch. The surviving records do not disclose on what terms, but it is probable that Tani stuck to his guns and refused to be responsible for the losses of the London branch in which

TABLE 71. SETTLEMENT OF ACCOUNTS BETWEEN LORENZO THE MAGNIFICENT
AND TOMMASO PORTINARI
FEBRUARY 15, 1481

	ducats	s.	d.	
Value of 11,000 cantara of alum chargeable to Tommaso Portinari....................................	56,000	0	0	debit
Deduct: value of four shipments of wool..............	35,716	5	0	credit
Balance of alum contract...........................	20,283	15	0	debit
Further adjustment on wool deliveries................	3,667	15	0	credit
Balance due from Portinari.........................	16,616	0	0	debit
	ducats	s.	d.	
Five deposit accounts to be paid by Portinari...........	16,404	0	0	credit
Interest (discrezione) at 8 percent for one year.........	1,312	0	0	credit
Total...	17,716	0	0	credit
Deduct: above balance.............................	16,616	0	0	debit
Balance due to Portinari by Lorenzo the M...........	1,100	0	0	credit

Source: MAP, filza 84, no. 76, fols. 153-154.

he was not a partner. He stayed in Bruges several months and returned to Florence by way of France, where Louis XI offered him the post of *contrôleur général des finances* and a pension of 4,000 francs, or about 2,500 écus. Tani, however, turned down this offer with the excuse that he was old, infirm, and not well versed in French.[192]

Cristofano Spini, the junior partner, readily cooperated with Ricasoli and was recompensed by being exonerated from any liability in connection with the deficit of the Bruges branch.[193] Tommaso Guidetti, the manager of the London office, was less lucky. After seventeen years of service with the Medici, he returned to Florence with the intention of settling down. He had scarcely arrived at his destination when he was apprehended and thrown into the debtors' prison, the Stinche, at the behest of Giovanni d'Orsino Lanfredini, the manager of the Venice branch, who sued him for payment of 3,549 ducats in connection with a shipment of currants consigned to the London office.[194] Although Guidetti claimed to have turned over the proceeds to Tommaso Portinari, he nevertheless lost the lawsuit and was sentenced by the *Mercanzia* — (Merchants' Court) to pay the full amount demanded by Lanfredini. In 1483 Guidetti left his pregnant wife in Florence and journeyed all the way to Bruges in order to recover the amount of 3,549 ducats from Portinari, who promised to supply fifty-five sacks of wool to the value of 3,465 ducats, but the wool was lost and never delivered.[195] Guidetti did not return to Florence until 1489. The sequel of this involved affair of currants and wool was a string of lawsuits which were still pending in the courts long after Guidetti's death in the second decade of the sixteenth century.[196]

Since the Medici withdrew completely, there is no basis for the story put into circulation by one historian and repeated by others that Lorenzo the Magnificent, after breaking off relations with Portinari, called Pierantonio di Guasparre Bandini-Baroncelli to the management of the Bruges branch.[197] This man was in 1478 the representative in Bruges of the Pazzi Bank and was closely related to Bernardo Bandini-Baroncelli, the murderer of Giuliano de' Medici, and to Portinari's wife, Maria Bandini-Baroncelli.[198] While Pierantonio himself undoubtedly did not participate in the Pazzi conspiracy, his behavior after this event was not such as to endear him to Lorenzo de' Medici. As soon as news of the abortive plot reached Bruges, Pierantonio fled to sanctuary, taking with him books and valuables belonging to the Pazzi Bank.[199] When Ricasoli presented himself with a mandate to seize any Pazzi property, Pierantonio Bandini-Baroncelli failed to cooperate and probably managed to prevent confiscation of some of the assets.[200] Under those circumstances, it is unlikely that he would be selected by Lorenzo to fill a position of trust. Moreover, all the available evidence shows that Portinari had no successor. Pierantonio continued to reside in Bruges and probably traded on his own account from 1478 onward. He was Florentine consul in 1490 and perhaps earlier.[201]

Lorenzo the Magnificent's withdrawal from business in Bruges deprived Tommaso Portinari of the renown that was still attached to the Medici name and left him in a precarious position with little or no working capital and creditors clamoring for payment. He spent the rest of his life trying to collect what was owing him and staving off creditors who were assailing him on all sides and threatening him with arrest. His principal debtor was Maximilian, Archduke of Austria and regent of the Low Countries after the death of Mary of Burgundy (1482). Spendthrift, and erratic in his diplomacy, Maximilian was about the worst debtor among all the princes of Europe. Nevertheless, about 1480, he pledged to Tommaso Portinari a costly jewel, the rich fleur-de-lys of Burgundy, set with precious stones and weighing at least nineteen pounds.[202] But crown jewels are a poor substitute for cash, especially when interest charges are piling up. The fleur-de-lys of Burgundy was carefully stored away at the Hospital of Santa Maria Nuova in Florence. Apparently Portinari was forced to give it as security to his own creditors. When, in 1500, the fleur-de-lys was finally released against payment of 4,000 ducats (or large florins) and 320 hundredweights of Cotswold wool, Portinari received nothing; everything, money as well as wool, was assigned directly to several creditors who had a lien on the jewel.[203] There are other indications that Portinari, after his break with Lorenzo, was constantly in financial troubles. In 1485 the toll of Gravelines was restored to him with permission to apply half the farm price to the extinction of Maximilian's debt. But this process was too slow, and Portinari, in 1487, obtained further relief out of pity for "the petitioner, his wife, and seven children" because accumulated arrears had "forced him out of business" and "involved him in heavy expense to maintain his credit." [204] To raise funds, Portinari was finally compelled to sell his claims on Maximilian and the Hanseatic League to his nephews, Benedetto and Folco di Pigello Portinari, most probably at a sacrifice.[205]

Not only was Portinari harassed by creditors; he also had trouble with unfaithful factors. It is true that he himself set a bad example by evading contracts and creating muddles which eventually led to unending litigation. One of the guilty factors was Bernardo Masi, who, in handling the accounts with Portugal, committed embezzlements extending over a period of years, presumably in complicity with Carlo Martelli. Masi was arrested and closely questioned but could not be brought to confess all his misdeeds; as a result, Portinari was never able to prove his case because records containing pertinent data mysteriously disappeared from the countinghouse in Bruges.[206] Another similar case was that of Folco d'Adoardo Portinari, who also perpetrated frauds and traded on his own while in Tommaso's employ.[207] Although a relative, he was apprehended and jailed from October, 1487, to April, 1488, despite the protests of his brothers Alessandro and Giovanni, who had both unstintedly supported Tommaso. This action probably caused a rift within the Portinari family.[208]

Driven to desperation by all kinds of difficulties, Tommaso himself lost all sense of business integrity and was not squeamish about means of raking up money or warding off creditors. After the expulsion of the Medici from Florence in 1494, he hastened to claim from the custodians of their property a sum of 15,445 florins which had allegedly been extorted from him in making the settlement with Ricasoli. This claim was awarded on December 24, 1498, but the money was retained on account of the 17,500 florins which the Commune had been compelled to pay to Guillaume

Bische when the French occupied Florence.[209] Another disappointment, and there were many!

Fortunately for Tommaso Portinari, he was able to secure employment as a diplomatic agent. Perhaps he was cut out to be a diplomat rather than a merchant. In 1487 Maximilian of Austria sent him as ambassador to Lodovico il Moro, regent of Milan, probably to negotate the investiture of this duchy.[210] Tommaso availed himself of this opportunity to visit Florence and make his peace with Lorenzo the Magnificent, protected against ill-intentioned creditors by a safe-conduct and his diplomatic status.[211] In 1489 Portinari with Cristofano Spini, his former partner, was sent as an envoy to England, this time by Lorenzo the Magnificent himself, to discuss the terms of a commercial treaty which established in Pisa the Mediterranean staple for English wool, a blow to the Venetians. The treaty also spelled the doom of Southampton as a port of call for the galleys.[212] In 1496 Portinari was among the negotiators of the *Intercursus Magnus*, the great treaty which for many years was to regulate commercial intercourse between England and the Low Countries.[213]

Nearly seventy, Tommaso Portinari finally retired and went to Florence. He died there four years later on February 15, 1501, in the Hospital of Santa Maria Nuova, founded in 1288 by his ancestor, Folco di Ricovero Portinari, the father of Beatrice.

Tommaso's son Francesco, named in the will as principal legatee, refused to accept the inheritance for fear that assets would not be sufficient to pay all the debts. In accordance with Roman law, by divesting himself of the inheritance, he did not become liable for the debts. Tommaso Portinari thus in the end paid the price of his own mistakes and his foolhardy conduct of business affairs.

XIV

THE DECLINE: 1464–1494

The decline of the Medici Bank embraces the period of thirty years stretching from the death of Cosimo in 1464 to the expulsion of the Medici from Florence in 1494. At this date the Bank was virtually in a state of bankruptcy, and the few branches still in operation (Lyons, Rome, and Naples) were struggling for existence against overwhelming odds. During these thirty years, leadership was assumed by three successive generations of Medici: Piero di Cosimo the Gouty (1464–1469), Lorenzo the Magnificent (1469–1492), and Piero di Lorenzo (1492–1494).

When Cosimo de' Medici died on August 1, 1464, his company had passed the peak of its prosperity and was already going downhill. The London branch had come to grief; other branches, too, were experiencing growing difficulties; and profits were falling off. Had Cosimo lived and retained his vigor, it is possible that he might have been able to retrieve the waning fortunes of the Medici Bank and to halt a descent that was leading to the abyss. His successors, unfortunately, lacked his ability and were ill-advised by those in whom they put their trust.

By a stroke of bad luck, Cosimo was survived by Piero, the elder of his two legitimate sons, who had been reared to rule but had received no practical training in the countinghouse.[1] To make matters worse, Piero suffered acutely from gout and was bedridden during most of the five remaining years of his life. Despite these handicaps, he did much better than expected and tried to stem the tide by initiating a policy of retrenchment which, however, was not carried through. Nonetheless, he was blamed for causing the wave of bankruptcies which shook the business world of Florence shortly after Cosimo's death.

According to Niccolò Machiavelli, Piero de' Medici, upon the perfidious advice of Dietisalvi Neroni, called in many loans from both foreigners and Florentines, thereby creating a great deal of discontent and making himself many enemies.[2] The odium incurred by Piero, Machiavelli adds, was increased by the number of business failures allegedly brought about by this credit contraction. Dietisalvi Neroni expected that Piero's unpopularity would favor the success of the plot to overthrow Medici rule which he was hatching with Messer Luca Pitti, Niccolò Soderini, and Messer Angelo Acciaiuoli. Instead of succeeding, this attempt was foiled and the chief conspirators were sent into exile, with the exception of Luca Pitti who had defected at the last minute and be-

11. Detail of the triptych "The Last Judgment," by Hans Memling. Tommaso
Portinari is the man kneeling in the scales. His wife is sitting in front of him.

12. Lorenzo the Magnificent

13. Entrance of Charles VIII of France and his Army into Florence, November 17, 1494, a few days after the expulsion of the Medici. The Medici Palace is the first building on the left.

trayed his accomplices.[3] His treachery brought him only ignominy and he was despised by all — Medici partisans as well as opponents.[4]

Machiavelli's story has been accepted at face value by some historians and rejected by others as improbable.[5] However, there never is any smoke without fire. While Machiavelli has somewhat twisted the facts, his story contains an element of truth. It is certain that Piero di Cosimo, shortly after his father's death, ordered a survey of his property and his business interests in order to know "in how many feet of water he was standing." This audit probably revealed that the affairs of the Medici company were not in as prosperous a state as was believed.[6] Piero, as a result, embarked upon a policy of retrenchment of which there is plenty of evidence in the Medici records. He took steps to terminate the Venice branch which was doing poorly, he made strenuous efforts to extricate himself from the muddle in London by sending Tani to negotiate a settlement with Edward IV, and he ordered Pigello Portinari in Milan to cut down the loans to the Sforza court. It is undoubtedly due to Piero's insistence that the partnership agreement of October 14, 1469, with Tommaso Portinari opposed any extension of credit to Charles the Bold and prescribed the liquidation of the Burgundian galleys. Piero was steadfast in this policy, but he unfortunately did not make sure that it was carried out in accordance with his intentions.

There is little doubt therefore, that Piero di Cosimo, in order to forestall increasing difficulties, adopted a policy of contraction instead of expansion. What remains doubtful is whether this policy provoked the epidemic of bankruptcies which broke out in Florence shortly after Cosimo's death. The first to fail was Matteo di Giorgio del Maestro Cristofano on November 13, 1464; he dragged down several other firms, including Giovanni and Angelo Baldesi, Bernardo Banchi and Brothers, and Pierozzo Banchi. These were concerns of minor importance with liabilities under 20,000 florins.[7] The first major crash was Piero Partini and Brothers, who owed 40,000 florins. Next came Lodovico Strozzi, whose liabilities amounted to about 32,000 florins, and Lorenzo d'Ilarione Ilarioni, who failed with a deficit of 160,000 florins. The latter was the grandson of Ilarione de' Bardi, who had been the general manager of the Medici Bank from 1420 to 1433.[8] In the last days of December 1464, news reached Florence that Gianfrancesco Strozzi, the son of Palla exiled by Cosimo in 1434, had suspended payments and was seeking an agreement with his creditors.[9] The same happened to Bartolomeo Zorzi, or Giorgi, the former farmer of the Phocea alum mines, who perhaps succeeded in retrieving his fortunes, since he recovered his rights in Asia Minor after conclusion of the peace treaty between Venice and Sultan Mohammed II in 1479.[10] The Salviati company also was tottering, and Borromei, its manager in Bruges, fled to sanctuary because he could not satisfy all the creditors demanding payment. However, the Medici came to the rescue and supplied 12,000 florins.[11] By April, 1465, the Salviati company was back on its feet.[12]

According to a letter of Angelo Acciaiuoli, the crisis of 1464–1465 was the worst calamity since 1339.[13] This may have been an exaggeration, but there is no doubt that unemployment was widespread and that lack of confidence caused business to come to a standstill. To what extent Piero's policy was responsible for the depression is quite another matter. The bankruptcies scarcely affected the Medici Bank; perhaps the hardest hit was its branch in Venice, which was involved to the amount of 1,000 ducats in the Partini crash. The Lyons branch had bought a bill of exchange of twelve gold marks, or 768 écus of 64, from the Strozzi; but Tommaso Portinari succeeded just in time in having it accepted by the drawee, the Salviati company in Bruges.[14]

Most of the bankrupt firms had connections in the Levant, and the occasion, if not the cause, of the slump seems to have been the outbreak of the war between Venice and the Sultan which was to last sixteen years, from 1463 to 1479. As soon as hostilities began, the Venetians in Constantinople and other parts of Turkey who had failed to make good their escape were either massacred or imprisoned, and all Venetian property was confiscated.[15] The result was that all firms with interests in the Levant were completely ruined or, at least, suffered huge losses. Although the Florentines in the Ottoman empire were not molested, they lost anything of theirs that was in the hands of Venetians.

Piero di Cosimo, as a matter of fact, did his best to alleviate the crisis. Not only did he come to the aid of the Salviati, but he helped Lorenzo Ilarioni and Lodovico Strozzi to come to terms with their creditors.[16] Strozzi eventually paid all claimants in full, thereby impoverishing himself, but Ilarioni settled for a few shillings in the pound and came out richer than before he had gone into business.[17]

After 1466 Piero di Cosimo continued to pursue the policy of retrenchment which he had adopted upon his father's death. However, he found it difficult to implement this policy because the granting of credit was to follow the line of least resistance and the calling in of loans was to run afoul of political imperatives. Branch managers showed no enthusiasm. Pigello Portinari, upon being reproached that he was too liberal in accommodating the Sforza court, promised to tighten his purse strings but pointed out all the same that, in an emergency, it was well-nigh impossible to turn down requests without losing favor and influence.[18] Once involved too deeply, the lender lost the strategic advantage to the borrower. To retreat was to court disaster. It was very well to enunciate the principle that one branch should not burden another, but to put this into practice was quite a different matter.[19] Branches short of resources were apt to draw on those having a surplus to lend or an easy access to funds seeking investment.

After warning Tommaso Portinari, Pigello's brother, against entanglements with the Burgundian court, Piero, for reasons of prestige and influence, inconsistently allowed him to farm the toll of Gravelines and to lend small sums for the sake of keeping "on good terms" with Charles the Bold. After taking this first step, would it be possible to stop and avoid further commitments? Then there was the problem of English wool, practically the only commodity in which Northern Europe could settle adverse balances in Italy as has been pointed out. The Bruges branch was even more dependent upon the fleece of English sheep than the London branch. But Italian exporters were more or less at the mercy of the king of England, who could turn the flow of supplies on or off by either granting or refusing licenses. And there were other aspects to the problem. Fine cloth was made of English wool, whose quality was unrivalled. It was an indispensable raw material for the Florentine woolen industry. As unofficial head of the state, Piero de' Medici was faced with the responsibility of supplying the looms and providing work for the "poor." Any period of prolonged unemployment was likely to foster unrest, touch off riots, and play into the hands of conspirators — and no one was fully trustworthy. Friends today were enemies tomorrow.

Piero di Cosimo was not in an enviable position. Occupied with affairs of state, he had little time to devote to the management of the Medici Bank and had to leave the conduct of business to his ministro, Francesco di Tommaso Sassetti (1421–1490). After serving for many years successfully as manager of the Geneva branch, Sassetti had been called to Florence in 1459 to help Giovanni di Cosimo in the discharge of his duties as general manager.[20] Upon Giovanni's death, the whole burden fell upon Sassetti, although the holding company as it existed prior to 1455 was never revived in his favor. While performing the functions of general manager for the Medici company as a whole, he was a partner only in the Avignon and Geneva-Lyons branches and had no share in either the capital or the profits of any other, except for a short period in the Tavola of Florence.

Piero de' Medici died on December 2, 1469, and was succeeded by two youths, Lorenzo aged twenty-one and Giuliano only sixteen. Because of their inexperience, per forza, they had to lean heavily upon their father's advisors. Lorenzo soon freed himself from their influence in political affairs and developed within a few years into one of the great statesmen of his time. But he was less interested in business matters and in this field continued to depend upon Francesco Sassetti, who became all powerful. Nothing was done without or against his advice. Any criticism of Sassetti's policy was brushed aside as inspired by envy or even less avowable motives.[21] Sassetti, however, did not have the stamina of the late Giovanni Benci. He lacked the latter's singleness of purpose or Cosimo's iron will. Intent upon pleasing everybody, if possible, he lived on expedients and delayed harsh decisions until it was too late to apply preventive measures.

Cosimo, in his time, had kept the branch managers tightly under control and never allowed them to deviate from his instructions, but Sassetti followed their lead instead of giving them guidance.[22] For example, he allowed himself to be hoodwinked by Tommaso Portinari and threw to the wind as twaddle any objections raised by the more cautious Angelo Tani.[23] In another instance, Sassetti remained deaf to any hint that Lionetto de' Rossi might be untrustworthy and did not take action until the damage done was beyond repair.[24] Eventually, Sassetti himself came to realize that he had followed a mistaken policy: at the end of his career, he wrote to Lorenzo, "I should not omit to tell you that, if your managerial staff is not ruled with more discipline and greater firmness than in times past, trouble will recur because any relaxation of authority is a tempting bait which leads to license and unruliness." [25] He should have taken a stand earlier, long before the Medici company was in desperate straits.

One may wonder how Sassetti came to assume a key position in the management of the Medici Bank. The son of a money-changer, in Mercato Nuovo, who had died while his children were still young, Francesco had entered the service of the Medici Bank around 1440 as a factor in Geneva and, within six years, had risen to branch manager, perhaps by intriguing against his chief, Ruggieri della Casa. Sassetti remained in Geneva until called to Florence in 1459 to relieve his friend, the overburdened Giovanni di Cosimo. Shortly thereafter he married Nera di Piero Corsi, a girl of only fifteen, who bore him five sons and five daughters.[26] By 1462, after twenty years with the Medici, he already had a sizable fortune of nearly 27,000 florins, which included a house in Florence, three poderi (farms), jewels, a library, and 18,000 florins invested in the Medici company, under the form both of deposits a discrezione and of shares in the equity of the Avignon and Geneva branches.[27] Four years later, this fortune had nearly doubled and amounted to 52,000 florins.[28] His business investments, chiefly in the Medici Bank, had increased to 45,000 florins. He also had bought more real estate and was building the beautiful villa on the heights of Montughi, from the terrace of which one looks out over the Mugnone valley with the hill of Fiesole rising in the background. This residence, it is said, cost him 12,000 florins or more.[29] Sassetti possessed a fine library of books, in both Latin and the vernacular. His ex libris displayed the significant motto, in French: *A mon pouvoir*.

But before Sassetti's death most of this large fortune was irretrievably lost, engulfed in the disastrous collapse of the Lyons branch and other bad investments. In 1489 he wrote from Lyons to Lorenzo the Magnificent that he was no longer affluent and regretted that he was unable to offer any financial assistance.[30] In another letter to the same correspondent, Sassetti expressed the desire to get out of debt as quickly as possible because interest was consuming his estate.[31]

As related earlier, Sassetti went to Lyons at the age of sixty-seven and stayed seven months to straighten out the muddle created by Lionetto de' Rossi's mismanagement. A few months after his return to Florence, on March 21, 1490, he had a stroke and was found by his valet lying unconscious on the floor of his room. He lived a few days longer with his right side paralyzed and without power of speech.[32] In all probability, he died on March 31, 1490, since Lorenzo the Magnificent on April 1 dictated letters to Lorenzo Spinelli, Philippe de Commines, Ymbert de Batarnay, and other clients in France to notify them of Sassetti's death.[33] The funeral took place the next day in the church of Santa Trinità, where Francesco Sassetti had acquired a family chapel, for which he had commissioned Domenico Ghirlandaio to paint an altarpiece, "The Adoration of the Shepherds," and the famous fresco representing the Pope approving the rules of the Franciscan Order.[34]

Fate had ceased to favor Sassetti despite his other motto, "May fate be kind to me" (*Mitia Fata Mihi*). His descendants in the sixteenth century were greatly impoverished; they kept the villa of Montughi as long as they could but they were finally compelled to sell it.[35] To retrieve the family fortunes, a great-grandson, Filippo Sassetti, entered the service of the Portuguese and went to the East Indies, where he died of tropical disease (1588). Although he succeeded in amassing a fortune, his heirs were robbed of their inheritance, and received next to nothing. Filippo's brother, Francesco, an impractical man, spent his days bending over old parchments, drawing up genealogies, and writing a history of his family in which he stressed its nobility and past wealth — a rather futile occupation.[36]

In the memorandum which Francesco Sassetti had dictated to his sons on the eve of his departure for Lyons in 1488, he attributed his misfortunes entirely "to the thoroughly bad and neglectful management" (governo) of Lionetto de' Rossi.[37] However, was Sassetti himself free from blame? His duty was to keep branch managers under control, to audit their accounts, to detect any frauds, and to lay down the rules to be followed. This he did not do. Sassetti erred in giving the branch managers too much leeway and in not examining more carefully their reports. Perhaps he sometimes had difficulty in convincing Lorenzo the Magnificent and did not have the strength of character to force the issue. In any case, the decline of the Medici Bank should not be traced to the shortcomings of one man. Lorenzo de' Medici has his share in the responsibility for the downfall. Besides, there were forces at work over which neither he nor Sassetti had any control.

According to Machiavelli, "Lorenzo the Magnificent had no luck in his commercial undertakings (*fu, quanto alla mercanzia, infelicissimo*); because of the mismanagement of his agents (*il disordine de' suoi ministri*) who conducted the business as if they were princes and not merely private persons, much of his wealth was lost in places abroad; as a result, the State had to support him with large sums of money." [38] Adam Smith, misunderstanding Machiavelli, made the most of this passage in order to illustrate the wastefulness and inefficiency of government enterprises and to prove that princes generally were unsuccessful as traders.[39] The example is poorly chosen, since the Medici Bank never was a public bank and Lorenzo was a private banker who also happened to be *de facto* chief of state without ever achieving princely status. Nevertheless, it is true that the behavior of some of the branch managers, for example, the Portinari brothers in Milan and in Bruges, was such as to excite the cupidity of princes by giving them the mistaken impression that the Medici Bank was able to lend unlimited amounts. Even the sophisticated Philippe de Commines marvels at Canigiani's ability to lend up to 120,000 écus to Edward IV and at Tommaso Portinari's readiness to stand surety for as much as 80,000 écus at one time.[40]

Enlarging upon Machiavelli, several chroniclers assert that Lorenzo the Magnificent not only had no luck but lacked aptitude for business. The humanist Francesco Guicciardini, for example, states that Lorenzo, having no understanding of business, failed to look carefully into the reports submitted by Tommaso Portinari and Lionetto de' Rossi and was thus deceived by them, with result that he was saved from bankruptcy only by appropriating public funds.[41] Lorenzo's own nephew, Alessandro de' Pazzi, is even more explicit and attributes the failure of the Medici company to his uncle's lack of business ability, lavish expenditures, and absorption with public and other affairs.[42] Giovanni Michele Bruto uses a bit of psychology when he tells us that Lorenzo blamed everything on the unfaithfulness of his agents and that they, to exculpate themselves, claimed his excessive spending to be the source of all the trouble.[43] Of course, such a claim cannot be sustained; it was not Lorenzo who, by his prodigality, caused the tremendous losses in Lyons, Bruges, or London: they were the result of mismanagement and excessive lending to sovereigns. This does not mean that Lorenzo the Magnificent was in no way responsible: upon Sassetti's advice, he made the fateful mistake of giving too much rope to his branch managers. As a result, his authority was undermined and he himself complained in 1478 to Girolamo Morelli that it grieved him very much that in Milan, where he would expect to enjoy great credit, he was not even able to prevent his managers (the Portinari brothers) from inciting hostility at the Sforza court.[44]

The available evidence concerning the maladministration of Lionetto de' Rossi and the Portinari brothers is so overwhelming that it cannot be brushed aside, but panegyrists of Lorenzo the Magnificent who regard him as a superman with only virtues and no defects have questioned the statement that he was devoid of business ability or, at least, took little interest in the affairs of his company.[45] The chroniclers who said so, these panegyrists contend, were blinded by either bias or partisanship.[46] What is the truth of the matter?

Like his father Piero, Lorenzo received a fine humanistic education, but his business training was rather neglected and he was not schooled in the practice of the countinghouse. It is true that a timid effort to remedy this defect was made in 1466, when Lorenzo, at the age of seventeen, went to Rome; he was urged by his father to listen attentively to Giovanni Tornabuoni, who would explain to him the state of the Rome branch so that Lorenzo, upon his return to Florence, would be able to report how matters stood.[47]

These casual contacts with the business world were, however, a poor substitute for systematic training.[48] After succeeding his father, Lorenzo the Magnificent took no interest in the management of his company and delegated all powers to Francesco Sassetti. When shortly after Piero's death, Angelo Tani, disagreeing with Sassetti's policy concerning the London branch, appealed to Lorenzo, the latter replied that "he did not understand such matters" (che lui non se n'intendeva).[49] Ten years later, in a memorandum dictated by himself, Lorenzo had to admit that, because of insufficient knowledge, he had been duped by Tommaso Portinari; Portinari's schemes, by the way, had been encouraged by Sassetti without consulting Tani, who would surely have withheld his consent.[50] The same story was repeated with reference to the Lyons branch, and Lorenzo did not recall Lionetto de' Rossi even after the latter's doings had aroused Sassetti's suspicions.[51] In 1487 Lorenzo Spinelli wrote the Magnificent: "It pleases me to see that you begin to take interest in your affairs and to manage them better than they have been in the past, because if you persevere benefits and credit will redound to you."[52] There is little doubt, therefore, that Lorenzo, at least in his early career, neglected his business interests and that he was prompted to pay more attention to them only after mounting losses had weakened his finances and were sapping the foundations of his rule.

The Pazzi conspiracy (April 26, 1478), in which Giuliano de' Medici was murdered and Lorenzo himself barely escaped with his life, was intended to topple the Medici Bank as well as the Medici regime. It burst out at a critical moment when financial difficulties were at their height because of the losses suffered in Apulia, Flanders, England, and Milan. Because the Pazzi Bank was perhaps the second largest in Florence and had branches in Rome, Lyons, and Bruges, its partners and managers were well aware of the fact that their most dangerous competitor was having serious trouble and resembled a colossus with clay feet. As a matter of fact, Renato de' Pazzi, the best mind in the family, had refused to take part in the plot because the Medici Bank was in such grave difficulties that he believed bankruptcy to be at hand.[53] In his view, if the Medici lost all credit, they would also lose all power. The failure of the plot only induced Pope Sixtus IV and his allies to redouble their efforts by striking at the Bank in order to bring down the Medici. "The King of Naples," Lorenzo complains in a letter to Girolamo Morelli, "seeks to destroy my business by insisting that I pay without allowing me to collect. I fear that the Pope, if he hears of this, will proceed in the same manner to cripple my business in Rome." [54] Lorenzo's fears were amply justified; the Pope sequestrated all Medici property, repudiated the debt of the Apostolic Chamber to the Bank, and expelled Giovanni Tornabuoni from Rome.

To meet the emergency, Lorenzo was constrained to mobilize all available resources. He wrote Morelli, the Florentine ambassador in Milan, to inquire whether Cecco Simonetta, the ducal secretary, could let him have 30,000 or 40,000 ducats, or from $120,000 to $160,000 in gold, a large sum then because the purchasing power of money was several times what it is today.[55] More serious, between May and September, 1478, Lorenzo de' Medici, being in desperate straits, at different times took a total of 53,643 florins in coin which belonged to Giovanni and Lorenzo, the minor sons of Pierfrancesco de' Medici, whose guardian he was.[56] This sum had not been repaid by 1485, when it was claimed by the two youths upon reaching majority. A compromise about this and other matters was concluded by arbitrators, but it gave satisfaction to neither of the two parties and was one of the main causes of the breach between the two branches of the Medici family descending from Giovanni di Bicci.[57] Although Lorenzo was forced to transfer to his cousins the ancestral villa of Cafaggiolo and other property in the Mugello, they complained of being charged with one third of the losses of the London branch and sumptuary expenses to which their father Pierfrancesco had not given his assent.[58]

Whether Lorenzo the Magnificent misappropriated public funds in 1478 or later has been for a long time a moot question argued back and forth between his eulogists and his detractors.[59] Chroniclers, among whom the most explicit is Pietro Parenti, have been disbelieved, allegedly because their assertions have not been confirmed by any documentary sources.[60] However, it seems likely that any incriminating evidence was suppressed when the Medici, after eighteen years of exile, returned to power (1512). In any case, a document has now been found among the Strozzi papers which establishes beyond the shadow of a doubt that Lorenzo the Magnificent diverted public funds to his own use.[61] On January 30, 1495, the Commune lodged a claim with the custodians of Medici property for 74,948 large florins, which had been paid out in several installments to Lorenzo or his agents by Francesco Della Tosa, steward of the Monte or the public debt. The document explicitly states that these payments were made "without the sanction of any law and without authority, to the damage and prejudice of the Commune." [62] In the absence of business records for the period after 1469, nothing indicates how the sum of 75,000 florins was actually used, whether to refloat the Bank or to bribe diplomats, a common practice in the age of Machiavelli. At any rate, not only the heirs of Lorenzo the Magnificent but also their partners in the Medici Bank, Lorenzo Tornabuoni and Giovambattista Bracci, were held liable for the sum of which the Commune had been defrauded. It is likely, therefore, that bankruptcy after the Pazzi conspiracy was averted only by dipping into the public treasury.

Even in those desperate circumstances, no heroic remedies were applied, and Sassetti was left to patch up the cracks, but his handiwork did not prevent the cracks from spreading until the entire structure was beyond repair. To rebuild the tottering edifice from the ground was not attempted; however, plans for a complete renovation of the decrepit structure were submitted to Lorenzo the Magnificent but apparently came to naught.

One such proposal was a reorganization plan which was formulated around 1482, certainly after the liquidation of the Bruges and Venice branches (1480) as terminus a quo and prior to the dismissal and arrest of Lionetto de' Rossi (1485) as terminus ad quem.[63] This plan contemplated the revival of the holding company form of organization as it had existed before the death of Giovanni d'Amerigo Benci (1455). In fact, the proposal involved the creation of two such companies: one placed under the management of Francesco Sassetti and the other under that of Giovanni Tornabuoni. The first would have controlled the Tavola in Florence itself and the branches in Lyons and Pisa, whereas the second would have comprised the banking establishments in Rome and Naples.

The plan was worked out in great detail down to the shares in the capital which each partner was to provide and the profit quotas to which he was entitled. However, since the plan never materialized, it would be purposeless to examine it with a magnifying glass. Suffice it to say that the planned capital of the two holding companies combined was set at a minimum of 48,000 ducats, of which Lorenzo the Magnificent was to supply only 18,000 ducats, Sassetti 15,000 ducats, and Giovanni Tornabuoni the same amount. In addition, junior partners were expected to contribute another 20,000 ducats. Aggregate capitalization, excluding deposits a discrezione, consequently reached the sum of 68,000 ducats, at least on paper. Notice that the share of Lorenzo de' Medici was reduced to a small fraction of this total, which proves the magnitude of his losses. In addition to banking, the project suggested the creation in Lyons of a special company to deal in silk fabrics and to be placed under the management of Francesco del Tovaglia. Its capital was to be supplied by the Lyons branch, so that there were to be three layers of superimposed partnerships, or companies: the partnership managed by Francesco del Tovaglia at the bottom of the pyramid, the Lyons branch in the middle, and the parent company with Francesco Sassetti and Lorenzo the Magnificent as partners at the top. To be complete, the reorganization plan also mentions the desirability of operating in Florence either a silkshop or a goldbeating establishment, but there is no longer any reference to a woolshop.

As managers of the Tavola in Florence, the reorganization plan suggests Giovanni d'Orsino Lanfredini and Lodovico Masi. The management of the Pisa branch would be entrusted to Simone Folchi, formerly in Montpellier, or to Francesco Spina. In Lyons, it was proposed to retain Lionetto de' Rossi, although, it is intimated, he did not deserve the confidence which Sassetti continued to have in him. At the head of the Naples branch, the author of the plan would have placed Francesco Nasi and Battista Pandolfini as joint managers, "if he had any hope that they would cooperate."

This plan, apparently, was designed to supply what had so long been lacking, control and coordination. One of the main troubles with the Medici Bank in later years was precisely lack of coordination. Cosimo de' Medici had always prevented the development of serious clashes, but Sassetti did not rule the branch managers with the same iron fist. As a result the Medici company was rent with dissension, and branch managers, instead of pulling together like a team, were often at loggerheads, each defending his own interests and disregarding those of the concern as a whole. For example, the irrepressible Giovanni Tornabuoni was in conflict with Bruges and Lyons, and Sassetti was unable to restore peace and to coordinate the activities of the different branches. He also allowed the weaker branches to drag down those who were still in a sound financial condition. Within the different branches, the clerical staff also was frequently torn by jealousies and discords which Francesco Sassetti sometimes encouraged instead of trying to dampen them. The best example of this is perhaps the disagreement between Angelo Tani and Tommaso Portinari, which Sassetti kept alive because he preferred to perpetuate a muddle in order to avoid an unpleasant decision apt to harm his own prestige.

The author of this reorganization plan was probably Giovambattista

Bracci, who was on the staff of the Tavola in Florence.[64] He was not influential enough to have his scheme accepted by Lorenzo de' Medici; if accepted, it is doubtful whether the plan would have made much difference or would have transformed the Medici company from a decaying body into a flourishing concern.

Nevertheless, the scheme, in somewhat different form, was revived in 1486 when Lorenzo Spinelli, writing to Lorenzo the Magnificent, approved the idea of creating a controlling partnership, from which all the other ragioni would emanate (*dal quale uscissino tutte l'altre ragioni*).[65] In other words, the purpose was to revive the holding company as it had existed prior to 1455, but with Lorenzo the Magnificent, Francesco Sassetti, and Giovanni Tornabuoni as maggiori. By so doing, it was hoped that Tornabuoni would cease to promote the interests of the Rome branch to the detriment of other branches and that he would be more inclined to consider the problems of the Medici company as a whole. Again, nothing was done and the project remained a dead letter. Moreover, one wonders whether it would have been possible to change the ingrained habits of Giovanni Tornabuoni who, with age, was becoming more and more set in his ways. What the Medici Bank needed was another Giovanni Benci, and there was nobody of his stature available.

When Sassetti died on March 31, 1490, he was succeeded by Giovambattista Bracci, a partner in the Tavola of Florence, probably assisted by Filippo da Gagliano. Of course, Uncle Tornabuoni continued to interfere, and his advice, whether good or bad, carried more weight than ever. Immediately after Sassetti's death, Lorenzo Spinelli expressed the pious hope that steps would now be taken to put the Lyons branch on a firm footing, presumably by liquidating past indebtedness and injecting new capital, because, he added, it was impossible to make profits as long as things were in a state of uncertainty and "without my knowing whether I am in heaven or on earth." [66] But, as usual, no action was taken. Lorenzo de' Medici was either unwilling to sink more money into a losing business or, more likely, unable to supply the capital needed to make a fresh start. During the remaining two years of his life, the Medici Bank was allowed to slide backward, ever closer to the pit of bankruptcy.

The descent became precipitous after the death of Lorenzo the Magnificent, which occurred at his villa of Careggi on April 8, 1492. His son Piero di Lorenzo (1472–1503), a young man of twenty, healthy, haughty, and fond of sports, possessed neither diplomatic skill nor managerial ability. His second son, Messer Giovanni (1475–1521), just made a cardinal at the ripe age of seventeen, was more gifted than Piero, but he was already displaying an inclination for extravagant spending that helped to accelerate the downfall of the family banking house as it later, after he became pope, wrecked the finances of the papacy. Lorenzo's third son,

Giuliano (1479–1516), was still a boy when his father died. It is reported
that Lorenzo the Magnificent used to say: "I have three sons: one is
foolish, one is clever, and one is kind." [67] Whether he actually said so
matters little. The epithets aptly depict the characters of Piero, Giovanni,
and Giuliano.

It was unfortunate for the Medici that the succession fell to the one
son who was the least fit to be either chief of state or head of a banking
house. Piero di Lorenzo left the care of public affairs in the hands of his
secretary, Piero Dovizi da Bibbiena, and the management of business
matters in those of his great-uncle, Giovanni Tornabuoni. This was not
the best choice. Tornabuoni was not a man endowed with any breadth
of vision or any capacity to see all the facets of a problem. He meant
well, but he was impulsive and swayed constantly between moods of
gloom and fits of unwarranted optimism.

If Medici rule had not been overthrown in 1494 because of Piero's
political ineptitude and the French invasion, it might have ended even
more disgracefully in a financial crash of the first order. The Medici Bank
was at this time on the brink of bankruptcy. Most of its branches had
been closed, and those still in existence were gasping for breath. Even
the Rome branch, for so long the main pillar of the Medici Bank, was
giving way because funds were immobilized in loans to the Camera Apostolica and to the Orsini family.[68] Besides, the debt of the Medici family
to the Rome branch exceeded their equity by 11,243 large florins. In
addition, Messer Giovanni, the youthful cardinal of Santa Maria in
Domenica, owed another 7,500 florins.[69]

After the Medici had been expelled from Florence, all their property
was seized by the new regime set up by their opponents. With regard
to the bank, an agreement was reached between the custodians of "rebel"
property and Giovanni Tornabuoni according to which he with his son
Lorenzo were to continue the business of the bank. Little or nothing is
known about the Tornabuoni company but, deprived of capital and
credit, it vegetated and was soon wilting. Although it would be difficult
to adduce texts in support of the humanist historian Francesco Guicciardini, he is probably right in asserting that Lorenzo di Giovanni Tornabuoni's participation in the plot to restore the Medici (1497) was actuated
by the dreadful prospect of imminent bankruptcy.[70]

Whatever the shortcomings of Lorenzo the Magnificent or of his "minister" Francesco Sassetti, it would be a one-sided point of view to attribute
the downfall of the Medici Bank exclusively to errors in judgment or
mistaken policies. Actually, the downfall is not traceable to a single cause
but to a complex of circumstances and a combination of interacting factors whose importance it is impossible to assess.[71] Some of the forces at
work, such as the diminishing supply of English wool, were entirely

beyond either Lorenzo's or Sassetti's control. Professor Robert S. Lopez goes so far as to assert that "even a skillful management would not have brought many dividends" and, presumably, would not have saved the Medici Bank from impending doom.[72] This opinion may be correct but is hard to prove. It is certain, however, that the financial structure of the Medici Bank made it very vulnerable to unfavorable trends, such as prevailed in the 1470's and 1480's.

As the surviving balance sheets show, the Medici were trading heavily on the equity. This policy allowed them to accumulate huge profits as long as the return on investment exceeded the interest (discrezione) paid to depositors. On the other hand, catastrophe was bound to ensue after mounting losses had wiped out the partners' rather slender equity.

A perusal of the extant balance sheets (Tables 33, 39, 41, 47, 51, 60, and 69) reveals another significant fact: the Medici Bank operated with tenuous cash reserves which were usually well below 10 percent of total assets. It is true that this is a common feature in the financial statements of medieval merchant-bankers, such as Francesco Datini and the Borromei of Milan.[73] The extent to which they made use of money substitutes is always a surprise to modern historians. Nevertheless, one may raise the question whether cash reserves were adequate and whether the Medici Bank was not suffering from lack of liquidity. The answer to this question should be cautious because medieval merchant-bankers, in a crisis, tended to rely a great deal on their private resources or hoards as the Medici did in 1433 and again in 1478 at the time of the Pazzi conspiracy. Another solution was to take up money by exchange, but this was an expensive form of borrowing. Reliance on it was a major factor in causing the heavy losses sustained by several Medici branches, especially Bruges, London, and Lyons.

During the prosperous years under Cosimo's management, the Medici Bank grew chiefly by plowing back earnings into the business and by setting aside generous reserves for bad debts. Profits, however, were so abundant that Cosimo was able to withdraw very large sums in order to expand his holdings of real estate or to display his munificence. He was a great builder. In addition to the Medici palace and the villa at Careggi which he built for his own use, he gave funds to erect the church of San Lorenzo, to complete the Dominican friary of San Marco, to enlarge the Badia of Fiesole, and to renovate the Church of the Holy Spirit in Jerusalem. It was really Cosimo who started the collection of manuscripts which came to be known as the Biblioteca Laurenziana. According to the *Ricordi* of his grandson, Lorenzo the Magnificent, the Medici family, between 1434 and 1471, spent the huge amount of 663,755 florins in buildings, charities, and taxes, not including household expenses.[74] Lorenzo continued to collect books and manuscripts and to patronize the arts, but not on the same scale as Cosimo had done. Apart from the villa of Poggio a Caiano, he built very little.[75] The reason is undoubtedly that he could no longer afford to spend money as freely as his grandfather had been in the habit of doing. Perhaps Lorenzo was unable to reduce his other expenses as well, to compensate him for his losses in business. At any rate, it is improbable that his lavishness as such would have caused the downfall of the Medici Bank if there had been no losses due to mismanagement.

A factor which deserves more serious attention is that the Medici were rulers *de facto,* if not legally. Because of their position, political considerations were often given priority over cool business judgment. A case in point is the establishment of the Milan branch, which from the very start was an undertaking intended to lend financial support to Francesco Sforza. It was unquestionably a move inspired by political motives but inconsistent with Cosimo's business policy which, because of the risks involved, opposed the making of loans to princes, magnates, or high churchmen. Furthermore, making an exception in Milan was setting a bad precedent for other branches to follow. As the Medici Bank increased in size, it also became increasingly difficult to find profit opportunities for idle funds. Tax-farming offered alluring opportunities for easy profits, but this step once taken almost inevitably led the farmer to grant anticipations on future revenues, a process which often ended with the debtor's default and the creditor's ruin. The toll of Gravelines, for example, was the wedge that drove Tommaso Portinari deeper and deeper into entanglements with Charles the Bold.

Sometimes it was impossible to do business at all without lending, as in England where licenses to export wool could be secured only by advancing money to the King. This was the dilemma which faced the Medici in their dealings with Edward IV. It is true that Gherardo Canigiani was a weakling, unable to resist pressure, who advanced far beyond the amount amortizable within a foreseeable future by obtaining licenses to export wool duty-free.

It was undoubtedly a congenital defect of what Professor N. S. B. Gras called "the financial type of sedentary merchant" to drift from private banking into government finance.[76] The Medici had before their eyes the example of the Acciaiuoli, the Bardi, the Frescobaldi, the Peruzzi, and other Florentine companies which had been wrecked by loans to English kings and other foreign sovereigns. Although the Medici were well aware of this danger, they were unable to steer clear of it and foundered on the same reef.

It is now generally accepted that the last decades of the fifteenth century were not a period of great prosperity, but witnessed a depression which was both lasting and profound. It played havoc with the Florentine economy and was certainly in part responsible for the straits of the Medici Bank. Lorenzo the Magnificent, in filing his return for the catasto of 1481, makes the sober statement: "In making out this report, I shall not follow the same procedure as my father in 1469 because there is a great difference between that time and the present with the consequence that I have suffered many losses in several of my undertakings, as is well known not only to Your Lordships but to the entire world." [77]

This statement, of course, implied that business conditions had taken a turn for the worse after the death of Piero the Gouty in 1469. What caused the slump is a matter of debate. Historians now fairly well agree in attributing to a declining population the downward trend which lasted for one hundred and fifty years from the Black Death to the Discoveries and which went into a trough during the last decades of the fifteenth century.[78] While demography may explain the general trend, it does not explain why the depression deepened. A major cause of the dip may have been the outbreak of the war between Venice and the Turks which raged from 1463 to 1479 and which, as already mentioned, caused a wave of bankruptcies. In spite of the fact that the Florentines remained neutral, it is likely that they suffered scarcely less than the belligerents from the disturbances brought about by the hostilities and the clogging up of the usual channels of trade. Restoration of peace, however, did not usher in a new period of prosperity, and the depression continued to run its course.

Besides demography and war, monetary instability also has been blamed for the slump. In fact, the silver currency continued to be debased, with the result that the rate of the large florin (fiorino largo) rose from about £4 di piccioli in 1455 to £7 di piccioli in 1497.[79] This rise was slow up to 1475 and then gained momentum. How far monetary disturbances affected the fortunes of the Medici Bank remains problematic. Probably only to a minor extent, if at all, because the change was gradual and was spread out over a period of more than twenty years. At all events, there is never any mention of monetary disturbances as a source of financial difficulties in the surviving letters. What is mentioned, however, is the problem of transferring funds from Northern Europe to Italy. As the century progressed, it seems that this problem became ever more acute and reached a critical stage after 1470. This would also explain why Lorenzo the Magnificent stated that the business climate had deteriorated since his father's death.

As already pointed out, wool was practically the major commodity which the Florentines were willing to buy in Northern Europe and which could be used to settle their claims and those of the Papacy, by no means a negligible item. The Low Countries' balance of trade with Italy, in particular, was very unfavorable because Flemish cloth, Dutch linens, and

Arras tapestries were far from equilibrating imports. Papal remittances, by adding to the deficit, made matters worse instead of better. Unfortunately, English wool became available in smaller and smaller quantities. Strangulation of foreign trade followed, because the Italians encountered increasing difficulties in making their returns and in withdrawing funds from England and the Low Countries. As the Medici correspondence plainly shows, credit balances tended to pile up in Bruges and London, and Giovanni Tornabuoni was constantly complaining because the branch managers in these cities failed to remit promptly to Rome or Florence. Of course, Tornabuoni, as usual, was shortsighted and failed to diagnose the source of the trouble. Another consequence was that Tommaso Portinari sought to borrow in Italy and to invest in England and the Low Countries.

In this connection, it should perhaps be noted that the Medici Bank contributed little to economic growth and that its funds, instead of being invested productively, were mainly used to finance either conspicuous consumption of royal courts or military campaigns from the War of the Roses to the exploits of Italian condottieri, such as Sforza.[80] It is not surprising that the Medici were unable to recover their money after it had been wasted in one way or another. Lack of investment opportunities was another weakness of commercial capitalism in the time of the Italian Renaissance.

The Medici Bank was not the only victim of the depression, which also hit the other Florentine banking houses with irresistible force. In 1478 the Pazzi Bank was perhaps doing better than its great rival but the catasto reports suggest that it was far from doing well. Giovanni di Paolo Rucellai, the second richest man in Florence, withdrew from banking before 1470 because of losses.[81] Between 1422 and 1470, the number of international banks (banchi grossi) fell from seventy-two to thirty-three.[82] By 1494 there were less than half-a-dozen bankers left, not enough to fill the offices of the Arte del Cambio. The decline was catastrophic. Thus the downfall of the Medici Bank coincided with the collapse of Florentine banking. Florence, it is true, re-emerged as a banking center in the sixteenth century, but it never regained its leading position as the financial capital of Western Europe.

To this dismal picture of general depression, there is one conspicuous exception, that of Filippo (1428–1491) and Lorenzo (1430–1479) degli Strozzi who, being in exile until 1466, were doing business in Naples. While the Medici Bank was going downhill, theirs prospered. The two Strozzi brothers, both before and after 1466, succeeded in accumulating a fortune which enabled Filippo, after his brother's death, to build the famous Strozzi palace.

Whether the Medici Bank, if it had been properly managed, could have survived the crisis, will remain forever a matter of conjecture. Perhaps the Medici should have done like Giovanni Rucellai and withdrawn from business before losses had engulfed their capital. However, there was nobody, least of all Francesco Sassetti, who dared take the responsibility for such a drastic step.

APPENDIX

General Managers

1402–1420	Benedetto di Lippaccio de' Bardi
1420–1433	Ilarione di Lippaccio de' Bardi
1433–1435	Lippaccio di Benedetto di Lippaccio de' Bardi
1435–1443	Antonio di Messer Francesco Salutati da Pescia and Giovanni d'Amerigo Benci
1443–1455	Giovanni d'Amerigo Benci alone
1455–1463	Giovanni di Cosimo de' Medici
1459–1463	Francesco di Tommaso Sassetti, assistant to Giovanni di Cosimo
1463–1490	Francesco di Tommaso Sassetti
1490–1494	Giovambattista Bracci with the assistance of Filippo da Gagliano

Branch Managers

Tavola of Florence

1406–1409	Giuliano di Giovanni di ser Matteo
1409–1420	Niccolò di Baldassare Buoni
1420–1431	Folco d'Adoardo Portinari
1431–1435	Lippaccio di Benedetto de' Bardi
1435–1440	Giovanni d'Amerigo Benci
1440–1454	Giovanni di Baldino Inghirami
1454–1470	Francesco di Baldino Inghirami
1460–1470	Tommaso Lapi, assistant manager
1470–1478	Francesco d'Antonio Nori with the assistance of Lodovico Masi
1478–1484	Lodovico Masi
1484–1487	Agostino di Sandro Biliotti
1487–1494	Giovambattista Bracci

Court of Rome

1400–1420	Ilarione di Lippaccio de' Bardi
1420–1429	Bartolomeo d'Andrea de' Bardi
1429–1435	Antonio di Messer Francesco Salutati da Pescia
1435–1438	Antonio di ser Lodovico della Casa
1439–1464	Roberto Martelli
1464–1494	Giovanni di Francesco Tornabuoni

Venice

1402–1406	Neri di Cipriano Tornaquinci
1406–1416	Giovanni di Francesco da Gagliano
1416–1435	Giovanni d'Adoardo Portinari
1435–1448	Lotto di Tanino Bozzi (Tanini) with the assistance of Antonio di Niccolò Martelli
1448–1465	Alessandro di Niccolò Martelli

1466–1469   Giovanni d'Oddo Altoviti
1469–1471   Discontinued
1471–1480   Giovanni d'Orsino Lanfredini
1481   Piero d'Antonio di Taddeo

Naples

1400   Castellano di Tommaso Frescobaldi
1400–1404   Adoardo di Cipriano Tornaquinci
1404–1407   Jacopo di Tommaso Bartoli
1407–1423   Jacopo di Tommaso Bartoli and Rosso di Giovanni de' Medici
1423–1426   Rosso di Giovanni de' Medici and Fantino di Fantino de' Medici
1426–1471   Naples branch discontinued
1471–1475   Agostino di Sandro Biliotti
1475–1489   Francesco Nasi
1490–1494   Bernardo Carnesecchi

Pisa

1442–1450   Ugolino di Niccolò Martelli and Matteo di Cristofano Masi
1450–1460 (?)   Ugolino and Antonio Martelli with the assistance of Matteo Masi
1460–1486   Pisa branch discontinued
1486–1489   Ilarione di Bartolomeo Martelli

Milan

1452–1468   Pigello di Folco Portinari
1468–1478   Accerrito di Folco Portinari, Pigello's younger brother

Geneva-Lyons

1426–1429   Michele di Ferro and Giovanni d'Amerigo Benci
1429–1435   Giovanni d'Amerigo Benci
1435–1447   Ruggieri di ser Lodovico della Casa
1447–1458   Francesco di Tommaso Sassetti
1459–1461   Amerigo di Giovanni Benci
1461–1470   Giuliano di Giovanni del Zaccheria with the assistance of Francesco
            Nori (1461–1468)
1470–1485   Lionetto de' Rossi
1486–1490   Lorenzo Spinelli
1490–1494   Lorenzo Spinelli with the assistance of Cosimo di Francesco Sassetti

Basel

1433–1438   Roberto Martelli
1438–1441   Giovenco di Lorenzo della Stufa
1441–1443   Lorenzo di Giovanni della Stufa

Avignon

1446–1448   Giovanni di Benedetto Zampini
1448–1456   Giovanni Zampini with the assistance of Verano di Bartolomeo
            Peruzzi
1456–1461   Giovanni Zampini and Francesco di Giovanni Benci
1461–1476   Giovanni Zampini
1476–1479 (?)   Michele Dini

Bruges

1439–1448 Bernardo di Giovanni Portinari
1448–1450 Gerozzo de' Pigli with the assistance of Simone Nori
1450–1465 Angelo Tani
1465–1480 Tommaso di Folco Portinari
1469–1471 Antonio di Bernardo de'Medici, assistant manager
1471–1473 Tommaso Guidetti, assistant manager
1473–1480 Cristofano Spini, assistant manager

London

1446–1450 Gerozzo de' Pigli with the assistance of Angelo Tani
1450–1466 Simone d'Antonio Nori
1460–1466 Gherardo Canigiani, assistant manager
1466–1469 Giovanni de' Bardi (?) and Gherardo Canigiani
1469–1472 Gherardo Canigiani
1473–1480 Tommaso Guidetti

Woolshop I

1402–1420 Michele di Baldo
1420–1439 Discontinued
1439–1480 Antonio di Taddeo Taddei
1480–1491 Discontinued
1491–1494 Paolo Benci

Woolshop II

1408–1429 Taddeo di Filippo
1431–1433 Giuntino di Guido Giuntini
1433–1465 (?) Andrea Giuntini

Silkshop

1433–1438 Piero di Domenico Corsi and Francesco di Francesco Berlinghieri
1438–1447 Francesco Berlinghieri with the assistance of Jacopo Tanaglia
1447–1480 Berlinghieri di Francesco Berlinghieri and Jacopo Tanaglia

1348	The Black Death ends a long period of demographic and economic growth
1363	Death of Averardo de' Medici called "Bicci"
1378	*Ciompi* revolt or uprising of the workers in the Florentine woolen industry
1384–1393	Giovanni, Bicci's son, is associated in business with a distant cousin, Vieri di Cambio de' Medici
1397	Giovanni di Bicci, already a banker in Rome, transfers his main office to Florence and, thereby, establishes the Medici Company
1406	Capture of Pisa by Florence
1414–1418	Council of Constance
1420	First reorganization of the Medici Bank. Giovanni di Bicci retires, leaving the management of the Bank to his son Cosimo
1422–1426	War between Florence and Milan
1429–1433	War for the conquest of Lucca, degenerating into another conflict with Milan
1429	Death of Giovanni di Bicci on February 20
1431–1443	Council of Basel, schismatic after 1437
1433	Cosimo de' Medici is arrested on September 7 and barely escapes being condemned to death. Instead, he and his brother are banished to Venice and Padua. Many of their followers, including Averardo di Francesco de' Medici, Cosimo's first cousin, are also exiled
1434	Cosimo is recalled on September 29 and, from then until his death, he controls the Florentine government without being the constitutional head of the state
1434–1443	Meeting of the ecumenical council: Florence (1434–1437), Bologna (1437), Ferrara (1438), and Florence again (1439–1443)
1435	Reorganization of the Medici Bank
1440	Death of Lorenzo, Cosimo's brother

1450	Milan is captured by Francesco Sforza with Medici support
1455	The death of Giovanni d'Amerigo Benci, general manager since 1435, ushers in the gradual decline of the Medici Bank
1464	Cosimo dies on August 1 and is succeeded by Piero, his only surviving son
1469	Piero dies on December 2 and is succeeded by two youths, Lorenzo (the Magnificent) and Giuliano. The management of the Bank is entrusted to Francesco Sassetti, who becomes all powerful
1478	The Pazzi conspiracy is hatched in Rome with the connivance of Pope Sixtus IV in order to overthrow the Medici as rulers of Florence and ruin their Bank. The plot miscarries: Giuliano is killed on April 26 while attending Mass in the cathedral of Florence, but Lorenzo the Magnificent escapes death, being wounded only slightly in the neck. Bloody reprisals follow: the Pazzi are either exterminated or exiled and their accomplices share the same fate. Even many innocents are executed. The crisis rocks the Medici Bank: Lorenzo de' Medici decides to dissociate himself from the Portinari brothers and to liquidate the Bruges and Milan branches
1485	Lyons branch in difficulties; its manager, Lionetto de' Rossi, is recalled to Florence and arrested upon arrival
1490	Francesco Sassetti dies from a stroke on March 30 or 31
1492	Death of Lorenzo the Magnificent on April 8 at his villa of Careggi
1494	The French invade Italy. Flight of Piero di Lorenzo de' Medici on November 9. A few days later, November 17, Charles VIII, King of France, enters Florence at the head of his army. All Medici property is confiscated and receivers are appointed. The Medici Bank, being virtually bankrupt, does not survive this blow

GENEALOGICAL TABLES

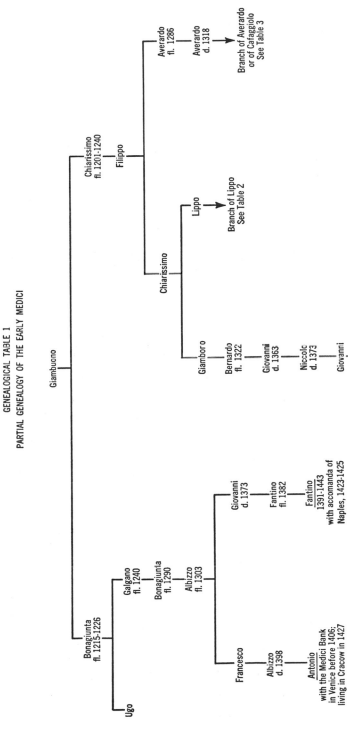

GENEALOGICAL TABLE 1
PARTIAL GENEALOGY OF THE EARLY MEDICI

Giambuono

Bonagiunta
fl. 1215-1226

Ugo

Chiarissimo
fl. 1201-1240

Filippo

Chiarissimo

Lippo

Branch of Lippo
See Table 2

Averardo
fl. 1286

Averardo
d. 1318

Branch of Averardo
or of Cafaggiolo
See Table 3

Giambono

Bernardo
fl. 1322

Giovanni
d. 1363

Niccolc
d. 1373

Giovanni

Rosso
1377-1429
with accomanda of
Naples, 1415-1425

Galgano
fl. 1240

Bonagiunta
fl. 1290

Albizzo
fl. 1303

Giovanni
d. 1373

Fantino
fl. 1382

Fantino
1391-1443
with accomanda of
Naples, 1423-1425

Francesco

Albizzo
d. 1398

Antonio
with the Medici Bank
in Venice before 1406;
living in Cracow in 1427

In these Tables the names underlined are those of persons connected with the Medici Bank.

383

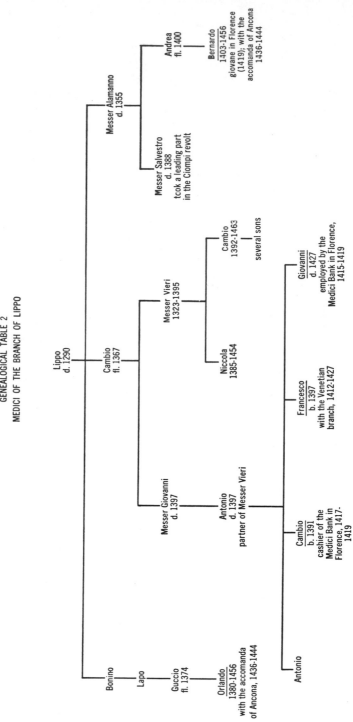

GENEALOGICAL TABLE 2
MEDICI OF THE BRANCH OF LIPPO

Lippo
d. 1290

Cambio
fl. 1367

Messer Giovanni
d. 1397

Messer Vieri
1323-1395

Messer Alamanno
d. 1355

Antonio
d. 1397
partner of Messer Vieri

Niccola
1385-1454

Cambio
1392-1463

several sons

Messer Salvestro
d. 1388
took a leading part
in the Ciompi revolt

Andrea
fl. 1400

Bonino

Lapo

Guccio
fl. 1374

Orlando
1380-1456
with the accomanda
of Ancona, 1436-1444

Cambio
b. 1391
cashier of the
Medici Bank in
Florence, 1417-
1419

Francesco
b. 1397
with the Venetian
branch, 1412-1427

Giovanni
d. 1427
employed by the
Medici Bank in Florence,
1415-1419

Bernardo
1403-1456
giovane in Florence
(1419); with the
accomanda of Ancona
1436-1444

Antonio

384

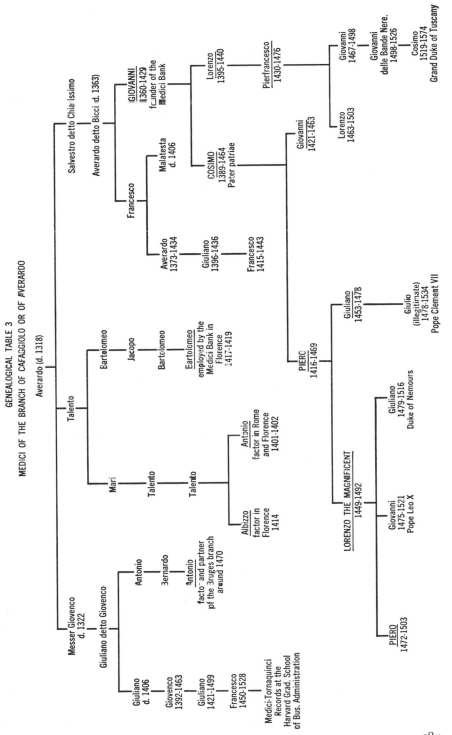

GENEALOGICAL TABLE 3

MEDICI OF THE BRANCH OF CAFAGGIOLO OR OF AVERARDO

385

GENEALOGICAL TABLE 4

PARTIAL GENEALOGY OF THE BARDI FAMILY

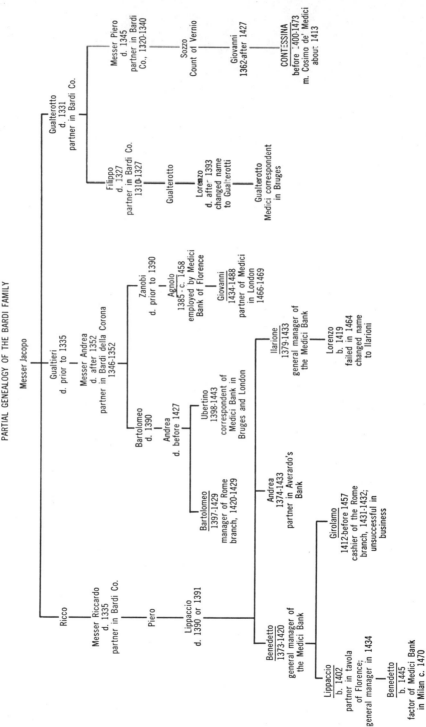

Messer Jacopo

Ricco

Messer Riccardo
d. 1335
partner in Bardi Co.

Piero

Lippaccio
d. 1390 or 1391

Benedetto
1373-1420
general manager of
the Medici Bank

Lippaccio
b. 1402
partner in tavola
of Florence;
general manager in 1434

Benedetto
b. 1445
factor of Medici Bank
in Milan c. 1470

Girolamo
1412-before 1457
cashier of the Rome
branch, 1431-1432;
unsuccessful in
business

Andrea
1374-1433
partner in Averardo's
Bank

Bartolomeo
1397-1429
manager of Rome
branch, 1420-1429

Andrea
d. before 1427

Ubertino
1398-1443
correspondent of
Medici Bank in
Bruges and London

Ilarione
1379-1433
general manager of
the Medici Bank

Lorenzo
b. 1419
failed in 1464
changed name
to Ilarioni

Bartolomeo
d. 1390

Gualtieri
d. prior to 1335

Messer Andrea
d. after 1352
partner in Bardi della Corona
1346-1352

Zanobi
d. prior to 1390

Agnolo
1385-c. 1458
employed by Medici
Bank of Florence

Giovanni
1434-1488
partner of Medici
in London
1466-1469

Gualterotto
d. 1331
partner in Bardi Co.

Filippo
d. 1327
partner in Bardi Co.
1310-1327

Gualterotto

Lorenzo
d. after 1393
changed name
to Gualterotti

Gualterotto
Medici correspondent
in Bruges

Messer Piero
d. 1345
partner in Bardi
Co., 1320-1340

Sozzo
Count of Vernio

Giovanni
1362-after 1427

CONTESSINA
before 1400-1473
m. Cosimo de' Medici
about 1413

GENEALOGICAL TABLE 5

PARTIAL GENEALOGY OF THE PORTINARI FAMILY

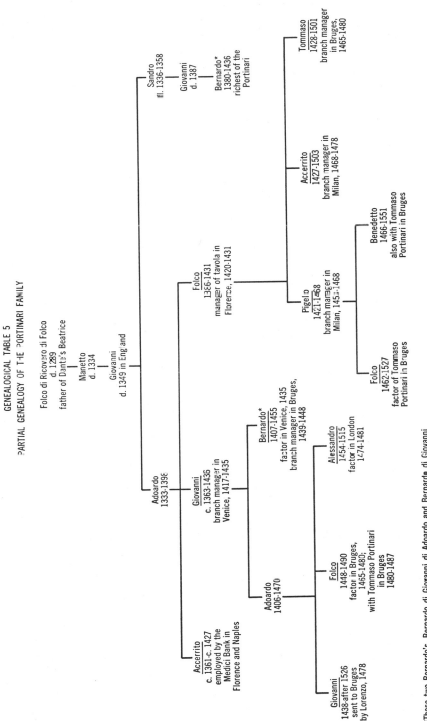

*These two Bernardo's, Bernardo di Giovanni di Adoardo and Bernardo di Giovanni di Sandro, should not be confused, as is often done by historians.

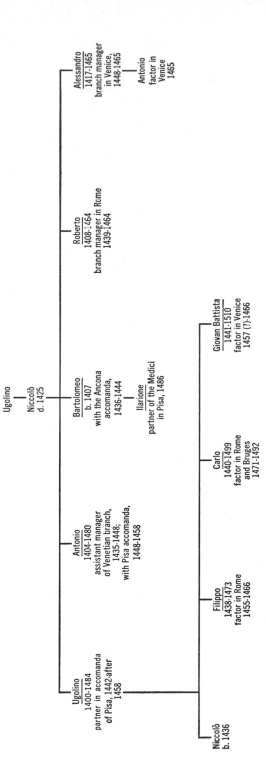

GENEALOGICAL TABLE 6
PARTIAL GENEALOGY OF THE MARTELLI FAMILY

388

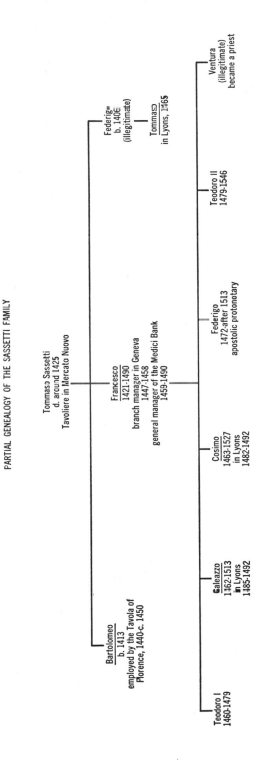

GENEALOGICAL TABLE 7
PARTIAL GENEALOGY OF THE SASSETTI FAMILY

Tommaso Sassetti
d. around 1425
Tavoliere in Mercato Nuovo

Bartolomeo
b. 1413
employed by the Tavola of
Florence, 1440-c. 1450

Francesco
1421-1490
branch manager in Geneva
1447-1458
general manager of the Medici Bank
1459-1490

Federigo
b. 1406
(illegitimate)

Tommaso
in Lyons, 1465

Teodoro I
1460-1479

Galeazzo
1462-1513
in Lyons
1485-1492

Cosimo
1463-1527
in Lyons
1482-1492

Federigo
1472-after 1513
apostolic protonotary

Teodoro II
1479-1546

Ventura
(illegitimate)
became a priest

389

BIBLIOGRAPHY

Manuscript Sources

The major source for a study of the Medici Bank is, of course, the collection of Medici papers called *Mediceo avanti il Principato* (MAP) in the State Archives of Florence (ASF). This collection consists of 165 bundles (*filze*) containing miscellaneous documents, chiefly letters. Unfortunately, this material has been put in bundles in the most haphazard fashion without any attempt at classification, except in a few instances. As a result, it is almost impossible to locate pertinent material without going through the entire inventory. For example, the letters of Giovanni Tornabuoni are scattered among 70 different bundles without regard to chronology. The entire collection should be reclassified, but the archivists shrank before this stupendous task and, moreover, hesitated to undo the work of their predecessors, however stupid. To remedy the situation somewhat, an inventory of the first hundred bundles has been published: *Archivio Mediceo avanti il Principato, Inventario*: Vol. I, filze 1–20 (Rome, 1951); Vol. II, filze 21–50 (Rome, 1955); Vol. III, filze 51–100 (Rome, 1957). A fourth volume, containing the inventory of the remaining 65 filze, was not published until 1963 after the first printing of this book. Changes in reference numbers have been corrected in this printing whenever possible.

Because of the confused state of the Medici papers, no attempt has been made to list the letters and the reader will have to rely on the references given in the footnotes. The dates indicated in all references are according to modern style and not the old Florentine style, according to which the year started March 25 (Incarnation) instead of January 1 (Circumcision). The printed inventory keeps the old style, so that there is a discrepancy of one year from January 1 to March 24.

Like other mercantile letters of the fourteenth and fifteenth centuries, Medici business letters often begin with a copy of the preceding letter. In other cases, letters include a postscript of a later date than the body of the text. Therefore it happens frequently that messages of different dates have the same reference, but this is not a mistake.

In addition to the Medici papers, extensive use was also made in the Archivio di Stato of the catasto records, the matriculation lists of the gilds, the Strozzi papers (*Carte Strozziane*), and the *pergamene* (parchment records), of the Medici, which form a separate collection (*Fondo diplomatico Mediceo*). Limited use was made of the Florentine statutes (*Balìa, Provvisioni*), the notarial archives (*Archivio notarile antecosimiano*), the tax records prior to the catasto (*Prestanze*), the prison records (*Archivio delle Stinche*), some Portinari family papers in the archives from the Hospital of Santa Maria Nuova, and the collection entitled "Manuscripts" (*Manoscritti*).

Occasionally, collections outside the State Archives were consulted, such as the manuscripts of the Biblioteca Riccardiana and the Biblioteca Nazionale in Florence, account books in the Archivio dello Spedale degli Innocenti, *Carte stranieri*, letters in the Datini Archives in Prato, and wardrobe accounts in the Archives Générales du Royaume in Brussels.

In Rome, many of the registers of the papal depositaries general are still extant in the Vatican Archives. Some of them date from the years when this office was in the hands of the Medici Bank. These records are not in the name of the Medici but in the name of their Rome manager or of the factor who was in charge of the papal business: a misleading fact. Three sets of *Entrate e Uscite* were made: one in Italian and two in Latin, one for the papal treasurer and one for the Apostolic Chamber. Sometimes only one copy is extant, but in other cases two or all three copies have survived, with the result that there is a great deal of duplication. This collection is called *Introitus et Exitus Camerae Apostolicae* and is preserved in the Archivio segreto del Vaticano. Only limited use was made of this material, since it concerns papal finance rather than the Medici Bank.

The Selfridge Collection of account books, letter books, and other business records belonging to the Medici-Tornaquinci are in the Baker Library at the Graduate School of Business Administration, Harvard University. Only limited use has been made of these records for this book, since the ancestors of the Medici-Tornaquinci (see Genealogical Table 3) were not closely related to Giovanni di Bicci, the founder of the Medici Bank. The Medici-Tornaquinci records are, nevertheless, of great historical value, especially for the study of the Florentine cloth and silk industries, less so for the history of banking.

For the convenience of the reader, systematic lists of partnership contracts, *ricordi*, account books, and balance sheets are given here:

PARTNERSHIP CONTRACTS

Place	Date	Reference in MAP		
		Filza	No.	fols.
Florence	September 1, 1420	153	2	4–5
	June 8, 1435	94	137	220–221
		153	3	2
	March 25, 1441	94	120	185–186
		153	3	50–51
Florence	October 16, 1420	153	2	5ᵛ–6ᵛ
(Tavola)	March 25, 1493	89	121	....
Ancona	May 1, 1436	94	153	282–283
	November 28, 1440	94	117	180–181
Bruges	December 21, 1448	88	391	505–506
	July 25, 1455	84	26	55
	August 6, 1465	84	22	47–49
	October 14, 1469	84	28	60
	December 15, 1469	84	29	61–62
	May 12, 1471	84	24	51–52
	March 26, 1473	84	25	53–54
Geneva	June 23, 1439	149	44	....
London	May 31, 1446	153	3	53–54
		82	178	552
		94	132	157–158
	March 25, 1454	83	95	537–538
	August 2, 1465	99	2	2–3
	August 13, 1467	148	32	....
Naples	January 1, 1423	153	2	8–9
	March 25, 1490	89	189	....

Pisa	December 26, 1442	153	3	52
Rome	March 25, 1416	94	166	305–306
	September 16, 1420	153	2	2–3
	March 10, 1429	94	89	238–239
	August 16, 1435	153	3	1
	March 24, 1465	16	149	. . . .
	July 22, 1487	94	152	280–281
Venice	April 25, 1406	89	190	. . . .
	October 23, 1420	153	2	7–8
	July 15, 1435	153	3	3
	January 20, 1455	146	. . .	176–182
	March 25, 1460	146	. . .	183–184
	March 25, 1465	82	22	118–120
Florence	July 1, 1439	94	138	222–223
(wool)	July 2, 1443	94	131	208–209
Florence	March 24, 1438	89	71	. . . .
(silk)	March 25, 1444	94	122	188–189
	March 25, 1447	94	135	216–217

RICORDI (INSTRUCTIONS)

			Reference in MAP		
Destination	Given to	Date	Filza	No.	fols.
Bruges	Marco Spinellini	December 23, 1430	68	2	. . . .
	Bernardo Portinari	1436	68	588	. . . .
	Tommaso Guidetti	May 23, 1471	94	198	357–358
	Cristofano Spini	May 13, 1472	82	112	320–323
	Rinieri da Ricasoli	September 14, 1479	89	308	. . . .
London	Gerozzo de' Pigli	May 31, 1446	94	134	214–215
Naples	Antonio de' Medici	July 8, 1481	89	154	. . . .
Rome	Bartolomeo de' Bardi	September 15, 1420	68	402	. . . .
Tunis	Schiatta Bagnesi	September 12, 1477	94	213	. . . .
Venice	Giovambattista Ridolfi	March 29, 1480	Bibl. Naz. Florence Mss. II. V. 13 (Carte Lanfredini) fols. 167–168		

ACCOUNT BOOKS

MAP, filza 153 contains three libri segreti (secret account books) of the Medici Bank:

No. 1. Libro segreto di Giovanni di Bicci de' Medici e compagni, Banco di Firenze, 1397–1427; 129 folios, first ten missing.

No. 2. Libro segreto bianco segnato A di Cosimo e Lorenzo de' Medici, e di Ilarione di Lippaccio de' Bardi, 1420–1435; 85 folios.

No. 3. Libro segreto giallo di Cosimo e Lorenzo de' Medici, di Giovanni di Amerigo Benci, e di Antonio di messer Francesco Salutati, 1435–1451; 100 folios. All three on parchment.

MAP, filza 133:
    No. 1. Libro grande (ledger) of the Bank of Averardo di Francesco de' Medici in Florence, 1395; fragment, fols. 17–110.
    No. 2. Libro di mercatantie (Warehouse ledger) of Averardo de' Medici in Rome, 1412–1413; fragment, fols. 151–166, blank from fol. 159 onward.
    No. 3. Ledger of the Bank of Averardo de' Medici in Pisa, 1424–1426; fragment, fols. 1–118.

MAP, filza 104, a bound volume of miscellaneous material, contains two fragments of records of bills of exchange issued, paid, or collected by the Tavola in Florence:
    Fols. 7–48. Quaderno di cambi mandati e ricevuti, April 2, 1440–24 March, 1441; 36 folios with writing, plus 5 blank fols.
    Fols. 541–559. Quaderno di cambi, 25 March, 1477–21 March, 1478.

MAP, Filza 131. This bundle contains seven different fragments of account books:
    No. 131 (sole designation). Giornale di lettere di cambi tratte e ricevute, segnato L (journal of bills of exchange issued, paid, or collected, marked L) kept by the Rome branch, March 26, 1429–March 24, 1430; 208 folios: fols. 1–84, lettere ricevute; fols. 103–198, lettere di cambio mandate; fols. 199–208, blank.
    (a) A small book of private accounts kept by a member of the Medici family, 1506–1511.
    (b) A wastebook kept in Basel, 1433; only fols. 2–19 have entries.
    (c) Expenses in connection with the building of a wall around a garden belonging to Cosimo and Lorenzo di Giovanni de' Medici, 1432; fols. 1–20, plus 7 blank.
    (d) Quadernuccio di cassa (cash book) kept by the Venice branch in 1459; only 10 folios written on.
    (e) Ricordi (memorandum book) kept in Geneva, 1421–1422, by Antonio di Lazzaro Bertini; fragment of 22 folios, corners damaged by fire.
    (f) Statement of account dated 1430.

MAP, filza 134 contains four items:
    No. 1. Entrata e uscita di cassa, a fragment of a cash book kept in 1436–1437 by the Medici branch in Venice; fols. 147–243.
    No. 2. Fragment of the ledger of the Bruges branch; 1441; fols. 147–243.
    No. 3. Quaderno di cambi (record of bills issued, paid, or collected) kept by the Florentine Tavola in 1455; fols. 1–48.
    No. 4. Fragment of the ledger of the Milan branch, 1459; fols. 1–113.

MAP, filza 135 contains two items:
    No. 1. Fragment of the ledger (libro grande giallo segnato L) kept by the Tavola in Florence, 1460; first 97 folios extant.
    No. 2. Quaderno di cambi e lettere, segnato D (record of bills of exchange and letter book, marked D) belonging to the Pisa branch, 1491–1492; fols. 1–230.

ASF, Conventi soppressi, Archivio 79, vol. 119:
Secret account book of Ilarione de' Bardi, 1420–1432; 257 folios.

ASF, Carte Strozziane, Series II, No. 20:
Secret account book of Francesco Sassetti, 1462–1472; 70 folios.

Florence, Archivio dello Spedale degli Innocenti, Estranei, No. 490:
    Medici Bank, Rome branch, Book of cash balances kept by Lodovico della Casa from March 25, 1424, to February 22, 1428; by Roberto di Niccolò Martelli, from March 25, 1428, to July 2, 1431; by Girolamo de'

Bardi, from July 2, 1431, to November 2, 1432; and by Giovenco della Stufa from November 25, 1432, to March 25, 1433.

BALANCE SHEETS

Ragione (branch)	Date	Reference
Medici Bank ...... (as a whole)	July 27, 1427	Catasto No. 51, fol. 1200.
Florence (Tavola)	July 12, 1427	Ibid., fols. 1162–1160.
	May 30, 1433	Catasto No. 470, fols. 521–546.
Basel	March 24, 1442	MAP, filza 104, fols. 599–603.
London	November 12, 1477	MAP, filza 99, no. 3, fols. 4–5.
Lyons	April 2, 1467	MAP, filza 83, no. 49, fols. 301–306.
Milan	March 24, 1460	MAP, filza 83, no. 9, fols. 34–42.
Naples	February 28, 1478	MAP, filza 99, no. 4, fols. 6–13.
Pisa	1486	MAP, filza 83, no. 7, fols. 26–31.
Rome	July 12, 1427	Catasto No. 51, fols. 1191–1200.
Venice	October 6, 1427	Catasto No. 51, fols. 1187–1190.
Florence (woolshop)	1427	Catasto No. 51, fols. 1170–1171.
Florence (silkshop)	1493	MAP, filza 136, fols. 79–81.

MISCELLANEOUS

The following documents are also very important for the history of the Medici Bank:

Report of Angelo Tani concerning the Bruges and London branches (after 1474), MAP, filza 82, no. 163, fols. 500–501.
Memorandum of Lorenzo de' Medici regarding losses in Bruges and London (1479), MAP, filza 84, no. 21, fol. 46.
Agreement between Tommaso Portinari and Rinieri da Ricasoli, regarding the liquidation of the Bruges branch, February 15, 1481, MAP, filza 84, no. 76, fols. 153–154.
Reorganization plan for the Bank as a whole (before September 1485), MAP, filza 83, no. 19, fols. 67–68.
Misappropriation of public funds by Lorenzo the Magnificent, Carte Strozziane, Series I, No. 10, fols. 190–191.
Use was made of two manuscript chronicles:
Cronaca di Benedetto Dei (died 1492), ASF, Manoscritti, No. 119.
Storia fiorentina, 1476–1518, di Pietro di Marco Parenti (died 1519), Biblioteca Nazionale, Florence, Manoscritti Magl. II, II, nos. 129–134; II, IV, 169–171.

Published Sources and Secondary Works

Aebischer, Paul. "Banquiers, commerçants, diplomates et voyageurs italiens à Fribourg (Suisse) avant 1500," *Zeitschrift für Schweizergeschichte (Revue d'histoire suisse, Rivista storica svizzera)*, 7:1–59 (1927).
Agnoletti, Anna Maria (ed.). See *Statuto dell'Arte della Lana*.
Aiazzi, G. degli (ed.). *Ricordi storici di Filippo di Cino Rinuccini dal 1282 al 1460 colla continuazione di Alamanno e Neri suoi figli fino al 1506*. Florence, 1840.
Antiqua ducum mediolani decreta. Milan, 1654.
Antonino, San. *Summa theologica*. Verona, 1740.

Archivio Mediceo avanti il Principato, Inventario. Ed. by Francesca Morandini and Arnaldo D'Addario. 3 vols. Rome: Ministero dell'Interno, 1951–1957.

Baix, François. *La Chambre Apostolique et les "Libri Annatarum" de Martin V (1417–1431).* Analecta Vaticano-Belgica, 14. Brussels: Institut historique belge de Rome, 1947.

Barbadoro, Bernardino. *Le finanze della Repubblica fiorentina, imposta diretta e debito pubblico fino all'instituzione del Monte.* Florence, 1929.

Barbieri, Gino. *Economia e politica nel ducato di Milano, 1386–1535.* Pubblicazioni della Università Cattolica del Sacro Cuore, ser. III, no. 18. Milan, 1938.

—— *Industria e politica mineraria nello stato pontifico dal '400 al '600 (lineamenti).* Rome, 1940.

Bauer, Clemens. *Unternehmung und Unternehmungsformen im Spätmittelalter und in der beginnenden Neuzeit.* Jena, 1936.

Becker, Marvin B. "Nota dei processi riguardanti prestatori di danari nei tribunali fiorentini dal 1343 al 1379," *Archivio storico italiano,* 114:741–748 (1956).

—— "Three Cases concerning the Restitution of Usury in Florence," *Journal of Economic History,* 17:445–450 (1957).

Below, Georg von. Review of Alfred Doren's *Die Florentiner Wollentuchindustrie* in *Jahrbücher für Nationalökonomie und Statistik,* 79:702–708 (1902).

Bensa, Enrico. *Francesco di Marco da Prato: Notizie e documenti sulla mercatura italiana del secolo XIV.* Milan, 1928.

Berlière, Dom Ursmer. *Inventaire analytique des Diversa Cameralia des Archives Vaticanes (1389–1590).* Rome: Institut historique belge de Rome, 1906.

Bernardino of Siena, San. *Quadragesimale de Evangelio Aeterno.* Vols. 3–5 of *Opera omnia.* Quaracchi-Florence, 1956.

Berti, Pietro. "Nuovi documenti intorno al catasto fiorentino per quali vien dimostrato che la proposta del medesimo non fu di Giovanni de' Medici," *Giornale storico degli Archivi toscani,* 4:32–62 (1860).

Bigwood, Georges. *Le Régime juridique et économique du commerce de l'argent dans la Belgique du moyen âge.* Mémoires de l'Académie Royale de Belgique, Classe des Lettres et des Sciences morales et politiques, ser. II, no. 14, 2 pts. Brussels, 1921–1922.

Biscaro, Gerolamo. "Il banco Filippo Borromei e compagni di Londra, 1436–1439," *Archivio storico lombardo,* 4th series, 19:37–126, 283–386 (1913).

Bloch, Marc. "Le Problème de l'or au moyen âge," *Annales d'histoire économique et sociale,* 5:1–34 (1933).

Boffito, Giuseppe and Attilio Mori. *Piante e vedute di Firenze.* Florence, 1926.

Borel, Frédéric. *Les Foires de Genève au quinzième siècle.* Genève, 1892.

Borlandi, Franco (ed.). See *El libro di mercatantie et usanze de'paesi.*

Braudel, Fernand and Ruggiero Romano. *Navires et marchandises à l'entrée du Port de Livourne (1547–1611).* Paris: S.E.V.P.E.N., 1951.

Brésard, Marc. *Les Foires de Lyon aux XVe et XVIe siècles.* Paris, 1914.

Brucker, Gene A. "The Medici in the Fourteenth Century," *Speculum,* 32:1–26 (1957).

Bruto, Giovanni Michele. *Istorie fiorentine.* Ed. by Stanislao Gatteschi. 2 vols. Florence, 1838.

Bullarium Romanum. Vol. 4. Turin, 1859.

Buser, Benjamin. *Die Beziehungen der Mediceer zu Frankreich während der Jahre 1434–1494 in ihrem Zusammenhang mit den allgemeinen Verhältnissen Italiens.* Leipzig, 1879.

Caggese, Romolo (ed.). See *Statuti della Repubblica fiorentina.*

Caizzi, Bruno. "Ginevra e Lione: un episodio di guerra fredda economica nel XV secolo," *Cenobio, rivista mensile di cultura* (Lugano), II (1953), no. 6, 39–46.

Calendar of the Patent Rolls, Edward IV–Richard III, 1461–1485. 3 vols. London, 1897–1901.

Cambi, Giovanni. *Istorie.* Delizie degli eruditi toscani, vols. 20–23. Florence, 1785–1786.

Camerani Marri, Giulia (ed.). *I documenti commerciali del fondo diplomatico mediceo nell'Archivio di Stato di Firenze (1230–1492), Regesti.* Prefazione di Raymond de Roover. Florence: Leo S. Olschki, 1951.

Camerani Marri, Giulia (ed.). See *Statuti dell'Arte del Cambio.*

Cameron, Annie I. (ed.). *The Apostolic Camera and Scottish Benefices, 1418–1488.* London, 1934.

Canestrini, Giuseppe. *La scienza e l'arte di stato desunta dagli atti ufficiali della Repubblica fiorentina e dei Medici.* Florence, 1862.

Caprariis, Vittorio de. "Sul Banco dei Medici," *Bollettino dell'Archivio storico del Banco di Napoli,* fasc. 1 (1950), pp. 45–54.

Carabellese, Francesco. "Bilancio di un'accomandita di casa Medici in Puglia del 1477 e relazioni commerciali fra la Puglia e Firenze," *Archivio storico pugliese,* 2:77–104 (1896).

——— See also Zambler.

Carocci, Guido. *I Dintorni di Firenze.* 2 vols. Florence, 1906–1907.

Casaregi, Giuseppe Maria. *Il cambista instruito per ogni caso de' fallimenti, o sia instruzione per le piazze mercantili.* Venice, 1737.

Casati, Dott. "Documenti sul palazzo chiamato 'il Banco Medice'," *Archivio storico lombardo,* 12:582–588 (1885).

Cassandro, Giovanni. "Vicende storiche della lettera di cambio," *Bollettino dell'Archivio storico del Banco di Napoli,* fasc. 9–12 (1955–1956), pp. 1–91.

Cassuto, Umberto. *Gli ebrei a Firenze nell'età del Rinascimento.* Florence, 1918.

Cavalcanti, Giovanni. *Istorie fiorentine.* 2 vols. Florence, 1838.

Ceccherelli, Alberto. *I libri di mercatura della Banca Medici, e l'applicazione della partita doppia a Firenze nel secolo decimoquarto.* Florence, 1913.

——— *Il linguaggio dei bilanci: Formazione e interpretazione dei bilanci commerciali.* Florence, 1939.

Charavay, Etienne. See Vaesen, Joseph.

Charpin-Feugerolles, Marquis de La Rivière, Hippolyte de. *Les Florentins à Lyon.* Lyon, 1893.

Chiaudano, Mario. "I Rothschild ·del Duecento: la Gran Tavola di Orlando Bonsignori," offprint from *Bullettino senese di storia patria,* New Series, VI (1935), fasc. 2, 40 pp.

Chiaudano, Mario and Raimondo Morozzo della Rocca (eds.). *Notai liguri del secolo XII: Oberto Scriba de Mercato (1190).* Turin, 1938.

Chomel, Vital and Jean-G. Ebersolt. *Cinq Siècles de circulation internationale vue de Jougne: un péage jurassien du XIIIe au XVIIIe siècle.* Paris: S.E.V.P.E.N., 1951.

Ciardini, Mario. *I banchieri ebrei in Firenze nel secolo XV e il monte di pietà fondato da Girolamo Savonarola.* Borgo San Lorenzo, 1907.

Cipolla, Carlo M. *Studi di storia della moneta,* I: *I movimenti dei cambi in Italia dal secolo XIII al XV.* Pubblicazioni della Università di Pavia, Studi nelle scienze giuridiche e sociali, no. 101. Pavia, 1948.

Codex diplomaticus lubecensis (Lübeckisches Urkundenbuch). Vols. V-VIII. Lübeck, 1877–1889.

Commines, Philippe de. *Mémoires*. Ed. by Joseph Calmette and G. Durville. 3 vols. Paris, 1925.

Corazzini, Giuseppe Odoardo. *I Ciompi, cronache e documenti*. Florence, 1887.

Corpus iuris canonici. Ed. by E. Friedberg. 2 vols. Leipzig, 1879–1881. Reprinted 1922.

Corpus juris canonici. Decretum Gratiani cum Glossis. Venice, 1584.

Corti, Gino. "Le accomandite fiorentine nel XV e XVI secolo." Unpubl. diss. University of Florence, 1937.

———— "Consigli sulla mercatura di un anonimo trecentista," *Archivio storico italiano*, 110:114–119 (1952).

Costa de Beauregard, Henri, Marquis. *Souvenirs du règne d'Amédée VIII, premier duc de Savoie*. Chambéry, 1859.

Cotrugli, Benedetto. *Della mercatura et del mercante perfetto, libri quattro*. 1st ed., Venice, 1573; 2d ed., Brescia, 1602.

Daniel, Gabriel, S.J. *Histoire de France depuis l'établissement de la monarchie française dans les Gaules*. Vol. VII. New ed., Paris, 1755.

Davanzati, Bernardo. "Notizia dei Cambi," *Scrittori classici italiani di economia politica, parte antica*. Vol. II. Milan, 1804.

Davidsohn, Robert. "Blüte und Niedergang der Florentiner Tuchindustrie," *Zeitschrift für die gesamte Staatswissenschaft*, 85:225–255 (1928).

———— *Geschichte von Florenz, IV. Die Frühzeit der Florentiner Kultur*. 2 pts. Berlin, 1922–1925.

Della Tuccia, Niccola. "Cronache di Viterbo e di altre città." published in *Cronache e statuti della Città di Viterbo*. Ed. by Ignazio Ciampi. Florence, 1872.

Del Piazzo, Marcello (ed.). *Protocolli del carteggio di Lorenzo il Magnifico per gli anni 1473–74, 1477–92*. Florence: Leo S. Olschki, 1956.

de Poerck, Guy. *La Draperie médievale en Flandre et en Artois: technique et terminologie*. 3 vols. Bruges, 1951.

Deroisy, Armand. "Les Routes des laines anglaises vers la Lombardie," *Revue du Nord*, 25:40–60 (1939).

de Roover, Florence Edler. "Early Examples of Marine Insurance," *The Journal of Economic History*, 5:172–200 (1945).

———— "Francesco Sassetti and the Downfall of the Medici Banking House," *Bulletin of the Business Historical Society*, 18:65–80 (1943).

———— "Lucchese Silks," *Ciba Review*, 80:2902–2930 (1950).

———— "A Prize of War: A Painting of Fifteenth-Century Merchants," *Bulletin of the Business Historical Society*, 19:3–12 (1945).

———— "Restitution in Renaissance Florence," *Studi in onore di Armando Sapori*. Milan, 1957. Pp. 775–789.

———— "Le Voyage de Girolamo Strozzi de Pise à Bruges et retour à bord de la galère bourguignonne 'San Giorgio'," *Handelingen van het Genootschap "Société d'Emulation" te Brugge*, 91:117–136 (1954).

de Roover, Raymond. "La Balance commerciale entre les Pays-Bas et l'Italie au quinzième siècle," *Revue belge de philologie et d'histoire*, 37:374–386 (1959).

———— "Cambium ad Venetias: Contribution to the History of Foreign Exchange," *Studi in onore di Armando Sapori*. Milan: Istituto Editoriale Cisalpino, 1957. Pp. 631–648.

———— "La Communauté des marchands lucquois à Bruges de 1377 à 1404," *Handelingen van het genootschap "Société d'Emulation," te Brugge*, 86:23–89 (1949).

———— "Le Contrat de change depuis la fin du treizième siècle jusqu'au début du dix-septième," *Revue belge de philologie et d'histoire*, 25:111–128 (1946–47).

—— "The Development of Accounting prior to Luca Pacioli according to the Account-books of Medieval Merchants," *Studies in the History of Accounting*, Ed. by A. C. Littleton and B. S. Yamey. London, 1956. Pp. 114–174.

—— "Early Accounting Problems of Foreign Exchange," *The Accounting Review*, 19:381–407 (1944).

—— *L'Évolution de la lettre de change, XIVᵉ–XVIIIᵉ siècles*. Paris: S.E.V.-P.E.N., 1953.

—— "A Florentine Firm of Cloth Manufacturers," *Speculum*, 16:1 33 (1941).

—— "I libri segreti del Banco de' Medici," *Archivio storico italiano*, 107:236–240 (1949).

—— "Lorenzo il Magnifico e il tramonto del Banco dei Medici," *ibid.*, 107:172–185 (1949).

—— *The Medici Bank: its Organization, Management, Operations and Decline*. New York: New York University Press, 1948.

—— *Money, Banking, and Credit in Mediaeval Bruges*. Cambridge, Mass.: The Mediaeval Academy of America, 1948.

—— "Monopoly Theory prior to Adam Smith," *Quarterly Journal of Economics*, 65:492–524 (1951).

—— "New Interpretations of the History of Banking," *Journal of World History (Cahiers d'histoire mondiale)*, 2:38–76 (1954).

—— "New Perspectives on the History of Accounting," *The Accounting Review*, 30:405–420 (1955).

—— "Oprichting en liquidatie van het Brugse filiaal van het Bankiershuis der Medici," *Mededelingen van de Koninklijke Vlaamse Academie voor Wetenschappen, Letteren en Schone Kunsten van België, Klasse der Letteren*, XV (1953), no. 7.

—— "The Origin of Endorsement," *South African Bankers' Journal*, 52:156–162, 205–212, 257–266 (1955).

—— "The Three Golden Balls of the Pawnbrokers," *Bulletin of the Business Historical Society*, 20:117–124 (1946).

—— "Il trattato di fra Santi Rucellai sul cambio, il monte comune e il monte delle doti," *Archivio storico italiano*, 111:3–41 (1953).

—— "What is Dry Exchange? A Contribution to the Study of English Mercantilism," *The Journal of Political Economy*, 52:250–266 (1944).

—— See also Camerani Marri, Giulia.

De Turri (della Torre), Raphael. *De cambiis, tractatus*. Frankfort-on-the-Main, 1645.

Di Tucci, Raffaele. *Studi sull'economia genovese del secolo decimo secondo: la nave e i contratti marittimi, la banca privata*. Turin, 1933.

Doren, Alfred. *Studien aus der Florentiner Wirtschaftsgeschichte: I. Die Florentiner Wollentuchindustrie vom 14. bis zum 16. Jahrhundert. II. Das Florentiner Zunftwesen vom 14. bis zum 16. Jahrhundert*. 2 vols. Stuttgart-Berlin, 1901–1908.

Dorini, Umberto. *L'arte della seta in Toscana*. Florence, 1928.

—— *I Medici e i loro tempi*. Florence, 1947.

——See *Statuti dell'Arte di Por Santa Maria*.

Ebersolt, J. See Chomel, Vital.

Edler, Florence. *Glossary of Mediaeval Terms of Business, Italian Series, 1200–1600*. Cambridge, Mass.: The Mediaeval Academy of America, 1934.

Ehrenberg, Richard. *Le Siècle des Fugger*. Abridged ed. trans. from the German. Paris: S.E.V.P.E.N., 1955.

———— *Das Zeitalter der Fugger*. 2 vols. 3d ed. Jena, 1922.

Einstein, Lewis. *The Italian Renaissance in England*. New York, 1902.

Emiliani-Giudici, Paolo. *Storia politica dei municipi italiani*. 2 vols. Florence, 1851.

Endemann, Wilhelm. *Studien in der romanisch-kanonistischen Wirtschafts- und Rechtslehre bis gegen Ende des 17. Jahrhunderts*. 2 vols. Berlin, 1874–1883.

Fabroni, Angelo. *Laurentii Medicis Magnifici Vita*. 2 vols. Pisa, 1784.

———— *Magni Cosmi Medicei Vita*. 2 vols. Pisa, 1789.

Fanfani, Amintore. *Le origini dello spirito capitalistico in Italia*. Milan, 1933.

Fantozzi, Federigo. *Pianta geometrica della città di Firenze*. Florence, 1843.

Filarete, Antonio Averlino. *Tractat über die Baukunst nebst seinen Büchern von der Zeichenkunst und den Bauten der Medici*. Ed. by Wolfgang von Oettingen. Vienna, 1890.

Fiumi, Enrico. "Fioritura e decadenza dell'economia fiorentina," *Archivio storico italiano*, 115:385–439 (1957); 116:443–510 (1958); 117:427–506 (1959).

———— *L'impresa di Lorenzo de' Medici contro Volterra (1472)*. Florence: Leo S. Olschki, 1948.

Forgeot, Henri. *Jean Balue, Cardinal d'Angers (1421?–1491)*. Bibliothèque de l'Ecole des Hautes Etudes, sciences philologiques et historiques, fasc. 106. Paris, 1895.

Fournier, Paul. *Les Florentins en Pologne*. Lyon, 1893.

Franceschini, Gino. "Il palazzo dei Duchi d'Urbino a Milano," *Archivio storico lombardo*, 8th ser., 2:181–197 (1950).

Gandi, Giulio. *Le corporazioni dell'antica Firenze*. Florence, 1928.

Gandilhon, René. *La Politique économique de Louis XI*. Rennes, 1940.

Gargiolli, Girolamo (ed.). *L'arte della seta in Firenze: trattato del secolo XV*. Florence, 1868.

Garner, S. Paul. *Evolution of Cost Accounting to 1925*. University, Ala.: University of Alabama Press, 1954.

Gascon, Richard. "Nationalisme économique et géographie des foires: la querelle des foires de Lyon, 1484–1494," *Cahiers d'histoire* (Clermont-Ferrand), 1:253–287 (1956).

———— "Un Siècle du commerce des épices à Lyon, fin XVe-fin XVIe siècles," *Annales (Economies, Sociétés, Civilisations)*, 15:638–666 (1960).

Gaupp, Frederic E. "De eerste Medici, Geldwisselaars — kooplieden — bankiers," *Wegbereiders der Renaissance*. Amsterdam, n.d. Pp. 13–51.

Gilliodts-van Severen, Louis (ed.). *Cartulaire de l'ancienne estaple de Bruges*. 4 vols. Bruges, 1903–1906.

———— *Cartulaire de l'ancien grand tonlieu de Bruges*. 2 vols. Bruges, 1908–1909.

———— *Inventaire des archives de la ville de Bruges*. Vol. VI. Bruges, 1876.

Ginori Conti, Piero. *Carte Cambi da Querceto (secoli XV–XVI): Inventario e descrizione*. Florence, 1939.

———— *Le magone della vena del ferro di Pisa e di Pietrasanta sotto la gestione di Piero dei Medici e Comp. (1489–1492)*. Florence: Leo S. Olschki, 1939.

Goldschmidt, Levin. *Universalgeschichte des Handelsrechts*. Stuttgart, 1891.

Goris, Jan A. *Etude sur les colonies marchandes méridionales à Anvers de 1488 à 1567*. Louvain, 1925.

Gottlob, Adolf. *Aus der Camera apostolica des 15. Jahrhunderts: ein Beitrag zur Geschichte des päpstlichen Finanzwesens und des endenden Mittelalters*. Innsbruck, 1889.

———— "Zwei 'instrumenta cambii' zur Uebermittelung von Ablassgeld (1468)," *Westdeutsche Zeitschrift für Geschichte und Kunst*, 29:204-212 (1910).

Gras, Norman Scott Brien. *Business and Capitalism: an Introduction to Business History*. New York, 1939.

Grunzweig, Armand. *Correspondance de la filiale de Bruges des Medici*. Only pt. 1 published. Brussels, 1931.

———— "La Filiale de Bruges des Médici," *La Revue de la Banque*, 12:73-85; 183-191 (1948).

———— "Le Fonds de la Mercanzia aux Archives d'Etat de Florence au point de vue de l'histoire de Belgique," *Bulletin de l'Institut historique belge de Rome*, 12:61-119 (Brussels, 1932); 13:5-184 (1933); 14:23 56 (1934).

———— "Le Fonds du Consulat de la Mer aux Archives d'Etat à Florence," *ibid.*, 10:1-120 (1930).

Guicciardini, Francesco. *Storie fiorentine dal 1378 al 1509*. Ed. by Roberto Palmarocchi. Bari, 1931.

Gutkind, Curt S. *Cosimo de' Medici, Pater patriae, 1389-1464*. Oxford, 1938.

———— *Cosimo de' Medici il Vecchio*. Florence: Marzocco, 1940.

Hanserecesse von 1431-1476. Zweite Abteilung. Ed. by Goswin Frhr. von der Ropp. Vol. VII. Leipzig, 1892.

Hanserecesse von 1477-1530. Dritte Abteilung. Ed. by Dietrich Schäfer. Vol. I. Leipzig, 1881.

Hart, Henry H. *Sea Road to the Indies*. New York: Macmillan, 1950.

Hauser, Arnold. *The Social History of Art*. 2 vols. New York: Alfred A. Knopf, 1951.

Heers, Jacques. *Gênes au XVᵉ siècle: Activité économique et problèmes sociaux*. Paris: S.E.V.P.E.N., 1961.

Heers, Marie-Louise. "Les Génois et le commerce de l'alun à la fin du moyen âge," *Revue d'histoire économique et sociale*, 32:31-53 (1954).

Hermes, Gertrud. "Der Kapitalismus in der Florentiner Wollentuchindustrie," *Zeitschrift für die gesamte Staatswissenschaft*, 72:367-400 (1917).

Heyd, Wilhelm. *Histoire du commerce du Levant*. 2 vols. 2d printing. Leipzig, 1923.

Holden, J. Milnes. *The History of Negotiable Instruments in English Law*. London: The Athlone Press, 1955.

Huvelin, Paul. *Essai historique sur le droit des marchés et des foires*. Paris, 1897.

Hyett, Francis A. *Florence: her History and Art to the Fall of the Republic*. London, 1903.

Janson, H. W. *The Sculpture of Donatello*. 2 vols. Princeton: Princeton University Press, 1957.

Kervyn de Lettenhove, Joseph, Baron. *Lettres et négotiations de Philippe de Commines*. 2 vols. Brussels, 1867.

Kristeller, Paul O. "Una novella latina e il suo autore, Francesco Tedaldi, mercante fiorentino del Quattrocento," *Studi letterari, Miscellanea in onore di Emilio Santini*. Palermo, 1955.

Kuske, Bruno. "Die Handelsbeziehungen zwischen Köln und Italien im spätern Mittelalter," *Westdeutsche Zeitschrift für Geschichte und Kunst*, 27:393-441 (1908).

Lane, Frederic C. *Andrea Barbarigo, Merchant of Venice, 1418-1449*. John Hopkins University Studies in Historical and Political Science, Series LXII, no. 1. Baltimore: The Johns Hopkins University Press, 1944.

———— "Venetian Bankers, 1496-1533: A Study in the Early Stages of Deposit Banking," *Journal of Political Economy*, 45:187-206 (1937).

———— *Venetian Ships and Shipbuilders of the Renaissance.* Baltimore, 1934.

———— "Venture Accounting in Medieval Business Management," *Bulletin of the Business Historical Society,* 19:164–173 (1945).

Lapeyre, Henri. *Une Famille de marchands: les Ruiz.* Paris: S.E.V.P.E.N., 1955.

———— "Une Lettre de change endossée en 1430," *Annales (Economies, Sociétés, Civilisations),* 13:260–264 (1958).

———— *Simon Ruiz et les Asientos de Philippe II.* Paris: S.E.V.P.E.N., 1953.

La Sorsa, Saverio. *L'organizzazione dei cambiatori fiorentini nel medio evo.* Cerignola, 1904.

Lastig, Gustav. "Beiträge zur Geschichte des Handelsrechts," *Zeitschrift für das gesamte Handelsrecht,* 23:138–178 (1878); 24:386–449 (1879).

Lattes, Alessandro. *Il diritto commerciale nella legislazione statutaria delle città italiane.* Milan, 1884.

Liagre, Léone. "Le Commerce de l'alun en Flandre au Moyen Age," *Le Moyen Age,* 61:177–206 (1955).

El libro di mercatantie et usanze de' paesi. Ed. by Franco Borlandi. Turin, 1936.

Lopez, Robert S. *Genova marinara nel Duecento: Benedetto Zaccaria, ammiraglio e mercante.* Milan, 1933.

———— "Hard Times and Investment in Culture," *The Renaissance, Medieval or Modern?* Ed. by Karl H. Dannenfeldt. Boston: Heath & Co., 1959. Pp. 50–61.

———— *Storia delle colonie genovesi nel Mediterraneo.* Bologna, 1938.

———— "The Trade of Medieval Europe: the South," *Cambridge Economic History.* Vol. II. Cambridge: Cambridge University Press, 1952. Pp. 338–354.

Lopez, Robert S. and Irving W. Raymond (eds.). *Medieval Trade in the Mediterranean World: Illustrative Documents translated with Introduction and Notes.* New York: Columbia University Press, 1955.

Lucas, Henry S. "Mediaeval Economic Relations between Flanders and Greenland," *Speculum,* 12:167–181 (1937).

Lunt, William E. (ed.). *Papal Revenues in the Middle Ages.* 2 vols. New York: Columbia University Press, 1934.

Luzzatto, Gino. "L'attività di un patrizio veneziano del Quattrocento," *Studi di storia economica veneziana.* Padua, 1954. Pp. 167–193.

———— *Storia economica d'Italia,* I: *L'antichità e il medio evo.* Rome: Leonardo, 1949.

Macinghi negli Strozzi, Alessandra. *Lettere di una gentildonna fiorentina del secolo XV ai figliuoli esuli.* Ed. by Cesare Guasti. Florence, 1877.

Machiavelli, Niccolò. *History of Florence from the Earliest Times to the Death of Lorenzo the Magnificent.* Ed. by Charles W. Colby. Rev. ed. New York, 1901.

———— *Istorie fiorentine.* Vol. I of *Opere.* Edited by Antonio Panella. Milan, 1938.

Mandich, Giulio. *Le Pacte de Ricorsa et le marché italien des changes au XVIIe siècle.* Paris: S.E.V.P.E.N., 1953.

Mansfield, Mildred. *A Family of Decent Folk, 1200–1741: the Lanfredini, Merchant-Bankers and Art-Patrons.* London, 1922.

Maréchal, Joseph. *Bijdrage tot de Geschiedenis van het Bankwezen te Brugge.* Bruges, 1955.

Martens, Mina. "Les Maisons de Medici et de Bourgogne au XVe siècle," *Le Moyen Age,* 56:115–129 (1950).

Martin, Alfred von. *Sociology of the Renaissance.* New York: Oxford University Press, 1944.

Mazzi, Curzio. "La compagnia mercantile di Piero e Giovanni di Cosimo dei Medici in Milano nel 1459," *Rivista delle Biblioteche e degli Archivi,* 18:17–31 (1907).

Mecatti, Giuseppe. *Storia cronologica della città di Firenze.* 2 vols. Naples, 1755.

Melis, Federigo. "Di alcune girate cambiarie dell'inizio del Cinquecento rinvenute a Firenze," *Moneta e credito,* fasc. 21. Rome, 1953. Offprint. Pp. 27.

———— "La formazione dei costi nell'industria laniera alla fine del Trecento," *Economia e Storia,* 1:31–60, 150–190. (1954).

———— "Una girata cambiaria del 1410 nell'Archivio Datini di Prato," *Economia e Storia,* 5: 412–421 (1958).

———— *Note di storia della banca pisana nel Trecento.* Pubblicazioni della Società storica pisana, no. 1. Pisa, 1955.

———— *Storia della ragioneria: Contributo alla conoscenza e interpretazione delle fonti più significative della storia economica.* Bologna: Cesare Zuffi, 1950.

Meltzing, Otto. *Das Bankhaus der Medici und seine Vorläufer.* Jena: Gustav Fischer, 1906.

———— "Tommaso Portinari und sein Konflikt mit der Hanse," *Hansische Geschichtsblätter,* 12:101–123 (1906).

Meyer, Alfred Gotthold. *Oberitalienische Frührenaissance: Bauten und Bildwerke der Lombardei.* 2 vols. Berlin, 1897–1900.

Mirot, Léon. "La Société des Raponde, Dine Raponde," *Etudes lucquoises.* Paris, 1930. Pp. 79–167. Also in *Bibliothèque de l'Ecole des Chartes,* 89:299–389 (1928).

Molini, Giuseppe. *Documenti di storia italiana copiati su gli originali autentici e per lo più autografi esistenti in Parigi.* 2 vols. Florence, 1836–1837.

Mollat, Michel. "Recherches sur les finances des ducs valois de Bourgogne," *Revue historique,* 219:285–321 (1958).

Mori, Attilio. See Boffito, G.

Müller, Karl Otto (ed.). *Welthandelsbräuche (1480 1540).* Deutsche Handelsakten des Mittelalters und der Neuzeit, V. Berlin, 1934.

Müntz, Eugène. *Les Arts à la cour des papes.* Vol. III. Paris, 1882.

Nelson, Benjamin N. "The Usurer and the Merchant Prince: Italian Businessmen and the Ecclesiastical Law of Restitution, 1100–1500," *The Journal of Economic History* VII (1947), Supplement, 104–122.

Noonan Jr., John T. *The Scholastic Analysis of Usury.* Cambridge, Mass.: Harvard University Press, 1957.

Origo, Iris. "The Domestic Enemy: the Eastern Slaves in Tuscany in the Fourteenth and Fifteenth Centuries," *Speculum,* 30:321–366 (1955).

———— *The Merchant of Prato, Francesco di Marco Datini, 1335–1410.* New York: Alfred A. Knopf, 1957.

Pagel, Karl. *Die Hanse.* Berlin: Deutsche Buch-Gemeinschaft, 1942.

Pagnini, Gian-Francesco. *Della Decima e di varie altre gravezze imposte dal Comune di Firenze, della moneta e della mercatura de' fiorentini fino al secolo XVI.* 4 vols. Lisbon-Lucca, 1765–1766.

Palmarocchi, Roberto. *Lorenzo de' Medici.* Turin, 1941.

Panella, Antonio. *Storia di Firenze.* Florence: Sansoni, 1949.

Paquet, Jacques. "Une Ébauche de la nonciature de Flandre au XVe siècle: les missions dans les Pays-Bas de Luc de Tolentis, évêque de Sebenico (1462–1484)," *Bulletin de l'Institut historique belge de Rome,* 25:27–144 (1949).

Partner, Peter D. "Camera Papae: Problems of Papal Finance in the Later Middle Ages," *The Journal of Ecclesiastical History,* 4:55–68 (1953).

—— *The Papal State under Martin V: the Administration and Government of the Temporal Power in the Early Fifteenth Century.* London: The British School of Rome, 1958.

Pastor, Ludwig von. *The History of the Popes from the Close of the Middle Ages.* Vol. I. 3d ed. St. Louis, 1906.

Pauli, Karl Wilhelm. "Ueber die frühere Bedeutung Lübecks als Wechesel-platz des Nordens," *Lübeckische Zustände in Mittelalter.* Vol. II. Lübeck, 1872. Pp. 98–171.

Pazzi, Alessandro de'. "Discorso al Cardinale Giulio de' Medici, Anno 1522," *Archivio storico italiano,* 1:420–436 (1842).

Pegolotti, Francesco Balducci. *La pratica della mercatura.* Ed. by Allan Evans. Cambridge, Mass.: The Mediacval Academy of America, 1936.

Peragallo, Prospero. "Cenni intorno alla colonia italiana in Portogallo nei secoli XIV, XV, e XVI," *Miscellanea di Storia italiana,* XL (Turin, 1904), 381–462. A later edition of 1907 was not accessible to me.

Perrens, François-Tommy. *The History of Florence under the Domination of Cosimo, Piero, Lorenzo de' Medicis, 1434–1492.* London, 1892.

Peruzzi, Simone Luigi. *Storia del commercio e dei banchieri di Firenze in tutto il mondo conosciuto dal 1200 al 1345.* Florence, 1868.

Peyronnet, Georges. "Il ducato di Milano sotto Francesco Sforza (1450–1466), politica interna, vita economica e sociale," *Archivio storico italiano,* 116:36–53 (1958).

Piattoli, Livio. "Il contratto d'assicurazione marittima a Venezia nel medio evo," *Rivista di storia del diritto italiano,* 8:327–337 (1935).

Picotti, Giovanni Battista. *La giovinezza di Leone X, il Papa del Rinascimento.* Milan, 1927.

Pieraccini, Gaetano. *La stirpe de' Medici di Cafaggiolo: Saggio di ricerche sulla trasmissione ereditaria dei caratteri biologici.* 3 vols. 1st ed., Florence, 1924; 2d ed., Florence: Vallecchi, 1947.

Piotrowski, Roman. *Cartels and Trusts.* London, 1933.

Pisani, Maria. *Un avventuriero del Quattrocento: la vita e le opere di Benedetto Dei.* Genoa, 1923.

Pitti, Buonaccorso. *Cronica.* Florence, 1720.

Pitti, Jacopo. "Istoria fiorentina," *Archivio storico italiano,* 1:xv–liii, 1–208 (1842).

Pius II (Aeneas Silvius Piccolomini). *Commentaries.* Trans. by Florence Alden Gragg, ed. by Leona C. Gabel. Smith College Studies in History, XXII, XXV, XXX, XXXV, XLIII (1937, 1939–1940, 1947, 1951, 1957).

Pöhlmann, Robert. *Die Wirtschaftspolitik der Florentiner Renaissance und das Prinzip der Verkehrsfreiheit.* Preisschriften der Fürstlich Jablonowski'schen Gesellschaft, Historisch-economische Sektion, no. 13, Leipzig, 1878.

Postan, Michael M. "Italy and the Economic Development of England in the Middle Ages," *Journal of Economic History,* 11:339–346 (1951).

—— "Report on the Middle Ages," in IXᵉ Congrès International des Sciences Historiques, I: *Rapports.* Paris: Colin, 1950. Pp. 225–241.

—— "The Trade of Medieval Europe: the North," *Cambridge Economic History.* Vol. II. Cambridge: Cambridge University Press, 1952. Pp. 119–256.

—— See Power, Eileen.

Postlethwayt, Malachy. "Venice," *The Universal Dictionary of Trade and Commerce.* Vol. II. London, 1755. Pp. 819–824.

Power, Eileen and M. M. Postan (eds.). *Studies in English Trade in the Fifteenth Century.* New York, 1933.

Prestage, Edgar. *The Portuguese Pioneers*. London, 1933.

Prims, Abbé Floris. "Heer Anselmus Fabri, onze tiende deken (1415–1449)," *Antwerpiensia, 1937; Losse Bijdragen tot de Antwerpsche Geschiedenis*. Antwerp, 1938. Pp. 19–26.

Pucci, Antonio. *Il Centiloquio che contiene la cronica di Giovanni Villani in terza rima*. Delizie degli eruditi toscani, vols. 3–6. Florence, 1772–1775.

Raymond, Irving S. (ed.). See Lopez, Robert S.

Redlich, Fritz. *De praeda militari: Looting and Booty, 1500–1815*. Beiheft 39 of *Vierteljahrschrift für Sozial- und Wirtschaftsgeschichte*. Wiesbaden, 1956.

———— "Military Entrepreneurship and the Credit System in the Sixteenth and Seventeenth Centuries," *Kyklos*, 9:186–193 (1957).

Remy, F. *Les Grandes Indulgences pontificales aux Pays-Bas à la fin du moyen âge, 1300–1531*. Louvain, 1928.

Renouard, Yves. "Lumières nouvelles sur les hommes d'affaires italiens du moyen âge," *Annales (Economies, Sociétés, Civilisations)*, 10:63–78 (1955).

———— *Les Relations des papes d'Avignon et des compagnies commerciales et bancaires de 1316 à 1378*. Bibliothèque des écoles françaises d'Athènes et de Rome, fasc. 151. Paris, 1941.

Reumont, Alfred von. "Di alcune relazioni dei Fiorentini colla città di Danzica; memoria," *Archivio storico italiano*, new scr., XIII, pt. 1 (1861), 37–47.

———— *Lorenzo de' Medici the Magnificent*. 2 vols. London, 1876.

Reynaud, Félix. "Le mouvement des navires et des marchandises à Port-de-Bouc à la fin du XVe siècle," *Revue d'histoire économique et sociale*, 34: 153–170 (1956).

Richards, Gertrude R. B. *Florentine Merchants in the Age of the Renaissance*. Cambridge, Mass., 1932.

Rinuccini, Filippo. See Aiazzi, G.

Rocha, Manuel. *Les Origines de "Quadragesimo Anno": Travail et salaire à travers la scolastique*. Paris, 1933.

Rodolico, Niccolò. *La democrazia fiorentina nel suo tramonto (1378–1382)*. Bologna, 1905.

———— *Il popolo minuto*. Bologna, 1899.

———— "The Struggle for the Right of Association in Fourteenth-Century Florence," *History*, new ser., 7:178–190 (1922).

Romano, R. See Braudel, F.

Ropp, Goswin, Baron von der. "Zur Geschichte des Alaunhandels im 15. Jahrhundert," *Hansische Geschichtsblätter*, Jahrgang 1900, pp. 117–136.

Roscoe, William. *The Life of Lorenzo de' Medici called the Magnificent*. 9th ed. London, 1847.

Ross, Janet (ed.). *Lives of the Early Medici as told in their Correspondence*. Boston, 1911.

Ruddock, Alwyn A. *Italian Merchants and Shipping in Southampton, 1270–1600*. Southampton: University College, 1951.

Rutenburg, Victor I. *Popular Unrest in Italian Cities (Fourteenth Century and Beginning of the Fifteenth)*. In Russian. Moscow, 1958.

Rymer, Thomas (ed.). *Foedera, conventiones, litterae, et cujuscumque generis acta publica inter reges Angliae et alios quosvis imperatores, reges pontifices, principes, vel communitates*. Vol. XII. London, 1727.

Salvemini, Gaetano. *La dignità cavalleresca nel Comune di Firenze*. Florence, 1896.

———— *Magnati e popolani in Firenze dal 1280 al 1295*. Florence, 1899.

Salzman, L. F. *English Trade in the Middle Ages*. Oxford, 1931.

Sapori, Armando. *La crisi delle compagnie mercantili dei Bardi e dei Peruzzi.* Florence, 1926.

────── "Gl'Italiani in Polonia nel medioevo," *Archivio storico italiano,* 83:125–155 (1925).

────── (ed.). *I libri degli Alberti del Giudice.* Milan: A. Garzanti, 1952.

────── (ed.). *I libri di commercio dei Peruzzi.* Milan, 1934.

────── "The Medici Bank," offprint from *Banca Nazionale del Lavoro Quarterly Review,* no. 11 (October 1949). 18 pp.

────── *Mercatores.* Milan: Garzanti, 1941.

────── *Studi di storia economica (secoli XIII–XIV–XV).* 3d enlarged ed. Florence: Sansoni, 1956.

Sassetti, Filippo. *Lettere edite e inedite.* Edited by Ettore Marcucci. Florence, 1855.

Savary, Jacques. *Le Parfait Négociant.* 2d ed. Paris, 1679.

Scaccia, Sigismund. *De commerciis et cambio.* 1st ed. Rome, 1619.

Schanz, Georg. *Englische Handelspolitik gegen Ende des Mittelalters mit besonderer Berücksichtigung des Zeitalters der beiden ersten Tudors Heinrich VII. und Heinrich VIII.* 2 vols. Leipzig, 1881.

Schevill, Ferdinand. *History of Florence from the Founding of the City through the Renaissance.* New York, 1936.

────── *The Medici.* London: Victor Gollancz, 1950.

Schick, Léon. *Un Grand Homme d'affaires au début du XVIe siècle: Jacob Fugger.* Paris: S.E.V.P.E.N., 1957.

Schulte, Aloys. *Geschichte des mittelalterlichen Handels und Verkehrs zwischen Westdeutschland und Italien mit Ausschluss von Venedig.* 2 vols. Leipzig, 1900.

Scofield, Cora L. *The Life and Reign of Edward the Fourth.* 2 vols. London, 1923.

Sieveking, Heinrich. "Bericht: das Hauptbuch von Averardo de' Medici," *Anzeiger der Kaiserlichen Akademie der Wissenschaften, Philosophisch-Historische Klasse,* 39:170–177 (1902).

────── *Aus Genueser Rechnungs- und Steuerbüchern: Ein Beitrag zur mittelalterlichen Handels- und Vermögensstatistik.* Sitzungsberichte der Kais. Akademie der Wissenschaften in Wien, Philosophisch-Historische Klasse, vol. 162, pt. 2. Vienna, 1909.

────── *Die Handlungsbücher der Medici.* The same series, vol. 151, pt. 5. Vienna, 1905.

Silva, Pietro. "L'ultimo trattato commerciale tra Pisa e Firenze," *Studi storici (Periodico trimestriale diretto da Amedeo Crivellucci),* 17:627–702 (1908).

Silvestri, Alfonso. "Sull'attività bancaria napoletana durante il periodo aragonese,' *Bollettino dell'Archivio storico del Banco di Napoli,* fasc. 6 (1953), pp. 80–120.

Singer, Charles. *The Earliest Chemical Industry: An Essay in the Historical Relations of Economics and Technology Illustrated from the Alum Trade.* London: The Folio Society, 1948.

Singer, Charles, et al. *History of Technology.* Vol. II. Oxford: Oxford University Press, 1956.

Smith, Adam. *An Inquiry into the Nature and Causes of the Wealth of Nations.* New York: Modern Library, 1937.

Solivetti, Guido. *Il banco dei Medici in Roma all'inizio del XV secolo.* Rome: Tipografia E. Pinci, 1950.

Statuta populi et communis Florentiae. 2 vols. Fribourg-Florence, 1778.

Statuti dell'Arte del Cambio di Firenze (1299–1316). Ed. by Giulia Camerani Marri. Florence: Leo S. Olschki, 1955.

Statuti dell'Arte di Por Santa Maria al tempo della Repubblica. Ed. by Umberto Dorini. Florence, 1934.

Statuti senesi scritti in volgare ne' secoli XIII e XIV. Ed. by Filippo-Luigi Polidori. Vol. I. Bologna, 1863.

Statuti della Repubblica fiorentina, vol. II: *Statuto del podestà dell'anno 1325*. Ed. by Romolo Caggese. Florence, 1921.

Statuto dell'Arte della Lana di Firenze (1317–1319). Ed. by Anna Maria E. Agnoletti. Florence, 1940.

Stefani, Giuseppe (ed.). *L'assicurazione a Venezia dalle origini alla fine della Serenissima*. 2 vols. Trieste: Assicurazioni Generali di Trieste e Venezia, 1956.

——— *Insurance in Venice from the Origins to the End of the Serenissima*. 2 vols. Trieste, 1958.

Stefani, Marchionne di Coppo. *Istoria fiorentina*. Delizie degli eruditi toscani, vol. 16. Florence, 1783.

Strieder, Jakob. *Studien zur Geschichte kapitalistischer Organisationsformen*. 2d ed. Munich, 1925.

Studi in onore di Armando Sapori. 2 vols. (paged contin.). Milan: Instituto Editoriale Cisalpino, 1957.

Symonds, John Addington. *Renaissance in Italy*. 2 vols. New York: Modern Library, 1935.

Tawney, Richard H. *Religion and the Rise of Capitalism*. New York: Harcourt, Brace, reprint 1952 of rev. ed., 1937.

Teja, Antonio. *Aspetti della vita economica di Zara dal 1289 al 1409*, Part I: *La pratica bancaria*. Zara, 1936.

Theiner, Augustin. *Codex diplomaticus domini temporalis S. Sedis*. Vol. III. Rome, 1862.

Trimble, Rufus. "The Law Merchant and the Letter of Credit," *Harvard Law Review*, 61:981–1008 (1948).

Unger, W. S. "Rekening van den Invoer van Aluin in de Schelde Delta, 1473–1475," *Economisch-Historisch Jaarboek*, 19:75–88 (1935).

Usher, Abbott Payson. *The Early History of Deposit Banking in Mediterranean Europe*. Harvard Economic Studies, 75. Cambridge, Mass.: Harvard University Press, 1943. (Only vol. I published.)

Uzzano, Giovanni di Antonio da. *La pratica della mercatura*. Vol. IV of G. F. Pagnini, *Della Decima*. Lisbon-Lucca, 1766.

Vaesen, Joseph and Etienne Charavay (eds.). *Lettres de Louis XI, roi de France*. Vol. III. Paris, 1887.

van Houtte, Jean A. "Bruges et Anvers, marchés 'nationaux' ou 'internationaux,' du XIVe au XVIe siècle," *Revue du Nord*, 34:89–108 (1952).

Vasari, Giorgio. *The Lives of the Painters, Sculptors, and Architects*. Trans. by A. B. Hinds. 4 vols. New York, Everyman's Library, n.d.

Verlinden, Charles. "La Colonie italienne de Lisbonne et le développement de l'économie métropolitaine et coloniale portugaise," *Studi in onore di Armando Sapori*. Milan, 1957. Pp. 617–628.

——— *L'Esclavage dans l'Europe médiévale*, vol. I: *Péninsule ibérique-France*. Bruges: "De Tempel," 1955.

Vespasiano da Bisticci. *The Vespasiano Memoirs: Lives of Illustrious Men of the Fifteenth Century*. Trans. by William George and Emily Waters. London, 1926.

Vettori, Francesco. *Il fiorino d'oro.* Florence. 1738.

Vigne, Marcel. *La Banque à Lyon du XVe au XVIIIe siècle.* Paris, 1903.

Villani, Giovanni. *Cronica.* 4 vols. Florence, 1845.

Villani, Matteo. *Cronica.* 2 vols. Florence, 1846.

Warburg, A. "Flandrische Kunst und Florentinische Renaissance," *Gesammelte Schriften.* Vol. I. Leipzig, 1932. Pp. 185–206, 370–380.

——— "Francesco Sassetti's letztwillige Verfügung," *Gesammelte Schriften,* same vol. Pp. 127–158, 353–365.

Warner, Sir George (ed.). *The Libelle of Englyshe Polycye: a Poem on the Use of Sea-Power (1436).* Oxford: Clarendon Press, 1926.

Zambler, A. and F. Carabellese. *Le relazioni commerciali fra la Puglia e la Republica di Venezia dal secolo X al XV.* Trani, 1898.

Zeno, Riniero. *Documenti per la storia del diritto marittimo nei secoli XIII e XIV.* Turin, 1936.

Zerbi, Tommaso. *Le origini della partita doppia: gestioni aziendali e situazioni di mercato nei secoli XIV e XV.* Milan: Marzorati, 1952.

——— *Studi e problemi di storia economica,* I. *Credito ed interesse in Lombardia nei secoli XIV e XV.* Milan: Marzorati, 1955.

Zippel, Giuseppe. "L'allume di Tolfa e il suo commercio," *Archivio della R. Società Romana di Storia Patria,* 30: 5–51, 389–462 (1907).

——— "Un cliente mediceo," *Scritti varii di erudizione e di critica in onore di Rodolfo Renier.* Turin, 1912. Pp. 475–490.

NOTES

CHAPTER I

Introduction

1. While the Florentines acquired Porto Pisano in 1406 when they conquered Pisa, they did not gain possession of the fortress and seaport of Leghorn until 1421 when they purchased it from the Genoese for the huge sum of 100,000 florins *di suggello*. The harbor of Porto Pisano was silting up, and, moreover, Leghorn commanded its access to the sea.

2. Armando Sapori, *Studi di storia economica (secoli XIII–XIV–XV)*, 3rd ed. (Florence, 1956), p. 55.

3. This figure is based on a list published by Sapori, pp. 718–729.

4. *Ibid.*, p. 667. The exact figure is £149,000 *affiorino*.

5. Giovanni Villani, *Cronica* (Florence, 1945) Libro XI, cap. 88.

6. According to Italian practice, Giovanni di Bicci de' Medici means Giovanni, son of Bicci, of the Medici family. Giovanni's son, Cosimo, was called Cosimo di Giovanni di Bicci (Cosimo, son of Giovanni who was the son of Bicci). The Italian practice will be followed throughout this study, since it is convenient in identifying individuals and in avoiding confusion between persons with the same given name. The prefix "dei" or "de' " is used only when preceded by a Christian name. When referring to the entire family, the Italians use the definite article without any prefix, *I Medici* (the Medici).

7. The Datini archives include about five hundred account books and more than 100,000 business letters, besides hundreds of miscellaneous items. A lifetime would not suffice to make a thorough study of this material.

8. Archivio di Stato, Florence (henceforth ASF), Mediceo avanti il Principato (henceforth MAP), No. 153.

9. This is, for example, the point of view of Arnold Hauser, *The Social History of Art* (New York, 1951), I, 283 ff. If the Medici are middle class, where is the upper class? Alfred von Martin, *Sociology of the Renaissance* (New York, 1944), classifies the Medici as *haute bourgeoisie*, which is more sensible, since they did not belong to the feudal nobility.

10. N. S. B. Gras, *Business and Capitalism; an Introduction to Business History* (New York, 1939), p. 145.

CHAPTER II

The Medici Bank and Its Institutional Background

1. *Corpus juris canonici, Decretum Gratiani*, Causa XIV, qu. 3, c. 1–4.

2. Gloss of Bartolomeo da Brescia to the *Decretum: Quod Autem*, Causa XIV, qu. 3.

3. San Bernardino of Siena, *Quadragesimale de Evangelio Aeterno*, sermon 36, art. 1, cap. 1 and art. 2, cap. 1 (*Opera omnia*, IV, Quaracchi-Florence, 1956, 205–207).

4. Such a contract was then a contract *in fraudem usurarum*.

5. In a case involving not the historic Medici but another branch of the family, restitution for usury was made only on secured loans. Florence Edler de

Roover, "Restitution in Renaissance Florence," *Studi in onore di Armando Sapori* (Milan, 1957), pp. 775–789. According to the theologians, credit risk did not justify the taking of interest. They based themselves on the ambiguous canon, *Naviganti* (*Corpus juris canonici, in X, V,* 19, 19).

6. According to the statutes of the Calimala Gild (1332), all interest was to be entered as a gift in the books of the merchants. Paolo Emiliani-Giudici, *Storia politica dei municipi italiani* (Florence, 1851), Appendix, p. 76, rubric 63 of the statute. Cf. Armando Sapori, *Mercatores* (Milan, 1941), pp. 113–121.

7. On this whole question, see Raymond de Roover, *L'Évolution de la lettre de change, XIVe–XVIIIe siècles* (Paris, 1953), 240 pp. One should also consult Henri Lapeyre, *Une Famille de marchands, les Ruiz* (Paris, 1955), pp. 275–335. These two authors fully agree except on a few points of detail, but Lapeyre makes some valuable supplementary remarks which should not be neglected.

8. Only a few canonists, among them Geoffrey of Trani (d. 1245) and Enrico Bartolomei, Cardinal Hostiensis (d. 1271), took the view that cambium was a form of mutuum.

9. San Bernardino of Siena, *De Evangelio Aeterno,* sermon 39 art. 3, cap. 2. (*Opera omnia,* IV, 291): *ubi nulla intervenit ratio mutui, nulla potest ibi esse usura.*

10. In this connection, see the pertinent remarks of Lapeyre, *Les Ruiz,* p. 326.

11. R. de Roover, *L'Evolution,* pp. 174, 176–177, 197.

12. Fra Santi Rucellai was the brother of Bernardo Rucellai, who married Nannina de' Medici, a sister of Lorenzo the Magnificent.

13. R. de Roover, "Il trattato di fra Santi Rucellai sul cambio, il monte commune e il monte delle doti," *Archivio storico italiano,* 111:3–41 (1953).

14. The treatise of Cotrugli was not published until 1573 and is entitled *Della mercatura et del mercante perfetto* (Venice, 1573).

15. This point of view is represented by Levin Goldschmidt, *Universalgeschichte des Handelsrechts* (Stuttgart, 1891), pp. 140–142. Goldschmidt attacked Wilhelm Endemann on this score, but received a rebuttal from Richard Ehrenberg, *Das Zeitalter der Fugger,* 3rd ed. (Jena, 1922), I, 32 n. Cf. the French translation, *Le Siècle des Fugger* (Paris, 1955), p. 16 n.

16. It was heresy to deny that usury was sin: *Corpus juris canonici, c. Ex gravi, in Clem.,* V. 5, 1. In 1346, the inquisitor, Piero of Aquila, began to fine those who whispered that usury was not a mortal sin, but the Florentine government quickly put an end to the activities of this overzealous friar. (Robert Davidsohn, *Geschichte von Florenz, IV: Die Frühzeit der Florentiner Kultur,* Pt. I, Berlin, 1922, p. 347.)

17. Benjamin N. Nelson, "The Usurer and the Merchant Prince: Italian Businessmen and the Ecclesiastical Law of Restitution, 1100–1500," *The Journal of Economic History,* VII (1947), Supplement, 104–122.

18. Iris Origo, *The Merchant of Prato: Francesco di Marco Datini, 1335–1410* (New York, 1957), pp. 157–159.

19. Vespasiano da Bisticci, *The Vespasiano Memoirs. Lives of Illustrious Men of the Fifteenth Century,* trans. William George and Emily Waters (London, 1926), pp. 218–219. The bull was anticanonical in so far as usury was concerned because canon law required restitution of usury to be made to the person aggrieved and not to charities (*Corpus juris canonici, Decretum:* c. *Nolitevelle,* Causa XIV, qu. 5, c. 1). Not even the pope himself was empowered to grant such dispensation.

20. The full text of the consultation of 1532 is given by Jan A. Goris, *Etudes*

sur les colonies marchandes à Anvers de 1488 à 1567 (Louvain, 1925), pp. 507–545. Cf. Lapeyre, *Les Ruiz*, p. 333.

21. Lapeyre, pp. 133–134.

22. Jacques Savary, *Le Parfait Négociant*, 2nd ed., (Paris, 1679), Part I, Bk. 3, chap. 11, pp. 265–277, especially pp. 265 and 274.

23. R. de Roover, "Early Accounting Problems of Foreign Exchange," *The Accounting Review*, 19:381–407 (1944).

24. Abbott Payson Usher, *The Early History of Deposit Banking in Mediterranean Europe* (Cambridge, Mass, 1943), I (only volume published), 73–109, especially p. 74.

25. This is the general thesis of Wilhelm Endemann, *Studien in der romanisch-kanonistischen Wirtschafts- und Rechtslehre* (Berlin, 1874–1883), I, 80. This thesis was rejected by Goldschmidt (see above note 15), who considers the bill of exchange only as a transfer instrument and not as a credit instrument, a cardinal mistake.

26. Nelson, "Usurer and Merchant-Prince," pp. 113, 120.

27. *Corpus juris canonici, Decretales:* c. *Quamquam usurarii manifesti, in VI*, V, 5, 2.

28. Umberto Cassuto, *Gli ebrei a Firenze nell'età del Rinascimento* (Florence, 1918), p. 369, No. ix: ". . . in quibus publice fenerari possi ut vulgo et communiter dicitur *a panello* sive ad velam rubeam."

29. Mario Ciardini, *I banchieri ebrei in Firenze nel secolo XV e il monte de pietà fondato da Girolamo Savonarola* (Borgo San Lorenzo, 1907) pp. 4, 15. The license issued to the Jews in 1437 specifies clearly: ". . . dum taxat ad pignus et seu ut vulgo dicitur *in sul pegno* et super bonis et rebus mobilibus et non aliis nec ad scriptam." This clause is reproduced word for word in later licenses.

30. Gloss of Giovanni d'Andrea da Rifredo to *Manifestos:* c. *Usurarum voragine, in VI*, V, 5, 1.

31. *Corpus juris canonici, Decretales:* c. *Ex gravi, in Clem*, V, 5, 1.

32. ". . . liberi et totaliter absoluti ab omni condempnatione, pena et gravamine." The text dates from 1354 and has been published by Alfred Doren, *Studien aus der Florentiner Wirtschaftsgeschichte*, Vol. II, *Das Florentiner Zunftwesen vom 14. bis zum 16. Jahrhundert* (Berlin, 1908), pp. 789–790.

33. *Ibid.*, II, 597, and Cassuto, *Gli ebrei*, p. 14. Cf. Martin B. Becker, "Three Cases concerning the Restitution of Usury in Florence," *The Journal of Economic History*, 17:445–450 (1957). A different but erroneous interpretation is given by Richard H. Tawney, *Religion and the Rise of Capitalism* (New York, 1952), pp. 37, 295. Mr. Tawney even jumps to the conclusion that "bankers" in medieval Florence were fined for usury "right and left."

34. Robert Pöhlmann, *Die Wirtschaftspolitik der Florentiner Renaissance und das Prinzip der Verkehrsfreiheit* (Leipzig, 1878), pp. 52–53, 84; Alessandro Lattes, *Il diritto commerciale nella legislazione statutaria delle città italiane* (Milan, 1884), p. 147.

35. The release of this miter from pawn gave rise to some difficulties and Pope Martin V had to threaten Giovanni di Bicci with excommunication if he failed to obey and restore the pledge. Giulia Camerani Marri, *I documenti commerciali del fondo diplomatico mediceo nell'Archivio di Stato di Firenze*, Preface by R. de Roover (Florence, 1951), p. 32, Nos. 48–49.

36. R. de Roover, "The Three Golden Balls of the Pawnbrokers," *Bulletin of the Business Historical Society*, 20:117–124 (1946).

37. R. de Roover, "New Interpretations of the History of Banking," *Journal of World History*, 2:38–39 (1954).

38. These account books are in the Medici-Tornaquinci archives at the Harvard Graduate School of Business Administration, MSS 520, 521, 523–524, 525 (2), 526–527, and 529–533. The articles of association are in MS 495.

39. Gino Corti, "Le accomandite fiorentine nel XV e XVI secolo," unpubl. diss. (University of Florence, 1937), p. 48.

40. Giulio Gandi, *Le corporazioni dell'antica Firenze* (Florence, 1928), pp. 8, 92.

41. Unlike the money dealers of Bruges, the bankers of Florence were not sharply divided into money-changers and merchant-bankers. In both cities, however, the pawnbrokers were in a class apart (R. de Roover, *Money, Banking, and Credit in Mediaeval Bruges*, Cambridge, Mass., 1948, 345–346).

42. G. Villani, *Cronica*, Libro XI, cap. 94.

43. Saverio La Sorsa, *L'organizzazione dei cambiatori fiorentini* (Cerignola, 1904), p. 63. The author gives 75 money-changers for 1350, but the figure must be a misprint for 57.

44. ASF, Arte del Cambio, No. 14, Libro di compagnie (1348–1399), fol. 117^v.

45. ASF, Arte del Cambio, No. 15, Libro di compagnie (1460–1487), fols. 2–4.

46. Gian-Francesco Pagnini, *Della Decima e di varie altre gravezze imposte dal Comune di Firenze* (Lisbon-Lucca, 1765–1766), II, 275; Maria Pisani, *Un avventuriero del Quattrocento, la vita e le opere di Benedetto Dei* (Genoa, 1923), p. 90.

47. Giovanni Cambi, *Istorie*, III, in Delizie degli eruditi toscani, XXII (Florence, 1786), 100, 176.

48. Frederic C. Lane, "Venetian Bankers, 1496–1533: A Study in the Early Stages of Deposit Banking," *Journal of Political Economy*, 45:187–206 (1937); R. de Roover, *Banking in Bruges*, pp. 338–341.

49. R. de Roover, "New Interpretations," p. 57.

50. *Ibid.*, pp. 61–67.

51. However, La Sorsa's thesis that merchant-bankers were not members of the Arte del Cambio is contradicted by the facts. It originates in a brief passage of Gaetano Salvemini, *Magnati e popolani in Firenze del 1280 al 1295* (Florence, 1899), pp. 38–39. On Salvemini's authority, it was even adopted by Gino Luzzatto, *Storia economica d'Italia*, I: *L'antichità e il medio evo* (Rome, 1949), 257.

52. G. Camerani Marri, ed. *Statuti dell'Arte del Cambio di Firenze (1299–1316)*, I (Florence, 1955), p. 39 (rubric 47): "Teneantur consules facere jurare omnes campsores qui hanc artem exercerent." On the other hand, those who did not operate a bank were excluded from membership.

53. *Statuti Arte del Cambio*, p. 41 (rubric 48 of the Statute of 1299). The text of this rubric is republished by Sapori, *Studi*, pp. 819–820. This regulation was never amended and applied only to partners and sons "qui cum eo starent ad tabulam," that is, who *stood* with the banker behind the counter or bench.

54. ASF, Arte del Cambio, No. 15, fol. 29^r.

55. La Sorsa, *Cambiatori*, pp. 17–19; *Statuti dell'Arte del Cambio*, pp. 4, 13, 34, 40, 55 (rubrics 2, 8, 40, 47, 72).

56. The tariff for money-changing was 6d. di piccioli per 100 florins according to Francesco Balducci Pegolotti, *La pratica della mercatura*, ed. Allan Evans (Cambridge, Mass., 1936), p. 196.

57. *Statuti Cambio*, pp. 28–29 and 160–161 (rubric 30 of the statute of 1299 and rubric 29 of that of 1313).

58. *Ibid.*, p. 70 (rubric 98 of the statute of 1299).

59. *Ibid.*, pp. 75–76 (rubric 105, which is an amendment enacted in 1300). The fiorini di suggello were so called because they circulated in sealed bags to prevent clipping.

60. *Ibid.*, p. 192 (rubric 106 of the statute of 1313).

61. For example, in Bruges (R. de Roover, *Banking in Bruges*, pp. 182–185),

62. *Statuti Arte del Cambio*, p. 19 (rubric 15 *in fine*).

63. On the use of oral contracts and orders to pay, see Usher, *Deposit Banking*, pp. 6, 18, 88, *et passim;* R. de Roover, *L'Évolution*, pp. 14, 24, 144.

64. *Statuti Cambio*, pp. 28, 43, 47, 48 (rubrics 29, 49, 58, and 60 of the statute of 1299). These provisions were never amended.

65. *Ibid.*, pp. 72–73 (rubric 102).

66. *Ibid.*, p. 61 (rubric 84).

67. *Ibid.*, pp. 8–9, 20 (rubrics 6 and 16).

68. *Ibid.*, pp. 23–24 (rubric 23).

69. Usher, *Deposit Banking*, pp. 287, 581.

70. This is clearly stated by Malachy Postlethwayt, "Venice," *The Universal Dictionary of Trade and Commerce* (London, 1755), II, 824. Cf. Giuseppe Maria Casaregi, *Il cambista instruito per ogni caso de' fallimenti, o sia instruzione per le piazze mercantili* (Venice, 1737), pp. 384, 387: Ordini e regole in materia del Banco del Giro.

71. Federigo Melis, *Note di storia della banca pisana nel Trecento* (Pisa, 1955), pp. 67–73.

72. A few of these checks were first published by Enrico Bensa, *Francesco di Marco da Prato*, pp. 352–358.

73. Melis, *Banca pisana*, pp. 74–116. Cf. Usher, *Deposit Banking*, pp. 89–94.

74. I would be a trifle less categorical than Professor Melis, *Banca Pisana*, p. 122.

75. *Statuta populi et communis Florentiae*, II (Fribourg-Florence, 1778), p. 164: Statute of 1415, Liber IV, rubr. 10, "Quod quilibet faciens scribi in libro tabulae sit absolutus a debito." Cf. A. Lattes, *Diritto commerciale*, pp. 127–128, 135 n.26; R. de Roover, *L'Évolution*, pp. 85–86, 206–207, 208, 212–213.

76. An assignment out of bank is a mode of payment according to which a creditor accepts, in settlement of a debt, a claim of his own debtor on a third party.

77. ASF, Carte Strozziane, Series II, filza 86, inserto 23: Consigli e ricordi alla Signoria di Firenze di Andrea di Francesco Arnoldi. According to the catasto, this Andrea Arnoldi was born around 1400.

78. Federigo Fantozzi, *Pianta geometrica della città di Firenze* (Florence, 1843), p. 104. Cf. ASF, Archivio del Catasto No. 51 (Gonf. Leon d'Oro, 1427), fol. 1141 and Catasto No. 1016 (Leon d'Oro, 1480), fol. 402^v.

79. ASF, MAP, filza 161, fols. 30–31.

80. Arezzo, Archivio della Fraternità dei Laici, filza 7, registro 55: Libro reale segnato E (1415–1425), fol. 36. The bill was for 200 florins at the rate of 14s. 11d., Barcelonese currency, per florin, which corresponds to £149 3s. 4d. in Barcelonese currency.

81. ASF, MAP, filza 154, fols. 35, 36. One of the entries reads: "Maso di Zanobi di ser Gino . . . ebe per me dalla tavola di Chosimo e Lorenzo de' Medici per paghamento di . . . ."

82. Origo, *Merchant of Prato*, pp. 75, 78, 148.

83. ASF, Arte del Cambio, No. 12, Matricole (1329–1598), fol. 50 and Arte della Lana, No. 20, Matricole (1352–1405), fol. 111.

84. ASF, Arte del Cambio, No. 12, fol. 86 and Arte della Seta No. 8,

Matricole (1433–1474), fol. 45. Cosimo's brother, Lorenzo di Giovanni, also was a member of the same two gilds, since he joined the Cambio in 1429 and the Seta in 1435.

85. ASF, Arte della Lana, No. 21, Matricole (1401–1456), fol. 124ᵛ.

86. ASF, Arte del Cambio, No. 12, fols. 94, 95.

87. ASF, Arte della Seta, No. 8, fol. 179 and Arte di Calimala No. 6, Matricole (1361–1495), fol. 52.

88. ASF, Calimala No. 6, fol. 62.

89. ASF, Arte del Cambio, No. 12, fol. 112.

90. Arte della Seta, No. 8, fol. 137ᵛ. Pierfrancesco di Lorenzo de' Medici belonged to the Silk and Wool Gilds only.

91. Bernardino Barbadoro, *Le finanze della Repubblica fiorentina* (Florence, 1929), pp. 75–76.

92. *Ibid.*, p. 87.

93. *Ibid.*, pp. 124, 159–161.

94. *Ibid.*, p. 156: ". . . . bene, juste et equaliter, ita quod quilibet extimum habeat secundum facultatem et possibilitatem suam" (Sapori, *Studi*, p. 677).

95. Barbadoro, *Finanze*, pp. 172–173, 187.

96. *Ibid.*, pp. 178–179.

97. In 1378, during the revolt of the *Ciompi*, the populace agitated in vain for reintroduction of the estimo on a permanent basis. Giuseppe Canestrini, *La scienza e l'arte di stato* (Florence, 1862), pp. 37–44, and Pagnini, *Della Decima*, I, 23.

98. Barbadoro, *Finanze*, pp. 623–624.

99. *Ibid.*, p. 632. The date of the second decree is February 22, 1345.

100. Matteo Villani, *Cronica* (Florence, 1846), Libro 3, cap. 106; R. de Roover, "Il trattato," pp. 14–19.

101. Canestrini, *L'arte di stato*, pp. 427–431.

102. M. Villani, *Cronica*, Libro 8, cap. 71.

103. Barbadoro, *Finanze*, p. 669.

104. *Ibid.*, p. 672.

105. Antonio Pucci, *Il Centiloquio*, Canto 91 in Delizie degli eruditi toscani, VI (1775), p. 185.

106. The law, dated January 19, 1390, is published in Pagnini, *Della Decima*, I, 201–210.

107. Prior to 1390, only those whose assessments was 2 florins or less were given this choice.

108. Niccolò Machiavelli, *History of Florence,* ed. Charles W. Colby (rev. ed., New York, 1901), Bk. IV, chap. 3, pp. 190–192; *Istorie fiorentine,* in *Opere,* ed. A. Panella (Milan, 1938), Bk. IV, §14–15, I, 245–247, Machiavelli states that the war with Milan alone cost 3,500,000 ducats, a plausible figure which agrees with contemporary estimates.

109. It is doubtful whether Machiavelli is right in asserting that the catasto was introduced because Giovanni di Bicci de' Medici and his popular following put pressure on the government. It seems that Giovanni was only a lukewarm advocate of the new tax and that the law was passed not over government opposition but with full government support (Pietro Berti, "Nuovi documenti intorno al catasto fiorentino," *Giornale storico degli Archivi toscani*, 4:32–62 (1860). Cf. Ferdinand Schevill, *History of Florence* (New York, 1936), p. 345.

110. Enrico Fiumi, "Fioritura e decadenza dell'economia fiorentina," *Archivio storico italiano*, 117:459 (1959).

111. Canestrini, *L'arte di stato,* pp. 319–320.

112. The text of the law is in Pagnini, *Della Decima,* I, 214–231, especially p. 229. Cf. Canestrini, pp. 146, 187.

113. Pagnini, *Della Decima,* I, 39 and Canestrini, pp. 319–320.

114. Heinrich Sieveking, *Aus Genueser Rechnungs- und Steuerbüchern: ein Beitrag zur mittelalterlichen Handels- und Vermögensstatistik* (Sitzungsberichte der Kais. Akademie der Wissenschaften in Wien, Philosophisch-historische Klasse, Vol. 162, Pt. 2, Vienna, 1909), p. 105, n. 1: ". . . per non alterare gli esercitii e traffichi della nostra città, de' quali tanto fiorito e si grande popolo per la maggior parte si pasce e nutricha."

115. Machiavelli, *History of Florence,* pp. 190 191 (Bk. IV, chap. 3).

116. Canestrini, p. 174.

117. Florence, Archivio dello Spedale degli Innocenti, Estranei, No. 77: Libro segreto di Andrea di Francesco Banchi e compagni all'Arte della Seta in Por Santa Maria, segnato A (1454–1460), fols. 5, 20.

118. For example, Folco d'Adoardo Portinari (1386–1431), junior partner of the Medici Bank in Florence, reported that he had f. 800 invested in this company and that his share in accrued profits amounted to f. 120 (ASF, Catasto No. 81, Campione, Gonf. Vaio, 1427, fols. 477ᵛ–478ᵛ).

119. The fifteenth century is the period during which domestic slavery was very common in Tuscany. In Florence, there was probably no prominent family without slaves, chiefly women. This includes the Medici, the Pazzi, the Strozzi, and even the decretalist, Messer Lorenzo d'Antonio Ridolfi. See Iris Origo, "The Domestic Enemy: the Eastern Slaves in Tuscany in the Fourteenth and Fifteenth Centuries," *Speculum,* 30:321–366 (1955).

120. Canestrini, *L'arte di stato,* pp. 115–116.

121. A division had been made in 1451, but it left some of the property in joint ownership (ASF, MAP, filza 161: Lodo per la divisione dei beni tra Cosimo di Giovanni e Pierfrancesco, suo nipote).

122. ASF, Catasto No. 924 (Leon d'Oro, 1469), fol. 312ᵛ–313ᵛ.

123. *Ibid.,* fol. 326ᵛ. With additions and head tax, his total tax was f. 243 16s. 9d. a oro.

124. Canestrini, pp. 139–140.

125. *Ibid.,* pp. 217, 224.

126. For example, Antonio di Taddeo di Filippo, a Medici partner, had a valsente of f. 3,288 7s. 4d. and, after deduction of 5 percent, a net amount of f. 3,066 19s. 0d. This figure at 7 percent gives an annual income of f. 214 13s. 9d. According to the scale (Table 2), Antonio's tax was 18 percent of this amount or f. 38 12s. 9d., which corresponds to the portata. The computations are not fully shown on the portata. Since I obtain the same results, my method of computing the tax must be correct (ASF, Catasto No. 1015, Leon d'Oro, 1481, fol. 204ᵛ).

127. Canestrini, p. 236.

128. Florence, Biblioteca Nazionale, Codice Magl. XIII, No. 72, item 2, fols. 34ᵛ–36ᵛ.

129. ASF, Catasto No. 16 (Gonf. Scala, 1427), fol. 325.

130. Canestrini, p. 151.

131. See above note 128.

132. The tax officials, in 1430–31, had Banchi submit his books for inspection, but they did not succeed in straightening out the matter, so they were forced to accept his figures: "Abiamo veduto il suo bilancio e i suoi libri e non ci pare

questa ragione bene chiara. Mettiamolla chome ci à dato per non aver tenpo a poterllo chiarire." This marginal comment is found in the Campione of Quartiere Santo Spirito, Gonf. Scala for 1430 (ASF, Catasto No. 393, fol. 3).

133. Ehrenberg, *Zeitalter*, I, 285, and *Siècle*, p. 137.

134. Carlo M. Cipolla, *Studi di storia della moneta*, I: *I movimenti dei cambi in Italia dal secolo XIII al XV* (Pavia, 1948), 56–62.

135. This is clear from a codification made in 1325: *Statuti della Repubblica fiorentina, II: Statuto del podestà, dell'anno 1325*, ed. Romolo Caggese (Florence, 1921), Bk. 3, rubric 128, pp. 279–80.

136. G. Villani, *Cronica*, Bk. 12, chap 97; Marchionne di Coppo Stefani, *Istoria fiorentina*, Bk. 10, rubric 877 (Delizie, XVI, Florence, 1783); san Antonino, *Summa theologica* (Verona, 1740), Part III, titulus 5, cap. 4, §4. The monetary system was an issue in the class struggle of 1378, since the mercantile interests resisted popular demand for improvement of the piccioli and stabilization of the florin. Niccolò Rodolico, *La democrazia fiorentina nel suo tramonto, 1378–1382* (Bologna, 1905), pp. 256–268.

137. Camerani, *Statuti*, p. 75 (rubric 105 of the statute of 1299). Cf. Pagnini, *Della Decima*, I, 120.

138. *Ibid.*, I, Table 4.

139. Francesco Vettori, *Il fiorino d'oro* (Florence, 1738), pp. 231–232.

140. ASF, Balie, No. 31, fols. 55–v56v.

CHAPTER III

The Antecedents and the Early Years of the Medici Bank under the Management of Giovanni di Bicci, 1397–1429

1. Gene A. Brucker, "The Medici in the Fourteenth Century," *Speculum*, 32:9 (1957). There are other examples of restitution for usury or ill-gotten gains in Medici testaments (*ibid.*, p. 12).

2. The importance of Vieri (or Veri) di Cambio as the first Medici to achieve outstanding success in business is emphasized by Frederic E. Gaupp, "De eerste Medici, Geldwisselaars — kooplieden — bankiers," *Wegbereiders der Renaissance* (Amsterdam, n.d.), p. 27. Cf. Machiavelli, *History of Florence*, Bk. III, chap. 7, pp. 166–167, and *Istorie fiorentine*, Libro III, §25. Machiavelli states that Vieri di Cambio could have made himself lord of Florence if he had been politically ambitious.

3. The word "factor," as used in the Florentine records, simply means a clerk or an employee.

4. He was one of the sixty-seven Florentine citizens knighted on July 20, 1378. Gaetano Salvemini, *La dignità cavalleresca nel Comune di Firenze* (Florence, 1896), p. 141, Appendix B, No. 4. Cf. Victor I. Rutenburg, *Popular Unrest in Italian Cities, Fourteenth Century and Beginning of the Fifteenth*, in Russian (Moscow, 1958), pp. 356–357.

5. ASF, Arte del Cambio, No. 12, Matricole, 1329–1598, fol. 24v.

6. This information is available in ASF, Arte del Cambio, No. 14. fol. 8v *et passim*.

7. S. L. Peruzzi, *Storia del commercio e dei banchieri di Firenze* (Florence, 1868), p. 221. Cf. Pietro Silva, "L'ultimo trattato commerciale tra Pisa e Firenze," *Studi storici*, 17:680 (1908).

8. Antonio Teja, *Aspetti della vita economica di Zara dal 1289 al 1409*, I: *La pratica bancaria* (Zara, 1936), pp. 74–75, 113.

9. ASF, Arte del Cambio, No. 14, fol. 80.

10. Riccardo del Maestro Fagno is mentioned in the Alberti account books. *I libri degli Alberti del Giudice*, ed. Armando Sapori (Milan, 1952), pp. 161, 199, 304.

11. Bensa, *Francesco di Marco*, pp. 327–328. An English translation of the bill is given in *Medieval Trade in the Mediterranean World*, eds. Robert S. Lopez and Irving Raymond (New York, 1955), p. 231, doc. 116.

12. Giovanni di Bicci joined the Arte del Cambio gild on February 14, 1386, at the age of twenty-six (ASF, Arte del Cambio, No. 12, Matricole, 1328–1598, fol. 50).

13. Brucker, "The Medici," p. 11.

14. Prato, Archivio Datini, Carteggi di Firenze, di Genova e di Pisa.

15. ASF, MAP, filza 153, Libro segreto No. 1 (1397–1420), fol. 114 (*dare*). Giovanni di Bicci claimed to have lost 860 cameral florins on this deal.

16. ASF, Arte del Cambio, No. 14, fol. 100ᵛ–108.

17. *Ibid.*, fols. 99ᵛ–101ᵛ. In 1398, Averardo di Francesco had as partners Francesco di Messer Alessandro de' Bardi and Lorenzo di Cione Buoni who, previously, had been doing business in Pisa with a relative, Gentile di Baldassare del Buono. This partnership of the del Buono was dissolved before 1397, when Gentile joined the bank founded by Giovanni di Bicci. See Alberto Ceccherelli, *I libri di mercatura della Banca Medici e l'applicazione della partita doppia a Firenze nel secolo decimoquarto* (Florence, 1913), pp. 28–29.

18. In his return for the catasto of 1430, Cambio di Vieri de' Medici mentions that his bank benefits from a moratorium granted by the Sei della Mercanzia, or Mercantile Court (ASF, Catasto No. 373, Leon d'Oro, 1430, fol. 704ᵛ).

19. The assets of these banks included uncollectible claims to the extent of 8,000 florins (ASF, Catasto No. 470, 1433, fol. 606).

20. Gaetano Pieraccini, *La stirpe de' Medici di Cafaggiolo* (1st, ed., Florence, 1924) I, 77; (2nd ed., Florence 1947), I, 82. Cf. Giuseppe Zippel, "Un cliente mediceo," *Scritti varii d'erudizione e di critica in onore di R. Renier* (Turin, 1912), p. 479 and n. 2.

21. ASF, MAP, filza 133, no. 1. Only fols. 17 to 110 (inclusive) are extant. This ledger was first described by Heinrich Sieveking in a communication to the Imperial Academy in Vienna, published in *Anzeiger der Kais. Akademie der Wissenschaften, Philosophisch-historische Klasse*, 39:170–177 (1902). Fragments of two other ledgers of the firm of Averardo di Francesco de' Medici & Co. are also extant: one for the Rome branch, 1412–1413, and one for the branch in Pisa, 1424–26 (MAP, filza 133, nos. 2, 3).

22. Ceccherelli is confused on this subject (*Libri di mercatura*, pp. 21–22).

23. Professor Tommaso Zerbi questions whether Averardo's ledger of 1395 is in double entry because of the absence of cross references in the case of cash transactions. *Le origini della partita doppia; gestioni aziendali e situazioni di mercato nei secoli XIV e XV*, (Milan, 1952), pp. 125–130). Such a query is difficult to refute because the surviving fragment does not show the procedure followed in closing and balancing the books (R. de Roover, "The Development of Accounting prior to Luca Pacioli according to the Account-Books of Medieval Merchants," *Studies in the History of Accounting*, eds. A. C. Littleton and B. S. Yamey (London, 1956), pp. 146–147. Cf. Ceccherelli, *Libri di mercatura*, p. 51.

24. Camerani, *Documenti*, p. 23, No. 9; Ceccherelli, *Libri*, pp. 44–45; Zerbi, *Partita doppia*, pp. 128–129; Heinrich Sieveking, *Die Handlungsbücher der Medici* (Sitzungsberichte der Kais. Akademie der Wissenschaften in Wien, Philosophisch-Historische Klasse, Vol. 151, Pt. 5, Vienna, 1905), p. 30.

25. ASF, MAP, filza 133, no. 1, fols. 23, 24, *et passim.*
26. Camerani, *Documenti,* pp. 22, 25, 26, *et passim.*
27. ASF, Catasto No. 60, Libro di Portate, Quartiere San Giovanni, Gonf. Vaio (1427), fol. 94.
28. A fragment of the ledger belonging to the Pisan branch and covering the years 1424–1426 is still extant (ASF, MAP, filza 133, no. 3).
29. ASF, Catasto No. 15 (Gonf. Scala, 1427), fols. 249–261 and No. 331 (Scala, 1430), fols. 145–159. These are the reports of Bardo di Francesco de' Bardi.
30. ASF, Catasto No. 331 (Scala, 1430) fols. 145–159 (Portata of Bardo de' Bardi).
31. Sieveking, *Handlungsbücher,* p. 5.
32. ASF, Catasto No. 410 (Campione, Vaio, 1430), fol. 5^v: ". . . uno abituro atto a fortezza posto in Mugello, luogho detto Cafaggiuolo. . . ."
33. ASF, Arte del Cambio, No. 14, Libro di compagnie, fol. 113^r.
34. The decision to open an office in Florence was evidently made early in 1397, because the first entries in the libro segreto show that the partnership was formed on March 26, 1397. ASF, MAP, filza 153, no. 1, fols. 10, 11. Later entries show that business in the Florentine office did not really begin until October of the same year.
35. ASF, Catasto No. 77 (Gonf. Leon Bianco), fol. 277^r. The catasto report further reveals that Gentile Buoni had been unable to pay any prestanze or forced loans. In the margin, one still sees the official annotation miserabile (pauper) and a cross to indicate that Gentile had died since handing in his report. The report of Baldassare, Gentile's son, for the catasto of 1430 (Catasto No. 390, fol. 182) relates that he was thrown in prison for his father's debt to Palla Strozzi and that some of his furnishings were pawned *alla Vacca,* the pawnshop near san Ruffilo, today via dei Pecori. In short, the whole family was in great distress.
36. ASF, Arte del Cambio, No. 14, fols. 115^r, 117^r.
37. *Ibid.,* fol. 113^r: ". . . Benedictus Lippaccii de Bardis (non matriculatus)." Giovanni de' Medici reported his newly formed partnership for Florence on April 7, 1397.
38. ASF, Arte del Cambio, No. 12, fol. 59^r.
39. ASF, MAP, filza 153, no. 1, fol. 11.
40. *Ibid.,* fol. 12.
41. *Ibid.,* fols. 21, 22.
42. *Ibid.,* fol. 14.
43. *Ibid.,* fols. 47, 48.
44. The partnership contract is extant: ASF, MAP, filza 89, no. 190.
45. ASF, MAP, filza 153, no. 1, fol. 14.
46. *Ibid.,* fols. 22, 46. The total capital was consequently 9,000 florins.
47. *Ibid.,* fols. 28, 48.
48. In other words, the profits of the Venetian branch were shared as follows:

Neri di Cipriano Tornaquinci	4 shares
Giovanni di Bicci de' Medici	9 shares
Benedetto di Lippaccio de' Bardi	3 shares
Total	16 shares

49. ASF, MAP, filza 153, no. 1, fols. 34, 40
50. *Ibid.,* fol. 65.

51. *Ibid.*, fol. 125.

52. ASF, MAP, filza 153, no. 1, fols. 86, 95. The creation of limited partnerships was permitted in Florence by a law passed in 1408.

53. ASF, MAP, filza 153, no. 1, fol. 15. He probably left the service of the Medici at the end of 1404 and was succeeded by Nanni di Nettolo Becchi who stayed with the Medici through 1414. He received, in 1405, a salary of 45 florins which was raised to a maximum of 50 florins in 1409 (*ibid.*, fols. 16, 72, 94). Nanni was dismissed apparently because he left his post during the plague and in other ways neglected his duties.

54. *Ibid.*, fol. 15.

55. *Ibid.*, fol. 74.

56. Origo, *Merchant of Prato*, pp. 107–108, 111.

57. ASF, MAP, filza 153, no. 1, fol. 18.

58. *Ibid.*, fol. 42.

59. *Ibid.*, fol. 62.

60. *Ibid.*, fol. 68.

61. *Ibid.*, fol. 16.

62. *Ibid.*, fol. 105.

63. *Ibid.*, fol. 106.

64. R. de Roover, "I libri segreti del Banco de' Medici," *Archivio storico italiano*, 107:236–240 (1949). The reference to the bundle is MAP, filza 153.

65. Profits fell from 2,000 florins in 1405 to 500 florins on the average between 1416 and 1420. Moreover, the downward trend took a turn for the worse after 1420.

66. ASF, Prestanze, No. 1523 (Gonf. Leon d'Oro), 1396, fols. 34ᵛ and 64.

67. ASF, Prestanze, No. 1999 (Quartiere S. Giovanni, 1403), fols. 102ᵛ, 104, 133ᵛ, 242.

68. ASF, Prestanze, No. 2904 (S. Giovanni, 1413), fols. 88ᵛ, 160ᵛ.

69. Florence, Biblioteca Nazionale, Codice Magl. XIII, No. 72, 2, fols. 34ᵛ–36ᵛ.

70. Benedetto di Lippaccio is recorded as deceased on April 13, 1420: ASF, MAP, filza 153, no. 1, fol. 110.

71. *Ibid.*, fols. 105, 106.

72. *Ibid.*, fols. 110, 125. The total loss was considerable and amounted to f. 2,187 28s. 5d. affiorino.

73. ASF, MAP, filza 68, No. 402.

74. These partnership agreements are all copied at the beginning of the second libro segreto (MAP, filza 153, no. 2).

75. ASF, MAP, filza 153, no. 2, fols. 8ᵛ–9ᵛ. Profits for three years were only 684 florins, or barely seven percent on an investment of 3,200 florins, a return which the Medici considered unsatisfactory, because they got a better yield on other investments.

76. *Ibid.*, fol. 40.

77. The libri segreti and other records of the Medici bank contain numerous references to specie shipments from Geneva to Rome.

78. Giovanni Cavalcanti, *Istorie Fiorentine* (Florence, 1838), I, 262 f. An English translation of the speech is given by Janet Ross, *Lives of the Early Medici* (Boston, 1911), p. 6.

79. Umberto Dorini, *I Medici e i loro tempi* (Florence, 1947), p. 31; Francis A. Hyett, *Florence, her History and Art to the Fall of the Republic* (London, 1903), p. 236.

80. Cavalcanti, I, 267. Cf. Alfred von Reumont, *Lorenzo de' Medici the Magnificent* (London, 1876), I, 37.

81. Ferdinand Schevill, *The Medici* (London, 1950), p. 59.

82. von Reumont, *Lorenzo de' Medici*, I, 35.

83. Machiavelli, *History of Florence*, Bk. IV, chap. 4, p. 194; *Istorie Fiorentine*, Libro IV §16.

84. ASF, MAP, filza 153, no. 1, fol. 125. The presence in Cracow of Neri Tornaquinci is reported as early as 1410. He must have gone there shortly after leaving the service of the Medici. Paul Fournier, *Les Florentins en Pologne* (Lyons, 1893), p. 339.

85. Angelo Fabroni, *Laurentii Medicis Magnifici Vita* (Pisa, 1784), II, 6; William Roscoe, *The Life of Lorenzo de' Medici called the Magnificent* (9th ed., London, 1847), p. 424, Appendix X.

86. ASF, MAP, filza 154, fol. 94^v.

CHAPTER IV

The Heyday of the Medici Bank: Cosimo at the Helm, 1429–1464

1. ASF, MAP, filza 153, no. 2, fols. 30, 44–47, 51, 59, 71.

2. ASF, MAP, filza 94, no. 89, fols. 238–239.

3. ASF, Catasto No. 830 (Chiavi, 1457/1458), fol. 685^v; No. 60 (Gonf. Vaio, 1427), fol. 94.

4. ASF, MAP, filza 153, no. 2, fol. 67.

5. *Ibid.*, fol. 59. Later Lotto changed his surname from Bozzi to Tanini.

6. *Ibid.*, fols. 67, 77.

7. *Ibid.*, fol. 71.

8. ASF, Catasto No. 497 (Leon d'Oro, Campione, 1433), fol. 192^r.

9. ASF, MAP, filza 88, no. 119. No exact date is given, but the letter was written shortly after February 5, 1433.

10. ASF, MAP, filza 153, no. 2, fols. 68, 72, and 78. These entries mention Ilarione de' Bardi as being dead.

11. *Ibid.*, fols. 60 and 79.

12. *Ibid.*, fols. 73 and 74.

13. This assertion is found in Sieveking (*Handlungsbücher*, p. 22) and is repeated by later historians. As reference Sieveking gives MAP, filza 131, which contains records of Antonio Bertini, Medici agent in Geneva (1421–1422), who had been sent there by the Rome branch. Among these papers, there are letters exchanged with Gualterotto de' Bardi & Co., who were the correspondents of the Medici Bank in Bruges, but there is no mention of a branch office in this city.

14. Two copies of this contract are available: one in Libro segreto, No. 3 (MAP, filza 153) and the other in filza 94, no. 137, fols. 220–221.

15. MAP, filza 153, no. 3, fols. 12, 13.

16. *Ibid.*, fols. 3, 14.

17. *Ibid.*, fols. 4, 32.

18. *Ibid.*, fol. 14.

19. *Ibid.*, fol. 15.

20. MAP, filza 153, no. 1, fol. 79.

21. MAP, filza 153, no. 2, fol. 3: partnership agreement of Rome branch (1420).

22. *Ibid.*, fol. 40.

23. ASF, Catasto No. 64 (Scala, 1427), fol. 272^v and No. 15 (Scala, 1427), fol. 799.

24. Camerani, *Documenti*, p. 44: Nos. 92, 94.

25. ASF, Catasto No. 832 (Vaio, 1457), fol. 217.

26. Catasto No. 608 (Scala, 1442), fol. 511.

27. Catasto No. 832 (Vaio, 1457), fol. 217.

28. ASF, Manoscritti, No. 624: Stefano Rosselli, "Sepultuario fiorentino" (1657), I, 463.

29. San Bernardino of Siena, *De Evangelio Aeterno*, sermon 33, art. 2, cap. 9.

30. ASF, Catasto No. 15 (Scala, 1427), fol. 799.

31. Catasto No. 832 (Vaio, 1457), fols. 213–218.

32. Roberto Martelli had been a factor in Rome since 1424 and later became the head of the Rome branch (1439).

33. Camerani, p. 59: Nos. 149, 150.

34. Two copies of the partnership agreement are extant: one in Libro segreto No. 3 (MAP, filza 153), fol. 5 and the other in filza 94, no. 153, fols. 282–283. The contract was extended with some changes in 1440 (MAP, filza 94, no. 117, fols. 180–181).

35. I wish to thank Professor Gaupp for this bit of information and for permission to use it. Sforza at that time was pontifical vicar in the Marches, but he was actually trying to carve for himself a principality to the detriment of the pope.

36. This is contrary to the thesis of Mina Martens, "Les Maisons de Medici et de Bourgogne au XVe siècle," *Le Moyen Age*, 56:115–119 (1950). The evidence presented, however, is unconvincing. Moreover, the Bruges branch was not founded in 1420 but in 1439, as the entries in the books of the Medici show.

37. ASF, MAP, filza 68, no. 588: Ricordo per Bernardo Portinari.

38. For a more detailed account of the foundation of the Bruges branch, see R. de Roover, "Oprichting en liquidatie van het Brugse Filiaal van het Bankiershuis der Medici," *Mededelingen van de Koninklijke Vlaamse Academie voor Wetenschappen, Letteren en Schone Kunsten van België, Klasse der Letteren*, Vol. XV (1953), No. 7.

39. ASF, MAP, filza 153, no. 3, fol. 30. This is the text of the entry in the libro segreto: Bernardo di Giovanni d'Adoardo Portinari a dì 24 di marzo 1438 f. semila [di] camera gli fecie buoni per noi più dì fa i nostri di corte per tanti gli asegniamo, perchè tengha nel trafficho della sua ragione di Brugia dove si trova, posto debino avere in questo c. 18 . . . . . . f. 6,420.

40. ASF, MAP, filza 84, no. 26, fol. 55.

41. MAP, filza 153, no. 3 fols. 38, 45.

42. *Ibid.*, fol. 9 and filza 94, no. 138, fols. 222–223.

43. MAP, filza 23, nos. 553, 554, 557, 558 and filza 29, nos. 614, 846, 1101.

44. MAP, filza 153, no. 3, fols. 29, 38. There had been a previous partnership with Piero Corsi, but it was of short duration. This Piero Corsi was the father-in-law of Francesco Sassetti.

45. MAP, filza 89, no. 71 and MAP, filza 153, no. 3, fol. 6.

46. MAP, filza 133, no. 3: Ledger of Averardo de' Medici & Co. in Pisa (1424–1426), fol. 106. The account is in the name of Donato di Niccolò, *intagliatore* (sculptor). Donatello's full name was Donato di Niccolò di Betto de' Bardi and he belonged to one of the poorer branches of this famous family. Sieveking (*Handlungsbücher*, p. 31) mentions this account but fails to identify the famous artist.

47. MAP, filza 153, no. 3, fol. 52.

48. Corti, "Le accomandite fiorentine nel XV e XVI secolo," pp. 132–133.

49. ASF, Catasto No. 823 (Leon d'Oro, 1457), No. 181: "Bilancio della

ragione d'Ugholino e Antonio Martelli e chonpangni di Pisa," February 28, 1458 (N.S.).

50. ASF, MAP, filza 94, no. 134, fols. 214–215: "Ricordo per Gierozzo de' Pigli."

51. ASF, Catasto No. 68 (Carro, 1427), fol. 100ᵛ.

52. Three copies are extant: see Chap. V n. 31.

53. MAP, filza 153, no. 3, fols. 78, 82.

54. Curt S. Gutkind, *Cosimo de' Medici, Pater Patriae, 1389–1464* (Oxford, 1938), pp. 191–193; *idem, Cosimo de' Medici il Vecchio* (Florence, 1940), pp. 255–257. This book is unfortunately unreliable for details.

55. He was not the brother-in-law of Giovanni di Bicci, as Gutkind states.

56. ASF, MAP, filza 153, no. 1, fols. 49–50.

57. Karl Wilhelm Pauli, "Ueber die frühere Bedeutung Lübecks als Wechselplatz des Nordens," *Lübeckische Zustände im Mittelalter,* II (Lübeck, 1872), p. 131, doc. no. 20. Baglioni was apparently residing in Lübeck already in 1411, when he made a trip to Italy. MAP, filza 83, no. 52, fols. 313–314.

58. After 1426, this "bank" or "exchange" was managed by Gherardo Bueri. Pauli, p. 150, doc. 51; *Codex diplomaticus lubecensis (Lübeckisches Urkundenbuch)*, VI (Lübeck, 1881) pp. 139, 610–11, docs. nos. 95 and 634.

59. He is already mentioned as burgher of Lübeck in 1430. *Codex lubecensis,* VI, 355, no. 379. In a Florentine document, he is still called *civis Florentiae. Codex lubecensis,* VIII (Lübeck, 1889), 707, no. 669.

60. Gutkind makes the fantastic supposition that he was connected with a Flemish banking house de Wale. In Low German, the designation *Wale* was applied to anyone speaking a Romance language.

61. Pauli, p. 114, No. 26.

62. *Ibid.,* p. 104.

63. ASF, Catasto No. 51 (Leon d'Oro, 1427), fols. 1167ᵛ, 1187–1190, 1191–1194.

64. Sieveking, *Handlungsbücher,* pp. 25–29; ASF, MAP, filza 153, no. 2, fols. 57, 58, 80. Pauli (p. 104) states that Baglioni disappeared from circulation in 1426, but the Medici records mention his partnership with Bueri in 1427 and still in 1433. Bueri was a member of a cartel which, in 1424, bought the entire output of the Lübeck rosary-makers for shipment to Venice, Nuremberg, Frankfort-on-the-Main, and Cologne (Pauli, p. 104).

65. *Codex lubecensis,* VIII, 432, doc. no. 396; Sieveking, *Handlungsbücher,* pp. 25–26.

66. *Codex lubecensis,* VIII, 707 ff., 745, docs. nos. 669 and 701.

67. Pauli, p. 115.

68. The popes would have liked to see the Italian banking houses establish branches in Northern and Eastern Europe, but the obstacles were unsurmountable. Armando Sapori, "Gl'Italiani in Polonia nel medioevo," *Archivio storico italiano,* 83:131 (1925).

69. Karl Pagel, *Die Hanse* (Berlin, 1942), p. 287.

70. Canestrini, *L'arte di stato,* p. 157; Ehrenberg, *Zeitalter,* I, 47; Alfred Doren, *Studien aus der Florentiner Wirtschaftsgeschichte,* I: *Die Florentiner Wollentuchindustrie vom 14. bis zum 16. Jahrhundert* (Berlin, 1901), 497–500, Appendix No. 3; Otto Meltzing, *Das Bankhaus der Medici und seine Vorläufer* (Jena, 1906), pp. 103 f. Doren gives more information than the others by listing the names of the partners, but all these historians are in error about the date.

71. If the date of 1431 were correct, some of the branch managers would still be young boys, which is impossible. Nevertheless, Armand Grunzweig used this

record to prove that the accomandite of Bruges and London existed already in 1431. Cf. Armand Grunzweig, *Correspondance de la filiale de Bruges des Medici* (Brussels, 1931), p. viii. I was unable to examine this *registro dei traffichi* consulted by Canestrini and Doren, because it could not be located.

72. ASF, MAP, filza 153, no. 3, fols. 80, 88.

73. *Ibid.*, fols. 7, 80, 88, 90.

74. *Ibid.*, fol. 90.

75. *Ibid.*, fol. 85.

76. *Ibid.*, fols. 90, 94.

77. R. de Roover, "Oprichting," p. 12; Grunzweig, *Correspondance*, pp. 34, 41, 52.

78. G. Villani, *Cronica*, Libro XI, cap. 88.

79. Angelo Fabroni, *Magni Cosmi Medicei Vita* (Pisa, 1789), II, 246.

80. Georges Peyronnet, "Il ducato di Milano sotto Francesco Sforza (1450–1466), politica interna, vita economica e sociale," *Archivio storico italiano*, 116:51 (1958); ASF, MAP, filza 8, no. 413.

81. Fabroni, *Magni Cosmi Medicei Vita*, II, 247.

82. The evidence is found in a letter of condolence written by Alessandro Martelli in Venice to Giovanni di Cosimo de' Medici on July 21, 1455. The writer tells his correspondent that the latter will have to brace himself if he is to carry out the will of Cosimo and to shoulder the responsibilities and duties heretofore assumed by Giovanni Benci. ASF, MAP, filza 9, no. 173.

83. ASF, Catasto No. 821 (Leon d'Oro, 1457/58), fol. 518^v.

84. ASF, MAP, filza 134, no. 3, fol. 42^v.

85. ASF, Arte del Cambio, No. 15: Libro di compagnie (1460–1487), fols. 7^v, 10, 14^v, 17, 20, 23, 26.

86. René Gandilhon, *La Politique économique de Louis XI* (Rennes, 1940), p. 362. This is the same Nori who was killed at the side of Giuliano de' Medici on the fateful day of the Pazzi conspiracy (1478).

87. ASF, Arte del Cambio, No. 15, fol. 79^v.

88. This statement rests on a comparison of the wording of the partnership contracts before and after 1455. Prior to 1455, such contracts usually either specifically mention Benci and Salutati (until 1443) as partners along with the Medici or include them implicitly under an "& Co." After 1455, the contracts name only the members of the Medici family with no reference to any other partner coming in for their share of the profits.

89. ASF, MAP, filza 82, no. 182, fol. 593^v. Cf. Sieveking, *Handlungsbücher*, p. 9.

90. ASF, Catasto No. 821 (Leon d'Oro, 1457), fols. 159, 160–163, 167–174. Francesco Neroni was exiled with his brothers Dietisalvi and Giovanni (archbishop of Florence) for participation in the plot to overthrow the Medici rule in 1466.

91. ASF, MAP, filza 82, fol. 595: "Se si fosse preso errore inn alchuna chosa, o in più o in meno, nonn è per malizia ne per inghanare, ma sarebbe errore, il quale siamo contenti sia richoretto sechondo che parrà alla vostra dischrezione."

92. ASF, MAP, filza 12, nos. 205, 232, 241. The letters are dated respectively February 18, March 4, and March 11, 1458 (N.S.).

93. MAP, filza 12, no. 232.

94. MAP, filza 146, fols. 176–182.

95. MAP, filza 12, no. 222. The false report was sent on February 18, 1458, at the same time as letter no. 205.

96. *Ibid.*, no. 232.

97. This discrepancy did not escape the notice of Sieveking (*Handlungs-bücher*, p. 9, n. 2). The florin at that time was worth about 50 Flemish groats.

98. One florin was equal to about £3 di imperiali. Greater accuracy is not necessary for this purpose.

99. One of the two or three correct figures in Cosimo's report seems to be the amount of 5,500 florins invested in the partnership with Neroni. Perhaps Cosimo distrusted Neroni and did not want him to know too much in the event of defection.

100. Marc Brésard, *Les Foires de Lyon aux XVe et XVIe siècles* (Paris, 1914), p. 19; Marcel Vigne, *La Banque à Lyon du XVe au XVIIIe siècle* (Paris, 1903), p. 59.

101. Schevill, *History of Florence*, p. 366.

102. *The Commentaries of Pius II*, trans. by Florence Alden Gragg, ed. by Leona C. Gabel, Smith College Studies in History, 25:163 (1939–1940).

103. Grunzweig, *Correspondance*, pp. 65–66, 70–72, 75–76.

104. Francesco Guicciardini, *Storie fiorentine dal 1378 al 1509*, ed. Roberto Palmarocchi (Bari, 1931), p. 12; Machiavelli, *History of Florence*, Bk. VII, chap. 1, and *idem, Istorie*, Libro VII, §6. Machiavelli does not state that the Sassetti and the Portinari, after each acquiring a fortune in Medici service, later lost it by being involved in the losses of the Bank.

CHAPTER V

The Legal Status and Economic Structure of the Medici Bank

1. Armando Sapori, *La crisi delle compagnie mercantili dei Bardi e dei Peruzzi* (Florence, 1926), p. 249.

2. Sapori, *Studi*, pp. 666–669, 678. In 1303 the Peruzzi family controlled 74 shares against 49 owned by outsiders.

3. However, the partners might rebel against weak leadership and claim their right to vote on all issues of any importance, as in the case of the Buonsignori (*ibid.*, pp. 784–788).

4. Sapori, *Studi*, pp. 665–670.

5. *Ibid.*, p. 684. In 1319 it was Giotto d'Arnoldo who reported to his fellow-partners about the financial condition of the company.

6. Mario Chiaudano, "I Rothschild del Duecento: la Gran Tavola di Orlando Bonsignori," reprinted from *Bullettino senese di storia patria*, VI (1935), fasc. 2, 17; Sapori, *Studi*, p. 681.

7. The word *ragione* had such an extensive meaning that it implied all these things, separately or taken together. Florence Edler, *Glossary of Mediaeval Terms of Business, Italian Series, 1200–1600* (Cambridge, Mass., 1934), p. 236.

8. Clemens Bauer, *Unternehmung und Unternehmungsformen im Spät-mittelalter und in der beginnenden Neuzeit* (Jena, 1936), p. 143.

9. Yves Renouard, *Les Relations des papes d'Avignon et des compagnies commerciales et bancaires de 1316 à 1378* (Bibliothèque des écoles françaises d'Athènes et de Rome, fasc. 151, Paris, 1941), pp. 49–50; R. de Roover, "La Communauté des marchands lucquois à Bruges de 1377 à 1404," *Handelingen van het genootschap "Société d'Emulation" te Brugge*, 86:64–69 (1949); Sapori, *Studi*, pp. 698–704.

10. Sapori (*Studi*, pp. 762 f.) gives an example of such a contract. This contract states the amount of the salary which the employers agreed to pay.

11. Sapori (*Studi*, pp. 712 f.) gives several examples from the Peruzzi records. The Alberti and the Medici followed the same policy.

12. *Ibid.*, pp. 755–762; Camerani, *Documenti*, p. 50, No. 115. According to the Statutes of the Calimala guild (1332), art. 66, any one, whether partner or factor, who was sent abroad by a trading company, had to be provided with a general or a special power of attorney (Emiliani-Giudici, *Storia politica*, II, 78).

13. ASF, Archivio notarile antecosimiano, G 620, Protocolli di ser Simone Grazzini da Staggia, 1472–1494, fols. 46–51ᵛ. This is a deed by which Lorenzo and Giuliano de' Medici appoint Giovanni d'Orsino Lanfredini, their partner in Venice, as their attorney and general representative (May 30, 1476).

14. Roscoe, *Life of Lorenzo de' Medici*, p. 425.

15. *I libri di commercio dei Peruzzi* (Milan, 1934), p. 160, ed. Armando Sapori.

16. Sapori, *Studi*, p. 704.

17. This was already pointed out by me in the first edition of this book published under a slightly different title: *The Medici Bank, its Organization, Management, Operations and Decline* (New York, 1948), pp. 6–7. Professor Armando Sapori agreed with these views with regard to the Medici, but rightly pointed out that the companies established by Francesco Datini around 1400 did not yet form a holding company. Sapori, *Studi*, pp. 162, 636–637, 1022–1023, and "The Medici Bank," *Banca Nazionale del Lavoro Quarterly Review*, fasc. No. 11 (October 1949), p. 9.

18. ASF, MAP, filza 94, no. 137, fols. 220–221.

19. *Ibid.*: ". . . vicitare gli altri traffichi i quali di questo uscissono chome paresse loro bisogno."

20. ASF, MAP, filza 153, no. 2, fols. 5ᵛ–6ᵛ.

21. ASF, MAP, filza 153, no. 3, fol. 3.

22. *Damiano Ruffini v. Tommaso Portinari*, Bruges, July 30, 1455. Louis Gilliodts-van Severen, *Cartulaire de l'ancienne estaple de Bruges*, II (Bruges, 1905), 36–37, doc. No. 958.

23. On the continent of Europe, partnerships, like corporations, have a legal personality distinct from the partners, a privilege which they do not enjoy according to English law.

24. The first to insist on this rôle was F. E. de Roover in her article, "Francesco Sassetti and the Downfall of the Medici Banking House," *Bulletin of the Business Historical Society*, 18:65–80 (1943).

25. Provisions to this effect are in all the partnership agreements and there is no doubt that they were carried out.

26. R. de Roover, "Accounting prior to Luca Pacioli," pp. 151 f.

27. Grunzweig, *Correspondance*, pp. 130 f. Cf. Biblioteca Nazionale, Florence, Mss. II, V, 13 (Carte Lanfredini), fol. 167. Ricordo (instructions) given by Giovanni Lanfredini, manager in Venice, to his factor, Giovambattista Ridolfi, going to Florence and carrying with him a copy of the balance sheet.

28. The usual practice was to give the copy drafted by the general manager to the branch manager and to have the latter make a transcript which was kept on file at headquarters.

29. These three contracts are: (1) the agreement of September 1, 1420, between Cosimo and Lorenzo di Giovanni de' Medici and Ilarione di Lippaccio de' Bardi (MAP, filza 153, no. 2, fols. 4–5); (2) the articles of June 8, 1435, between Cosimo and Lorenzo, on the one hand, and Giovanni Benci and Antonio Salutati, on the other hand (two copies extant: MAP, filza 153, no. 3, fol. 2, and filza 94, no. 137, fols. 220–221); (3) the articles of March 25, 1441, sub-

scribed by Cosimo, Benci, and Salutati (two copies extant: MAP, filza 153, no. 3, fol. 50, and filza 94, no. 120, fols. 185–186).

30. The original text is available in Grunzweig, *Correspondance,* pp. 53–63, with a summary in French; also in Gutkind, *Cosimo de' Medici,* pp. 308–312; *idem, Cosimo de' Medici il Vecchio,* pp. 407–413. The English translation will be found in *Medieval Trade in the Mediterranean World,* ed. Lopez and Raymond, pp. 206–211.

31. Perhaps this text should be compared with an earlier contract of 1446 relating to London instead of Bruges, but also involving Pigli. It states in its preamble that it is concluded between Cosimo de' Medici and Giovanni Benci, on the one hand (*d'una parte*), and Gerozzo de' Pigli, on the other hand (*dall'altra parte*). Consequently, the partnership between Cosimo and Benci was party to the contract. Three copies are extant: MAP, filza 153, no. 3, fols. 53ᵛ–54; filza 82, no. 178, fol. 552; filza 94, no. 132, fols. 211–212. See also Lewis Einstein, *The Italian Renaissance in England* (New York, 1902), p. 242.

32. As the Zwyn was silting up and becoming more and more unsafe, the galleys usually anchored in the roadstead of Arnemuiden (Ital. Remua) on the island of Walcheren. Bergen-op-Zoom is a Dutch town, north of Antwerp, on an arm of the Scheldt River. Its fairs, famous in the fifteenth and early sixteenth centuries, declined after 1550. Calais was important because it was the staple town for English wool.

33. An excellent analysis of this contract is given in Einstein, *Italian Renaissance,* pp. 242–245.

34. Clauses forbidding gambling or carnal relations with women are also found in employment contracts of factors (Sapori, *Studi,* p. 762). Whether such clauses were strictly observed is doubtful, according to other evidence.

35. The galleys were considered such a safe mode of transportation that many merchants did not deem it necessary to take out insurance. Frederic C. Lane, *Venetian Ships and Shipbuilders of the Renaissance* (Baltimore, 1934), p. 26.

36. Grunzweig, *Correspondance,* p. xxv.

37. The total capital was 4,000 florins, of which 800 florins were put up by Rosso and Fantino. ASF, MAP, filza 153, no. 2, fols. 8ᵛ–9ᵛ.

38. ASF, MAP, filza 68, no. 402.

39. MAP, filza 94, no. 134, fols. 214–215.

40. A description of Pigli's instructions is given by Einstein, *Italian Renaissance,* pp. 245–249.

41. Many of the bills of exchange drawn on the firm Giovanni Venturi and Riccardo Davanzati by the Venice branch were returned with protest (Camerani, *Documenti,* pp. 64–71). Simone Nori sent one of his factors, Attaviano Altoviti, from Bruges to Barcelona in an effort to get favored treatment in the settlement of the bankruptcy. Raimondo Mannelli to Giovanni Benci, Barcelona, January 31, 1448 (MAP, filza 82, no. 73, fol. 237). With regard to the Avignon branch, also involved in the failure of Venturi and Davanzati, there is a file of correspondence extant (MAP, filza 86, nos. 10 and 29, fols. 110–111, 225–228).

42. In 1451 Raimondo Mannelli became involved in a lawsuit with the Avignon branch before the Mercanzia in Florence (MAP, filza 129, fols. 116–142).

43. The ricordo for Pigli does not give Alessandro's family name, but it was undoubtedly Rinuccini (Camerani, *Documenti,* p. 73, No. 201). Alessandro di Filippo di Cino Rinuccini (1425–1493) left the service of the Medici to become a Dominican friar at San Marco, where he distinguished himself by his piety and religious zeal and served as prior for two years. *Ricordi storici di Filippo*

di Cino Rinuccini dal 1282 at 1460, ed. G. degli Aiazzi (Florence, 1840), p. 138.

44. Grunzweig, *Correspondance,* pp. xxv-xxvii.

45. In a Latin document dated January 21, 1468 (N.S.), Portinari called himself *socius et gubernator societatis egregii domini Petri de Medicis ac sociorum.* This document was published by Adolf Gottlob, "Zwei 'instrumenta cambii' zur Uebermittelung von Ablassgeld (1468)," *Westdeutsche Zeitschrift für Geschichte und Kunst,* 29:208 (1910). An Eng. trans. is available in William E. Lunt, *Papal Revenues in the Middle Ages* (New York, 1934), II, 469–474. The translation sometimes lacks accuracy. Thus *socius et gubernator* should have been "partner and manager" instead of "colleague and governor." *Procuratore* would have been better translated by "proxy" or "attorney" than by "proctor."

46. Gutkind (*Cosimo,* p. 183) states that Cavalcanti was "an expert on French connections" and was selling silk stuffs to the "French" court. This statement is puzzling. The French court was in Paris, not in Bruges. The Burgundian court of Philip the Good and Charles the Bold was "French-speaking." Cf. Gutkind, *Cosimo il Vecchio,* p. 243.

47. ASF, MAP, filza 134, no. 2: Ledger of the Bruges branch, 1441, fols. 227–251.

48. Antonio Tornabuoni was a son of Filippo di Filippo and a first cousin once removed of Giovanni, manager of the Rome branch.

49. Grunzweig (*Correspondance,* p. xxv) confuses this Folco di Adoardo di Giovanni di Adoardo with Folco di Pigello di Folco di Adoardo. The latter, born in 1462, would have been a factor in Bruges at the age of four, an impossibility!

50. Tommaso Portinari to Piero di Cosimo, December 1, 1464 (ASF, MAP, filza 12, no. 379). Referring to the ill-trained youth Portinari states: "il quale non sapeva tenere la penna in mano quando me fu dato."

51. Tommaso Portinari to Piero di Cosimo, February 13, 1467 (N.S.) (MAP, filza 12, no. 312). The text is as follows: ". . . Ma che sia di qualità da potersene aiutare e non averlo a mandare alla schuola."

52. Tommaso Portinari to Lorenzo di Piero, June 9, 1470 (ASF, MAP, filza 4, no. 501).

53. As pointed out before, the Medici always had the right to terminate prematurely an agreement.

54. ASF, MAP, filza 84, no. 24, fols. 51–52.

55. Pagnini, *Della Decima,* II, 304. Lorenzo Tanini mentioned in the chronicle was the son of Lotto di Tanino Bozzi, manager in Venice. This family changed its name from Bozzi to Tanini. Lorenzo was in Bruges as early as 1462 (Camerani, *Documenti,* pp. 112 ff.)

56. The chronicle of Benedetto Dei mentions: (1) Francesco Nasi (2) Francesco Capponi (3) Berto Tieri (4) Pierantonio Bandini-Baroncelli (5) Bartolomeo Nasi (6) Niccolò Capponi (7) Dionigi Nasi (8) Filippo Bucelli with the Pazzi in Bruges.

57. The names of the Milan staff members are given in a balance sheet dated March 24, 1460 (N.S.): ASF, MAP, filza 83, no. 9, fols. 34–42.

58. ASF, MAP, filza 153, no. 3, fol. 17.

59. *Ibid.,* fol. 19.

60. Pagnini, *Della Decima,* II, 305. The Dei chronicle lists the following: (1) Gherardo Canigiani (2) Giovanni d'Angelo de' Bardi (3) Jacopo del Zaccheria (4) Lorenzo Ottavanti.

61. Grunzweig, *Correspondance,* pp. xlv-xlix.

62. ASF, Catasto No. 51 (Leon d'Oro, 1427), fols. 1162–1200.

63. Another example is given by R. de Roover, "Accounting prior to Luca Pacioli," pp 149–150.

64. Zerbi, *Origini,* pp. 125, 130.

65. ASF, Catasto No. 51 (Leon d'Oro, 1427), fol. 1200: "†1427, a dì 27 di luglo. Apresso scriveremo i debitori e creditori di libro segreto di Cosimo e Lorenzo de' Medici e Ilarione de' Bardi di Firenze."

66. The Medici were by no means the first to practice this policy.

67. This is stated clearly in the preamble of the Libro segreto, No. 3: ". . . e tegniallo alla viniziana nell'una faccia il dare e nell'altra l'avere e lle due faccie mettiamo per una charta."

68. Edler, *Glossary,* pp. 130, 274.

69. "E dì 24 di marzo 1447 [1448] posto debi dare in questo c. 61, per resto di quella ragione che tanto ci si truova di *sopracorpo.*"

70. Edler, "Francesco Sassetti," p. 71.

71. ASF, MAP, filza 83, no. 49, fol. 304. In 1471, Sassetti had a deposit of 7,285 fiorini larghi with the Avignon branch. Instead of being in his own name, it was placed in the name of the Monastery of the Celestines. In his libro segreto, he states this clearly: ". . . tenghono *di mio* in disposito in nome del Convento de' Cilestrini." ASF, Carte Strozziane, Series II, No. 20, fol. 39.

72. ASF, Catasto No. 373 (Leon d'Oro, 1430), fol. 745. Cf. Sieveking, *Aus Genueser Rechnungsbüchern,* p. 97.

73. ASF, MAP, filza 134, no. 4, fols 9, 11. Cf. Sieveking, *Handlungsbücher,* p. 37.

74. This meaning is given in a contract concluded on March 12, 1433, between the Medici company of Venice and Jacopa, wife of Malatesta de' Baglioni of Perugia. In this contract, the Medici acknowledge the receipt of a deposit of 2,000 florins to be used in business at their discretion (*ricevuti in deposito a nostra discrezione*). The same document uses the word "discretion" in its second meaning and states that the deposit will be repaid on request after at least one year, together with a suitable "discretion," or return (. . . *e dobiano provederlo della discrezione per tutto il tempo gli avessino tenuti*). ASF, MAP, filza 94, no. 83, fols. 230–231.

75. Edler, *Glossary,* p. 107; Grunzweig, *Correspondance,* p. 131; Sieveking, *Aus Genueser Rechnungsbüchern,* p. 97; R. de Roover, *The Medici Bank,* 1st. ed., p. 71.

76. Raffaele Di Tucci, *Studi sull'economia genovese del secolo decimo secondo; la nave e i contratti marittimi, la banca privata* (Turin, 1933), p. 88; Mario Chiaudano and Raimondo Morozzo della Rocca, eds., *Notai liguri del secolo XII: Oberto Scriba de Mercato, 1190* (Turin, 1938), p. 223, No. 565.

77. Armand Grunzweig, "Le Fonds de la Mercanzia aux Archives d'Etat de Florence au point de vue de l'histoire de Belgique," *Bulletin de l'Institut historique belge de Rome,* 12:92–93 (Brussels, 1932).

78. Grunzweig, *Correspondance,* p. 131; Amintore Fanfani, *Le origini dello spirito capitalistico in Italia* (Milan, 1933), p. 41.

79. *Summa theologica* (Verona, 1740), Part II, cols. 109–110: title 1, cap. vii, §34 and 35.

80. Luke 6: 35 (Douai version). Cf. John T. Noonan, Jr., *The Scholastic Analysis of Usury* (Cambridge, Mass., 1957), pp. 32–33, 104–105.

81. ASF, Catasto No. 51 (Leon d'Oro, 1427), fols. 1191–1194. The balance sheet lists the following cardinals among the depositors of the Medici bank:

Articino della Porta from Novara; Branda da Castiglione, bishop of Piacenza; and Henry Beaufort, bishop of Winchester.

82. Grunzweig, "Mercanzia," p. 93. Cf. Edler, "Restitution Florence," p. 785; G. Lastig, "Beiträge zur Geschichte des Handelsrechts," *Zeitschrift für das gesamte Handelsrecht*, 23:143 ff. (1878).

83. Joseph, Baron Kervyn de Lettenhove, *Lettres et négotiations de Philippe de Commines* (Brussels, 1867), II, 69–70.

84. *Ibid.*, pp. 70–71. Cf. ASF, MAP, filza 96, no. 197.

85. "Le dit appointement est bien mègre pour moi," Commines to Lorenzo, March 5, 1490/91: ASF, MAP, filza 43, no. 45; Kervyn, *Lettres de Commines*, II, p. 72. Cf. von Reumont, *Lorenzo*, II, 336.

86. Kervyn, *Lettres*, II, 83.

87. ASF. MAP, filza 84, no. 45, fol. 95.

88. Kervyn, *Lettres*, II, 147, 248–249, 255–256, 269, 271–273. The last request bears the date of August 25, 1511. Commines died the same year.

89. This is the impression I myself give in the first edition of this book (pp. 56–57), but it does not agree with newly discovered documents.

90. ASF, Carte Strozziane, Series I, filza 10, fol. 288. This is a certificate dated March 9, 1474 (N.S.).

91. ASF, MAP, filza 94, no. 83, fols. 230–231.

92. *Documenti di storia italiana*, ed., Giuseppe Molini. I (Florence, 1836), 13–16.

93. It is impossible to figure out the rate with accuracy because the *écu sans soleil* was worth a little less than the *écu au soleil*.

94. *The Heirs of Tommaso Soderini v. Tommaso Portinari*, September 11, 1487. Gilliodts-van Severen, *Cartulaire de l'estaple*, II, 260, No. 1240.

95. Another example is that of a Medici customer who wanted to place 6,250 ducats on deposit at 8 percent. Since he strongly objected to using the words deposito or discrezione because it was "manifest usury," it was decided to make out the contract in such a way that it provided for the payment of an annuity or *pensione* of 500 ducats with the understanding that the capital was repayable only after three years' notice. Whether or not a contract was usurious thus came to depend to a large extent upon the drafting of the contract. Letter of Paolo di Sandro in Avignon to Lorenzo the Magnificent, January 19, 1489 (ASF, MAP, filza 40, no. 198).

96. Kervyn, *Lettres*, II, 39, 68.

97. ASF, MAP, filza 89, no. 124. ·

98. There were two deposits standing to the credit of Bische: one of £3,000 groat, Flemish currency, and one of £10,000 Artois of 40 groats each, equivalent to £1,666 13s. 4d. groat. Grunzweig (*Correspondance*, p. xxxvi) obtains the wrong total of £13,000 groat by adding large pounds of 240 groats with small pounds of 40 groats. The pound groat was equal to £6 Artois.

99. Lionetto de' Rossi in Lyons to Lorenzo de' Medici, August 11, 1484 (ASF, MAP, filza 39, no. 280); September 30, 1484 (*ibid.*, no. 339); December 8, 1484 (*ibid.*, no. 398). Also letter of Antonio Mellini in Paris to Lionetto de' Rossi in Lyons, March 30, 1485 (MAP, filza 89, no. 147).

100. Sometimes the rate is explicitly stated and sometimes not. "E deono dare ∇ 480 vecchi per providigione d'uno anno di ∇ 6,000 a 8 per cento l'anno." This is a deposit at 8 percent with the Geneva branch. Sassetti received 10 percent from the Milan branch on a deposit of 5,000 large florins: "E deono dare fior. cinquecento larghi per discretione de' detti danari insino a tutto l'anno

1463 d'accordo con loro, posti in questo a c.20 fior. 500." These entries are taken from Sassetti's private account book: ASF, Carte Strozziane, Series II, No. 20, fols. 11, 12.

101. ASF, MAP, filza 134, no. 4, fol. 9. Cf. Sieveking, *Handlungsbücher,* p. 37.

102. Tani in London to Lorenzo de' Medici, May 9, 1468 (MAP, filza 20, no. 391).

103. ASF, Catasto No. 51 (Leon d'Oro, 1427), fols. 1191–1194.

104. *Ibid.,* fols. 1162–1168, 1187–1190.

105. MAP, filza 83, no. 9, fols. 34–42.

106. *Ibid.,* no. 49, fols. 301–306.

CHAPTER VI

Banking and the Money Market at the Time of the Medici

1. Grunzweig, *Correspondance,* p. 55; Lopez and Raymond, *Medieval Trade,* p. 206. The contract of the holding company concluded with Giovanni Benci on June 8, 1435, states that the purpose of the partnership was to exercise well and honorably "the art and craft of exchange" with the funds invested by the partners and those that will be entrusted to them by way of deposit or other honest means (ASF, MAP, filza 153, no. 3, fol. 2 and filza 94, no. 137, fols. 220–221). The emphasis, it should be noted, is on exchange.

2. R. de Roover, *L'Évolution,* p. 19.

3. They could do so because the taking of interest up to 10 percent was allowed by statute after 1571.

4. R. de Roover, "Le Contrat de change depuis la fin du treizième siècle jusqu'au début du dix-septième," *Revue belge de philologie et d'histoire,* 25:119 (1946–1947); *idem, L'Évolution,* pp. 43, 144, 209. This definition is already given by Gaspare Calderini in the fourteenth century: *contractus venditionis certae pecuniae pro alia certa pecunia recipienda alio loco.* Cf. R. de Roover, "New Interpretations," p. 49.

5. Already, in 1896, Ehrenberg had seen this point and stated it very clearly *(Das Zeitalter der Fugger,* I, 52). Nevertheless, his statement made no impression on later historians.

6. *De cambiis* (Frankfort-on-the-Main, 1645), Index (Distantia) and Disp. 1, qu. 11, No. 9. Cf. Lapeyre, *Les Ruiz,* pp. 325–335.

7. De Turri, *De cambiis,* Disp. 1, qu. 11, No. 6: ". . . eius scilicet, qui dat pecunias, eius, qui recipit, eius, cui fit tracta, et eius cui fit remissa." Cf. *ibid.,* Disp. 1, qu. 2, No. 10.

8. This terminology was still in use in the sixteenth century: in Elizabethan documents and early mercantilist pamphlets, the words "taker" and "deliverer" were consistently used in the meaning indicated above. Today prenditore (Fr. *preneur)* designates the beneficiary of a bill, but this meaning was not introduced until the seventeenth century, when the practice of endorsement changed entirely the original features of the cambium contract. Cf. Lapeyre, *Les Ruiz,* p. 276; R. de Roover, *L'Évolution,* p. 117, and his *Money, Banking, and Credit,* pp. 53, 69–70. In the Datini and Medici correspondence, the words datore and prenditore were always used in the meaning indicated above in the text and prenditore was never synonymous with beneficiary.

9. L. F. Salzman, *English Trade in the Middle Ages* (Oxford, 1931), p. 35. To my knowledge, Salzman is the first modern historian who saw this point clearly. He is absolutely right.

10. For information on usance, consult Giovanni di Antonio da Uzzano, *La pratica della mercatura* (Pagnini, *Della Decima*, IV) pp. 100–103; and *El libro di mercatantie et usanze de' paesi*, ed. Franco Borlandi, (Turin, 1936), pp. 169–172 *et passim*.

11. This is correctly stated in *El libro di mercatantie*, pp. 6–7 and in Pegolotti, *La pratica della mercatura*, p. 195. Uzzano (*Pratica*, pp. 100, 102) gives misinformation; the text should be emended to read: "Da Firenze a Vinegia, dì 5 vista la lettera, di là qui dì 20 alla fatta."

12. R. de Roover, "Cambium ad Venetias: Contribution to the History of Foreign Exchange," *Studi in onore di Armando Sapori* (Milan, 1957), pp. 634–635.

13. ASF, Fondo diplomatico mediceo, October 22, 1463. See Camerani, *Documenti*, p. 119, No. 361. The annotation on the rear of the protest reads as follows: "Protesto di ducati 500 facto a Francesco Giorgi e Piero Morosini per lettera di Bartolomio Zorzi e Jeronimo Micheli a sterlini 44 per ducato tornorono e più con soldi 4 di sterlini per costo d'esso, ducati 535, 5 grossi a oro."

14. There were a few exceptions, among them Tommaso de Vio, Cardinal Cajetan (1468–1534) and Fra Santi (Pandolfo) Rucellai (c. 1436–1497). R. de Roover, "Cambium ad Venetias," p. 645, and his "Il trattato," pp. 9, 24–28. For later scholastic writers, see Lapeyre, *Les Ruiz*, pp. 326–335. Ehrenberg was well aware of this fact since he states that interest was stealthily inserted in the exchange rate (*Zeitalter der Fugger*, I, 33).

15. This was first noticed by Salzman (*English Trade*, pp. 34–35) who examined the exchange rates published in the *Calendar of State Papers, Venice*.

16. Bernardo Davanzati, "Notizia dei Cambi," *Scrittori classici italiani di economia politica, parte antica*, II (Milan, 1804), 63.

17. The total of 23,500 is computed by taking 47×500. The amount of 534 ducats is obtained by dividing 44 into 23,500.

18. An example is the ill-fated attempt made in 1400 by the Flemish authorities who, in order to force gold into circulation, decreed that bills of exchange were to be paid one third in gold and two thirds in silver. The result was to tighten the money market and to precipitate a crisis (R. de Roover, *Money, Banking, and Credit*, pp. 78–81).

19. The remark applies to dry exchange, but it does not matter in the least, since the mechanism of the money market is unaffected by the "dryness" of the exchange (R. de Roover, "Cambium ad Venetias," p. 641).

20. Gino Corti, "Consigli sulla mercatura di un anonimo trecentista," *Archivio storico italiano*, 110:119 (1952).

21. The best and most detailed description is in a manual still in manuscript: Biblioteca Nazionale, Florence, Codice Palatino, No. 601, Pt. 3: Zibaldone di notizie utile a' mercatanti (c. 1443).

22. Uzzano, *Pratica*, cap. xlvii, p. 153.

23. Bibl. Naz., Florence, Cod. Palatino, No. 601, Pt. 3, fol. 72^v.

24. The letter itself is dated September 25, 1453 (ASF, MAP, filza 88, no. 111, fols. 118–119). Only the postscript is published by Grunzweig, *Correspondance*, pp. 24–26.

25. Francesco Sassetti & Co. in Lyons to Piero de' Medici & Co. in Florence, May 16, 1468 (ASF, MAP, filza 137, no. 248).

26. Cosimo de' Medici & Co. in Venice to Bernardo Portinari in Bruges, May 20, 1441 (MAP, filza 84, no. 91, fol. 182).

27. Cosimo de' Medici & Co. in Venice to Bernardo Portinari in Bruges,

February 22, 1441 (MAP, filza 98, no. 379), May 20, 1441 (filza 84, no. 91), and June 14, 1441 (filza 88, no. 104).

28. Bernardo Portinari in Bruges to Antonio Salutati in Ferrara, May 23, 1438 (MAP, filza 94, no. 146, fol. 241).

29. MAP, filza 153, no. 2, fol. 78, and no. 3, fols. 70, 74 (1443–1445). Giovanni Benci and Francesco Sassetti & Co. in Geneva to Giovanni and Pierfrancesco de' Medici & Co. in Florence, July 29, 1455 (MAP, filza 138, no. 445).

30. Piero de' Medici, Gerozzo de' Pigli & Co. in London to the tavola of the Medici in Florence, October 25, 1455 (MAP, filza 84, no. 93, fol. 185). There are passing references in other letters.

31. Piero and Giovanni de' Medici & Co. in Rome to the banco of the Medici in Florence, June 6 and 8, 1461 (MAP, filza 138, nos. 438, 439). Cf. Rome branch to Venice branch, May 16, 1455 (MAP, filza 138, no. 106).

32. R. de Roover, *The Medici Bank*, 1st ed., pp. 73–74, 76. The evidence is based on entries in the ledger of the Bruges branch for the year 1441 (MAP, filza 134, no. 2, fol. 250).

33. R. de Roover, *Money, Banking, and Credit*, p. 65.

34. Giovanni Altoviti in Venice to Piero di Cosimo de' Medici & Co. in Milan, November 6 1467 (MAP, filza 16, no. 302).

35. MAP, filza 153, no. 3, fol. 19.

36. It is untrue that "billbroking does not appear before the eighteenth century" (Gutkind, *Cosimo de' Medici*, p. 281). The Italian translator, presumably unable to translate billbroking, even asserts that the dealings in bills of exchange do not antedate the eighteenth century (Gutkind, *Cosimo il Vecchio*, p. 373), which is complete nonsense.

37. Thus in 1386 Jacopo di Ubaldino Ardinghelli sent a bill on Zara to his correspondents in Venice. Teja, *Aspetti della vita economica di Zara*, p. 114.

38. According to the Libro segreto No. 2, 1650 florins di camera were equal to 1740 florins di suggello in 1420 (fol. 36). Cf. Uzzano, *Pratica*, p. 136; MAP, filza 138, nos. 430, 433, 434, 435.

39. Usher, *Early History*, pp. 6–7.

40. Prato, Datini Archives, No. 854 (Bruges-Barcelona correspondence): Giovanni Orlandini and Piero Benizi & Co. in Bruges to Francesco di Marco & Co. Barcelona, September 3, 1400.

41. ASF, MAP, filza 134, no. 3, fols. 42^v–43^r.

42. MAP, filza 104, no. 2 fols. 8–48, and filza 134, no. 3, fols. 42–48.

43. Bruno Kuske, "Die Handelsbeziehungen zwischen Köln und Italien im spätern Mittelalter," *Westdeutsche Zeitschrift für Geschichte und Kunst*, 27:414–415 (1908). Cf. Sieveking, *Handlungsbücher*, pp. 24–25, 41.

44. *Ibid.*, pp. 23–24.

45. In general, any mention of interest is carefully avoided in medieval account books, probably because merchants, according to canon law, could be convicted of usury on the strength of their own books. *Corpus juris canonici*, canon *Ex gravi*, in *Clement.*, V, 5, 1.

46. A detailed technical study on this subject is available: R. de Roover, "Early Accounting Problems of Foreign Exchange," pp. 381–407.

47. Sieveking, *Handlungsbücher*, pp. 34, 41. The text of a Nostro and a Vostro account is available in the first edition of this book, Appendices IV and V, pp. 73–81.

48. The text is available, *ibid.*, Appendix VI, pp. 82–85.

49. This diagram was first published in an article: R. de Roover, "What is Dry Exchange? A Contribution to the Study of English Mercantilism," *The*

Journal of Political Economy, 52:263 (1944). I wish to thank the editor of this journal for giving permission to reproduce this diagram here.

50. The meaning of this phrase is explained and its importance emphasized by Giulio Mandich, *Le Pacte de Ricorsa et le marché italien des changes au XVIIe siècle* (Paris, 1953), pp. 129–131.

51. The recambium amounted to 401 ducats and 6 grossi.

52. The recambium called for repayment of 461 ducats and 19 grossi, so that there was a total profit of 19 ducats and 10 grossi.

53. Dry exchange, still tolerated by Messer Lorenzo Ridolfi, was censured by most of the later theologians, including San Bernardino, San Antonino, and Cardinal Cajetan. The latter condemns dry exchange whether or not bills of exchange are actually issued and sent to a foreign correspondent (Mandich, *Pacte de Ricorsa,* p. 133). The text of *In eam* is published, among others, by Sigismund Scaccia, *De commerciis et cambio* (1st ed., Rome, 1619), §9.

54. Summaries of the protests have been published by Camerani (*Documenti,* pp. 111–121, Nos. 334, 335, 338, 342, 350, 363, 371). The text of one of the bills has been published by R. de Roover (*L'Évolution,* p. 150). It was issued in Milan on February 25, 1462, payable at the Easter Fair, and protested in Geneva on May 14, 1462. The comments of Mandich (*Pacte de Ricorsa,* p. 132) are based on the same text.

55. According to Professor Mandich, the above bill was protested to exonerate the Medici of Geneva of all responsibility in redrawing, since the Milan branch had given them no guarantee of this kind.

56. Fanfani, *Origini,* p. 101; Lattes, *Il diritto commerciale,* p. 189. There are two Milanese statutes dealing with the matter: the earlier statute of April 2, 1439, declared all bills not based on a real exchange transaction to be void and forbade commercial courts to grant remedy on such instruments; the later statute of 1444 allowed the courts to receive the action of creditors who swore that a bill was not fictitious but based on real exchange. *Antiqua ducum Mediolani decreta* (Milan, 1654), pp. 282–283, 308.

57. The balance sheet of the Tavola in Florence for the year 1433 lists several items relating to *cambio senza lettera* or fictitious exchange without bills. ASF, Catasto No. 470 (Leon d'Oro, 1433), fols. 541–545.

58. R. de Roover, "Cambium ad Venetias," p. 634.

59. ASF, Provvisioni, No. 126, fols. 313^v–314: Law of November 19, 1435.

60. ASF, MAP, filza 138, no. 324.

61. Floris Prims, "Heer Anselmus Fabri, onze tiende deken (1415–1449)," *Antwerpiensia 1937; Losse Bijdragen tot de Antwerpsche Geschiedenis* (Antwerp, 1938), pp. 19–26; Dom Ursmer Berlière, *Inventaire analytique des Diversa Cameralia* (Rome, 1906), pp. 52, 72, 90, Nos. 222, 318, 400.

62. ASF, MAP, filza 134, no. 2, fol. 245.

63. Bensa, *Francesco di Marco,* pp. 323, 326, Nos. 16, 20. The letter of credit is a neglected subject and the only study available is that of Rufus James Trimble, "The Law Merchant and the Letter of Credit," *Harvard Law Review,* 61:981–1008 (1948).

64. ASF, MAP, filza 134, no. 3: Ricordanze e lettere di cambio, fol. 33^v.

65. Federigo Melis, "Di alcune girate cambiarie dell'inizio del Cinquecento rinvenute a Firenze," *Moneta e Credito,* fasc. No. 21 (Rome, 1953), pp. 1–27.

66. *Idem,* "Una girata cambiaria del 1410 nell'Archivio Datini di Prato," *Economia e Storia,* 5:412–421 (1958).

67. Teja, *Aspetti della vita economica di Zara,* pp. 68, 75–77, 113–115.

68. Henri Lapeyre, "Une Lettre de change endossée en 1430," *Annales*

(*Economies, Sociétés, Civilisations*), 13:260–264 (1958). Cf. Sieveking, *Aus Genueser Steuerbüchern,* pp. 99–100.

69. ASF, Notarile antecosimiano, S. 636 (ser Silvano Frosini, atti 1437–1439), fols. 87ᵛ–88ᵛ. In English the text is as follows:

In the name of God, on the 5th of May, 1438. Pay by this first of exchange, sixty days from date, to Cosimo and Lorenzo de' Medici & Co. three hundred florins, that is 300 florins, for the value at 14s. 9d. [per florin received] from Filippo Borromei & Co. and charge this to your account. May Christ protect you.
Francesco Tosinghi and Vanni Rucellai & Co.
in Barcelona

In two different hands:
Accepted on the 6th of June 1438.
We, Cosimo and Lorenzo de' Medici & Co., order you, at maturity, to pay for us to Adoardo Giachinotti & Co.
On the back:
Pierantonio e Jacopo Pierozzi & Co. in Florence.
First

70. Giovanni Cassandro, "Vicende storiche della lettera di cambio," *Bollettino dell'Archivio storico del Banco di Napoli,* fasc. 9–12 (Naples, 1955–1956), pp. 47–52.

71. The text of this assignment is as follows: I, Bernardino de Carnago, am satisfied [in receiving payment] for the said bill of exchange in the Tornabuoni bank. (*Io, Bernardino de Carnago, sono contento del dicto cambio per lo bancho de Tornabuoni*).

72. Alfonso Silvestri, "Sull'attività bancaria napoletana durante il periodo aragonese," *Bollettino dell' Archivio storico del Banco di Napoli,* fasc. 6 (Naples, 1953), p. 112.

73. R. de Roover, Banking in Bruges, pp. 334–335; *idem, L'Évolution,* pp. 85–86.

74. The junior partner and local manager, Bernardo di Francesco Carnesecchi, owned only a minor part of the capital: 500 ducats out of 9,500 ducats. This partnership agreement of 1490 is extant: ASF, MAP, filza 89, no. 189.

75. This statement is based on the author's acquaintance with collections of bills of exchange in Antwerp and Italian archives.

76. R. de Roover, "The Origin of Endorsement," *South African Bankers' Journal,* 52:156–162, 205–212, 257–266 (1955). For an example of a bill with five endorsements, see the photograph opposite p. 209.

77. Usher, *Early Deposit Banking,* pp. 94–109; R. de Roover, *L'Évolution,* p. 83–118; J. Milnes Holden, *The History of Negotiable Instruments in English Law* (London: 1955), pp. 4–65.

78. Usher, *Early Deposit Banking,* p. 89; R. de Roover, *L'Évolution,* pp. 92–93.

79. Pigello Portinari in Milan to Piero di Cosimo de' Medici in Florence, June 29, 1467: MAP, filza 17, no. 569. According to this letter, the debt of the Duke of Milan and his mother, Bianca Maria Visconti, amounted to 115,000 ducats secured by assignments on diverse taxes. In addition, there was a loan of 64,000 ducats secured by jewels, which the Medici were trying to sell.

CHAPTER VII

The Medici As Merchants and As Dealers in Alum and Iron

1. Gras, *Business and Capitalism*, p. 122.

2. Such temporary partnerships were usually based on informal agreements and limited to a single lot, which the partners bought in common. They traded publicly under their own names, so that the persons with whom they dealt were not aware of the existence of any agreement to share risks and profits. After conclusion of the venture, the partners settled accounts and the partnership was dissolved. *Ibid.*, p. 165.

3. MAP, filza 134, no. 2, fol. 250. The value was £50 16s. 4d. di grossi or 508 ducats and 4 grossi, Venetian currency, worth in Bruges £110 2s. groat, Flemish currency, at 52 groats per ducat.

4. Tommaso Portinari to Piero di Cosimo de' Medici, February 13, 1467 (MAP, filza 12, no. 312). Cf. Grunzweig, *Correspondance*, p. 11.

5. John Addington Symonds, *Renaissance in Italy* (Mod. Lib. ed.), I, 393.

6. Sieveking, *Handlungsbücher*, p. 28. This is doubtless the complete copy of Pliny mentioned by Vespasiano da Bisticci in his life of Niccolò de' Niccoli (*The Vespasiano Memoirs*, p. 397).

7. Pigello Portinari to Giovanni di Cosimo de' Medici, April 9, 1456 (MAP, filza 9, no. 203).

8. Grunzweig, *Correspondance*, pp. 28, 40, 42, 82.

9. *Ibid.*, pp. 79–80.

10. The Bruges branch also bought tapestries already woven. Thus they purchased a set representing the Story of Samson for Astorre Manfredi, lord of Faenza. It was not of the best design, but the customer presumably did not want to spend more. *Ibid.*, pp. 27–28.

11. *Ibid.*, pp. 40, 42, 82, 99.

12. *Ibid.*, pp. 27–28, 40, 82. In 1460, a fardel containing tapestries for Giovanni di Cosimo was stolen from the Florentine galleys in the port of London (*ibid.*, pp. 100–101).

13. Sieveking, *Handlungsbücher*, p. 43.

14. *Correspondance*, pp. 11–13, 63–64, 78, 82–83. See also Tommaso Portinari to Pierfrancesco de' Medici, December 17, 1464 (MAP, filza 12, no. 370).

15. Tommaso Portinari to Piero di Cosimo de' Medici, January 11, 1466 (MAP, filza 12, no. 306).

16. Tommaso Portinari to Piero, July 14, 1464 (MAP, filza 73, no. 315).

17. Francesco Sassetti to Giovanni di Cosimo, January 29 and May 16, 1450 (ASF, Carte Strozziane, Series I. 3, fols. 57, 60).

18. MAP, filza 134, no. 2, fol. 246. See 1st edition of this book, Appendix VIII, pp. 87–90.

19. The Flemish sterling, not to be confused with the English penny, was equal to 8 mites or one third of a Flemish groat. On bills of exchange, the rate of consular fees was 2 mites per pound groat or approximately one third per mille. In 1461, these rates were increased to one-half groat per pound on merchandise and 3 mites or one eighth groat per pound on bills of exchange. In 1498, they were doubled and raised to one groat and one fourth groat respectively, an indication that the volume of business of the Florentines was steadily shrinking. Armand Grunzweig, "Le Fonds du Consulat de la Mer aux Archives d'Etat à Florence," *Bulletin de l'Institut historique belge de Rome*, 10: pp. 111–112, 120 (1930).

20. Nicolas de Drijl or van Drijl also had dealings with the Medici in connection with pontifical indulgences. F. Remy, *Les Grandes Indulgences pontificales aux Pays-Bas à la fin du Moyen Age, 1300–1531,* diss. (Louvain, 1928), p. 65.

21. Borlandi, ed., *El libro di mercatantie,* p. 126. The price was sometimes set in Flemish sterlings equal to one-third groat, so that a price of £10 10s. sterling corresponded to £3 10s. groat.

22. MAP, filza 134, no. 2, fol. 242.

23. J. van Houtte, "Bruges et Anvers, marchés 'nationaux' ou 'internationaux,' du XIVe au XVIe siècle," *Revue du Nord,* 34:89–108 (1952).

24. F. C. Lane, "Venture Accounting in Medieval Business Management," *Bulletin of the Business Historical Society,* 19:164–173 (1945).

25. Guglielmo Querini (c. 1400–1468), a Venetian merchant, lost the major part of his capital because he was either ill-advised or unlucky in selecting his commission agents. He sometimes sold bills of exchange to the Medici Bank. G. Luzzatto, "L'attività di un patrizio veneziano del Quattrocento," *Studi di storia economica veneziana* (Padua, 1954), pp. 167–193. Andrea Barbarigo (c. 1399–1449), another Venetian, was more fortunate, but he too had his share of troubles with an agent in Syria named Dolceto who gave him unsatisfactory service and cheated his principal on prices. F. C. Lane, *Andrea Barbarigo, Merchant of Venice, 1418–1449* (Baltimore, 1944), pp. 109–113.

26. Pigello Portinari in Milan to Cosimo de' Medici, March 18, 1458 (MAP, filza 12, no. 251).

27. Cosimo de' Medici & Co. in Venice to Bernardo Portinari in Bruges, October 16, 1441 (MAP, filza 88, no. 95).

28. Accerrito Portinari in Florence to Lorenzo and Giuliano de' Medici & Co. in Milan, March 11, 1475 (MAP, filza 138, no. 336).

29. Piero de' Medici and Gerozzo de' Pigli & Co. in London to the Medici company in Florence, October 8, 1455 (MAP, filza 84, no. 93, fols. 184–185). This letter is not in Grunzweig, *Correspondance.*

30. Tommaso Portinari in Bruges to Giovanni Altoviti, manager in Venice, October 8, 1466 and July 10, 1467 (MAP, filza 10, nos. 582 and 583).

31. Angelo Tani in London to Lorenzo the Magnificent in Florence, January 12, 1468 (MAP, filza 23, no. 102). Some of the wool apparently belonged to the Medici and some to Sir John Crosby, one of the leading wool merchants and a member of the Staple of Calais. In 1467, he was granted a license to ship wool by the "Straits of Marrock." Tani's letter undoubtedly refers to wool exported under this license. Eileen Power, "The Wool Trade in the Fifteenth Century," *Studies in English Trade in the Fifteenth Century,* ed. Eileen Power and M. M. Postan (New York, 1933), pp. 47, 366 n.39.

32. The Rome branch had to pay for the alum as soon as it was taken from the warehouse in Civitavecchia and to credit the papal treasury as soon as collections were made in England or Flanders. After 1470, the pope was forced to accept part payment in Flemish and English cloths and other goods.

33. Grunzweig, "Consulat de la Mer," p. 95.

34. *Ibid.,* p. 96.

35. *Ibid.,* pp. 99–100.

36. For further evidence about the exportation of feathers (*piume*), see F. E. de Roover, "Le Voyage de Girolamo Strozzi de Pise à Bruges et retour à bord de la galère bourguignonne 'San Giorgio'," *Handelingen van het Genootschap "Société d'Emulation" te Brugge,* 91:124 (1954).

37. *Hanserecesse (1431–1476)*, Zweite Abteilung, ed. Goswin, Baron von der Ropp, VII (Leipzig, 1892), 115, No. 41.

38. L. Gilliodts-van Severen, *Inventaire des archives de la ville de Bruges*, VI (Bruges, 1876), 410–417, doc. No. 1262 (August 5, 1496).

39. One of the altarpieces was Memling's "Last Judgment" commissioned by Angelo Tani. The presence of goose feathers for beds may seem puzzling, but there is no mistake. This commodity came from the Baltic. Also Girolamo Strozzi bought feathers in Bruges.

40. After several interruptions, the Consuls of the Sea decided in 1480 to abandon the galley voyages for four years; they were never resumed. Alwyn A. Ruddock, *Italian Merchants and Shipping in Southampton, 1270–1600* (Southampton, 1951), p. 211.

41. Tommaso Portinari in Bruges to Piero di Cosimo de' Medici in Florence, June 8, 1464 (MAP, filza 12, no. 383).

42. Ruddock, *Italian Shipping in Southampton*, pp. 214–215.

43. Small parcels of furs and goose feathers from Prussia were perhaps the only exception, but this trade was of little importance. For a fuller discussion of the balance of trade between Flanders and Italy, see R. de Roover, "La Balance commerciale entre les Pays-Bas et l'Italie au quinzième siècle," *Revue belge de philologie et d'histoire*, 37:374–386 (1959).

44. MAP, filza 148, no. 13: policies dated April 29, 1444 and January 20, 1445 (N.S.)

45. MAP, filza 84, no. 83, fol. 165. This contract was published by Livio Piattoli, "Il contratto di assicurazione marittima a Venezia nel medio evo," *Rivista di storia del diritto italiano*, 8:327 337 (1935). Piattoli misread pounds groat, lire di grossi, as fiorini di grossi. This contract was republished with the same error in *L'assicurazione a Venezia dalle origini alla fine della Serenissima* ed. Giuseppe Stefani (Trieste, 1956), I, 221–222.

46. MAP, filza 84, no. 72, fol. 140. This policy also was published by Piattoli and republished by Stefani, I, 222–223. In the English edition, *Insurance in Venice from the Origins to the End of the Serenissima* (Trieste, 1958), the text of the two policies is found on pp. 230–232.

47. On the rates of marine insurance premiums in the fifteenth century, one should consult F. E. de Roover, "Early Examples of Marine Insurance," *The Journal of Economic History*, 5:192–193 (1945). The first known examples of undisguised premium insurance date from 1350 and are found in Palermo notarial records. Riniero Zeno, *Documenti per la storia del diritto marittimo nei secoli XIII e XIV* (Turin, 1936), 229–231, 242–243, Nos. 190, 192, and 202.

48. Camerani, *Documenti*, pp. 13, 122–123, 125–126, Nos. 374, 383; MAP, filza 97, no. 7, fols. 7–11.

49. In my opinion, Canigiani was entitled to keep the premium because there was clearly an attempt to defraud. Frauds were common in the insurance field until the organization of Lloyd's put a stop to dishonest practices.

50. Charles Verlinden, *L'Esclavage dans l'Europe médiévale* (Bruges, 1955), I, 748–833. The second volume has not yet appeared.

51. G. Aiazzi publishes excerpts from the diary (ricordi) of Cino di Filippo Rinuccini in his introduction to the diary of Cino's father, *Ricordi storici di Filippo di Cino Rinuccini dal 1282 al 1460* (Florence, 1840), p. 252.

52. MAP, filza 82, no. 182, fol. 595 (catasto of 1457, Leon d'Oro). Florentine slavery was domestic and most of the slaves were women used in lieu of maids.

53. Charles Singer, *The Earliest Chemical Industry: An Essay in the Histori-*

cal Relations of Economics and Technology Illustrated from the Alum Trade (London, 1948), p. 90 *et passim;* Wilhelm Heyd, *Histoire du commerce du Levant* (2d printing, Leipzig, 1923), II, 565–571; Pegolotti, *Pratica,* pp. 43, 293, 367–370, 411; R. S. Lopez, *Genova marinara nel Duecento: Benedetto Zaccaria, ammiraglio e mercante* (Milan, 1933), pp. 276–80.

54. Save for a short interruption from 1340 to 1346 when the mines were reoccupied by the Greeks. Heyd, *Commerce du Levant,* I, 489, 493; Maria Louise Heers, "Les Génois et le commerce de l'alun à la fin du moyen âge," *Revue d'histoire économique et sociale,* 32:31 (1954).

55. Heyd, *Commerce du Levant,* II, 565.

56. The alum from Ischia was of such poor quality that its use was forbidden in Bruges and Paris by the gild statutes. G. de Poerck, *La Draperie médiévale en Flandre et en Artois, technique et terminologie* (Bruges, 1951), I, 170.

57. Already Benedetto Zaccaria (d. 1307), the first Genoese owner or lessee of the alum mines of Phocea, had set up a monopoly to prevent overproduction and to maintain prices. Lopez, *Zaccaria,* pp. 26–27, 33–38.

58. R. S. Lopez, *Storia delle colonie genovesi nel Mediterraneo* (Bologna, 1938), pp. 414–415.

59. Adolf Gottlob, *Aus der Camera apostolica des 15. Jahrhunderts* (Innsbruck, 1889), pp. 279–280. Giovanni da Castro was a godson of Pius II and the son of Paolo da Castro (d. 1441), a famous civilian who taught law at the University of Padua. The father had been a friend of the humanist Aeneas Silvius Piccolomini long before his elevation to the papacy. In 1460, the son, Giovanni da Castro, being harassed by creditors, was living in Rome under his godfather's special protection and took advantage of his leisure to indulge in his hobby, prospecting for minerals. *The Commentaries of Pius II,* trans. by Florence Alden Gragg, ed. by Leona C. Gabel, Smith College Studies in History, 35:505–507 (1951).

60. Giuseppe Zippel, "L'allume di Tolfa e il suo commercio," *Archivio della R. Società Romana di Storia Patria,* 30:21, 437–438 (1907), Appendix No. 1. Zippel publishes the full text of the bull ratifying the contract.

61. Gottlob, *Camera apostolica,* pp. 283–285. The text of this second contract is published in full by Zippel, "L'allume di Tolfa," pp. 438–444 (Appendix No. 3).

62. Gottlob, *Camera apostolica,* pp. 285–286. A summary is given by Zippel, "L'allume di Tolfa," p. 405.

63. This royalty was reduced later, on December 27, 1474, from two ducats to one ducat, a sure indication that the Pope had not been entirely successful in setting up a monopoly (Gottlob, *Camera apostolica,* p. 288).

64. This assertion is made by Niccola Della Tuccia, "Cronache di Viterbo e di altre città" in *Cronache e statuti della Città di Viterbo,* ed. Ignazio Ciampi (Florence, 1872), p. 268. Cf. E. Fiumi, *L'Impresa di Lorenzo de' Medici contro Volterra, 1472* (Florence, 1948), p. 27.

65. In 1471, output was about 70,000 *cantara* or approximately 3,500 metric tons, the cantaro weighing about 50 kilos. It is improbable that 8,000 workers would be needed to extract and to process 3,500 tons of alum, less than half a ton per worker in a year.

66. This figure of 8000 is questioned by Zippel, ("L'allume di Tolfa," p. 20) but accepted by Singer (*Chemical Industry,* p. 143).

67. Gottlob, *Camera apostolica,* p. 289.

68. These payments were usually made by the Medici company in Venice to representatives of King Mathias Corvinus (*reg.* 1458–1490).

69. *Corpus juris canonici: in X,* canons *Ita quorumdam* and *Ad liberandam,* V, 6, 6 and 17; *Extravag. comm.,* canon *Multa mentis,* V, 2, 1. These canons were confirmed by decrees not included in the canon law, among others, by the bull *Adaperiat Dominus* issued by Gregory X on March 11, 1272 (*Bullarium Romanum,* IV Turin, 1859, 11–13) and the bull *Olim tam* issued by Nicholas V on August 23, 1449 (*In VII,* V, 2, 1).

70. The date of this decretal is April 11, 1465. Gottlob, *Camera apostolica,* p. 295.

71. Jakob Strieder, *Studien zur Geschichte kapitalistischer Organisationsformen* (Munich, 1925), pp. 168–183; Roman Piotrowski *Cartels and Trusts* (London, 1933), pp. 153–164. Piotrowski rejects Strieder's thesis (pp. 69–70) that the alum cartel was a fiscal rather than a private cartel. The text of the cartel agreement was published by Augustin Theiner, *Codex diplomaticus dominii temporalis S. Sedis,* III (Rome, 1862), 463–467, No. 398.

72. Strieder, *Studien,* p. 173.

73. Fanfani, *Le origini,* pp. 109–10, 123. This is the doctrine of San Bernardino di Siena, San Antonino of Florence, and Tommaso de Vio, better known as Cardinal Cajetan. Cf. R. de Roover, "Monopoly Theory prior to Adam Smith," *Quarterly Journal of Economics,* 65:498–499.

74. *Corpus juris canonici, Decretum Gratiani:* c. *Quicumque tempore messis,* Causa XIV, qu. 4, can. 9.

75. Zippel, "L'allume di Tolfa," pp. 36–38. This author is of the opinion that the contract was revised on a more equitable basis as a result of improved relations between the papacy and the kingdom of Naples after the accession of Sixtus IV.

76. Fiumi, *L'impresa contro Volterra,* pp. 33–37.

77. *Ibid.,* pp. 37–43.

78. The story is told in great detail in Fiumi's book. A different interpretation is given in Roberto Palmarocchi, *Lorenzo de' Medici* (Turin, 1941), pp. 58–63. This author tries to exonerate Lorenzo from all responsibility for the sack of Volterra. According to the rules of war then prevailing, the mercenary troops had the right to sack any city or town taken by assault after a siege. This was not exactly the case of Volterra, but Montefeltro did not succeed in keeping under control his soldiery embittered by a long siege and deprived by the terms of the surrender from their right to the spoils. On the rules of war regulating the matter, see Fritz Redlich, "De praeda militari, Looting and Booty, 1500–1815," *Vierteljahrschrift für Sozial- und Wirtschaftsgeschichte,* Beiheft No. 39 (Wiesbaden, 1956), p. 23.

79. Fiumi, *L'impresa di Volterra,* pp. 162–67; Zippel, *L'allume di Tolfa,"* p. 409; Doren, *Wollentuchindustrie,* p. 375.

80. Alum was used in the making of Venetian glass.

81. Heyd, *Commerce du Levant,* II, 328.

82. Six thousand *cantara* corresponds to about 300 metric tons.

83. Zippel, "L'allume di Tolfa," pp. 46–47.

84. Gottlob, *Camera apostolica,* p. 297.

85. *Ibid.,* p. 300.

86. *Ibid.,* pp. 297–298; Zippel, "L'allume di Tolfa," pp. 396–397.

87. Jacques Paquet, "Une Ébauche de la nonciature de Flandre au XVᵉ siècle: les missions dans les Pays-Bas de Luc de Tolentis, évêque de Sebenico (1462–1484)," *Bulletin de l'Institut historique belge de Rome,* 25:27–144 (1949).

88. Zippel, "L'allume di Tolfa," p. 390. The text of this treaty is available in Theiner, *Codex diplomaticus,* III, 451–455, No. 391, and in Berlière, *Diversa*

440 NOTES TO CHAPTER VII

Cameralia, pp. 235–243, annex No. 40. A subsequent ordonnance of Charles the Bold (June 24, 1468) forbade not only the importation of any other than papal alum but even the use of any substitute (Berlière, pp. 243–246, No. 41).

89. The carica was 400 lbs., Flemish weight, and corresponded to about 180 kilos. It was consequently three and a half times as heavy as the cantaro of 150 Roman lbs or about 50 kilos.

90. Zippel, "L'allume di Tolfa," pp. 393–394.

91. Léone Liagre, "Le commerce de l'alun en Flandre au Moyen Age," *Le Moyen Age,* 61:202–203 (1955).

92. See the report of the papal nuntius, Luke de Tolentis, written on July 3, 1473. Paquet, "Les Missions de Luc de Tolentis," p. 107, No. 13.

93. *Ibid.,* pp. 43, 113.

94. Report of the nuntius, de Tolentis, on June 29, 1472 (*ibid.,* p. 87, No. 8).

95. Gilliodts, *Cartulaire de l'estaple,* II, 164, No. 1108

96. W. S. Unger, "Rekening van den Invoer van Aluin in de Schelde Delta, 1473–1475," *Economisch-Historisch Jaarboek,* 19:75–88 (1935).

97. Gottlob, *Camera apostolica,* p. 111.

98. Tommaso Portinari to Cosimo de' Medici, February 15, 1464 (Grunzweig, *Correspondance,* pp. 106–107).

99. Tommaso Portinari and Angelo Tani to Cosimo, March 28, 1464 (*ibid.,* pp. 107–108, 111–112). Cf. Singer, *Chemical Industry,* p. 149.

100. Tommaso Portinari to Cosimo, April 29, 1464: Grunzweig, *Correspondance,* pp. 109, 118–119.

101. Letter of May 14, 1464 (*ibid.,* pp. 129, 132).

102. Gottlob, *Camera apostolica,* p. 287.

103. The report was started in Antwerp on June 8, 1464, and completed in Bruges on June 17 (MAP, filza 12, no. 383).

104. Three ducats per cantaro in Italy corresponded to about ten and a half ducats per carica in Bruges, since one carica was about 3½ cantara. The selling price being £4 groat or about 16 ducats, there was a gross margin of 50 percent, which was ample to cover transportation charges from Italy to Flanders and leave a generous net profit.

105. Tommaso Portinari to Piero de' Medici, July 1 and 14, 1464 (MAP, filza 73, no. 315.

106. Portinari to Piero, November 3, 9, and 10, 1464 (MAP, filza 12, no. 375).

107. Portinari to Piero, November 27, 1464 (MAP, filza 12, nos. 374, 379).

108. Portinari to Piero, December 18 and 26, 1464 (Map, filza 12, nos. 378, 381, 395).

109. Giovanni Tornabuoni to Piero de' Medici, January 31, 1465 (MAP, filza 14, no. 78).

110. Tornabuoni to Piero, February 16, 1465 (MAP, filza 17, no. 400).

111. Tornabuoni to Piero, April 23 and May 10, 1465 (MAP, filza 17, no. 444 and filza 16, no. 180). Cf. Gottlob, *Camera apostolica,* p. 287.

112. Tommaso Portinari to Piero de' Medici, May 3, 1465 (MAP, filza 12, no. 321).

113. Letter by the same of November 11, 1465 (MAP, filza 12, no. 371).

114. Letter of January 11, 1466 (MAP, filza 12, no. 306).

115. Letter of March 4, 1466 (MAP, filza 12, no. 314).

116. Giovanni Tornabuoni to Piero de' Medici, April 2, 1466 (MAP, filza 16, no. 355). Cf. Gottlob, *Camera apostolica,* p. 285; Zippel, "L'allume di Tolfa," pp. 404–405. The contract was signed in the presence of the young Lorenzo: "Lorenzo fu in Camera Apostolica e accepto in vostro nome."

117. ASF, MAP, filza 84, no. 27, fol. 56.

118. Yearly payments were consequently 15,000 ducats.

119. Giovanni Tornabuoni to Lorenzo the Magnificent, February 23, 1471 (MAP, filza 22, no. 234). Zaccherelli was master of the household of the Greek Cardinal John Bessarion, archbishop of Nicaea.

120. Giovanni Tornabuoni to Lorenzo the Magnificent, June 26, 1473 (MAP, filza 61, no. 156).

121. Gottlob, *Camera apostolica,* p. 288.

122. G. Tornabuoni to Lorenzo the Magnificent, March 18, 1475 (MAP, filza 21, no. 535).

123. Lorenzo the Magnificent to Tommaso Portinari, July 21, 1473 (Map, filza 84, no. 32, fol. 66).

124. G. Tornabuoni to Lorenzo the M., July 1, 1475 (MAP, filza 32, no. 381).

125. Tornabuoni to Lorenzo, October 23, 1477 (MAP, filza 26, no. 192).

126. Gottlob, *Camera apostolica,* p. 111.

127. Gino Barbieri, *Industria e politica mineraria nello Stato pontifico dal '400 al '600* (Rome, 1940), p. 24.

128. Berlière, *Diversa Cameralia,* pp. 260–261, Annex No. 46.

129. The stocks of alum in possession of the Medici were confiscated by Sixtus IV on January 25, 1479, according to Goswin, Baron von der Ropp, "Zur Geschichte des Alaunhandels im 15. Jahrhundert," *Hansische Geschichtsblätter,* 1900, p. 129.

130. Zippel, "L'allume di Tolfa," p. 415.

131. Jacques Heers, *Gênes au XVᵉ siècle, activité économique et problèmes sociaux* (Paris, 1961), p. 220.

132. Camerani, *Documenti,* p. 133, No. 411.

133. There is on this subject a study by Prince Piero Ginori Conti, *Le magone della vena del ferro di Pisa e di Pietrasanta sotto la gestione di Piero de' Medici e Comp., 1489–1492* (Florence, 1939), 110 pp. The author unfortunately did not know how to extract useful information from account books.

134. *Ibid.,* p. 94.

135. Gras, *Business and Capitalism,* p. 123, remarks that this development should be made the object of further study.

Chapter VIII

The Medici As Industrial Entrepreneurs

1. ASF, MAP, filza 153, no. 1, fols. 11, 34, 40. This partnership began on April 1, 1402. The Medici's bank's share in the capital was 3,000 florins, of which 2,250 belonged to Giovanni di Bicci and 750 to Lippaccio de' Bardi. Whether Michele di Baldo invested any money is not made clear by the records, but he probably put up the sum of 1,000 florins, since profits were to be divided equally.

2. *Ibid.,* fol. 65. This partnership with Taddeo started on March 25, 1408, with a capital of 4,000 florins supplied entirely by the Medici Bank, as explained above in Chap. III.

3. ASF, Catasto No. 497 (Gonf. Leon d'Oro, 1433), Campione, fol. 192, where it is stated that the officials of the Catasto dealt with Andrea and no longer with Giuntino.

4. Two copies of the contract of 1439 are still extant: MAP, filza 153, no. 3, fol. 9 and filza 94, no. 138, fols. 222 f. See Chap. IV, n. 42.

5. This woolshop is still mentioned in the catasto report of 1458 (Chap. IV, n. 89) but is no longer mentioned in the one made out by Piero in 1469 (Catasto No. 924, fol. 310ᵛ).

6. ASF, Catasto No. 1015 (Leon d'Oro, 1481), fol. 204.

7. ASF, Carte Strozziane, Series I, No. 10, fols. 186ᵛ–187ʳ.

8. ASF, MAP, filza 153, no. 3, fols. 24, 27. The Medici Bank was entitled to two thirds of the profits, but no information on the amount of capital is available.

9. The profits were to be divided as follows: three fifths to the Medici Bank, seven twenty-fifths to Francesco Berlinghieri, and three twenty-fifths to Jacopo Tanaglia.

10. Two copies of this contract of 1444 are still extant: MAP (1) filza 153, no. 3, fol. 52ᵛ and (2) filza 94, no. 122, fols. 188–189.

11. Consequently, Berlinghieri Berlinghieri's share in the capital was reduced from 1,900 florins to 1,800 florins and in the profits from one-third to one-fourth. The share of the Medici Bank, both in the capital and in the earnings, remained unchanged. A copy of this contract concluded on March 25, 1447, is extant: MAP, filza 94, no. 135, fols. 216–217.

12. ASF, Catasto No. 924 (Leon d'Oro), fol. 310ᵛ.

13. Camerani, *Documenti*, p. 134.

14. Giuseppe Mecatti, *Storia cronologica della città di Firenze* (Naples, 1755), P. II, p. 417, No. 920.

15. January 11, 1480 (MAP, filza 37, no. 12).

16. MAP. filza 129, fols. 80–97.

17. More details about this silkshop are given in the last pages of this chapter.

18. ASF, Carte Strozziane, Series I, No. 10, fol. 186ʳ.

19. Libro reale segnato E (1415–1425). Arezzo, Archivio della Fraternità dei Laici, filza 7, reg. 55, fols. 27, 67, 114.

20. *Ibid.*, fols 91, 118. Cf. R. de Roover, "Cambium ad Venetias," p. 648.

21. MAP, filza 153, no. 1, fols. 109, 110. The loss, according to the books, was £2,517 19s. 5d. aff., which corresponds to 1,736 florins 15s. 5d. aff. There is some doubt whether this figure refers to two or four years, because the entries on folios 109 and 110 give two different dates, 1418 and 1416.

22. MAP, filza 153, no. 1, fols. 124, 125.

23. MAP, filza 153, no. 3, fols. 9, 52ᵛ and filza 94, nos. 122, 131, 135, and 138.

24. MAP, filza 89, no. 71 and filza 94, nos. 122, 135.

25. Edler, *Glossary*, p. 411 and Doren, *Wollentuchindustrie*, pp. 220–221. The latter exaggerates when speaking of large workshops in which the woolsorters, combers, and carders toiled like slaves.

26. Doren's *Wollentuchindustrie* is supplemented by the appendices of F. Edler's *Glossary*, pp. 335–426; F. Melis, "La formazione dei costi nell'industria laniera alla fine del Trecento," *Economia e Storia*, 1:31–60, 150–190; (1954); and R. de Roover, "A Florentine Firm of Cloth Manufacturers," *Speculum*, 16:1–33 (1941).

27. Georg von Below, rev. of Doren's *Wollentuchindustrie* in *Jahrbücher für Nationalökonomie und Statistik*, 79:703 (1902). Von Below complains because Doren fails to give precise information about the size of a typical firm. Perhaps his sources did not enable him to answer this question.

28. *Wollentuchindustrie*, pp. 249–254, 262–263, 290. Of course, the gild went too far by having filchers excommunicated; but perhaps it was the only effective way of preventing this practice.

29. *Ibid.*, pp. 25, 34, 202, 249, 327, 400, 447, *et passim*, and *Zunftwesen*, pp.

505, 560, and 721.

30. Gertrud Hermes, "Der Kapitalismus in der Florentiner Wollenindustrie," *Zeitschrift für die gesamte Staatswissenschaft*, 72:367–400. (1917). This article contains pertinent criticism and has not received the attention which it deserves. The arguments presented by Dr. Hermes were rather curtly dismissed by R. Davidsohn, "Blüte und Niedergang der Florentiner Tuchindustrie," *Zeitschrift für die gesamte Staatswissenschaft*, 85:225–255 (1928). His attempted refutation, however, is weak and unconvincing and to a large extent beside the point.

31. Doren (*Wollentuchindustrie*, p. 216) asserts the contrary: "Die Medici — deren Reichtum ursprünglich aus ihren Bankgeschäften erwachsen war — haben später ein fast gleich grosses Kapital im Tuchgeschäft" (the Medici, whose wealth originated in the banking business, later invested nearly as large a capital in the cloth business). The records, however, do not substantiate this contention. In 1451 investments in industry (10,800 florins) were slightly over one sixth of the amount invested in banking and foreign trade (58,459 florins including 12,952 florins in the Tavola in Florence).

32. Doren, *Wollentuchindustrie*, pp. 526–527.

33. ASF, Catasto No. 51 (Leon d'Oro, 1427), fols. 1170–1171.

34. Edler, *Glossary*, p. 338. This agreement went into effect on June 30, 1434.

35. *Ibid.*, pp. 339–340. Such a shop could not have been very large even if one assumes that less capital was required because cheaper wool was used.

36. Bk. I, chap. 6 (Mod. Lib. ed., p. 48).

37. A list with terminology in English and Italian is given in Edler, *Glossary*, pp. 324–329.

38. Doren, *Wollentuchindustrie*, p. 220; Edler, *Glossary*, p. 411; San Antonino, *Summa theologica*, Pt. III, title 6, chap. 4, §4.

39. R. de Roover, "A Florentine Firm," p. 11. A Boston wool merchant told me that this is very plausible and that a woolsorter would be well qualified to act as consultant.

40. Edler, *Glossary*, pp. 409–410.

41. This is the reason why the gild passed drastic regulations to prevent cabbaging and to punish negligence or sabotage. *Statuto dell'Arte della Lana di Firenze (1317–1319)*, ed. Anna Maria E. Agnoletti (Florence, 1940), pp. 24, 27, 94–95, 122, 169–170, 173–174, 179–180, 182–185 (Lib. I, arts. 7, 8, 9, 10; Lib. II, arts. 2, 30; Lib. III, arts. 32, 37, 43, 44, 45; Lib. IV, arts. 1, 2).

42. Edler, *Glossary*, pp. 411–412. Michele di Lando, one of the leaders of the Ciompi revolt in 1378, was a capodieci or fattore sopra i lavoranti.

43. Doren, *Wollentuchindustrie*, p. 221. They are so represented by Boccaccio in his *Decameron*.

44. *Summa theologica*, Pt. III, title 8, chap. 4, §4.

45. The gild statutes of the fourteenth century give the impression that the woolsorters, the beaters, the carders, the combers, and the others who worked on the premises were journeymen and received day wages, but the Medici account books of a later period show definitely that these workers were paid by the piece, i.e., pounds of wool, and not by the day.

46. Doren, *Wollentuchindustrie*, pp. 221, 235.

47. R. de Roover, "Florentine Firm," p. 13.

48. Doren, *Wollentuchindustrie*, p. 249.

49. Edler, *Glossary*, p. 413.

50. R. de Roover, "Florentine Firm," p. 15.

51. R. de Roover, "New Perspectives on the History of Accounting," *The Accounting Review*, 30:417 (1955), and "Florentine Firm," p. 33. In using the

figures given by Melis ("La formazione," pp. 56–57, 152), I obtain spinning, 10.1% and weaving, 8.1% of industrial cost.

52. Doren, *Wollentuchindustrie*, p. 259.

53. Doren (*ibid*, p. 220) declares that the warping was done in the shop, but this statement is contradicted by the text of the *Trattato dell'Arte della Lana,* which he himself published (*ibid.,* p. 490).

54. Edler, *Glossary*, pp. 413, 422.

55. Doren, *Wollentuchindustrie*, p. 280.

56. The Italian expression, *andare alle telerie,* is found in articles of partnership dated 1434 and 1437. The earlier of these articles have been published by Gertrude Randolph Bramlette Richards, *Florentine Merchants in the Age of the Medici* (Cambridge, Mass., 1932), p. 237.

57. Doren, *Wollentuchindustrie*, pp. 264–277. Doren assumes without adequate evidence that only a small minority of the weavers managed to retain their own looms and thus to preserve their independence.

58. Harvard Graduate School of Business Administration, Selfridge Collection, Ms. 558/5, fol. 4.

59. Edler, *Glossary*, p. 421. It is true that the evidence applies to the sixteenth century when loans to weavers were forbidden by statute.

60. R. de Roover, "Florentine Firm," pp. 16, 32.

61. Melis, "La formazione," p. 162 and R. de Roover, "Florentine Firm," p. 27.

62. Davidsohn, *Geschichte von Florenz*, IV, Pt. II, 53.

63. Giuseppe Boffito and Attilio Mori, *Piante e Vedute di Firenze* (Florence, 1926), pp. xxiv–xxv, 40–43.

64. In the fourteenth century, the *tiratoi* were still privately owned, but after 1400 the gild succeeded in acquiring all those still in existence: Doren, *Wollentuchindustrie,* pp. 390–393; Davidsohn, *Geschichte,* IV, pt. II, 52; Gandi, *Corporazioni,* pp. 136–137.

65. R. de Roover, "Florentine Firm," p. 17.

66. *Ibid.,* pp. 17–18.

67. Doren, *Wollentuchindustrie,* pp. 286–313. Doren contradicts himself in declaring on p. 290 that the dyer was a worker and in showing on p. 310 that he was a small master employing several wage earners. Only the latter statement corresponds to the truth.

68. Edler, *Glossary,* pp. 335, 345.

69. R. de Roover, "Florentine Firm," p. 18.

70. Edler, *Glossary,* p. 298.

71. Doren, *Wollentuchindustrie,* p. 290.

72. A description is given in Edler, *Glossary,* Appendices II-IX, pp. 348–426, and in "Florentine Firm," pp. 3–32. This article deals with the later books belonging to the sixteenth century, when methods of bookkeeping reached their climax of perfection.

73. Evidence is found in the del Bene account books of the fourteenth century and the Datini records toward 1400. Cf. S. Paul Garner, *Evolution of Cost Accounting to 1925* (University, Alabama, 1954), pp. 15–21 and F. Melis, *Storia della ragioneria* (Bologna, 1950), pp. 553–574.

74. Melis, *Ragioneria,* pp. 558–560. Cf. R. de Roover, "New Interpretations," pp. 416–417.

75. R. de Roover, "Florentine Firm," p. 29. Doren (*Wollentuchindustrie,* p. 218) shows little understanding of business in assuming the organization of production to be an easy task which did not require the constant attention of the

management. Moreover, the bottega of a clothier was not a training school for the factors of banking and trading companies: they were trained in the branches abroad. The Medici records give decisive evidence which contradicts Doren's thesis.

76. Davidsohn, "Blüte und Niedergang," p. 230.

77. Statuto dell'Arte della Lana, Lib. II, art. 19, pp. 114–115 and Lib. IV, art. 32, p. 203. Cf. Doren, Wollentuchindustrie, pp. 460, 525. Florence was not the only city where similar provisions were incorporated in the gild statutes. In Siena, for example, the statutes (Dist. VIII, cap. 1) of the clothiers' gild forbade the woolworkers to join any subversive secret society or "conjuration." See Statuti senesi scritti in volgare nei secoli XIII e XIV, ed. Filippo-Luigi Polidori, I (Bologna, 1863), 260.

78. N. Rodolico, Il popolo minuto (Bologna, 1899), pp. 58–62 and 157–160, doc. No. 14.

79. Idem, "The Struggle for the Right of Association in Fourteenth-Century Florence," History, new Ser., 7:183–184 (1922).

80. San Antonino, Summa theologica, Pt. II, tit. 1 (De avaritia), cap. 17, §8; Manuel Rocha, Les Origines de "Quadragesimo Anno": travail et salaire à travers la scolastique (Paris, 1933), p. 58. Rocha's interpretation is open to question.

81. San Antonino, Summa, Pt. II, tit. 1, cap. 17, §7 and 8; Pt. III, tit. 8, cap. 4, §4 and 5. Cf. Doren, Wollentuchindustrie, pp. 458–459.

82. G. Villani, Cronica, Lib. XII, cap. 97. Cf. Rodolico, Democrazia fiorentina, pp. 262–263.

83. Giuseppe Odoardo Corazzini, I Ciompi, cronache e documenti (Florence, 1887), p. 137; Doren, Wollentuchindustrie, pp. 466–468; Hermes, "Der Kapitalismus," p. 371; Davidsohn, "Blüte und Niedergang," p. 247.

84. Statuto dell'Arte della Lana, Lib. III, art. 10, pp. 154–155. Cf. Doren, Zunftwesen, pp. 659–660.

85. Statuto dell'Arte della Lana, Lib. III, art. 40, pp. 176–177.

86. A list of these steps in the manufacture of silk cloth with the terminology in English and Italian is given in Edler, Glossary, pp. 330–331.

87. L'arte della seta in Firenze: trattato del secolo XV, ed. Girolamo Gargiolli (Florence, 1868), pp. 108–109.

88. Ibid., pp. 102–108.

89. F. E. de Roover, "Lucchese Silks," Ciba Review, 80:2917–2919 (1950); Charles Singer et al., History of Technology, II (Oxford, 1956), 206–207.

90. In each row there were sixteen reels and six spindles per reel. F. de Roover, "Lucchese Silks," p. 2918.

91. I am indebted for this information to my wife; it is based on the business records of the silk manufacturer, Andrea di Francesco Banchi, preserved in the Archives of the Spedale degli Innocenti.

92. F. de Roover, "Lucchese Silks," p. 2918.

93. Gargiolli, Trattato, p. 117: "Piero di Giovanni Ciriagi e compagni tintori ànno da noi a cuocere. . . ." Cf. Statuti dell'Arte di Por Santa Maria al tempo della Repubblica, ed. U. Dorini (Florence, 1934), p. 407.

94. F. de Roover, "Lucchese Silks," p. 2919.

95. Gargiolli, Trattato, pp. 63–64.

96. Ibid., pp. 30–63.

97. Statuti dell'Arte di Por S. Maria, p. 459. Further evidence is found in the records of Andrea Banchi (see n. 91 above).

98. F. de Roover, "Lucchese Silks," p. 2920.

99. There are several examples in the records of Andrea Banchi.

100. Gargiolli, *Trattato,* p. 98. The editor uses by mistake the symbol F., designating florins, instead of the pound sign £: wages were always paid in moneta di piccioli. The braccio was about 60 centimeters or two feet.

101. This information is based on the business records of Andrea Banchi.

102. *Statuti dell'Arte di Por S. Maria,* pp. 487–488.

103. *Ibid.,* p. 83 (art. 56 of the Statute of 1335), p. 256 (art. 18 of the amendments of 1352), and p. 407 (art. 3 of the amendments of 1411).

104. In 1460, this practice, it was alleged, inflicted intolerable damage (*ibid.,* p. 598).

105. Rubric 53 of the Statute of 1335 (*ibid.,* p. 80).

106. Rubrics 25 and 136 of the same statute (*ibid.,* pp. 49, 155). These provisions were confirmed in 1352 (*ibid.,* p. 253).

107. Rubric 56 of the Statute of 1335 (*ibid.,* p. 83).

108. Umberto Dorini, *L'arte della seta in Toscana* (Florence, 1928), p. 28 and *Statuti,* pp. 590–591.

109. Amendment of 1411 (*Statuti,* p. 408).

110. Amendments of 1353 and 1411 (*ibid.,* pp. 255, 407).

111. The truck system was first banned in 1411 (*Statuti,* pp. 408–409) and this provision was renewed in 1420, 1429, 1438, 1458, and 1460 (*ibid.,* pp. 459–460, 496–497, 540–541, 590–591, and 613).

112. In 1429, it was enacted that not more than one fourth of the wage might be paid in kind (*ibid.,* pp. 459–460, 497).

113. Archivio dello Spedale degli Innocenti, Estranei, No. 85 (Libro tessitori B, 1459–1462, di Andrea Banchi), fols. 61, 87, 96, 179, 239, *et passim.* Banchi even paid all kinds of things for his weavers from hose to medical care and thus acted as the banker of his employees (*ibid.,* fols. 87, 96).

114. This statement is based on Banchi's extant business records in the Spedale degli Innocenti, especially his libri segreti and his *ricordanze.*

115. Information is found in the fragment of a ledger of the Milan branch (MAP, filza 134, no. 4, fol. 96). Cf. Sieveking, *Handlungsbücher* p. 39. The Milan branch did not act as agent for the Medici silk shop exclusively, but also for other Florentine manufacturers.

116. R. de Roover, "La Communauté des marchands lucquois à Bruges," p. 37, gives some details about the Rapondi. From 1445 to 1464, Arnolfini was the chief supplier of the court of Burgundy according to the Comptes des recettes générales de Flandre in the Lille and Brussels State Archives.

117. Tommaso Portinari to Piero di Cosimo de' Medici, July 1, 1464 (MAP, filza 73, no. 315).

118. Brussels, Archives générales du Royaume, Chambre des comptes, No. 1923, fol. 352 ff.

119. The King bought silks for about £1,000 sterling: Angelo Tani to Piero de' Medici, September 1, 1468 (MAP, filza 22, no. 174).

120. Ruddock, *Italian Merchants,* pp. 73, 82.

121. Florence, Biblioteca Nazionale, Mss. II, V, 11 (Carte Lanfredini), fol. 143.

122. Several account books of *setaiuoli,* among others, those of Andrea Banchi, are in the archives of the Spedale degli Innocenti, or Foundling Hospital, of Florence.

123. ASF, MAP, filza 136a, fols. 79ᵛ–81ʳ. It was published in summary form with errors in dates, in names, etc., by A. Ceccherelli, *Libri di mercatura* pp. 64–67, and republished by the same author in his later book, *Il linguaggio dei bilanci* (Florence, 1939), pp. 50–53.

124. The document is probably a copy made in 1497 when the activities of Lorenzo Tornabuoni were being investigated. He was beheaded for plotting the overthrow of the existing government and the restoration to power of the Medici.

125. See also note 31 of this chapter.

Chapter IX

The Medici and the Financial Business of the Papacy: The Rome Branch of the Medici Bank

1. ASF, MAP, filza 153, no. 3, fol. 19. The house they rented belonged to Roberto di Giovanni Aldobrandini.

2. Uzzano, *Pratica*, p. 157.

3. Greenland made remittances in whalebones which were sold in Bruges for the benefit of the Apostolic Chamber. Henry S. Lucas, "Mediaeval Economic Relations between Flanders and Greenland," *Speculum*, 12:167–181 (1937). In 1492, the Bishop of Greenland, on account of the poverty of his see, was exempted from the payment of the annates and other tributes. Lunt, *Papal Revenues*, II, 296–298, No. 398.

4. Renouard, *Relations des papes d'Avignon*, p. 470.

5. In the 14th century, remittances from Poland to Rome were usually made by sending furs and other commodities to Bruges, where these goods were sold and the proceeds delivered to papal bankers. Renouard, *Relations*, pp 210–213, 310–311.

6. Aloys Schulte, *Geschichte des mittelalterlichen Handels und Verkehrs zwischen Westdeutschland und Italien mit Ausschluss von Venedig* (Leipzig, 1900), I, 342.

7. *Codex diplomaticus lubecensis*, V (1877), pp. 633–634. Filippo Rapondi was an important merchant-banker, well in favor at the Burgundian court.

8. Peter D. Partner, *The Papal State under Martin V: The Administration and Government of the Temporal Power in the Early Fifteenth Century* (London, 1958), pp. 131–136. Cf. Lunt, *Papal Revenues*, I, 65.

9. Lunt, *Papal Revenues*, I, 16.

10. Partner, *Papal State*, p. 136.

11. This was already so in the fourteenth century. Renouard, *Relations*, p. 6.

12. Partner, *Papal State*, p. 137; Lunt, *Papal Revenues*, I, 19.

13. Gottlob, *Camera apostolica*, p. 132. Cf. Partner, *Papal State*, p. 187 and *The Apostolic Camera and Scottish Benefices, 1418–1488*, ed. Annie I. Cameron (London, 1934), pp. lxxxix–xc.

14. Vatican Archives, Introitus et Exitus Camerae Apostolicae, Nos. 376–540 are for the 15th century. Cf. Gottlob, *Camera apostolica*, pp. 31–57, 111–112.

15. Lunt, *Papal Relations*, II, 508, No. 550; ASF, Conventi soppressi, Archivio 79, vol. 119: Libro segreto di Ilarione de' Bardi, fol. 11.

16. It would be difficult to give full page references here, since these data were obtained by piecing together small bits of information from the account books examined in the Vatican Archives and from the works of Adolf Gottlob, A. I. Cameron, and William E. Lunt. The list of depositaries given by Gottlob (pp. 111–112) is far from accurate.

17. Paul II (Pietro Barbo) was a nephew of Eugene IV (Gabriele Condolmer).

18. Giovanni Tornabuoni to Lorenzo the Magnificent, January 27, 1472 (N.S.), ASF, MAP, filza 31, no. 1.

19. On June 8, 1476, Bartolomeo Maraschi, bishop of Città di Castello and Meliaduce Cigala are named as depositaries. Cameron, *Apostolic Camera,* p. 249.

20. Vatican Archives, Introitus et Exitus, No. 428: Account book of Roberto Martelli, April 1, 1454–April 3, 1455, fols. 42ᵛ, 114ᵛ, 115ʳ⁻ᵛ. The vice-treasurer, whom Calixtus III ordered to make the special audit of Martelli's accounts as depositary, wrote in the Italian account book for September 1, 1448 to March 14, 1450 (N. S.) a statement that he had examined seven account books of Martelli and was satisfied that the contents were correct. The date is March 30, 1457 (Introitus et Exitus, No. 416, fol. 86ᵛ). Cf. Gottlob, *Camera,* p. 165.

21. Vatican Archives, Introitus et Exitus, No. 487, Accounts of Giovanni Tornabuoni, August 16, 1471-July 15, 1472. Cf. Gottlob, *Camera,* p. 262.

22. Letters of Giovanni Tornabuoni to Lorenzo de' Medici, February 6, 1473 (N. S.) and June 26, 1473 (ASF, MAP, filza 61, nos. 151, 156). The Latin text of the settlement ratified by the Pope, March 12, 1473 (Vatican Archives, Diversa Cameralia, 1472–1476, fol. 80) is published by Eugène Müntz, *Les Arts à la cour des papes,* III (Paris, 1882), pp. 63–64. Gottlob (*Camera,* p. 172, n. 3) gives most of the text. The English translation is in Lunt, *Papal Revenues,* I, 322–323, No. 169.

23. The reason why the Pope intervened and ratified the settlement of March, 1473, referred to in n. 22, was that the employees of the Apostolic Chamber disagreed with the Medici over the prices charged for silks and woolens and other commodities furnished for the funeral of Paul II in July 1471 and the coronation of Sixtus IV in August.

24. There are many examples in Cameron, *Apostolic Camera,* pp. 26, 52, 54, 55, 58, 59, 60, *et passim.*

25. This was already the procedure followed in the fourteenth century according to Renouard (*Relations,* pp. 464–469). There does not seem to have been any change after 1400. In Central and Eastern Europe, there were no banks, with the consequence that transfers were difficult and hazardous. Gottlob, *Camera apostolica,* pp. 210–214.

26. Gottlob, "Instrumenta cambii," pp. 204–212. A trans. in English is available in Lunt, *Papal Revenues,* II, 469–474, No. 521. The translation lacks accuracy, because the translator was unacquainted with business terminology. Christopher Spini was at that time assistant manager. Cf. above, Chap. V, n. 45.

27. Remy, *Indulgences pontificales,* pp. 94–95.

28. Partner, *Papal State,* pp. 104, 141. In 1429, warrants were issued on several provincial treasurers in favor of Antonius de Piscia (Antonio Salutati), the Depositary General, presumably to extinguish an overdraft. *Ibid.,* p. 141, n. 2.

29. Lunt, *Papal Revenues,* I, 33–34, II, 26. In 1429, the Treasurer of the March of Ancona is ordered to consign all the monies collected by him to Giovanni Cavalcanti, who will receive them on behalf of Cosimo and Lorenzo de' Medici. A receipt is to be secured each time (Partner, *Papal State,* p. 112, n. 1). For a payment to Luigi de Verme, captain, see *ibid.,* p. 213.

30. Cameron, *Apostolic Camera,* pp. xiii and lx-lxi; François Baix, *La Chambre apostolique et les "Libri Annatarum" de Martin V (1417–1431)* Analecta Vaticano-Belgica, XIV, (Brussels, 1947), pp. xxxiv-xxxv; Lunt, *Papal Revenues,* I, 95–96.

31. *Ibid.,* I, 98–99.

32. Cameron, *Apostolic Camera,* pp. xxviii-xxxvii. This procedure involved, of course, an advance by the banker to the Apostolic Chamber.

33. This was a general rule applying to all revenues due the Church. Lunt, *Papal Revenues*, I, 50, 284, 289, 291–292.

34. Cameron, *Apostolic Camera,* see Index.

35. Grunzweig, *Correspondance,* pp. 13–15, No. 8.

36. *Ibid.,* pp. 2–4, No. 2. The bishop's name was Jean Vivion.

37. Gottlob, "Instrumenta cambii," p. 205.

38. ASF, MAP, filza 94, no. 166, fols. 305–306.

39. Camerani, *Documenti,* p. 29, No. 36.

40. ASF, MAP, filza 153, no. 1, fol. 107: ". . . posto i nostri di Corte di Firenze debino dare . . . che sono per li avanzi di quatro anni, fatti a Ghostanza e qui in Firenze al bancho si tenea a Santa Maria Novella."

41. The inscription on the tomb states: *Joannes quodam papa XXIII* (John XXIII, once pope).

42. Vespasiano, *Memoirs,* p. 214.

43. MAP, filza 153, no. 2, fol. 2ᵛ–3ᵛ. Bartolomeo de' Bardi supplied 1,000 florins and was to receive one fourth of the profits.

44. This is further evidence that the usury doctrine had practical consequences. The Italian text reads as follows: ". . . deba il detto Bartolomeo traficare in detto traficho o chanbio di Corte di Roma secondo che Messer Dominedio ne presterà la grazia e come si richiede a simile mestiere di bancho e *sopratutto deba fare buoni e liciti contratti.*" (Italics mine).

45. MAP, filza 68, no. 402: "Ricordo dato a Bartolomeo de' Bardi di mano di Ilarione." The extant copy is in the handwriting of Bartolomeo.

46. This expression is a puzzle and probably refers to merchants who were skippers as well and operated coastal vessels bringing supplies to Rome.

47. Maguelonne, once a Gallo-Roman *civitas,* is today a small hamlet, but it had a cathedral until 1536 when the see was transferred to Montpellier. Later, Louis Aléman became archbishop of Arles; he entered into conflict with Eugene IV and was deprived of his cardinalship which was restored by Nicholas V.

48. ASF, MAP, filza 153, no. 2, fols. 52, 59; MAP, filza 94, no. 89, fols. 238–239.

49. MAP, filza 153, no. 2, fol. 3ʳ.

50. Guido Solivetti, *Il banco dei Medici in Roma all'inizio del XV secolo* (Rome, 1950), p. 14. Antonio is mentioned in a deed dated August 14, 1420, as being in the employ of the Medici.

51. *Ibid.,* pp. 11, 24. In a document dated July 10, 1405, it is stated that the tavola of Giovanni di Bicci is located in *regione Pontis.* San Giovanni was not built until the pontificate of Leo X, the Medici pope.

52. ASF, MAP, filza 68, no. 402.

53. MAP, filza 153, no. 2, fols. 35, 47.

54. This aspect of war finance has been studied only by Dr. Fritz Redlich, and he deals with the 16th and 17th centuries alone. The financing of condottieri goes back to the fifteenth century. See Fritz Redlich, "Military Entrepreneurship and the Credit System in the Sixteenth and Seventeenth Centuries," *Kyklos,* 9:186–193 (1957).

55. Ludwig von Pastor, *The History of the Popes from the Close of the Middle Ages,* I (3rd ed., St. Louis, 1906), 243–244.

56. P. D. Partner, "Camera Papae: Problems of Papal Finance in the Later Middle Ages," *The Journal of Ecclesiastical History,* 4:67 (1953).

57. Cameron, *Apostolic Camera,* pp. 227, 231; Partner, *Papal State,* pp. 141, 167; Gottlob, *Camera apostolica,* p. 111; Baix, *Chambre apostolique,* p. cccxliv; Camerani, *Documenti,* pp. 43, 48. Salutati is called "Antonius de Piscia, mercator

Florentinus Romanam Curiam sequens," that is, a Florentine merchant following the Roman curia.

58. ASF, MAP, filza 94, no. 89.

59. The text of art. 3 is as follows: "E sono d'achordo che 'l detto Cosimo, Lorenzo e Ilarione per ragione di più creditori asegniono al detto trafficho e compagnia non debino mettere in detta compagnia ne tenere alchuno chorpo. . . ."

60. MAP, filza 153, no. 3, fol. 4.

61. Ibid., fol. 7.

62. Martin V had ended the Great Schism and reconquered and pacified the Papal States.

63. Camerani Documenti, p. 44, No. 92. This is a residence permit issued on March 22, 1433. Giovanni Benci was still in Basel on September 9, 1433 (ibid., pp. 44–45, No. 94).

64. He was in Basel from December 1433 onward (MAP, filza 131, item e). He wrote from Ferrara to Cosimo about his first interview with the Pope on August 26, 1438 (MAP, filza 13, no. 15).

65. Giovenco della Stufa is mentioned as having been in Basel for some time on March 26, 1439 (Camerani, Documenti, p. 54, No. 131). He was still there in December 1440 (ibid., p. 56, No. 138).

66. R. de Roover, "La Balance commerciale entre les Pays-Bas et l'Italie," p. 378. In 1444, he wrote to Cosimo from Sluys to report about the arrival of the galleys.

67. Camerani, Documenti, p. 59, Nos. 148–150. One of these three documents relates to the transfer of the proceeds of indulgences in the kingdom of Sweden.

68. Camerani, Documenti, p. 46, No. 102 and p. 55, No. 136.

69. Ibid., p. 55, No. 134. Heyd (Commerce du Levant, II, 487) relates that Giovenco della Stufa was sent to Egypt as Florentine ambassador.

70. Camerani, Documenti, p. 47, No. 105. In another contract, dated November 7, 1435, the same cardinal received 2,000 ducats and transferred to them bills of exchange payable in Venice (ibid., p. 49, No. 111).

71. Ibid., p. 46, No. 102.

72. Ibid., p. 48, No. 109 and p. 55, Nos. 134, 135.

73. ASF, MAP, filza 104, fol. 599^r.

74. MAP, filza 153, no. 3, fol. 21.

75. MAP, filza 104, fols. 599–603.

76. MAP, filza 153, no. 3, fol. 18.

77. Roberto Martelli, Ferrara, to Giovanni Benci, November 28, 1438 (Map, filza 94, no. 121, fol. 187).

78. Ricordo for Gerozzo de' Pigli, MAP, filza 94, no. 134, fols. 214–215.

79. MAP, filza 153, no. 3, fols. 18, 30.

80. Ibid., fols. 18, 19.

81. An English translation of this letter is available in Ross, The Early Medici, pp. 14–15. The author, however, gives a wrong date, 1430 instead of 1438. The correct date is given in the printed inventory, Archivio Mediceo avanti il Principato, Inventario, I, 74.

82. Pieraccini, Stirpe de' Medici, I (1st ed.), 77; (2 ed.), 82. Ser Giovanni Caffarecci is often called Johannes de Vulterris (MAP, Inventario, I, 74, et passim). The reference for this letter is MAP, filza 5, no. 327.

83. Giovanni Tornabuoni to Piero di Cosimo de' Medici, Rome, May 13, 1458 (MAP, filza 17, no. 172).

84. ASF, Catasto No. 818 (Leon Bianco, 1457), fols. 178–179.

85. Leonardo Vernacci to Cosimo de' Medici, Rome, March 4, 1458 (MAP, filza 12, no. 233).

86. Giovanni's first job was to keep the quaderno di cassa. Giovanni Tornabuoni to Piero de' Medici, Rome, October 5, 1443 (MAP, filza 17, no. 31).

87. Tornabuoni claimed that he was attending to the company's business better than to his own. Giovanni Tornabuoni to Piero de' Medici, Siena, August 24, 1449 (MAP, filza 16, no. 44).

88. The text is as follows: "Questa chompagnia soleva tirare innanzi ciaschuno che bene faceva, e non avere avertenza a parentado nè altro." Leonardo Vernacci to Giovanni di Cosimo de' Medici, Rome, June 21, 1453 (MAP, filza 138, no. 387).

89. "Al facto tocchato a Giovanni Tornabuoni . . . io gl'ò sempre prestato afezione, si per amore di voi e per le sue virtù." Leonardo Vernacci to Piero di Cosimo, Rome, March 18, 1458 (MAP, filza 17, no. 150).

90. "Apreso mi vuol dare a intendere io sia in diferenza con Giovanni Tornabuoni, e noi siamo come fratelli e secho conferisco delle facende del bancho, sechondo achade." Vernacci to Cosimo, Rome, May 21, 1458 (MAP, filza 17, no. 179). The complaints of Tornabuoni about Vernacci's obstructive tactics are in a letter addressed to Piero on May 13, 1458 (MAP, filza 17, no. 172).

91. Roberto Martelli is mentioned as having died recently in a letter dated March 28, 1464, written in Bruges. Grunzweig, Correspondance, p. 111.

92. Giovanni Tornabuoni to Piero de' Medici, Rome, March 23, 1465 (MAP, filza 16, no. 141).

93. ASF, Catasto No. 922 (Leon Bianco, 1470), fol. 73. Vernacci was married to Maddalena di Messer Marcello Strozzi.

94. Cameron, Apostolic Camera, pp. 69, 174, 248, 249.

95. The contract is certainly antedated, because it was not ratified by Piero de' Medici and Giovanni Tornabuoni until October 31, 1465. MAP, filza 16, no. 149.

96. Giovanni Tornabuoni to Lorenzo de' Medici, Rome, December 10, 1481 (MAP, filza 38, no. 171).

97. Tornabuoni to Lorenzo, Rome, January 5, 1482 (MAP, filza 38, no. 69); March 5, 1482 (ibid., no. 166); March 23, 1483 (ibid., no. 448).

98. See the letters of March 23, 1483 (cited above), April 4, 1483 (MAP, filza 51, no. 227), April 20, 1483 (ibid., no. 231), June 15, 1483 (ibid., no. 244), and August 11, 1487 (MAP, filza 40, no. 114).

99. Letter of September 3, 1487 (MAP, filza 40, no. 133).

100. Letter of August 11, 1487 (ibid., no. 114).

101. Letter of June 15, 1487 (MAP, filza 51, no. 434).

102. Letter of May 17, 1477 (MAP, filza 34, no. 147).

103. Letter of February 28, 1478 (ibid., no. 58).

104. ". . . E benchè gli amici nostri siano fermi nella usata fede." Letter of December 10, 1481 (MAP, filza 38, no. 171).

105. Letters of January 5 and March 5, 1482 (ibid., nos. 69 and 166).

106. Letter of April 4, 1483 (MAP, filza 51, no. 227).

107. ". . . et tireremo questa ragione in luogho che sare' d'aspetarne chol tempo grand' onore e hutile," Letter of June 15, 1483 (ibid., no. 244).

108. Letter of April 1, 1488 (MAP, filza 40, no. 237).

109. ". . . e che sendo usciti di tanta sfortuna, non anneghiamo in un bicchiero d'acqua." Letter of April 12, 1489 (MAP, filza 41, no. 103).

110. MAP, filza 94, no. 152, fols. 280–281.

111. MAP, filza 135, no. 2: Ricordanze di cambi, segnato D, del filiale di Pisa, 1491–1492.

112. In a letter dated August 11, 1487, Tornabuoni begged Lorenzo to intervene personally and ask the Orsini to reduce an excessive debit. MAP, filza 40, no. 114.

113. ". . . E perchè tu sai quanto in ogni chosa Tommaxo è dificile," Letter to Lorenzo de' Medici, February 23, 1471 (MAP, filza 22, no. 234).

114. MAP, filza 40, no. 180. The printed inventory gives the date of a postscript as that of the letter itself. *Inventario,* II, 410.

115. The date of this agreement is June 4, 1495. Two copies are extant: (1) Harvard University, Baker Library, Selfridge Collection, Ms. 195, Sec. C, pp. 17–37, and (2) MAP, filza 82, no. 145, fols. 446–462.

116. Tornabuoni's wife was the daughter of the builder of the Pitti Palace, Messer Luca Pitti (1395–1472), who participated in a plot against the Medici in 1466 and was pardoned after betraying his accomplices.

CHAPTER X

Medici Establishments in Italy: The Tavola in Florence and the Fondaco in Venice

1. See above Chap. II, n. 80.

2. ASF, MAP, filza 153, no. 1, fol. 73: "Avanzi . . . E deono dare a dì detto f. dugiento d'oro i quali diamo a Giuliano di Giovanni di ser Matteo, nostro conpagno, l'anno 1408 per lo settimo li toccha di f. 1400 d'oro. . . . E deono dare a dì detto f. mille dugiento d'oro, i quali tochano a Giovanni de' Medici e Benedetto de' Bardi per resto degli avanzi fatti l'anno 1408, posto avanzi che s'apartenghono a loro propri, debino avere a c. 74 f.1200."

3. MAP, filza 154 (account book of Rosso de' Medici), fols. 35, 36.

4. Arezzo, Archivio della Fraternità dei Laici, filza 7, reg. 55: Libro reale segnato E di Lazzaro Bracci, 1415–1425, fol. 36.

5. The first known examples of checks date from 1374; they were drawn on a Pisan bank. Numerous early checks were also found in the Datini archives. Cf. Melis, *Banca pisana,* pp. 69–128. Professor Melis believes that by 1400 the check was widely used in Florence. This may be true of Florence or Pisa, but in Venice the use of checks was still strictly forbidden in the eighteenth century.

6. ASF, Catasto No. 51 (Leon d'Oro, 1427), fols. 1162^v–1168^v.

7. See the balance of Datini's firm in Barcelona, published by R. de Roover, "Accounting prior to Luca Pacioli," pp. 142–143.

8. ASF, MAP, filza 153, no. 2, fols. 5^v–6. This is a copy of the partnership agreement dated October 16, 1420.

9. The item of the balance sheet reads as follows: "Michelozzo e Donatello, intagliatori, per una sepultura del Cardinale Branchacci, carta 7, 188 fiorini 1s. 11d. aff." This tomb still stands today in the Brancaccio chapel of the church of Sant' Angelo a Nilo in Naples. The work was done in Pisa from 1426 to 1428.

10. ASF, Catasto No. 470 (Leon d'Oro, 1433), fols. 541^r–546^v.

11. *Ibid.,* fol. 539^r.

12. One entry reads as follows: "Chostantino e Antonio di Brancha per £120 di grossi sanza lettera . . . . . . f. 1281 4s. 4d. affiorino."

13. ASF, MAP, filza 153, no. 2, fols. 73, 76.

14. MAP, filza 153, no. 3, fol. 24.

15. A summary of the balance of 1433 is published by R. de Roover, "Accounting prior to Luca Pacioli," pp. 149–150.

16. ASF, MAP, filza 153, no. 1, fol. 15.

17. *Ibid.*, fols. 59 and 74: ". . . i quali gli diano per sua provedigione, cioè di suo salaro, tratandolo come compagno."

18. *Ibid.*, fols. 73, 74.

19. *Ibid.*, fol. 76. During the pestilence of 1412, Niccolò Buoni deserted his post to the great displeasure of his masters. Before assuming some of the duties of manager, he was keeping the books and taking care of correspondence.

20. *Ibid.*, fols. 108, 112.

21. ASF, Catasto No. 77 (Leon Bianco, 1427), fols. 157–158.

22. ASF, MAP, filza 153, no. 1, fols. 84, 96, 98.

23. MAP, filza 153, no. 2, fols. 5^v–6^v.

24. *Ibid.*, fols. 4–5^r.

25. *Ibid.*, fols. 47, 51.

26. MAP, filza 153, no. 2, fols. 30, 31.

27. *Ibid.*, fols. 44, 45.

28. *Ibid.*, fols. 47, 51.

29. *Ibid.*, fols. 53, 59, 62, 71, 73, 76. At this time, the Tavola was sharing in the profits of the Geneva branch. Thus, in 1429, the profits of the Tavola were 1,287 florins 11s. 4d. aff., after deducting 1,200 florins representing its share in the profits of the Geneva branch.

30. MAP, filza 153, no. 2, fols. 73, 76.

31. ASF, Catasto No. 410 (Vaio, 1431), fols. 233^v–235^r.

32. ASF, MAP, filza 104, no. 2, fol. 37^v.

33. MAP, filza 81, no. 3, fol. 7.

34. MAP, filza 153, no. 3, fol. 36.

35. *Ibid.*, fol. 81.

36. Grunzweig, *Correspondance*, p. 44. This is a reference to a letter sent from Bruges on July 8, 1454.

37. ASF, MAP, filza 153, no. 3, fols. 24, 25, 26, 41.

38. *Ibid.*, fol. 73.

39. *Ibid.*, fols. 81, 85, 88.

40. Sieveking, *Handlungsbücher*, p. 27.

41. ASF, MAP, filza 134, no. 3, fol. 42^v.

42. ASF, Arte del Cambio, No. 15, fol. 7^v.

43. ASF, Catasto No. 821 (Leon d'Oro, 1458), fol. 518^v: "Trovomi essere chompagno di Giovanni e Pierfrancesco de' Medici solo a la chompagnia di Firenze nel bancho e ghoverno cho' la mia persona e trovomi di corpo nella mia proprietà fiorini quatrociento."

44. Sieveking, *Handlungsbücher*, p. 9.

45. ASF, MAP, filza 135, no. 1, 97 fols. Cf. Sieveking, *Handlungsbücher*, pp. 33–35.

46. This remittance was routed via the fairs of Geneva (MAP, filza 135, no. 1, fol. 26).

47. Sieveking, *Handlungsbücher*, p. 35. The account of Piero di Peralto, major-domo of the King of Navarre, is inactive and apparently overdue (MAP, filza 135, no. 1, fol. 31).

48. *Ibid.*, fols. 24, 73, 79.

49. See the accounts of Antonio di Taddeo (fol. 18) and Bardo d'Agnolo Vernacci (fol. 25) who receive, respectively, 6 and 7 percent. The Milan branch,

on the other hand, pays 180 florins in six months that is, 12 percent, on a deposit of 3,000 florins (fol. 17).

50. The Easter fair yielded a profit of 254 florins (fol. 37), the August fair a profit of 508 florins (fol. 48).

51. The Medici sometimes speculated for the account of customers and earned only a small commission on such transactions. See the account on fol. 54 relating to exchange dealings for Castello Quaratesi who made a profit of 75 florins.

52. MAP, filza 135, no. 1, fols. 33, 36.

53. *Ibid.*, fol. 23.

54. *Ibid.*, fols. 5, 50, 63.

55. Ricordo di Schiatta Bagnesi, September 12, 1477 (MAP, filza 94, no. 213).

56. MAP, filza 135, no. 1, fols. 10, 12, 15, 82.

57. *Ibid.*, fol. 82. Cf. Sieveking, *Handlungsbücher*, p. 35.

58. ASF, Arte del Cambio, No. 15, fols. 7–26.

59. *Ibid.*, fols. 29^r, 32^v.

60. *Ibid.*, fols. 79^v, 85^r.

61. *Protocolli del carteggio di Lorenzo il Magnifico per gli anni 1473–74, 1477–92*, ed. Marcello del Piazzo (Florence, 1956), p. 300.

62. ASF, MAP, filza 89, no. 121.

63. R. de Roover, *Money, Banking, and Credit,* pp. 338–341.

64. Lane, "Venetian Bankers," p. 189.

65. Lapeyre, *Les Ruiz,* p. 251. Cf. R. de Roover, "History of Banking," p. 57.

66. ASF, MAP, filza 153, no. 1, fols. 21, 22.

67. *Ibid.*, fol. 25: "Nela sopradetta somma sono li avanzi fatti a Vinegia ne' detti anni tre, che per conto de' detti di Roma faceano." See also fol. 20: ". . . e per lo tenpo i nostri di Vinegia tenono il conto pe' nostri di Roma."

68. Ibid., fols. 14 and 22: "Neri di Cipriano Tornaquinci dè dare . . . E dì 27 di maggio (1402) f. mille d'oro . . . che deba tenere nel corpo di Vinegia, secondo i patti che abiamo co' lui."

69. *Ibid.*, fol. 21: Giovanni de' Medici received 1,290 florins and his partner, 430 florins.

70. ASF, MAP, filza 153, no. 1, fols. 22, 28, 30.

71. *Ibid.*, fols 22, 29, 30, 44.

72. *Ibid.*, fols. 46, 47. The profits reported amounted to 8,730 florins.

73. *Ibid.*, fols. 47, 48, 50.

74. *Ibid.*, fol. 47.

75. ASF, MAP, filze 153, no. 1, fols. 103, 112.

76. *Ibid.*, fol. 103: ". . . fu per danari avea rischoso per noi di ser Piero Bichierano in Carcovia, nostro debitore, i quali ci avea tenuti oculti più tenpo."

77. *Ibid.*, fol. 125.

78. ASF, MAP, filza 89, no. 190.

79. MAP, filza 153, no. 1, fols. 55–57, 67–68.

80. MAP, filza 89, no. 190.

81. MAP, filza 153, no. 1, fol. 88.

82. *Ibid.*, fols. 61, 91.

83. *Ibid.*, fol. 103: "Giovanni d'Adoardo Portinari dè avere a dì 15 di luglio f. trecento d'oro, i quali li diano per suo salario per l'anno 1417 e 1418 stato per noi a Vinegia . . . f. 300."

84. Biblioteca Riccardiana, Ms. 2009: Genealogia degli Huomini e delle Donne della Famiglia de' Portinari di Firenze, fols. 328, 331.

85. ASF, MAP, filza 153, no. 1, fols. 104, 107. The investment of the maggiori was £700 groat or 7,000 ducats, Venetian currency.

86. *Ibid.*, fols. 98, 102, 107. Profits before reserves and adjustments were 1,100 florins in 1417 and 1,560 florins in 1418.

87. MAP, filza 153, no. 2, fols. 7r–8r.

88. *Ibid.*, fols. 59, 67, 77.

89. Giovanni Portinari died the next year, April 11, 1436.

90. Vervi or Wervicq in Flanders was a very important cloth-producing center on the Lys where this river today forms the boundary between Belgium and France. Vervi is often wrongly identified as Verviers, the center of the Belgian woolen industry in modern times.

91. In connection with the Neri Tornaquinci affair, the Medici paid 180 florins to Lodovico Baglioni for traveling expenses when he made a trip through Germany to collect overdue claims. ASF, MAP, filza 153, no. 1, fol. 102.

92. MAP, filza 153, no. 3, fols. 2, 3.

93. *Ibid.*, fol. 17.

94. Harvard University, Baker Library, Selfridge Collection of Medici Manuscripts, Ms. 495, Sec. C, pp. 13, 15.

95. ASF, MAP, filza 153, no. 3, fol. 85: ". . . vi si truovino tanti debitori non buoni che montano più che gli avanzi."

96. Camerani, *Documenti*, pp. 64–71, Nos. 167–192.

97. The wording of the note in Libro segreto, No. 3, fol. 85, suggests that the maggiori were dissatisfied with his performance.

98. No contract has survived, but this inference may be drawn from an entry in Libro segreto No. 3, fol. 87, which states that Alessandro became a partner at the beginning of 1448, Florentine style. See also fol. 91 for profits of 1449–1450.

99. F.-T. Perrens, *The History of Florence under the Domination of Cosimo, Piero, Lorenzo de' Medicis, 1434–1492* (London, 1892), p. 103.

100. ASF, MAP, filza 146, fols. 176–182. The date of the contract is January 20, 1455. It went into effect on March 25 following.

101. *Ibid.*, fols. 183–184.

102. Alessandro Martelli to Cosimo de' Medici, Treviso, June 23, 1464 (MAP, filza 12, no. 310).

103. MAP, filza 82, no. 22, fols. 119v–120r.

104. Alessandro Martelli to Piero di Cosimo de' Medici, Venice, January 22, 1465: MAP, filza 17, no. 655.

105. MAP, filza 82, no. 22, fol. 119v.

106. The principal debtors were Piero Guidiccioni, ser Marco Corner, and Marino and Francesco Dandolo. Guidiccioni was a buyer of alum.

107. Letter of Giovanni Altoviti to Piero de' Medici, Venice, October 26, 1466 (MAP, filza 17, no. 463). The printed inventory gives No. 643, probably a typographical error. (*Inventario*, I, 304).

108. G. Altoviti to Piero, August 9, 1466 (MAP, filza 17, no. 498).

109. Giovanni Tornabuoni to Piero de' Medici, January 16, 1468 (MAP, filza 16, no. 217).

110. The return was filed with the authorities in November or December 1469 while Piero di Cosimo was still alive. Sieveking, *Aus Genueser Rechnungsbüchern*, p. 101. The statement reads: "La mia ragione di Vinegia ch'è finita e più non vi tegniamo trafficho."

111. In 1470, the collection of the claims on the Dandoli was in the hands of

a representative or solicitor called Francesco di Bartolomeo del Vigna. See his letter to Lorenzo the Magnificent, April 14, 1470: MAP, filza 21, no. 181. This letter is not mentioned in the printed inventory (*Inventario*, II, 5).

112. ASF, MAP, filza 82, no. 22, fols. 118–120. The Martelli presented a claim for £680 groat: £300 capital, £335 undistributed profits, and £45 representing a credit in current account.

113. The claims are listed and include £150 groat due from Francesco di Nerone and £54 from Antonio Partini.

114. This partnership is mentioned incidentally in the ricordo for Tommaso Guidetti (MAP, filza 94, no. 198, fols. 357–358). It did business under the style of Pierfrancesco e Giuliano de' Medici & Co.

115. Lanfredini is better known as a diplomat than as a merchant-banker. In a book on the family, there is scarcely any mention of his business career, except that he was trained in his father's firm. Mildred Mansfield, *A Family of Decent Folk, 1200–1741: The Lanfredini, Merchant-Bankers and Art-Patrons* (London, 1922), pp. 62–64.

116. Del Piazzo, *Protocolli*, pp. 83, 96.

117. *Ibid.*, p. 112, 117–118. However, on December 4, 1480, Giovanni Lanfredini is still called "socius et gubernator societatis cantantis sub nomine Laurentii de Medicis et sociorum de Venetiis." ASF, Archivio notarile antecosimiano, G 620, ser Simone Grazzini, fol. 164ʳ.

118. Lorenzo announces the arrival of Piero d'Antonio di Taddeo in two letters dated April 7, 1481, one to Moro Arrighetti and the other to Agnolo Baldesi. Del Piazzo, *Protocolli*, p. 141.

CHAPTER XI

Medici Establishments in Italy: The Branches in Naples, Milan, and Pisa

1. ASF, MAP, filza 153, no. 1, fol. 14: "Il detto morì a Napoli nel tenpo dela mortalità 1400." Frescobaldi's salary was only sixty florins per annum.

2. *Ibid.*, fol. 15. Adoardo Tornaquinci had been in the service of Giovanni di Bicci in Rome since 1396.

3. *Ibid.*, fol. 16. Accerrito Portinari was the first of that family to be employed by the Medici. He served in the Florentine tavola from 1398 to 1401 before being sent to Naples.

4. *Ibid.*, fol. 23: "Francesco Barucci, nostro giovane a Ghaeta. . . ." In 1405, Barucci was taken by pirates and ransomed for 171 florins (*ibid.*, fol. 38).

5. *Ibid.*, fols. 16, 17.

6. *Ibid.*, fols. 17, 35.

7. ASF, MAP, filza 153, no. 1, fol. 35: "Jacopo di Tommaso Bartoli che sta ne' Rengno per noi."

8. *Ibid.*, fols. 38, 39, 51.

9. ASF, MAP, filza 148, fol. 44; Catasto No. 60 (Vaio, 1427), fol. 94ʳ.

10. MAP, filza 153, no. 1, fol. 43. Profits were 451 ounces, 17 *tari*, 17 grains, Neapolitan currency, including 80 ounces for Gaëta.

11. *Ibid.*, fols. 43, 54. Gross income was 396 ounces, 7 tari, and 16 grains, Neapolitan currency, equivalent to 2,507 florins in Florence. This amount includes 91 ounces representing the profits made in Gaëta.

12. *Ibid.*, fol. 69: ". . . aveano ragionato fosse d'avanzo in dette due anni che poi quando vennono a saldare del conto, no' vi furono."

13. MAP, filza 153, no. 1, fol. 80.

14. *Ibid.*, fol. 62.

15. *Ibid.*, fols. 86, 95.

16. *Ibid.*, fol. 37.

17. MAP, filza 153, no. 2, fols. 8ᵛ–9ᵛ.

18. *Ibid.*, fols. 20, 32.

19. *Cronica* (Florence, 1720), pp. 131, 138. Rosso de' Medici married Buonaccorso Pitti's daughter, Maddalena, on May 30, 1423. His first wife was a Spaniard, Margherita Rodrigues.

20. Fantino de' Medici *di Barzalona* appears in the balance sheet of the Tavola of Florence as creditor for an amount of nearly 1,500 florins, probably a consignment of wool (ASF, Catasto No. 51, Gonf. Leon d'Oro, 1427, fol. 1167ᵛ. See also MAP, filza 153, no. 2, fols. 52 and 94 relating to an account with Fantino de' Medici in Barcelona.

21. Ricordo for Tommaso Guidetti, May 23, 1471, MAP, filza 94, no. 198, fol. 358: "A Napoli, come sapete, s'è posto Agustino Billiotti a chui avete a commettere accadendovi avere a far nulla in quelle parti."

22. Biliotti had served for several years as *patronus* (skipper) on board of the Florentine galleys, but he apparently had no training in bank management.

23. Biliotti still wrote from Naples on April 4, 1475. MAP, filza 26, no. 157.

24. Camerani, *Documenti,* p. 95, No. 273; Pagnini, *Della Decima,* II, 304.

25. Francesco Carabellese, "Bilancio di un'accomandita di casa Medici in Puglia del 1477 e relazioni commerciali fra la Puglia e Firenze," *Archivio storico pugliese,* 2:77–104 (1896).

26. The Venetian Republic maintained a consul in Apulia with residence in Trani. A. Zambler and F. Carabellese, *Le relazioni commerciali fra la Puglia e la Republica di Venezia dal secolo X al XV* (Trani, 1898), pp. 110–122.

27. ASF, MAP, filza 99, no. 4, fols. 6–13.

28. MAP, filza 26, no. 169.

29. Silvestri, "Sull'attività bancaria," pp. 102–103.

30. The date of these instructions is July 8, 1481 (MAP, filza 89, no. 154).

31. Ricordo for Giambattista Ridolfi, March 29, 1480, Biblioteca Nazionale, Florence, Mss. II, V, 13 (Carte Lanfredini), fols. 167–168.

32. Tornabuoni to Lorenzo the Magnificent, December 10, 1481 (MAP, filza 38, no. 171).

33. MAP, filza 51, no. 222.

34. *Ibid.*, no. 226.

35. Tornabuoni to Lorenzo the Magnificent, April 4, 1483 (MAP, filza 51, no. 227).

36. Silvestri, "Sull'attività bancaria," pp. 104, 109.

37. Giovanni Tornabuoni to Lorenzo, June 15, 1487 (MAP, filza 51, no. 434).

38. Silvestri, "Sull'attività bancaria," p. 110.

39. MAP, filza 89, no. 189.

40. Silvestri, "Sull'attività bancaria," pp. 111–113.

41. Cassandro, "Lettera di cambio, pp. 50–51.

42. Some of the persons who testified were the employees of the Tornabuoni bank in Naples: Giuliano di Giorgio Ridolfi, the principal factor, Lorenzo Acciaiuoli, the cashier, Vittorio Caiano or Caggiano, a factor. Another witness was Pier Antonio Bandini, formerly connected with the Pazzi bank in Bruges. *Ibid.*, p. 50.

43. *El libro di mercatantie,* ed. Borlandi, pp. 7, 12, 14. However, on p. 169, it is indicated that usance between Milan and Florence was 10 days after sight and not 10 days from date. Cf. Uzzano, *Pratica,* p. 100.

44. Fabroni, *Magni Cosmi Medicei Vita*, II, 246.

45. Letters of Pigello Portinari in Florence to Giovanni di Cosimo in Treviso, July 24, 1434 (MAP, filza 5, no. 297); August 7, 1434 (Carte Strozziane, I serie, filza 3, fol. 51); and September 25, 1434 (MAP, filza 5, no. 298). The two boys, being exactly the same age, were apparently close friends. The letters were written while the Medici were in exile.

46. MAP, filza 153, no. 3, fol. 17.

47. He was also granted Milanese citizenship without losing Florentine citizenship (Fabroni, *Cosmi Vita*, II, 246. G. Barbieri exaggerates, however, when he states that Pigello Portinari was practically the Duke's minister of finance. *Economia e politica nel ducato di Milano, 1386–1535* (Milan, 1938), p. 212. The document reproduced by Fabroni is in the *pergamene* of the Fondo diplomatico mediceo, ASF (Camerani, *Documenti*, p. 113, no. 343).

48. Dott. Casati, "Documenti sul palazzo chiamato 'il Banco Mediceo'," *Archivio storico lombardo*, 12:582–588 (1885).

49. Antonio Averlino Filarete, *Tractat über die Baukunst*, Wolfgang von Oettingen, ed. (Vienna, 1890), pp. 679–686.

50. Giorgio Vasari, *The Lives of the Painters, Sculptors, and Architects* (Everyman's Library, New York, n. d.), I, 323. The general plan was Michelozzi's, but much of the details of the interior decoration was done by local artists carrying out this design. Alfred G. Meyer, *Oberitalienische Frührenaissance: Bauten und Bildwerke der Lombardei*, I (Berlin, 1897), 99–110.

51. Sforza's wife, Bianca Maria, was the natural daughter (legitimatized) and only child of the last Visconti duke, Filippo Maria.

52. Filarete, *Tractat*, p. 686: ". . . Pigello Portinari, huomo degnio e da bene. El quale lui regge e guida tutto el traffico che [i Medici] ànno a Milano."

53. ". . . uno chassone di nocie chon serrature e suoi fornimenti, compramo da maestro Piero Stremeto, legnamaro per nostro uso e per tenervi dientre libri e schriture sechrete del nostro bancho." Curzio Mazzi, "La compagnia mercantile di Piero e Giovanni di Cosimo dei Medici in Milano nel 1459," *Rivista delle Biblioteche e degli Archivi*, 18:22 (1907). Sieveking, *Handlungsbücher*, pp. 36–37.

54. Pigello Portinari to Giovanni di Cosimo, March 9, 1461 (MAP, filza 8, no. 413).

55. Already in 1458, Portinari mentions in a letter to Cosimo that the public had an exaggerated idea of the profits made by the Milan branch of the Medici, March 18, 1458 (MAP, filza 12, no. 251).

56. MAP, filza 83, no. 9, fols. 34–42.

57. *Ibid.*, fol. 40^v: "Venghano a montare più i chreditori che i debitori come si vede di sopra £914 16s. 5d. d'inperiali che chon destro modo rischontreremo il libro e troverassi l'errore, che Idio per l'avenire ci ghuardi da magiori."

58. MAP, No. 134, no. 4, fol. 97.

59. Letter of February 22, 1458 (MAP, filza 12, no. 176): "Come sapete il fatto nostro di qui consiste sul chredito; e con fare con quello d'altri, dà in modo che gl'utili non possono esser troppi, rispetto alle condizioni di qua."

60. Pigello Portinari to Cosimo, letter of April 12, 1460 (MAP, filza 83, no. 8, fol. 33). "Mandovi con questa e' conti saldi di questa ragione: prima non si sono potuti mandare. Vedrete per essi come l'abiamo fatto questo anno passato, che batte circha il segnio di quelli dinanzi. Iddio non ci concede pegio per l'avenire."

61. Pigello Portinari to Cosimo, February 22, 1458 (MAP, filza 12, no. 176): ". . . Signore, donde dipende tutto quello pocho si fa qui."

62. Letter of April 12, 1460 (MAP, filza 83, no. 8, fol. 33).

63. The same is found in the Datini account books. R. de Roover, "Accounting prior to Luca Pacioli," p. 144.

64. There is another rivedimento della cassa among the Medici papers: it dates from 1464 when Andrea Petrini was cashier. MAP, filza 83, no. 15, fols. 61–62. Because of the steady deterioration of the Milanese currency, the ducat had risen from 82s. to 84s. imp. between 1460 and 1464.

65. Camerani Documenti, pp. 115, 119, 121. All bills relate to dry exchange concluded with Angelo Simonetta, the ducal secretary.

66. Interest paid was charged to the account Discrezione and interest received was credited to the same.

67. The leniency is also noted by Tommaso Zerbi, Studi e problemi di storia economica. I. Credito ed interesse in Lombardia nei secoli XIV e XV (Milan, 1955), p. 70.

68. The reference number of this fragment is MAP, filza 134, no. 4.

69. Several deposits at 8% are mentioned in a letter of the Tavola in Florence to the Milan branch, November 19, 1462 (MAP, filza 138, no. 305).

70. MAP, filza 134, no. 4, fols. 9, 11.

71. Ibid., fol. 34.

72. Ibid., fol. 30: ". . . overo che li ragioniamo li tochi d'utilità nel tenpo si sono esercitati."

73. Mazzi, "Medici in Milano," p. 18. These local treasurers were: Amaretto Mannelli in Pavia, Difendente Baliotti in Novara, Giovanni da Erba in Como, and Manfredotto da Cornazzano in Parma. Sieveking, reading tessitore (weaver) for tesoriere (treasurer), erroneously identifies these men as weavers and comes to the amazing conclusion that weavers were often tax collectors (Handlungsbücher, pp. 39, 40, 42).

74. Ibid., pp. 40–41.

75. Ibid.

76. MAP, filza 134, no. 4, fols. 96, 100.

77. Mazzi, "Medici in Milano," p. 26; Sieveking, Handlungsbücher, pp. 39, 43.

78. Ibid., p. 41; MAP, filza 134, no. 4, fol. 12.

79. Sieveking, Handlungsbücher, p. 43; MAP, filza 134, no. 4, fol. 82.

80. Mazzi, "La compagnia dei Medici in Milano," p. 18; Sieveking, Handlungsbücher, pp. 38–39.

81. Mazzi, "Medici in Milano," pp. 24–25. This author misreads grossi as guadagni. The text should read: ". . . lb. 80. 13. 10 di grossi di Brugia che li faciamo valere a grossi 54 per ducato, duc. 360." Florentine cloth was sold to Cicco Simonetta or Cicco da Calabria (this is the same person). Cf. Sieveking, Handlungsbücher, p. 43.

82. In a letter dated May 4, 1455, Pigello Portinari informs the Venice branch that he is sending them 300 ducats in a sealed package and another 400 florins to Florence for account of Gerozzo de' Pigli, the Medici manager in London. Further shipments are announced. (MAP, filza 5, no. 740). A letter of November 19, 1462, mentions two shipments, one of 400 ducats and another of 600 ducats, sent from Milan to Florence (MAP, filza 138, no. 305).

83. Mazzi, "Medici in Milano," p. 20.

84. Borromei received £955 19s. 5d. imp. for his salary of three years. This was a good salary, comparable to that paid by competing firms. Alessandro da Castagnuolo, the main employee of the Borromei bank, received only £200 imp. a year. Zerbi, Le origini, p. 313.

85. Camerani, Documenti, p. 98, No. 286.

86. MAP, filza 83, no. 15. This number is the *rivedimento della cassa* mentioned above in n. 64.

87. Accerrito Portinari to Lorenzo de' Medici, March 24, 1470 (MAP, filza 21, no. 138).

88. Same correspondents, May 15, 1473 (MAP, filza 26, no. 127).

89. His father, Piero Petrini, had been a partner of Andrea Banchi.

90. Del Piazzo, *Protocolli*, p. 9.

91. Mohammed II granted the request and caused the arrest of Bandini who was brought back to Florence in chains and executed.

92. Accerrito Portinari to Lorenzo, May 15, 1473 (MAP, filza 26, no. 127). Perhaps Antonio dal Canto did not take the advice, since Benedetto Dei, in 1477, wrote from Bruges to an "Antonio di Dino" who stayed with the Medici bank. Pisani, *Un avventuriero*, p. 117.

93. *Handlungsbücher*, p. 41.

94. Letter of February 22, 1458 (MAP, filza 12, no. 176).

95. ". . . manchando i guadagni, manchino anche le spese, se si potrà."

96. Letter of February 11, 1456 (MAP, filza 9, no. 130).

97. Letter of June 29, 1467 (MAP, filza 17, no. 569).

98. "Noi qui faciamo al modo passato e questo è perdere." (MAP, filza 23, no. 188).

99. Sieveking, *Aus Genueser Rechnungsbüchern*, p. 101.

100. Accerrito Portinari in Venice to Messer Bartolomeo in Florence, March 1454 (MAP, filza 84, no. 20, fol. 45).

101. Accerrito Portinari to Piero di Cosimo de' Medici, July 2, 3, 5, 6, 14, 1464 (MAP, filza 12, nos. 357, 359, 360, 362; filza 17, nos. 423, 426.

102. Francesco Nori was expelled from France in August, 1468 and was probably detained in Milan by the last illness of Pigello. Benjamin Buser, *Die Beziehungen der Mediceer zu Frankreich während der Jahre 1434–1494 in ihrem Zusammenhang mit den allgemeinen Verhältnissen Italiens* (Leipzig, 1879), p. 141; Gandilhon, *Politique économique*, p. 362.

103. Francesco Nori in Milan to Lorenzo de' Medici, November 13, 1468 (MAP, filza 137, no. 254). This letter contradicts another sent two days previous in which Nori has only praise for Accerrito and reports that everything is going smoothly. The first letter was probably written to be shown to Accerrito and appease him.. (MAP, filza 20, no. 427).

104. Tommaso Portinari in Bruges to Piero di Cosimo in Florence, November 12-December 6, 1468, (MAP, filza 12, no. 380). The printed inventory (*Archivio Mediceo*, I, 236) gives the wrong year.

105. Accerrito Portinari to Lorenzo the Magnificent, March 24, 1470 (MAP, filza 21, no. 138).

106. Lorenzo and Giuliano de' Medici & Co. in Milan to the Bishop of Conca (Cuenca), April 27, 1471 (MAP) filza 88, no. 90). The printed inventory (III, 345) states erroneously that the letter was addressed to Raffaele Riario who, in 1471, was only nine years, too young to be a bishop.

107. Letters of Lorenzo to Morelli, October 16 and November 14, 1478 (MAP, filza 96, nos. 91, 92, 93).

108. Lorenzo to G. Morelli, October 23, 1478 (MAP, filza 124, fol. 293); Tommaso Portinari in Milan to Lorenzo in Florence, October 21, 1478 (MAP, filza 137, no. 425).

109. Ricordo da Matteo Ghini a Folco d'Adoardo Portinari, November 22, 1486, ASF, Spedale di Santa Maria Nuova, no. 130.

110. The contract or lease is in MAP, filza 148, no. 59.

111. Letter to Lorenzo from Jacopo Guicciardini, Florentine ambassador in Milan, March 3, 1486 (MAP, filza 26, no. 334). This letter is published by Gino Franceschini, "Il palazzo dei Duchi d'Urbino a Milano," *Archivio storico lombardo*, Serie 8, II (1950), 190, n. 17.

112. Del Piazzo, *Protocolli*, pp. 343, 345.

113. Franceschini, "Il palazzo . . . ," p. 191.

114. Casati, "Banco Mediceo," p. 587.

115. Fernand Braudel and R. Romano, *Navires et marchandises à l'entrée du Port de Livourne, 1547–1611* (Paris, 1951), pp. 16–17.

116. A fragment of the ledger kept in Pisa by Averardo de' Medici & Co (1424–1426) is extant in the Florentine archives (MAP, filza 133, no. 3). On folios 106 and 113, it has the account of Donato di Niccolò, sculptor, that is, of the famous Donatello. According to this account, 110 florins were placed to his credit by the Medici of Florence and were spent in small sums to meet current living expenses, purchases of marble, and other items. Donatello was then working on the tomb of Cardinal Brancaccio, with the collaboration of Michelozzi. H. W. Janson, *The Sculpture of Donatello,* (Princeton, 1957), II, 89.

117. Sieveking, *Handlungsbücher*, pp. 30–31.

118. ASF, MAP, filza 153, no. 3, fol. 52.

119. Corti, "Le accomandite," pp. 132–133.

120. According to numerous letters emanating from this firm (Map, filza 138, nos. 389–427).

121. The catasto report is in Archivio del Catasto, No. 823, (Catasto of 1457, Leon d'Oro), portata No. 181.

122. MAP, filza 83, no. 7, fols. 26–31.

123. Ginori-Conti, *Le magone della vena del ferro*, pp. 24–30.

124. *Idem, Carte Cambi da Querceto (secoli XV–XVI), Inventario e descrizione* (Florence, 1939), tav. II facing p. 48.

125. *Ibid.*, pp. 43–44.

CHAPTER XII

Branches of the Medici Bank outside Italy: Geneva, Lyons, and Avignon

1. V. Chomel and J. Ebersolt, *Cinq Siècles de circulation internationale vue de Jougne* (Paris, 1951), pp. 94–95.

2. Frédéric Borel, *Les Foires de Genève au quinzième siècle* (Geneva, 1892), pp. 54–61. Cf. Paul Huvelin, *Essai historique sur le droit des marchés et des foires* (Paris, 1897), p. 290. This author believes that the fair of SS. Peter and Paul (June 29) was more important than the one of St. Peter in Chains (August 1), but this may be wrong, since the third fair was later called the August fair.

3. Huvelin, pp. 291–292. In the seventeenth century, the fairs of Besançon were actually held in Piacenza and Novi. These fairs were no longer trading centers, but became international clearing centers exclusively. Cf. Ehrenberg, *Zeitalter der Fugger*, II, 226.

4. Marc Bloch, "Le Problème de l'or au moyen âge," *Annales d'histoire économique et sociale*, 5:28 (1933).

5. For example, in May, 1438, Bernardo Portinari, writing from Bruges to Antonio Salutati, suggests sending large amounts of English nobles to Geneva. Such shipments were usually concealed in bales of cloth. It was more profitable to send coins than to remit because the exchanges were high, that is, presumably

above the export specie point. (MAP, filza 94, no. 146, fols. 241–242.) Examples of specie shipments from Geneva to Florence in 1443, 1444, and 1445 are found in the Libro segreto No. 3, fols. 69, 70, 74. They were entrusted to Medici factors: Giovanni di Betto [Zampini], Lorenzo Nettoli, Attaviano Altoviti, and Perino di Giusto (MAP, filza 153, no. 3). Between March 24, 1443 and December 30, 1445, Geneva shipped to Florence a total of at least 35,000 florins di suggello in gold coins, most of which were sent to the Florentine mint to be recoined.

6. Léon Schick, *Un Grand Homme d'affaires au début du XVI⁶ siècle: Jacob Fugger* (Paris, 1957), p. 271; *Welthandelsbräuche, 1480–1540*, ed. Karl Otto Müller (Berlin, 1934), pp. 268–271.

7. *El libro di mercatantie*, pp. 6, 8. This mark corresponded to about 245 grams.

8. The manual of da Uzzano mentions as a recent event the trade privileges granted by the sultan of Egypt in the year 825 of the Hegira, or 1422 of the Christian Era, to the Florentine merchants trading at Alexandria. The exchange rates listed in the Libro di mercatantie are those prevailing in 1450, or there-abouts, according to the data given in Camerani, *Documenti*.

9. *El libro di mercatantie*, p. 8: ". . . chanbiasi da Vinegia a Ginevra per la prima fiera che v'è."

10. Besides the Medici, there were in Geneva branches of the following Florentine banks: Alberti, Baroncelli, Guadagni, and Pazzi. Borel, *Foires de Genève* pp. 134–137, 237.

11. Perhaps his real name was Fabri. In any case, he was not a Florentine. On February 5, 1436 (N.S.), in Florence, he matriculated as a setaiuolo grosso: the entry states that he was from Geneva in Savoy.

12. According to entries in Libro segreto No. 1, he received in 1414 a salary of 85 ducats for seventeen months of service, which corresponds to 60 ducats per annum, and in 1420, 63 ducats and 9 grossi (groats) for an unspecified period (MAP, filza 153, no. 1, fols. 88, 105–111).

13. This information is based on a book of memoranda (ricordi) kept by Bertini (MAP, filza 131, item e). This manuscript is in a bad state of preservation, some of the folios are in shreds and all of them are partly burned.

14. *Ibid.*, fol. 5ᵛ.

15. *Ibid.*, fol. 19ᵛ. Herenthals is a small town, east of Lierre, in the province of Antwerp. *Panni di Rintalzo*, or cloths from Herenthals, are also mentioned in Uzzano's manual (p. 3).

16. Henri, Marquis Costa de Beauregard, *Souvenirs du règne d'Amédée VIII, premier duc de Savoie* (Chambéry, 1859), p. 169.

17. According to the records of Bertini, Michel di Ferro was paid 450 florins for commission (provigione) and room and board (MAP, filza 131 item e, fol. 5ᵛ).

18. MAP. filza 153, no. 2, fols. 35, 36.

19. *Ibid.*, fols. 40, 41.

20. This accomanda is mentioned in an entry dated May 10, 1427 (*ibid.*, fol. 41).

21. *Ibid.*, fols. 47, 51. In other words, the Rome branch and the Tavola each received three eighths of the profits.

22. *Ibid.*, fol. 57: ". . . sono per lo corpo per la nostra parte abiano a tenere a Ginevra."

23. ASF, Catasto No. 487 (Scala, 1433), fol. 234ʳ: "Truovasi conpangno a Ginevra di Cosimo e Lorenzo de' Medici, dove è conpangno con la persona sanza danari."

24. MAP, filza 153, no. 2, fols. 52, 53.

25. *Ibid.*, fol. 72.

26. MAP, filza 153, Libro segreto, No. 3, fol. 14.

27. *Ibid.*, fols. 12, 14. The capital was first set at 8,000 florins only, but was increased to 10,000 florins within less than a year, or on March 20, 1436 (*ibid.*, fol. 15).

28. MAP, filza 149, fol. 94. Another copy is in MAP, filza 153, Libro segreto No. 3, fol. 8.

29. MAP, filza 153, no. 3, fol. 79.

30. *Ibid.*, fol. 85.

31. The date of his matriculation as a silk manufacturer is December 18, 1447, but his contract ran to March 24, 1448.

32. Letter of May 16, 1450 (ASF, Carte Strozziane, Series I, filza 3, fol. 60).

33. MAP, filza 153, no. 3, fols. 32, 33. Domenico Salvestri's salary was 45 écus per annum and Pietro Malzi's, 32 écus.

34. ASF, Catasto No. 621 (Leon Bianco, 1442), fol. 348: "Francesco detto d'età 21 e truovasi di cinquina f. 14 d.3 a oro. Il detto Francesco è a Ginevra nella conpagnia di Cosimo de' Medici overo di Giovanni Benci e conpagni, e però io, Bartolomeo, suo fratello, ò data per lui questa scritta."

35. Sieveking, *Handlungsbücher*, p. 9.

36. A first example occurs in 1432 and concerns a reserve of 3,240 florins di suggello which was retransferred to avanzi (profits) and distributed among the partners (MAP, filza 153, no. 2, fol. 72). The second case dates from 1445 and concerns an amount of ▽8,687 or 9,653 florins remitted to Florence in several shipments (MAP, filza 153, no. 3, fol. 60).

37. Paul Aebischer, "Banquiers, commerçants, diplomates et voyageurs italiens à Fribourg (Suisse) avant 1500," *Zeitschrift für Schweizergeschichte,* 7:29–30 (1927).

38. Borel, p. 135.

39. Bruno Caizzi, "Ginevra e Lione: un episodio di guerra fredda economica nel XV secolo," *Cenobio,* II (1953), no. 6, 39–46.

40. Camerani, *Documenti,* p. 76, Nos. 208, 209. Cf. Letter of Giovanni Benci e Francesco Sassetti e conpagni in Geneva to Giovanni e Pierfrancesco de' Medici e conpagni in Florence, July 20, 1455 (MAP, filza 138, no. 439).

41. Sieveking, *Handlungsbücher,* p. 9; Camerani, *Documenti,* pp. 79–112.

42. A new partnership without Amerigo Benci as one of the partners began on March 26, 1462. This information is based on Sassetti's private ledger: ASF, Carte Strozziane, Series II, No. 20, Libro segreto di Francesco Sassetti, 1462–1472, fol. 13. The breach occurred between August 14 and November 17, 1461, when the new style omitting Amerigo Benci's name is already used (Camerani, *Documenti,* pp. 100–102, Nos. 294–301).

43. Jacopo Pitti, "Istoria fiorentina," *Archivio storico italiano,* 1:24 (1842). The two brothers went into partnership with each other and established themselves as setaiuoli in Florence.

44. Libro segreto di Francesco Sassetti (Carte Strozziane, Series II, No. 20), fol. 13; henceforth Sassetti's libro segreto.

45. Francesco Nori was in the employ of the Medici at least from 1452 onward (Aebischer, p. 29). At the time of Giovanni Benci's death, in July 1455, he happened to be in Florence where he had been sent by the Geneva branch to deliver a shipment of 1,400 ducats in specie (Geneva branch to maggiori, July 29, 1455, MAP, filza 138, no. 440). Giuliano del Zaccheria had been a factor in Geneva since 1456 and probably earlier (Camerani, *Documenti,* p. 81, No. 225).

46. *Ibid.*, p. 102, No. 301. Cf. Sassetti's libro segreto, fol. 13.

47. *Ibid.*, fol. 12.

48. *Ibid.*, fols. 17 and 19: "E a dì 10 di marzo 1463 ▽1500 vecchi i quali ci mandorono contanti in oro di più raxoni per Pippo della Veduto vetturale, de' quali ritraemo f. 1455¼ larghi, ebbi io Francesco Sassetti, posto debbi dare a c. 19 . . . . ▽1500, f. 1680."

49. The existence of a suboffice in Geneva is mentioned in the balance sheet of the Lyons branch for the year 1466, Florentine style (MAP, filza 83, no. 49, fols. 301–306).

50. Caizzi, "Ginevra e Lione," pp. 39–46.

51. Vigne, *Banque à Lyon*, pp. 66–67; Brésard, *Foires de Lyon*, pp. 9–12.

52. Vigne, *Banque*, pp. 58–63; Brésard, *Foires*, pp. 19–21.

53. Vigne, *Banque*, pp. 67–70.

54. Brésard, *Foires*, p. 111; Vigne, *Banque*, p. 71.

55. R. de Roover, *L'Evolution*, p. 126.

56. Vigne, *Banque*, pp. 68, 70.

57. *Ibid.*, pp. 71–72. This privilege aroused many complaints because it allegedly allowed the Italian bankers to operate with impunity in denuding France of its gold and silver. The complaints grew so loud and had so much effect that they led in 1484 to the temporary suppression of the fairs of Lyons. On this question, see Richard Gascon, "Nationalisme économique et géographie des foires: la querelle des foires de Lyon (1484–1494)," *Cahiers d'histoire*, 1:253–287 (1956).

58. Brésard, *Foires*, pp. 24–28.

59. Geneva tried to work out a compromise which would have given her two fairs and Lyons also two. This solution was opposed by the merchants on the grounds that it would increase expenses, especially cartage. Brésard, *Foires*, pp. 29–36; Vigne, *Banque*, p. 59.

60. MAP, filza 83, no. 49, fols. 301–306.

61. See, for example, the balance sheets of the Borromei in London and Bruges as published by Zerbi, *Origini*, pp. 420–421, 440–441.

62. Richard Gascon, "Un Siècle du commerce des épices à Lyon, fin XVe-fin XVIe siècles," *Annales (Economies, Sociétés, Civilisations)*, 15:638 (1960). However, the Medici branch in Lyons does not seem to have participated to any extent in the trade in spices. Perhaps this line of business was entirely in the hands of the Milanese and the Venetians.

63. ASF, Manoscritti, No. 119, Cronica di Benedetto Dei, fol. 34r. According to the same source, his three sons were doing business in Avignon. Pagnini, *Della Decima*, II, 305. He is mentioned as being in Avignon in 1444. Aebischer, "Banquiers à Fribourg," p. 28.

64. Borel, *Foires de Genève*, pp. 36–38. Amédée de Pesmes was also an official in the service of the Duke of Savoy.

65. Sassetti's libro segreto, fol. 22: "Annomene creditore a llor libro segreto a c. 8 in nome della raxone vecchia di Ginevra" and ". . . in nome di Ami di Pemes."

66. *Ibid.*, fol. 39: ". . . tenghono di *mio* in deposito in nome del convento de' Celestrini."

67. Gandilhon, *Louis XI*, p. 359. Cardinal Balue had been, before his arrest, pontifical collector general of the crusade and was in touch with Jean de Cambray, one of his collectors, who had funds on deposit with the Medici Bank. Henri Forgeot, *Jean Balue, cardinal d'Angers, 1421?–1491* (Paris, 1895),

pp. 26–27, 213.

68. A biographical notice on Antoine de Châteauneuf is found in Père Gabriel Daniel, *Histoire de France,* VII (new ed., Paris, 1755), pp. 692–694.

69. ASF, MAP, filza 83, no. 49, fol. 305; "E per più stangni lavorati ci mandarano i nostri di Londra piu fa che furono rubati da quelli di Lièggio." A sister, Isabella of Bourbon, was the second wife of Charles the Bold and the mother of Mary of Burgundy.

70. Vigne, *Banque,* p. 85; Brésard, *Foires,* p. 282.

71. Although Clavel or Clavelli is mentioned as a servant in the balance sheet of 1467, he later joined the clerical staff. In 1476, he was sent into Piedmont to collect revenues assigned to the Medici by the Duke of Savoy (Letter of Lionetto de' Rossi, July 28, 1476, MAP, filza 34, no. 355). In 1496, after the expulsion of the Medici from Florence, as burgher of Fribourg he received the support of the local authorities in pressing a claim on the liquidators of the Medici Bank (Aebischer, "Banquiers à Fribourg," p. 31).

72. Lionetto de' Rossi to Lorenzo the Magnificent, October 20, 1476 (MAP, filza 34, no. 386). Terrino Manovellozzi was still with the Medici on July 15, 1481. as appears from a letter he wrote on that date to Lorenzo the Magnificent (MAP, filza 38, no. 263). In an earlier letter (June 4, 1481), he claims to have been in the service of the Medici for twenty-six years (MAP, filza 38, no. 203).

73. Pagnini, *Della Decima,* II, 304.

74. Buser, *Beziehungen,* pp. 141–142. Cf. Gandilhon, *Louis XI,* pp. 362–363.

75. *Lettres de Louis XI, roi de France,* eds. Joseph Vaesen and Etienne Charavay, III (Paris, 1887), 251–252, No. 375. The King's letter, dated August 10, 1468, is explicit as to the reasons for his resentment. Nori was given ten days to leave France.

76. *Ibid.,* pp. 260–261, No. 378. The letter to the duke of Milan is in Italian and bears the date of August 12, 1468. Nori might have fared worse had it not been for Sforza's friendship with Piero.

77. Hippolyte de Charpin-Feugerolles, marquis de la Rivière, *Les Florentins à Lyon* (Lyons, 1893), p. 132. Cf. Camerani, *Documenti,* p. 109, No. 327.

78. ASF, Archivio notarile antecosimiano, G 620, fols. 44–45. The contract is dated May 31, 1476, with an apostil of June 18 following.

79. Camerani, *Documenti,* pp. 76, 83, 130, Nos. 207, 233, 397.

80. Charpin-Feugerolles, *Les Florentins à Lyon,* p. 174.

81. Sassetti's libro segreto, fol. 28.

82. Lionetto de' Rossi to Lorenzo the Magnificent, October 20, 1476 (MAP, filza 34, no. 386).

83. Same to Lorenzo, May 22, 1476 (MAP, filza 34, no. 338). "Reputation," it is explained in another letter, means the readiness to do business and to undertake new ventures (*la riputazione è dimostrazione d'essere disposti a fare faciende*). This definition is given by Lorenzo Spinelli in a letter to Lorenzo the Magnificent, October 30, 1487 (MAP, filza 40, no. 153).

84. Lionetto de' Rossi to Lorenzo the Magnificent, July 11, 1481 (MAP, filza 38, no. 257): ". . . visto che chosì è la intenzione vostra che io facci, della quale per nulla non voglio uscire."

85. Report of Lorenzo Spinelli, August 30, 1481 (MAP, filza 38, no. 312). Lionetto was relatively well disposed toward Spinelli.

86. Lionetto de' Rossi to Lorenzo the Magnificent, May 28, 1481 (MAP, filza 38, no. 240).

87. The same, June 28, 1482 (MAP, filza 34, no. 341).

88. MAP, filza 39, no. 30.

89. Lionetto de' Rossi to Lorenzo the Magnificent, December 4, 1482 (MAP, filza 10, no. 610).

90. Letter of June 23, 1483 (MAP, filza 39, no. 30).

91. Lionetto to Lorenzo, March 30, 1484 (Carte Strozziane, Series I, filza 3, fol. 106).

92. Letter of Lorini at Cléry to Lionetto de' Rossi in Lyons, July 3, 1482 (MAP, filza 137, fol. 455). Lorini spent most of his time at the French court. The expression used is *cazzatello,* which is vulgar and obscene.

93. Lionetto de' Rossi to Lorenzo the Magnificent, December 8, 1484 (MAP, filza 39, no. 499). For Tornabuoni's side of the story, see the report to Lorenzo, January 4, 1485 (MAP, filza 39, no. 52). Lionetto also complains because Rome allegedly makes no effort to sell the goods he has sent on consignment.

94. Francesco Sassetti to Lorenzo, April 4, 1485 (MAP, filza 39, no. 422). Lionetto de' Rossi also drew on Naples and Venice and expected the Medici branches in those cities to honor his drafts.

95. Giovanni Tornabuoni to Lorenzo, June 15, 1483 (MAP, filza 51, no. 244).

96. See above, note 93.

97. Tornabuoni writes on January 4, 1485: "Ho letto quanto vi scrive Lionetto de' Rossi, che à gran torto e parmi si governi al buio. . . ."

98. Jules Thierry, his father, and his grandfather had been the Medici correspondents in Brittany for many years. See Lionetto's letter to Lorenzo, May 27, 1485 (MAP, filza 26, no. 385). In a letter of June 5, 1485, Lionetto complains about another protest and charges that the managers in Rome tell fables to cover up their mistakes (*dichono molte frasche per choprire gl' errori che fanno*) (MAP, filza 26, no. 395).

99. Lionetto de' Rossi to Lorenzo, June 19, 1484 (MAP, filza 51, no. 282): "E mi doluto e duole solo una chosa: el non mostrare voi avere in me quella fede che debitamente doverresti, ma mi chonforto che l'arete chom tempo."

100. The date of Lionetto de' Rossi's report is July 11, 1484 (MAP, filza 39, no. 253).

101. Lionetto de' Rossi to Lorenzo the Magnificent, August 4, 1484 (MAP, filza 39, no. 276).

102. Lorenzo Spinelli to Lorenzo the Magnificent, February 11, 1485 (MAP, filza 39, no. 83).

103. Francesco Sassetti to Lorenzo the Magnificent, March 26, 1485 (MAP, filza 26, no. 342).

104. Del Piazzo, ed., *Protocolli,* pp. 326, 328.

105. He was still in Lyons on June 5 (MAP, filza 26, no. 395).

106. His arrest took place before July 5 when Lorenzo ordered Lodovico de' Rossi, Lionetto's nephew, to deliver his uncle's papers to Cosimo Sassetti (Del Piazzo, *Protocolli,* p. 330). On September 17, Lionetto wrote from the Stinche that he had been in jail eighty days (MAP, filza 26, no. 443).

107. Lorenzo Spinelli in Lyons to Lorenzo the Magnificent, December 4, 1485 (MAP, filza 26, no. 491). Since this is a reply to a letter from Lorenzo dated November 10, Lionetto de' Rossi was freed shortly before this date.

108. ASF, Stinche, No. 111, fol. 42. This is a record of the keeper of the Stinche. Cf. Lorenzo Spinelli in Lyons to Lorenzo de' Medici in Florence. October 30, 1487 (MAP, filza 40, no. 153). Lionetto de' Rossi was released only upon condition that he would not leave Florence.

109. Spinelli writes in this connection: ". . . detta ritenzione aveva dato più alterazione alle chose vostre non ne istimavi." See above note 107.

110. "Conseillers de la ville de Lion" to Lorenzo de' Medici and Francesco Sassetti, July 23, 1485 (MAP, filza 137, no. 473). To Lorenzo personally (ibid., no. 474). A similar letter was received from Dominique Panisse in Avignon (MAP, filza 73, no. 355).

111. Agostino Biliotti in Lyons to Lorenzo the Magnificent, August 1, 1485 (MAP, filza 26, no. 409).

112. Same correspondents, September 5, 1485 (MAP, filza 26, fol. 425).

113. Letters of October 1, 12, and 22, 1485 (MAP, filza 26, fols. 455, 460, 466).

114. The same note is struck in a letter of Giovanni Tornabuoni, September 25, 1485 (MAP, filza 26, no. 449). Tornabuoni states that the loss will probably amount to several hundred marks.

115. A mark is eight ounces or $280. I do not take into account the fact that the mark troy in question was a couple of grams lighter than its present English namesake.

116. Biliotti to Lorenzo, September 5, 1485 (MAP, filza 26, no. 425).

117. Galeazzo and Cosimo Sassetti to Lorenzo the Magnificent, December 11, 1485 (MAP, filza 26, no. 498).

118. Lorenzo Spinelli in Lyons to Lorenzo the Magnificent, December 4 and 11, 1485 (MAP, filza 26, nos. 491 and 496).

119. "Questa ragione si truova sui chanbi, et il bisongnio per acquistare credito sarebbe l'opposto." Lorenzo Spinelli to Lorenzo the Magnificent, September 6, 1486 (MAP, filza 39, no. 558) and September 2, 1487 (MAP, filza 40, no. 136).

120. "E anchora che a voi parrà fussi molto meglio pensare a stralciare, e nonne cierchare altre faciende." The same correspondents, October 30, 1487 (MAP, filza 40, no. 153).

121. Same correspondents, April 28, 1486 (MAP, filza 39, no. 472). The same complaint in a letter of January 29, 1490 (MAP, filza 41, no. 45).

122. Spinelli to Lorenzo the Magnificent, August 13, 1487 (MAP, filza 40, no. 120).

123. Same correspondents, April 9, 1488 (MAP, filza 40, no. 257). This letter was not dispatched until April 14.

124. Francesco Sassetti in Lyons to Lorenzo the Magnificent, May 20, 1488 (MAP, filza 40, no. 327). Pellegrino Lorini, for example, cost ∇500 and could get along on ∇50. Letter of June 6, 1488 (MAP, filza 40, no. 340).

125. Spinelli to Lorenzo, May 29, 1488 (MAP, filza 40, no. 348).

126. Sassetti to Lorenzo, December 1488 (MAP, filza 40, no. 217).

127. The most recalcitrant of all was Louis of Bourbon-Montpensier, Dauphin d'Auvergne, called "Conte-Dalfino" in the Medici records.

128. "Fate conte che anno bixongno di gran ghoverno." (Same reference as note 126.)

129. Sassetti, after a few months of experience in working with Spinelli, admits frankly that the latter is a devoted servant of the Medici Bank.

130. F. Sassetti to Lorenzo, February 12, 1489 (MAP, filza 40, no. 204).

131. Letter of February 20, 1489 (MAP, filza 40, no. 209).

132. Ibid.

133. Vigne, Banque, p. 64; Brésard, Foires, pp. 49–50; Gascon, "Nationalisme économique," p. 259.

134. Gascon, "Epices à Lyon," pp. 640–642.

135. Brésard, Foires, p. 61.

136. Letter of May 20, 1484 (MAP, filza 39, no. 182).

137. Lorenzo Spinelli to Lorenzo the Magnificent, April 28, 1486 (MAP, filza 39, no. 472).

138. Same correspondents, September 2, 1487 (MAP, filza 40, no. 136).

139. Same correspondents, February 8, 1489 (MAP, filza 7, no. 363).

140. Francesco Sassetti to Lorenzo the Magnificent, May 13 and 24, 1489 (MAP, filza 138, no. 185 and filza 88, no. 199).

141. One of the merchants in trouble was Michele Dini, former manager of the Medici bank in Avignon. Spinelli to Lorenzo, February 15, 1491 (MAP, filza 42, no. 18).

142. G. B. Picotti, *La giovinezza di Leone X* (Milan, 1927), pp. 70–72. This book gives an excellent and accurate account of the hunt for benefices. Cf. von Reumont, *Lorenzo de' Medici*, II, 398–399.

143. Antonio Mellini to Lionetto de' Rossi, March 7, 1484 (MAP, filza 96, no. 476). On account of the abbey of Fontdouce, the Medici became involved in a lawsuit with Monsignor of Saint-Pons before the Parlement of Paris (Lionetto de' Rossi to Lorenzo, July 11, 1484, MAP, filza 39, no. 253). The income of the abbey was only 250 ducats a year, the buildings were badly in need of repairs, and the monks were undisciplined. Letter from Cosimo and Galeazzo Sassetti, December 23, 1485 (MAP, filza 26, no. 501).

144. Picotti, *Leone X*, p. 73. The name of the archbishop was Olivier de Pennart.

145. The monks of La Chaise-Dieu also tenaciously clung to their right of electing their abbot and had little use for the Pope! Spinelli to Lorenzo, October 30, 1487 (MAP, filza 40, no. 153); Picotti, *Leone X*, p. 80.

146. *Ibid.*, p. 78.

147. Lionetto de' Rossi to Lorenzo de' Medici, December 4, 1482 (MAP, filza 10, no. 610).

148. Spinelli to Lorenzo, May 9, 1489 (MAP, filza 41, no. 117).

149. Same correspondents, April 4, 1490 (MAP, filza 42, no. 37).

150. Same correspondents, June 9, 1490 (MAP, filza 42, no. 96).

151. Same correspondents, April 4, 1490 (MAP, filza 42, no. 37). When this letter was written, the news of Sassetti's death had not yet reached Lyons, but it was known that he had had a stroke and was not expected to survive.

152. Spinelli to Lorenzo, July 6, 1490 (MAP, filza 42, no. 111).

153. This Francesco Nori is probably Franceschino or Francesco-Antonio, born in 1464, the legitimitized son of the Francesco Nori killed in the Pazzi conspiracy (1478). The latter had a posthumous son also named Francesco, but he was too young to be a factor in Lyons in 1490.

154. Francesco Sassetti to Lorenzo the Magnificent, May 24, 1489 (MAP, filza 88, no. 199). One of the grandsons of Matteo di ser Giovanni was cashier. This Matteo was with the Tavola of Florence in the 1440's. Guglielmo da Gagliano is probably the same as Guglielmo di Niccolò. Avaretto and Pagolo Palmieri were with the Lyons branch when Lionetto de' Rossi was manager (1485) and drew a salary of ∇30 each. Letter of Lionetto to Lorenzo, May 24, 1486 (MAP, filza 39, no. 513).

155. Pagnini, *Della Decima*, II, 304. Cf. Ehrenberg, *Fugger*, I, 284–285. This author's information is sometimes inaccurate.

156. Spinelli to Lorenzo, September 2, 1487 (MAP, filza 40, no. 136): ". . . il male vostro giova loro."

157. Buser, *Beziehungen*, pp. 332, 548.

158. Spinelli in Chambéry to Lorenzo Tornabuoni in Florence, February 10, 1495 (MAP, filza 137, no. 550). Cardinal Barbiano wrote in the same vein to Lodovico il Moro, July 3, 1494. Text in Buser, *Beziehungen*, p. 550.

159. Y. Renouard, "Lumières nouvelles sur les hommes d'affaires italiens du moyen âge," *Annales (Economies, Sociétés, Civilisations)*, 10:70 (1955).

160. Félix Reynaud, *Histoire du commerce de Marseille*, II (Paris, 1951), pt 2, 565–573.

161. Port-de-Bouc's location was more favorable in relation to Avignon than that of Marseilles which lies farther east.

162. The counts of Anjou and Provence were claimants to the throne of Naples.

163. MAP, filza 153, no. 3, fols. 33, 78, 82.

164. Archivio dello Spedale degli Innocenti, Estranei, No. 488, fol. 338: "1442, Giovanni Zampini dimora a Vingnone per chonto nostro dè avere."

165. MAP, filza 153, no. 3, fol. 78.

166. *Ibid.*, fols. 82, 85.

167. *Ibid.*, fol. 96.

168. *Ibid.*, fols. 85, 86, 90, 94.

169. This total is made up as follows:

	f.	s.	d.
1446–1447	3556	14	6
1448	1972	0	0
1449–1450	3420	0	0
Total	8948	14	6

170. Sieveking, *Handlungsbücher*, p. 10.

171. This information is based on the portate reports of Baldovini and Benci (Catasto No. 832 (Vaio), fols. 213–218 and 651–653).

172. Sieveking, *Handlungsbücher*, p. 10.

173. Sassetti's libro segreto, fol. 14: "La compangnia et trafficho di Vingnone che debbe dire in Francesco Sassetti et Giovanni Zampini, ma per ancora dicie in Giovanni Zampini."

174. Sassetti's libro segreto, fol. 26: "Giovanni Zampini di Vingnone per conto nuovo d'avanzi appartenenti a llui e a me, perchè i Medici ne trassono il corpo loro e gli avanzi insino di dicembre. 1468."

175. Sieveking, *Aus Genueser Rechnungsbüchern*, p. 101.

176. Sassetti's libro segreto, fol. 28.

177. There are references to King René in the few extant letters of the Avignon branch.

178. Michele Dini to Lorenzo the Magnificent, June 29, 1476 (MAP, filza 33, no. 497). Cf. Catasto No. 1019 (Drago 1481), fol. 335.

179. "Solevo avere parte a Vingnone nel trafficho di Giovanni Zanpini che finì già fa circha a 2 anni et disse in nome di Michele Dini dove s'attende a ritrarre et non si fa nulla perchè è finita già fa più tenpo," Catasto No. 1013 (Leon Bianco 1481), fol. 320v.

180. MAP, filza 34, no. 387.

181. The last conjecture is the more likely. Dini to Lorenzo, October 13, 1489 (MAP, filza 73, no. 424).

182. Spinelli to Lorenzo, February 15, 1491 (MAP, filza 42, no. 18).

183. Pagnini, *Della Decima*, II, 304–305.

184. In 1470, Francesco Sassetti had a deposit of 14,000 petty florins or 7,305 florins di suggello with Lionardo Mannelli & Co. of Avignon (Libro segreto, fol. 30).

185. Letter of Giovanni Zampini & Co. in Avignon to Giorgio e Paolo Cigallo in Majorca, July 29, 1463 (MAP, filza 68, no. 60). Letter of the same firm to Antonio Zordano, captain of the Venetian galleys (MAP, filza 82, no. 25).

186. MAP, filza 73, no. 355.

187. Rosso da Sommaia was in Montpellier in 1466, according to the balance sheet of the Lyons branch (*Rosso da Sommaia, per nostro chonto, in Montpellieri,* MAP, filza 83, no. 49, fol. 304ᵛ). There also are extant three letters of his addressed to Lorenzo in 1471, 1476, and 1477. The last of the three, dated February 18, 1477, deals with the helmet of Charles the Bold picked up on battlefield of Nancy and offered for sale by a retainer or a vassal of the seneschal of Toulouse (MAP, filza 33, fol. 118).

188. Rosso da Sommaia in Montpellier to Lorenzo the Magnificent, November 15, 1471 (MAP, filza 27, no. 565). In this letter, Rosso claims to belong to a family of "poor gentlemen."

189. Catasto No. 1005 (Leon Nero, 1481), fol. 423: "Lorenzo sta a Monpolieri nella ragione che disse in Giovanni Zampini loquale Giovanni è morto e la detta ragione finita et atendono a ritrarsi."

190. Michele Dini to Lorenzo, January 12, 1483 (MAP, filza 38, no. 387).

191. Catasto No. 1019 (Drago, 1481), fol. 335. By the way, Rosso's son was called Giovanni Zampini after his great-uncle.

CHAPTER XIII

Medici Branches outside Italy: Bruges and London

1. *Codex diplomaticus lubecensis,* V, 633–634. The date is May 27, 1416. See also the letter of Giovanni de' Medici & Co. in Florence to Lodovico Baglioni in Lübeck, December 11, 1415 (ASF, MAP, filza 83, no. 51, fol. 312).

2. Léon Mirot, "La Société des Raponde, Dine Raponde" in *Etudes lucquoises* (Paris, 1930), pp. 79–169; also in *Bibliothèque de l'Ecole des Chartes,* 89:299–389 (1928). Cf. R. de Roover, "Communauté des marchands lucquois," pp. 74–79.

3. Catasto No. 51 (Leon d'Oro, 1427), fols. 1162ʳ–1168ʳ, 1187ʳ–1190ᵛ, 1191ʳ-1200ʳ. This branch of the Bardi family changed its name to Gualterotti in 1393.

4. Camerani, *Documenti,* pp. 29, 31, Nos. 35, 45. Cf. Martens, "Les Maisons de Medici et de Bourgogne," pp. 115–129. Mlle Martens, however, confuses the two competing Medici banks.

5. In addition, Ubertino de' Bardi owed £500 groat, Venetian currency, or 5,000 ducats, to the Venice branch, according to the balance sheet of 1427. His total debt, therefore, exceeded 20,000 florins, a sizeable sum. On the other hand, Totto Machiavelli and Ubertino de' Bardi were creditors of the Florentine Tavola to the extent of 3,600 florins, probably for wool shipped to Florence through the Straits of Gibraltar. Gualterotto Gualterotti of Bruges, on the contrary, owed 3,800 florins to the Tavola of Florence.

6. R. de Roover, "Oprichting van het Brugse filiaal," p. 7. This is the author's inaugural address as a member of the Royal Flemish Academy of Science, Letters, and Fine Arts (Belgium) and contains a slightly different and more detailed narrative.

7. MAP, filza 68, no. 2: Ricordo a te Marcho Spinellini, Verona, December 23, 1430.

8. Scottish, Northumberland, and other northern wools were "slight" wools that could not bear high export duties. Eileen Power, "The Wool Trade" pp. 43, 50.

9. Letter of October 4, 1432 (MAP, filza 68, no. 472). The printed inventory states that this letter emanates from Averardo de' Medici, but this is questionable.

10. Origo, "The Domestic Enemy," p. 363, n. 81.

11. MAP, filza 153, no. 3, fol. 17.

12. MAP, filza 68, no. 588: Ricordo per Bernardo Portinari.

13. Camerani, *Documenti*, p. 50, No. 115.

14. The duke of Burgundy had left the English alliance and made peace with the king of France by the treaty of Arras (1435). As a result, the French were able to resume the offensive and reconquered Paris (April 13, 1436). The English considered themselves betrayed by the duke of Burgundy and took sanctions against him and his subjects. For a time, trade intercourse between England and Flanders was suspended.

15. His presence in Antwerp is attested in a document of March 11, 1439 (MAP, filza 68, no. 5) and in a letter written in Brussels by one Imbert de Plaine on August 30 or 31 (MAP, filza 93, no. 612).

16. MAP, filza 68, no. 5 and filza 94, no. 159.

17. MAP, filza 94, no. 146, fols. 241–242. The letter is dated from Bruges, May 23, 1438. The standard value of the English noble was 6s. 8d. st. or three nobles to the pound sterling.

18. He is still called factor, not partner, in a notarial deed dated March 13, 1439 (Camerani, *Documenti*, p. 54, No. 129).

19. MAP, filza 153, no. 3, fols. 18, 30. Grunzweig (*Correspondance*, p. vii) asserts that such a branch existed in 1421, but there is not a shred of evidence to support this assertion. The document, a catasto report (mentioned p. viii), dates from 1451 instead of 1431. In this connection, see also R. de Roover, "Oprichting van het Brugse filiaal,'" p. 5, n. 5 and p. 6, n. 6.

20. MAP, filza 153, no. 3, fol. 46.

21. See above, Chap. V, n. 41.

22. Tani was not a good linguist. He never learned English or French.

23. MAP, filza 94, No. 134: instructions for Gerozzo de' Pigli.

24. MAP, filza 153, no. 3, fol. 83. The tenor of this contract is ably discussed by Lewis Einstein, *Italian Renaissance in England*, pp. 242–245.

25. The evidence is found in the entries of the libro segreto (MAP, filza 153, no. 3, fols. 86, 89).

26. Einstein also discusses Pigli's instructions (pp. 245–249).

27. By April, 1448, Angelo Tani seems to have been in charge of the Bruges branch (Camerani, *Documenti*, p. 71, No. 194).

28. MAP, filza 88, no. 391, fols. 505–506.

29. MAP, filza 153, no. 3, fol. 83.

30. MAP, filza 153, no. 3, fols. 94, 96.

31. Grunzweig, *Correspondance*, pp. 19, 24, 26.

32. Evidence is given in a letter of the London branch, dated October 4, 1453, which mentions several times the firm "Agniolo Tani e chompagni di Brugia" (MAP, filza 84, no. 89, fol. 178).

33. There is also a legal aspect: if the Medici had kept their name in the style of the two accomandite, they would have been fully liable.

34. Simone Nori to Giovanni Benci, September 25, 1453 (MAP, filza 88, no.

111): "la brighata grachiava." This is the first part of a letter of which Grunzweig (*Correspondance,* pp. 24–26, No. 13) published a postscript (*arroto*) dated October 4, 1453 (MAP, filza 98, no. 377).

35. Pigli announces his safe arrival in Bruges in a letter dated November 10, 1453. Almost a year later, on October 20, 1454, he writes that he is about to leave but awaits news from Angelo Tani, who was then in Florence and expected to rejoin his post (Grunzweig, *Correspondance,* pp. 26–27, 46–47).

36. Letter of September 25, 1453, quoted in note 34: "Io ci ò credito e ben visto e amato quanto Italiano."

37. Power, "The Wool Trade," p. 46.

38. *The Libelle of Englyshe Polycye, 1436,* ed. Sir George Warner (Oxford, 1926), pp. 18–21.

39. A letter of Simone Nori, dated October 4, 1453, mentions a small bale containing ten pieces of suantoni shipped to Florence (MAP, filza 84, no. 89). Grunzweig (*Correspondance,* p. 23) refers to the same shipment, which also included one kersey. Cf. Ruddock, *Italian Merchants in Southampton,* p. 93.

40. Power, "The Wool Trade," pp. 41–45. Cf. Grunzweig, *Correspondance,* pp. 70–72.

41. Armand Deroisy, "Les Routes des laines anglaises vers la Lombardie," *Revue du Nord,* 25:40–60 (1939). Some wool also reached Milan by way of Gibraltar and Genoa (Grunzweig, *Correspondance,* pp. 136–37, No. 43).

42. Power, "The Wool Trade," p. 46.

43. The Medici saw the struggle coming. In a letter of September 25, 1453, Nori reported that the Queen (Margaret of Anjou) had gone to Westminster because of her approaching confinement, and he added: "God grant that it be for the good of this Realm" (MAP, filza 88, no. 111). Prince Edward, later slain at the battle of Tewkesbury (1471), was born on October 13, 1453.

44. R. de Roover, "Balance commerciale," p. 377.

45. Peruzzi, *Storia del commercio,* Appendices, p. 82; Grunzweig, "Consulat de la Mer," pp. 24–25, 32, 53; F. E. de Roover, "Voyage de Girolamo Strozzi," pp. 135–36; R. de Roover, "Balance commerciale," pp. 377–379.

46. This contrast is brought out very clearly in *The Libelle* pp. 17–21. The Genoese, in 1436, the date of the *Libelle,* were still in control of the alum mines in Asia Minor of which they retained possession until 1455 (Heyd, *Histoire du commerce du Levant,* II, 320).

47. R. de Roover, "Balance commerciale," p. 381. Sources give various estimates as to the value of the cargo but fully agree as to its composition.

48. Letter of October 4, 1453, addressed to the Medici Tavola in Florence: ". . . perchè di danari, chome sapete, al chontinovo di chostà abiano di bixogno" (MAP, filza 84, no. 89).

49. ". . . trovando in Inghilterra una somma di lane a ddare a l'incontro d'alumi" (MAP, filza 12, no. 375).

50. Nori to Giovanni Benci, September 25, 1453 (MAP, filza 88, no. 111).

51. Unfortunately, the letter does not disclose whether Nori bought the wool from woolgrowers or from middlemen.

52. Some Dutch linens which Nori commissioned Tani to send to Geneva were so badly packed that three fourths were frayed upon arrival at destination.

53. Letter of September 25, 1453 (MAP, filza 88, no. 111): "Agnolo à le forbici a cintola e a Tommaso salta tropo presto il fummo al naso."

54. "Al chontinovo sono stato e sono obrigato per loro in £2,000 sterlini per tenpi di lane e danari trattimi."

55. MAP, filza 83, no. 95, fols. 537–538.

56. Statutes at Large: 3 Edward IV, c. 1 (1463). Ruddock (*Italian Merchants in Southampton*, p. 208) mentions this statute but gives a different version of the sequence of events. There is no question that licenses continued to be issued after 1463. No wool was shipped in 1464 either on the Florentine or on the Venetian galleys (Grunzweig, *Correspondance*, p. 133).

57. 4 Edward IV, c. 2 (1464). See also 12 Edward IV, c. 5 (1472). This statute makes it clear that wool and woolfells to be shipped "towards the West" in galleys or carracks were not subject to the rules of the staple.

58. *Calendar of the Patent Rolls, Edward IV and Henry VI, 1467–1477*, II (London, 1900), 11, 132, 160, 273, 547, *et passim*. Cf. Cora L. Scofield, *The Life and Reign of Edward the Fourth* (London, 1923), II, 423, 424, 426.

59. ASF, Catasto No. 798 (Carro, 1457), fol. 651. Cf. Grunzweig, *Correspondance*, pp. 65, 68–69.

60. *Correspondance*, pp. 119, 131. The winding up of the partnership lasted until 1464.

61. *Ibid.*, pp. 116, 121. The dowager of Hungerford refused to pay a single penny. Castillon was the last battle of the Hundred Years' War. As a result of this defeat, the English lost their last strongholds in Guyenne and kept only Calais. Lord Hungerford was beheaded after the battle of Hexham, in which the supporters of Henry VI were routed (May, 1464). The matter of his ransom was still in abeyance (Grunzweig, *Correspondance*, p. 132). It is highly probable, though there is no evidence, that the Medici were unable to collect anything.

62. Nori left London in November or December 1460 (Grunzweig, *Correspondance*, p. 95) and did not resume his duties until October 1461 (Scofield, *Life of Edward IV*, I, 196). The dates of the second trip are given in Grunzweig, *Correspondance*, pp. 106, 108, 115 and in a letter of Tommaso Portinari of May 3, 1465 (MAP, filza 12, no. 321). He reached Bruges on March 30, 1465 (MAP, filza 12, no. 316).

63. Grunzweig, *Correspondance*, p. xxviii.

64. Promemoria a Lorenzo de' Medici per Francesco Nori (MAP, filza 20, no. 622).

65. Scofield, *Life of Edward IV*, II, 421. This license, it should be noted, was issued while the statute forbidding the shipment of wool from Southampton (3 Edward IV, c. 1) was in effect.

66. Two hundred times four marks equals 800 marks, the principal of the loan. The duties were as follows:

subsidy 43s. 4d. per sack of wool or 240 woolfells
customs 10s. 0d. per sack
————
53s. 4d. or four marks at 13s. 4d. *per mark*.

(*Calendar of the Patent Rolls, Edward IV and Henry VI*, II, 239).

67. MAP, filza 99, no. 2, fols. 2–3. There is also a brief discussion of this contract in Einstein, *Italian Renaissance in England*, pp. 256–257. This discussion, however, is not very enlightening.

68. These figures correspond to 41.6, 25, and 16.7 percent, respectively.

69. Scriptà dell' achordo e fine fatta con Gierozzo de' Pigli, 1467 (MAP, filza 148, no. 32).

70. *Correspondance*, p. xxviii.

71. The letter is addressed to Lorenzo the Magnificent (MAP, filza 20, no. 459).

72. *Calendar of the Patent Rolls, Edward IV and Henry VI,* II, 239. The mention of an establishment composed of three clerks and four servants would suggest that his firm was important.

73. *Calendar of the Patent Rolls, Edward IV, Edward V, Richard III, 1476–1485,* III (London, 1901), pp. 251, 296. The other license was issued to permit the exportation of 15½ sacks in settlement of a small debt of £41 6s. 8d. or 62 marks.

74. ASF, Conventi Soppressi 78, Familiario, vol. 316, fol. 54: Lettere a Benedetto Dei.

75. Pagnini, *Della Decima,* II, 305. See also Camerani, *Documenti,* pp. 78, 85, 88, 91 *et passim.* Jacopo del Zaccheria was a brother of Giuliano del Zaccheria, manager of the Lyons branch. He was in London from 1460 onward (Camerani, p. 94, No. 268). Lorenzo Attavanti or Ottovanti served first in Bruges where he was a giovane in 1458 (*ibid.,* p. 85, No .240).

76. *Calendar of the Patent Rolls, Edward IV,* II, 160 (May 29, 1469).

77. Camerani, *Documenti,* pp. 78, 97, 123, 125, *et passim.*

78. Scofield, *Life of Edward IV,* I, 453–454 and II, 423–424.

79. According to a letter of Angelo Tani to Giovanni d'Agnolo de' Bardi, January 10, 1480/81 (in the private Guicciardini Archives, Florence, No. 49).

80. The date of the grant is December 20, 1467. The king's debt amounted exactly to £8,468 18s. 8d. or £8,500 in round figures (*Calendar of the Patent Rolls, Edward IV,* II, 11). Cf. Scofield, *Life of Edward IV,* II, 423. This figure given in the English sources corresponds to that given in Tani's reports: "Con questa vi mando il bilancio di questa ragione che, come per esso potrete vedere, dalle £8,500 in fuori che s'ànno avere dalla Maestà di questo Re, non v'à altra detta che non s'àbino a ritrarre in brieve." Letter of January 12, 1468 (MAP, filza 23, no. 102). The same figure is also given in two later letters of January 23 and February 12, 1468 (MAP, filza 137, no. 192 and filza 22, no. 105).

81. Letter of January 23 cited above: ". . . e restono avere in una partita dalla Maestà di questo Re £8,500 in circha, che attenghono a lloro, di che n'ànno asengnamenti sulle chostume e credo chol tenpo s'àbino a ritrarre, ma fieno lunghi perchè sono asengniati sulla mezza e non più." In fact, one needed to export more than 3,000 sacks of wool to cancel the debt, since £8,500 corresponds to 12,750 marks.

82. These data are based on the information given in Tani's reports cited above in n. 80.

83. Tani to Piero di Cosimo, February 12, 1468. In this letter, Tani expresses the hope of getting part of the subsidies, fifteenths and tenths, to be voted by Parliament and the clergy in order to finance a planned invasion of France which the writer does not expect to materialize. The prediction became true: Edward IV never carried out his intended invasion. On May 9, 1468, Tani reports that Edward IV promised to give him from £3,000 to £4,000 if the subsidies were voted by Parliament (MAP, filza 20, no. 391). They were actually voted (Scofield, *Life of Edward IV,* I, 452).

84. Tani to Piero, September 1, 1468 (MAP, filza 22, no. 174).

85. Scofield, *Life of Edward IV,* II, 423.

86. Scofield, II, 423 and Tani's letter of September 1, above n. 84. The £2,000 secured by pledges had not been repaid.

87. Cora Scofield thinks that this patent refers to a new loan, but this interpretation, in the light of the Medici correspondence, is extremely doubtful (*Life of Edward IV,* II, 421).

88. Angelo Tani to Piero di Cosimo, May 9, 1468 (MAP, filza 20, no. 391).

89. These statements are found in a letter, dated May 23, addressed to Lorenzo di Piero and attached to a copy of the above letter of May 9, 1468.

90. Tornabuoni apparently refused to take cloth in payment of the balance due from the London branch. Tani to Piero, September 1, 1468 (MAP, filza 22, no. 174).

91. Reports of Angelo Tani, no date, but after 1474 (MAP, filza 82, no. 163, fols. 500–501).

92. Joint letter written from Ghent by Tommaso Portinari and Angelo Tani, June 18, 1469 (MAP, filza 17, no. 711).

93. Scofield, *Life of Edward IV*, II, 424.

94. *Calendar of the Patent Rolls, Edward IV*, II, 273.

95. Thomas Rymer's *Foedera* (London, 1727), XII, 7–9.

96. MAP, filza 82, no. 163; A. Warburg, "Flandrische Kunst und florentinische Renaissance," *Gesammelte Schriften* (Leipzig, 1932), I, 375–376.

97. Sieveking, *Handlungsbücher*, p. 51. This figure is quoted in a settlement of accounts between Lorenzo and Giuliano di Piero de' Medici and the heirs of their first cousin, Pierfrancesco de' Medici (MAP, filza 99, no. 8, fols. 30–31).

98. *Calendar of the Patent Rolls, Edward IV*, II, 401. For a more detailed biography of Canigiani, see Scofield, *Life of Edward IV*, II, 420–428.

99. The marriage took place between November 3 and November 30, 1473, since it is mentioned on this latter date in a letter of Cristofano Spini (MAP, filza 26, no. 133). Cf. *Calendar of the Patent Rolls, Edward IV*, II, 466.

100. Scofield, *Life of Edward IV*, II, 420.

101. *Ibid.*, II, 425–427. I disagree with Cora Scofield's statement that it was Canigiani's change of allegiance — instead of mismanagement — that got him into trouble with the Medici.

102. *Calendar of the Patent Rolls, Edward IV*, II, 481. Cf. Grunzweig, *Correspondance*, p. xxx.

103. The total purchase price of the wool was £6,795 16s. 5d. plus £952 for packing and incidentals. The exact figure of the customs was £1,738 12s. 3d. The sack thus came to £9 11s., which is quite plausible.

104. Letter of July 1, 1475: "Egl'à mancho fede che un Turcho" (MAP, filza 26, no. 160).

105. MAP, filza 99, no. 3, fols. 4–5.

106. Pigello Portinari to Cosimo de' Medici, May 19, 1464 (MAP, filza 12, no. 328): "Sechondo mi scrive Tommaso, la ragione loro finiscie per tutto questo anno" (According to what Tommaso writes me, the partnership will last through this year). This means through March 24, 1465.

107. Grunzweig (*Correspondance*, p. xiii) states that Tommaso Portinari came to Bruges in 1437, but this is certainly incorrect, since the Bruges branch was not founded until 1439. Moreover, Tommaso, according to his father's catasto report was not born in 1425, but in 1428 or perhaps 1429.

108. Grunzweig, *Correspondence*, p. xviii.

109. According to Grunzweig (*ibid.*), this appointment dates back to 1464. At any rate, he is designated as the Duke's councilor in a charter dated May 18, 1465 concerning the toll of Gravelines. In 1468, Tommaso Portinari marched in the parade for the wedding of Charles the Bold at the head of the Florentine nation, "dressed as a councilor of Monseigneur the Duke" (R. de Roover, *Money and Banking in Bruges*, p. 21).

110. Tommaso Portinari to Piero di Cosimo, November 10, 1464 (MAP, filza 12, no. 375), December 18, 1464 (MAP, filza 12, nos. 381 and 395), and a postscript of uncertain date, but before January 9, 1465 (MAP, filza 12, no. 392).

111. Tommaso Portinari to Cosimo de' Medici, July 1, 1464 (MAP, filza 73, no. 315).

112. Grunzweig, *Correspondance*, pp. 109, 117.

113. The text of Tommaso's letter is in Grunzweig, *Correspondance*, pp. 122–125. It is quoted in Singer, *The Earliest Chemical Industry*, p. 150.

114. Pigello Portinari to Cosimo de' Medici, May 19, 1464 (MAP, filza 12, no. 328).

115. Portinari was invited to come to Florence in order to discuss the terms of the new contract. He left Bruges late in June 1465, traveled through Lorraine and reached Milan on July 23. (Portinari from Milan to Piero, July 24, 1465, MAP, filza 17, no. 576. He rejoined his post in Bruges on October 5, 1465 (MAP, filza 12, no. 372).

116. MAP, filza 84, no. 22, fols. 47–49.

117. Tommaso Portinari to Piero de' Medici, March 4, 1466 (MAP, filza 12, no. 314). The purchase price was payable in six yearly installments.

118. Joseph Maréchal, *Bijdrage tot de Geschiedenis van het Bankwezen te Brugge* (Bruges, 1955), pp. 61–62.

119. Letter to Piero, March 29, 1466 (MAP, filza 12, no. 314).

120. Scofield, *Life of Edward IV*, I, 405.

121. ". . . non sarebbe bene che altri prendessi la lepre che per noi è stata levata" (letter cited above, n. 119).

122. Grunzweig, *Correspondance*, pp. xxiii-xxiv.

123. The farm of Gravelines was offered to Portinari by Antoine de Croy, who was at that time the all-powerful advisor of Philip the Good. Tommaso Portinari to Piero de' Medici, July 1, 1464 (MAP, filza 73, no. 315).

124. Portinari to Piero, November 9, 1464 (MAP, filza 12, no. 375) and December 1, 1464 (filza 12, no. 379).

125. Georg Schanz, *Englische Handelspolitik gegen Ende des Mittelalters* (Leipzig, 1881), I, 445. In reprisal, products of the Low Countries were barred from England by statute (4 Edward IV, c. 5). Cf. Scofield, *Life of Edward IV*, I, 357–358, 367.

126. Louis Gilliodts-van Severen, *Cartulaire de l'ancien grand tonlieu de Bruges*, I (Bruges, 1908), 341–343.

127. The toll of Gravelines was temporarily abolished after the death of Charles the Bold but was reestablished by Maximilian of Austria and restored to Portinari in 1485 (Grunzweig, *Correspondance*, pp. xxxv-xxxvii).

128. The pound groat of 240 groats was worth six pounds Artois of 40 groats or 20 stivers. This smaller pound is the origin of the Dutch guilder.

129. Georges Bigwood, *Le Régime juridique et économique du commerce de l'argent dans la Belgique du moyen âge*, I (Brussels, 1921), 663.

130. Armand Grunzweig, however, states that there were three galleys and that one of them was shipwrecked on the first voyage. "La Filiale de Bruges des Médici," *La Revue de la Banque*, 12:79 (1948).

131. Portinari in Bergen-op-Zoom, Nov. 27, 1464 (MAP, filza 12, nos. 374, 379).

132. Grunzweig, *Correspondance*, pp. 108, 114, 129, 133; Tommaso Portinari in Brussels to Piero di Cosimo, February 14, 1465 (MAP, filza 12, no. 313). The galleys had not been sold by May 1465 (MAP, filza 12, no. 321).

133. Grunzweig, "La Filiale de Bruges des Médici," p. 79.

134. Grunzweig, *Correspondance*, p. xxi. Cf. F. E. de Roover, "A Prize of War: A Painting of Fifteenth-Century Merchants," *Bulletin of the Business Historical Society*, 19:4 (1945).

135. In a letter of January 9, 1469, Portinari is still pleading with Piero to

keep the galleys (MAP, filza 12, no. 307). Cf. Letter of January 31, 1469 (MAP, filza 12, no. 307 and filza 17, no. 607).

136. Letter of Tani and Portinari to Piero di Cosimo, June 18, 1469 (MAP, filza 17, no. 711).

137. MAP, filza 84, no. 28, fol. 60.

138. MAP, filza 84, no. 29, fols. 61–62. This contract was not signed in Florence, so one copy was sent to Bruges for Portinari's signature.

139. Tommaso Portinari in Milan to Lorenzo de' Medici, October 27, 1469 (MAP, filza 22, no. 227).

140. Sieveking (Handlungsbücher, p. 50) saw the implications of these clauses very well and it is only fair to give due credit to this pioneer of business history.

141. Tommaso Portinari in Bruges to Piero di Cosimo, December 7, 1469 (MAP, filza 17, no. 465).

142. Warburg, "Flandrische Kunst," pp. 197, 377.

143. ASF, Diplomatico, Santa Maria Nuova di Firenze, September 7, 1470: ". . . dictus Thomas . . . vendidisse dicto Johanni . . . septem octavas partes duarum galearum que comuniter appellantur galee Burgundie."

144. Tommaso Portinari to Lorenzo, June 9, 1470 (MAP, filza 4, no. 501). Antonio di Bernardo de' Medici, after his recall to Florence, went into the diplomatic service. In 1479, he was sent by Lorenzo the Magnificent as a special envoy to Constantinople in order to procure from Sultan Mahomet II the arrest and extradition of Bernardo Bandini-Baroncelli, one of the murderers of Giuliano de' Medici. Bandini, as is well known, was brought in chains to Florence and executed.

145. MAP, filza 84, no. 24, fols. 51–52: contract of 1471.

146. Sieveking, Handlungsbücher, p. 52.

147. MAP, filza 94, no. 198, fols. 357–358.

148. MAP, filza 84, no. 25, fols. 53–54.

149. MAP, filza 82, no. 112, fols. 320–323.

150. Memorandum of Lorenzo the Magnificent (MAP, filza 84, no. 21) and report of Angelo Tani (MAP, filza 82, no. 163): ". . . lo feciono per loro sanza dirmi nulla."

151. Quite a few articles have been published on this affair of the Burgundian galleys: A. von Reumont, "Di alcune relazioni dei Fiorentini colla città di Danzica; memoria," Archivio storico italiano, New Series, XIII, pt. I (1861), 37–47; G. von der Ropp, "Zur Geschichte des Alaunhandels," pp. 130–136; Otto Meltzing, "Tommaso Portinari und sein Konflikt mit der Hanse," Hansische Geschichtsblätter, 12:101–123 (1906). F. E. de Roover, "A Prize of War," pp. 3–12; idem, "Le Voyage de Girolamo Strozzi," pp. 117–136.

152. This Francesco Tedaldi was quite a colorful personality: he was the author of a Latin novel and a humanist besides being a merchant and a navigator. Paul O. Kristeller, "Una novella latina e il suo autore, Francesco Tedaldi, mercante fiorentino del Quattrocento," offprint from Miscellanea in onore di Emilio Santini (Palermo, 1955), 24 pp. Francesco Tedaldi is sometimes called Francesco Sermattei (von Reumont, "Relazioni," p. 39; Ruddock, Italian Merchants, pp. 198, 210, 214).

153. Some of the injured were cast pitilessly into the sea. A. von Reumont, "Relazioni," p. 42; Hanserecesse (1431–1476), Zweite Abteilung, VII, 63.

154. Hanserecesse (1431–1476), 2. Abt. VII, 115.

155. F. E. de Roover, "Voyage de Girolamo Strozzi," p. 136.

156. Hanserecesse (1431–1476), 2. Abt., VII, 115, No. 41; Gilliodts-van Severen, Inventaire des archives de la ville de Bruges, VI, 417, No. 1262.

157. *Hanserecesse (1431–1476)*, 2. Abt., VII, 65, No. 41. Incidentally, in answering the claim, the Hansa towns disclaimed being a federation; they were only a *corpus* with regard to the privileges they enjoyed in certain countries.

158. See the complaint of Master Jehan Halewijn, the Duke's envoy, at the Conference of Utrecht (*Hanserecesse (1431–1476)*, VII, 82, No. 106).

159. von Reumont, "Relazioni," pp. 37–47.

160. Hamburg and Lübeck claimed at the Conference of Utrecht that they forbade the sale of the loot within their walls, but Spini replied that this prohibition was observed by day and not by night (*Hanserecesse (1431–1476)*, VII, 65, No. 41). It is clear from the records that the Hansa towns were not acting in good faith.

161. *Ibid.*, pp. 381–382, No. 168. This attitude did not change between 1474 and 1495. *Hanserecesse (1477–1530)*, Dritte Abteilung, ed. D. Schäfer, I (Leipzig, 1881), 425, No. 552.

162. *Hanserecesse (1431–1476)*, 2. Abt., VII, 234–35, No. 135. In January 1474, Portinari impounded the goods of the German merchants, their bank accounts, and their credits with furriers.

163. Meltzing, "Portinari," p. 120. The exact date of this decision is August 5, 1496.

164. *Hanserecesse (1477–1530)*, 3. Abt., I, 249, No. 327.

165. Meltzing, "Portinari," p. 121.

166. von der Ropp, "Alaunhandel," p. 136.

167. F. E. de Roover, "Early Examples of Insurance," pp. 191–194.

168. Michel Mollat, "Recherches sur les finances des ducs valois de Bourgogne," *Revue historique*, 219:318–319 (1958).

169. Lionetto de' Rossi in Lyons to Francesco Nori in Florence, June 26, 1476 (MAP, filza 34, no. 342). The Medici evidently hoped that the Duke would be forced to negotiate and to make peace — which course he did not follow — because there was so much of their money at stake.

170. Gilliodts-van Severen, *Cartulaire de l'ancien grand tonlieu*, I, 343; Bigwood, *Commerce de l'argent*, I, 89, 470, 663. Grunzweig (*Correspondance*, p. xxxi) states that the debt amounted to £57,000 groat, which is incorrect, since the text refers to small pounds of 40 groats, not to large pounds of 240 groats.

171. MAP, filza 84, no. 21.

172. *Ibid.*: "Et lui, per entrare in grazia del prefato Ducha et farssi grande alle nostre spese, non se ne churava."

173. Edgar Prestage, *The Portuguese Pioneers* (London, 1933), p. 188; Henry H. Hart, *Sea Road to the Indies* (New York, 1950), p. 28.

174. Tommaso Portinari in Milan to Lorenzo the Magnificent, November 28, 1478 (MAP, filza 137, no. 425).

175. Prestage, *Portuguese Pioneers*, pp. 216–217, 234.

176. Marchionni later helped to finance the first voyages to the East Indies (Heyd, *Histoire du commerce du Levant*, II, 512–514). In Portuguese records, Bartolomeo Marchionni is sometimes called "Bartholomeu Florentim." Prospero Peragallo, "Cenni intorno alla colonia italiana in Portogallo nei secoli XIV, XV, e XVI," *Miscellanea di Storia italiana*, XL (Turin, 1904), 417–420; Charles Verlinden, "La Colonie italienne de Lisbonne et le développement de l'économie métropolitaine et coloniale portugaise," *Studi in onore di Armando Sapori* (Milan, 1957,) pp. 621, 623.

177. The contract is no longer extant but is mentioned among the papers which Rinieri da Ricasoli took to Bruges when he was sent there by Lorenzo to effect a final settlement with Tommaso Portinari (MAP, filza 89, no. 241).

178. The wool business was managed by Cristofano Spini who was entitled to 2s. in the pound or ten percent, so that the share of the Medici was the same as Portinari's, 45 percent (Map, filza 84, no. 21).

179. The Italian text says: ". . . e questi sono i ghuadangni grandi che ci à assengniati il ghoverno di Tommaxo Portinari" (MAP, filza 84, no. 21, fol. 46).

180. The ducats are reckoned at the rate of sixty groats apiece.

181. Antonio di Bernardo de' Medici to Giuliano di Piero de' Medici, April 11, 1478 (MAP, filza 103, no. 109). Tommaso Portinari was probably in Florence at the time of the Pazzi conspiracy (April 26, 1478).

182. Giovanni d'Adoardo Portinari in Milan to Lorenzo de' Medici, October 21, 1478 (MAP, filza 137, no. 422).

183. Lorenzo the Magnificent to Girolamo Morelli, ambassador in Milan, October 16 and November 14, 1478 (MAP, filza 96, nos. 91 and 93).

184. Tommaso Portinari in Milan to Lorenzo de' Medici, November 28, 1478 (MAP, filza 137, no. 429).

185. Lorenzo de' Medici in Florence to Girolamo Morelli in Milan, December 22, 1478 (MAP, filza 50, no. 6).

186. Rinieri da Ricasoli was a resident of Bruges in 1448 (Gilliodts-van Severen, *Cartulaire de l'estaple,* I, 692, No. 863). He was still there in 1453 when he was fined for removing a tombstone in the Florentine chapel at the Friars Minor (Grunzweig, *Correspondance,* pp. 29, 33, 36–37). According to the records of the Arte del Cambio, Rinieri da Ricasoli was a partner in the firm Antonio da Rabatta and Bernardo Cambi from 1465 through 1477 (Arte del Cambio, Libro di compagnie, No. 15, fols. 14ᵛ, 45ᵛ, 60ʳ). He apparently withdrew while he was in Bruges, from 1478 to 1481, and rejoined the same firm upon returning to Florence in 1481 (*ibid.,* fol. 80ʳ). His daughter Lisa married Tommaso Guidetti on October 2, 1481 (ASF, Carte Strozziane, Series IV, No. 418: Libro di ricordi di Tommaso Guidetti, fol. 3ᵛ).

187. ASF, Archivio notarile antecosimiano, G 620: Protocollo di ser Simone Grazzini da Staggia, 1472–1494, fols. 126–128. The date is September 1, 1479.

188. MAP, filza 89, no. 308: Ricordi e istruzioni di Lorenzo de' Medici a Rinieri Richasoli, September 14, 1479.

189. Rinieri da Ricasoli in Bruges to Lorenzo de' Medici, August 7, 1480 (MAP, filza 137, no. 449): ". . . che avendo queste ultime vostre, per le quali dite si tagli le parole del fare di nuove et si vadi drieto al chontarsi tutta la ragione." See also the letter of Angelo Tani of August 2, 1480 (MAP, filza 26, no. 293).

190. Only Ricasoli's letter accompanying the agreement has survived (see n. 189).

191. MAP, filza 84, no. 76, fols. 153–154.

192. Angelo Tani in Tours to Lorenzo de' Medici, April 9, 1481 (MAP, filza 38, no. 156).

193. Rinieri da Ricasoli in Bruges to Lorenzo de' Medici, August 19, 1480 (MAP, filza 137, no. 450).

194. Carte Strozziane, Series IV, No. 418: Libro di ricordi di Tommaso Guidetti, fols. 2–7.

195. The wool was valued at sixty-three ducats per sack, according to a loose sheet in the libro di ricordi of Guidetti.

196. ASF, Archivio dello spedale di Santa Maria Nuova, No. 130. It seems that the proceeds of the currants were embezzled by Folco d'Adoardo Portinari.

197. Warburg, "Flandrische Kunst," p. 202; Sieveking, *Handlungsbücher,* p. 53; Meltzing, *Bankhaus der Medici,* p. 137; Gutkind, *Cosimo de' Medici,* Eng.

ed., p. 186, Ital. ed., p. 247. Grunzweig (*Correspondance*, p. xxxiv) refutes the assertion of these writers.

198. Gilliodts-van Severen, *Cartulaire de l'estaple*, II, 224, No. 1181. In this document dated August 19, 1475, Bandini-Baroncelli is called: "Pierre Antoine Banding, marchand de Florence, facteur et compaignon de la compaignie de Francisque et Andrea de Pacis." Cf. Pagnini, *Della Decima*, II, 304.

199. Letter of Folco d'Adoardo Portinari in Bruges to Tommaso Portinari in Florence, May 23, 1478 (ASF, Spedale di Santa Maria Nuova, No. 130).

200. Grunzweig, *Correspondance*, p. xxx.

201. Gilliodts-van Severen, *Cartulaire de l'estaple*, II, 270, No. 1253.

202. Ehrenberg, *Zeitalter der Fugger*, I, 277.

203. Pagnini, *Della Decima*, II, 299–302.

204. Gilliodts-van Severen, *Cartulaire de l'ancien grand tonlieu*, I, 343–345.

205. Grunzweig, *Correspondance*, p. xxxvii.

206. MAP, filza 89, no. 197. The frauds were probably discovered in auditing the books for the settlement of accounts between Lorenzo the Magnificent and Tommaso Portinari.

207. Folco d'Adoardo Portinari was indicted on ten different counts before the Court of the Sei di Mercanzia, April 10, 1488 (ASF, Spedale di Santa Maria Nuova, No. 130).

208. See the letter written from London by Alessandro d'Adoardo Portinari, July 13, 1481 (Spedale di Santa Maria Nuova, No. 130).

209. Grunzweig, *Correspondance*, p. xxxviii.

210. Pierantonio Bandini-Baroncelli in Bruges to Lorenzo de' Medici, April 23, 1487 (MAP, filza 82, no. 41, fol. 179).

211. Tommaso Portinari stayed in Florence for several months until 1489. See Libro di ricordi di Tommaso Guidetti, fol. 7ᵛ (Carte Strozziane, Series IV, No. 418).

212. The mayor of Southampton insisted upon addressing Parliament and said that his town would be ruined if the Venetian galleys ceased to come there. Letter of Portinari and Spini, London, November 11, 1489 (MAP, filza 41, no. 388). Cf. Ruddock, *Italian Merchants*, p. 222. The text of the treaty is in Pagnini, *Della Decima*, II, 288–289.

213. Grunzweig, *Correspondance*, pp. xxxix-xl.

CHAPTER XIV

The Decline: 1464–1494

1. The evidence is found in a letter of ser Giovanni Caffarecci da Volterra to his pupil, Giovanni di Cosimo, who was being trained for business in the countinghouse of the "Rome" branch at Ferrara (May 5, 1438). Pieraccini, *La stirpe de' Medici*, I, 77. See above Chap. IX, n. 82.

2. Machiavelli, *History of Florence*, Bk. VII, chap. 2, pp. 353–355; *idem*, *Istorie fiorentine*, Libro VII, §10–11.

3. The defection of Messer Luca Pitti was apparently secured by Francesco Sassetti, who was Piero's emissary in this business. Jacopo Pitti, "Istoria fiorentina," p. 22.

4. Among the plotters was Amerigo di Giovanni Benci, the son of the former general manager.

5. Among those who question Machiavelli's veracity is Dorini (*I Medici*, p. 77). Those who accept Machiavelli's tale are Gino Capponi, F. A. Hyett, and

Panella (*Storia di Firenze*, p. 154). The most reliable account is given by Perrens (*History of Florence*, p. 231) who used the correspondence of Nicodemo Tranchedini, Milanese ambassador in Florence, a false friend of the Medici.

6. This was, of course, standard practice among Florentine business men. The only doubtful point is whether this audit was entrusted to Dietisalvi Neroni who already was inimical to the Medici in Cosimo's lifetime.

7. Alamanno Rinuccini (Ricordi, p. 94) gives a list of the business firms that failed. See also the letters of Alessandra Macinghi negli Strozzi to her son Filippo Strozzi in Naples: *Lettere di una gentildonna fiorentina*, ed. Cesare Guasti (Florence, 1877), pp. 333, 336, 354, 379, 421.

8. This branch of the Bardi family changed its name to Ilarioni in the fifteenth century.

9. Macinghi, *Lettere*, p. 336.

10. See also the letters of Tommaso Portinari written on December 18 and 26, 1464, and January 9 and 25, 1465 (MAP, filza 12, nos. 378, 381, and 311).

11. Tommaso Portinari in Bruges to Piero di Cosimo, January 25, 1465 (MAP, filza 12, no. 311).

12. The same to the same, April 5, 1465 (MAP, filza 12, no. 316).

13. Macinghi, *Lettere*, p. 350. Messer Angelo was in a pessimistic mood and went on to lament the fact that "the poor were without bread, the rich without brains, and the learned without common sense"; so the future was not bright.

14. Grunzweig, *Correspondance*, pp. xxiv-xxv; Tommaso Portinari in Bruges to Piero de' Medici, December 26, 1464 (MAP, filza 12, no. 381).

15. Heyd, *Commerce du Levant*, II, 328; Pagnini, *Della Decima*, II, 235–236.

16. Perrens, *History of Florence*, pp. 231–232. Perrens exaggerates: it is certainly untrue that Piero was the author of Lorenzo Ilarioni's ruin.

17. Macinghi, *Lettere*, pp. 358, 379. Gianfrancesco Strozzi (*ibid.*, p. 421) also came to an agreement with his creditors and promised to satisfy them in full, but only in installments extending over eight years.

18. See the important letter of Pigello Portinari to Piero di Cosimo, June 29, 1467 (MAP, filza 17, no. 569).

19. *Ibid.*: "Io ho molto bene inteso della deliberazione avete fatta e del'ordine dato per tutto, che non si dia graveza l'una ragione al'altra, che, come vi dissi per altra mia, lo lodo e commendo."

20. It is untrue that Sassetti around 1440 entered the service of the Medici Bank as a factor in Avignon, since the Avignon branch was not founded until 1446. He was always in Geneva. The mistake was first made by his descendant and copied by others: "Notizie dell'origine e nobilità della famiglia dei Sassetti raccolte da Francesco di Giambatista Sassetti, 1600," *Lettere edite e inedite di Filippo Sassetti* (Florence, 1855), p. xxxv.

21. R. de Roover, "Lorenzo il Magnifico e il tramonto del Banco dei Medici," *Archivio storico italiano*, 107:185 (1949).

22. F. E. de Roover, "Francesco Sassetti," p. 76.

23. Warburg, "Flandrische Kunst," pp. 375–376. This note is based on Tani's memorandum (MAP, filza 82, no. 163): "Ragione che Agniolo Tani allegha per lequale e' dicie la ragione di Bruggia non avere a partire nè a fare niente chon Gherardo Chanigiani di Londra, e che lui non à chompagnia chol detto Gherardo." Warburg's note summarizes this memorandum very well. It shows plainly that Sassetti was partial to Tommaso Portinari whose proposals, although pernicious, saved him from embarrassment.

24. Project of Reorganization (MAP, filza 83, no. 19): "Resta che il Xaxetti si fidi di Lionetto."

25. Francesco Sassetti in Lyons to Lorenzo the Magnificent in Florence, May 24, 1489 (MAP, filza 88, no. 199).

26. One of Sassetti's sons (Teodoro I) died in his youth, Federigo became a priest, Cosimo and Galeazzo joined the staff of the Medici Bank. I do not know what became of Teodoro II, the youngest son, born in 1479 after the death of Teodoro I. One of the daughters, Violante, married Neri Capponi, who headed a rival bank in Lyons and, through his wife, was well informed about the difficulties of the Medici Bank. Francesco Sassetti also had an adulterine son named Ventura who entered the priesthood. In this respect Francesco was like Giovanni Benci. Warburg, "Francesco Sassetti's letztwillige Verfügung," *Gesammelte Schriften*, I, 131–132.

27. F. E. de Roover, "Francesco Sassetti," pp. 69–70. Business investments represented 68.6 percent of the estate. These figures are based on the valsente (inventory) found in Sassetti's libro segreto, fol. 2 (ASF, Cart Strozziane, 2d Series, No. 20).

28. *Ibid.*, fol. 71. Business investments minus debts represented sixty-four percent of this total. The books are today in the Biblioteca Laurenziana.

29. Warburg, "Letztwillige Verfügung," p. 133.

30. Sassetti in Lyons to Lorenzo de' Medici in Florence, December 9, 1488 (MAP, filza 40, no. 217): ". . . dolgo mi di nonn esser riccho et pechunioxo come io solevo." Same statement in a letter of February 12, 1489 (MAP, filza 40, no. 204).

31. Same correspondents, May 24, 1489 (MAP, filza 88, no. 199).

32. Letter of Francesco di ser Barone in Florence to Piero Pandolfini, Florentine ambassador in Rome, March 22, 1490 (Florence Biblioteca Nazionale, Manoscritti, II, IV, 371, fol. 105). Letter of Lorenzo Spinelli in Lyons to Lorenzo de' Medici, April 4, 1490 (ASF, MAP, filza 42, no. 37). Spinelli had heard about the stroke and did not expect Sassetti to live. News of Sassetti's demise had not yet reached Lyons.

33. Del Piazzo, *Protocolli*, p. 414.

34. Warburg, "Letztwillige Verfügung," p. 131, n. 2.

35. The villa was sold by Sassetti's descendants in 1546 to Piero di Gino Capponi. Guido Carocci, *I dintorni di Firenze* (Florence, 1906), I, 183.

36. Warburg, "Letztwillige Verfügung," p. 129. In 1581, Filippo Sassetti is mentioned as concluding an *asiento* with the Spanish crown. H. Lapeyre, *Simon Ruiz et les Asientos de Philippe II* (Paris, 1953), p. 43.

37. Warburg, "Letztwillige Verfügung," p. 141.

38. *History of Florence*, Bk. VIII, chap. 7. The original reads as follows (*Istorie fiorentine*, Libro VIII, §36): "Nelle altre sue private cose fu, quanto alla mercanzia, infelicissimo; perchè per il disordine de' suoi ministri, i quali non come privati, ma come principi le sue cose amministravano, in molti parti molto suo mobile fu spento; in modo che convenne che la sua patria di gran somma di danari lo suvvenisse." The Bohn translation of this passage is not reliable. From the Medici correspondence, it is clear, for instance, that *disordine* means mismanagement and that ministri is the term often used for branch managers, today we would say executives.

39. *The Wealth of Nations*, Bk. V, chap. 2, pt. 1 (New York: Modern Library ed., 1937), p. 771.

40. Philippe de Commines, *Mémoires*, eds. Joseph Calmette and G. Durville (Paris, 1925), III, Bk. VII, chap. 6, 41–42.

41. *Storie fiorentine*, chap. 9, pp. 76 and 81: ". . . nelle mercatantie e cose private non ebbe intelligenzia."

42. Alessandro de' Pazzi, "Discorso al Cardinale Giulio de' Medici, Anno 1522," *Archivio storico italiano*, 1:422 (1842).

43. Giovanni Michele Bruto, *Istorie fiorentine*, ed. Stanislao Gatteschi (Florence, 1838), II, 499.

44. Lorenzo the Magnificent to Girolamo Morelli, November 14, 1478 (MAP, filza 96, no. 93): ". . . et non posso fare che io non scoppi di dolore quando io penso che a Milano, dove io doverrei havere tanta reputatione et favore, non possa havere ragione co' mie' ministri."

45. Meltzing, in 1906, attributed the decline of the Medici Bank to Lorenzo's laxity and the mismanagement of his agents, especially Tommaso Portinari (*Bankhaus der Medici*, pp. 123, 132, 134–135).

46. Roberto Palmarocchi, *Lorenzo de' Medici* (Turin, 1941), pp. 37–42.

47. Piero de' Medici in Florence to his son Lorenzo in Rome, March 15, 1466 (MAP, filza 20, no. 142). The text of this letter is published in A. Fabroni, *Laurentii Medicis Magnifici* II, 47–49 and in Roscoe, *Lorenzo de' Medici*, p. 417, Appendix VI.

48. For making the same statement elsewhere, I have been branded as an enemy of humanism. This is a misunderstanding. All I mean to say is that a banker needs to know banking and I do not object to his knowing Latin besides. I presume that my critics do not go twice to a restaurant where the cook burns the food while reading Virgil or Homer. See Emilio Cristiano in *Lo Spettatore Italiano*, 4:267–268 (1951).

49. Report of Angelo Tani (MAP, filza 82, no. 163).

50. Memoria di Lorenzo de' Medici (MAP, filza 84, no. 21).

51 Lionetto de' Rossi in Lyons to Lorenzo the Magnificent, June 19, 1484 (MAP, filza 51, no. 282).

52. Lorenzo Spinelli to Lorenzo the Magnificent, September 2, 1487 (MAP, filza 40, no. 136).

53. Guicciardini, *Storie fiorentine*, chap. 4, p. 36; Perrens, *History of Florence*, p. 298.

54. July 25, 1478 (MAP, filza 124, No. 2). Translated in Ross, *Lives of the Early Medici*, pp. 207–208.

55. *Loc. cit.*

56. MAP, filza 104, fols. 454–469: November 8, 1485. The amount of 53,643 florins is made up as follows:

1478 May 1	20,043	florins
May 3	5,000	
June 2	8,000	
August 8	8,000	
August 13	1,600	
September 27	11,000	
Total	53,643	florins

57. MAP, filza 99, No. 8, fols. 30–31.

58. Guicciardini refers to these differences in *Storie fiorentine* (p. 76).

59. Perrens, *History of Florence*, p. 409; Palmarocchi, *Lorenzo de' Medici*, p. 38.

60. Guicciardini, *Storie fiorentine*, pp. 77, 81; Pietro di Marco Parenti, "Storia fiorentina, 1476–1518," Florence, Biblioteca Nazionale, Manoscritti, Magl. II, II, 129, fol. 105ʳ.

61. ASF, Carte Strozziane, Series I, No. 10, fols. 190–191. Louis Marks, who found this document, kindly called my attention to it.

62. ". . . perchè detto scrivano e huficiali per leggie veruna non ànno alturità nessuna, ànnolo fatto in danno e progiudicio del Chomune."

63. MAP, filza 83, no. 19, fols. 67–68.

64. Bracci is designated as the author of the plan in a letter written by Lionetto de' Rossi on September 23, 1485, while imprisoned in the Stinche (MAP, filza 26, no. 447).

65. Letter of September 6, 1486 (MAP, filza 39, no. 558).

66. Letter of April 9, 1490 (MAP, filza 42, no. 38).

67. Hyett, *Florence*, p. 475.

68. MAP, filza 84, no. 46, fol. 96.

69. MAP, filza 82, no. 145, fols. 446–462. Another copy is in Harvard University, Baker Library, Selfridge Collection of Medici Mss., No. 495, Section C.

70. *Storie fiorentine,* chap. 15, p. 143.

71. F. E. de Roover, "Francesco Sassetti," p. 80. Cf. Vittorio de Caprariis, "Sul Banco dei Medici," *"Bollettino dell'Archivio storico del Banco di Napoli,* fasc. 1 (1950), p. 51. This author, inspired by the ideas of his father-in-law, Benedetto Croce, thinks it is futile to search for the causes of the downfall of the Medici Bank. He may be right to a certain extent, but it is nevertheless worthwhile to make an attempt, to point out the probable causes, and to discard any circumstances without influence.

72. R. S. Lopez, "Hard Times and Investment in Culture," *The Renaissance, Medieval or Modern?* ed. Karl H. Dannenfeldt (Boston, 1959), p. 61.

73. R. de Roover, "Accounting prior to Luca Pacioli," p. 142; Tommaso Zerbi, *Le Origini della partita doppia,* pp. 420, 440.

74. The text of these *Ricordi* is in Roscoe, *Lorenzo de' Medici,* p. 426 (Appendix X).

75. This is pointed out by Guicciardini, *Storie fiorentine,* p. 81.

76. Gras, *Business and Capitalism,* p. 166.

77. ASF, Catasto No. 1016 (Leon d'Oro, 1481), fol. 474^r: ". . . non oservo l'ordine di mio padre del 69 per essere grande differenzia da quel tempo al presente. Et per avere ricievuto molti danni in diversi mie traffichi chome ch'è noto non solamente alla Signoria Vostra, ma a tutto il mondo." Cf. Sieveking, *Aus Genueser Rechnungsbüchern,* pp. 102–103.

78. M. M. Postan, "The Trade of Medieval Europe: the North," *Cambridge Economic History,* II (Cambridge, 1952), 191–216; Robert S. Lopez, "The Trade of Medieval Europe: the South," *ibid.,* II, 338–354. Lopez, however, stops in 1453, but the capture of Constantinople and the depredations of the Turks in the eastern Mediterranean were not conducive to prosperity. See also Professor Postan's report to the International Congress in Paris (1950), published in IXe Congrès International des Sciences Historiques, I. *Rapports* (Paris, 1950), pp. 225–241.

79. See the chart on p. 61 of the first edition of this book. Cf. Cipolla, *Studi della moneta,* pp. 60–64, 99. Cipolla's chart and mine correspond.

80. M. M. Postan, "Italy and the Economic Development of England in the Middle Ages," *Journal of Economic History,* 11:339–346 (1951). There is no evidence, however, that the Medici bank ever received extensive deposits from English lords. The only exception perhaps is Henry Beaufort, Cardinal of Winchester, who was a creditor of the Rome branch.

81. ASF, Catasto No. 919 (Leon Rosso, 1469/70), fol. 406. Rucellai had a tavola with Piero Soderini as partner.

82. Pagnini, *Della Decima,* II, 65.

INDEX